Continuity and Change in World Politics

Continuity and Change in World Politics:
Competing Perspectives

Fourth Edition

Barry B. Hughes

University of Denver

Prentice Hall, Upper Saddle River, New Jersey 07458

Library of Congress Cataloging-in-Publication Data

HUGHES, BARRY B. (date)
　　Continuity and change in world politics : competing perspectives /
Barry B. Hughes. — 4th ed.
　　　p.　cm.
　　Includes bibliographical references and index.
　　ISBN 0130835781 (pbk.)
　　1. International relations.　2. World politics—1945-　I. Title.
JZ1242.H84　2000
320.9′045—dc21
99–33795
CIP

Editorial Director: Charlyce Jones Owen
Editor-in-Chief: Nancy Roberts
Senior Acquisitions Editor: Beth Gillett Mejia
Associate Editor: Nicole Conforti
Editorial Assistant: Brian Prybella
Project Manager: Joan Stone
Prepress and Manufacturing Buyer: Ben Smith
Creative Design Director: Leslie Osher
Interior Design: Thomas Nery
Cover Design: Thomas Nery
Cover Art Credit: Jean-Luc Wang/Superstock, Inc.
Line Art Coordinator: Guy Ruggiero
Electronic Art Production: Hadel Studio
Marketing Manager: Christopher DeJohn

Maps in text by Central Intelligence Agency. Maps made available for downloading by the Perry-Castaneda Library Map Collection, University of Texas at Austin, Texas. Available: http://mahogeny.lib.utexas.edu.

This book was set in 10/12 Palatino by Carlisle Communications, Ltd., and was printed and bound by RR Donnelley & Sons Company. The cover was printed by Phoenix Color Corp.

Printed in the United States of America
10　9　8　7　6　5　4　3　2　1

ISBN　0-13-083578-1

PRENTICE-HALL INTERNATIONAL (UK) LIMITED, *London*
PRENTICE-HALL OF AUSTRALIA PTY. LIMITED, *Sydney*
PRENTICE-HALL CANADA INC., *Toronto*
PRENTICE-HALL HISPANOAMERICANA, S.A., *Mexico*
PRENTICE-HALL OF INDIA PRIVATE LIMITED, *New Delhi*
PRENTICE-HALL OF JAPAN, INC., *Tokyo*
PEARSON EDUCATION ASIA PTE. LTD., *Singapore*
EDITORA PRENTICE-HALL DO BRASIL, LTDA., *Rio de Janeiro*

To Bernard and Jean Hughes,
who encouraged a boy from Punkin' Center
to grapple with global issues

Contents

Preface   xvii

Part I   INTRODUCTION

CHAPTER ONE   Forces of Change   1

Demographic Transition   3
Growing Food Sufficiency   7
Energy Transition   9
Increased Environmental Impact   11
Global Economic Restructuring   13
   Geographic Diffusion of the Industrial Revolution   14
   The Information Revolution   15
   Globalization   17
Rise and Fall in Global Position   18
Growth of Destructive Potential   20
Increased Social Mobilization   22
Uncertain Implications of Trends   25

CHAPTER TWO   Elements of Analysis   27

Three Subject-Matter Categories for Analysis   28
   Political-Military Aspects   28
   Economic Aspects   31
   Broader Environment   32
The Importance of All Three Subject-Matter Categories   33
A Structure of Understanding   33
Clash of Perspectives: Competing Worldviews   36
   Realism, Liberalism, and Constructivist Perspectives   37

Commercial Liberalism, Mercantilism, and Neo-Marxism   *38*
Modernism and Eco-Wholism   *39*
Organization of the Book   39

Part II   THE WORLD OF POLITICS

CHAPTER THREE   Realist, Liberal, and Constructivist Views   41

Realism   41
Concepts   41
Theories   42
Values and Prescriptions   44
Important Contributions to Realist Thought   45
Liberalism   46
Concepts   47
Theory   48
Values and Forecasts   49
Prescriptions   49
Important Contributions to Liberal Thought   50
Constructivism   52
Concepts   53
Theory   56
Forecasts, Values, and Prescriptions   56
Important Contributions to Constructivist Thought   58
Worldview Overlap   59

CHAPTER FOUR   States and the Pursuit of Interest   61

State Systems   63
Historic State Systems   64
The Modern State System   66
Early Polarity   66
Contemporary Polarity   67
Hegemonic Leadership   68
State Interests   70
Power   72
Definition and Measurement   72
Demographic Size   72
Economic and Military Capabilities   74
Aggregate Capabilities and Power   75
Other Capabilities   77
Power and the Interest of States   78
Instruments of Power: Statecraft   79

Diplomacy   79
Economic Instruments   82
Instruments of Violence   87
The Decision to Go to War   90
Conclusion   92

CHAPTER FIVE   Dynamics of State Systems   94

Patterns of Conflict   97
  Studies of War   97
  Crises and Serious Interstate Disputes   101
Insights from Bilateral Analysis   104
Bilateral Relations and Nuclear Arms   106
  The Players and Their Equipment   106
  Strategic Concepts and Theory: State Behavior   109
Insights from Multilateral Analysis   110
  Balance of Power Advocacy   111
  Definition   111
  Balance of Power and State Behavior   112
  Alliances   112
Change in Polarity and Its Consequences   113
Insights from Hegemonic Analysis   114
  Rise and Fall of Hegemons   114
  Advantages of Hegemonic Leadership   116
  Changing of the Guard   117
Post–Cold War Uncertainties   118
  The Role of NATO   119
  The Systemic Role of Russia   120
  The Systemic Role of China   121
Conclusion   122

CHAPTER SIX   Interaction in the Pursuit of Cooperation   124

A Framework for Interaction: International Law   125
  Rights of States   126
  Obligations of States   127
A Logic of Interaction: Delivering the Goods   130
  Basic Characteristics of Private and Public Goods   130
  Categories of Goods   131
  Collective Action and Problems of Underprovision   135
  Trade and the Logic of Collective Action   136
  An Approach to Repetitive Interaction: Regimes   137

A Focus of Interaction: Arms Control   139
   Arms Control and Disarmament Efforts   140
Conclusion   150

CHAPTER SEVEN   Opening the State   152

Levels of Analysis   153
   State System   154
   The State   154
   Society   156
   Individual   157
   Government   157
Society   158
   Public Opinion   158
   Interests   161
   Ideas   167
Individuals   168
   Leadership and Vision   169
   Gender and Foreign Policy   171
   Psychology and Foreign Policy   172
   Risk Aversion and Acceptance   173
   Perception and Crisis   174
   Crisis Management   175
   Individuals in Groups   176
Government   177
   Decision Making   177
   Differential Power of Decision-Making Models   178
   Government Character and Foreign Behavior   180
On Rational, Unitary Actors   180

CHAPTER EIGHT   An Emergent Liberal World Order?   183

Actor Proliferation and Empowerment   185
Global Community   187
   Normative Community: Global Culture   188
   Normative Community: Human Rights Law   189
   Community of Understanding   194
   Global Governance: The Spread of Democracy   194
   Global Community: Peaceful Interaction   196
Institutional Development   199
   Beyond the State?   201
Conclusion   206

CHAPTER NINE   Organizations and Governance   207

United Nations   208
  Transformation   210
  Performance: Peace and Security   211
  Performance: Social Development   214
  Controversies Facing the United Nations   215
European Union   216
  Transformation   217
  Performance and Controversies   219
  Other Regional Economic Organizations   220
A Liberal Governance Model?   221
Conclusion   225

CHAPTER TEN   Constructing Global Society: Identities and Ideas   227

Social (De)Construction   230
Nations and Nationalism   230
  The Modern Nation System   233
  Nationalism Within States   234
  Nationalism and Interstate Relations   236
  Problem Cases   236
Religion and World Politics   241
Family   244
Race   245
Gender   246
Class   247
Humanity: Universalisms   248
  Historic Universalism   249
  Modern Universalism: Roots of the Cold War(s)   249
Terrorism: Instrument of the Disadvantaged   251
  Foundations of Terrorism   251
  Trends in Terrorism   252
Social Construction   253
Conclusion   255

Part III   THE GLOBAL POLITICAL ECOMONY

CHAPTER ELEVEN   Commercial Liberalism, Mercantilism, and Neo-Marxism   256

Commercial Liberalism   257
  Concepts   257
  Theory   257

Values and Prescriptions   262
Mercantilism   263
Neo-Marxism   267
   Marxist Conceptual Roots   267
   Imperialism   268
   Neo-Marxist Theory   269
   Values and Prescriptions   271
Worldviews and Methodology   271

CHAPTER TWELVE   The Globalization of the World Economy   274

The Irregular Growth of an Open Global Economy   274
Liberalism Ascendant Again: Bretton Woods   277
   Institutions of Bretton Woods   277
   Early Challenge and Change   280
Trade: The Shadow of Mercantilism   281
   Bases of Neomercantilism   281
   Confronting the Challenge of Neomercantilism   282
   The Fear of Spoilers   283
   The Heavy Trade Agenda   285
Managing Explosive Financial Flows   287
   The Volume and Pattern of Flows   288
   Consequences of Global Flows   292
   Policy Options   294
The Leadership Question   294

CHAPTER THIRTEEN   A World Divided   296

Imperialism and Decolonization   297
Economic Gaps   299
   North-South Gap   299
   Gaps Within Countries   302
Global Structures   304
   Global Division of Labor   305
   Political-Economic Institutions and Regimes   306
   Multinational Corporations   312
   Military-Power Differentials   316
Development Strategies   319
   Inward-Looking Policy   319
   Collective and Structural Reform   320
   The Liberal Rebuttal: Growth-Enhancing Participation   322
Conclusion   325

Part IV   THE BROADER ENVIRONMENT

CHAPTER FOURTEEN   Modernism and Eco-Wholism   327

Modernism   328
   Sketch of the Worldview   328
   Important Contributions to Modernist Thought   329
Eco-Wholism   331
   Challengers in Brief   331
   Values and Prescriptions   333
   Important Contributions to Eco-Wholist Thought   333

CHAPTER FIFTEEN   Technological Advance and Human Interaction   337

Intensity and Patterns of Interaction   337
   Transportation   338
   Communications   339
Technology and Human Well-Being   341
Technology and War   343
Technological Advance and Diffusion   345
   Long Waves of Technological Advance?   346
   State Efforts to Control Technology   348
   Are States Losing Control?   353
Technology and Social Organization   354
   Penetration of States   354
Transformation of Global Order?   355
Conclusion   356

CHAPTER SIXTEEN   Environmental Context and Constraints   358

Microenvironment   359
Population Pressures   361
   Competing Perspectives   362
   Migration and Refugees   363
   Population Control Efforts   364
Resource Scarcities: Food   367
   Competing Perspectives on Global Food Supply   368
   Competing Perspectives on Food Distribution   373
   Global Attention to Food Problems   375
Resource Scarcities: Energy   377
   Competing Perspectives on Energy Supply   378
   Energy Policy Issues   381

Ecosystem Vulnerability   385
   The Range of Human Impact   385
   Interstate Policy Approaches   388
Conclusion   393

Part V   THE COMPLEXITY OF UNDERSTANDING

CHAPTER SEVENTEEN   Continuity and Change in World Politics   395

Understanding Change   396
   Stability or Unpatterned Change   396
   Progressive Change   400
   System Transformation   404
   Cycles   407
Putting the Perspectives Together   408
Conclusion   410

CHAPTER EIGHTEEN   Alternative Futures: The Clash of Perspectives   411

Business as Usual for States   412
The Evolution of Global Governance   414
The Clash of Peoples   415
The Global Market   417
Evolving Global Division of Labor   418
Technological Advance   420
Environmental Limits   421
Last Words   422

Glossary   423

References   445

Index   469

Preface

Welcome to new readers and to professors who have used previous editions! This fourth edition continues to emphasize provision of a solid and substantial kit of analytic tools for long-term use. And it continues to use those tools to convey an understanding of continuity and change in the tumultuous contemporary era. This edition also, however, completely updates all material and significantly improves its presentation. My goal is to help students of the early twenty-first century (for whom the Cold War is nearly "ancient" history) not just survey, but *understand* their world.

The presentation builds on the premise that an *understanding* of world politics has four principal elements. The first is an extensive foundation of information including knowledge of the current world and some familiarity with its history. The book provides a significant base of factual knowledge—not abstractly, but as needed to give flesh to a broader framework of understanding.

The second element is analysis. Large numbers of important concepts and theories allow a serious student of world politics to move from particularistic description to generalization, from knowledge to analysis. This book extensively and systematically introduces those concepts and theories (bold or bold italic type emphasizes their use and a glossary elaborates textual definitions). At the end of each chapter you will find the items in bold repeated within a listing of selected key terms; those will be the terms for which most instructors will assign students responsibility prior to examinations. Some instructors may wish to extend that list by assigning responsibility also for the additional terms in bold italic type. Terms in bold italic are generally defined and used more extensively in other chapters.

The third element is interpretation. In world politics we can never say "these are the facts and here is how to interpret them." Anyone who reads the opinion page of a daily newspaper or who watches the debates on issues of world politics knows that analysts choose facts selectively and that their interpretations of even the seemingly most basic ones vary. All students of world politics need to understand that the field combines science and controversy, insight and competing interpretations. This text maps the primary competing worldviews on the "big questions" and helps the reader understand that the contributions of scientific analysis have often been within, not across, those worldviews.

The fourth and final element of understanding is insight into dynamics. Perhaps because the Cold War froze global politics into a fairly rigid pattern for more than four decades, analysis and interpretation of world politics have frequently failed to emphasize how rapidly the global system can change and have neglected to consider the bases of change. This book seeks to convey an understanding of the forces that transform our world.

There is much continuity in this edition with previous ones. There is also much change. The last edition broke free of the straitjacket that "idealism" had imposed on the discussion of what the book (and broader scholarship) now elaborates more fully and analytically as the "liberal" worldview. The change allows much more coherent discussion of global developments in democracy, human rights, and institutional development.

This edition takes another large step by introducing the "constructivist" worldview (as a replacement for what the last edition rather clumsily called "communitarian"). This makes it possible to give gender, race, class, ethnic/nationalist, and religious issues and perspectives more of the attention they deserve. The study of world politics increasingly recognizes the importance of identity, culture, and other ideas (or social constructions) and is finally bringing those elements into its understanding of continuity and change in the global system. Scholarship in the field has fastened with remarkable speed in recent years on the "constructivist" label and has begun to elaborate the content of this "third" worldview.

Readers of past editions will note a variety of other important changes, including much more extensive treatment of that key phenomenon, globalism. I have also consolidated the three brief "reprise" chapters on change into a single more integrated treatment. Throughout the book I have tried to make what needs to remain a challengingly analytic treatment of world politics as accessible as possible to students. I have cut back footnotes considerably, more carefully defined key concepts when the text introduces them, added a glossary, and otherwise rewritten material to help students understand.

With respect to our understanding of world politics, I firmly remain one of the optimists—we have made great intellectual progress during the last few decades. I have always tried to write a text that not only collects and synthesizes our growing understandings of the world, but also contributes to them.

The Graduate School of International Studies (GSIS) was an exceptional environment in which to undertake a work that covers as much ground as this one does. The GSIS brings together congenial, intellectually stimulating colleagues from a mixture of disciplines, and it attracts first-class students with whom to develop ideas interactively. My intellectual debts in the preparation of this book are, of course, much broader. It is only really possible to thank specifically some of those who saved me from some of my errors and confusions, by commenting on substantial parts or all of this or previous editions: Carina A. Black, *University of Nevada, Reno*; Mark A. Boyer, *University of Connecticut*; Patrick Boyle, *Loyola University, Chicago*; Stuart A. Bremer, *Pennsylvania State University*; Emily Copeland, *Florida*

International University; James A. Caporaso, *University of Washington*; Harold Damerow, *Union County College*; Richard C. Eichenberg, *Tufts University*; Peter M. Haas, *University of Massachusetts*; William Hazleton, *Miami University, Ohio*; W. Ladd Hollist, *Brigham Young University*; David P. Levine, *University of Denver*; Michael McGinnis, *Indiana University*; Brian M. Pollins, *Ohio State University*; Michael Niemann, *Trinity College*; Susan Northcutt, *University of South Florida*; James Lee Ray, *Vanderbilt University*; Neil Richardson, *University of Wisconsin*; Peter J. Schraeder, *Loyola University, Chicago*; Dale L. Smith, *Florida State University*; Marvin S. Soroos, *North Carolina State University*; and Roland Stephen, *North Carolina State University*. In addition, James Chung, Steven Durand, Shannon Brady, and Michael Ferrier provided invaluable research assistance.

With more time and additional advice, I hope in future editions to enhance still further the understanding that students obtain from this book; I welcome suggestions. Finally, I offer my thanks for the time you spend in reading and thinking about this book and convey my hopes that it will reward you.

Barry B. Hughes

University of Denver

Continuity and Change in World Politics

Forces of Change

The political equivalents of earthquakes periodically restructure global politics. World War II and events of the years immediately following it shook the world with devastating force. Most of the surface features of the early twentieth century world still stood in 1938 when World War II began. That world was highly Eurocentric. Britain was the dominant country in many parts of the globe, but Germany posed an increasingly strong challenge to it. European empires divided much of the world among themselves. The United States and Russia were important but somewhat peripheral powers.

Pressures for change, however, had built below the surface throughout the first half of the twentieth century. The war revealed many of the discrepancies between the old surface forms and the new underlying realities. In particular, the United States and the Soviet Union emerged as the dominant military powers. An event in the final months of fighting confirmed the U.S. position: On August 6, 1945, the United States dropped an atomic bomb on Hiroshima, Japan, and thereby initiated the atomic weapons era.

⊙ **KEY WEB LINKS**

www.igc.org/wri/enved/
trends.html
www.nytimes.com/
www.economist.com/index.html

Many aftershocks followed the earthquake of the war. The wartime alliance of the United States and the Soviet Union, formed to combat Germany and Japan, quickly disintegrated. Decolonization proceeded rapidly. The war had temporarily reduced or eliminated control by the Western European states over their extensive colonial empires in Africa and Asia; Britain and France tried to reestablish imperial positions. They failed and the empires disappeared.

The two new superpowers rapidly drew much of the rest of the world into new relationships. By 1949, the United States, Britain, and France forged alliances with former enemies Germany (the Western two-thirds) and Japan; together they faced former allies, the Soviet Union and China, across an "iron curtain." The **Cold**

War, a 40-year-long political, economic, and military struggle without direct military confrontation, had begun. The United States led the North Atlantic Treaty Organization (NATO), and the Soviet Union soon dominated the Warsaw Pact. Relative stability returned.

Even with the building of new global surface structures during the Cold War, underlying pressures for more change did not stop building. A variety of demographic, economic, environmental, and technological forces continued to operate. For instance, world population more than doubled by 1990. Germany and Japan rose from the ruins of World War II to engage the United States and other new friends in intense economic competition. Humanity put increasing pressures on its biological and physical environments. New communications technologies linked the peoples of the world as never before.

The world continued to experience small shocks throughout the 1960s, 1970s, and 1980s. Then, in 1989–1991, another large-scale earthquake rocked it (Chapter 2 provides more details). The epicenter was the Soviet Union, which installed a reforming leadership in 1985, but shock waves rapidly radiated to Central Europe. In 1989 and 1990 the dominant role of Communist parties in the Soviet Union and all of its Eastern allies crumbled. By 1992 the Warsaw Pact had fallen and the Soviet Union had broken into fifteen countries.

The ramifications of the new shock spread globally. Rapid movement toward both unilateral and negotiated reductions in arms developed. The United States and Russia began to see opportunities for cooperation in the resolution of problems around the world. Long-standing political configurations in the Middle East, Central America, and elsewhere in the globe shifted.

Other developments added to the pace of change during this period. Twelve countries in Europe, which had fought an almost uncountable number of wars during the preceding 400 years, met a 1992 deadline for the development of a common economic market and added three more members in 1994. Rapid economic growth in China signaled its movement into a prominent role on the world stage. South America completed a movement toward democratization, at one time boasting democratic governments throughout the continent for the first time ever. South Africa moved to dismantle its apartheid system.

The sum total of changes wrought by these two extraordinary periods is astounding. Yet beneath the mosaic of change, many patterns of continuity persist. Two are especially apparent. First, countries remain the dominant actors in world politics. Some, like the United Kingdom, France, or Portugal, can trace their existence back several centuries. Even in the roster of countries there is, of course, change. The United States came onto the scene little more than 200 years ago, Germany has been united for scarcely more than 100 years, and Bangladesh will not celebrate its fiftieth anniversary until 2021. Schoolchildren around the world must now learn the location of new countries such as Croatia, Belarus, and Georgia.

Second, warfare predates our historic knowledge and appears to be a constant of human existence. In a typical year 30 or more conflicts are underway, and not a day passes without a war-related death somewhere in the world. Economic competition among countries is a related constant, and many of the methods by which countries seek relative advantage today are little changed from those of 300 years ago.

What are the major forces of global change and the primary elements of continuity in world politics? What kind of world are they jointly creating? The years since the beginning of World War II, which encompass two political earthquakes and much other dramatic change, fall short of an average lifetime. How dramatically might world politics evolve during the lives of the students reading this book?

We cannot foresee the future world, any more than someone in early 1939 or even in 1988 could have forecast the world of today. In this volume we can convey an understanding of important forces at work, however, and present alternative and often clashing perspectives for considering the implications of those forces. The rest of this chapter sketches eight forces that appear especially potent in their contribution to global change. Each force has potentially both positive and negative consequences; often the implications for individual human beings will depend on the country of their citizenship or on their social position.

The simultaneous operation of several forces, with substantial and complex interaction among them, presents tremendous difficulty for anyone attempting to understand the present state of world politics or to anticipate its future—it is perhaps impossible to know even the relative importance of these forces, much less to comprehend the product of their interplay. We have seen that world politics is a bit like the surface of the earth, which often exhibits long periods of relative calm even while massive "tectonic plates" continue their long-term drift just below the surface. Periodically, and as yet unpredictably, the underlying forces dramatically disrupt surface features. Identification of geologic plates was a critically important step for geologists toward understanding the effects of their movement including the location of earthquake zones. Identification of the forces that gradually reshape world politics, and that periodically lead to massive restructurings, has comparable significance.

Demographic Transition

People are our core interest. That alone might justify placing demographic change first on our list of important long-term forces. More to the point, the numbers and geographic distributions of populations affect most other patterns of global development. Dramatic global change in human numbers and distribution has recently occurred and continues. Specifically, *the world is undergoing a demographic transition from small populations with short life expectancies to large populations with long life expectancies.*

A millennium ago global population was a fraction of the 6.0 billion current world inhabitants (specifically about 250 million or 4.2 percent), and it required high birthrates to offset the prevailing high mortality rates and to allow very slow net population growth. Mortality rates of European populations gradually fell, and growth rates accelerated during the last 500 years because of advances in transportation of both food and people, changes in agricultural technology, and progress in sanitation and health care. Yet only in the last century have we seen really dramatic improvement in life expectancy. At the end of the seventeenth century life expectancy at birth in England was only 32; by 1860 it had advanced just to 45 (United Nations 1973, 23–24); it has now reached 77. In countries like

England, birthrates gradually eased in the wake of lower mortality rates until the two again became approximately equal. The European and North American **demographic transitions** from high mortality and fertility rates to low mortality and fertility rates, and the surges of population growth that accompanied the temporary surplus of births relative to deaths, are therefore now largely complete.

The demographic transitions of most non-European peoples began only in the twentieth century, for the most part after World War II. Mortality declines, because of the rapidity of transfer of modern medical technology throughout the world, were much more rapid than the earlier ones in Europe. In fact, life expectancies at birth outside of Europe and North America increased from 43 years in 1950–1955 to 63 today. As earlier in Europe, mortality declines preceded those in fertility, so that a significant gap between mortality and fertility rates opened, and population growth accelerated.

Figure 1.1 portrays the demographic transitions in economically developed and developing countries by showing fertility and mortality rates over time. Demographers measure fertility in various ways, frequently with the **crude birth rate** or total annual births per 1,000 population. Similarly, they often capture mortality by the *crude death rate* or total annual deaths per 1,000. The difference between the crude birth and death rates is the net population growth per 1,000. For instance, the Democratic Republic of Congo (Zaire) is one of the fastest-growing countries in the world. Its crude birth rate is 48, and its crude death rate is 16. The difference of 32 per 1,000 is equivalent to a 3.2 percent annual rate of population growth.

In light of these high fertility rates and low mortality rates, global population growth rates are now increasing, right? No. Global gaps between fertility and mortality, driven especially by the post-World War II mortality declines in Africa, Asia, and Latin America, reached a peak in the 1960s. At that time the world passed a critically important demographic *turning point.* Specifically, global population growth rates, which had been increasing indefinitely, reached a peak of approximately 2 percent per year and began to decline (as fertility moved lower and began to catch up with mortality declines). In the early 1980s the global rate eased to about 1.7 percent, and now, at 1.4 percent, it is poised for sharper declines.

The world has, in fact, now passed a second important demographic turning point. After 1970 the declines in annual percentage growth rates were initially so small that, when the growth rates were applied to higher and higher world population totals, they still yielded increasing year-to-year additions to world population (see the bottom half of Figure 1.2). That is, the actual number of people added to world population each year continued to grow to nearly 90 million each year in the late 1980s (about the population of Mexico). World population growth rates are now slowing more quickly, and annual increments have fallen to about 80 million.

Even after crossing these two critical divides in human demographic history, world population will grow far into the twenty-first century, reaching perhaps 10 billion before any kind of stability is attained. Although future numbers are highly speculative, it is nearly certain that most population growth in the next century will occur outside of North America and Western Europe—in fact, practically all of it will (see Figure 1.2). Populations are fundamental to economic and military capabilities, and to pressures on land and other resources (that is, potentially to both

Figure 1.1   Demographic Transition

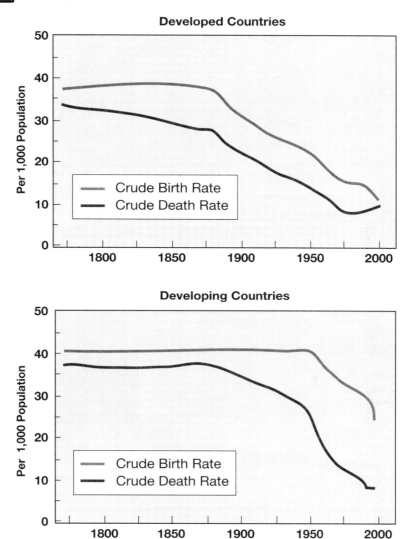

Source: Nancy Birdsall, *Population and Poverty in the Developing World.* World Bank Staff Working Paper No. 404. (Washington, DC: World Bank, 1980), 4; Population Reference Bureau, *World Population Data Sheet.* (Washington, DC: Population Reference Bureau, 1986, 1988, 1992, 1995, 1998).

strength and weakness). For better or for worse, Europe and North America will have considerably smaller shares of a much larger global population.

Demographic changes will bring both challenges and opportunities. Many of the costs of increased world population are obvious: greater congestion with respect to land, air, water, and biological resources. Assuming that fertility rates continue to drop in most of the world, however, the growth in pressure on food

Figure 1.2   Global Distribution of Population and Annual Population Growth

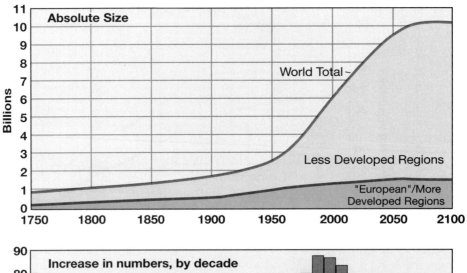

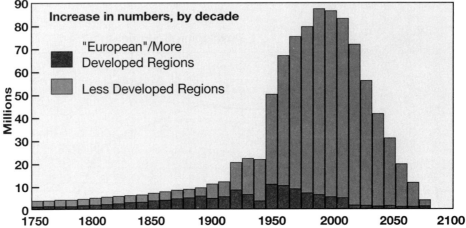

Source: Thomas W. Merrick, "World Population in Transition," *Population Bulletin* (Population Reference Bureau, Inc.), 41, no. 2 (April 1986), 4. Reprinted with permission.

supplies, raw materials, and employment opportunities should slow. Because younger people require health care, food, and education, while often making little contribution to production, demographers call them **dependent population.** In general, a large percentage of the population in a rapidly growing country is under the age of 15. For instance, that age group constitutes 36 percent of the total in Mexico compared with 22 percent in the United States. Declines in fertility reduce the size of the dependent population relative to the more economically productive population, facilitating economic growth.

Yet even the countries that successfully navigate the demographic transition face significant potential problems. In Germany, for instance, population could decline for years, because fertility rates have fallen below mortality. Many European countries may follow this pattern. An aging, longer-lived population (a second category of dependent population) puts increasing demands for medical care and pension benefits on those who work. In the United States, 13 percent of the population already exceeds 65 years of age compared with 4 percent in Mexico. Whereas the United States now has about five people working for each retiree, by the year 2050 that ratio may fall to 2-to-1. In Germany and France it may be 1.2-to-1.

Growing Food Sufficiency

Population growth puts pressure on food supplies. With rapid population growth, food per capita has been decreasing, right? Wrong. *The world has increasingly gained the physical ability to feed itself.* Throughout the post-World War II period, growth in global food production regularly equaled or outstripped growth in the global population. In 1997 world food production per capita exceeded that of 1950 by 46 percent. Between 1970 and 1990 the portion of the population in less-developed countries that was malnourished fell from 35 percent to 20 percent—although the absolute number declined only from 900 to 840 million (World Resources Institute [WRI] 1998, 155). Since the 1950s the green revolution has developed strains of grain that can respond to fertilizers, pesticides, and irrigation with dramatically increased yields. Beginning with research on wheat in Mexico under the sponsorship of the Rockefeller Foundation and the direction of Nobel-laureate Norman Borlaug, the green revolution has spread to a variety of grains and to all continents.

Averages, however, can conceal much. Although the global average of food production per capita has increased, the economically more developed countries, rather than the poorer countries, attained the largest per-capita gains. Western Europe, long a food-importing region, now has significant food surpluses and faces food disposal problems comparable with those of the United States. At the other extreme, Africa has experienced long-term declines in food production per capita (see Figure 1.3), offset for consumers only by increasing imports (and gifts) of food. The United Nations estimated that 250,000 died of starvation in the Sudan during 1988, when civil war disrupted food production and imports.

Two problems stand in the way of food sufficiency for all humans—and even challenge the gains to date. Environmental constraints pose the first. The pressures that agriculture places on forest areas, grazing areas, and the oceans continue to intensify. For example, increased grazing of animals on neighboring grassland is causing the Sahara and other deserts to expand. Production gains on currently cultivated land come from applications of fertilizers, pesticides, and irrigation water that extend the impact of food production well beyond the farm gates. For instance, fertilizer and pesticide runoffs are the most significant sources of water pollution over most of the globe. Second, great disparities exist in access to food between and within countries. Although surpluses increase in Western Europe, shortages climb in Africa. Although India has exported grain for several years since 1980, many Indians remain malnourished. Food sufficiency requires not only adequate production globally, but adequate incomes locally.

Figure 1.3 Food Production per Capita: Percent of 1961–1965

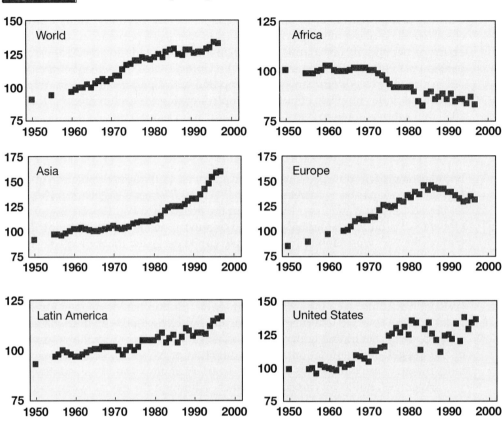

Sources: United Nations FAO, *FAO Production Yearbook* (Rome: United Nations Food and Agriculture Organization, 1965, 1975, 1985, 1987, 1991); United Nations FAO. *FAOSTAT Agriculture Data, Production Indicies.* [http://apps.fao.org/lim500.nph-wrap.pl?Crops.Primary&Domain=PIN]. November 1997.

We may be seeing the implications of these two problems in recent data on food production. Whereas global production per capita grew 11 percent in the 1970s, it has increased at only about half that rate in the last two decades. The fact that food prices have not increased suggests, however, that income is currently a more important constraint than environmental limits.

A considerable international effort now focuses on eliminating hunger. At the World Food Summit in 1996, 186 countries adopted a declaration resolving to cut the number of the world's malnourished population in half by 2015. Massive government-supported or privately supported international and intranational transfer programs could eliminate hunger, but such programs are unlikely. The best long-term solution would assist the malnourished in earning enough income to buy food on the world food market, rather than indefinitely converting them into welfare recipients.

The opportunities are spectacular. Nothing is a more basic human need than food. The world has the potential to eliminate hunger, that seemingly eternal scourge, within the lifetimes of children today. The elimination of hunger would also assure great progress against the diseases that prey on the malnourished and against the lifelong physical debilitation that can result from a single childhood bout with hunger. If humans were to slay famine, one of the four horsemen of the apocalypse, the impact on our collective self-image and our willingness to tackle other global problems could also be dramatic.

Energy Transition

In the year 1850, the burning of wood supported approximately 90 percent of the inanimate energy budget in the United States. By 1910 coal provided roughly 70 percent of U.S. energy. In 1970 the United States relied on oil and gas for close to 70 percent of its energy. Thus by 1970 the United States, and much of the rest of the world, had completed two **energy transitions** (wood to coal and coal to oil and gas), each lasting approximately 60 years. *A third energy transition is underway, and the world will be far into it by 2030–2050.* Since 1970 the global use of conventional oil as a percentage of total energy has declined, whereas coal, nuclear, and solar energy contributions have increased. Because of physical limits on resources of conventional oil and gas, by 2030–2050 they may provide less than half of our global energy budget. Although a third energy transition is underway, it is not at all clear what the dominant energy form or energy mix will be on completion.

Important turning points have marked the current transition. One that few noted at the time, the peak of oil production in the United States, occurred in 1970. Its significance became clear in 1973–1974 when global oil prices quadrupled, in part because the United States had begun to increase oil imports and compete in the world market. The global energy system will reach another turning point sometime in the first half of the twenty-first century when *global* conventional oil production will peak. In fact, the rise of global oil production to a peak and its subsequent fall, tracing a bell-shaped pattern like that of Figure 1.4, characterize the energy transition better than most other descriptions.

Past energy transitions had dramatic social and political consequences. Coal is geographically less dispersed than wood. The transition to coal thus led to greater concentrations of labor and of capital (facilitating the growth of labor movements and corporations). The energy quality of coal is also higher, in that it provides more heat per unit of weight; movement to a coal-based economy allowed the growth of steel and railroad industries. Oil and gas deposits are even more concentrated globally than coal, and their production requires still more capital and technology. The necessity of mobilizing substantial capital and high technology in the oil and gas industry supported the growth of corporations that are among the largest in the world (3 of the largest 20 corporations by sales are energy companies). The political and military importance that the world places on desert real estate in the Middle East (such as Kuwait) is obviously linked to oil and gas. So, too, is growth in the automobile industry (and the two largest industrial corporations of the world), U.S. interstate and trans-European highways, and the suburbanization of the world.

Figure 1.4 Hypothetical Oil Production and Resource Depletion Profile

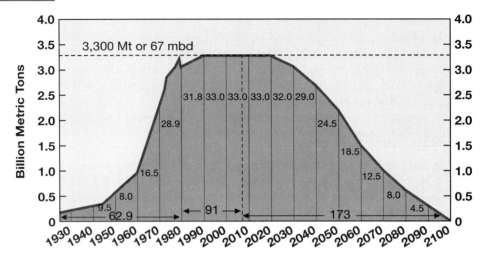

Source: International Energy Agency, *World Energy Outlook* (Paris: OECD, 1982), 215. Reprinted with permission.

In short, the nature of the energy system interacts with (it is too strong to say "causes") important developments in economic, social, and political structures. One basis for opposition to the nuclear industry, in addition to the environmental dangers of the plants and fuel cycles, is the linkage between a potentially dangerous, highly capital- and technology-intensive industry (even more so than oil and gas), and government regulation and control. Many nuclear opponents prefer local and distributed energy supplies, as rooftop solar collectors provide, to the concentrated power (electrical, economic, and political) of corporations and government (Lovins 1976). Thus the current transition will continue to be a focal point of political debate as well as of environmental and economic argument.

The energy transition poses substantial challenges. Capital investments in existing energy systems, and domestic and international political-economic arrangements based on them, will constitute an anchor, dragged along by the forces of the transition process. The anchor will periodically and grudgingly jerk loose, and then grab hold again. For example, rapid and substantial increases and decreases in oil prices (**oil shocks**) have occurred several times, and we can expect them again. Those in turn have set in motion massive international movements of capital, which can destabilize entire countries. Although the energy sector constitutes only 5 to 10 percent of the economy of most developed countries, there would be no modern economies without energy. No individual metals, manufactured products, or services can be the source of as much disruption to modern economies as changes in the availability or price of energy.

Opportunities also exist. The world's energy system has become highly concentrated geographically, with dependence of the world on the Persian Gulf. This has been a source of global political instability and conflict for many years. Whatever the newer energy system will be, it appears highly likely that such geographic concentration will decline. It is also possible, although by no means certain, that the intensive research and development efforts that accompany this energy transition will provide environmentally cleaner, less expensive, and even "eternal" energy sources.

Increased Environmental Impact

Human beings have long affected their local and regional environments in important ways, but *we now increasingly and adversely alter our global environment.* As hunters and gatherers, humans put pressure on, and probably exterminated, some food sources (Bower 1987, 284). With fixed agriculture (starting about 10,000 years ago), we began to alter the vegetation of sizable areas. Our reliance on wood for fuel and building materials, and our conversion of forests to fields, caused extensive change in woodland extent. Humans have yet to reverse the large-scale destruction, centuries ago, of forests in Lebanon (the famous cedars) and on the Dalmation coast of Croatia. In the twentieth century, forest cover in Haiti declined from more than 40–50 percent of land area to about 2 percent, whereas that in Ethiopia shrank from 40 percent to 4 percent.

In fact, large-scale deforestation may well be the first of the major global changes that humans made to their biological and physical environment. Between the initiation of significant agricultural activity and today, global forest area fell by approximately 50 percent.[1] Concerns about deforestation have shifted from the more-developed countries, where the process is stabilizing or reversing, to less-developed countries, and in particular to tropical rain forests in the Amazonian basin and in Africa. Why do we worry globally about local rain forests? Shrinking rain forests destroy habitat for local species and can lead to their extinction. Rain forest loss may also change global climate patterns.

With the industrialization of the last 200 years, the ability of humanity to wreak havoc with air, water, and biological systems grew dramatically. Initial impact was geographically limited, as with the famous coal-based smogs of London and the contemporary petroleum-based smogs of Mexico City. Damage to the world oceans was once specific to coastlines that suffered from local failure to control sewage, industrial pollution, and other effluents.

Burning fossil fuels, especially high-sulphur coal, releases sulfur and nitrogen compounds into the air; in combination with water these create **acid rain.** It is a problem crossing country borders. Scandinavians complain of damage to their lakes from acid rain originating in the heavily industrialized Ruhr area of Germany and elsewhere in Eastern and Western Europe. The Canadians complain of acid rain in their maritime provinces, traceable to steel and electric plants of the U.S. Midwest.

British scientists discovered an annually reappearing **ozone hole** in the upper atmosphere over the Antarctic that appears to be growing. Subsequent studies found that ozone depletion is also occurring globally and scientists discovered that

---

[1]Forest definitions vary so much across sources that absolute land areas in forest are difficult to specify. This estimate of reduction combines information from the World Resources Institute (1986, 61–62) and the Council on Environmental Quality (1981, 117–118).

depletion is a result of the increasing global use of chlorofluorocarbons (CFCs) and halons, which chemically interact with ozone in the upper atmosphere. Ozone in the upper atmosphere helps protect humans from ultraviolet radiation and the skin cancers that it can cause. Depletion would harm plants and animals as well.

Still another global environmental problem is the increase in atmospheric carbon dioxide (CO_2), to which burning of fossil fuels contributes most (Figure 1.5). Atmospheric CO_2 allows sunlight (short-wave solar radiation) to penetrate it, but traps the long-wave infrared or heat radiation much as glass in a greenhouse does. The **greenhouse effect** is the resultant global warming. CFCs, methane, and other gases also contribute to lesser degrees. Estimates suggest that a doubling in the atmospheric level of carbon dioxide, which could well occur near the middle of the twenty-first century, will cause a 1.5°C to 3.5°C increase in average global temperatures. We have already measured increases of about 0.7°C since 1880. In fact, 10 of the 11 warmest years ever recorded have occurred since 1987, and 1998 was the warmest on record. The greenhouse effect may cause more substantial warming of the ice-covered poles and have somewhat less effect in equatorial regions. In 1995 the prestigious Intergovernmental Panel on Climate Change released a report concluding that the earth's heating might well lead to enough melting of ice caps to increase ocean levels three feet by 2100. Recent studies of ice cores carrying temperature records of the last 100,000 years have indicated, however, that global temperature can swing by 7.0°C to 10.0°C in just a few years. Thus there is great uncertainty in forecasts.

It is difficult to see many opportunities in the increasing scale of human environmental impact. One example, however, is our ability to organize global attacks on diseases (part of our biological environment) through coordinated vaccination programs. In 1977 the United Nations World Health Organization (WHO) announced that, because of precisely such activity, it had globally eliminated smallpox infection. With a technological revolution occurring in the biological sciences, other diseases will follow smallpox. In 1994 polio was eradicated from the Western Hemisphere. "River blindness," which has taken the eyesight of more than 300,000 people, especially in equatorial regions, is a target. The opportunities lie in coordinated international attacks against problems either created by humankind (like polluted water) or predating our ability to create them (like disease).

The challenges of human impact on the environment are, however, more obvious and are very substantial. Even with respect to disease, the widespread emergence of quinine-resistant malaria and the appearance of a form of staph infection that resists all current antibiotics are frightening. With larger human numbers and greater economic activity, the scope of many environmental problems must inevitably expand. Only collective international action can handle some, like the release of CFCs. In September 1987, representatives of 22 countries met in Montreal and agreed to reduce the use of CFCs by 50 percent, no later than the year 1998; they and other countries subsequently raised the target to a complete phase-out. That is an almost unique international agreement and could serve as the prototype for others.

CFCs have substitutes, however, and the economic cost of switching to them is much lower than that of accepting large numbers of additional human cancers from ozone depletion (plus damage to crops and animal life). Reduction in use of

Figure 1.5   Increase in Atmospheric Carbon Dioxide

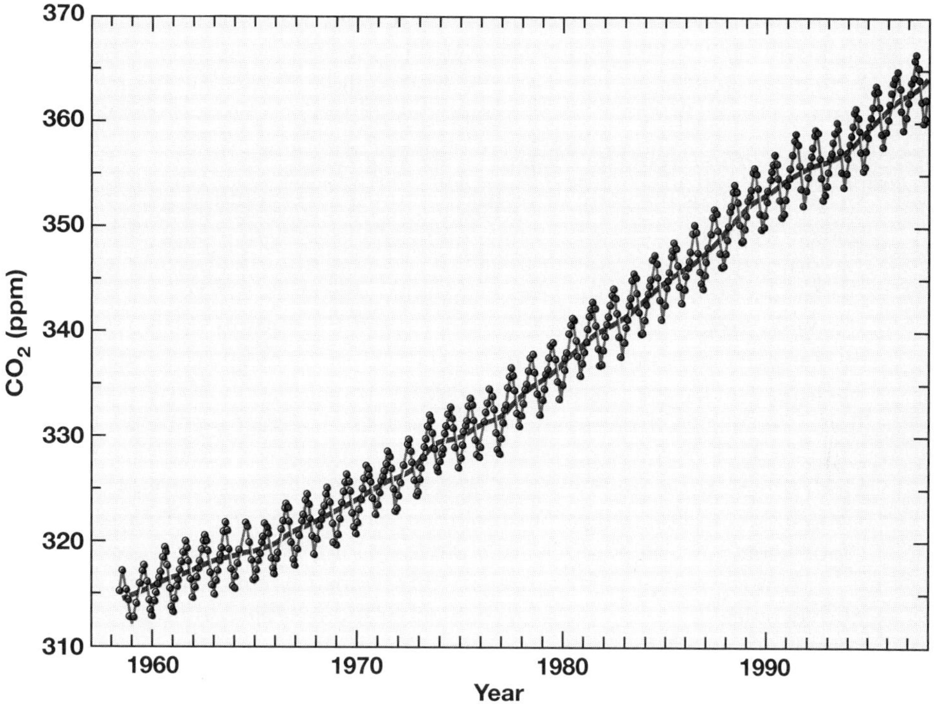

Sources: Data prior to May 1974 are from the Scripps Institution of Oceanography; data since May 1974 are from the National Oceanic and Atmospheric Administration. Principal investigators are Pieter Tans, NOAA CMDL Carbon Cycle Group, Boulder, Colorado, and Charles D. Keeling, SIO, La Jolla, California. Data courtesy of Pieter Tans.

fossil fuels and thus in creation of CO_2 is much more difficult, because the economic costs could be extraordinary. Humanity is now in the early stages of a global climate experiment. We almost certainly will double the atmospheric level of CO_2 by the middle of the twenty-first century. Our scientists now have the ability to measure the increase, the resultant change in global temperatures, and the subsequent rise in global oceans. Although some confounding factors (such as changes in atmospheric dust levels) will make direct causal linkages somewhat ambiguous, other scientists will report to humanity on the results of this grand and dangerous experiment.

Global Economic Restructuring

The world-wide economic restructuring initiated by the industrial revolution continues, but an information revolution now proceeds simultaneously in much of the world, and "globalization" of the world economy is rapid. The **industrial revolution,** which began about 200 years ago, refers generally to the social and economic changes surrounding the widespread substitution of complex machinery for the simpler tools of craft production. It continues even in the most advanced economies and is spreading throughout the world. Overlaying that process is the **information revolution,** a new phase of technological and organizational advance that both extends and supersedes the industrial revolution. Together the industrial and information revolutions have increasingly integrated the global economy through trade, financial, and technological flows in a process called globalization.

Geographic Diffusion of the Industrial Revolution

In the late 1700s the early stages of the industrial revolution transformed England and, to a somewhat lesser degree, France. Although beginning earlier in each case, the primary surge of industrialization occurred after the Civil War (1861–1865) in the United States, after the Franco-Prussian War (1870–1871) in Germany, and after the Meiji Restoration (1867) in Japan. One of the aims of the Soviet revolution in 1917 was the industrialization of Russia. Other European economies and countries of British settlement (like Canada and Australia) also underwent the transformation, primarily in the late nineteenth and early twentieth centuries. In the last half of the twentieth century a new group of industrialized countries emerged. It includes some additional European and European-settler countries (Spain, Portugal, Greece, Yugoslavia, Israel, South Africa, Brazil, Mexico, and Argentina) and the "four tigers" of Asia (South Korea, Taiwan, Hong Kong, and Singapore) (Table 1.1).

Among common requirements for industrialization are educated, literate, and technically trained workers, extensive and reliable communication and transportation capabilities, some initial investment in one or more important economic

Table 1.1	World Industrial Production	
Year	Index Value (1913 = 100)	Average Annual Growth Rate During Period (percent)
1710	0.6	
1790	1.8	1.4
1840	7.4	2.9
1913	100.0	3.6
1938	182.7	2.4
1973	1,116.0	5.3
1980	1,321.5	2.4
1990	1,636.0	2.2
1996	1,859.5	2.2
1710–1996		2.9

Sources: W. W. Rostow, *The World Economy: History and Prospect* (Austin: University of Texas Press, 1978), 49, 662; United Nations, *Statistical Yearbook 1983/84* (New York: United Nations, 1986); United Nations, *Monthly Bulletin of Statistics,* March, 1998, 250.

sectors, and a government apparatus that is supportive of industrialization internally and protective of it externally. Countries that now meet these requirements include China and India. China already is the fifth largest producer of manufactured goods in the world, and India is twelfth (World Bank 1998, 184–186). As these two demographic giants clearly join the ranks of the industrialized, they jointly have brought nearly one-third of humanity with them, roughly doubling the portion of the world living in industrialized countries.

Even in the most advanced economies, the amount of physical capital per worker and the quality of that capital continue to increase (capital consists of machinery and buildings for production). Advanced countries still experience consistent rises in manufacturing productivity (output per worker) and declines in the price of capital relative to the price of labor. For example, annual working hours in advanced industrial countries fell from about 3,000 in 1820 to 1,600 in 1992, whereas per-capita output grew by a factor of 15, implying that productivity per hour worked increased nearly 30 times during this period (Maddison 1982, 4; Maddison 1995, 248). The productivity gains and the industrial revolution continue.

The Information Revolution

The ongoing productivity trend has, however, begun to diminish the relative size of the industrial sector of advanced countries in a fashion reminiscent of earlier decline in agriculture. In the United States the agricultural sector's claim on the country's work force declined from approximately 80 percent at the time of the American revolution to 3 to 4 percent today. The industrial work force increased its share steadily until about 1910 (surpassing the agricultural work force in 1905) and remained above 30 percent of the total until the mid-1960s. Since then the industrial share of the work force has dropped steadily, to about 18 percent of the U.S. nonagricultural work force in 1996, and manufacturing as a percentage of the gross domestic product (GDP) fell from 29 percent to 18 percent.[2]

In the last 25 years, several other industrialized countries (including the United Kingdom, Belgium, France, and Germany) have experienced relative declines in the share of work force employed in manufacturing and industry. Services provide most growth in these advanced economies. Services are "things you can buy and sell, but not drop on your foot"; they include wholesale and retail trade, banking, insurance, advertising, accounting, education, and government. The service sector has become considerably more than half of the economy in what we still sometimes mistakenly call the industrialized countries (Figure 1.6).

Some portions of the service sector exhibit many of the same characteristics as blue-collar manufacturing: division of labor into simple, repetitive tasks and relatively low skill requirements. These service jobs, like fast-food processing or dry cleaning, are much like manufacturing jobs and produce or process countable things (like hamburgers). More and more white-collar jobs, however, such as teaching or scientific research, process information and do not have easily measured output.

[2]*The 1998 Information Please Almanac* (1997, 134). See also World Bank (1997), which indicated slightly slower rates of manufacturing decline in the United States and verifies similar declines in most other industrial countries.

Figure 1.6   Distribution of GNP by Development Level

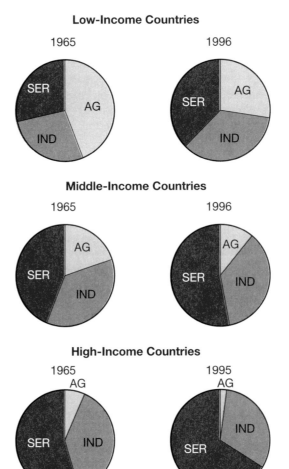

Low-Income Countries

1965   1996

Middle-Income Countries

1965   1996

High-Income Countries

1965   1995

Sources: World Bank, *World Development Report 1988* (New York: Oxford University Press, 1988); World Bank, *World Development Indicators 1997* (Washington, DC: World Bank, 1997), p. 136; World Bank, *World Development Indicators 1998* (Washington, DC: World Bank, 1998), p. 182.

Computer and communications technologies are especially important to handling information. The explosion of the World Wide Web and the movement to digital storage of information in our libraries illustrate where this revolution is taking us and the speed with which it is happening. Computer processing speeds (and memory capacity) have been doubling every 18 months for the last 30 years, one indicator of productivity growth (a phenomenon known as Moore's Law). Although still in its infancy, the information age has arrived.

| **Figure 1.7** | World Exports as Portion of World GDP |

Note: Maddison's calculations are for 56 countries, goods only. World Bank figures are for the entire contemporary world and include services.

Sources: Angus Maddison, *Monitoring the World Economy, 1820–1992* (Paris: Organization for Economic Cooperation and Development, 1995), 227, 239; World Bank, assorted issues of the *World Development Report* and *World Development Indicators.*

Globalization

The two drivers of global economic restructuring, diffusion of the industrial revolution to additional countries and the emergence of an information revolution, present wide-scale opportunities. Together they have brought some unambiguous improvements in the quality and even length of life to inhabitants of currently industrialized countries. It is likely that few would choose to live almost anywhere, at anytime before 1700, if they could live in Western Europe or North America today (assuming they could not in advance know their station in life). In addition, the communications technology of the information age is creating a growing sense of global community—it is difficult not to empathize with starving children or war-torn bodies on television.

The economic restructuring forces jointly drive a process called globalization. *Globalization* is world-wide integration of economies in the face of substantially increased transborder trade and investment. Countries of the world are more extensively and intensively linked now than ever in the past (see Figure 1.7). These ties cannot help but also to connect and perhaps even blend societies and cultures.

The challenges of the global economic restructuring and of globalization are also significant. In the more recently industrialized or industrializing countries, environmental quality has suffered. Like Mexico City, with air quality that makes Los Angeles appear pristine, the most polluted cities in the world now lie scattered across the economically less-developed portion of the globe. Another major problem is distribution of income, which generally deteriorates in at least the early stages of both industrial and information revolutions (creating problems like the Chiapas revolt in Mexico and growing income inequalities throughout Europe and North America). Underlying that problem is inequality in the ownership of the complex machinery, capital, or skills so fundamental to the industrial or information processes.

Rise and Fall in Global Position

Russia has fallen, American power and wealth are in slow relative decline, but China and the European Union are rising.[3] Although we will see that it is not easy to assign global position to particular countries, much of this book will elaborate the implications of this particular force of global change.

A primary source of clout in the world is economic strength. The United States produced considerably more than 40 percent of the world's goods and services at the end of World War II. Although the wartime destruction of many other economies inflated that number, the figure was still well over 30 percent in 1960. In the 1980s and 1990s the U.S. share varied between 22 percent and 28 percent (see Figure 1.8). This economic decline does not reflect a failure of the United States to grow, but rather a long-term tendency for it to grow more slowly than the rest of the world.[4] Similarly, in spite of very considerable absolute growth, the U.S. share of global stock markets fell from 66 percent in 1970 to 44 percent in 1997.

Net exports of goods and of capital to the rest of the world also measure global economic influence. Powerful, productive nations typically export more goods and capital than they import. The United States capped a long decline in its trade surplus (exports minus imports) with a trade deficit (more imports) in 1971; since then, deficits have been the rule. Similarly, the United States moved from a net capital exporting country to a net capital importer. Residents of other countries have greater investments in the United States than Americans do abroad.

While the U.S. share of the global economy has declined on many measures, two other global powers have risen. Between 1980 and 1995, the gross domestic product of China grew by an average of 11 percent per year, causing its share of the global economy to nearly double. The second global economy on the rise is not Japan (its economy stalled in the 1990s), but that of the European Union. Although the economic growth rates of most members of the European Union have not been exceptional, the grouping's expansion from 6 to 15 countries (with more to come) has raised it to the same global economic rank as the United States.

---

[3]Not everyone agrees that the U.S. position is in relative decline (Huntington 1988; Kugler and Organski 1989; Nau 1990).

[4]While U.S. manufacturing productivity grew by 130 percent between 1960 and 1989, that in France, Italy, and Japan grew by 239, 319, and 623 percent, respectively (National Science Foundation 1991, 111).

Figure 1.8   World Position: Global Shares

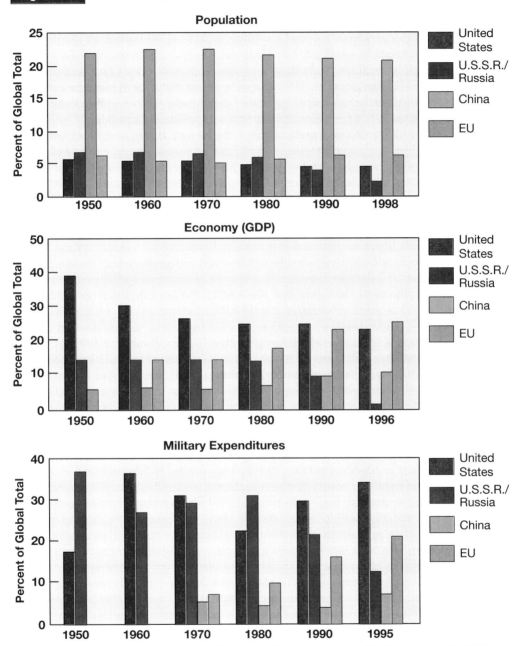

Note: Soviet/Russia economic and military expenditure estimates are highly uncertain. Pre-1991 economic size was probably overestimated and post-1991 economic size is possibly underestimated.

Sources: Assorted Publications from the United Nations, World Bank, Population Reference Bureau, U.S. Arms Control and Disarmament Agency, Stockholm International Peace Research Institute, and the U.S. Central Intelligence Agency.

An additional foundation of power is population. Although 5.9 percent of the world's population resided in the United States in 1950, the figure has fallen to 4.7 percent. Again, the European Union is now larger. China is, of course, the clear demographic giant of the world, home to more than 20 percent of the global population.

When most people think of global power, however, they focus on military strength. It is in this arena that U.S. global dominance remains most pronounced. At one time Russia, as the core of the Soviet Union, seriously threatened that global position. From an initial monopoly on nuclear capabilities (which lasted from 1945 to 1949), the U.S. advantage gradually but steadily gave way to rough parity with the Soviet Union at the end of the 1970s. In conventional forces the Union of Soviet Socialist Republics (U.S.S.R.) was the premier world power throughout the Cold War period, with the possible exception of the peak of U.S. buildup during the Vietnam War (around 1968–1970). China now maintains the largest military forces, but the United States spends by far the most.

The reference point for this discussion of global position has been the United States, primarily because its relative power was so strong at the end of World War II. Its dominant early postwar share of the global economy and nuclear military power made the United States a **hegemonic power** (the term implies an ambiguous combination of leadership and control). The collapse of the U.S.S.R. led many to argue that, contrary to the rumors of its decline, the United States had become stronger than ever. Relative to other "Great Powers" in the global system it is, in fact, exceptionally strong; any potential military threat to the United States has greatly diminished with the Soviet Union's demise. The world has, however, become increasingly integrated, and in a global context the U.S. relative decline continues slowly and irregularly on many measures, especially economic ones. That global decline cannot help but affect its ability to dominate the global system.

Many in the world probably react to gradually declining U.S. hegemony and the collapse of Soviet power with pleasure. Even many Americans may feel more comfortable in a less-commanding global role. The other side of the coin is that the U.S. position made it possible to provide important leadership on a variety of environmental, economic, and security issues; no single country can in the foreseeable future replace it in that leadership role. We will return often to some of the possible consequences of declining leadership ability.

Growth of Destructive Potential

The ability of human beings to injure or kill others continues to increase rapidly. One measure of that "progress" is explosive power. In 1500, near the beginning of the gunpowder era, the maximum explosive power of weaponry was equivalent to about 0.001 ton of trinitrotoluene (TNT). Growth was slow but steady and in World War I the cannon called Big Bertha packed a punch near one ton of TNT. The blockbuster bombs of World War II raised the power to about ten tons (see Table 1.2). The atomic bomb dropped on Hiroshima in 1945, with a force of 20 thousand tons of TNT, shifted the explosive power growth curve dramatically

Table 1.2	Milestones in Military Potential

Year	Tons of TNT Equivalent	Weapon
1500	0.001	Gunpowder "bomb"
1914	1.0	Large cannon
1940	10.0	Blockbuster bomb
1946	20,000.0	Hiroshima atomic bomb
1961	50,000,000.0	Largest hydrogen bomb

Year	Maximum Range (miles)	Weapon
1453	1.0	Cannon
1830	3.0	Coastal artillery
1915	200.0	Zeppelin raid on London
1938	750.0	European bombing formation
1949	5,000.0	Bombing plane
1959	Global	Satellite-launching missile

Sources: Robert U. Ayres, *Technological Forecasting and Long-Range Planning* (New York: McGraw-Hill, 1969), 22; *The Columbia Desk Encyclopedia,* 3rd ed. (New York: Columbia University Press, 1963), 1237, 966; Harold Sprout and Margaret Sprout, *Toward a Politics of the Planet Earth* (New York: Van Nostrand Reinhold, 1971), 403.

upward. In 1961 the Soviets tested a 50-megaton (50-million-ton) hydrogen bomb. Actual weapons of that size make little sense, given that much smaller ones can adequately destroy large cities, so countries primarily build warheads of less than one megaton.

"Quality" of weaponry is only part of the story. In 1946 the American arsenal held only nine atomic warheads, and the Soviet Union did not test its first bomb until 1949. In 1990 the United States and the former U.S.S.R. each had more than 10,000 strategic warheads and together possessed more than one million times the destructive power of the bomb that killed 140,000 in Hiroshima, Japan. There has also been a spread of the weaponry to other countries. Great Britain joined the nuclear club in 1952, France followed in 1960, China entered in 1964, and both India and Pakistan officially joined by testing bombs in 1998. Together these seven countries constitute the declared nuclear powers. Experts suspect that Israel and possibly North Korea have unannounced supplies of nuclear warheads or weapons-grade plutonium. In addition the Iraqi effort was far along when the UN coalition destroyed and dismantled it in 1991–1992, and Iran appears to harbor desires for its own weapons.

Atomic warheads are best exploded at some distance from the country deciding to use them. The Soviet Union launched a small satellite named Sputnik in October 1957 and thereby announced the impending capability of delivering warheads to targets anywhere on the globe. Canada, Germany, Israel, Japan, and all declared nuclear powers except Pakistan have now demonstrated the capability of launching satellites and therefore delivering nuclear warheads around the globe. Several other countries are also developing such missiles.

In spite of reductions in the levels of nuclear arms in the 1990s, the world remains well above an important threshold in destructive capability: Humanity has gained the ability to destroy industrial society (and some say humanity itself) with a fairly brief military exchange. Salvos of perhaps 200 warheads could paralyze the economies of the United States and Russia (by destroying, for instance, major energy facilities such as oil refineries). Full use of their thousands of strategic warheads would extensively burn cities and forests; the resulting smoke in the atmosphere around the world could block sunlight for long enough to create a **nuclear winter** (Sagan 1983). Many of those whom the initial explosions did not kill would die from radiation burns or starve as crops failed and social structures deteriorated. Few turning points and thresholds listed in this chapter can be as important.

Increased Social Mobilization

Another important global transition is the *rapid social mobilization of peoples around the world.* **Social mobilization** is the process of transforming the conditions and attitudes of people from the traditional to the modern (Deutsch 1961). Among the many conditions that modernization transforms are educational and literacy levels and the extent of social interactions. Attitudinally, people come to believe that their own actions can improve their conditions of life. These changes frequently precede increased demands for social, economic, and political participation.

Education is a high priority in societies around the world. Global education expenditures take approximately 5 percent of total economic output, about the same as that absorbed by health spending and now considerably more than the military (Sivard 1996, 44). In 1960 5 of every 1,000 people globally were teachers, whereas that figure now approximates 8 (those bearing arms have declined from 6 to about 4 per 1,000). In the poorest countries of the world, only 37 percent of primary school-aged populations attended school in 1950; that number grew to 51 percent in 1960, and it is now near 100 percent (Figure 1.9).[5] Literacy rates reflect the educational effort. In 1955 a majority of the people of the world older than 15 years of age were literate for the first time (Deutsch 1988, 313) and now the global rate approximates 70 percent. The advance of literacy in the economically least-developed countries is especially rapid; it is now near 65 percent.

Exposure to print media has increased with literacy. Access to electronic media (radio, movies, and television) is increasing even faster. For instance, the number of radios per 1,000 population globally has climbed from 159 in 1965 to 364 (Figure 1.10). Televisions per 1,000 increased from 55 to 228 since 1965.

The exposure of human beings to a broad range of other humans, and to their ideas, also rises with urbanization. More than 46 percent of humans live in cities. The portion of humanity dwelling in cities increases by nearly 5 percent each decade and should reach 50 percent around 2006. The total is already 76 percent in the high-income countries (World Bank 1998, 30).

[5]Meyer and others (1979, 40); World Bank (1979 and 1992a). These figures suffer from significant measurement problems. The true numbers could be as much as 20 percent lower.

Figure 1.9 School Enrollment in Low-Income Countries

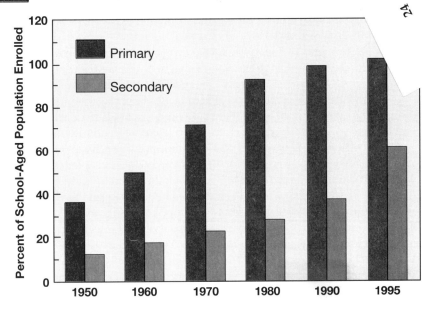

Sources: John W. Meyer, Francisco O. Ramierez, Richardson Rubinson, and John Boli-Bennett, "The World's Educational Revolution, 1950–70," in *National Development and the World System,* ed. John W. Meyer and Michael T. Hannon (Chicago: The University of Chicago Press, 1979), 37–55; World Bank, *World Development Report* (Washington, DC: World Bank, 1979, 1983, 1989, and 1992); World Bank, *World Development Indicators* (Washington, DC: World Bank, 1998), 78.

Karl Deutsch expressed the importance of these changes:

> In all these respects, and many others, the patterns of thousands of years are breaking in our lifetime. Some of these changes seem slow on the time scale of a busy year or two, but they are dramatically swift when seen on a scale of decades or generations. Faster than ever before, humanity is being transformed in its social and economic structures and informed by its mass communications. . . . The upshot of many of these changes is a thrust of people toward politics. (Deutsch 1988, 313–314)

The implications of social mobilization for political participation are difficult to measure. On the average, however, the societies with the highest levels of social mobilization are those with the most open and democratic political processes. The pressures for greater democracy in South Korea, Taiwan, Russia, and China illustrate how economic advance underlies social mobilization, which in turn calls forth demands for greater control over one's own destiny. Political systems do not always accommodate the increased pressures gracefully. Both violent and nonviolent political protest have been increasing over time around much of the world.

In addition, social mobilization often expresses itself in nationalism, a force that both created and destroyed countries over the last 100 years and is far from spent. Ethnic groups, as they mobilize, often seek to establish control over their

Figure 1.10 Exposure to Communication

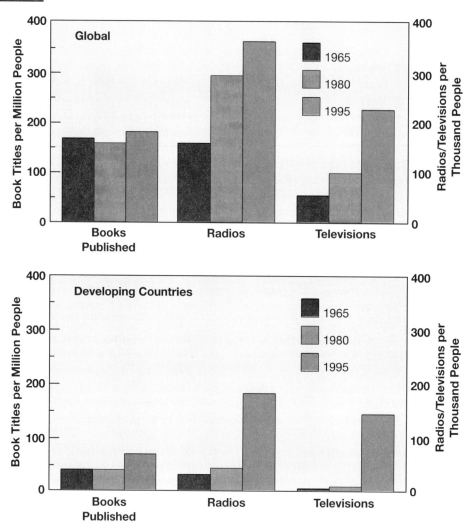

Note: Data for books published is 1994, not 1995.

Sources: Statistical Yearbook 1992 (Paris: United Nations Educational, Scientific, and Cultural Organization), 6–11, 6–19, 6–20; United Nations Development Program, *Human Development Report, 1998* (New York: United Nations, 1998), 167.

own government and sometimes attempt to expel or subjugate others. It is possible that when historians look back on the twentieth century they will describe it primarily in terms of the power of nationalism and the breakdown of the nineteenth-century empires.

Another and generally more peaceful manifestation of social mobilization is the rapid proliferation in developing countries of grass-roots organizations for self-help activities ranging from building a school or health clinic, to reforesting a hillside, to establishing a credit union. The organizations include co-operatives, mothers' clubs, religious groups, neighborhood federations, and many others.

Social mobilization also spills across the borders of countries. The internationalization of media and the expansion of global travel and personal communication create worldwide communities with shared interests and often with collective political agendas. There are now more global actors, with broader issue interests than ever before in world politics. Voluntary organizations such as Greenpeace (environmental protection), Amnesty International (protection of human rights), and Beyond War (nuclear war avoidance) translate increased mobilization into global political pressure. They act upon an increasing recognition of collective human interests and of failure by individual countries to satisfy them.

Uncertain Implications of Trends

This chapter sketched eight global forces or megatrends.[6] There is no way to identify the most important global development forces scientifically, so any list will be subjective and probably incomplete. For instance, the chapter considered the advance of technologies like electronics only as implicit in other trends. Other analysts might point to the buildup of debt in economically less-developed countries or of financial surplus in China as important trends. In fact, throughout this book we will direct considerable attention to technology, debt, and still other forces and trends.

The many interacting forces of change, with the multiple opportunities they present and challenges they pose, create a base on which widely varying understandings of global relations rest. For instance, pessimists point with alarm to the growing global population and slowing gains in food supply per capita, to growing human ability to damage the environment, and to the insecurity that nuclear weapons have brought to the world, an insecurity that proliferation amplifies. Optimists see hope in the declining rate of global population growth, in long-term growth of physical ability to feed that population, in the spread of the information revolution, and in the mobilization of peoples on behalf of human rights and democracy.

Are you relatively pessimistic about global futures or more optimistic? Why? This book, in addition to presenting the reader with basic information about world politics, constitutes an exploration of such competing understandings of the world—of a clash of perspectives. More specifically, this text presents multiple images of the global superstructure that rests on the substructure of the eight forces this chapter identified. The multiple understandings present generally coherent but sometimes quite limited views of the world. Many readers will find one or more especially compatible with their own interpretations. This author does not seek to convert you, but asks only that you look seriously at the possibility that other perspectives can supplement and enrich your own.

---

[6]Naisbitt (1982) coined the expression *megatrends,* but elaborated a very different set from that of this chapter.

Selected Key Terms

Cold War

demographic transitions

dependent population

energy transitions

oil shocks

acid rain

ozone hole

greenhouse effect

industrial revolution

information revolution

hegemonic power

nuclear winter

social mobilization

CHAPTER 2

Elements of Analysis

The Central and Eastern European revolutions of 1989–1991 have already entered global history alongside the American and French Revolutions of 1775–1783 and 1789–1792, the European revolutions of 1848, and the Russian Revolution of 1917–1918 that established a communist government. In December 1988 the Supreme Soviet of the Union of Soviet Socialist Republics (U.S.S.R.) changed the country's constitution to create a new legislature (the Congress of People's Deputies), to be elected in a partially democratic process involving multiple candidates for many seats. The rewriting also strengthened the presidency. These developments signaled a potential shift of power from the institutions of the Communist party to those of the government proper and to a broad electorate. In January 1989 Poland legalized Solidarity, the trade-union movement that had become an important noncommunist opposition force in the early 1980s and was then banned. These actions, and many others, set in motion a period that only the word "revolutionary" can describe. Subsequent events have dramatically transformed the area that we once called the Soviet bloc and which we now call Central and Eastern Europe: the former U.S.S.R., Poland, the former Czechoslovakia, Hungary, united Germany, Romania, Bulgaria, the former Yugoslavia, and Albania.

In March 1989 opposition and reform candidates stunned the Soviet leadership with their elections for the new Congress of People's Deputies— even many unopposed communist candidates lost because voters struck their names from ballots. Hungary, already farther along in political and economic change than other countries of the region, began in May to remove the barbed wire from its 150-mile-long border with Austria. After this first tangible lifting of the

KEY WEB LINKS

www.aber.ac.uk/~inpwww/
resour.html

www.refdesk.com/facts.html

www.clark.net/pub/lschank/
web/country.html

www.etown.edu/home/selchewa/
international_studies/firstpag.htm

www.ntu.edu.sg/library/
statdata.htm

"iron curtain," East Germans began to use Hungary as an escape route to Austria and then on to West Germany. Liberalization progressed rapidly.

Solidarity made an agreement with the Polish regime that allowed it to contest about half of Polish Parliamentary seats, and it then swept all but one of those open seats. In August it took control of the government—the first non-communist government in the region. Protests in East Germany and continued flight of its citizens to the West led to a decision on November 9, 1989, to open the walls between East and West Germany. Massive demonstrations in Czechoslovakia and even Bulgaria swept hard-line leaderships from office; Vaclav Havel, a noncommunist, who had been imprisoned not much earlier, took the presidency in Czechoslovakia. A bloody but quick revolution in Romania toppled the dictatorship there.

In February 1990 the Central Committee of the Communist party in the Soviet Union voted to suggest the elimination from the constitution of Article 6, which guaranteed the leading political and social role to the party. Most Central European leaderships had already renounced similar articles. Throughout Eastern and Central Europe, elections and leadership turnover extended into 1990 the revolutionary change of 1989. Astounding agreements between East and West allowed German reunification at the end of the year. By the end of 1990, economic and political conditions had changed so much that the United States began to offer food aid to its major adversary.

In 1991 the earth shaking continued. The Warsaw Treaty Alliance of European communist countries dissolved itself in July. The United States and the Soviet Union signed a major conventional arms-control treaty with countries throughout Europe and signed a bilateral agreement to reduce nuclear arms very substantially. After a coup attempt by the Communist party and army in the fall, Russian president Yeltsin barred activities of the party. Most dramatic, on December 25, the Russian flag replaced the Soviet flag above the Kremlin, announcing the end of the U.S.S.R.

By the end of 1991 the world had changed fundamentally. Russia and the 14 other former republics of the U.S.S.R. joined the United Nations, World Bank, and International Monetary Fund, and they appealed for a major Western aid package.

Three Subject-Matter Categories for Analysis

We have described what happened in the revolution of 1989–1991. But why did it happen? The purpose of this book is not to give you dates and facts to memorize. The purpose is to provide you with analytical tools for the understanding of these events and many others. The purpose of this chapter is to introduce many of these tools to you. The rest of the book elaborates and uses them. We start with a division of our subject matter into three categories and a delineation of some of the specific elements that we typically look for in each category.

Political-Military Aspects

This period of revolution demonstrates much that is at the core of world politics. The power of the Soviet Union dominated Central Europe following World War II, when Soviet armies remained in place after pushing out the Germans. That mili-

Figure 2.1   The Subject Matter of World Politics

Central Subject Focus	Important Forces/Trends

Politics

Rise and Fall in Global Position

Growth of Destructive Potential

Increased Social Mobilization

Economics

Global Economic Restructuring:

1. Industrial Revolution

2. Information Revolution

3. Globalization

Broader Environment

Demographic Transition

Growing Food Sufficiency

Energy Transition

Increased Environmental Impact

tary strength allowed the U.S.S.R. to install governments subservient to it throughout the region. Soviet military force subsequently crushed reform movements in Hungary in 1956 and in Czechoslovakia in 1968 and discouraged other efforts to escape Communist domination.

Thus, leadership changes in the U.S.S.R. and decreased willingness and ability of that leadership to continue the use of repressive force were critically important factors in the revolutions of 1989–1991. In March 1985 Mikhail Gorbachev took the reins of the Soviet Communist party and articulated a vision of economic and political reform—a vision of peaceful revolution. One debate that will occupy historians for many years is whether the changes would have occurred more slowly, or perhaps not at all, with different top leadership. Another is whether the military buildup of the United States in the 1980s intensified the pressure for reform in the Soviet Union or whether internal forces in that country would have inevitably given rise to it (Risse-Kappen 1991). On one issue there can be little debate: The decreasing power of both the United States and the Soviet Union, relative to many other global actors, had gradually weakened the ability of both to play dominant roles in Western and Central Europe.

The events forced large numbers of new power and security (war and peace) questions onto the agendas of the United States and countries in Western Europe. How should countries sympathetic to the democratic reforms of the East react? How actively should they provide economic support to encourage the process but not signal an attempt to dominate the region? What is the role of NATO after the lifting of the "iron curtain"? What forces, in armies, secret services, communist parties, or nationalistic movements might reverse some or all of the changes, and how can the outside world reduce the danger of reversal? It will be many years before answers to all these questions become clear.

A focus on power politics alone, however, cannot help us fully understand the events of 1989–1991 and their aftermath. Ideas and ideals play a critical role. For instance, communist thought evolved as communists examined their record of structuring political and economic systems and found it wanting. Many former communist parties in Central and Eastern Europe increasingly looked to the social democratic parties of Western Europe for models of success.

Similarly, a belief by many people in universal human rights was important. In 1975 the members of both military alliances (NATO and the Warsaw Pact) and a number of neutral countries in Europe signed an agreement (the Helsinki Final Act) that pledged their attention to such rights as access to communication, freedom of travel, and freedom of political organization. Although the Eastern countries often ignored or repressed these rights, the pressures built both internally and externally for serious commitment to them. In fact, Mikhail Gorbachev, the last leader of the U.S.S.R., reported in his memoirs that

> The principal reason for the changes is not to be found in the machinations of the imperialist West. What lay behind them was the irresistible striving by all peoples for freedom, and their desire to liberate themselves from the presence of foreign military bases and foreign troops on their territory; in effect to be freed from the caprice of Big Brother. (*The Economist,* August 12, 1995, 73)

Many ideas and ideals define the appropriate boundaries of community in different ways from traditional borders of countries (just as advocates of human rights focus on values *they* believe are common to a global community, not just to those on one side or the other of the Cold War). It is impossible to understand the developments of recent years without understanding commitments to both national (ethnic) and religious communities. For example, the Soviet Union forcibly incorporated Lithuania, Latvia, and Estonia, collectively known as the Baltic Republics, into the union in August 1939. In August 1989, on the fiftieth anniversary of that occasion, one million citizens of the Baltic Republics peacefully formed a human chain across the region to demonstrate solidarity and to protest for independence.

Throughout the entire region, many borders failed and often still fail to conform to the historic homelands of peoples. The pressure for unification of the Germanies originated in the shared belief that the citizens of both were Germans—not East Germans or West Germans. Non-Russian peoples constituted half of the population in the Soviet Union, and most wanted their independence. Similarly, the formation of Yugoslavia at the end of World War I unified Serbs, Slovenes, Albanians, Croatians, and others, and pressures for autonomy of those nationalities date from that event.

Religious communities also crisscross the area. Orthodox, Catholic, and Moslem loyalties divide former Yugoslavia as clearly as nationalistic ones do. The southern portions of the former Soviet Union contain many Islamic peoples. Traditional disputes between them and Christian Armenians and Georgians intensified after 1990.

Although many look at the revolutionary events in this region and see issues of power and security, war and peace, many others look and see issues of autonomy and independence, freedom and community. A relatively complete understanding requires examination through both sets of lenses. Comprehension, however, requires even more.

Economic Aspects

A period of poor economic performance preceded and accompanied the revolutions. Economic growth of the region was weaker throughout the 1980s than it had been earlier. Exact figures are uncertain, because the communist governments often used statistics to trumpet achievements, including nonexistent ones. The fact that the East was falling steadily behind the West was, however, apparent to anyone who could make comparisons through books and magazines, television and movies, or travel.

The communist governments had many real economic success stories in earlier years. They built heavy industry and infrastructure (for instance, highways, railroads, and power grids). In the mid-1960s the Soviet Union boasted of its achievements in industrialization and pointed to a growth rate that surpassed that of the United States. As the nature of the leading world economies shifted from industry to services and information, however, communists proved much less competent. Central planning had been more capable of replicating large industrial complexes than it was of establishing systems to serve either producers or consumers quickly and flexibly.

In the late 1970s and early 1980s several Eastern European countries began to look to the West for economic assistance in the form of loans to help them overcome relative economic stagnation. Several took on substantial debt. The repression that the Romanian leadership, later overthrown in bloodshed, applied to its people grew in part from an effort to repay that debt quickly. Poland and Hungary had especially substantial burdens and continued efforts to reorganize their economies so as to repay those debts. That helps us understand why those two countries blazed the trail toward market economies during this revolutionary period.

Given the economic precursors of the revolution, it is not surprising that many new economic questions appeared on the agenda of countries by the end of this period. How rapidly should formerly communist countries with state ownership of all major economic assets shift those assets and the responsibility for economic decision making to private individuals and firms? How should they balance the benefits of reform against the probable unemployment that would result from it? How rapidly should they open their economies to those of the West, risking dependence to gain the benefits of foreign trade and technology? On the Western side, should the United States and Western Europe provide massive programs of economic aid? What should the conditions be? These questions raise perennial issues of economic well-being and growth and of distribution (within and between countries).

Broader Environment

A fuller understanding of these spectacular events also requires that we look at a broader environment including developments in population, food, energy, and the biological-physical environment. A focus on demographic factors provides some insights. For example, in Romania a negative population growth rate led the regime to ban abortion and to actively encourage births. The repressive methods it used in this effort were among the factors that encouraged the revolt. Similarly, in the Soviet Union, the greater birth rates of non-Russian peoples, especially the Islamic populations, both strengthened their position and raised Russian fears of becoming a minority in their own country.

Food, another aspect of the broader environment, was especially important in setting the stage for the revolutions. The systems of collective agriculture in the East proved incapable of improving the diets of the people, much less of sustaining the region's traditional position as the breadbasket of Europe. In general, access to a diverse and attractive diet improved as one traveled from East to West in the communist region and approached the conditions available in Western Europe. Citizens were aware of this pattern and saw the West as a model for their own agriculture.

Energy was a factor of great importance. The Soviet Union (especially Russia) was the world's largest producer of both oil and natural gas. It still supplies a large portion of the energy of Central Europe and exports to Western Europe. This provided Russia with a basis for considerable leverage over its neighbors. For many years it paid a cost to maintain that leverage, however, because it effectively subsidized the energy systems of its fellow Soviet republics and allies by trading its oil at reduced prices for inferior goods (by world standards) from Central Europe. One reason Russia not only became willing to allow its former Central European "satellites" and sister republics to improve relations with the West, but effectively encouraged them to do so, is that this allowed Russia to begin charging Central Europe for oil and other raw materials at world prices in Western currency. In short, Russia began to use its energy for the purchase of Western goods rather than for the purchase of political-economic control. The change also opened access to Western technology for its oil fields at a time when the state of Russia's own technology proved inadequate to sustain production levels.

The condition of the biological-physical environment also enters into a more complete understanding of the revolutions. The emphasis of communist governments on heavy industry using rather old technology, combined with a suppression of mechanisms that people might have used to protest deteriorating local environmental conditions, led to wide-scale abuse of the environment throughout Central and Eastern Europe. Some of the first opposition parties throughout the region were "greens"—environmental activists. In Bulgaria, "Ecoglasnost" played an important role in overthrowing the communist leadership of Zhikov. In Hungary, the struggle against a dam on the Danube honed political skills later used for more general reform efforts (French 1990).

The Importance of All Three Subject-Matter Categories

Scholars of world politics often refer to questions of military and strategic significance—questions of war and peace—as **high politics.** Economic or environmental issues are **low politics.** Stark separation of these issues is somewhat recent; for centuries studies of politics and economics were inextricably linked because the dominant perspective was that a country's economic performance and external power were highly interdependent.

In 1776, however, Adam Smith published *The Wealth of Nations* and laid the foundations for a view that wealth of countries could best be increased without the active intervention of governments. Adam Smith's philosophy of laissez faire (nonintervention by the government in the economy) gradually came to be a powerful force in intellectual and policy communities and in establishing boundaries between politics and economics. Simultaneously, European and North American economies industrialized, left predominantly agricultural societies behind, and pushed back threats of starvation. With these developments the once all-encompassing study of political economy split into more and more specialized subdivisions: Not only did demography emerge as a separate field, but politics and economics parted company and further split into subfields such as agricultural economics or world politics.

The revolutions of 1989–1991 suggest that, in spite of these intellectual divisions, economics and politics remain tightly connected in reality. Moreover, that discussion and the forces outlined in Chapter 1 suggest the need to extend the subject matter of world politics even beyond politics and economics. The onset of the energy transition exposed the linkages between resource availability and the power and security of countries; such linkages had been of great concern to students of politics early in the century but were downplayed thereafter. In addition, the emergence of human ability to damage the global environment has created an entirely new and important arena of global policy concern. Three interconnected foci or subject matters thus organize the discussion here: politics, economics, and the broader environment.

A Structure of Understanding

Only combined attention to strictly political elements (both domestic and foreign), economic factors, and a broader environment can provide a fairly complete understanding of events and issues in world politics. Each of these categories, however, contains a tremendous mass of potential information—the preceding sketch of the background and aftermath of the revolutions of 1989–1991 conveyed only a small part of it. And each category draws our attention to truly fundamental and important questions. How can we more systematically approach world politics, so that in attempting to understand a new issue or episode we know what to look for and how to organize it? You need more tools.

A systematic study of world politics cannot consist solely of individual case studies, like the discussion of the revolutions of 1989–1991, treating every episode of global relations in isolation. Fundamentally, we want to generalize. For instance,

we want a more general understanding of dramatic transformations in political relations, one that might allow us to see the similarities and differences between contemporary events and those at the end of World War II. We want more general understanding so that we might anticipate such transformations and so that we can
make them as peaceful as possible. Yet as the physicist Frank Oppenheimer
pointed out, "Understanding is a lot like sex; it's got a practical purpose, but that's
not why people do it normally." That is, we also seek to generalize concerning
crises, alliances, treaties, wars, and other interactions among countries for the pure
pleasure of better understanding.

Figure 2.2 portrays a hierarchy of understanding that structures our knowledge about global politics and our generalizations concerning it. At the most basic
level are raw data or unpatterned **facts.** Gorbachev came to power in the Soviet
Union in 1985. Reagan led a substantial U.S. military buildup in the 1980s. The Soviet Union revised its constitution in late 1988. The Hungarians initiated economic
reforms earlier than other Central European countries.

Such facts are critical to our understanding, but they are only a beginning.
If our knowledge about the revolutions of 1989–1991 were limited to facts, we
might be good at answering trivia questions about them, but we would have no
basis for saying anything about the period after World War II. One of the most
basic ways in which we organize facts and extend our knowledge is via concepts. **Concepts** are labels for general categories of phenomena. An important
concept in both periods (post-World War II and the late 1980s) is power. A discussion of the power of the United States, the U.S.S.R., and countries in Western
and Central Europe helps organize facts important to our understanding of the

Figure 2.2   Hierarchy of Understanding

Levels	Elements/Capabilities Introduced
World Views	Values Prescriptions
Theories	Dynamics Forecasts
Propositions	Relationships
Concepts	Generality
Facts/Data	Unpatterned Information

events and outcomes. Defining and measuring power satisfactorily pose considerable difficulty (see Chapter 4), but are essential for discussion of a broad range of phenomena in world politics.

Just as facts have little or no meaning without concepts, concepts individually have limited use. Assume for the moment that we have defined power in terms of military capabilities, and we agree that the U.S.S.R. had several times as much power as the countries of Central Europe in the late 1980s. This concept of power takes on real meaning only when it is linked in **propositions** to other concepts, such as success or failure in the accomplishment of objectives. Voltaire nicely summarized a proposition linking the two concepts (power and success) when he supposedly said that "God is always on the side of the larger battalions" (Ray 1990, 198). That is, greater power most often facilitates accomplishment of objectives. The fact that the U.S.S.R. failed to sustain its domination of the region seems to contradict this proposition. Soviet power had, however, slipped relative to that of countries in Western Europe, which competes in many ways for influence in Central Europe. Such analysis might lead us to a second, related proposition: Third parties often enter into power struggles in support of the weaker party, thereby offsetting the power of the stronger party.

Propositions, when linked together in clusters and used to explain or predict, constitute **theory.** A theory such as one that clusters related propositions on the utility of power provides explanations of world events. Theory often assists in understanding the unfolding of events over time—that is, understanding the dynamics of the events. It should, if the theory is "good," also carry some predictive capability, for instance, the ability to foresee the most probable outcomes of future power struggles. As it does with key concepts, this text also highlights, in boldface type, names of theories, such as the greenhouse effect or the balance of power, when it first explains them. (*The glossary provides full definitions.*)

Worldviews selectively choose among competing theories. Two bases for the selection stand out. First, *alternative* worldviews emphasize different basic agents or units of analysis. Although one may emphasize states (countries) and their interactions, another may draw our attention to individuals, and a third to economic actors and markets.[1] Second, and related, *competing* worldviews highlight different values (both those of agents and those of worldview adherents). While one worldview may stress the value that countries place on security, another may focus on the desire of ethnic communities for independence or autonomy.

Values add a prescriptive element to worldviews that is missing from theories.[2] Theories explain and perhaps predict, but worldviews also prescribe. When we combine an emphasis on theory concerning the efficacy of power with a value

---

[1]Analysis within each worldview often proceeds at more than one level of analysis, for instance at both an individual level (state, class, individual, or firm) and systemic level (state system, class structure, community, or market). That is, levels of analysis do not distinguish worldviews.

[2]Worldviews have much in common with paradigms but the typical definition of paradigms (Kuhn 1970) recognizes neither the attention to the different agents nor the role of values. Ferguson and Mansbach (1988) correctly stressed the necessity of addressing values in social science (see also Holsti 1985, 132–133). Banks (1984) summarized how the study of world politics evolved toward the formulation of competing worldviews and how it needs a more integrated perspective; this book seeks to move toward such integration.

judgment that the use of force is not inherently wrong, the combination becomes a worldview. That particular worldview led some observers of the revolutions in 1989–1991 to interpret them as a successful outcome of pressure applied on the U.S.S.R. by the United States and its European allies, especially by the U.S. military buildup of the 1980s.

Conversely, it is possible to reject the utility of theory based on power in understanding what happened during this period. An observer could instead reasonably argue that the transformation was the result of growing global commitment to basic human rights, including democracy, and a communication of that same attachment to Central and Eastern Europe by interstate agreements and interpersonal contacts. These views appeared to strongly influence Gorbachev and many other communist leaders. In other words, a theoretical understanding of how the world works that downplays power, emphasizes growing global community, and values protection of individual rights, provides a very different "understanding" of the period.

Clash of Perspectives: Competing Worldviews

The hierarchy of understanding should make somewhat clearer the constant tension that exists in the study of world politics between facts and interpretation. If our study of the subject matter required only facts, we could potentially all have the same understanding of world politics. *Facts do not, however, speak for themselves.* They are organized by concepts, structured by theories, interpreted by worldviews, and evaluated in the light of individual and subjective value systems.

Some argue that this places students of world politics in the position of the blind men and the elephant, with each man touching a different part of the elephant and interpreting the entire beast in terms of the treelike leg, the ropelike tail, or the fanlike ear. But that is a poor analogy. We can exchange facts and thereby gain a broader perspective. We can argue about concepts and definitions and generally agree on some useful ones. We can build, present, debate, and test theories, ultimately expanding the understanding of all engaged in the enterprise. We can even attempt to identify our own values and the worldviews linked to them, and to communicate those to others. In all these ways, knowledge and understandings become more scientific and more nearly universal.

We will, however, never all come to share the same values or perspectives, and there will always be a clash of perspectives. As a result, in policy debates we will continue to choose differentially among bodies of theory, concepts, and facts. Our task in the study of world politics is complicated. We want to identify as large a body of "knowledge" as possible. Yet we never want to forget that perspectives clash strongly, even in the face of our large and growing knowledge. We clearly need to study competing perspectives. As an aid, this text identifies three sets of worldviews that dominate interpretation of world politics for many North Americans and Europeans. Both scholars and practitioners recognize these views to be coherent and important. Identifying them allows us to proceed further to outline the theories, concepts, and facts on which they draw. Each of the three succeeding parts of this volume, on world politics, political economy, and the broader environmental context of world politics, elaborates a small number of primary worldviews.[3] We only preview them here.

Realism, Liberalism, and Constructivism

Realism portrays the world political system as an anarchic struggle for power and security among competing states (countries). No higher authority (at least none with any real capability to enforce its judgment) exists than these states. Thus states individually, or in alliance with other states, provide for their own defense. Power is the only effective means of assuring security. Because each state's efforts to increase its own power and security pose a potential threat to all other states, regular conflict among states is inevitable. This description of the world also frames the realist's prescription—security and peace follow only from vigilance and willingness to act individually or in concert to prevent any state from achieving a preeminent and threatening position.

If you see the outlines of the power struggle between the U.S.S.R. and the United States after 1945 in this portrayal of the world, you are right. In the United States, the prevailing wisdom was that it should maintain sufficient military power (in alliances, if not alone) to prevent any significant gains by the U.S.S.R. "The price of freedom [or peace] is eternal vigilance." The U.S.S.R. obviously had its own realists. A principal lesson that both countries drew from World War II was that leaders had not mobilized adequately and early enough against the enemy, in that case Hitler.

Liberalism portrays the world in terms of individuals seeking more freedom and better living conditions, as well as physical security and other values (in one excellent summary, "life, liberty, and the pursuit of happiness"). Lest the term be confusing, we should note immediately that it does not refer to "liberal" in the sense of the American liberal-conservative political spectrum. It means liberal in a "classical" sense, that is, those who focus their attention on the individual.

Both those who support relatively active assistance by the state to individuals (as do modern American liberals) and those who oppose it (as do American conservatives) may fall within the general rubric of liberalism as defined here, because of their emphasis on improving the lot of the individual. Classical liberalism is, in fact, a dominant perspective in the United States. Many Americans are liberal domestically and realist internationally. We shall see, however, that highly developed realist and liberal understandings of the world can come into conflict, especially when liberals believe that states are restrictive of individual action.

Constructivism portrays the world in terms of identity groupings and social structures, rather than states or individuals. Ethnic or national groups define identity for many people and attract their intense loyalty. Religious groupings command similar devotion from many others. Gender, race, and class often define the

---

[3]There is considerable variation in the field of international relations concerning the major worldviews or paradigms and their relationships to each other. For a brief but useful summary of proposed typologies, see Holsti (1985, 5–7). Lapid (1989) indicated the confusion that alternative paradigms, competing underlying premises, and pluralism in methodology have introduced to the field. The presentation in this volume may help clarify the issue through its specification of conceptual, theoretical, and value bases of each worldview.

identity of and position of people both within and across societies. When states reinforce the boundaries of identity groupings, realist and constructivist aspirations very happily coexist. The relationship between these two lenses on the world is complicated. The same is true for constructivist and liberal perspectives.

Commercial Liberalism, Mercantilism, and Neo-Marxism

When we move from predominately political subject matter to greater emphasis on political economy, we will find that a similar set of worldviews dominates discussion. **Commercial liberalism** is a strand of liberalism that focuses on economics. It dates back to Adam Smith, who argued that markets free of government control provide economic benefits for all participants and maximize aggregate economic well-being. It emphasizes *individuals* in their economic roles as producers and consumers.

Mercantilism is similarly an extension of realism to political economy. It portrays the state not as just a political actor interested in security, but as an economic actor interested in wealth. Mercantilists argue that states can, do, and should use the economy as a tool for their own purposes. If economic strength contributes to military capability, and such contribution is difficult to dispute, then perhaps states should consciously strengthen their economies. The states might accomplish this, for example, through higher tariffs (taxes on imports) to keep the goods of other economies out and to encourage higher production of domestic factories. Although commercial liberals disagree that such "help" actually improves economic performance in the long run, states have a long history of engaging in just such activity. Japan and South Korea are only recent examples of countries where the governments played an active role in building the economies.

Yet there is complementarity as well as conflict between realist-mercantilist and liberal perceptions of the world. Both place a premium on rational, self-interested action by major actors. From the viewpoint of realists and liberals, that behavior not only provides benefits to individual actors, but provides collective benefits for all. This is best known in the liberal theory of laissez faire. By attempting to maximize profit as a producer or utility as a consumer, these actors assure greater production and more efficient use of resources. For instance, a producer might develop a new technology or discover a low-cost resource from which it profits handsomely and that may also provide real benefits to others who eventually adopt the technology or profit from the low production costs associated with it. Similarly, in interstate politics, states may attempt to provide only their own security, but in so doing may maintain a broader balance of power that can benefit other states.

Neo-Marxism is a third worldview on political economy. Because it builds a model of society up from socially constructed economic classes, there are ties between neo-Marxism and constructivism. In contrast to realism and mercantilism, it does not portray the economy as the instrument of the state but sees instead the state as an instrument of economic agents. Many variations on this challenge have roots in the Marxist argument that the nature of economic production determines social and political relations. A traditional agricultural society generates a feudal division between those who work the land and the aristocrats who own it and who, simultaneously and derivatively, hold political control. The rise of capitalism creates a division between those who work in the new industries and the capitalists or bourgeoisie who own them; capitalists supplant the aristocrats in political leadership. Once in control of the state, this class uses state power to protect its domestic prerogatives and to expand its foreign opportunities (markets, raw material access, and investment outlets). Thus, a global structure arises in which those who own capital and those who do *not* remain bound together and at the same time in natural opposition.

Modernism and Eco-Wholism

Modernism is a worldview that provides an environmental context for world politics and global economics. Modernists draw our attention to the concept of progress—to the increasing human mastery of physical and biological environments. Regular breakthroughs in technology play a central role in this advance.

Modernists point to the steady extension of life spans, initially in Europe but now worldwide, as a key indicator of progress. Life spans respond to progress in diverse arenas, especially conquering or controlling diseases and ensuring adequate shelter and food to greater percentages of humans globally. Modernism is optimistic, because technology or knowledge is easily transmitted and potentially provides benefits to all who share in it. Prescriptively, modernists argue that states and economic actors should not impede technological progress and should, in fact, further it.

Challengers to modernism point to environmental problems against which technology appears to be making little progress or which technology may actually exacerbate, and they emphasize the close, holistic relationship between humans and their ecosystem; we call this view **eco-wholism.** Of central importance in many challenges is the global population explosion accompanying the demographic transition. According to eco-wholists, increased population has created or intensified many environmental problems—not just pollution but pressure on food production capability and raw material availability. Human beings, they argue, are part of an ecosystem on which they now place demands that are too great.

Eco-wholists have a less optimistic view of the world. Raw materials like oil, natural gas, copper, and chromium have fixed material endowments, and thus their use deprives others, including future generations, of them. Land, too, is in fixed supply as are the inputs, such as fertilizers, that allow more productive use of the land. Clean air and water exist in limited quantity. Both increased population and increased economic activity accelerate depletion or despoliation of the broader environment.

Organization of the Book

The structure of this book builds on the presentation of this chapter. It has three primary parts of unequal length. Part II (the longest) focuses centrally on political-social issues, such as war and peace, freedom and justice, and community. In Part III the spotlight shifts to economic issues of growth and equity, and to their relationships with world politics. Finally, Part IV takes us to the broader environment, to the issues of progress and scarcity, and to the linkages between these issues and both global politics and economics. Each major part of the book allows the primary worldviews to elaborate, in turn, their understanding of global politics.

There was a period in the study of world politics when the belief in an emerging science was so strong that scholars might have considered the introduction of competing, value-laden worldviews an admission of defeat. There is only one world, the scientist argues, and therefore we need seek only a single accurate description of it. This author, like many others, refuses to abandon the attempt to discover that one true world—but must simultaneously recognize two realities. First, the world may be so complex that we can benefit from looking at it through different lenses or at different angles. Second, accidents of our birth and upbringing (for instance, country of origin and social position) leave us predisposed to adopt only one perspective and to be certain that we have the best view. *Both realities suggest the importance of consciously identifying and separately considering a variety of viewpoints.* All you need do is read a newspaper or watch the evening news to discover the ongoing clash of perspectives concerning world politics. This book should help you understand that clash.

Selected Key Terms

high politics	worldviews	mercantilism
low politics	realism	neo-Marxism
concepts	liberalism	modernism
propositions	constructivism	eco-wholism
theory	commercial liberalism	

Realist, Liberal, and Constructivist Views

Т he world is a dangerous place. Wars have killed more than 142 million people since 1500 and more than 110 million in the twentieth century alone (Sivard 1991, 20; Sivard 1996, 7). The world is also unfair. While Europeans and North Americans worry about their waistlines, approximately 800 million people suffer from malnutrition that devastatingly affects their health and life prospects. Moreover, those who are born female or with a skin that is not white are considerably more likely to live among the impoverished and hungry. Some of the most pressing questions facing humanity are: What causes war? What brings peace or at least some basic level of security? How do the disadvantaged and oppressed of the world obtain fairness or justice?

KEY WEB LINKS

www.artsci.lsu.edu/poli/
theoryx.html

Three worldviews, the realist, liberal, and constructivist, help us address those questions; this chapter sketches the way in which they do. Then Chapters 4 through 10 will elaborate the manner in which these three worldviews interpret the world.

Realism

Realism offers a reasonably parsimonious (simple) worldview that explains a large portion of world politics.[1] Although realists share a relatively simple framework, they elaborate their understanding in individualistic and often complex ways. This chapter portrays the *basic* worldview, and subsequent chapters indicate the diversity.

Concepts

Two types of concepts help define realism (and the worldviews to follow): agents and the structures that frame the interaction among those agents. Theories within worldviews build on these fundamental units.

[1]See Morgenthau (1973, originally 1948) and E. H. Carr (1964, originally 1939, vii).   **41**

The agent at the core of realism is the **state.** A state is fundamentally what we normally call a country, and we use the terms interchangeably (and define state more precisely later). Realists portray the state as a unitary actor that speaks with one voice and acts without internal dissent on interstate issues (as if no interest groups competed within states). In addition, they suggest that states are rational in the pursuit of their interests, primarily security and autonomy. Realists know both the unitary and rationality assumptions are simplifications of reality—but do not view them as brutal ones; in fact, they believe that such simplification adds power to their theory (see Gilpin 1981, 18–19). Many extensions to the basic realist perspective are friendly relaxations of these two assumptions.

Although realist thought begins with the state, much of that thought focuses not on individual states but rather on the structure in which they function, the state system.[2] A *system* is a set of units or actors and the interactions among them; the **state system** is the collection of states in the world and their interactions. For analysts who believe that the system determines the behavior of the individual components, rather than the reverse, the state system becomes the central unit of analysis. System-oriented realists (Waltz 1979) emphasize that a state system without central authority is a world of **anarchy,** a world in which no central authority exists to set rules for state behavior. That systemic condition, and particularly the requirement it places on states to guard their own interests, shapes much of realist thought.

What are *state interests?* Most fundamentally they are autonomy and security. More immediately, however, the basic interest is often power.[3] Realists say that "power is the currency of politics." That is, **power,** the ability to influence outcomes, is the basis of interaction among states (the next chapter elaborates this central concept). States rationally use power in pursuit of their more fundamental interests. Obviously, there are times when the interests of states collide, and at such times conflict is possible.

States vary in their power and a small number commonly dominate the global system. We can describe the **polarity** (number of major powers) of the system in terms of a single dominant actor (unipolar), two dominant actors (bipolar), and multiple dominant actors (multipolar). We might reasonably expect polarity to affect interstate behavior patterns.

Table 3.1 summarizes the conceptual basis of realism and two other perspectives. It organizes the entire discussion of this chapter and should be a useful reference throughout.

Theories

Theories explain the dynamic interactions of rational, self-interested states in an environment of anarchy. Foremost among these is the security dilemma. Even fundamentally good individuals, in an anarchic environment, act from self-

---

[2]Each of the worldviews of this text draws attention to an agent and a structure. Relative emphasis on agents and structures varies, even within worldviews. Hence "structural realism" stresses the state-system level of analysis and more traditional realism focuses on the state.

[3]Realists often claim that states primarily seek power (not security or autonomy). As Keohane (1983b, 515) points out, that assertion is inconsistent with their own balance of power theory in which states "moderate their efforts when their positions are secure."

Table 3.1	Political Behavior Worldviews		
Worldview Name(s)	Realism	Liberalism	Constructivism
Central Concepts: Agents/ Structures	States State system Anarchy	Individuals Groups Institutions	Social constructs Institutions Ideas, culture
Values of Agents	State interests: Security Autonomy Power	Utility: Freedom Economic well-being	Identity Relationships
Central Concepts: Bases of Interaction	Rational individualistic behavior Power Polarity	Learning Mutually beneficial exchange Group formation Institution formation	Identity creation Coordination power Cultural struggles
Theories: Systematic Descriptions	Security dilemma Action-reaction dynamic Balance of power Coalition behavior Hegemonic theory Cooperation under anarchy	Nonstate actors play roles in global politics States represent domestic actors State preferences determine behavior	Agents and structures co-create each other
Theories: Typical Forecasts	Same as past	Spread of human rights and democracy Expansion of democratic peace	Social world can change dramatically and fundamentally
Values of Worldview Proponents	Stability Relative peace	Progress Economic well-being Peace	Action programs of ideologies, "isms"
Typical Prescriptions	Protect, enhance power	Support education Protect human rights Pursue democracy Build global community	Position dependent: Autonomy Justice Dominance

interest in ways that endanger the interests of others (for instance, by becoming better with a gun in the American West). Similarly, an innocent attempt by a state to assure its own security by increasing its power will invariably threaten the security of other states. This inability to protect oneself without threatening others is known as the **security dilemma.** The security dilemma gives rise in turn to the **action-reaction dynamic.** States in an environment of anarchy (and therefore in a security dilemma) often view security-enhancing acts of other states as threatening and react by increasing their own defense. Arms races frequently result.

More than two states interact in most state systems, and they often counter the actions of others not simply with their own reactions, but through the building of alliances. Either unilaterally or collectively states seek to counter power with power, to pursue a *balance of power.*

As noted earlier, polarity may affect system dynamics. For example, in some cases, like that of the United States after World War II, states may assume a hegemonic or dominant position of power in a unipolar system. Realists seek theoretically to explain both fluctuations in position within the state system and their consequences for the conflict level in the system.

Although much of the emphasis of realists has traditionally been on conflict among states, they recognize that even self-serving states can rationally cooperate in pursuit of mutual interests—there can be *cooperation under anarchy.* Cooperation can extend to various security (arms control), economic (trade), and environmental (pollution control) issues. Much realist thought in recent years addresses such cooperation.

Change is important to realists, but they place greater emphasis on continuity. Realist views of history often begin and end with characterizations of power, power balances, and struggles for security. Realists foresee the same kind of interstate struggle in the future.

Values and Prescriptions

Values are fundamental to politics, which by definition involves struggles over them. To do justice to the subject we must attempt to distinguish between the value orientations of the participants in the processes we describe and those of the observer or analyst. With respect to realism, this means identifying both the values of states (the central actors for realists) and the normative orientations of realists themselves.[4]

Because realists emphasize security and autonomy goals of states, critics sometimes mistakenly characterize realists as insensitive to the value of peace—even as amoral (distinguishing "amoral," which means *without morality,* from "immoral," which means *contrary to morality*). Actually, there are few in this world who do not value peace highly. Realists argue, however, that attention by states to peace above cautious and realistic attention to preservation of security often leads to the loss of both. Power deters other states from aggression better than do declarations of peaceful intent.

Fundamental to an understanding of the morality of realists is recognition that the clashes of the world do not always involve right versus wrong, or the "good guys" versus the "bad guys" as in an American movie about the old West. They often pit right against right, as in the mutual historical claims of Jews and Palestinians to the same land in the Middle East, or wrong against wrong, as in the war between Nazi Germany and the Stalinist Soviet Union. For diplomats, choices may be almost impossible to sort out in moral terms. Attempts to base state action on morality will often create conflict rather than ameliorating it. These considerations drive realists back to security and autonomy as the legitimate bases for state action.

[4]The importance of values is a reason this book uses "worldview" in preference to "paradigm" (Kuhn 1970).

Important Contributions to Realist Thought

Thucydides (ca. 460 to ca. 400 B.C.), the chronicler of the Peloponnesian Wars between the alliances led by ancient Athens and Sparta, has become the spiritual father of realism. The most often cited sentence of Thucydides is "What made war inevitable was the growth of Athenian power and the fear that this caused in Sparta." That one sentence emphasized his attention to power, to the city-state level of analysis (within a systemic context), to the fundamental importance of security, and even to the security dilemma. This early realist also recognized the limited role of moral behavior in the relationships among states. The destructive demands by Athens on Melos, a city-state that refused Athenian insistence on contribution to its alliance, stripped away any pretense of morality from the bases of interstate relations:

> We on our side will use no fine phrases, since you know as well as we do that, when these matters are discussed by practical people, the standard of justice depends on the equality of power to compel and that in fact the strong do what they have the power to do and the weak accept what they have to accept. (quoted in Smith 1986, 6)

Thucydides may have had misgivings about that aspect of interstate relations, and he was by no means constrained only to realist thought. The infamous advice that Machiavelli (1469–1527) provided his prince, however, further stamped early realist thought as amoral:

> it is honourable to seem mild, and merciful, and courteous, and religious, and sincere, and indeed to be so, provided your mind be so rectified and prepared that you can act quite contrary on occasion. [A prince is] oftentimes necessitated, for the preservation of his State, to do things inhuman, uncharitable, and irregular. . . . (Machiavelli 1513)

The security interests of the state (its *raison d'état*) justified for Machiavelli nearly any action by its leader. A republican in much of his writing, his life experiences explain Machiavelli's support for a strong and amoral prince. He entered public life in 1494, the year of the French king Charles VIII's invasion of Machiavelli's state, Florence. He eventually served Florence as defense minister and in many other capacities. Throughout his career he faced and opposed the French occupation of Northern Italy and the growing intrusion of Spain. In 1502 he went as envoy to Cesare Borgia, then at the peak of his power and cunning. Borgia, despite Machiavelli's early reservations about him, became the model of his ideal prince because he proved successful in consolidating several Italian city-states. In short, Machiavelli believed that Italy needed unification to withstand foreign force and that only a strong prince could realistically provide it.

Thomas Hobbes (1588–1679) elaborated the systemic perspective in the realist worldview through his thought experiments concerning a "state of nature." He asked us to imagine the anarchy in a society without central government to provide order, and he described the wretchedness of existence in such a society. His major work *Leviathan* appeared in 1651, following many years of English civil war and the execution of the king in 1649. The book called for society to give over control to central government, even if that government is a leviathan or monster, in return for an order that makes life not only bearable but possible.

Hobbes rooted his thought about the state of nature in an understanding of human nature, which he argued flowed from the working of appetites. Some realists even more strongly tie their thought to a negative characterization of human nature. Theologian Reinhold Niebuhr, who wrote before and after World War II, referred to human nature as "the rock bottom problem" (Smith 1986, 17). He influenced Hans Morgenthau, who in turn wrote in the most widely read world politics textbook of the Cold War:

> The history of modern political thought is the story of a contest between two schools that differ fundamentally in their conceptions of the nature of man, society, and politics. One believes that a rational and moral political order, derived from universally valid abstract principles, can be achieved here and now. It assumes the essential goodness and infinite malleability of human nature. . . .The other school believes that the world, imperfect as it is from the rational point of view, is the result of forces inherent in human nature. To improve the world, one must work with these forces, not against them. (Morgenthau 1973, 3)

Two infamous tyrants, Hitler and Stalin, and the events surrounding World War II, reinforced this common realist emphasis on a fundamentally bad human nature.

The basic concepts and theories of realism do not, however, require a negative view of human beings, individually or within states. We earlier discussed the security dilemma. States acting innocently to enhance their own security may threaten that of others and set up an action-reaction dynamic. The insight by realists that structure may matter more than human nature and intentions emerges in a variant called *structural realism* or *neorealism* (new realism).[5] Neorealists focus more heavily and theoretically than traditional realists on systemic structures and the influences these have on state behavior. They direct attention to systemic anarchy, to distribution of capabilities within the system, and to the implications these systemic conditions have for individual state behavior. Neorealists need not assume an evil human nature to analyze ongoing conflicts of interest. Greater attention to system structure and theory also provides neorealists with a basis for somewhat more extensive consideration of change, an issue to which we will return. Neorealists have also broadened their interests to the study of cooperation.

Liberalism

Realists identify states as the central actors in world politics. Liberals remind us that the agents who ultimately practice politics are actually individuals. Obviously, an understanding of world politics centered on approximately 6 billion individuals cannot be as parsimonious as a worldview focused on about 180 states. Nonetheless, the basic liberal model, which Table 3.1 summarizes, is not much more complicated than the realist worldview.

The terms *liberal* and *liberalism* will confuse many readers unless we immediately address terminology. In European politics, and in academic or intellectual writing around the world, a liberal is one who favors limited governmental intervention

---

[5]Waltz (1979) most clearly developed neorealism, without so labeling it.

in the economy. Most European countries have a liberal party with exactly that platform. In the contemporary political discourse of the United States, however, a liberal
is one who often favors considerable governmental intervention, both efforts to manage the economy and use of economic resources on behalf of less privileged members of society. Stated in this way, the European and American liberals appear to be
near opposites.

We will sometimes use the expression **classical liberalism** to designate the
European variant, because this definition goes back about 200 years. When we refer to the liberal position in the modern American sense, we will always label it
modern liberalism (in European terms modern liberals are social democrats, not
liberals). All liberalism, classical and modern, converges in its attention to the well-
being of the individual (as does a "liberal" education), and it is this broad, encom-
passing liberal tradition that interests us here.

Concepts

Like states, individuals have interests. Economists, who commonly adopt a classical liberal view, speak of individuals pursuing *utility.* They rarely attempt to
define that synonym of interest, preferring to focus on the preferences that individuals indicate in their behavior. When pressed, liberals generally rank both the
pursuit of personal freedom and of economic well-being (or, as some famous liberals once said, "life, liberty, and the pursuit of happiness") at the top of the list
of interests or values. Merquior (1991, 6–7) found that liberals put varying em-
phases on four concepts of freedom: (1) freedom from oppression, (2) freedom
to participate, (3) freedom of conscience and belief, and (4) freedom of self-
fulfillment. Classical liberals in the Anglo-American tradition attach special
weight to the first.

Individuals act and interact in the liberal world. We can identify three particular kinds of action. First, individuals learn. Learning is both a strictly individual action and a collective accumulation and sharing of knowledge over time.
Learning is of great importance because it facilitates more intelligent pursuit of
interest. Second, individuals acquire capabilities or physical goods that allow
them to satisfy their needs and also to enter into mutually beneficial exchange of
goods and services. Third, individuals enter into associations and create institutions for assistance in the pursuit of their interests. These may be private, voluntary associations such as domestic interest groups, or they may be formal governmental structures.

These basic concepts of what individuals desire and how they pursue those
desires (see again Table 3.1) suggest a very important difference between realist
and liberal thought. Realists perceive a relatively fixed amount of security in the
system and view shifts in power and security on the part of one state as mirror images of shifts in power and security of other states. This is called a win-lose or **zero-
sum** perspective, because the value of changes sum to zero across all actors. In contrast, liberals believe all actors can *simultaneously* increase their economic and more
general well-being (a win-win or **nonzero-sum** orientation). Individuals do so by
learning how to do things more efficiently and effectively, through mutually beneficial exchange and through collective action.

Theory

The concepts of liberalism form the basis for its theory. Although liberals join realists in recognizing the key place of states in global politics, liberal theory concerning states is quite different from that of realists in at least three ways.[6]

First, liberals argue that nonstate actors also play important roles in global
politics. Charismatic individuals and insightful scientists, influential interest
groups and corporations, and intergovernmental organizations work alongside
states and through markets and politics to determine the life conditions of humans
around the world.

Second, although states clearly remain the most important global actors, they
represent the domestic actors and forces at work within them, rather than having
agendas that are as simple, consistent, and easily predictable as realists suggest.
Different domestic actors, with widely varying interests, compete to capture the
state's external agenda. Sometimes the agenda of a single (and not always rational)
individual will dictate the preferences of the state. At other times an economic or
ethnic faction with either minority or majority status may control it. Frequently, internal actors compromise concerning the state's external preferences.

Third, state preferences determine behavior in the state system. This may
seem obvious, but remember that the realist model emphasized the capabilities
or power of the interacting states as the determinant of behavior in the system
(their seeking to enhance domestic capabilities, reacting to the power of other actors, forming alliances, and so on). One of the important consequences flowing
from a theory that preferences drive state behavior, in combination with a theory
that those preferences reflect the varying interplay of domestic interests, is that
state behavior patterns will also vary. Consider, for instance, the difference in behavior of a state with a preference for territorial expansion, dictated by a small
group of people actually unlikely to die in any war of expansion, relative to the
behavior of a state with a preference for increased trade with its neighbors, due
to the internal influence of a business community and a democratic political
process. Consider further the differences between a state system dominated by
states of the former type (authoritarian *territorial states* in the terminology of
Rosecrance 1986) and a state system populated by states of the latter type (democratic *trading states*).

Some neorealists argue that states pursue only *relative gain* (Gilpin 1987, 33;
Grieco 1988 and 1990). That is, a state will cooperate only if it minimally gains as
much as other states. A liberal believes, however, that a state will often cooperate
if it can obtain *absolute gain* from doing so, even if other states might gain more.
We should not exaggerate this difference between the two worldviews, because realists can generally imagine acceptance of limited unequal cooperation and liberals can understand some inequalities of outcome that would prevent cooperation.

It is important to reiterate that while realists generally see consistency in
global politics across time, liberals believe that many of the important forces within
states are changing, therefore potentially changing state preferences and behavior.

---

[6]Moravcsik's presentation (1997) of liberal theory influenced the discussion here.

For instance, technologies of transportation and communication continue to advance, facilitating movement of both goods and information across borders and, at least potentially, favoring the interests of that trade-oriented business community relative to those who are territorially oriented.

Values and Forecasts

In fact, liberals generally portray history as progressive and value that characteristic of it (Adler and Crawford 1991). We see much progress in cumulative improvements in the technological capability of humanity and the material advance that technology makes possible. Some progress—and here liberals disagree among themselves—may independently take the form of moral improvement. It has been suggested, for instance, that the abolition of slavery represented moral progress and not simply changed economic conditions (Ray 1989). Some liberals even see a combination of progress in material well-being and moral progress ultimately leading to the obsolescence of major war (Mueller 1989).

Progress will occur also, liberals believe, in political arrangements. Within states, democracy will increasingly become the preferred form of government. Those governments will protect human rights, the social and political freedom of individuals. They will also support private property and the commercial freedom of individuals, both domestically and internationally. Among states, mutually beneficial exchanges will flourish. Moreover, states will learn how to interact in additional ways that advance their mutual interest in security, welfare, and human rights of their citizens (Adler, Crawford, and Donnelly 1991).

Liberals see a set of mutually reinforcing relationships among these progressive phenomena: more educated and competent citizens, active interest groups both within countries and across state boundaries, prosperity and democracy within countries, and commerce and peaceful relationships among them. For instance, they argue that democracies do not fight one another, an assertion that is close to a law of global politics. Writing at the end of the 1700s, just as the first modern democracies were beginning to appear, Immanuel Kant (1724–1804) argued that "republican" governments would not make war on each other because the citizens would bear the cost and be loathe to incur it. He predicted a "zone of peace" among democracies. Many contemporary authors (Doyle 1983 and 1986b; Rummel 1983; Chan 1984) have elaborated the argument and found it empirically valid. That leads at least some liberals to believe that the *democratic peace* of recent years will expand.

Prescriptions

Realists reject such argument that "all good things go together," arguing, for instance, that trade among countries can be as much a source of conflict as of cooperation. In fact, the belief that the world could experience such progress leads realists to apply the label *idealism* (and even "utopianism") to liberalism, obviously implying that liberals pursue unattainable ideals. In truth many liberals have simply *prescribed* peaceful behavior by states, rather than viewing global politics through an *analytical* lens, thereby meriting the idealist label. Some idealistic liberals argued on behalf of extensive arms control between World Wars I and II,[7] more recently called for general and complete disarmament of the superpowers, and continue to prescribe a world federal government. In contrast, more analytical liberals investigate increasing global literacy, growing protection of individual human rights, spread of democracy, rising trade levels, decreasing incidence of wars among great powers, and the relationships among these changes.

Still, even analytical liberals often risk appearing idealistic by going beyond simply analyzing progressive global change in order to prescribe active pursuit of it. Specifically, they prescribe educating individuals around the world and providing them with basic sanitation and medical care, including childhood immunizations. They prescribe working to protect the basic rights of all humans, including the right to own property and to live in a democracy. They prescribe active involvement in both domestic and global politics, through participation in groups with other individuals pursuing the same goals. They prescribe the active pursuit of interstate cooperation on a wide range of issues, even when the gains may not be equal for all participating states. And they prescribe the development of regional and global institutions in support of cooperation among states.

Important Contributions to Liberal Thought

Emphasis on the individual is central to the definition of the liberal worldview. The antecedents of liberalism developed as a challenge to the feudal order of the late Middle Ages. In that order, the individual had a diminished role, greatly limited by religious, secular, and economic authorities (in the form of the feudal aristocracy and clergy). For instance, salvation required the assistance of the Church and its personnel. Martin Luther (1483–1546) helped set in motion the forces that ultimately generated liberalism by arguing that the relationship between an individual and God was personal. He rejected the claim that only the church's representatives could interpret the scriptures. Similarly, Francis Bacon (1561–1626) and René Descartes (1596–1650) placed the individual at the heart of a new search for knowledge about the universe (rather than accepting that knowledge from ancient authority). Descartes made this revised role of the individual clear in the famous statement at the foundation of his philosophic enterprise: "I think, therefore I am."[8]

Enlightenment thought of eighteenth-century Europe provided the real foundations of liberalism. The scientific and intellectual advances of the seventeenth and eighteenth centuries shaped that thought. Philosophers of the Enlightenment saw in the rationality and learning of humans the basis for progress, human perfectibility, and the discovery of universal social and political principles. Immanuel Kant helped define the era: "*Sapere aude*, have the courage to know: that is the motto of enlightenment" (*The Economist*, March 16, 1996: 85). Since the Enlighten-

---

[7]In an interwar golden period for idealistic liberalism, international conferences and agreements sought to codify armament balances and to restrict state actions. The Kellogg-Briand Pact (or Pact of Paris) in 1928 bound 15 states (among them France, Britain, the United States, Germany, Japan, and Italy) to use only pacific methods for dispute settlement and to renounce war. The failure of this international superstructure to prevent World War II tainted the entire liberal enterprise and set the stage for the post–World War II dominance of realists.

[8]Which reminds me. René Descartes walked into a bar. He ordered and drank a glass of wine. The bartender asked him if he wanted another. René pondered, said "I think not," and disappeared.

ment, liberals have elaborated various theoretical traditions. Although these traditions interact so much that it is difficult to draw lines among them or their developers, it is useful to distinguish two:[9]

1. Protection of individual rights via law and democracy. Some historians regard John Locke (1632–1704) as the founder of liberal democratic thought. Basing his argument on a belief that God created humanity, he concluded that humans have certain natural rights, including self-preservation. He extrapolated natural rights into the right to sell one's own labor and to own additional property, justifying a capitalist society. He also made a strong case that the government should not interfere with the exercise of these rights. In a step toward "modern liberalism," Locke, Rousseau, and Kant further argued that states should promote education as a foundation of a virtuous citizenry and a better government. Many others, including Jeremy Bentham, John Stuart Mill, and James Madison, gradually created a body of politically liberal thought based on universal suffrage and the protection of individual rights.

A belief in the universal rule of law, applicable to all individuals and states, developed early in liberal thought. The Dutch jurist Hugo Grotius (1583–1645) founded modern international law. Grotius based his thought about international law both on deep religious conviction and on a concept of human nature. Specifically he believed that human beings possess reason, goodness, sociability, and the ability to learn and improve. On these religious and philosophical foundations, very different from those of early realism, he built his belief in the law, applicable to both individuals and to states as groupings of individuals.

At the domestic level, liberals have gradually elaborated a model of governance that combines two elements: (1) a strong state, so as to overcome the anarchy in interpersonal affairs that realists so powerfully describe in interstate affairs; and (2) a separation of powers within a constitutionally constrained state that helps protect individual rights in the same manner that balance of power preserves state autonomy. For example, James Madison urged incorporation of a separation of powers into the American constitution. He also strongly advocated the bill of rights to protect individuals.

At the interstate level, an idealistic liberalism has sometimes argued analogously for immediate development of strong global institutions. For instance, in 1712 the Abbé de Saint-Pierre proposed a European Union with representation from 24 states. A long line of legal scholars and federalists have maintained these idealistic traditions. More commonly, however, liberals have either proposed the strengthening of global society with cooperation based on international law or advocated the gradual transformation of the global system via institutions that constrain the state.[10] Because the strong-state option is closed to liberals internationally, they often support a complex system of governance in which states maintain an important role, but in which they both balance one another and delegate increasing amounts of legitimate authority to large numbers of international organizations. We might call the model one of "power diffusion and circumscription" rather than "power separation."

---

[9]Keohane (1990, 175–180), Caporaso (1993, 466–467), Zacher and Matthew (1995, 120–137), and Hughes (1995a) provided other lists.

[10]Martin Wright (1991) argued that there are only three traditions in global political thought: (1) states in anarchy (realism); (2) a society of states capable of cooperation (rationalism or Grotianism); and (3) world society (revolutionism or Kantianism).

2. Focus on interactions (exchange, group formation, and interdependence). Adam Smith (1723–1790) provided the classic statement of the value of commercial interaction. He argued that the mutual benefit of exchange was a key to the wealth of nations. Immanuel Kant, Thomas Paine, and Jeremy Bentham are only a few of those who have elaborated the merits of trade and have also linked commerce to improved interstate relations. In 1857 the British diplomat Richard Cobden wrote that "Free trade is God's diplomacy, and there is no other certain way of uniting people in the bonds of peace."

In-depth attention to pluralistic social groupings and their interaction is fairly recent, but Alexis de Tocqueville (1805–1859) pointed to the role of such groupings in American democracy. As a counterweight to excessive individualism, de Tocqueville emphasized the give and take of collective social groupings in what has come to be known as **civil society.** Frequently, groups arise as a result of common interests in exchange, but a variety of mutual interests can motivate them.

The rapid growth of corporations doing business across borders and of international organizations (including many like Amnesty International, based not on states but on individual membership) has encouraged the enunciation of a variant of liberalism that we can call *transnationalism* (Keohane and Nye, 1970 and 1977). Transnationalists describe and analyze an inevitable growth in global interactions and institutions, driven by advances in communications and transportation technology. For instance, David Mitrany (1966) argued that, driven by the needs of their citizens and facilitated by the increasing sophistication of communication and transportation systems, states would come together to form an increasingly large number of functionally specific institutions. Examples range from the very early Universal Postal Union (1874) to the very modern World Trade Organization (1995). Mitrany argued that the ties that such institutions place upon states would ultimately restrict their ability to engage in conflictual interactions.

The most significant contribution to liberalism in recent years has been the strengthening of its analytical and empirical content. We have already noted the very extensive work by many researchers on the concept and theory of democratic peace. As we saw earlier, liberalism's concept of state preferences may be richer than that of realism and, Moravcsik (1997) argues, could encompass much of realist understanding. Similarly, by building an understanding of politics up from the individual, liberalism could potentially encompass thought about groups and societies, the focus of the constructivist perspective to which we now turn. As we will see, however, liberalism has been limited in ability to explain the formation and behavior of identity groups. Therefore "constructivist" perspectives will further enrich our ability to analyze world politics.

Constructivism

Throughout the 1990s, about 30 wars raged at any given time (Stockholm International Peace Research Institute [SIPRI] 1997, 17). With very few exceptions, they had a domestic or civil-war character. Thus realism, which treats states as impermeable wholes (like billiard balls), and liberalism, which tells us practically nothing about violent conflict among ethnic, religious, or social-class based groups, do not adequately explain those wars. In fact, there is a great deal about which realism and liberalism tell us relatively little. How did states come to have their dominant position in world politics and might the world someday be constructed/structured in a very different way? Where are women in global politics?

We therefore introduce a third worldview, one to which scholars until recently have paid less attention. Because this perspective directs our attention to the construction of social structures and argues that they take on roles independent of the agents that help create them, we label this perspective *social constructivism* or simply **constructivism.**[11] Because the perspective emphasizes the role of ideas and culture, we could also call it the "ideational" or "cultural" perspective.

Both realism and liberalism focus on agents (the states of realism and the individuals or individual-based groupings of liberalism). Both perspectives portray those agents as rational and interest-seeking actors who create and maintain social structures only insofar as they serve the interests of the agents. The similarities between the two perspectives are sufficiently strong that in some respects realism is merely a manifestation of liberalism, restricted in attention to states. It is important to stress that constructivism differs from both realism and liberalism in positing that agents and structures interact in a process of mutual creation and recreation. Social structures, both formal institutions (or organizations) like governments and informal "institutions" like widely shared beliefs or norms, substantially affect individuals and states.[12]

Concepts

Constructivists see the world in terms of *social constructs* (or "social facts"). Instead of the world being a stable reality that we need only describe and analyze (like the physical world of the natural scientists), the social world is what we make it, and it is very dynamic. For instance, we cannot really build up to the concept of human rights from the biology of a human being. Instead, those rights are defined and redefined by social convention. Do women have an equal role with men in politics? Do blacks have the same inherent rights as whites? Does anyone really have a right to a job or to health care? Roles and rights are social constructions.

Whereas realism and liberalism take rational, interest-seeking states or individuals as a given and then elaborate theory around those agents and their interaction, constructivists ask how states came to be dominant social actors and suggest that the interests of individuals are not a universal given, but a function of social definition. Consider, for instance, the variation across societies (as between Confucian and the Western) in relative emphasis on social obligations and self-sacrifice versus individual development and the acquisition of material goods. Social structures help define the basic agents and their preferences.

---

[11]The previous edition called the third perspective "communitarian" (Alker and Biersteker 1984, 124). Communitarian inappropriately evokes, however, the American social movement by the same name (Etzioni 1988; Daly 1994). The professional literature increasingly juxtaposes (social) constructivism with neorealism and neoliberalism (Onuf 1989; Wendt 1992; Lapid and Kratochwil 1996; Katzenstein 1996; Wæver 1997; Ruggie 1998; Walt 1998; Hopf 1998; Checkel 1998; Kubálková, Onuf, and Kowert 1998) and more generally takes culture seriously (Desch 1998).

[12]Liberals seek to explain institutions partly in terms of the rational efforts of their creators to reduce transaction costs (in Williamson's 1985 analogy, "the economic equivalent of friction in physical systems"). Institutionalists in the constructivist tradition look to "path dependence" in which institutions carry distant historical factors and events.

Thus agents and structures shape each other. Moreover, and very importantly, constructivists claim that social structures have an existence and influence independent of the actions of the agents who help create them. Neorealists also recognize that state systems structure interaction of states, but they portray the state system as a manifestation of its member states. A neorealist would not expect two state systems with identical numbers of member states (with identical capabilities) to differ in implicit rules about the acceptability of violating territorial borders or the use of particular weapons in warfare. Constructivists, in contrast, would expect such variations in rules or what one might call systemic culture. Even anarchy, that basic concept of realism, is not a true constant across time or geography, but a varying construct of states and constraint on them (as Wendt 1992 said, "anarchy is what states make of it"). Because structures have this independence, constructivism does not fit with complete comfort into the framework of Table 3.1. Nonetheless, we shall use that framework to help us elaborate the perspective and compare it with realism and liberalism.

Constructivists see identity and interest as social constructs to explore with particular care. Some kind of community or **identity group** (Burton 1985) attracts the loyalty of all humans. Many different bases, including race, ethnicity, gender, social condition, beliefs/ideology, and religion, individually or interactively structure our identities. One of the most important identity groups in world politics is the **nation,** an ethnic community with a shared sense of self-identity, like that of Germans or Palestinians. The conflict between Kosovars and Serbs derives, as does that between the Iraqi government and the Kurds, from **nationalism**—from a desire by peoples with a sense of self-identity to control their own affairs. Both liberals and realists frequently dismiss nationalism as irrationality.[13] Constructivists look for roots of particular nationalisms in long-term historical and cultural evolution, and they give nationalism serious attention.

When liberals do analyze nationalism, they look to its individualistic, as opposed to its ideational or cultural roots. For liberals, the basis of most all identities is the seemingly basic, biological need for connection with others. That need probably exists because humans cannot really survive as individuals. They need communities in which they can share the duties of reproduction, food provision, and self-defense. Hardin (1995) suggested that while liberals usually focus on the power of exchange (or **exchange power**), realized when individuals interact to trade goods and services, they pay too little attention to **coordination power.** Coordination power is the bringing of people together for collective action on activities such as hunting, building irrigation systems and roads, or stockpiling food. Hardin further suggested that what often appear to be irrational social rituals, even ones as extreme as dueling, may serve individual interests by reinforcing the social bonds that underly coordination power.

---

[13]Morgenthau illustrated the relative inattention by realists to the important concepts of nation and nationalism. Not only did he use nation throughout as a synonym for state, but his brief discussion of nationalism portrayed it as aberrant behavior:

> The intellectual and political excesses of nationalism and its degenerate offspring, racism, have shocked and repelled the non-nationalistic mind to a much greater degree than have the excesses of geopolitics. . . . The excesses of nationalism . . . are the logical outgrowth of a secular religion that has engulfed in the fanaticism of holy wars of extermination, enslavement, and world conquest only certain countries, yet has left its mark on many everywhere. (Morgenthau 1973, 161)

Yet while there may be clearly identifiable individual motives for creating and being part of identity groups, it is often far from clear within a framework of individual rationality how particular identity groups come into being, how certain social practices or rituals rationally serve individual needs and therefore persist (for example, the immolation of widows on funeral pyres or the practice of female genital mutilation), or why group interaction sometimes leads to genocidal violence.

Consider, for instance, the ebbs and flows of Serbian or Yugoslavian, Spanish or Catalonian, Swiss or German, Canadian or Quebecois, and Mexican or Mayan identities. Although there are some objective bases for identities in language, race, religion, or other characteristics, the truth is that it appears impossible to consistently build up to ethnic identities from such factors. It appears that there is a strong element of social construction in identities, creating a need for the contextual, historical, and particularistic explanation of them that constructivists offer.

Beyond nations, many other identity groups interest us. Like the Kosovo conflict, the long-running one within the Sudan has religious components as well as ethnic ones. The Christians of the south objected strongly when the northern-controlled central government imposed Islamic Law on them. That law violated Christian ideals concerning their community. Religious idealism therefore also demonstrates social construction.

Although nations and religious groups often interact with states fairly closely and may even help define states, other identity groups or communities routinely exist within or across states. Three such identities—gender, race, and class—all combine elements of objective character and/or interest with social construction. Tickner has argued that

> identity has been a central concern in contemporary feminist theory. Since women have generally been outsiders, excluded from historical processes that have framed contemporary political and economic life, as well as from the development of knowledge that has interpreted these processes, most contemporary feminist approaches take identity as a starting point for their theoretical constructions. Conscious of the exclusion of women, feminists have been particularly concerned with the question of who are the collective "we" about whom the historical understanding of our world has been constructed. (Tickner 1997, 148)

Social construction creates not only identity groups and their definitions of interest, but the broader structures in which they operate. For instance, states and the state system came to organize European politics only in the 1600s after the breakdown of the Medieval system. Until then Europe was a patchwork of overlapping empires, kingdoms, and other assorted fiefdoms. With the evolution of the European Union in recent years, Europe again has become a mosaic of political units or polities (Ferguson and Mansbach 1998) within which states function very differently from 100 years ago.

Similarly, economic systems have undergone tremendous change over time and vary greatly around the world at any point in time. Although variable economic "realities" such as production technology explain much such variation, ideas and beliefs play an important role. As John Maynard Keynes said:

> The ideas of economists and political philosophers, both when they are right and when they are wrong, are more powerful than is commonly understood. Indeed,

the world is ruled by little else. Practical men [people], who believe themselves to be quite exempt from any intellectual influences, are usually the slaves of some defunct economist.

Theory

Again, social constructivists do not identify agents and then proceed to analyze their interaction, but rather portray agents, larger structures or institutions, and the co-determination of agents and structures. Consider, for instance, the realist concepts of state sovereignty and anarchy. Realists portray the interstate system as one in which states do not interfere in the internal affairs of other states and in which no meaningful constraints, other than fear of counteraction by other states, exist on the actions of states. Constructivists point out that constraints in the relationships among North American and European states appear fundamentally different than those between many other states in the system. Moreover, in recent years the global system increasingly accepts intervention in states that suppress socially defined "human rights." States and other actors constructed the patterns or rules of these relationships (often called informal institutions), but those institutions now shape state behavior.

Similarly, constructivists point out that studies have long found that the level of social trust among citizens and therefore the extent and character of interaction varies greatly across countries (Banfield 1958; Almond and Verba 1963). In fact, social trust constitutes a kind of **social capital,** along with networks and norms, for societies (Putnam 1993). Along the same lines, some religions can be relatively intolerant of other traditions (seeking to define sharply their differences with them to convert others into their own traditions), while other religions seek to blur distinctions among faiths and to cooperate actively with others. These variations in rules or patterns of relationship within and across social institutions often appear inexplicable except in terms of long histories and basic cultural traditions.

An emphasis on ideational or cultural factors in social relationships does not preclude attention to material factors. For instance, interaction of a community and the outside world will depend on the relational conditions in which the community finds itself. Those whose identity lies in groupings (like gender and class) that cannot pursue separation from a broader society, logically pursue justice or fairness in their treatment. In contrast, nationalists can draw sharp boundaries (based on race, language, or culture), and they therefore sometimes seek separation from those outside the nation.

Constructivist thought is generally not as self-consciously theoretical as realist or liberal thought. In part this is because it is considerably easier to look for patterns of relationship among agents (and to describe, for instance, the action-reaction dynamic) than to look for patterns among ideas or between agents and ideas. Yet there are at least two theoretical statements that constructivists make: (1) Agents and structures shape each other; and (2) social constructs have a degree of independence from the more material world.

Forecasts, Values, and Prescriptions

Many constructivists themselves identify with one or more socially constructed identities and with specific interests. Many feminists, for example, came to constructivist perspectives because they objected strongly to the subordinate role of women in domestic and global politics. They saw no attention to that subordination in realism and inadequate concern in liberalism. Like Enloe (1990), they asked "Where are the women?" Many nationalists have come to the perspective for exactly the same reason. Thus large numbers of "isms" and ideologies elaborate the values and prescriptions of particular constructivists. Some, like feminism and many nationalisms, articulate cries for equality and justice. Others, like fascism and racism, can be desires for and even brutal defenses of superior positions in the social order.

A handful of specific constructivist orientations are **universalisms.** When an idealistic commitment to a particular form of social organization, whether it be Marxist, capitalist-democratic, or religious, supports extension of that form to a larger, ultimately global community, that viewpoint is universalist.[14] Ironically, universalism lies behind large numbers of local and regional conflicts over governmental forms. Universalisms periodically also give rise to some extremely large-scale conflicts. For instance, a clash of universalisms (specifically Marxism versus Western liberalism) interacted with the power and security considerations of realists to sustain the Cold War.

From the viewpoint of a constructivist, Western liberalism is an especially interesting universalism. We have explained that liberals tend to view liberalism in terms of a set of processes and institutions (such as democratic governments) that individuals rationally and universally create to serve their needs. Those who take a cultural perspective, however, may be more likely to see liberalism as often prior to and determinative of individual action, rather than determined by them. "It creates actors; it is not created by them" (Finnemore 1996, 333). In this perspective, the increasingly powerful Western culture effectively dictates adherence to individualism, even when collective action might better serve those individuals, and leads to the creation of democratic governments, even when they are too weak to protect or serve their citizens.

Proponents of attention to constructs sometimes foresee a fragmented world, quite different from the increasingly integrated world predicted by liberals. It has become almost a cliché in the post–Cold War era to point simultaneously to the (liberal) forces of integration and (identity-based) forces of disintegration. A few, like Huntington (1993), suggest ominously that cultural orientations may divide the world into a handful of primary cultural competitors, and even that a new bipolar division may appear between Christian and Islamic societies.

Whether they foresee fragmentation and conflict or the more integrated world of liberalism, most constructivists agree that the social world can change quite quickly and fundamentally, in ways that realists and liberals may downplay or completely ignore. Thus constructivists embrace ideas and anticipate developments like global government, a Kurdish state, socialist revolution, gender equality, or racial harmony much more easily than can those in other traditions.

This complex of challenges by constructivists to realism and liberalism lacks the unity and coherence of thought that helps give realism or even liberalism their

---

[14]Although liberals can be universalistic, they need not be. Kant argued forcefully against interference in the constitutions or governance of others. In fact, he thought that the republican state would only be "painfully acquired" after "multifarious hostilities and wars" (Lynch 1994, 54–56).

power. Social scientists often relegate the seemingly "irrational" pursuit of various community ideals to the unexplained fringes of our understanding of the world, preferring assumptions of rational behavior by unitary actors, whether states or individuals.[15] As George Will (1983, 17) stresses, however, ideas have consequences and thus the contemplation of ideas is an intensely practical undertaking.

Important Contributions to Constructivist Thought

We have seen that those who laid the foundations for major worldviews often did so in reaction to the political events around them. This is true also for constructivism, but the antecedents of the perspective are more difficult to identify, more diverse, and often more academic.

One variety of social constructivism has roots in two French and German sociologists of the late 1800s, Émile Durkheim and Max Weber.[16] Durkheim stressed the importance of ideational factors and of social facts. Weber emphasized that humans are cultural beings and that actions have social (not simply individual) significance. Although both wanted to study ideational factors as scientifically as possible, they argued for the mutual influence of material and ideational factors.

It would be very useful to place the thought of Karl Marx high on the list of antecedents to constructivism. When this book moves to a discussion of political economy, it will note the links between the Marxist and some constructivist perspectives. Yet Marx insisted that material factors, particularly the character of economic production, determined social ones, an essentially anticonstructivist perspective. It has been the contemporary followers of Marx who have managed to embrace both his legacy and constructivism. Their doing so makes sense, because the important concept of "class" is, in fact, a social construction and in significant part independent of life condition. Marxists have often identified the need to create a "class consciousness" as a precursor to social change.

Constructivism is a large tent that covers many related but still diverse perspectives. For instance, the "English school" generally fits within it (Wright 1991, Bull 1977, Watson 1992). A primary contribution of the English school has been to identify elements of global society that reflect a normative and structured overlay on the anarchy that realists emphasize. Realists tend to assume that concepts like "state interests," "sovereignty," and "anarchy" have clear-cut and constant meanings. Constructivists in the English school point out that states can define their interests to include sanctions against South Africa even when they have economic costs for those who impose them, can disregard the traditional notions of sovereignty in countries like Somalia or Bosnia, and can embrace a wide range of international laws that explicitly attempt to dampen anarchy.

Post-modernism is another relative of constructivist thought. Drawing upon more recent French scholars such as Michel Foucault and Jacques Derrida, but reaching back also to the Austrian philosopher Ludwig Josef Johann Wittgenstein, this perspective emphasizes linguistic construction. Not simply our particular understanding

---

[15]It is much easier to theorize about a world in which all actors have the same preference structures and values than one in which actors vary dramatically with respect to both. For the sake of simplifying theory, classical liberals and realists both choose to ignore real-world diversity.

[16]Ruggie (1998) attributes classical social constructivism to them and we draw on his discussion.

of society, but our language itself reflects social construction and power relations. Our discourse is fundamentally political. Consider, for instance, the designation of "terrorists." It is the powerful who identify terrorists to the world. The terrorists characterize themselves as "freedom fighters," struggling against injustice. It is also the powerful who created the convention of using masculine rather than feminine or gender-neutral pronouns for abstract individuals. The pervasiveness of "hegemonic discourse" discourages many post-modernists from believing that social science is truly possible; it encourages them to focus on "deconstructing" the meaning of language and reconstructing it in order to challenge the power behind it.

Worldview Overlap

The three worldviews of this chapter (and most of the book) bring both competing and complementary insights to our study of world politics. Figure 3.1 suggests how they have both overlapping and discrete content. For instance, realism and liberalism share an attention to how individual actors rationally interact, while both realism and constructivism emphasize power relationships throughout international relations. Liberals and constructivists both identify numerous social

Figure 3.1   Relationships Among Worldviews

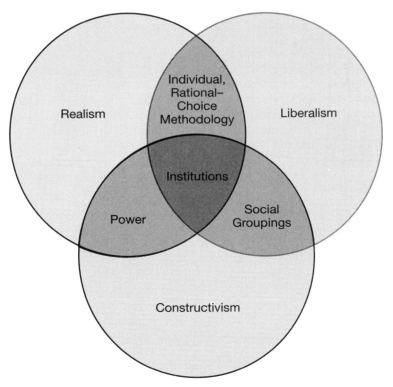

groupings, although liberals portray them as individuals pursuing shared interests while constructivists focus on the manner in which they shape and react to broad social structures. All three perspectives draw our attention to institutions, although constructivists attribute the most independent influence to them.

More than one perspective aids in understanding global politics. Leaving aside the fact that one worldview might be closer, even considerably closer, to the truth than another, realism, liberalism, and constructivist thought could not hold sway for so long over so many, if each did not make important contributions to our understanding of the world and to our involvement in it. In the coming chapters we pursue the insights of each perspective. First, we sketch a largely realist view of global relations, elaborating fundamental concepts and theory. Later chapters further develop liberalism. We then return to the important role that social constructs play in world politics.

Selected Key Terms

state	classical liberalism	nation
state system	modern liberalism	nationalism
anarchy	zero-sum	exchange power
power	nonzero-sum	coordination power
polarity	civil society	social capital
security dilemma	constructivism	universalisms
action-reaction dynamic	identity group	

States and the Pursuit of Interest

Much of world history is a story of empires. Their boundaries were often less well defined than modern states as they struggled to expand and to fight off the "barbarians" on their periphery. Many such empires viewed themselves as the entire civilized world and had no concept of other basically equal political units. An often overlapping part of world history, not just in Europe but in many geographic areas, has been feudal. Feudal governments are not fully in charge of their own fates—they are embedded in larger units (like empires), answerable in part to a king, an emperor, outside religious authorities, or all of those.

Europe in 1600 was a fundamentally feudal system, officially structured by the Holy Roman Empire. This meant that local "sovereigns" were sometimes in reality, and always in theory, accountable to both the Pope and a secular emperor. This feudal character contributes to the difficulty most of us have in developing strong mental pictures of politics during the Middle Ages—it becomes a blur of expanding and contracting papal and imperial authority, further complicated by the fact that marriages and heredity merged or divided large pieces of territory. For instance, in 1500 Mary of Burgundy married Maximilian of Austria; in the bargain the Netherlands of today became part of the Hapsburg family domains. Later the Netherlands came under the control of the Spanish branch of the Hapsburg family. Perhaps it was this kind of sequence that led Harry Truman to conclude that "History is just one damn thing after another."

In the 1500s, however, underlying forces were creating increasing tensions that would ultimately lead to change. One important tension was the increased questioning of papal and other clerical authority. Martin Luther nailed his 95 theses

KEY WEB LINKS

www.nationalsecurity.org/
www.odci.gov/cia/publications/
pubs.html
www.popnet.org/texts/
governmt.htm
www.state.gov/index.html
www.info.usaid.gov/
www.oecd.org/dac

to the church door in Wittenberg in 1517. Jean Bodin in France published *Six Books on the State* in 1576, arguing the case for the divine right of the French king to rule in an absolute manner, free of outside authority.[1]

The feudal system broke in the Thirty Years War (1618–1648). A mosaic of warfare engulfed much of Europe, especially the modern German and Bohemian (western Czechoslovakian) territories, where the wars reduced population levels by one-third to one-half. The participants in the Peace (or Treaties) of Westphalia in 1648 officially created a new system of decentralized, sovereign, and equal units, responsible to no higher authority. Choice of religion, a central issue of the wars, devolved to local sovereigns.

The new European structures thereby formalized one of the key characteristics of a modern state, the dominant and sovereign role of government. By the end of the 1500s England was a defined and relatively fixed territory with an effective monarch. France, Spain, Russia, and Austria followed. These states did not, of course, emerge from feudalism full-grown; they evolved with considerable turmoil.

According to Tilly (1985), potential kings with some initial power acted to resist their opponents (competitors in the power and security game) and to expand their own power within their current territory and beyond. New military technology helped them expand. Early in the process, there was little distinction between the violence of bandits, pirates, the king's representatives, regional authorities, and professional soldiers. The emerging king relied on bandits and pirates, used professional soldiers who looted for their payment, and played various regional authorities against one another. State building bore much resemblance to modern protection rackets. Only gradually did a king obtain a monopoly on the "legitimate" use of violence. More succinctly, Tilly said "the state makes war, and war makes the state."

Successful states provided incentives and examples for latecomers. Portugal, the Netherlands, and England were relatively early. Spain, France, Germany, Russia, and Japan reacted in self-defense and built states through emulation and innovation (Modelski 1978). The colonial process and subsequent decolonization extended the European state system to the rest of the world.

What exactly is a state? According to widely accepted convention, a **state** has four characteristics: (1) territory, with clear boundaries; (2) a population; (3) a government, not answerable to outside authorities, with control over the territory and population; and (4) **sovereignty,** or recognition by other states as a legally equal player in the global environment. In other words, what scholars of world politics call a state is essentially what the rest of the English-speaking world knows as a *country,* and we will use the terms interchangeably. There is, however, important reason for insistence on precision in definition. For example, Taiwan is a country that many other countries do not recognize as a sovereign equal. Both the Republic of China (ROC) on the island of Taiwan and the People's Republic of China (PRC) on the mainland agree that there is a single China and demand that other states recognize only one of them as the legitimate government of the Chinese

---

[1]Hinsley (1986) traced the rise and fall of the concept of sovereignty during the Roman empire period and the reemergence of it with Bodin.

state. Governments around the world gradually chose to recognize the government that took control of the mainland in 1949. Taiwan lost its membership in the United Nations to the PRC in 1971 and no longer even exchanges ambassadors with most countries. It falls short of being a full state.

State Systems

The modern state system developed during a period of about 300 years, beginning in Europe and expanding around the world. According to one count, there were 23 members in 1816, 42 in 1900, 64 in 1945, and 161 in 1985.[2] In 1997 UN membership reached 185.

Because the state system consists wholly of states, it might seem that analysis of it would simply involve studying the behavior and interactions of individual states. Because of the number of possible interactions (for example, alliance combinations) in even a small state system, that quickly becomes a difficult task; in a system of about 190 states it is overwhelming. Thus scholars often make the leap from analyzing individual states to considering the structure of the state system as a whole and considering how that structure influences individual state behavior.

Polarity describes the distribution of power in the state system. Polarity first distinguishes between great powers and lesser powers. **Great powers** or *major powers* have systemwide interests and sufficient power to pursue them.[3] Second, polarity identifies the number and relative size of the great powers. Historically, great powers have constituted a limited subset of total states, seldom more than five or six. Third, polarity sometimes specifies relationships between great and lesser (or minor) powers. Among theoretically possible systemic polarities are[4]

1. The **unipolar system.** When a single political entity dominates the system, it is unipolar.

2. The **bipolar system.** In any bipolar system, two great powers stand above all other states in power capabilities. In the bipolar system of the Cold War, the United States and the Soviet Union had such great nuclear and conventional capabilities relative to other great powers that they became **superpowers.** The system is loosely bipolar when the two primary poles do not organize the remaining states (great or lesser powers) into strong alliance structures and tightly bipolar when the two dominant great powers do organize the system into strong and opposing alliances.

3. The **multipolar system.** In this system, only the great powers are serious players, and there are but a handful (often five or six) relatively equal ones. The **unit veto system** is a variant of multipolar systems. This configuration requires that all great powers

---

[2]Singer and Small data (see Small and Singer 1982) provided by Thomas Cusack. The Singer and Small count has its critics. Bennett and Zitomersky (1982) pointed out that the Singer and Small interstate system is Eurocentric, requiring that either France or Britain diplomatically recognize all member states. In contrast, Bennett and Zitomersky counted 305 "autonomous political units" in 1816, only 76 in 1916 (after the spread of European empires), and 149 in 1970 (data again from Cusack).

[3]The expression "great power" acquired widespread usage in the mid-eighteenth century and first appeared in a treaty in 1815, at which time it referred to Great Britain, France, Austria, Prussia, and Russia (Craig and George 1983, 3). See Stoll (1989) for definition and discussion of major powers.

[4]Kaplan (1957, 21–85) distinguished six polarities and posited "rules" of state behavior in each of these systems.

have the ability to defend themselves individually from all others. It would in effect require that all have weapons such as nuclear arsenals, the use of which could not be denied to them. Each actor would have a veto on the actions of all others. Should the current system evolve into a world of many relatively equal nuclear powers, the unit veto system could appear—there is the skeleton of such a system already.

These categories are ideal types and simplify reality. Nonetheless, polarities offer a powerful way of grasping the structure of power in historic and contemporary systems.

Polarity structures emphasize political-military power relations among states, especially great powers. Yet other characterizations of global structures exist. For example, world-systems theory grows out of neo-Marxist economic analysis and portrays the world in terms of an economic class structure:

> For these world-system theorists, the fundamental units in their model of world order are high-wage, capital-intensive, developed countries specializing in manufactures—the *core*—and low-wage, labor-intensive, underdeveloped countries usually, but not always, specializing in raw materials for export—the *periphery*. A semiperipheral zone, which is something of a mix of core and peripheral economic activities, is also discussed. (Bergesen 1983, 45)

Such a predominantly economic perspective still emphasizes the power relations among states that are so important to realists. And it potentially supplements the realist military-political polarity characterizations of state-system structure by describing relations between more- and less-economically developed countries. The world-systems approach, however, clashes with realist understanding of the world for two reasons. First, it suggests that class-based distributions of power globally may be significantly independent of state borders and that classes may be a better unit of analysis than states. Second, it posits that political-military power analysis depends on economic power analysis. Neither of these images fits the realist world. This book will return to the world-systems perspective when we present and evaluate economic perspectives on world politics.

Many realists have, however, increasingly accepted some of the emphasis by the world-systems theorists on economics and on a truly global world system, while reasserting the primacy of politics over economics and rejecting any implication of diminished state role. Reexamining the interstate system with eyes better attuned than before to economic power relationships, some realists have begun to argue that an important structural pattern is the existence of a single leading or *hegemonic state* that dominates the political-economic system. These analysts describe the United States not as a superpower but as a hegemon.

Historic State Systems

The modern state system differs in important ways from historic ones, especially in the technology available to states. Yet, striking similarities appear with earlier eras. Holsti (1988, 23–51) surveyed three earlier systems: the Chinese system of the Chou Dynasty period (1122 B.C. to 221 B.C.), the Greek city-state system (800 B.C. to

322 B.C.), and the Renaissance Italy system (fourteenth and fifteenth centuries A.D.). We draw here on his review of the latter two systems.

In the Greek city-state system of 800 B.C. to 322 B.C., the basic unit was the city-state or *polis*. Considerable growth in intrasystem and extrasystem trade (especially by the fifth century B.C.) assured regular contact among the units. War was recurrent and frequently brutal. The city-states developed mechanisms such as arbitration and conciliation (reliance on third parties for conflict resolution) to deal with conflict. They normally respected the immunity of diplomats from harm, even during warfare.

The *polis* celebrated a philosophy of independence and small size. Although that might seem to preclude desire for empire, stratification grew. In the period 492 B.C. to 477 B.C., the city-states created the Hellenic League under the leadership of Athens and Sparta to resist the external power of the Persians. Thereafter fear of Athenian imperialism led competitors to form the Peloponnesian League under Spartan direction, whereas Athens established the Delian League to formalize its empire. In addition to the Delian League, Athens held an even more extensive hegemonic position in the system, built on its commercial and naval superiority; the attractiveness of its laws, courts, and currency; and the services it performed for other city-states. The system appeared simultaneously to be bipolar militarily and hegemonic economically. The Peloponnesian wars between the two Leagues erupted in 431 B.C. and lasted nearly 30 years. Athens lost the war. In 338 B.C. the weakened system succumbed to an outside power, Alexander the Great's Macedonia.

We see in this description a number of features that reoccur in other state systems. These include a multipolar to bipolar evolution. States also developed diplomatic techniques to allow some peaceful conflict resolution. Commerce among units was extensive, with Athens taking on an economic leadership role.

In the fourteenth and fifteenth centuries a set of relatively well-defined political entities appeared in northern Italy, somewhat isolated from the rest of Europe by mountains. Venice had been an important trading state for several centuries. In fact, in terms of the larger, extra-Italian system, it had many characteristics of a hegemonic power (Modelski 1978, 218). An oligarchy that received considerable popular support ruled Venice as a republic.

In contrast, most city-state governments earned relatively less popular support and therefore were less stable. They proved fairly easy targets for subversion and political intrigue sponsored from without. Frequent mercenary wars characterized the period. The states invented permanent embassies as a mechanism for maintaining diplomatic contact. Moreover, a rough multipolar balance of military power among actors during this period helped maintain relative tranquility. The French ultimately destroyed the system by invasion from without in 1494, on invitation of Milan.

Adam Watson (1992) surveyed the history of all state systems since ancient Sumer (about 2000 B.C.). He argued that state systems fall on a spectrum from absolute independence of states to absolute empire. While the periods of the Chinese warring states, Greek city-states, and Italian Renaissance fall at or near the absolute independence end of the spectrum (and thereby illustrate the anarchy of realists), it has been more common that hegemony, "dominion" (the dominant actor influences the internal character of states), and even empire organize them. Watson argued that most analysts therefore underestimate the degree to which interstate order and society existed historically and exist today.

Whatever characterization of historic state systems we accept, should we believe our era to be unique in the evolution of the modern state system, history refutes that belief. Should we believe that the history of the last few hundred years is a story of progress toward an ultimately cooperative, peaceful world, attention to earlier history raises doubt. Realist history is repetitive history.[5]

The Modern State System

Two portrayals of the evolution of the modern state system coexist. The first relies on the descriptive concepts of alternative military-political polarities (bipolar, multipolar, and so on). The second traces changing hegemonic leadership in the modern system. We consider each in turn.

Early Polarity

The birth of the modern state system, meaning the birth of a multipolar state system, is often said to be the Treaty of Westphalia in 1648, which ended the Thirty Years War and the pretensions of a Holy Roman Empire. Thereafter, at least until World War II, the European state system politically and militarily remained a generally multipolar one. The states of Portugal, Spain, the Netherlands, Britain, and France were fairly well established by 1648, and they persisted.

The Treaty of Utrecht in 1713, which presented terms to France after the defeat of its attempt to dominate much of Western Europe, contained the first explicit reference to balance of power (Craig and George 1983, 8). At the Congress of Vienna in 1815, after the defeat of France again, the great powers gave even more deliberate attention to balance and equilibrium. They established the Concert of Europe to facilitate discussions among governments and efforts to maintain the status quo. The following century encompassed the golden age of multipolar power balancing. For most of that period, Britain played an exceptional role as the balancer in the system. Britain maintained a flexibility in its dealings with other states that allowed it to mediate disputes and prevent disruptions to the European balance.

Before the outbreak of World War I in 1914, however, the once-flexible system had evolved into two fairly fixed alliance structures led by Britain and Germany. The apparent failure of balancing mechanisms to prevent World War I (1914–1918) gave rise to a surge of globalist idealism and search for international cooperation in the period following it. For instance, states established the first global political institution, the League of Nations. Nonetheless, the League of Nation's primary purpose, like that of the Concert of Europe, was to assist in management of a multipolar balance of power, not to replace it with a world government. It remained a realist world.

---

[5]Science fiction fans will recognize the same basic pattern in Isaac Asimov's Foundation series—a breakup of the galactic empire, an anarchic period in which local units develop and establish a galaxy-wide "state system," premature and abortive attempts to reestablish a universal system (the Mule is a kind of Napoleon), and even an essentially bipolar system under the leadership of the two foundations. A single power, Gaia, provides unity once again.

One critical difference characterized the war settlements of 1815 and 1919. Although victors restored France to a place of equality and participation after 1815, they reduced Germany to a position of inferiority and subordination after 1919. They stripped it of military power and territory, forced it to pay heavy reparations, and did not allow it to join the League until 1926. Although many reasons explain subsequent German aggression and the reinitiation of hostilities in 1939, the desire of Germans to regain what they had lost ranks high on the list.

Contemporary Polarity

World War II (1939–1945) again reduced Germany to impotence, this time partitioning it physically among four great power victors (France, Great Britain, the United States, and the Soviet Union). The occupation zones of the first three eventually became the Federal Republic of Germany (West Germany), whereas the Soviet zone became the German Democratic Republic (East Germany). As the sarcastic saying went, "The great powers love Germany so much that they are glad to have two of them."

The victorious great powers (joined by China) moved cooperatively to set up a multipolar base for the postwar international order. They established the United Nations, in which each would sit on the Security Council and hold veto power. The emergence of conflict, however, between the two largest of the powers, the United States and the Soviet Union, rapidly disrupted the plans of the major powers for the postwar management of international power.

Although their conventional military strength also vastly exceeded that of all other great powers except China, nuclear capability of the two superpowers assured their superior positions. The United States exploded its first atomic weapons in 1945, including the two used to win the war with Japan; the Soviet Union exploded its first in 1949. By the time other states acquired nuclear weapons, the lead of the superpowers was overwhelming, and the organization of the globe into two competing blocs or **spheres of influence** was very far along.

Formal organization followed, and the system quickly became tightly bipolar. In 1949 NATO came into being with 12 members including the United States, France, and Britain. In 1951 the United States concluded bilateral security or mutual defense treaties with Japan and the Philippines, and a trilateral one with Australia and New Zealand. Further treaties bound the United States to South Korea (1953) and Taiwan (1954), and established the Southeast Asia collective defense group (1954). The Federal Republic of Germany entered NATO in 1955. Many other agreements and treaties extended the network, centered on the United States, around the globe. On the Soviet side, formalization included establishment of the Warsaw Treaty Organization in 1955, linking the Soviet Union to most of the East European states. Various agreements allied the U.S.S.R. and China after the communist revolution of 1949 in China.

The subsequent transformation of the interstate system from a tightly bipolar to loosely bipolar structure was more gradual. Stalin died in 1952, and already by 1956 General Secretary Khrushchev undertook a de-Stalinization campaign. Superpower tensions eased a bit, and they held a summit meeting in 1955. Those changes and the desires of Eastern Europeans for greater local autonomy caused unrest within the Soviet bloc.

In the late 1950s DeGaulle challenged the privileged U.S. position in the Western alliance, initially through resistance to U.S. economic leadership. France sought military independence as well. In 1966 it withdrew from NATO's integrated military command and created its own nuclear strike capability. It remained an observer in NATO.

In 1958 six European states signed the Treaty of Rome and began a long process of integrating their economies that inevitably involved some distancing of Europe from the United States. Breakdown of the European colonial empires further weakened the coherence of U.S.-centric global alliance structures. In the early 1960s many economically less-developed countries, especially in Africa, gained independence. They rapidly raised voices of opposition to domination by either superpower. For instance, in 1960 alone, 17 new states entered the United Nations, and the U.S. dominance of that institution suffered a body blow.

As a much larger power, China began to distance itself in small ways from the Soviet Union by the middle of the 1950s. The break between the two communist powers became overt in the early 1960s. China entered the ranks of nuclear powers in 1964.

Gorbachev became general secretary of the Soviet Communist party in 1985, and began to loosen the reins of control in Eastern Europe and to release the pent-up pressure. His design for controlled change, however, gave way to the sudden shocks that Chapter 2 described. By 1990 all Soviet allies in Eastern Europe had removed hard-line communist governments and Soviet troops were departing. On December 31, 1991, the U.S.S.R. formally dissolved. Eastern and Western Europe began to grope toward new relationships, perhaps even unity.

By the late 1960s the modern state system had already become loosely bipolar. There is now evidence of real multipolarity. The visit by Nixon to China in 1972 was part of an active strategy to accommodate and even facilitate that evolution. Nixon's secretary of state, Henry Kissinger, was a serious student and admirer of the Austrian Chancellor Prince Metternich, who convened the 1814–1815 Congress of Vienna to regularize the nineteenth-century multipolar balance of power. Nixon and Kissinger believed that a new five-power multipolar system was developing, with the United States, U.S.S.R., Japan, China, and a partially unified Europe playing great power roles.

This brief review of the modern state system, emphasizing the evolution of polarity, illustrates the utility of describing the world in such terms. It was for a long time the dominant approach to characterizing the modern state system. (See, however, the box entitled "Categories of States.")

Hegemonic Leadership

A second characterization of historical and contemporary state systems has gained popularity in recent years. Instead of a multipolar world, many scholars describe the European system as a traditionally hegemonic one with a single dominant power at any one point in time. For example, Modelski (1978; 1987) argued that Venice was the dominant or hegemonic state during roughly the fifteenth century, followed by Portugal in the sixteenth, the Netherlands in the seventeenth, Britain in the eighteenth and nineteenth, and the United States in the twentieth. Thus he

Categories of States

The state system numbers about 190 states, so that the concepts of great powers, lesser powers, and hegemonic states are inadequate to describe the position of states.

Much terminology conveys economic differences among countries. The *North* means the economically more-developed countries (MDCs), and the *South* refers to the economically less-developed countries (LDCs). It is an interesting phenomenon that the more-developed countries are generally located above the equator and the less-developed countries are often near or below the equator. The typology of the World Bank introduces an intermediate category: high-income countries, middle-income countries, and low-income countries. In addition, a subcategory of less-developed countries called **newly industrialized countries (NICs),** or sometimes newly industrialized economies (NIEs), is common. Countries within it, like Israel, Brazil, Mexico, Taiwan, and South Korea, have experienced especially rapid economic growth and have strong industrial sectors. Many NICs have moved from low-income into middle-income status, and some, like Singapore and South Korea, have moved into high-income status.

Other terminology conveys more political differences. The *West* refers to the traditionally noncommunist countries of the world (primarily in the Western Hemisphere and Western Europe), whereas the *East* (seldom used now) designates the countries that came under communist governments after World War II. Although most of those countries have thrown out communist governments, they still share common problems in restoring Western democracy and market systems. Eastern countries are now countries in transition. We see increasingly heavy use of the political categories of the Freedom House: free, partly free, and not free.

One typology remaining from the days of the Cold War carries both economic and political content. The First World contains economically more advanced, Western countries (a subset of the West). The Second World (basically the East) consists of the one-time communist countries of Central and Eastern Europe, including the Soviet Union. This category is now archaic, economically, and much of the old Second World looks surprisingly like the Third World. The Third World is a residual category, generally equivalent to the South. As the great heterogeneity of the Third World grouping became increasingly clear to the category makers of the First World, they gave it a subcategory, the Fourth World (also least-developed countries). The Fourth World consists of those countries, like Bangladesh, Haiti, and Burkina Faso, that have experienced little or no economic advance in the post–World War II period.

presented even the nineteenth century, supposedly that golden period of multipolarity, as a time in which England was more than a simple balancer; it was a leading, dominant, or hegemonic state.

When we try to reconcile the multipolar and hegemonic characterizations, we might imagine an Orwellian state system, a collection of equals, among whom one is considerably "more equal" than others. A superior reconciliation of this apparent conflict lies, however, in understanding the movement of realist thought from purely military-political analysis into economic analysis. Britain's military superiority in the nineteenth century (especially in any continental conflict) was not as striking as its economic superiority (especially outside the continent). Britain's overwhelming sea power allowed it to establish a predominant commercial position in the world economy.

Similarly, attention to the concept of economic hegemony alters our perception of the post–World War II period. Instead of seeing the United States as a superpower opposed by one of roughly equal size, we see a world in which the United States unilaterally dominated world trade and finance. The Soviet Union remained largely separate from this system, engaging in relatively little trade, two-thirds of which was with other communist countries (Central Intelligence Agency 1988, 217). The collapse of the Soviet empire exposed the real hegemony of the United States.

Modelski and Thompson (1987) argued, however, that hegemonic global leadership was always as apparent in military power, especially seapower, as in economic size and trade. Figure 4.1 traces five long cycles in hegemonic leadership using seapower concentration. (Note that at the end of World War II the United States had a near monopoly on seapower and never lost that leadership.)

State Interests

Realists posit that states are the key actors in world politics. They further argue that states pursue key interests; while common terminology designates those to be "national interests," we will refer to them as **state interests.** Realists claim that those interests provide the only legitimate basis for state action. Two British diplo-

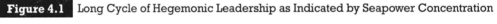

Figure 4.1 Long Cycle of Hegemonic Leadership as Indicated by Seapower Concentration

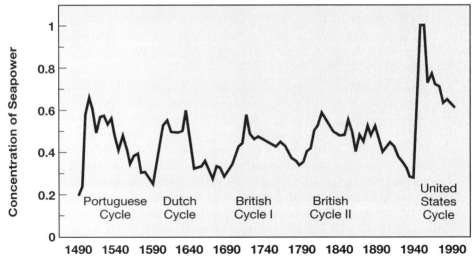

Source: Data courtesy of William R. Thompson.

mats gave us popular quotations concerning the centrality of interests to interstate politics. Lord Salisbury claimed that "the only bond of union that endures [is] the absence of all clashing interests" (Morgenthau 1973, 9). Palmerston provided the dictum that "Britain has no permanent friends or enemies, only permanent interests."

What, then, are these all-important interests of states? It is curious, given the presumed importance of state interests to the understanding of interstate behavior, that realists seldom devote much attention to defining them. Morgenthau went little further than equating state interest with power and security. A useful first step is to divide state interests into *core interests* and *instrumental interests.* The core interests of the state flow from its desire to preserve its essence: territorial boundaries, population, government, and sovereignty. Territorial disputes are almost certainly the most fundamental of all interstate conflicts, especially when, as in the case of the Iraqi claim to all of Kuwait, they threaten the continued existence of the state. States will, however, resist even the smallest redefinition of borders with the greatest of intensity. India and China fought in 1962 over a remote, mountainous, and largely uninhabitable territory called Ladakh. India and Pakistan have repeatedly clashed over the disposition of the much richer region of Kashmir. Japan and Russia proved unable to resolve their dispute over the Kurile islands, delaying the kind of post–Cold War reconciliation that came with remarkable ease to Russia and the United States, even while their nuclear weapons remained targeted on each other's population.

It may appear cynical to suggest that territory has greater importance to states than do people, but examples of the sacrifice by states of people for territory (for instance, via warfare) come more easily to mind than do those involving trades of territory for the security of people. Nonetheless, states also rank protection of their citizenry among core interests. Israel has been especially willing to take great risks and pay high costs to protect even small numbers of its citizens that terrorism threatened.

It should surprise no one that states also take threats to their governments seriously. The Iraqi government of Saddam Hussein regarded the effort by the United States in the 1990s to overthrow it as the most fundamental threat to core state interests. In the contemporary world more interstate conflicts have their roots in attempts to subvert a government than in attempts by external states to change territorial boundaries.

Protection of territory, people, and government (and thereby of sovereignty as well) thus emerge as fundamental to security and become the bedrock of state interest. Yet as Waltz (1979, 134) pointed out, "to say that a state seeks its own preservation or pursues its national interest becomes interesting only if we can figure out what the national interest requires a state to do." Unfortunately that is not simple. Consider, for example, the state interest of Israel and debates over whether or not it should trade land in the occupied West Bank for peace with its neighbors. What do core interests require Israel to do? Would a sacrifice of territory save lives by dampening conflict with neighbors or ultimately cost lives by making the remaining territory of Israel less secure from attack?

States routinely face such fundamentally important uncertainties about the definition of their interest and the demands that definition places upon action. Yet states need to act (even inaction is obviously a choice). Realists help address this dilemma in part by shifting much attention to instrumental interests, notably power. If a state protects and enhances its power, it stands a good chance of deterring threatening action by other states, of maximizing its ongoing options for action, and even of reducing the damage inflicted by mistaken action or inaction.

Power

Definition and Measurement

A common and succinct definition of **power** is the ability of A to get B to do X. More generally, power is the ability to influence outcomes to an actor's satisfaction. Unfortunately, it is not at all simple to translate this definition into any clear measurement of power. For instance, when the United States does something that Mexico wants (such as signing a free trade agreement), does it indicate that Mexico has power over the United States?

Your first reaction might be "no"—the United States signs such an agreement only if it wants to do so. The United States, however, may pay a penalty (higher costs of imported goods or greater illegal immigration) if it does not sign, just as it would pay a penalty if it decided to forego oil from the Persian Gulf. The size of those penalties suggests the amount of power that Mexico and Saudi Arabia have over the United States. That Mexico might pay an even larger penalty if the United States refused to ratify a free trade agreement suggests that both sides have power, and that it may not be equal. The extent and complexity of such vulnerability relationships in the modern world are staggering.

Frequently when we think of power, however, we focus less on such vulnerability to the withdrawal of a relational benefit than on the ability to coerce another actor with overt force. Clearly, the ability of the United States to bomb Libya or to invade Panama gives it some control of policies in those countries. Here, too, however, power is complex. Libya, although militarily weaker, has the ability to train terrorists for attacks on targets valued by Americans. The presence of the canal in Panama could potentially either deter U.S. military action (for fear of its being shut down) or invite it (because of its strategic importance).

That power is such a central concept in interstate politics motivates us to measure and compare the aggregate power of various states. How can we possibly undertake such measurement? Although the linkage is sometimes tenuous, much power grows ultimately out of capabilities: military strength, demographic size, economic production, resource bases, and even geographic position. Because much wisdom lies in the aphorism that "God is always on the side of the larger battalions," let us greatly simplify the issue and look at battalions and other measures of capabilities. We return to the issue of interactions and outcomes later.

Demographic Size

Table 4.1 ranks states on four capabilities: population, GNP, military spending, and military personnel. Two states stand above all others in terms of population: China with about 1.2 billion people and India with about 1.0 billion. The United States

Table 4.1   Selected Measures of State Power

Population 1998 (millions)		Gross National Product 1996 (billions)	
China	1,243	United States	7,433
India	989	China	4,047
United States	270	Japan	2,945
Indonesia	207	Germany	1,729
Brazil	162	France	1,256
Russia	147	United Kingdom	1,173
Pakistan	142	Italy	1,141
Japan	126	Brazil	1,023
Bangladesh	123	Canada	641
Nigeria	122	Russia	619

Military Spending 1995 (millions of U.S. dollars)		Military Personnel 1995 (thousands)	
United States	278	China	2,930
Russia	76	United States	1,620
China	64	Russia	1,400
Japan	50	India	1,265
France	48	North Korea	1,040
Germany	41	Turkey	805
United Kingdom	33	South Korea	655
Italy	19	Pakistan	587
Saudi Arabia	17	Vietnam	550
South Korea	14	France	504

Sources: (Population) Population Reference Bureau, *World Population Data Sheet* (Washington, DC: Population Reference Bureau, 1998). (GNP at Purchasing Power Parity) World Bank, *World Development Indicators 1998* (Washington, DC: World Bank, 1998). (Military Data) U.S. Arms Control and Disarmament Agency, *World Military Expenditures and Arms Transfers, 1996* (Washington, DC: U.S. Arms Control and Disarmament Agency, 1997).

ranks a quite distant third. Moreover, the gap between it and the rest of the pack is comparatively narrow; given the high growth rates of countries like Indonesia and Brazil, the gap is also closing rapidly.

Over long periods, other capabilities frequently accrue to states with large populations. For instance, at the end of the nineteenth century, the newly unified Germany could boast a population greater than that of the United Kingdom or France. It took little time for Germany to pose an economic and military challenge to the older states. The reunified East and West Germany once again boasts a larger population (about one-third) than either of its two long-term rivals.

The astute French social observer, de Tocqueville, used population trends in his study of the United States in 1835 to foresee the world politics of the twentieth century. At that time he examined U.S. census data from 1830 that reported a U.S.

population of 12.9 million including more than 2 million slaves (de Tocqueville 1945, originally 1835, 386f and 412f). On the basis of past growth and the amount of land available he argued that

> The time will therefore come when one hundred and fifty million men [people] will be living in North America,[6] equal in condition, all belonging to one family, owing their origin to the same cause, and preserving the same civilization, the same language, the same religion, the same habits, the same manners, and imbued with the same opinions, propagated under the same forms. The rest is uncertain, but this is certain; and it is a fact new to the world, a fact that the imagination strives in vain to grasp.
>
> There are at the present time two great nations in the world, which started from different points, but seem to tend to the same end. I allude to the Russians and the Americans. Both of them have grown up unnoticed; and while the attention of mankind was directed elsewhere, they have suddenly placed themselves in the front rank among the nations, and the world learned of their existence and their greatness at almost the same time.
>
> All other nations seem to have nearly reached their natural limits, and they have only to maintain their power; but these are still in the act of growth. . . . Their starting-point is different and their courses are not the same; yet each of them seems marked out by the will of Heaven to sway the destinies of half the globe. (de Tocqueville 1945, originally 1835, 451–452)

China and India now have cutting-edge technology and rapidly developing economic systems. They each have populations two to four times as large as those of Western Europe or the United States. Their economic growth rates are considerably faster than those European-based populations. Their natural resources and land areas are extensive. Should we perhaps now foresee that in the twenty-first century they will come to sway the destinies of the globe?

Economic and Military Capabilities

Table 4.1 also indicates the structure of global economic capabilities. The United States has a unique place at the pinnacle of the measure. In fact, its economic size is much greater than that of China or Japan. Table 4.1 represents GNP at **purchasing power parity,** that is, in terms of the volume of goods and services that the GNP of countries can provide. Were the more common representation at "exchange rates" used, the Chinese GNP would be much smaller and Japan's would be somewhat larger. In any case the U.S. lead in GNP is commanding and reinforces our identification of the United States as an economic hegemon.

GNP (gross national product) may be the best single measure of current power because states can fairly readily convert economic capabilities into military ones.[7] In 1940, before the U.S. entry into World War II, Germany outproduced the

---

[6]He reported 205 million in Europe at that time, in a lesser geographic area; there are now over 270 million people in the United States and about 580 million in all of Europe, excluding Russia.

[7]Measuring GNP and GDP is difficult. Increasingly, estimates are based on purchasing power parity (PPP) rather than exchange rates, for enhanced comparability. But in 1996 the World Bank reduced its PPP estimate of the Chinese economy by nearly 30 percent as it learned more about the extent of poverty there (*The Economist* October 12, 1996, 35).

United States by six to one in combat munitions (Deutsch 1988, 21). Because of the inherent strength of the U.S. economy, American production of munitions thereafter increased six-fold in only three years as the economy mobilized for war. Few doubt today that Japan could similarly turn its economy to military production with remarkable speed, should it decide to do so.

Military power is more difficult to measure than population or economic size. Military spending and military personnel often serve as indicators. The United States outspends all of its nearest rivals combined. Before placing much trust in military spending figures, however, consider just two of the problems in comparing that of the military great powers. First, although the United States does not put into its military budget all items that could be argued to be military expenditures (for example, veteran's benefits and interest on government debt, much of which it incurred for military purposes), China has long consciously concealed a significant portion of its military budget (as did the former U.S.S.R.). Second, the United States has voluntary and relatively highly paid armed forces in contrast to the Russian and Chinese use of low-paid conscripts. In military personnel China is the superpower. In general, attention to personnel raises the ranking of Third World countries. But military personnel is clearly an inadequate military power measure by itself. Debates inevitably rage concerning "true" military capabilities. Furthermore, we have not addressed the difficulty that nuclear weapons add to the issue.

Aggregate Capabilities and Power

Despite measurement problems, the Correlates of War Project at the University of Michigan added the variables of Table 4.1 into an overall index of power capabilities; the index provides a sketch of changes in relative power over time (Ray 1987, 193). The original composite index relied on two demographic measures (total population and urban population), two economic indicators (steel production and fuel consumption, now both replaced by GNP), and two military figures (personnel and expenditures), combined with equal weight. Table 4.2 reports that index for great powers at selected intervals in the twentieth century (immediately before and after World Wars I and II and in recent years). The absolute numbers have limited credibility; we should focus on general patterns and on changes over time.

Several patterns are especially notable in Table 4.2. One is the placement of the United States in first or very close second position throughout the twentieth century, the "American century." Second, the challenge that Germany made to the leading powers and especially to Britain, preceding both world wars, shows clearly in the index. Before both wars German power had risen above British. Coalitions vanquished Germany in both world wars, and Britain reemerged above all other European states, its position of the nineteenth century. Third, the failure of the European great powers of 1900 (especially Germany, Great Britain, and France) to recover serious ability to challenge the superpowers after World War II indicates the fundamental transformation of the system that occurred in that war. Finally, China and India, which the Michigan scholars did not even consider for inclusion in the power rankings through 1946, rank above the European states by the mid-1980s. Dramatic global changes marked the "quiet" years after World War II.

Table 4.2	Aggregate Power Index		

1913 (pre–World War I)		1920 (post–World War I)	
United States	26	United States	46
Russia	18	United Kingdom	22
Germany	18	France	13
United Kingdom	14	Italy	11
France	9	Japan	8
Japan	6		
Austria-Hungary	6		
Italy	4		

1938 (pre–World War II)		1946 (post–World War II)	
U.S.S.R.	25	United States	45
United States	24	U.S.S.R.	34
Germany	20	United Kingdom	14
United Kingdom	10	France	7
Japan	10		
France	6		
Italy	5		

1984 (pre–U.S.S.R. collapse)		1993 (post–U.S.S.R. collapse)	
United States	27	United States	27
U.S.S.R.	24	China	22
China	18	Japan	12
India	10	India	12
Japan	8	Russia	11
West Germany	5	Germany	6
France	4	France	5
United Kingdom	4	United Kingdom	4

Note: GNP was substituted for both steel production and energy consumption in the index computation beginning in 1984.

Sources: James Lee Ray, *Global Politics*, 3rd ed. (Boston: Houghton Mifflin, 1987), 193–195. Calculations for 1984 and 1993 from sources of Table 4.1.

Although not trustworthy, the absolute numbers are provocative. The gap between the United States and all other states is substantial. China ranks high, however, because of its strength on many measures, including demographic. Russia has fallen very sharply in recent years. India achieves its position primarily for demographic reasons. Japan surpasses the individual power totals of the traditional European great powers but would fall considerably short of the total for a united Western Europe. It is also interesting that most of the largest powers now have Pacific Ocean coastlines.

In addition to the superpowers and great powers, many other states hold significant military capabilities. Table 4.3 presents some information on the power capabilities of states in regional arenas; it groups sets of states with historic conflicts. Note especially the Asian pairs. In recent years arms expenditures in that region have jumped; Chinese expenditures on advanced arms have even caused Japanese anxiety.

Regions and Competitive States	Population 1998 (millions)	GNP 1996 (billions)	Military Spending 1995 (billions)
Asia			
India	988.7	1,493.3	7.8
Pakistan	141.9	213.6	3.7
China	1,242.5	4,047.3	63.5
India	988.7	1,493.3	7.8
North Korea	22.2	20.9	6.0
South Korea	46.4	595.7	14.4
China	1,242.5	4,047.3	63.5
Taiwan	21.7	315.0	13.1
Europe			
Greece	10.5	133.3	5.1
Turkey	64.8	379.9	6.6
Latin America			
Argentina	36.1	335.6	4.7
Brazil	162.1	1,023.1	10.9
Middle East			
Israel	6.0	103.0	8.7
Egypt	65.5	169.5	2.7
Syria	15.6	43.8	3.6
Iran	65.1	335.0	4.2
Iraq	21.8	42.0	NA

Table 4.3   Regional Balances of Power, 1995–1998

Sources: (Population) Population Reference Bureau, *1998 World Population Data Sheet* (Washington, DC: Population Reference Bureau, 1998); (GNP) World Bank, *World Development Indicators 1998* (Washington, DC: World Bank, 1998) and CIA *World Factbook* (http://www.odci.gov/cia, June 16, 1998). (Military Spending) U.S. Arms Control and Disarmament Agency, *World Military Expenditures and Arms Transfers 1996* (Washington, DC: U.S. Arms Control and Disarmament Agency, 1997).

Other Capabilities

Still other capabilities contribute to overall power. Alliances frequently play determining roles in the outcomes of wars. On the basis of demographic and economic size, Table 4.3 shows that Iran should have easily beaten Iraq in their war (Iranian advantages are more than three-to-one). Yet Iran was largely isolated in the international community, whereas Saudi Arabia and others (including the United States) gave Iraq considerable support. Similarly, the slight edge given the United States over the Soviets in the overall power rankings of Table 4.2 during the 1980s did not reflect the important strength of its alliance structure. In the case of an East-West conflict, the Eastern European forces were unreliable allies for the U.S.S.R.

One reason for the greater appeal of the United States in alliances is its **soft power** (Nye 1990). The political and economic institutions and the popular culture of the United States have great appeal around the world. This gives the country an intangible edge in all sorts of interactions with other states.

Territory and natural resources also contribute to power. Both the United States and Russia have considerable autarky (economic independence), because they possess vast territory and abundant supplies of many natural resources, especially energy. Germany suffered in World War II from its much greater dependence on outside resources. Other geographic factors make contributions to capabilities, however hard to measure. For instance, natural borders, such as the mountains of Switzerland or the seas surrounding Britain, Japan, and the United States, confer advantages.

Geopolitics (theory that attributes a substantial role to geographic factors in world politics) heavily influenced both scholars and practitioners in the early part of the twentieth century. In 1890 Alfred Mahan attributed the rise of British power to the country's island position and its related development of naval power. His writings encouraged President Theodore Roosevelt to develop U.S. naval power in the first decade of the twentieth century (Kennedy 1983, 43–85). Sir Halford Mackinder retorted in 1904 that history alternates between land and sea power (which he said had been dominant for four centuries) and argued that modern industry and the railroad would favor the great land powers in the twentieth century.

Neither scholars nor practitioners devote as much attention to geopolitics as they did a century ago. This is as it should be, because industrialization and technological advance reduce the potence of geographic barriers to human movement in commerce or military action. The United States and Russia, separated by the major oceans of the world, are fully able to destroy each other.

Power and the Interest of States

We began this discussion of power by noting that realists frequently shift the focus of interstate politics to power because the instrumental approach appears to offer a definition of state interest with potentially fewer problems than that based on core interests. In the course of our discussion, however, at least one key problem should have become obvious—it is not easy to define and measure power.

Measurement difficulty does not make a concept less important, as a realist would be quick to point out. It does, however, make a concept less useful as a guide to action. For instance, throughout the 1990s a central foreign policy debate in Russia concerned the appropriate size of the defense budget, which fell precipitously after the overthrow of communism. Because both military capabilities and economic health are important to overall power, we cannot easily determine an optimal level of Russian military spending. Many Russian realists, looking at possible threats from China or from the West, argue for maintenance of considerable military expenditures. Clearly military expenditures compete, however, with other governmental and private expenditures and can reduce economic growth. Therefore many other Russian realists argue for reduced expenditures. Power is an important but complicated concept.

Instruments of Power: Statecraft

The previous discussion focused on power capabilities. Although it would be convenient to continue elaboration of the theoretical argument of realists by assuming that states use their power capabilities skillfully, in reality they do not always do so. Thus many (especially traditional) realists take time out to instruct policy makers on the proper use of power. We will similarly digress here to discuss the *art* of statecraft.

Statecraft is the artful application of state power, guided by an understanding of the contemporary state system and a *vision* of desirable change in it. State action should not be ad hoc reaction to daily events, but rather purposeful long-term pursuit of state interests. The tools of statecraft fall generally into the categories of diplomacy, economic instruments, and the use of force. We consider each in turn.

Diplomacy

Simpson (1987, 6) defined diplomacy as "the process by which policies are converted from rhetoric to realities, from strategic generalities to the desired actions or inactions of other governments." Lester Pearson put it more colorfully when he said that "Diplomacy is letting someone else have it your way." **Diplomacy** involves three activities: representation, reporting, and negotiation (Van Dinh 1987, 4). The first two, representation and reporting, center on the conveyance and acquisition of information, of which rational policy making and implementation require large volumes.

Representation   It is important to governments that other states adequately understand their policy concerns and objectives. For instance, one factor contributing to the North Korean invasion of South Korea on June 25, 1950, may well have been inadequate communication by the United States of its commitment to defend South Korea from attack. On January 12, 1950, Secretary of State Dean Acheson gave a speech to the National Press Club in Washington in which he identified the defense perimeter of the United States in terms of a line from the Aleutians to Japan to the Ryukyus (islands of southwest Japan) to the Philippines (Dougherty and Pfaltzgraff 1986, 80). Although South Korea was not specifically excluded, it was not included. During his presidential campaign, Dwight Eisenhower subsequently argued that this definition virtually invited the attack.

States regularly attempt to clarify their policy positions in a variety of ways. One approach in the United States is the statement by presidents of doctrines. The Monroe Doctrine (1823) declared the Western hemisphere off-limits to European powers. The Truman Doctrine (1947) enunciated an intent to support any country resisting communist pressure. On issues of special importance, governments also periodically issue "white papers," which generally review a policy problem and state official positions. On a day-to-day basis, foreign ministries routinely brief diplomats from other countries about their policy objectives and intent.

Although states normally wish to communicate clearly, and rely on skilled diplomats to avoid miscommunication, countries also deliberately obfuscate and conceal. With respect to the scope of concerns and intensity of interest, states commonly overstate them to avoid the kind of problem the United States had in Korea. The routine proclamation that a government would "view with serious concern" a particular action by another government deliberately creates some ambiguity about the actual extent of concern and potential counteraction.

Thus governments play a cat-and-mouse game with one another seeking to inform, misinform, and obfuscate. Still another twist is disinformation including the propagation of forged documents supposedly originating with one's opponent and intended to discredit that opponent. The former Soviet Union used this technique frequently. For instance, one Soviet forgery of a letter, supposedly from the American undersecretary of state to the ambassador in Greece, suggested that the United States was willing to support a military coup in Greece, if necessary, to maintain its military bases there (Holsti 1988, 211–212). The purpose of the letter was to cause an intense anti-American reaction in Greece.

Propaganda is another form of representation, targeting foreign populations rather than governments. It has been so often tainted by untruths that the term itself has a negative connotation; many prefer to call it information services. The United States Information Agency, which has a good reputation for accuracy, staffs more than one hundred libraries and information centers abroad. The United States uses a global radio network called the Voice of America and other vehicles including Radio Marti, which broadcasts specifically for Cuba. TV Marti began in 1990. The British Broadcast Corporation's World Service has a large global audience because of a very well-deserved reputation for accuracy.

Reporting   Gathering intelligence and providing it to decision makers is a central activity of diplomats and foreign diplomatic missions. When, in 1979, Iranian radicals labeled the American embassy in Teheran a "Den of Spies," they were in a most general sense correct. All embassies seek information on the objectives and interests of the states in which they are located. Much of the information search is open and, as discussed earlier, the host country even facilitates it. Because much information given freely omits or even obfuscates important details concerning intent and capabilities, however, states supplement it with clandestinely obtained knowledge.

Historically, the most important clandestine tool was human espionage. The advent of sophisticated electronic eavesdropping extended abilities dramatically. Although as recently as 1929 an American Secretary of State, Henry Stimson, huffed that "Gentlemen do not read each others' mail," governments now routinely monitor conversations and read "electronic mail." American evidence in 1988 that Libya was building a chemical weapons factory came in part from eavesdropping on a telephone conversation between Libyan and German scientists.

The sophistication of electronic measures complicates the relationships between embassies and the host governments. In the 1980s, the United States and the former U.S.S.R. built and sought to open new embassies in Moscow and Washington, respectively. The United States found that Soviet surveillance equipment so permeated the structure of its new embassy in Moscow that it could never be secure. The United States refused to let the Soviets occupy their new Washington embassy until they resolved problems in Moscow. In late 1991, as the Cold War was ending, the chief of the Soviet KGB helped break the logjam by giving the U.S. ambassador full plans of the Moscow bugging.

Governments around the world maintain extensive intelligence operations, sometimes under the cloak of diplomatic function and sometimes more openly. Among the most famous or notorious are the Russian Foreign Intelligence Service (IVR)—part of the former KGB, the American Central Intelligence Agency (CIA), the Israeli Mossad, and the British MI-6. The bulk of the budgets for such organizations supports a range of electronic and human intelligence gathering. Electronic intelligence gathering and protection of communication has become such a large-scale activity that the U.S. Department of Defense also maintains a huge National Security Agency (NSA) devoted solely to it (its existence was a state secret until 1992). Electronic intelligence using reconnaissance satellites, spy ships, special aircraft, and ground stations falls into its domain. The public notoriety of the intelligence organizations comes, however, from their covert actions, which include psychological, political, military, and economic activities.

In the 1990s economic espionage on behalf of domestic firms moved to a more prominent place on the spying agenda. High-tech companies are special targets of French, German, and Japanese espionage. The French Direction Générale de la Sécurité Extérieure (DGSE) has been accused of bugging airline seats and hotel rooms of businessmen and of planting moles in companies. In 1995 the French expelled five U.S. citizens for spying, perhaps because American spies had discovered bribery by French firms pursuing contracts in Saudi Arabia and Brazil.

Negotiation   The third diplomatic activity, and the one we most often associate with diplomats, is negotiation. Obviously, an important function of negotiation is to reach agreement among two or more countries over issues on which they have partly overlapping but also competing interests. Each side seeks to attain agreement as close to its own preferred position as possible and the skill of diplomats plays an important role. For instance, diplomats seek to conceal their minimally acceptable position or *resistance point* so as to achieve more. It is partly for this reason that the quotation from Sir Henry Wotton, an English official (1568–1639) is so popular. He defined a diplomat as "an honest man sent abroad to lie for the good of the country."

Negotiation most often involves the iterative narrowing of the gap between initial positions within or at least toward the **zone of overlap** defined by the minimally acceptable positions. For instance, Henry Kissinger flew repeatedly in 1974 between Aswan, Jerusalem, and Damascus so as to secure an agreement among Egypt, Israel, and Syria that defused the military situation remaining from the 1973 Mideast War (Stoessinger 1976, 190–200). His technique became known as **shuttle diplomacy.** President Jimmy Carter accomplished the same feat in 1978, when he brought Egyptian President Sadat and Israeli Prime Minister Begin to Camp David (the U.S. presidential retreat) and shuttled between their cabins until an agreement was obtained.

Diplomacy can, however, be a "velvet glove" that conceals the iron hand of power. Weaker powers must frequently make concessions at the table to avoid losses in a test of power. The close relationship between diplomacy and force gives rise to a combination that Alexander George (1991) calls **coercive diplomacy.** For instance, the United States threatened the use of force against Iraq in 1998, should it not resume compliance with UN sanctions, and moved almost in slow motion to prepare for the use of force, while it searched for a diplomatic settlement. The Secretary General of the United Nations ultimately negotiated compliance by Iraq.

Negotiation also sometimes has functions other than the apparent one of attaining agreement. It may have a propaganda function. Countries periodically put forward arms control proposals that appear sincere, but that are patently unacceptable to the other side and that seek only to convey a peace-loving image to publics around the world. Soviet calls over many years for general and complete disarmament fell into this category. Another function is to stall for time in the hope that the external power balance will shift in one's favor. In early 1999 both the Albanians (initially) and the Serbians rejected proposals from the United States for a settlement in Kosovo because both sides believed they could win on the battlefield.

Negotiating styles differ considerably across time and by country. In the nineteenth century, diplomats commonly conducted discussions covertly and even kept important mutual defense treaties secret. This *old diplomacy* had some advantages. Practitioners could conduct it in a somewhat genteel atmosphere, unconstrained by the passions of public opinion. The contribution of secret treaties to the spread of World War I, by committing states to actions of which other states were unaware, and the democratization of government in the twentieth century, brought a new, public diplomacy. With few but sometimes very productive exceptions, like the secret dispatch of diplomats by Bush to China in 1989, the Oslo agreement between Israel and the Palestinians in 1994, or various rounds of discussion between North and South Korea, diplomats conduct the *new diplomacy* quite openly.

Bargaining styles also differ across countries. More powerful states can afford "sincere" and "pragmatic" styles aimed at finalizing agreements. Less powerful states are more likely to bluster and posture, and to rely on tactics to wear down the other side.

Economic Instruments

Countries also draw on a wide range of economic instruments in their interactions with other countries (Baldwin 1985). For example, both the former U.S.S.R. and the United States have used their contributions to international organizations as leverage for policy influence. In 1990 the United States reduced its contribution to the United Nations Food and Agricultural Organization in protest against its support for the Palestine Liberation Organization. The best-known and perhaps most frequently applied economic instruments are trade restrictions and foreign aid; we concentrate our attention on them.

Trade Restrictions   The most common trade restrictions or sanctions, applied with the intent of influencing the behavior of other states, are **boycotts** (the restriction of imports from a country or countries) and **embargoes** (the prohibition of exports) to a country. **Tariffs** (taxes on imports) can also reward and punish other states, but more often raise revenue or protect domestic industry. **Quotas** (numerical limitations) on imports or exports sometimes also constitute application of economic power.

Trade restrictions have a long and controversial history. Athens applied a trade boycott to Megara, a Spartan ally in 432 B.C. (Baldwin 1985, 150–154). That use of economic power may have precipitated the Peloponnesian War. The League of Nations directed both a boycott and limited embargo at Italy in 1935–1936 in reaction to its invasion of Ethiopia. Most analysts characterize that effort as a failure, and the episode contributed to negative assessments of both the league and economic instruments.

The United States, the leading economic power of the century, often uses trade restrictions in its foreign policy. For instance, the United States embargoed exports of anything with strategic value to the Soviet Union and its allies. After the communist government of Fidel Castro took over in Cuba, the United States applied sanctions and gradually raised them to the level of a total embargo. Because Cuba had been highly integrated with the U.S. market, the embargo dealt a severe blow to the island economy. It did not, however, achieve a change in the Cuban government. The sanctions and the controversy over them continued into the 1990s, when the United States further intensified them. In 1995 the UN voted 117 to 3 on a resolution condemning the U.S. embargo. Even strong U.S. allies like Canada chafed under efforts by the United States to prevent them from trading with Cuba.

In 1994 the United States led an embargo against the Haitian military government. That government ultimately stepped aside, perhaps more from fear of an invasion (and promises of personnel relocation) than from effects of the embargo. In the early 1990s, the United States attempted to use sanctions, especially the denial of trade privileges, to push China toward acceptance of human rights conventions. Ultimately, it abandoned the effort in favor of subtler pressures. In 1997 and 1998 China did sign the two primary UN conventions on human rights.

In the 1980s South Africa faced increasing restrictions on its trade and international capital flows from countries around the world, because of its Apartheid policy of racial separation. A debate raged over whether intensified sanctions would weaken the South African economy and force change, or whether they would create a "bunker mentality" among South African leaders and cause them to resist change even more strongly. Also, some argued that economic sanctions hurt blacks more than whites.

The United Nations has also sought to organize economic sanctions. In the early 1990s, the Security Council imposed "mandatory" sanctions eight times, compared to only twice from 1945–1990. Prior to the use of military action against Iraq for its takeover of Kuwait, the UN Security Council ordered tight boycotts and embargoes on Iraq. By some estimates, the GNP of Iraq dropped 50 percent due to the sanctions and was still collapsing when the United States and UN decided to use force. And in 1992–1993 the UN imposed and tightened an embargo on Serbia. It contributed to hyperinflation and considerable economic pain. Serbia initially appeared to backpedal on its military support for a "Greater Serbia." However, supplies of many goods, including Russian weapons, continued to arrive in Serbia via Greece, Bulgaria, and Romania.

Assessment of Trade Restrictions   Although some analysts argue that trade restrictions are effective political instruments, many others dispute that assessment. One comprehensive study concluded that they were successful in 34 percent of 115 cases since World War I (Hufbauer, Schott, and Elliot 1990, 93). Pape (1997) reviewed the data from the same study and concluded that "sanctions do not work." There are two fundamental methodological problems in evaluating success and failure. First, the aims of the sanctions are not always clear. Second, we have no "control" case against which to evaluate the application of economic power—we do not know what would have happened had it *not* been applied.

Two factors limit the effectiveness of trade restrictions. The first is that with exceptions such as highly sophisticated technology, most goods are **fungible.** That is, goods produced in one country are nearly indistinguishable from goods originating in another. This is especially true of raw materials like crude oil or grain. Thus restrictions on trade by one country or a group of countries generally elicits offsetting supplies or markets in others. Governments can easily "cheat" by simply failing to monitor carefully the actions of companies that can, if caught, be blamed for undertaking actions of which the government officially disapproves.

The second problem is that governments often use trade restrictions to apply pressure on issues so important that the states facing sanction will accept considerable sacrifice rather than buckle to that pressure. This is a failure in statecraft, because the declared goals are unreasonable. Despite lack of access to U.S. markets, Cuba was unwilling for more than 40 years to change its system of government. In 1998 the United States imposed strong economic sanctions on both India and Pakistan following their tests of nuclear weapons, but both states brushed aside proposals to renounce nuclear weapons. In fact, Pakistan's leadership renewed claims, dating from 1965, that its population would "eat grass" rather than forgo nuclear weapons development. In some cases outside pressure can, at least for a time, be a rallying point for governmental efforts to secure popular support—the "rally around the flag" effect.

Further complicating assessment, the declared goals (or "apparent" goals, because states often act without a clear goal declaration) frequently differ from the real goals. Many embargoes simply satisfy domestic pressures to "do something," and embargoes threaten all parties less than military action. The U.S. grain embargo against the Soviet Union, imposed after it invaded Afghanistan in 1979, fell into this category.

Recently, **smart sanctions** have begun to attract much attention (Lopez and Cartwright 1998). Trade sanctions can actually be blunt instruments, hurting innocent civilians as much or more as those in power. For instance, UN sanctions against Iraq in the 1990s, in spite of efforts to exempt food and medicine, led to significant malnutrition and health problems and to many thousands of deaths. Smart sanctions include freezing the foreign assets of those in power, limiting travel abroad of the elite and their families, denying access to international telephone connections (including the Internet), banning sports and cultural exchanges, prosecuting leadership for war crimes in international tribunals, and refusing access to international financial institutions. For instance, in 1997 the UN voted to prohibit air travel to the areas of Angola controlled by Savimbi's forces, banned contracts to maintain his forces, and asked governments to close his overseas offices.

Foreign Aid   Foreign assistance is another economic instrument available to states and includes monetary grants, commodity gifts, loans, technical assistance, and emergency humanitarian relief. The Marshall Plan was the most spectacular aid program of the post–World War II period. In 1948, three years after the war, the

European economies were still in bad shape, with energy shortages and hunger characterizing both the victors and the vanquished. Communist movements in Western Europe gained strength. In a speech at Harvard, U.S. Secretary of State George Marshall proposed a substantial aid program for Europe. Although officially named the European Recovery Program, it is much better known as the Marshall Plan. It channeled $12 billion to Europe. Between 1946 and 1952 the United States devoted more than 2 percent of its GNP to foreign aid (Baldwin 1985, 296) compared with less than 0.2 percent in recent years. It helped precipitate the "economic miracles" of European growth in the 1950s and 1960s; it tied Western Europe to the United States politically and economically; and it even provided some initial impetus to the economic integration of Europe by requiring the states to plan the use of aid collectively.

In the 1950s and 1960s U.S. aid shifted from Europe to the less-developed countries (LDCs). The newly recovered countries in Europe increasingly joined in giving aid. The Development Assistance Committee (DAC) now monitors foreign aid programs of major Western donors. Its membership consists of most Western European countries and the United States, Canada, Australia, and New Zealand. According to the DAC, **official development assistance (ODA)** should meet two criteria: It should promote economic development and welfare; and it should be concessional in character, with a grant component of at least 25 percent. The concessional, nongrant element of aid consists of loans that LDCs can repay during long periods and with low interest rates (averaging about 2 percent).

In the 1990s some observers called for aid similar to the Marshall Plan to the former republics of the U.S.S.R. and to countries of Eastern Europe. Nothing remotely equivalent to the Marshall Plan ever materialized.

Aid Donors and Channels   The United States was the dominant Western donor of all types of aid through the 1950s and 1960s. In 1965 it still gave over 60 percent of total development assistance. As the economies of its allies strengthened and their aid grew, however, the U.S. commitment weakened. In 1996 its share was 21 percent, not much more than the 17 percent that Japan provided (World Bank 1997, 306). Figure 4.2 traces the U.S. and DAC aid history as a percentage of GNP.

In an effort to balance a desire to provide aid against the more competitive economic environment in which countries increasingly find themselves, they have turned to mechanisms that help serve domestic as well as foreign interests. For example, to meet the need for food in LDCs, and simultaneously to help dispose of U.S. surpluses, the United States initiated the Food for Peace Program (Public Law 480) in 1954. Global trade agreements now restrict such disposal of surpluses, but the United States remains the principal source of emergency food relief when starvation threatens Africa or other areas of the world. Another mechanism adopted by all donors is **tied aid,** distributions that recipients must spend in the donor country. That rule helps maintain some domestic support for aid programs (Figure 4.3).

Most foreign assistance is bilateral aid (country to country) and donor countries distribute it through their own institutions. Both donors and recipients see this as a way of maximizing political and economic control of donors. Recipients have urged greater multilateral aid, support directed through global institutions. Multilateral aid grew from a negligible portion of the total aid effort (5.9 percent in 1965) to about one-fourth of the total.

Figure 4.2   Foreign Aid Donation Rates

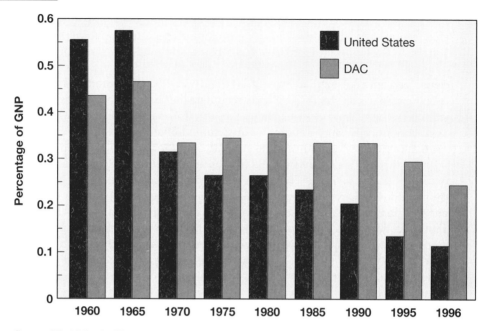

Source: World Bank, *World Development Report 1992* (Washington, DC: Oxford University Press, 1992), 254; World Bank, *World Development Report 1995* (Washington, DC: Oxford University Press, 1995), 198, World Bank, *World Development Indicators 1997* (Washington, DC: World Bank, 1997), 306; World Bank, *World Development Indicators 1998* (Washington, DC: World Bank, 1998), 340.

Foreign-assistance activities of nongovernmental organizations and even private individuals have become increasingly important over time. NGOs from the United States and Britain now channel more than $7.5 billion in aid funds, more than 10 percent of what governments spend (*Economist* June 22, 1996, 44). Participants include the Red Cross Societies, CARE, Save the Children Fund, and OXFAM. That they raise about one-third of their money from government, and that they compete aggressively for private donations does not detract from the importance of their activities. In addition, one individual, billionaire financier George Soros, played a key role in supporting the transitions to democracy and free markets throughout the former communist world via his Soros Foundation.

The Impact of Aid   For the lowest-income countries of the world, excluding China and India, foreign aid provides nearly one-third as much foreign exchange as do export sales (World Bank 1997, 212, 316). Because it is highly concentrated, it has a much greater impact on selected countries. Of the $12.8 billion in official aid given by the United States in 1996, just two countries, Israel and Egypt, received about $5 billion. As deserving as these two states may be, the U.S. effort to maintain peace in the Middle East obviously takes priority over Southern economic development (Table 4.4).

Figure 4.3   Foreign Aid Donation Levels

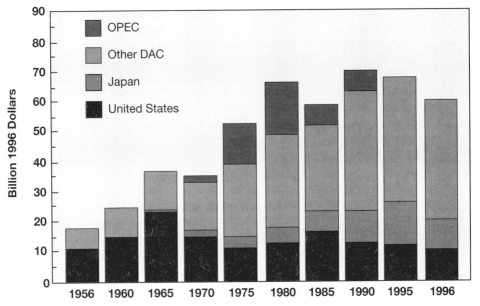

Source: World Bank, *World Development Report 1992* (Washington, DC: Oxford University Press, 1992), 254–255; World Bank, *World Development Indicators 1998* (Washington, DC: World Bank, 1998), 340.

What effect does aid have on the recipients? Partly as a result of the Marshall Plan's success, expectations for success in fostering development within the Third World were high. Studies of the relationship between aid receipts and economic growth, however, are indecisive (Bremer and Hughes 1990, 38–43). Moreover, recipients understand the mixture of motives behind aid, and they resent efforts to control them. For example, U.S. aid recipients have very often voted against it in the United Nations. In reality, aid has achieved neither rapid economic growth nor close and enduring political relationships. In this climate of pessimism about aid, the West has exhibited special reluctance about giving large amounts of it to the former communist countries. Some cynics say that aid means that "poor people [taxpayers] in rich countries help rich people in poor countries."

It would, however, be inappropriate to end the discussion of aid on a sour note. Many aid donors truly are beneficent, and much aid has saved lives and improved living standards. It is relative to inflated expectations that aid has frequently failed. Nevertheless, *aid fatigue,* a disillusionment with the results of aid and resultant lessening of commitment to it, has led to a substantial retrenchment by donors.

Instruments of Violence

States and other actors have a wide range of coercive instruments available to them, many involving overt violence and others incorporating the threat of it. Powerful states select from the full gamut of options, whereas weaker states and

Table 4.4	U.S. Foreign Aid by Type and Recipient 1996		

Country	Total Receipts	Economic Assistance	Military Assistance
Israel	3,000,000	1,200,000	1,800,000
Egypt	2,118,454	817,445	1,301,009
Bosnia-Herzegovina	245,584	245,325	259
Russia	178,820	178,060	760
India	157,532	157,175	357
Rwanda	120,770	120,527	243
South Africa	117,175	116,709	466
Ethiopia	110,763	110,436	327
Jordan	108,401	7,199	101,202
Ukraine	101,790	100,771	1,019
Haiti	99,281	99,112	169
Peru	85,322	84,942	380
Bolivia	75,389	74,842	547
Armenia	70,724	70,724	0
West Bank/Gaza Strip	63,448	63,448	0
Angola	62,940	62,940	0
Mozambique	59,028	58,825	203
Liberia	57,912	57,912	0
El Salvador	56,971	53,436	3,535
Bangladesh	54,940	54,614	326
Poland	51,029	50,008	1,021
Philippines	43,252	42,042	1,210
Ghana	42,957	42,700	257
Uganda	38,775	38,586	189
Guatemala	35,173	35,173	0
Total (25 countries)	7,156,430	3,942,951	3,213,479
Total (all 144 recipients)	12,783,473	9,515,730	3,267,743

Note: Ranked by amount of total assistance; units are thousands of U.S. dollars.

Source: U.S. Agency for International Development FY98 Congressional Presentation, FY 1996 U.S. Economic & Military Assistance—Actual Obligations (http://www.info.usaid.gov/pubs/cp98/summtables/96actual.htm, July 23, 1998).

other actors more often choose from the menu of clandestine and unconventional instruments.

Nonstate actors find themselves restricted primarily to **unconventional warfare,** a use of force that generally involves hit-and-run tactics (sometimes only isolated attacks on property, killings, or bombings) by actors who then fade into a larger population. One significant manifestation of unconventional warfare in the Cold War was the guerilla warfare of communist movements. Since the Cold War we have seen guerilla warfare by nationalist forces in places such as Chechnya and Kosovo. Guerilla war generally incorporates a range of unconventional activities, up to large-scale battles. In the future, one increasingly likely type of unconventional attack on property will be "cyber-terrorism." By one estimate, there were as many as 250,000 "attacks" on U.S. defense computer systems in 1995 (*Christian Science Monitor* June 7, 1996, 5). Although domestic hackers are responsible in almost all cases, the fear is of sophisticated and hostile action.

States generally consider unconventional warfare illegitimate, a status they logically extend to the actors that threaten them with it. Nonetheless, states frequently engage in essentially identical activities themselves. Often they do so covertly and via *proxies,* actors working in the interests of others. The Reagan administration of 1980–1988 significantly increased prior American support for use of unconventional force, directing it through proxies against Marxist governments in Afghanistan, Angola, and Nicaragua. In the first case the United States was unwilling to oppose Soviet forces directly. In the other two cases, the administration did not have congressional or popular support sufficient to allow overt application of more substantial force.

Even superpowers prefer to use lesser force when accomplishment of desired objectives seems probable with it. Covert operations, under the leadership of intelligence services, are a favored instrument. During 1975 the United States cut off support for Kurdish forces that the CIA had supported on behalf of Iran against Iraq. In explaining the subsequent slaughter of one-time allies, realist Henry Kissinger said that "Covert action should not be confused with missionary work." Sadly, the United States again abandoned covert Kurdish allies to Saddam Hussein's power in the mid-1990s. Although officially highly secret, the United States spent about $30 billion on covert activities in 1996 (*Christian Science Monitor* June 6, 1996, 19).

The instruments available to states, however, extend beyond proxy and unconventional violence. States often engage directly in low-level violence, activities short of full-scale war. For instance, great powers periodically use *demonstration force* as an instrument of policy. In April 1986 the United States selectively bombed Libya in retaliation for governmental support of terrorist incidents, including a bombing of a discotheque in Berlin. Although the United States denied that leader Muamar Khadafi was himself a target, precision bombing struck his tent and reportedly killed one of his children. Only a strong state, such as the United States, appears likely to succeed with demonstration force, because the intention is to demonstrate both capability and willingness to inflict even more harm.

Gunboat diplomacy is a broader category, into which demonstration force falls. It involves the demonstration, threat, or actual use of limited military (originally naval) force. In an earlier era, the Soviet Union used military maneuvers near the borders of Poland and Czechoslovakia to indicate displeasure concerning internal governmental developments and to threaten actual invasion. The United States did the same to Iraq in 1998 and 1999. Again, such behavior is predominantly that of great powers.

In addition to low-level violence such as demonstration force, states obviously do have full-scale warfare available to them. Given the importance of war, in subsequent chapters and particularly the next one, we will return to issues surrounding it, such as its frequency, intensity, and relationship to power configurations. Because of the great destruction it wreaks and the aversion most of us have to it, you might think that war is aberrant behavior, either an unintentional consequence of actions or irrationality in action. The fact is, however, that war is an instrument of statecraft and states do *choose* to make war. Because it is such an important decision, we will use the rest of this chapter to explore how states make it.

The Decision to Go to War

According to realists, states have power and interests, and they rationally use that power, in the form of diplomatic, economic, and military instruments, to pursue their interests. Although more often than not they treat each other peacefully, in some instances states make the decision to abandon cooperative interaction and go to war. This section advances three interrelated propositions with respect to that important decision. Each assumes the rationality that realists attribute to states. Realists cannot, of course, deny that sometimes states act irrationally, but irrational behavior is by definition difficult to analyze.

First, *states sometimes find war beneficial.* When a state expects to win and when the costs of battle appear less than the fruits of victory, it should logically be prepared to fight (unless it can achieve equivalent gains simply by threat or demonstration force). For instance, Iraq invaded Kuwait in 1990 because it expected relatively easy victory against a small state. Success promised Iraq a doubling of oil resources and more than $100 billion in financial assets. Similarly, Serbia supported the attack by fellow nationals on the government of Bosnia, because it foresaw an easy victory and set a high priority on a "Greater Serbia."

Second, *states will generally settle conflicts short of large-scale warfare.* Very often, the probable victor of a war is apparent to both sides, and the probable loser will make concessions. Especially when the more powerful state has demonstrated the existence of its power and the determination to use it, the weaker state will find it profitable to negotiate a settlement rather than fight and face imposition of a potentially similar or even worse settlement. In 1962 the Soviets withdrew nuclear missiles they had placed in Cuba rather than fight a war with the United States. At that time, the nuclear capabilities of the United States vastly exceeded those of the U.S.S.R.

Third, *when states fight, one side has frequently miscalculated.* In some cases both sides calculate themselves to be the stronger (the Iran-Iraq war in 1980 may illustrate this). In other cases, the demands of the stronger party may so threaten the most basic interests of the weaker that the weaker will risk probable defeat rather than peacefully accept dictated terms; Vietnam would not accept its division in the Geneva Accords, and Kosovo would not accept its treatment by the Serbs. When the stakes of conflict are not so high for the stronger, the willingness of the weaker to battle may eventually force the stronger to withdraw.

For example, Germany initiated large-scale hostilities in both World Wars I and II. It lost both soundly. In 1913, before the onset of World War I (see again Table 4.2), the American, British, and French alliance together had a fairly striking advantage over the German and Austrian-Hungarian combination. In 1938, before World War II, the American, Russian, British, and French alliance overwhelmed Germany and Japan. On the basis of the power index in Table 4.2, neither outcome should have been in serious doubt after complete involvement by all parties. These cases indicate especially the considerable complexity for a state like Germany in assessing where the larger battalions actually lie, because it was uncertain that the United States would enter either war.

Let us consider some of the conflicts since World War II. The U.S.S.R. invaded Hungary in 1956, Czechoslovakia in 1968, and Afghanistan in 1979. The United States responded to the North Korean invasion of the South in 1950 and slid gradually into Vietnam in the early 1960s. Both superpowers have mixed records in these large-scale conflicts. In recent years the United States has picked its fights with great care. The invasions of Grenada (1983) and Panama (1989) were tremendous mismatches. The United States organized a 28-state coalition against Iraq and used the UN to assure that no significant state opposed its intervention; it then relied on airpower for 26 days to maximize the probability of success in a brief land war.

Lesser powers have also applied substantial force with mixed consequences. Tanzania successfully invaded Uganda in 1979 to overthrow the vicious government of Idi Amin. Vietnam invaded Cambodia in 1978 with the announced intention of ending the vicious rule of the Khmer Rouge. Libya invaded Chad initially in 1973 and intermittently into the 1980s to annex part of its territory; it ultimately withdrew. In 1998 Ethiopia initiated a border war with Eritrea, the primary aim of which was probably to protect its access to the sea, but which did not accomplish that. The most deadly interstate war since World War II (leaving aside the civil wars in which superpowers became involved) was the war between Iraq and Iran, which broke out in 1979 when Iraq thought that the revolutionary disruption in Iran would allow easy settlement of a long-standing territorial dispute. The ceasefire in 1988 left the territorial issues unresolved. The Iraqi invasion of Kuwait similarly proved a major disaster for Iraq.

Although war initiators often win, many lose. What is the overall quantitative record? Wang and Ray (1994) found that initiators won 60 percent of wars involving Great Powers between 1495 and 1991, and they won 72 percent in the last two centuries. Sivard (1987, 28) argued, however, that the odds moved against all sizes of initiators in the twentieth century, falling to a 39 percent chance that the initiating state would ultimately win.

Is there basis for an argument that "times have changed since the nineteenth century"? Two factors support the claim. First, a major reason for the success rate of great powers in the nineteenth century was the tremendous power differential between modern industrial states and the minor states of the day. Today the power differentials between North and South have considerably narrowed. Second, in the nineteenth century, warfare still involved relatively simple weapons and few troops. Today even "weak" states can field machine guns, tanks, jet aircraft, and other highly destructive weaponry. In addition they can mobilize much of their adult population to the battle. Thus war-initiating states are bound to pay a substantial cost, if their victims choose to resist. This may cause more of them (very rationally) to break off the contest than in the past.

Consider, for instance, the wars in Vietnam and Afghanistan. How does one explain the withdrawal by the United States from Vietnam after the loss of 47,000 Americans in battle and without the accomplishment of its objectives? How does one explain the failure of the U.S.S.R. to accomplish its objectives in Afghanistan, directly on its own border? It admits loss of 15,000 soldiers. That seeming failure of the larger battalions to prevail is the **paradox of unrealized power** (Baldwin 1979, 163), and it has several explanations (see Ray 1987, 166–177, for a similar list).

First, apparently bilateral interactions in world politics seldom in reality involve only two parties. Both superpowers were significantly involved (through arms shipments and advising roles, if not troops) in both the Vietnam and Afghanistan wars, even though the world considered the first a U.S. war and the second a Soviet war. These were in essence **proxy wars**—both of the superpowers used other parties to fight on their behalf and thereby avoided direct confrontation. There are, on closer examination, few real "two-party" international conflicts.

A second explanation expands on some elements of the first. In part because the conflicts were not simple one-on-one wars, the superpowers were reluctant to commit more than a fraction of their power potential to them. They feared escalation by the other power were they to do so. Additionally in the case of the United States, internal dissension made it impossible for the government to use its power potential fully.

Third, power based in one capability may not translate into power based in other capabilities. Power types are not fully **fungible** (easily convertible from one to another). Most important, the nuclear forces of the United States and U.S.S.R. were essentially useless in both conflicts.

Fourth, the stakes for Vietnam and Afghanistan were much higher than the stakes for the United States or the U.S.S.R. Threats to control of one's own territory generally bolster willpower and morale much more effectively than more abstract ideological challenges. The superpowers suffered many fewer casualties than their opponents, and in terms of population percentages, the Vietnamese and Afghan losses were dramatically greater. For example, the Vietnamese lost perhaps 2.3 million people during the U.S. involvement and Afghanistan lost about 1.5 million before the Soviets withdrew (Sivard 1993, 21). The strength of will was tremendously strong in those resisting the superpowers.

If the world consisted purely of two-party interactions and each interaction called forth the full capabilities of the two states with equal, or at least calculable stakes, outcomes would be much more predictable, and statecraft would be a fairly pure science of power application. We could rely on what March (1966, 54–61) calls a "basic force model." States can seldom predict, however, exactly which other states will become involved in an interstate issue, what their objectives will be, and what resources they will bring to bear. We need instead a "force activation model." Statecraft is much more an art than a science.

Conclusion

This chapter elaborated some of the basic elements of realism. Specifically, it defined state and explored the concept of state interest. It pursued the definition and measurement of power in considerable detail because of the centrality of that concept to realism and the deeper understanding power distributions give us of our world. It explored the complexity of translating power into state action by examining the varied instruments of statecraft. Finally, it considered the implications of the assumption by realists of rational state use of those instruments in conflict.

Realism promises much more, however, than this analysis primarily of individual states, their power, and their instruments. It potentially offers considerable insight into their *interactive behavior.* The next chapter pursues that promise.

Selected Key Terms

state	purchasing power parity	quotas
sovereignty	soft power	fungible
great powers	geopolitics	smart sanctions
unipolar system	statecraft	official development assistance (ODA)
bipolar system	diplomacy	tied aid
superpowers	zone of overlap	unconventional warfare
multipolar system	shuttle diplomacy	paradox of unrealized power
unit veto system	coercive diplomacy	proxy wars
spheres of influence	boycotts	
state interests	embargoes	
power	tariffs	

CHAPTER 5

Dynamics of State Systems

The world is a dangerous place for states. It is an environment of anarchy, in which each state holds ultimate responsibility for its own defense. Allies help, but they are unreliable. Neighboring states may promise nonaggression and even friendship, but a change in leadership and a quick flaring of old passions can convert an erstwhile friend into an invader.

Consider Turkey. Since 1700 it has fought 15 wars (Sivard 1987, 30). As its Ottoman Empire gradually disintegrated (a process completed in 1918), Russia moved to expand its influence in the areas of weakened control, especially the Balkan states. Russia and Turkey fought six times. Churchill had good reason for saying that the Balkan region is known "for producing more history than it can consume."

Greece is a second traditional adversary and battled Turkey in two wars since 1700. Greece possesses most of the islands near the Turkish coast, giving rise to continued disputes over fishing and mineral rights in the areas immediately adjacent to Turkey. The two countries rattled sabers in 1996 over the island of Imea. In addition, Turkey traditionally ruled Cyprus, which has a population about 80 percent Greek. The island is now divided, and an uneasy truce prevails between Greek and Turkish populations, both supported by respective mother countries (Table 5.1).

KEY WEB LINKS

www.cfcsc.dnd.ca/links/

www.nato.int/

www.fsk.ethz.ch/

www.seas.gwu.edu/nsarchive/
index.html

www.seas.gwu.edu/nsarchive/
nsa/cuba_mis_cri/
cuba_mis_cri.html

cwihp.si.edu/default.htm

As if these traditional problems with its Russian and Greek rivals were not enough, tempers flare periodically in relations with Bulgaria because of that country's treatment of its large Turkish minority. Also, Turkey has had to keep a wary eye on the conflicts involving Iraq and other countries on its southern border. It is linked to Syria, Iraq, and Iran in many ways, including watersheds, a resurgence of Islamic fundamentalism, and the fact that all four host a Kurdish minority that desires an independent homeland.

Table 5.1	Conflicts Involving Turkey	
Years	**Identification of Conflict**	**Total Deaths**
1730–1730	Janissaries revolt	7,000
1806–1812	Russia vs. Turkey	45,000
1826–1826	Janissaries massacred	20,000
1828–1829	Russia vs. Turkey	191,000
1877–1878	Russia vs. Turkey	285,000
1889–1889	Cretan revolt vs. Turkey	3,000
1894–1897	Armenians vs. Turkey	40,000
1897–1897	Greece vs. Turkey over Crete	2,000
1909–1910	Massacres in Armenia	6,000
1911–1912	Italy vs. Turkey	20,000
1912–1913	First Balkan War vs. Turkey	82,000
1914–1918	World War I	1,450,000
1915–1916	Armenians deported	1,000,000
1919–1920	France vs. Turkey	40,000
1919–1922	Greece vs. Turkey	100,000
1977–1980	Terrorism; military coup 1980	5,000

Source: Ruth Leger Sivard, *World Military and Social Expenditures 1991* (Washington, DC: World Priorities, 1991), 23.

Finally, Turkey now finds itself embroiled in the affairs of the Southern republics of the former Soviet Union. For example, Armenia borders Turkey and the Christian Armenians have not forgotten their genocidal expulsion from Moslem Turkey in 1915–1916—perhaps 1 million Armenians died. The conflict between Armenia and Azerbaijan over pockets of territory and population has drawn Turkish concern and even troop mobilization.

To survive, and in an effort to prosper, Turkey relies on a complex mixture of military, diplomatic, and economic initiatives—the statecraft of the last chapter. Militarily, it is an active member of NATO and strong ally of the United States. The United States understands that Turkey occupies a pivotal position between the Islamic countries of the Middle East, the Turkish former republics of the Soviet Union, and Europe. The NATO alliance has unfortunately not eliminated tensions with Greece, which is also a member. Because of their mutual hostility, Greece and Turkey both spend much more heavily on defense than the average NATO member. In an effort to defuse tensions, the leaders of Greece and Turkey met in Switzerland in 1988 and opened direct, top-level discussions. Yet the basic areas of disagreement remain, and in 1995 Greece sought to block Turkish accession the following year to a customs-union arrangement with Europe.

Turkey became an active member of the military coalition that united against the Iraqi invasion of Kuwait. It closed its border with Iraq (see Map 5.1). There has been tension between Turkish interest in dampening Kurdish nationalism and the

Map 5.1

anti-Iraq coalition's interest in protecting the Kurdish population in Iraq. Yet when Turkey has invaded Northern Iraq in pursuit of Kurdish forces, the United States has muted its reaction in part because of Turkish service to the coalition.

On the economic and diplomatic front, Turkey has applied for membership in the European Union. It leads a movement to establish a free-trade zone around the Black Sea (including Russia). With respect to the Asian republics of the former U.S.S.R., Turkey began broadcasting Turkish television throughout the region via satellite (on a channel formerly used by Moscow). It has given extensive aid to those new countries. In dealing with its neighbors to the South, Turkey has used its relatively plentiful water resources as both a carrot and a stick.

No matter how skillfully the leadership of Turkey has pursued its interests, however, the harsh reality is that Turkey is only one member of the interstate system, not a particularly powerful one, and one buffeted by the larger patterns of the system. The end of the Cold War dramatically affected the parameters framing Turkish policy. The purpose of this chapter is to explore the structure of the world in which states like Turkey find themselves and the interaction of that structure with the self-help efforts of states.

Methodologically, this chapter shifts our primary focus from individual states to the state system. Understanding Turkey's role in the state system, its historic position as a one-time great power, its geographic position on the front-line of the old Cold War, and its strategic political-economic position between a Christian and democratic Europe and an Islamic and often undemocratic Asia, is important to the study of global politics. It is, however, almost impossible to simultaneously consider the detailed histories and behavior of close to 200 states. Many disciplines shift approach when they move to a study of larger numbers of agents, introducing new methods of study as well as new concepts and theories. Physics has long recognized that it needs different tools to describe the interaction of many bodies than it does to study one or two. The discipline of economics divides its subject matter into microeconomics (the study of individual firms and households) and macroeconomics (the study of the entire economy). In essence the study of world politics similarly profits from division into the study, as in the last chapter, of individual states ("micro-world politics") and the study of the state system ("macro-world politics").[1]

Realists describe systemic structure in terms of constant anarchy but changing power distributions. What theory can they offer us concerning the implications of these characteristics for state behavior and systemic stability? To answer that question this chapter will consider, in turn, theory concerning bipolarity, multipolarity, and hegemonic leadership. Before we do that, however, it is useful to devote some attention to conflict, the general phenomenon that realists most frequently attempt to explain.

Patterns of Conflict

In the world of states, conflict is inevitable. The constant threat of nuclear war between the superpowers during the Cold War and the recurrent crises that took humanity to the brink of that war have largely receded in memory. Global politics today pays, as it should, increased attention to economic, social, and environmental issues. Yet we *must* remain attentive to conflict and war in our study of global politics. Why? Because there have been earlier long periods of relative peace that have ended with brutal speed and consequences. Because wars are, in fact, still taking lives around the world every day. Because the nuclear arsenals that remain are still sufficient to destroy civilization and perhaps the species. And because we still suffer the crises that sometimes precipitate war, even between countries that do not believe it will happen. This section examines the historic record of two types of conflict—war and crisis.

Studies of War

Lewis Fry Richardson, a mathematician and meteorologist, undertook some of the earliest systematic measurements and analysis of war, beginning his work in 1919. He counted 317 wars between 1820 and 1949, in work published posthumously (Richardson 1960a, 1960b).[2] While Richardson worked, Sorokin (1937) published his analysis of 862 European wars between 1100 and 1925. Independent of both

---

[1]This chapter does not, however, make a clean shift to macropolitics. It continues to devote much attention to the behavior of individual states. The limited number of really important actors at the systemic level makes it impossible to ignore the individual state (as macroeconomics can largely ignore even Exxon or Microsoft).

[2]Which reminds me—after a lecture by an eminent professor, a student excitedly told him that the "lecture was simply superfluous." To which the professor sarcastically retorted that he hoped "to have it published posthumously." The student had the final words: "Great. The sooner the better!"

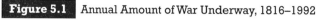

Figure 5.1   Annual Amount of War Underway, 1816–1992

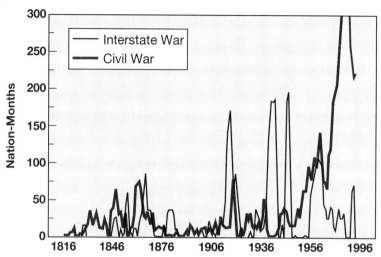

Source: Courtesy of the Correlates of War Project and J. David Singer. Reprinted with permission.

Richardson's and Sorokin's efforts, Quincy Wright (1965) identified 200 wars between 1480 and 1941. Given their substantially different war totals, these three scholars obviously defined war differently. Scholars of world politics have been extremely fortunate to have had a modern, even more intensive project on war measurement and analysis in place since 1963. J. David Singer and Melvin Small directed the Correlates of War project at the University of Michigan in an ongoing effort to identify and explain international conflict.[3] Defining war as conflict involving at least 1,000 battle deaths, Singer and Small found 224 wars during the 1816–1980 period, of which 67 were interstate, 51 were extrasystemic (that is imperial or colonial), and 106 were civil wars.

Numbers of wars during long periods are interesting but not very useful. We want to know whether there are any patterns in such characteristics as frequency, cyclic occurrence, and intensity. Most importantly, we want to know why wars occur. We look now in turn at frequency, cycles, and intensity. The bases of war, however, is a subject that we address throughout the chapter and book.

Frequency   According to the Correlates of War project, the number of total interstate and civil wars has increased irregularly since 1815 (see Figure 5.1). When adjusted by the increasing number of states in the interstate system, however, the frequency of war involvement for an average state exhibits no clear trend in these two centuries. The uncertain trend for overall warfare frequency in recent decades

---

[3]Small and Singer (1982, 1985). The Correlates of War project also collected data on "militarized international disputes," conflict that may fall short of warfare. Another important project focused on 119 wars involving great powers between 1495 and 1975 (Levy 1983). Claudio Cioffi-Revilla (1990) reviewed contemporary data projects on conflict and has created a data set on war since 3000 B.C. as part of his Long-Range Analysis of War Project.

is discouraging for those who value peace. It is, however, consistent with the basic realist belief in continuity of political behavior.

Studies of warfare among great powers find a clear downward trend since 1495, and some claim that the great powers have fought no wars since 1945.[4] Yet, the postwar great powers that Table 4.2 identified have fought each other on two occasions since World War II: in the Korean War (China versus the UN forces led by the United States) and in the Chinese-Indian border dispute of 1962. In addition, the two superpowers warred frequently through support for lesser states that served as their proxies (as in Korea, Vietnam, and Afghanistan). In brief, the evidence for trends in great power war frequency is generally positive, but somewhat ambiguous.

A very clear trend is the near elimination of imperial wars in the post–World War II period. Whereas a high proportion of wars in the 1800s pitted a great power against a prospective or actual colony in the Third World, that era is effectively over. The conflict in 1982 between Britain and Argentina over the islands that the former calls the Falklands and the latter labels the Malvinas (and considers a colonial outpost of Britain) seemed a real anachronism.

Most dramatically, however, conflicts around the world have increasingly become civil wars, with and without intervention from outside (see again Figure 5.1). Throughout the 1990s about 30 armed conflicts (involving 1,000 or more deaths over their entire duration) raged or simmered at any one time, and almost all were civil wars. Realists focus our attention on interstate war, especially those among the major powers. Clearly, limiting attention to interstate conflict overlooks essential elements of global politics. Although we continue our discussion here of interstate conflict, we must return later to the issue of intrastate conflict.

Cyclic Occurrence   The notion that wars occur in some kind of regular cycle has long intrigued scholars and the public. A glance at historic patterns of interstate warfare like that in Figure 5.1 strongly suggests such cycles. The problems are twofold. First, what is the length of the cycle? Singer and Cusack (1981) searched the Correlates of War data from 1816 through 1965 and found no cycles of any regular length, either for individual countries or at the systemic level.

Such studies do not disprove that warfare has a cyclical dynamic, however, because a repetitive dynamic need not result in highly regular warfare occurrence. Thus, a second problem surrounding cyclical-war hypotheses becomes central: What is the explanation for the cycles? War outbreak "could be related, among other things, to the time needed to 'forget' the last bloody conflict" (Small and Singer 1985, 13). Forgetting could interact with other factors, however, including leadership personality, weapons technology advance, and the severity of the most recent conflict. Instead of warfare every 20 years, the "forgetting dynamic" could contribute to increased conflict propensity in as little as 10 years or as many as 40. The generational memory explanation has an appeal to Americans because they can look back on the Spanish American War (1898), First World War (1914–1918), Second World War (1939–1945), Korean War (1950–1953), and Vietnam War (ca. 1964–1973). Without the Korean War, the cyclical pattern is remarkably regular.

---

[4]See Levy (1983) and Wright (1965). Gaddis (1987) wrote of *The Long Peace,* while Mueller (1989) saw a *Retreat from Doomsday.*

Table 5.2	War Fatalities in Britain, France, Austria-Hungary, and Russia		
Century	Military Deaths	Population Mid-Century	Deaths as Percent of Mid-Century Population
Twelfth	29,940	11,500,000	0.26
Thirteenth	68,440	15,500,000	0.44
Fourteenth	166,729	21,500,000	0.78
Fifteenth	285,000	30,000,000	0.95
Sixteenth	573,020	40,000,000	1.43
Seventeenth	2,497,170	55,000,000	4.54
Eighteenth	3,622,140	90,000,000	4.02
Nineteenth	2,912,771	171,530,000	1.70
Twentieth	33,525,000	288,717,000	11.61

Source: (Compilation of Sorokin Data) Francis A. Beer, *Peace Against War* (San Francisco: W. H. Freeman, 1981), 45; (subsequent twentieth-century casualties) Ruth Leger Sivard, *World Military and Social Expenditures* (Washington, DC: World Priorities), assorted issues; *United Nations, World Population Trends and Prospects by Country, 1950–2000* (New York: United Nations, 1979).

The Soviet economist Kondratieff identified 50- or 60-year economic cycles, and others have associated warfare with the economic cycles, in some cases arguing that warfare peaks in every second economic cycle (Goldstein 1985, 123–141). In reference to this cycle length, the famous political economist Kindleberger said that "Kondratieff is like astrology." Beck's analysis (1991) found no such cycles in warfare. Pollins (1992 and 1994) not only identified warfare cycles, but linked them to economic ones. The jury on cycles of warfare is still out.

Intensity Trends in interstate warfare frequency are generally ambiguous (although great-power warfare appears to have fallen and civil war has clearly increased). Cycles in warfare outbreak are too irregular and poorly understood to provide either explanatory or predictive capability. Most study of warfare does, however, agree on one long-term and powerful pattern: The intensity of the worst wars has increased over several hundred years. Table 5.2 lists the numbers killed in warfare in France, England, Austria-Hungary, and Russia over nine centuries. Large increases in casualties relative to population occurred in the seventeenth and eighteenth centuries and again in the twentieth century. Advances in military technology and increased ability of governments to mobilize populations and economies explain those increases. The twentieth century easily takes the prize for bloodiest. Major participants suffered 8.4 million military deaths in World War I, and 17 million of their troops and 34 million civilians (2 percent of world population) perished in World War II.

The United States has generally not suffered as much as Europe in the great wars of the last two centuries. Table 5.3 shows U.S. casualties in all its wars since independence. In total numbers of deaths, and especially in the percentage of population dying, the Civil War was the greatest catastrophe the United States has ever

Table 5.3	U.S. Fatalities in War		
War	**Battle Deaths**	**Total Deaths**	**Percent of Population**
Revolutionary War (1775–1783)	6,824	25,324	0.645
War of 1812 (1812–1815)	2,260	2,260	0.031
Mexican War (1846–1848)	1,723	13,283	0.057
Civil War (1861–1865)	214,938	498,332	1.585
Spanish American War (1898)	385	2,446	0.003
World War I (1917–1918)	53,513	116,708	0.110
World War II (1941–1945)	292,131	407,316	0.311
Korean War (1950–1953)	33,629	54,246	0.036
Vietnam War (1964–1973)	47,321	58,021	0.029

Source: *The World Almanac and Book of Facts 1987* (New York: World Almanac, 1987), 321, 337.

suffered. For reference only, and not to minimize the suffering of Americans in any war, we should compare U.S. deaths with the casualty totals suffered by the U.S.S.R. in three wars of the twentieth century. They lost 6 million in World War I, 800,000 in the 1918–1920 civil war, and about 15 million in World War II (Sivard 1987, 30).

The increased severity of the worst wars may well explain the apparent decrease in frequency of general war pitting great powers against each other. Should we ever suffer a full-scale and nuclear World War III, casualties could reach 1 billion. The certainty of major slaughter in great-power warfare should give pause to rational, unitary actors.

Crises and Serious Interstate Disputes

Wars do not simply start. Almost invariably a crisis precipitates war. Although the frequency of full-scale war among great powers may have declined as the consequences become less acceptable, crises among great powers, with the threat of war, were common in the Cold War and still occur. They have more than once taken the world to the brink of nuclear war. Hermann (1969) developed the most widely used definition of **crisis:**

> Crisis is a situation that (1) threatens the high-priority goals of the decision-making unit; (2) restricts the amount of time available for response before the situation is transformed; and (3) surprises the members of the decision-making unit when it occurs. (Hermann 1969, 29)

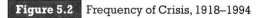

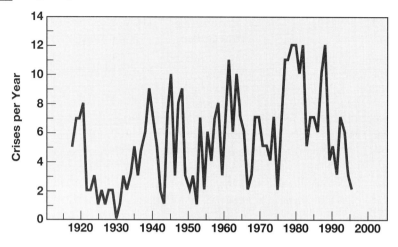

Figure 5.2   Frequency of Crisis, 1918–1994

Source: Courtesy of Michael Brecher and Jonathan Wilkenfeld, from *A Study of Crises* (Ann Arbor: University of Michigan Press, 1997).

Crises are of great importance because they obviously can lead to war. One of the most famous and best studied began on June 28, 1914, when a Serbian nationalist in Sarajevo assassinated the Austrian Archduke and heir to the throne, Francis Ferdinand. Austria sent an ultimatum to Serbia on July 23. Although Serbia met most demands of the ultimatum, Austria declared war against it on July 28; Russia mobilized its army, and Germany declared war on Russia (August 1) and France (August 3). Within a relatively brief time after the beginning of the crisis, a global conflict was underway. It is possible that better crisis management after the assassination could have avoided war. We will never know.

Trends in Crises   Crisis management may have improved, and we return to that subject later. Improvements are important because the number of crises has actually been increasing. In their study of militarized disputes since 1815, Gochman and Maoz (1984, 593) discovered an increasing trend in absolute numbers. After controlling for the number of states in the system, no clear long-term trend remains; however, even when controlling for state numbers, crises surged during the first 25 years of the post–World War II period. Brecher and Wilkenfeld (1997) studied crises since 1918 (Figure 5.2) and identified a slight upward trend.

Which countries are most often involved in crises? Since 1815 the ten countries most likely to have initiated or to be the target of disputes are all major powers except one, Turkey. Great powers were involved in about two-thirds of all disputes, with Great Britain, the United States, and the U.S.S.R. leading the list (Gochman and Maoz 1984, 609). Surprisingly, given the danger of nuclear weapons, great-power participation in disputes since World War II may actually have increased relative to their numbers in the interstate system—they have become regularly embroiled in (and often caused) the problems of the lesser powers.

Objectives of Crisis Initiators   Lebow (1981) classified crises into three major categories by objective of the initiator. *Some crises justify the broader hostility* of the state beginning them. For instance, in 1964 the Johnson administration in the United States had decided that it needed to bomb North Vietnam, if it were to pursue the war in South Vietnam successfully. Although uncertainty lingers over the degree to which the United States provoked and anticipated North Vietnamese patrol boat attacks on U.S. destroyers in early August,[5] the administration used the attacks to garner the domestic support necessary to launch the bombers (Lebow 1981, 30–31).

Many crises are spin-offs of activities pursued for other objectives. For example, the German submarine campaign against British shipping in 1915 was a blunt instrument and sunk many neutral ships in the war zone. The Germans believed that the danger of confrontation with neutral powers, like the United States, was less than the advantage to be gained by cutting British sea lanes. On May 7 a U-boat sank the Lusitania with many Americans on board. This was the first of several German-American crises that ultimately helped bring the United States into the war on the British side in April 1917.

Some crises involve aggressive brinkmanship. **Brinkmanship** occurs when "a state knowingly challenges an important commitment of another state in the hope of compelling its adversary to back away from his commitment" (Lebow 1981, 57). Iraq created such a crisis in 1998 when it refused access by UN weapons inspectors to sites they demanded to visit. The United States mobilized for war to force a policy change. One particularly famous superpower crisis, possibly the most dangerous of the Cold War era, also falls into this category. It was the Cuban missile crisis.

After Castro came to power in 1959 and Cuba moved into the Soviet orbit, concern grew in the United States that any Soviet nuclear weapons on the island could strike U.S. targets without warning, leaving no time for retaliation. The Kennedy administration explicitly warned the U.S.S.R. against placing such weapons there and received assurances that the Soviets would not do so. Apparently in an effort to overcome a position of nuclear inferiority (they had only 20 operational missiles on Soviet territory), and because they believed that an American invasion of Cuba was a serious threat, the Russian leadership decided to install nuclear missiles there secretly.

After discovering construction of nuclear missile sites in October 1962, the United States issued an ultimatum demanding their removal and a guarantee that no missiles would be put into Cuba (Chapter 7 discusses the U.S. policy-making approach in more detail). A naval blockade of Cuba and the threat to use nuclear weapons reinforced the ultimatum. After a few tense days, the Soviets backed down, securing a guarantee against U.S. invasion of Cuba. Many of the U.S. participants in the crisis decision making later reported that they felt the world to be quite near nuclear war—one assessment was a 50 percent probability. Conferences at Harvard in 1988 and in Moscow in 1989 brought together some of the principals from both countries to talk about the crisis. The Soviets revealed that their

---

[5]Weather conditions and visibility were poor; the attacks, monitored electronically, may not even have occurred. Johnson later quipped that "For all I know, our Navy was shooting at whales out there." (Foster and Edington 1985, 148).

leadership had actually given the order to run the blockade, and that they countermanded it only an hour before the confrontation. In addition, they had completed delivery of 20 warheads to Cuba. The world has almost certainly never been closer to nuclear war.

Post–Cold War Crises   Crises did not disappear with the Cold War. Nor did the possibility that one could lead to nuclear war. Crises are frequent and often involve nuclear power.

We have already noted that Turkey and Greece frequently threaten conflict. In 1997 Turkey reacted to a decision by the Greek-dominated Cypriot government to purchase Russian missiles by threatening to attack it. Throughout the 1990s, Israel and the new Palestinian government (not quite yet a state) clashed over territorial issues, including new Israeli settlements.

India and Pakistan have already fought three wars, two over the Kashmir region. Both are nuclear powers. Kashmir has a Muslim majority population, but was split between India and Pakistan in 1947 when the British left the subcontinent. Pakistan gives the separatist movement in Indian Kashmir at least moral support, and India claims that it provides weapons and training. In 1990 an intensification of rebellion against the Indian government led to a significant crisis. Although there is debate among analysts over how close the region was to nuclear war, there is no question that both countries mobilized forces and that the United States rushed an emergency mission to the region to help dampen passions.

Several other post–Cold War crises have involved still another nuclear power, namely China. In 1994 the United States granted a visa for a private visit by the president of Taiwan to the United States, about the same time that campaign rhetoric in Taiwan was touching on the highly sensitive issue of independence from China. In early 1995 China reacted strongly and held military exercises in the Taiwan Strait that involved "testing" missiles within 100 miles of the island. The United States sent into the same strait the largest naval force that it had put together since the Vietnam War. Although the tension ultimately passed without incident, the status of Taiwan has led to so many confrontations between the United States and China over the years that another is always possible.

States resolve most crises, about 90 percent, short of war (Gochman and Maoz 1984, 601). Happily nuclear powers have to date achieved a perfect record in their direct confrontations. The memory of that remaining 10 percent, however, when deep-seated hostility, unintended consequences, or brinkmanship did lead to war, haunts anyone who thinks about it seriously.

Insights from Bilateral Analysis

Self-interested states in interaction engage in both conflict and cooperation. In fact, interaction of states almost invariably consists of a mixture of both. Realism offers a considerable body of theory relevant to both the conflict on which we focus in this chapter and the cooperation to which we turn in the next. In our elaboration of that important theory, we begin with elements attentive to the interaction of two states. Thereafter we will broaden the discussion.

In the pursuit of their own security interests, states seek to increase their power. Chapter 4 emphasized, however, that power is relative. Increases in the power of one country automatically diminish that of others. Even if the attempts by China to secure control over as much of the South China Sea as possible are purely defensive, such an increase in Chinese power poses a threat to all neighboring states. Such countries find themselves in a classic **security dilemma.** That is, actions that may be intended defensively appear offensive to another state. They do not seek conflict, but the zero-sum character of power pushes them into it.

The security dilemma often sets up an *action-reaction dynamic* between two parties. The action of one state to improve its security elicits a reaction from its rival. The most common manifestation of this pattern is the *arms race.* Often each country sees itself as threatened by the other and acting purely in its own defense by increasing its military capabilities. The other state has the same perception.

States sometimes recognize the influence of the security dilemma on them and the mutual harm it can cause. When they do, they may adopt strategies to dampen the action-reaction dynamic and to reassure their opponent/partner that they intend no threat. Such strategies rely on the recognition that the action-reaction dynamic can also work in reverse—that reduction in threat to an opponent can give rise to matching action by that state.

Consider the parallel with human beings who also interact repeatedly and find it useful to abide by a variety of rules, such as not hitting each other, even when interacting in the absence of any authority to enforce those rules. They do so because they know that violation of the rules would destroy an existing pattern of cooperation that is a basis for further beneficial interaction. They live in the "shadow of the future" (Axelrod 1984). Individuals therefore often apply the principle of **reciprocity,** captured in the Golden Rule of "do unto others as you would wish them to do unto you." Most religions codify the principle, and a large portion of cooperative human behavior involves expectations of reward in the form of reciprocated cooperation. States find themselves in the same situation.

The Golden Rule is balanced in human interaction by the principle of "an eye for an eye, a tooth for a tooth." When we behave cooperatively, we expect cooperation in return, but we are often prepared to retaliate when we receive hostility. The deeper the relationship (implying a long record of cooperation), the greater the temporary deviation from cooperative reciprocity we will accept. Axelrod examined the benefits of this pattern of reciprocity in behavior, reciprocating either positive or negative behavior. He did so to answer fundamentally important questions for those directing the foreign policy of any state: "When should a person cooperate, and when should a person be selfish, in an ongoing interaction with another person? Should a friend keep providing favors to another friend who never reciprocates?" (Axelrod 1984, vii)

In an analysis (involving a computerized tournament) of a variety of strategies for two-party interaction, Axelrod found the reciprocity-based strategy that encouraged the most cooperation in the long run to be the simplest one tested: **tit for tat.** Beginning with a cooperative stance toward the other party, this strategy rewards cooperation with further cooperation and punishes once each negative action by the other side. Moreover, Axelrod argues that this "winning" strategy tends to evolve naturally in many situations of repeated interaction, implying social learning that eliminates other, less successful strategies. That evolution occurs even in unlikely situations, such as the trench warfare of World War I. "Cooperative" behavior often grew without communication between the infantrymen of the two sides, despite efforts by officers to suppress it. A British officer noted that:

> It was the French practice to "let sleeping dogs lie" when in a quiet sector . . . and of making this clear by retorting vigorously only when challenged. In one sector which we took over from them they explained to me that they had practically a code which the enemy well understood; they fired two shots for every one that came over, but never fired first. (Axelrod 1984, 61)

We can make a further distinction between **specific reciprocity** and **diffuse reciprocity.** In situations of specific reciprocity "partners exchange items of equivalent value in a strictly delimited sequence" (Keohane 1989, 134). The cooperation across the trenches of World War I illustrates specific reciprocity. So does international law restricting the use of certain weapons and practices during war. Diffuse reciprocity involves more delayed and less precise exchange, in which obligations accrue and greater trust exists. "In personal life, bargaining over the price of a house reflects specific reciprocity; groups of friends practice diffuse reciprocity" (Keohane 1989, 134). The relations of the United States and Canada illustrate diffuse reciprocity.

While tit-for-tat interaction implements specific reciprocity, a second strategy for interacting with other states, graduated reciprocation in tension-reduction (GRIT) builds on the concept of diffuse reciprocity. Charles Osgood (1962) made the argument that states could elicit cooperative actions from other states by announcing and undertaking a series of unilaterally cooperative steps. He proposed the policy specifically to reduce the arms race of the Cold War. We will discuss in the next chapter some limited attempts to implement this strategy.

In summary of insights from bilateral analysis, states often find themselves trapped in a security dilemma and a cycle of increased arms spending or even of increased overt violence. They can, however, attempt to dampen such cycles via reciprocity-based strategies, such as tit for tat and GRIT. Before turning to realist insights concerning multilateral environments, we will extend the bilateral discussion into a specific and important arena, that of interaction between nuclear powers.

Bilateral Relations and Nuclear Arms

The United States and Russia possess far more nuclear weapons than other states. We review the development of those weapons more generally, but then return to bilateral analysis of them.

The Players and Their Equipment

Nuclear forces have two components: nuclear warheads and delivery vehicles. Seven states officially have and plan to maintain nuclear forces. The United States tested and used its first bombs in 1945. The U.S.S.R. followed it into the era of

Table 5.4	Declared Nuclear Strategic Capabilities (1996)				
	United States	**Russia**	**U.K.**	**France**	**China**
Delivery Vehicles					
ICBMs	595	727	0	48	113
SLBMs	384	440	64	64	12
Bombers	166	113	96	87	180
Total	1145	1280	160	199	305
Warheads					
ICBMs	2075	3565	0	48	113
SLBMs	3072	2272	198	384	12
Bombers	2800	1398	100	80	150
Total	7947	7235	298	512	275

Note: ICBMs are intercontinental ballistic missiles and SLBMs are submarine-launched ballistic missiles.
Source: Stockholm International Peace Research Institute, *SIPRI Yearbook 1996* (New York: Oxford University Press, 1996), 613, 615, 616, 618, 619, 634–635.

nuclear weaponry (1949), as did Great Britain (1952), France (1960), and China (1964). Each of these states moved from the simpler and less destructive atomic bomb technology that the United States used against Hiroshima and Nagasaki, to the much more devastating power of hydrogen bombs. India openly exploded a "peaceful nuclear device" in 1974 but claimed to have assembled no bombs. Both India and Pakistan tested multiple bombs in 1998 and officially declared their membership in the nuclear club. Hindu nationalists cheered the Indian tests, and Pakistani crowds celebrated the birth of an "Islamic bomb."

At the peak of their arsenals in the late 1980s the United States and the former Soviet Union each deployed about 11,000–12,000 strategic warheads. Together the superpowers maintained more than 16,000 megatons (millions of tons of TNT equivalent) in their strategic arsenals, more than three tons per human. Both countries have significantly reduced warhead totals via arms control agreements that are discussed in Chapter 6. The French possess about 500 warheads, the British about 300, and the Chinese about 300 (see Table 5.4). Russia inherited most of the warheads of the former Soviet Union, but Kazakhstan, the Ukraine, and Belarus found themselves with about 2,300 warheads. Those three new states agreed in early 1992 to disable their missiles within three years and to eliminate them within seven.

Several countries may now be in the category of *undeclared nuclear powers.* South Africa covertly built six weapons, cancelling the program in 1989 and dismantling the bombs by 1993 (Gray 1993, 9). Israel probably crossed the nuclear threshold in the late 1960s and may have 50 to 100 atomic warheads plus hydrogen bomb technology (Spector 1990, 6). Iraq apparently was well on its way to nuclear capability when Israel bombed and destroyed its Osisraq test reactor in 1981, exactly for that reason. It resumed its march toward nuclear capability, only to be interrupted again in 1991 when the United States mobilized forces against its invasion of Kuwait (again, in part because of its nuclear ambitions). North Korea was minimally very close to nuclear weapon completion in 1994 when it reached an agreement with the United States to close its plutonium-producing power plants in exchange for the financing of less dangerous ones by the United States. The United States argued that Iran was well on its way to nuclear status in 1994–1995, thereby justifying a request that Russia and others deny the country all possible nuclear weapon technology. Several other Third World countries (including Libya) have indicated interest in nuclear weapons but appear years away from the capability of developing their own.

Other countries have arrived at the threshold and stepped back. Argentina and Brazil both have the basic capabilities and had classified nuclear programs in the early 1980s. In 1985 they signed a mutual inspection agreement to ease fears of a regional nuclear arms race. As it had with South Korea in 1976, the United States pressured Taiwan in 1988 to stop work on a secret nuclear facility that could have produced plutonium for warheads (*New York Times,* March 23, 1988, 1). Almost all First World countries have the technology to produce nuclear weapons but refrain from undertaking programs. For example, the Swiss ratified the Nuclear Non-Proliferation Treaty in 1977, but continued a secret project to build nuclear weapons until 1988 (*Christian Science Monitor,* June 11, 1996, 1).

Delivery vehicles fall into three classes: land-based missiles, submarine-based missiles, and aircraft. The United States and Russia maintain all three types, and the United States refers to its delivery system as the **triad.** Table 5.4 shows the delivery vehicles in each leg of the superpower triads and also indicates the warheads dedicated to them. India also has advanced missile technology (it has launched satellites) and Pakistan's capability is improving rapidly. In 1998 the United States claimed that Russia was helping India develop a sea-launched ballistic missile and that China continued to assist the Pakistani missile program.

All potential undeclared nuclear powers minimally have combat aircraft that could carry nuclear warheads into neighboring states, and missile technology is advancing rapidly in most of these states. Although the United States and six other industrial countries established a "control regime" in 1987 to slow proliferation of missile technology, it may not succeed. Israel has launched space satellites since 1988, joining the declared nuclear powers and Japan in that exclusive club. In 1989 Iraq demonstrated a missile with that capability. Such states have the capability of delivering nuclear warheads by missile for distances of at least 1,000 miles. The potential availability to still additional states (like Libya) of nuclear-capable missiles with shorter ranges, provided by countries like North Korea, further adds to the complicated picture of nuclear delivery capability. Proliferation of nuclear capabilities is proceeding more slowly than before the Cold War ended, but it nonetheless continues.

Although the nuclear world is obviously multipolar, the bipolar relationship between the United States and Russia has long dominated it. In addition, much other interaction among nuclear powers, like that between India and Pakistan, is essentially bilateral. Thus it is not surprising that most strategic thought around the weapons focuses on two-party interactions. We consider now the conceptual and theoretical framework developed to understand that world.

Strategic Concepts and Theory: State Behavior

A state has a **first-strike capability** when it can preemptively launch nuclear weapons against an opponent. It also has a **second-strike capability** when it can launch a devastating attack after absorbing one itself. A second-strike capability requires that the warheads available for retaliation be protected in hardened missile silos, in submarines at sea, or in planes aloft. A second-strike capability greatly reduces the possibility during a crisis that a country will fear losing its retaliatory capability, should the other side strike first, and thus itself be tempted to launch first. When either or both sides harbor such fears, there is an **unstable nuclear balance.**

Every country with nuclear weapons wants to convince its actual or potential enemies that it is willing to use those weapons. It also wants to minimize the danger that either side will actually use them. These two objectives led to the development of a deterrence strategy called **mutual assured destruction (MAD).** It requires that both sides have second-strike capabilities. Thus both sides can destroy the other, but they can also afford to wait and see how the other side handles a crisis situation. This creates a relatively *stable nuclear balance.* Although it may seem anachronistic in the post–Cold War world, MAD remains central to strategic thought on nuclear weapons.

It is no accident that each of the first five declared nuclear powers has a force of missile-launching submarines. These are the least vulnerable leg of modern triads. Thus even secondary nuclear powers have a second-strike capability that could, as France has said, "tear off an arm" of a superpower. India, Pakistan and the undeclared nuclear powers currently do not have second-strike capabilities and live in a world of unstable nuclear balance.

Students of world politics study the logic of deterrence and MAD with the help of techniques from game theory. A game called the **prisoner's dilemma** illustrates the instability of solely first-strike situations. In one hypothetical example, a district attorney seeks to convict two suspects, Pat and Mike, of armed robbery. She keeps them apart to eliminate communication and offers each the same deal. (Ignore any ethical and legal restrictions the district attorney might face in this example.) Should either one confess and the other not confess, the district attorney will request freedom for the confessor and ten years of imprisonment for the other. If both confess, she will ask an eight-year sentence for both. If neither confesses, she will prosecute both on the charge of illegally carrying concealed weapons (found when they were arrested) and should be able to send each to prison for one year.

The matrix of Table 5.5 indicates the payoffs for the two prisoners, dependent on whether or not they confess. The first payoff in each cell is for Mike. Thus should Mike confess and Pat not (bottom left corner), Mike will go free and Pat will spend ten years behind bars. Mike considers his options, based on what Pat might do. Should Pat confess (second column), confession would better serve Mike, cutting his losses from ten years to eight. Should Pat not confess (first column), confession again better serves Mike, improving his prospects from one year in jail to none. Thus no matter what Pat does, Mike improves his prospects by confession and decides to do so. Unfortunately, Pat faces exactly the same logic. They both confess, and both serve eight years. Had they been able to somehow cooperate and avoid any confession, they could have cut their prison terms to one year each. The

Table 5.5	The Prisoner's Dilemma		

		Pat	
		Not Confess	Confess
Mike	Not Confess	−1, −1	−10, 0
	Confess	0, −10	−8, −8

Table 5.6	An Unstable Nuclear Balance		

		Pakistan	
		Wait	Attack
India	Wait	-10, -10	-1,000, -5
	Attack	-5, -1,000	-800, -800

dilemma is that without being able to communicate and somehow assure each other that they will not confess (or threaten each other should they do so), they cannot reach the superior outcome. Even with communication, trust may be so low that each will defect to confession in a vain attempt to cut their losses.

When India and Pakistan (or any other pair of nuclear powers) have only first-strike capabilities, they face the same kind of situation that Mike and Pat did. Table 5.6 portrays a payoff matrix for the two powers in an unstable nuclear balance. Although some readers may think such a portrayal trivializes the stakes of mutual destruction, it is nevertheless helpful in understanding the logic of the situation.

In this gaming representation, both parties can choose to wait (not attack at least for now) or to attack now. If both wait, there are costs because they prolong the tension and expense of the arms race and continue to live under the threat of future destruction. Should they both attack, the destruction is devastating on both sides. If one should attack and the other not, the aggressor damages the other side even more heavily than in a mutual attack (which prevents some planes and missiles from getting through), while suffering limited damage because the other side is (in this example) unable to retaliate. The reader should analyze the matrix in Table 5.6 and verify the pressure of "rationality" on both sides to strike immediately. It should not surprise us if some of the "older" nuclear powers help India and Pakistan develop second-strike capabilities as well as assisting them with crisis management.

Insights from Multilateral Analysis

Strictly speaking, balances of power obviously occur in bipolar systems as well as in multipolar ones. Because multipolar analysis devotes so much attention to balance, however, we have saved discussion of it until now.

Balance of Power Advocacy

Traditional realists advocate attention by decision makers to maintenance of the systemic balance of power as a necessary foundation for security and relatively peaceful interactions. British leaders actively pursued an interstate balance of power for generations. Winston Churchill, who guided Britain through World War II, described that pursuit as "the wonderful and unconscious tradition of British foreign policy." Former American Secretary of State Henry Kissinger similarly gave the argument his blessing: "The balance of power, a concept much maligned in American political writing—rarely used without being preceded by the pejorative 'outdated'—has in fact been the precondition of peace" (Chan 1984, 119).

Advocates of the politics of balance of power frequently look back to the nineteenth century interlude between the Napoleonic Wars and World War I as the "golden age" of the policy. As Central Europe and the Middle East were throughout the Cold War (and as Turkey and the South China Sea may be today), there were in that century two principal focal points of interstate politics at which the balance operated.

The first was Belgium, strategically located between France, the United Kingdom, and Germany. When Germans marched through Belgium on the way to France in 1914, that violation of Belgium neutrality helped lead Britain to fight alongside France. The second focal point was in the Balkans (in the front yard of Turkey). The other great powers resisted Russian efforts to expand into the territory once controlled by the dying Ottoman empire. When the balance of power system finally came apart in 1914, the immediate issues centered on Serbia, a longtime ally of Russia.

Balance-of-power enthusiasts argue that the system was unable to control the tensions in the Balkans at that point because, instead of fluid alliance structures directed against whichever power might seek gains, two fairly rigid alliances had evolved among the great powers. Thus instead of containing the conflict locally and protecting the status quo, the alliances propagated it throughout the system. Critics suggest, however, that the outbreak of World War I (in which Turkey perhaps inevitably became a major battlefield) proved the essential bankruptcy of the idea that a balance-of-power system could maintain relative peace.

Definition

One of the problems faced by those who prescribe a politics of **balance of power** lies in definition of it. As a static description, it means (1) any distribution of power (the balance of power is . . .); (2) an equal distribution (there is an equivalence of power among . . .); and (3) a superior position (country X holds the balance of power). As a dynamic, policy-oriented concept, it either (1) operates automatically (all states will oppose aggressive power) or (2) requires conscious attention to balance by states (Britain adopted a balancing role).[6]

---

[6]Haas (1953) and Claude (1962) elaborated various definitions. Realists have done little to clarify the issue; Morgenthau consciously used four definitions:

> The term "balance of power" is used in this text with four different meanings: (1) as a policy aimed at a certain state of affairs, (2) as an actual state of affairs, (3) as an approximately equal distribution of power, (4) as any distribution of power. (Morgenthau 1973, 167ff.)

Balance of Power and State Behavior

Realpolitik describes how individual states and leaders are supposed to behave in a balance of power. In brief, "success is the ultimate test of policy, and success is defined as preserving and strengthening the state." (Waltz 1979, 117)

Kaplan elaborated rules for states in balance-of-power systems and tailored them to different system polarities. Although they fundamentally reduce to acting so as to preserve and strengthen the state, Kaplan's (1957, 23) specific rules for states in a multipolar system are

1. Act to increase capabilities but negotiate rather than fight.
2. Fight rather than pass up an opportunity to increase capabilities.
3. Stop fighting rather than eliminate an essential national actor.
4. Act to oppose any coalition or single actor that tends to assume a position of predominance with respect to the rest of the system.
5. Act to constrain actors who subscribe to supranational organizing principles.
6. Permit defeated or constrained essential actors to reenter the system as acceptable role partners or act to bring some previously inessential actor within the essential actor classification. Treat all essential actors as acceptable role partners.

Anyone who has played board games of interstate politics, such as Risk, Diplomacy, or Axis and Allies, will recognize how the seemingly automatic adoption by players of such rules prolongs the games (the existence of the states) interminably.

Alliances

Alliances help maintain the balance of power in a multipolar system. They allow weaker states to counter the power of stronger ones. As Kaplan's rules suggest, states tend collectively to oppose threats to dominate the system. The alliances against Napoleon early in the nineteenth century, against Hitler in the mid-twentieth century, and against the Soviet Union in the Cold War demonstrated that dynamic at work.

The alliance against Nazi Germany showed that ideology need not prevent the formation of interstate ties when power relations dictate them. The United States and Stalinist Russia cooperated extensively after Germany invaded the Soviet Union. More recently, we saw the strange combination of authoritarian Pakistan, communist China, and a democratic United States all supporting an Islamic guerrilla movement in Afghanistan against the Soviet Union's puppet state. In power struggles, "the enemy of my enemy is my friend" (and my arms supplier).

Rational power calculations should explain not just the formation but the size of alliances. When an alliance brings together a large portion of interstate power (significantly more than 50 percent), its members normally have less to gain by remaining within it. If one views the terms imposed on the vanquished as spoils (as when territory is divided or reparations are imposed), then the larger the coalition the smaller the share any member will receive. Thus alliances should logically be large enough to win but not so large as to dilute the fruits of victory. Riker (1962) labeled the tendency for movement toward minimum winning coalitions the *size principle* or the **minimum winning coalition principle.**

As a corollary, when opposition power weakens, old disagreements among alliance partners will resurface, causing either dissension in the alliance or coalition breakdown. Holsti, Hopmann, and Sullivan (1973, 17) concluded that "Probably the most widely stated proposition about alliances is that cohesion depends upon external danger and declines as the threat is reduced." For instance, after the defeat of Nazi Germany, the United States and the Soviet Union were unable to sustain cooperation.

The logic of power and the size principle do not, however, completely explain the post–World War II history of alliances. Because the United States was the larger and stronger of the two superpowers, pure power considerations should have led to a larger coalition around the Soviet Union. Explanations beyond the size principle are needed. **Bandwagoning** (joining forces with the stronger coalition) can occur in alliances and cause their size to exceed minimum winning level. In particular, weak states may jump on the bandwagon because they really cannot affect the outcome and should rationally just pick the probable winner. In a bipolar system dominated by superpowers, many other states find themselves in that position. In addition, U.S. power actually paid for the development of extensive alliances through the strength of its economy, and the aid and trade it could offer. Another factor is ideology—many Western states were more comfortable with the United States despite its extensive power in the system.

More recently, the failure of NATO to collapse following the disbanding of the Warsaw Pact and the disintegration of the Soviet Union creates an even greater anomaly for realist theory (McCalla 1996). In fact, NATO (an issue we address later in the chapter) has even given Russia partnership status. Without an apparent threat and without clear benefits to collective action, NATO's cohesion should rapidly decline. If it does not, then nonrealist theories of alliance behavior, including liberal emphasis on the affinities of economically advanced, democratic countries, will gain considerable support.

Change in Polarity and Its Consequences

Although the military superpowers and their nuclear arsenals dominated the global system after World War II, some observers believe that the balance of power has moved from bipolar to multipolar character. The growing demographic, economic, and military strengths of China; the ongoing unification of Western Europe; and the economic rise of Japan may herald a new system. If so, it behooves us to consider how such a systemic transformation might affect world politics.

There is a long-running argument among scholars about the relative stability of bipolar and multipolar systems. Deutsch and Singer (1969) claimed that multipolar systems are more stable. They argued that **cross-cutting cleavages** in such systems can result in shifting coalitions on different issues. Thus in the five-power world that might be evolving, communist China might find itself opposed by the capitalistic United States, Western Europe, and Japan on some issues. The United States and Japan have a built-in propensity for disagreement on some high-technology and industrial trade issues, whereas the United States and Europe often disagree about agricultural policies. Shifting coalitions and disagreements mean that there are more potential alliance partners (and perhaps no fixed alliances), and that there is more uncertainty about power configurations and the possibility of winning in any conflict. As the last chapter discussed, states are rationally averse to entering conflicts unless there is a high probability of success.

Waltz (1969; 1979, 161–193) disagreed and argued that bipolarity is more stable and less conflict-prone for two reasons. First, states exhibit considerable conservatism when stakes are large. In bipolar systems, direct conflict between the two powers has often destroyed one or both (as in the Chinese and Greek state systems, and as in the wars between Rome and Carthage). Second, he argued that in a two-power system there is a considerable certainty about power balances that eliminates the risk of miscalculations. Both sides know who would win an overt conflict and settle differences accordingly. The Cuban missile crisis illustrates that.

It is a frustration for realists, but research concerning the relative stability of multipolar and bipolar systems has been inconsistent (Midlarsky 1988). The most dangerous times may be when polarity is changing, and power balances and alliance commitment are least certain. If true, this is not comforting, because polarity is now changing.

Insights from Hegemonic Analysis

To this point in the chapter we have examined selected realist insights into bipolar and multipolar worlds. We have discussed, for example, the security dilemma and reciprocity, the prisoner's dilemma, the interaction of multipolar state systems and state behavior, the formation and dissolution of alliances, and the implications of change from bipolarity to multipolarity.

As Chapter 4 discussed, however, another way of looking at the contemporary state system is to see the United States as a hegemonic power. "Winning the Cold War" appears to reinforce its hegemony. Yet Chapter 1 showed that the United States no longer has the margin of economic superiority over other states that it once did—both superpowers are exhibiting signs of relative decline, and Russia has simply set a much more rapid pace. Especially for those who look at the system not in terms of political-military balance of power but in terms of economic leadership (hegemony), the period of U.S. leadership may be coming to an end. Such speculation raises at least three questions. First, what forces cause the rise and fall of hegemons? Second, what advantages might attend a stable leadership or hegemony? Third, are there any particular consequences for world politics of changing leadership?

Rise and Fall of Hegemons

Those who study economic leadership over the centuries note a regularity in the rise and fall of hegemons. Although British leadership lasted two centuries (the seventeenth and eighteenth), earlier hegemons, like the Dutch, remained dominant for approximately one century. Several explanations exist for the transition of hegemons.

Although analysts devote less attention to the rise of hegemons than to their fall, Gilpin (1981, 10–11) suggested an explanation for rise. Gilpin assumed that states are rational utility-maximizers. Expansion of control over their environment (more territory, greater security, greater wealth, more prestige and influence over others) normally provides benefits and encourages that expansion. Gilpin (1981, 106) concluded that a state will expand until the "marginal costs of further change are equal to or greater than the marginal benefits." When states achieve such a balance they seek to maintain it. In reality, however, they eventually decline.

The Gilpin argument draws nicely on the realist logic of power. A second argument looks below the self-contained superstructure that realists build to the long-term force of underlying technological change. According to this argument, leadership is closely related to technological capability and often arises when some technological breakthrough (or cluster of breakthroughs) provides an edge:

> The Portuguese edge was associated with shipbuilding, navigation, and the Indian Ocean spice trade. The Dutch had herring, shipbuilding, and textiles, and they controlled much of the intra-European and European-Asian maritime commerce. The British claim was first predicated on shipbuilding, Atlantic commerce, and wool textiles. Later cotton textiles, coal, steam engines, and iron products, and then railroads lay at the heart of Britain's nineteenth century centrality in the world economy. The American rise, in its turn, was based on automobiles, steel, and petroleum. More recently, these products were superseded to some extent by plastics, electronics, and aerospace industries (Rasler and Thompson 1994, 8–9)

Once in place, however, technological leadership is vulnerable because technology is less expensive to copy than it is to innovate. Other states, like Japan in the early post–World War II period, can adopt and even improve U.S. technology.

Primary among explanations that focus on the decline of hegemons is the cost of hegemony. Maintaining military power is expensive. In 1997, the United States spent about 3.6 percent of its GDP on defense. West European allies spent 2.2 percent of their GDP on defense. Japan has a constitutionally based commitment to limit defense forces and holds spending to 1 percent of GDP.

Why does the United States not only spend more than its allies on defense but devote a larger portion of its economy to it? U.S. congressmen repeatedly raise this question, noting also that much U.S. spending supposedly defends those same allies or supports their interests, as in Bosnia. The principle of **exploitation of the big by the small** supplies part of the explanation (Olson and Zeckhauser 1966). Luxembourg and Iceland are both NATO countries. Luxembourg directs less than 1.0 percent of GDP to defense, and Iceland has no military at all (it provides base sites to NATO). From the viewpoint of these countries, even defense spending of 10 percent of GNP would make no real contribution to NATO, because their economies together are only 0.2 percent that of the United States. Why bankrupt themselves when they can obtain the defense of NATO anyway? Middle-sized countries, like Belgium and Denmark, which spend less than 2 percent of GDP on defense, can make the same argument, but less strongly.

The defense that NATO provides against attack is a collective good, available to all NATO members. The alliance cannot deny that good to any member, and each

Table 5.7		NATO Members and Expenditures		
Country	GNP (billion $)	Defense Expenditures (percent of GNP)	Educational Expenditures (percent of GNP)	Investment (percent of GNP)
United States	7,434	3.6	5.3	18
Germany	2,365	1.6	4.7	23
France	1,534	3.0	5.9	18
UK	1,152	2.8	5.5	16
Italy	1,141	1.9	4.9	18
Canada	570	1.3	7.3	18
Spain	563	1.4	5.0	21
Netherlands	403	1.9	5.3	19
Belgium	267	1.6	5.7	17
Turkey	178	4.3	3.4	24
Denmark	169	1.7	8.3	17
Norway	151	2.2	8.3	20
Greece	120	4.6	3.7	14
Portugal	101	2.6	5.4	25
Luxembourg	17	0.8	4.0	—
Iceland	7	0.0	5.6	—
Average	1,010	2.0	5.0	19

Sources: (GNP at exchange rates, 1996; Investment, 1996; Educational Expenditures, 1995) World Bank, *World Development Indicators 1998* (Washington, DC: World Bank, 1998) and Ruth Leger Sivard, *World Military and Social Expenditures, 16th ed.* (Washington, DC: World Priorities, 1996); (Military spending, 1997) *NATO Review* (Spring 1998), D15.

thus has an incentive to be a **free rider**—to take the good but contribute as little as possible. The United States cannot make the same argument that Luxembourg or Belgium can; without the U.S. share, about two-thirds of NATO expenditures, there would be no collective defense system. Table 5.7 verifies the tendency for the largest members of NATO to spend near or above the average level, and for the smallest to spend near or below the average (Turkey and Greece spend more than the average NATO member on defense because of their historic regional enmity).

Advantages of Hegemonic Leadership

The preceding discussion suggested some of the systemic advantages of hegemonic leadership, particularly the provision by hegemons of defense, technology, and other benefits to secondary powers. The **theory of hegemonic stability** pursues this line of thought (Keohane 1980, 136). The theory posits that a combination of control and leadership by the hegemon facilitates free trade systems, free flow of technology, agreements on environmental issues, and a range of peaceful, cooperative relations among states. Many theorists of hegemonic stability especially emphasize the collective benefits of the free markets that the British and Americans have provided for two centuries. The decline of the hegemon could mean the loss of such benefits (Kindleberger 1973). The next chapter will explore in more detail the relationship between hegemony and systemic cooperation. In fact, this volume will return often to the theme of systemic leadership by a hegemon.

The word "hegemon" does not always, however, have such a positive connotation. It can imply a domineering power, even an imperial one. Other perspectives raise the possibility that the existence of a hegemon has many negative consequences for other members of the global system. We will also return later in this volume to such arguments.

Changing of the Guard

The history of transition from one hegemon to another has been a history of conflict. **Hegemonic transition theory** focuses on the reasons for the transition (extending our earlier discussion about the rise and fall of hegemons) and on the conflict engendered by the transition. The conflict arises because hegemons seldom voluntarily surrender systemic leadership; a challenging state usually forces the issue.

Although leadership may be of value to the system, the hegemon also presumably benefits. As Gilpin (1981, 200) emphasizes, what is at stake is "governance of the international system." During the period of the Portuguese and Spanish empires, governance gave the right to plunder and take tribute. In the mercantile empires of the Dutch and early British periods, it established extensive areas in which the hegemon had exclusive rights to obtain food and minerals and to sell manufactured goods. Even in free-trade eras, the hegemon has retained some exceptional privileges relative to other states. As French President de Gaulle pointed out, only the United States had the ability to spread its currency freely around the system, effectively making loans to itself. When Mexico repays its international debt, it must do so in U.S. dollars over which it has no control. When the United States repays its debt, it can do so in dollars and can, if it wishes to accept the inflationary consequences, issue more of them. The United States also has extensive military bases, dominant voting rights in international financial institutions, locations for its satellites in a few prime orbital positions, and other advantages of being number one.

When a challenging power wants some or all of these advantages for itself, conflict is possible. A century from now, historians may look back at World Wars I and II and describe a Germany that had surpassed Britain in economic strength, but held a decidedly secondary position in the international order. They may conclude that this tension caused the "Two German Wars," and that the British-German issue disappeared only when outside powers (the United States and the U.S.S.R.) decisively transformed the system from a Eurocentric one to a truly global one, something they failed to do after World War I.

Along these lines, the **power-transition theory** (Organski 1968; Organski and Kugler 1980) posits that war is most likely when the balance of power is changing, and a challenging state has reduced the power gap between it and the dominant state. Considerable debate surrounds the power configuration that creates the greatest danger of conflict. It appears that conflict probability is relatively low when power preponderance is great and when power is quite equally balanced and stable. Conflict can increase when power is moderately unbalanced and especially when there is power convergence between challenger and hegemon (Mansfield 1994).

The challenger normally initiates the war. Surprisingly, the challenger does not usually win the transition war and become the new leader (Modelski 1978). Instead, the transitional war frequently weakens both the leader and challenger and allows a third party to rise in a relatively peaceful transformation of the system after the war. That third party is often an ally of the old leader. For example, England was an ally of the Dutch at the end of the Netherlands' leadership period, and the United States was similarly associated with the British during the transition wars preceding U.S. leadership.

One difficulty in applying hegemonic transition theory to the current period is identifying the most likely challenger to U.S. leadership. Japan's economic rise has given it an economy about one-half that of the United States, but it appears to have lost momentum. China remains preoccupied with political transition and demographic pressures. Nonetheless, it is growing so rapidly that among the war games played in American defense academies is one pitting China against the United States in 2010 (Segal 1996, 124). Russia is now a declining military giant and an economic weakling.

It is also possible that a united Europe could eventually emerge as the new systemic leader (see again Figure 1.8). It is now larger economically than the United States and has considerably greater military capability than Japan. The European Union is the only political unit in the postwar world that has grown geographically and that has great potential for still further expansion. Perhaps historians will one day identify the Cold War as the war of transition, and a United Europe will follow in the hegemonic footsteps of the United Provinces (the Netherlands), the United Kingdom, and the United States.

We have now considered what theorists tell us about interstate dynamics in bipolar, multipolar, and hegemonic systems. The post–Cold War system appears to combine features of a new multipolarity and continued U.S. hegemony, but the character of that system is still taking shape. There remain many uncertainties about critical actors and dynamics in the emergent system.

Post–Cold War Uncertainties

In December 1994, Russian troops invaded the Republic of Chechnya, in the southwestern portion of the Russian Federation called the Caucasus. Only about 20 percent of the population of Chechnya is ethnically Russian, the bulk of the Chechens are Muslim, and the region has long sought greater autonomy or independence. Russian forces pounded the capital of Grozny for weeks, destroying the city and killing perhaps 20,000. Fighting then moved into the countryside.

The Western world did not know how to react. Since the collapse of the Soviet Union in 1991, the members of NATO had searched for a strategy to deal with the new Russia. Their hope was that the country would move unambiguously toward democracy, free markets, and the Western alliance. They hoped that NATO

and the former communist countries would jointly and cooperatively address security issues throughout Central and Eastern Europe. Their fear was that Russia
would, after a period of transition, reassert its traditional regional power, especially in the countries of the former Soviet Union, which Russia called its **near
abroad.** A second fear compounded the first, namely that nationalists would overthrow the new and fragile Russian democracy, should those elements perceive outsiders as threatening to basic Russian interests. The fact that NATO considered
Chechnya to be part of Russia tempered their reaction.

On the other side of Asia, in early 1995 China built a token facility on Mischief
Reef of the Spratley Islands in the South China Sea. That reef is within the 200-mile
economic zone of the Philippines and much further from the mainland of China.
In what appears to be a pattern, China seized the Paracel islands in 1974 (where it
has now built an airfield), and in 1988 a brief naval battle between China and Vietnam over other Spratley Islands set three Vietnamese ships on fire. Chinese maps
lay claim to still other islands that Indonesia believes to be its own and that sit
above large natural gas fields. Through such actions China has encouraged many
of its Southeast Asian neighbors to increase their own arms spending.

These developments illustrated some of the issues that leaped onto the world
political stage early in the post–Cold War era. How will the West organize its security structure and what will be the relationship between that system and the former communist states? What should be the role of NATO and the future of arms
control? Will Russia and China have cooperative relationships with the Western
powers or will new conflicts arise? The rest of this chapter will elaborate on some
of these questions.

The Role of NATO

Immediately after the end of the Cold War many analysts declared that NATO no
longer had a role and that dissolution was imminent. This position was, of course,
consistent with realist theory that alliances serve to balance power. When the opposing power collapses, the alliance should end.

Instead of dissolving, NATO turned to the definition of a new role with two
major elements. First, NATO has given itself the option of supporting "out-of-area"
missions. Already in the war of 1991 following Iraq's invasion of Kuwait, NATO
coordinated its members' contribution to the war. In 1994 NATO supported the
United Nations peace-keeping forces (UNPROFOR) in Bosnia with 25,000 personnel and air support. In 1995 NATO placed an implementation force (IFOR) of
60,000 into Bosnia to enforce a peace treaty signed in Dayton, Ohio. In 1996 NATO
further reinforced out-of-area capabilities like IFOR by authorizing combined joint
task forces (CJTFs). They allow a subset of members (rather than all of NATO) to
integrate forces for such missions. In 1999 NATO bombed Serbia.

Second, and even more important, NATO defined for itself the role of creating an integrated security community stretching from Vancouver to Vladivostok.
It would reach out to the countries of the former Soviet bloc and offer them association with NATO, but it would not dilute the core strengths of the alliance. A significant step involved the issuance in early 1994 of an open invitation by the 16

NATO countries for members of NACC to join a Partnership for Peace. Partners join with NATO members in planning, training, and exercises. They can cooperate in peacekeeping and humanitarian missions. They open their own national defense planning and budgeting to the outside world and guarantee democratic control of military forces. They can also act to align their defense structures (organization and weaponry) with NATO. By 1995, 26 states had applied for partnership status, which many in Central Europe eagerly viewed as a way station on the road to full NATO membership. Russia wavered, but signed on in 1995. Another major step came in 1999 when the Czech Republic, Hungary, and Poland joined NATO itself.

Why has NATO survived the Cold War? One key reason is that the United States, while toying with unilateralism in foreign policy, has generally embraced **multilateralism,** an approach to external affairs that relies upon allies. President Bush put together the broadest coalition possible against Iraq after it invaded Kuwait. Many military contributions were so small that coordination costs may well have exceeded military value. It was political value that Bush sought. The expansion of NATO is also a political action and an expression of multilateralism.

Many uncertainties remain. Will NATO expansion collapse from within as a Western European pillar gains strength relative to the United States? Will the U.S. public support continued foreign involvement and multilateralism, or will it force a retreat into isolationism? Will an expanded NATO give rise to exactly the threat it seeks to prevent by engendering hostility from Russia? Or will NATO continue to expand and consolidate a zone of Western peace and democracy?

The Systemic Role of Russia

Although realists periodically warn of a resurgent Russia, the general approach that the West has taken toward Russia is one of assisting its leadership to build a market economy and to consolidate democratic institutions. To that end the West put together a variety of financial aid packages. Because of fairly stringent conditions attached to release of funds, the bulk of which came as loans, many in Russia and elsewhere in Eastern and Central Europe perceived the assistance as grudging and insignificant. At the same time, the pace of economic reform in Russia and other former republics of the Soviet Union did not always impress the Western powers and their corporations.

More troubling for the West, Russia began already in 1992 to flex its muscles with respect to the other former members of the Soviet Union. Russia initially led 12 of 15 former Soviet Republics into the Commonwealth of Independent States (CIS), a kind of common market. It then began maneuvering for military roles in many of those states. In 1992 Tadzhikistan allowed Russia to station 24,000 troops along its border with Afghanistan, effectively ceding its defense policy to the Russians. In 1995, four years after the dissolution of the U.S.S.R., Russia had troops in 13 countries in its "near abroad" and plans to withdraw from only 3. After 1996 its foreign policy tilted more openly against the United States and toward some of its former client states, including countries like Iraq and Iran that the Western world viewed as "rogues" on the global stage. The Russian parliament refused to ratify the nuclear arms control treaty, START II, and Russian arms exports began to climb again. Its historically close relationship with Serbia prevented the Western powers from more clearly identifying Serbians as aggressors in the Bosnian and Kosovo conflicts and from tilting support more openly toward Muslim forces.

However, Russia also moved to liberalize both its domestic and external relations. Internally, it essentially completed the privatization of state-owned industry and political democracy limped along. Externally, Russia reached an agreement with the Ukraine in 1998 to respect existing borders and to divide the Black Sea Fleet. Some officials even began to recognize that the "near abroad" was not a popular expression in much of the rest of the CIS.

Even with the weakening of Russian military power during the early 1990s and the downsizing of nuclear forces, Russia will remain a formidable military power; its definition of state interest and its sphere of influence will be of great significance and debate in the West. Its desire for a status appropriate to its past and present power will be fundamentally important, both in NATO and in the Group of Eight leading Western economies. Key questions remain: Will Russia regress to authoritarianism? Will it define interests that conflict with those of NATO? How fast will it rebuild military strength?

The Systemic Role of China

Although Chinese economic reforms generated economic growth rates averaging nearly 10 percent annually throughout the 1990s, its leadership remained officially communist. That combination of change and continuity frames many of the issues that the rest of the world faces with respect to China.

One issue is human rights. China's dictatorship continued to suppress political dissent. A second issue is trade. China's foreign-account surpluses grew increasingly large throughout the decade. In 1995, major economic powers pressed China for substantial opening of its markets and protection of their firms' copyright and patent rights as a precondition for allowing China to join the new World Trade Organization.

The main issues, however, concern China's place in the global security structure and the community of major powers. Throughout the 1980s Chinese military expenditures declined considerably in real-dollar terms. The government reversed that decline in 1990 and in the next decade those expenditures not only grew with the booming economy, but outstripped it. Such expenditures would, by themselves, be of concern to its neighbors and major world powers. China combined them, however, with an increased external assertiveness that caused even greater concern. We noted earlier China's consistent push into the South China Sea. That even brought it into conflict with Japan, the major regional power, over the islands near Taiwan that Japan holds and calls the Senkaku Islands, but China calls the Diaoyu Islands.

Finally, the future status of Taiwan remains perhaps the most dangerous issue. For many years after the flight in 1949 of the anticommunist government from the mainland to Taiwan, all parties agreed that Taiwan was ultimately an integral part of China. On Taiwan, however, a movement for long-term independence from China continues to grow. China threatens invasion should Taiwan declare independence and strongly resents any actions by other states that appear to recognize Taiwanese independence. It has dramatically increased the number of missiles aimed at Taiwan. During his visit to China in 1998, U.S. President Clinton affirmed U.S. acceptance of Chinese assertions that there is only one China and that Taiwan should not receive UN membership or other diplomatic recognition.

How should the outside world treat China during this difficult period of growing regional and even global strength? One suggestion has been a policy of *constrainment,* a combination of engagement on issues where China will cooperate with the outside world and containment, as in the Cold War, where it will not (Segal 1996). **Conditional engagement** is another term for the policy of attempting to involve China in world trade and weapons agreements, but not capitulating to territorial demands in the South China Sea or elsewhere.

Like containment, conditional engagement is meant to buy time and facilitate internal change. China is changing. In 1998 it signed the key UN human rights accords. Little-noticed age and term limits set on party and government officials in 1982 facilitated a drop in their average age and a transition to a new, much more educated generation (Pei 1998). Village level politics became more democratic. And during the Clinton visit of 1998 the Chinese telecast a joint press conference with Chinese president Jiang Zemin and Clinton in which Clinton openly challenged the record of the regime on human rights. At the same time, however, China continued to spend almost 10 times its official military budget and to modernize its armed forces rapidly. Key questions remain. Will Chinese economic and military growth continue at the pace of the 1990s and, if so, what strains will that cause in external relations? Will China liberalize politically? Will China pursue an aggressive policy outside its borders?

Conclusion

States are dominant actors in world politics and interact in an interstate environment of anarchy, little controlled by interstate law. They seek to preserve and extend their power and to limit that of other states. Conflict is inevitable in this system, although strategies of reciprocity and balances of power limit it, and hegemony may even create zones and periods of considerable cooperation. This realist worldview explains a great deal about world politics and constitutes a powerful initial basis for understanding.

Yet the early performances of states in the post-Cold War era do not clearly follow the realist script of increased interstate conflict (Mearsheimer 1990). Although the conflict of power politics could quickly re-emerge in either Asia or Europe, the survival and even strengthening of NATO, and the efforts to create security structures that incorporate the former communist states rather than exclude them, suggest that leaders believe quite extended cooperation among states to be possible. It is to the model of an often cooperative society of states, rather than pure anarchy, that the next chapter turns.

Selected Key Terms

crisis

brinkmanship

security dilemma

reciprocity

tit for tat

specific reciprocity

diffuse reciprocity

(delivery system) triad

first-strike capability

second-strike capability

unstable nuclear balance

mutual assured destruction
  (MAD)

prisoner's dilemma

balance of power

minimum winning
  coalition principle

bandwagoning

cross-cutting cleavages

exploitation of the big by
  the small

free rider

theory of hegemonic
  stability

hegemonic transition
  theory

power-transition theory

near abroad

multilateralism

conditional engagement

CHAPTER 6

Interaction in the Pursuit of Cooperation

Cold War and regional conflicts were especially intense throughout the 1960s. At the beginning of the decade the Soviet Union and the United States faced off over Cuba, threatening nuclear war during the Missile Crisis of 1962. Near the end of the decade, U.S. involvement in Vietnam was at its peak and Soviet antiaircraft advisors in North Vietnam fired at U.S. bombers. At the regional level India and Pakistan battled in 1965 and the Middle Eastern states fought the Six-Day War in 1967.

Yet throughout the decade, there was a great deal of cooperation. A substantial number of agreements strengthened international law in general and arms control in particular. In 1963 the Limited Test-Ban Treaty prohibited testing of nuclear weapons in the atmosphere by the United States, U.K, and U.S.S.R. Seven years of negotiation led in 1968 to the Treaty on the Non-Proliferation of Nuclear Weapons. That treaty has without doubt slowed the expansion of the club for nuclear powers. In 1969 the United States and the Soviet Union began Strategic Arms Limitation Talks (SALT) in Helsinki. Their agreement in 1972 put the first limits on nuclear-weapon numbers and paved the way for subsequent talks that substantially reduced those numbers.

KEY WEB LINKS

www.tufts.edu/fletcher/
multilaterals.html
www.un.org/Depts/Treaty/
www.pitt.edu/~ian/resource/
law.htm
cns.miis.edu/
www.fas.org/nuke/control/
index.html
www.acda.gov/

Cooperation proceeded on nonnuclear issues as well. More- and less-developed countries met in 1964 for the first of periodic United Nations Conferences on Trade and Development (UNCTAD). The LDCs presented the idea for a general system of preferences (GSP) to give their goods easier access to the markets of the North; UNCTAD II reached agreement on the system in 1968. Malta called in 1967 for a new conference on law of the sea that began in 1973.

As important as war and crisis are, they account for only a small fraction of the interactions among states. Although by one estimate England has been involved in wars for 56 of every 100 years since A.D. 901 (Blainey 1988, 3), more than one-half of all states have fought no interstate wars at all since 1816 (Small and Singer 1985, 15).

It is important to understand that cooperation requires interaction and that interaction brings both cooperation and conflict. This chapter analyzes interaction in the pursuit of cooperation, but does not assume that only cooperation results. First, it examines the framework within which states interact, what they call international law. Second, it investigates the logic of interaction as states seek the possible benefits of cooperation. Finally, it describes a particular kind of cooperation, that on arms control.

A Framework for Interaction: International Law

If what we call international law dealt routinely with the interaction of Kurds and Turks or with ethnic Albanians (including those in Kosovo) and Serbs, the label would be accurate. It deals, however, primarily with the interaction of Turkey and Iraq or of Albania and Yugoslavia. It is actually interstate law. What we call international law does, however, increasingly include global covenants that tell China how it should deal with political dissidents and that pose constraints on how the Turks should deal with the Kurds. We normally refer to such aspects of international law as "human rights" law. We hold until a later chapter most of our discussion of human rights law. Here we focus primarily on the interstate elements of international law.

What is international law? Article 38 of the Statute of the International Court of Justice defines it as:

1. International conventions [treaties], whether general or particular, establishing rules expressly recognized by the contesting states;
2. International custom, as evidence of a general practice accepted as law;
3. The general principles of law recognized by civilized nations;
4. Subject to the provisions of Article 59, judicial decisions and the teachings of the most highly qualified publicists of the various nations, as subsidiary means for the determination of the rules of law. (Couloumbis and Wolfe 1986, 257)

This listing reflects a **positivist view of international law,** the largely realist position that law is what states make it. An earlier, more idealistic tradition called **naturalist** argued that divine law or human nature is the true source of international law, and the task of legal scholars is to discover those fundamental principles. The naturalist view owes much to religious thought and scholars of the Middle Ages, like St. Augustine, but is making a comeback with human rights law. Grotius, the "father of modern international law," built on the naturalist tradition but began also to modify it by documenting state practice. In fact his work illustrated a confusion about the ultimate sources of law:

> He will tell us, often with regard to the same question, what is the law of nature, the law of nations, divine law, Mosaic law, the law of the Gospel, Roman law, the law of charity, the obligations of honour, or considerations of utility. But we often look in vain for a statement as to what is *the* law governing the matter. (Lauterpacht 1985, 12)

To reduce the confusion and to limit the idealistic element of international law and its vulnerability to conflicting universalisms, international legal scholars at the turn of the century expounded international legal positivism (see, for example, Oppenheim 1908). The positivist tradition, now dominant, moves international law as a field of study away from prescription and toward description.

Domestic legal systems typically incorporate three major elements: law making, law adjudication, and law enforcement. Although the strength of the international legal system falls short of domestic systems in all three areas, the greatest failing is in *enforcement*. International law is decentralized law, relying on the individual or group behavior of states for much of its creation and interpretation and essentially all of its enforcement. As a result, individual state interests influence strongly the character of international law.

Most of international law, created by states and for states, spells out their rights and obligations. States' rights correspond in general to their attributes (defined in Chapter 4): sovereignty (recognition by other states), territory (with boundaries), government, and population.[1] The Charter of the United Nations, part of international law, incorporates four elements concerning states, three that reinforce these attributes of statehood, and one that refers to states' obligations. In the words of one of its drafters:

> first, States are juridically equal; second, . . . each State enjoys the right inherent in full sovereignty; and third, . . . the personality of the State is respected as well as its territorial integrity and political independence. . . . And the fourth element [is] that the States should, under international order, comply faithfully with their international duties and obligations. (cited in Cassese 1986, 129)

The rest of this section considers in turn the rights of states (the protection of their sovereignty, territory, and government) and their obligations.

Rights of States

States are like the animals in George Orwell's *Animal Farm:* All are equal, but some are more equal than others. Most international organizations, including the United Nations, recognize this formal equality through their one-state, one-vote decision rules. Although some organizations (like the World Bank and IMF) vary from that principle and weight voting by economic contribution and thus effectively by economic power, *none* weights votes by population. This fact reemphasizes that states, not human beings, are the bases of most international law.

The fundamental principle of sovereign equality underlies much of international law. It makes the granting of recognition by one state of another an important and sometimes controversial act. The United States denied the sovereign equality of the People's Republic of China (PRC) from 1949–1979 simply by refusing to recognize it, continuing instead to recognize the government on Taiwan as that of all China. The broader international community reinforced that denial of sovereignty by excluding the PRC from the United Nations until 1971.

---

[1]Much of the discussion here is based on Cassese (1986).

The issue of territoriality also underlies a considerable amount of international law. Debates repeatedly surface concerning the limits of territorial waters, rights of passage through straits, and control over the resources of the continental shelf or other offshore extensions of states, such as island chains.

Sovereign equality and the right of states to their own government jointly produce the legal principle of *nonintervention* in the internal affairs of other states. International law at one level is a mutual agreement of governments to legitimize and protect their rule within their own territories. States are not to bring pressure to bear on the domestic institutions of another state, even though they might find the government repugnant. Should civil war break out, states are to refrain from intervention on the side of the rebels. In practice, of course, they frequently violate this. Of 106 civil wars between 1816 and 1980, 21 drew overt military intervention by another country that caused at least 100 battle deaths (Small and Singer 1982, 234). Many others attracted economic or military aid.

In an attempt to comply at least officially with international law, states most often attempt to justify interventions that they undertake. For instance, the U.S.S.R. insisted that the legitimate government of Afghanistan invited its military involvement in 1979. In reality, the Soviets entered on request of a communist government that their embassy helped install in a coup during April 1978. Moreover, on entering in December 1979, Soviet special forces killed the leader who supposedly invited their involvement (Klass 1988, 925–926). Similarly, the Soviet Union said that the Czechoslovakian government requested the very intervention in 1968 that ousted it and brought an end to the Prague Spring. In Vietnam, the United States maintained that South Vietnam was a separate state from North Vietnam and argued that it was assisting the South in self-defense against aggression from the North.

Obligations of States

Another and overlapping category of international law defines the obligations of states in their dealings with each other and constitutes an effort to manage anarchy. We can usefully divide it into three subcategories: (1) laws that treat the interactions of states during peacetime, (2) laws that seek to avoid or resolve conflict, and (3) laws that specify the rules of warfare.

Peacetime Behavior   The status and treatment of diplomats is of great importance during both peace and war. The Italian city-states of the fifteenth century developed the permanent mission, or legation, and established professional corps of diplomats. As the modern European state system developed, so did conflicts among diplomats. Coachmen were killed and duels fought over rank in the court to which they were posted (Holsti 1983, 165). The Congress of Vienna in 1815 established the ranking system with four categories that we still use: ambassadors and papal nuncios, envoys extraordinary and ministers plenipotentiary, ministers resident, and finally *chargés d'affaires*. In 1818 states agreed that, within a rank, they would accord status on the basis of time in post. Thus the dean of the diplomatic corps in Washington is the ambassador from abroad who has served longest in the United States, regardless of the size and importance of the country from which he or she comes.

The principle of **diplomatic immunity** from punishment also has a long history. The ancient Indian *Mahabharata* specifies that "The King who slays an envoy sinks into hell with all his ministers." (Holsti 1983, 166). Should a diplomat commit any crime while abroad, the host country can declare the individual *persona non grata* and insist that he or she be withdrawn, but prosecution can only occur in the diplomat's own country. On the other side, diplomats are supposed to abide by the laws and customs of the receiving country and refrain from intervention in the affairs of that country.

During its capitalist expansion, Britain established many laws of international commerce that still apply throughout the world. For instance, international laws protect shipping from pirates and protect navigation through straits. They also specify that contracts and indebtedness are binding.

International law divides treaties into two categories, specific and law making (Couloumbis and Wolfe 1986, 267). *Specific treaties* most often settle specific issues bilaterally and have no regional or global implications. They become part of international law for the signatories only. Multilateral conventions are **law-making treaties** and, as a result of United Nations action, are increasingly universal. In international law such a convention cannot be binding on states that have not ratified it, but considerable pressure for compliance does build on states that do not sign law-making treaties with widespread support. International legal scholars increasingly refer to such nonbinding, but influential, law as **soft law** (Ratner 1998). It is a growth area.

The Legality of War   Deadly force is legal in world politics, so debate is only about *when* war is legal. Historically, scholars and practitioners placed great emphasis on the concept of **just war.** St. Augustine and other medieval scholastics argued that war was just when fought in self-defense or to punish wrongdoers (Couloumbis and Wolfe 1986, 254). The designation of wrongdoers was a prerogative of God and the pope as his representative, but left a great deal to the interpretation of those who decided to do God's will.

There are two dominant modern traditions on war as an instrument of policy. Machiavelli defined the realist tradition: The state determines when war is appropriate to state aims (the *raison d'état*). Grotius sketched the idealist tradition, which denies the unrestricted right of war implied in the concept of *raison d'état* (Lauterpacht 1985, 22). Instead it restricts just war primarily to self-defense or redress of injury (punishing religious wrongdoers is not included).

Legal texts since 1815 have increasingly characterized war as unacceptable. International reaction to recent wars provides further evidence of growing rejection of the just war and *raison d'état* views: There was widespread condemnation of Vietnam for its invasion of Cambodia in 1978 (despite the overthrow by that invasion of the vicious Pol Pot government), most of the world rejected the Soviet invasion of Afghanistan in 1979, and many of its allies did not stand behind the U.S. invasions of Grenada in 1983 and Panama in 1989. On the other hand, almost all states in the global system supported the "just war" against Iraq in 1991, because Iraq had clearly violated the sovereignty of Kuwait by its invasion and annexation.

Law of War   Once war is underway, there is a large body of international law that supposedly regulates its conduct. That corpus evolved gradually through custom during the eighteenth century and with greater speed after the Congress of Vienna in 1815. The basic principle is reciprocal cooperation to limit the destructiveness of war, especially its impact on noncombatants. Examples of law regulating warfare include:

> Wars ought to be declared prior to their initiation. Combatants ought to wear distinctive uniforms so as to be differentiated from noncombatants—in other words, the wider civilian population. Damage, killing, and destruction should be limited to what is required by "military necessity." Only military targets should be marked for bombing and destruction. Prisoners of war should not be harmed or molested, should be fed and clothed, and should be kept in good physical condition throughout their captivity. Hospital crews and Red Cross and Red Crescent vehicles should be exempted from military attacks. Museums, historic edifices, and shrines should not be bombed or destroyed. Cities declared to be open (i.e., undefended) should be spared from bombing attacks. Populations in occupied territories should be properly administered and cared for. Women and children should not be raped or molested. Private property should not be looted. (Couloumbis and Wolfe 1986, 270)

The Hague conferences of 1899 and 1907 and the Geneva conference of 1949 codified such elements of the law of war. The technology of the twentieth century rendered many of these principles immediately obsolete, however. Modern war is total war, involving full-scale mobilization of personnel, conversion of economies to war making, and use of weaponry so destructive that states simply cannot restrict it to military targets (which, in an economy geared to providing military support, are difficult to identify in any case).

The international community continues to struggle with the law of war. The Nuremberg trials, convened by the victorious allies in November 1945, are the most famous attempt to enforce international law governing its initiation and pursuit (Chan 1984, 333–345). The allies tried 22 individual Germans for crimes against peace and humanity and executed 11. Similar trials in Tokyo investigated 28 individuals and sentenced 7 to be hanged. The arguments of defense and prosecution attorneys illustrated many of the principles of international law that we have discussed. Among the elements of the defense were appeals to the rights of states. Specifically, defenses included references to the principle of territoriality (which allows a government to prosecute crimes only in its own borders), local law, military necessity, and sovereign rights and immunity from prosecution of states. The allies countered with references to the universality of law and precedence of natural law over local law. Moreover, the allies treated the defendants as individuals rather than representatives of their states. One additional defense that they denied was **respondent superior,** acting under orders. They ruled that an individual has the obligation to reject illegal orders.

The Nuremberg trials focused not just on warfare and the action of states. They essentially put the *leadership* of the German state on trial for massive violations of human rights in the killing of 6 million Jews during the Holocaust. The international community increasingly differentiates leaders from their states and condemns inhumane actions within as well as across state borders, overriding claims of territoriality. Examples include the global opposition to South African apartheid, to Latin American death squads, to Chinese political repression, and to "ethnic cleansing" in Bosnia. All of these concerns fall within the rubric of human rights, a topic to which we return in Chapter 8, and one which increasingly subverts state control of international law.

Even without pushing further now into a discussion of human rights law, it seems apparent that the international legal system creates an environment that affects state behavior (the constructivist argument), even while states continue to reshape law. Hedley Bull (1995) wrote of a global society in which the law we have described for states in peacetime and in war has evolved historically and helps define the actors in the global system (the states) and their interactions. It is to some of those interactions that we now turn.

A Logic of Interaction: Delivering the Goods

It would be a mistake to believe that interstate law somehow abstractly shapes interstate cooperation. The reality (as legal positivists proclaimed) is that the interests of states largely determine law. Those interests extend, however, well beyond protecting their existence and immediate security. States *benefit from interaction*—they can obtain goods (for instance, imports, capital, technology, improved air and water quality, and even cultural enrichment) from interaction. International law often grows up around such interaction in the pursuit of benefit. This section introduces some new concepts and theory that offer a wealth of insight into state interaction and both the cooperation and the conflict that result. The concepts and theory build largely on the self-interested behavior of realist politics. Just as we can understand most individual human behavior, even seemingly altruistic action, as self-serving (by establishing mutually beneficial patterns of reciprocity), we can explain fairly elaborate interstate cooperation from selfish motives. These concepts and theory stretch realism toward liberalism, however, because they move us away from strict attention to relative gain and from consideration of state interests to "human interests."

Basic Characteristics of Private and Public Goods

When states interact they want something. They may want a piece of territory, an agreement on opening of markets, a treaty on reduction of arms, a global postal system, unimpeded access to the radio frequency spectrum, or the knowledge to control malaria. In short they want some kind of "good" that interaction (not necessarily cooperation) of states can provide.[2] This list suggests a wide variety of such goods, and we benefit from differentiating them according to some key characteristics. After doing that we will consider how those characteristics might set up typical patterns of interaction among states pursuing the goods.

Rivalry characterizes a good when only one individual or state can benefit from a specific unit of the good. For instance, when a state controls a piece of territory (a good), no other state can do so. When one fishing fleet kills a herd of whales,

---

[2]Soroos (especially 1986 and 1997) provided good treatments of global public policy based on the concept of commons.

no other can do so. Rivalry creates zero-sum situations.[3] In contrast, however, access to radio waves or television transmissions is nonrivalrous—no one's access precludes that of anyone else (rivalry does, however, characterize radio frequencies upon which to transmit). We would expect more conflict when there is more rivalry.

Congestion characterizes a good when the consumption of units of a good interferes with the ability of others to obtain units of it (generally when it becomes "scarce"). For instance, whales already possessed the characteristic of rivalry in the eighteenth century: Consumption of a specific whale prevented consumption of it by anyone else. At that time, however, there were so few who had the equipment and capability to hunt whales that there was no congestion. Currently, however, the killing of whales limits availability to others. In essence, congestion makes manifest or obvious the rivalry for a good (consider traffic on a freeway as it becomes more congested). We would expect congestion initially to increase conflict, but also potentially to increase cooperation toward relief of the congestion.

Nonexcludability characterizes a good when all states or individuals have access to it. For instance, it is impossible to fence the atmosphere—air moves across borders and anyone can use it for breathing or for disposal of pollutants. Similarly, it is difficult or impossible to restrict access to knowledge. Even high-school students can compile the basic knowledge involved in building an atomic bomb. In contrast, it is possible to exclude countries from the world postal system or from Antarctica. Robert Frost said that "good fences make good neighbors." In reality, if good fences exist, they tend to reduce both cooperative and conflictual interaction—except when it comes time to rebuild or (especially) to move the fence. When fences do not exist, interaction often intensifies, *for better or for worse.*

Nonexcludability is sometimes a physical property of a good (like the atmosphere) and sometimes a legal choice (like the open range of the Wild West). When it is a legal choice, ***privatization*** can create excludability. For instance, a city golf course or even a national forest can be privatized and the new owners may restrict access and exclude the general public.

This discussion emphasizes that we should not always expect that cooperation and conflict in an interstate relationship will vary inversely (as one goes up, the other goes down). Often, low levels of state interaction result in limited cooperation or conflict, and high levels of interaction may lead to increased levels of either or both.

Categories of Goods

Table 6.1 uses rivalry and excludability to categorize and illustrate four types of goods: private goods, coordination goods, common property resources, and pure public goods (Samuelson 1955; Weimer and Vining 1989).

Private goods (in the upper left cell of Table 6.1) exhibit rivalry and excludability. Territory is the best example of a private good. During the expansion of empires in the nineteenth century, Britain, France, Portugal, and Germany grabbed pieces of African territory. In the early part of the century they had limited ability to exploit that continent (in part because malaria stopped

---

[3]The term "jointness" is sometimes used instead of nonrivalry.

them from penetrating it), and there was little congestion with respect to claims of interior territory. By the end of the century there was a great deal of congestion and much conflict.

One typical solution to the problem of congestion is privatization of the good to which ownership was earlier vague or contested. The imperial powers met at the Berlin Conference of 1884–1885 and divided claims in Africa. Similarly, most countries of the world attended the Third United Nations Law of the Sea Conference between 1973 and 1982 and extended their control over ocean resources to a distance of 200 miles from their coastlines.

A second approach is to establish some form of collective control with a fairly explicit statement of privileges and obligations concerning use. For instance, the Antarctic Treaty of 1959 neither recognizes nor denies previous territorial claims, but prohibits all military activity on the continent. Various agreements on the law of the sea guarantee free shipping on the high seas more than 12 miles offshore of states and through key straits even when within 12 miles of shore. The global community has declared the seabed beyond 200 miles of coasts to be the collective property of humanity.

A third approach would potentially be to reduce congestion and thereby eliminate conflict about access to goods. For instance, agreements like that in Berlin over colonies never ultimately resolved imperial disputes, but when countries decided that the costs of colonies were greater than the benefits, the demand fell sharply and eliminated congestion.

Coordination goods lie in the upper right corner of Table 6.1 and exhibit nonrivalry and excludability. For instance, all countries can benefit simultaneously from the World Wide Web. In fact, the more states that partake of the good, the greater the benefit for other states. Yet it would be possible to exclude a country (like Iraq) from any established system. Global postal and telecommunications systems have the same character. Cooperation on a "permanently" inhabited space platform falls also into this category. Russia, Europe, the United States, Japan, and Canada plan to build one collectively and must cooperate closely on equipment compatibility in the modular structure.

The core problem associated with provision of coordination goods is the establishment of initial standards and procedures (Snidal 1985). Interstate cooperation is frequently easy to obtain on coordination goods because the benefits are great, and costs are often low—interests are fundamentally harmonious. It is hardly an accident that the Universal Postal Union and the International Telegraph Union were among the very first modern international organizations.

Yet cooperation is seldom automatic. For instance, the world now is moving toward high-definition television, and there has been competition among European, American, and Japanese firms to define the global specifications. The winning firm and country benefit by being able initially to dominate the market for the system. Think about Microsoft and the benefits that it accrues from having Windows as an unofficial global standard in computer operating systems.

The lower left corner of Table 6.1 contains goods characterized by rivalry and nonexcludability. Because access is unimpeded, we often call them **common property resources.** Biological resources of the high seas, like whales or tuna, illustrate these goods. While rivalry is a generally physical attribute of goods, we have al-

Table 6.1	Classification of Goods	

	Access Rivalrous?	
	Yes	No

Access Excludable? Yes	**Private Goods**
	Core problem: defining
	  property rights
	Examples
	  Alsace-Lorraine
	  The West Bank
		Coordination Goods
		Core problem: establishing
		  standards
		Examples
		  World Wide Web
		  International postal service
		  Global telecommunication
		    systems

No	**Common Property Resources**
	Core problem:
	  overexploitation
	Examples
	  Fish and whales
	  Global atmosphere
	  Geostationary orbits
	  Radio frequency spectrum
		Pure Public Goods
		Core problem: underprovision
		Examples
		  Knowledge to control
		    malaria
		  Radio/television
		    transmissions

Privatization →

Zero-sum   Nonzero-sum

← Congestion

ready stressed that excludability can be partly a legal concept. Theoretically, we could brand (privatize) whales in the same way that ranchers once branded cattle on the open range, thus legally excluding access to them by others and converting them to a private good.

Similarly, geosynchronous orbital space and the spectrum of radio frequencies have the character of common property resources. Again, although there will always be rivalry, because only one satellite can efficiently use a given location, there need not always be nonexcludability. The global community can legally allocate slots and convert them into private property, even allowing purchases and sales by new owners.

The core problem facing states in their provision of common property goods is overexploitation. Fishing on the open ocean illustrates the logic of individuals in a congested common property situation. Each fishing state seeks to obtain as much of the good as possible (there is rivalry) and cannot exclude others from doing the same. Each fleet acts rationally to take additional fish every year. The individual fleet fully captures the benefits of taking more fish. The cost of doing so is smaller future harvests, and all fishing fleets share that cost. That is, the cost is largely external to the individual calculation—each fleet creates what economists call an **externality** for other fleets, in this case a negative one.

This result has come to be known as the **tragedy of the commons** (Hardin 1968), in reference to the ancient tradition of a communal grazing area called a commons

Figure 6.1 Global Fish Catch

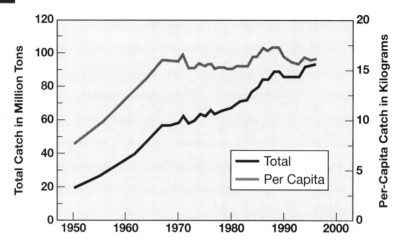

Source: Lester R. Brown, Michael Renner, and Christopher Flavin, *Vital Signs 1998* (New York: W. W. Norton, 1998), 35.

(still seen in some places). As long as the population of grazing animals on the commons is small, sharing poses no problem because the grass is an uncongested good. As population increases and congestion develops, however, the individual interest comes into conflict with that of the group. Animals overgraze the commons and destroy the vegetation, to the detriment of all community members.

Figure 6.1 shows the result of such logic. The UN Food and Agriculture Organization (FAO) estimates that 20 percent of the world's fish are fully exploited or overexploited. In spite of rapid development of LDC fishing fleets (now 60 percent of the global total), global fish catch peaked about 1989. In 1995 there was a "fish war" between Canada and Spain in which Canada impounded one Spanish boat and cut the nets of another, insisting that Spain was overfishing turbot in international waters.

Again we see the same three possible approaches to congestion. First we can privatize the good. The International Whaling Commission (IWC) could theoretically adopt the same approach that most states use domestically with big game: Sell a certain number of hunting licenses, rationing them among potential hunters by lottery or price to create a private good. Instead the IWC chose the second approach, collective regulation. It once set global quotas for the total harvest of various whale species. Because it did not allocate these to particular countries, however, it created a situation like that of access to many concert tickets in the United States, namely a scramble to be first—a "Whale Olympics" (Soroos 1986, 278). Using the same approach, the Alaskan herring-roe fishery was open in the early 1990s for only 40 minutes per year. In 1986 the IWC declared a moratorium on commercial whaling. Third, some activists work to reduce congestion. For instance, they attempt to eliminate public and commercial demand for products of whales, or for tusks, or for furs of endangered animals, and thereby to lessen the pressure on the commons.

The final quadrant of Table 6.1 includes pure **public goods,** which exhibit neither rivalry nor excludability (we call goods exhibiting only nonrivalry or nonexcludability *partially public goods*). For example, your use of knowledge about how to dance the electric slide does not interfere with the provision of that knowledge to anyone else, and it is effectively impossible to deny access to that knowledge.

This last category of international goods is very small. For instance, it was once traditional to cite air or the atmosphere as a pure public good. In reality, however, your use of the oxygen in a given unit of air for breathing or polluting precludes my effective use of the same unit. Thus although I cannot exclude you from that use, we are rivals for it. The atmosphere is actually a common property resource that once was abundant or uncongested relative to demands on it. As long as congestion is low, many common property resources (including whales, radio frequencies, and the atmosphere) appear much like pure public goods. When congestion increases, however, the underlying element of rivalry becomes obvious.

Collective Action and Problems of Underprovision

Although many pure and partially public goods, like whales and clean air, are at least initially "natural" and simply free for the taking, others, like knowledge and "free markets" exist only as a result of human action. Moreover, when "natural" goods become congested and needs for regulatory systems arise, only collective action will assure consistent access to the good.

Especially when excludability of others is not an option (as with many common property resources), states have little incentive to contribute to the costs of the collective action and the provision of the **collective good** (both pure and partially public goods are collective goods, in contrast with private goods). Instead, states prefer to be **free riders,** to partake of the good without contribution. There are even sometimes costs associated with the initial provision of a coordination good that states would prefer someone else paid (the U.S. defense department helped pay the start-up costs of what is now the World Wide Web). If all states decided to "let Denmark do it," there would be no collective action. More commonly, states limit their share of the contribution and the result is underprovision.[4]

When this problem appears within countries, the typical solution is collective coercion. For instance, travel on highways is a good that most of us would like to use without payment. If we were asked to make voluntary contributions to a national highway fund, we might kick in a few dollars, but it is unlikely that we would pay in proportion to our use. We would starve the fund for money, and it would underprovide highways. Instead, we collectively agree to tax ourselves and to force everyone to pay. For instance, collective payment with gasoline taxes or tolls is roughly in proportion to highway use.

In the global arena, there is no central authority to administer collective coercion. In a **privileged group** (Olson 1965, 49–50), however, one or more members has a private incentive to provide some level of the collective good, to the benefit

---

[4]Olson (1965) provided a classic elaboration of this argument. Russett and Starr (1989, 505) quoted a statement of the problem by Aristotle: "What is common to the greatest number has the least care bestowed upon it. Everyone thinks chiefly of his own, hardly at all of the common interest."

of all. Returning to our highway example, if one extremely large trucking firm existed or a small group of firms could collaborate, the firm or group might determine that its own interest lay in paying the costs of a basic national highway system and tolerating some free riding by private individuals. Although the system might still underprovide the public good, there would be a basic supply of it.

Privileged groups sometimes appear globally. For instance, the agreement by 24 countries in Montreal in 1987 to reduce CFC production and use, even in the absence of commitment by other countries, illustrates the principle. These economically advanced countries produce most of the problem, so they could assure significant provision of the collective good of CFC reduction. In fact, a somewhat smaller subgroup, the 12 countries of the European Union, subsequently decided to eliminate production totally by 2000. These leaders in the provision of the collective good do, however, worry about free riders. The production and use of CFCs in China, for example, is growing so rapidly that it could significantly offset reductions elsewhere. If so, China would become a **spoiler,** a free rider so large that it frustrated efforts by a privileged group.

One of the ways in which privileged groups overcome the problem of spoilers is through side payments. **Side payments** are "exchanges among the members of a coalition to equalize any inequalities arising from their cooperation" (Luce and Raiffa 1957, 180). The richer countries will provide some CFC-replacement technology to China as a side payment to encourage Chinese cooperation on the ozone issue; they even established a fund to assist China and other LDCs in its acquisition.

In some cases, a single country can create a privileged group. For instance, a hegemonic world leader, like the United States today or the United Kingdom earlier, may be willing and able for private reasons to provide a collective good. In the security arena, the Pax Britannica of the nineteenth century or the Pax American of the post–World War II period, long periods of unusually peaceful interstate relations, may illustrate the beneficent functioning of a hegemon. The hegemon obtains such a large benefit from an era of peace that it may individually be willing to foot the bill. These same hegemons have also made critical contributions to the provision of free markets that benefit other states, including those that free ride by exporting into the free markets while protecting their own. We referred earlier to such benefits in the theory of hegemonic stability.

Trade and the Logic of Collective Action

Most states want for their citizens the good of access to extensive markets. Western economic theory often describes open markets as if they possessed the public good characteristics of nonrivalry and nonexcludability (Snidal 1985). Specifically, there need be no rivalry because all countries gain by participating in free trade, and there should be no excludability because that would contradict the principle that all have free access to the market.

In reality, however, excludability is legally simple—countries impose tariffs or simply deny access to their domestic markets. Moreover, there is a common perception by states around the world that markets are congested, and they therefore act as rivals in them. Specifically, greater access by Japan to European markets may lessen American access. Thus there is a tendency for states to treat trade as a private good, excluding others from domestic markets and preemptively capturing external markets. At the extreme this privatization logic would result in only intrastate markets. Short of the extreme it might lead to rigid trade blocs, generally centered on one large country.

Thus an extensive free market is not a "natural" public good, with clear-cut characteristics of nonexcludability and nonrivalry. Instead it is a collective good that states must create, essentially by controlling excludability and dampening rivalry. States must overcome the problem of underprovision. How can they do that?

Once again, a hegemon can be useful. For instance, Great Britain and the United States have at times reduced systemic rivalry over market access by opening their extensive markets to smaller powers. Perhaps as important, these hegemons exerted pressure on other states to maintain open markets themselves, thus increasing the supply of the collective good. The hegemon can, however, also selectively deny access to the good. During the Cold War the United States limited access, and in some cases completely *excluded* communist countries from its markets.

A second approach is collectively to regulate access, as global institutions have done since the late 1940s. These international organizations again attempt to expand the supply of the good by maintaining open markets and dampening rivalry over them. With respect to dampening rivalry, they exert pressure on countries that have taken too much of the good (for instance, the large surplus of Japanese exports over imports) to reduce their trade surpluses. With respect to controlling excludability, they make it more difficult for countries not willing to free their own markets by requiring that they do so as a condition for access to the markets of others.

An Approach to Repetitive Interaction: Regimes

Interstate interaction on private and public goods is seldom a one-time phenomenon. The level of congestion changes, supply and demand patterns shift, and states find themselves revisiting old issues. One approach to facilitating ongoing cooperation among states is the creation of a regime. Although in common parlance regimes refer to domestic governments (and often to repressive ones), international **regimes** are the "principles, norms, rules, and decision-making procedures around which actors' expectations converge" in a given issue area (Krasner 1983, 2). Regimes may or may not involve formal organizational structure and formal international law. The international oceans regime, although building on treaties from three UN Law of the Sea Conferences, does not have a standing international organization dedicated to the regime. Nonetheless, fundamental principles, norms, and rules, such as freedom of the high seas, and state rights in the 12-mile territorial seas and 200-mile exclusive economic zones, guide most interstate behavior concerning the oceans. When international organizations and codified international law do exist, however, they help structure regimes. For instance, the WHO strongly shapes and directs the world health regime.[5]

---

[5]Oran Young (1986, 107) usefully put regimes into the category of social institutions like marriages, markets, or electoral processes. Thinking of them in this way helps us understand how they combine institutional structures (like marriage or sales contracts) with informal, process-based patterns (cooperation, trust, and reciprocity). Coercion, too, is associated with all social institutions.

States are willing to pay some start-up costs for regimes, because once in place they lower the *transaction costs* (the costs of striking deals) for further cooperation:

> By transaction costs are meant the irretrievable costs occurred in realizing an exchange of goods and services. Potential partners for exchange have to be sought out, costly bargaining occurs until the terms of exchange are agreed upon, the contracting parties have to monitor the performance of each other and, if the contract is not kept, further costly actions are necessitated by renegotiating, by applying sanctions or by other actions limiting the loss from the other party's reneging on the contract. (Keck 1993, 39)

Regimes also provide negotiating forums, precedents, and easier access to information.

Because states recognize their persistence, regimes establish linkages among decisions over time. In so doing they extend the **shadow of the future**—because states expect that they will return to the same regime structures wanting cooperation from other states in the future, they will more likely cooperate in the present in a bid to generate reciprocity across time.

We can also look at regimes from the supply side, focusing particularly on the behavior of a systemic hegemon. The desires of a hegemon, if one exists, strongly influence the character of the regime. In the arena of international trade, which regime theorists study actively, the Dutch commitment to mercantilism in the seventeenth century imposed a mercantilistic regime on world trade (Ruggie 1983, 198). The British and Americans subsequently opted for liberal or free-trading regimes.

The character of a regime imposed by a hegemon depends in large part on the self-interest (and on the causal beliefs concerning that self-interest) of the hegemon. British and American leaders have believed that free markets allow their economically efficient producers to capture markets globally; the Soviet Union, as a regional hegemon, used barter trade to pursue its security interests in Eastern Europe.

Yet the persistence of regimes suggests that states, even hegemons, may lose control of them once they are established. Although economists disagree, many Americans believe that the rise in productivity among its economic competitors has made U.S. support of free trade anachronistic. In the last quarter of the nineteenth century and the first quarter of the twentieth, Britain did hold onto a free-trade system in which it was no longer fully competitive (Cohen 1987). The Soviet ideological commitment to Socialist barter exchange patterns also continued long after the evidence showed them to be highly inefficient. Although states develop regimes, regimes also shape the expectations and behavior of states (as social constructivists would argue).

Regimes emerge in nonhegemonic environments as well. States bargain and reach agreements even when the extent and distribution of gains from agreement remain somewhat unclear. In fact, states negotiating in multilateral settings on an agreement likely to be in place for decades, such as the creation of a World Trade Organization, often cannot calculate the implications for themselves—they function under a "veil of uncertainty" (Young 1994, 43–54). Therefore, they cannot fully exhibit the rational, self-interested negotiating behavior that realists expect, and they must instead seek fairness and equity.

A Focus of Interaction: Arms Control

The good that people and states perhaps find most difficult to obtain reliably is security. What kind of good is security? It is clearly subject to rivalry. An effort by one state to increase its security can reduce the security of its neighbors (the zero-sum situation described in the classic security dilemma).[6] In an interstate system, security also demonstrates nonexcludability. That is, it is impossible to deny access to more of the good by a state determined to increase its security by spending more on its military. Security in this environment thus exhibits characteristics of a common property resource subject to overexploitation. As each state attempts to take more of the good for itself (with negative externalities for other states), arms races are a common result.

There are many variations on and policy approaches to this unfortunate security environment. One variation is hegemony. If one state is sufficiently powerful, it may unilaterally be able to determine whether other states have security or not. A hegemon effectively makes property-right decisions about security, obviously protecting its own, but granting some to other, nonchallenging states.

An approach called **collective security** calls for cooperative action of all other states against any aggressor. It seeks to dampen rivalry by collectively protecting all weaker states against that aggressor and therefore removing the need of those weaker states to strengthen individually their armed forces. Collective security in essence pushes security into the public good quadrant of Table 6.1. We have seen that the problem in that quadrant is a tendency to free ride, resulting in collective underprovision of the good. What if other states expect us to come to their rescue against an aggressor, but fail to come to our defense?

A collective security arrangement looks inward to punish wayward members of the state system. The UN correctly described its action against Iraq after the invasion of Kuwait as a collective security action. Alliances, like NATO, sometimes call themselves collective security organizations to obtain the respectability that the term conveys. They traditionally have, however, been outward-looking *collective defense* organizations, not collective security arrangements.

The first global effort to create a collective security organization was the League of Nations in 1919. Article 16 of the League Covenant provided that boycotts and embargoes would apply to aggressor states and authorized the council to recommend the use of collective force by member states should that prove necessary. The machinery of the League of Nations did assist in preventing the escalation to warfare of border disputes between Albania and Yugoslavia in 1921, and between Greece and Bulgaria in 1925 (Brown 1987, 157). It failed in several other important cases, however. The league repudiated Japan's establishment of a puppet government in Manchuria in 1931, but Japan withdrew from the league rather than from Manchuria—and suffered no sanctions. In 1935 the council declared Italy's invasion of Ethiopia illegal. For the first time in history, most countries of

---

[6]Congestion is important here. Rousseau posited a state of nature in which humans had little contact with each other, and therefore the rivalry characteristic was less important. He noted, however, that as they increased in numbers and began to come into regular contact, the competition for security grew (the kind of state of nature that Hobbes posited).

the world embargoed arms and "strategic materials" to an aggressor. The embargo, however, was porous and exempted oil, so it did not significantly weaken the Italians. The full-scale Japanese invasion of China in 1937–1938 elicited practically no league response.

There were several reasons for the failure of collective security to work during this period. One was the failure of the United States to join the league and associate its power with the principle. A second was the complete unacceptability of the World War I settlement to Germany, one of the key global powers. That settlement took substantial territory from Germany (in both the East and the West), required heavy economic reparations, and dictated restrictions on the German military (including demilitarization of territory west of the Rhine). The spoilers were too large and numerous.

Still another approach to the security dilemma in the collective regulation tradition is the creation of a multilateral arms-control regime. Arms control is essentially an effort to establish common standards with respect to security. It attempts to make security something more like a coordination good. By obligating all participants to forgo or limit certain weapons systems, it dampens rivalry, at least temporarily. It also attempts to allocate set shares of security to individual states (for instance, by specifying warhead numbers), excluding access to more. As we have seen, the core problem with coordination goods is establishing the standards. That is particularly difficult with respect to arms control, because there is always the possibility that states will revert to treating security as a good over which there is intense rivalry. The rest of this chapter reviews the efforts of states to set those standards via international law.

Arms Control and Disarmament Efforts

Arms-control efforts have proceeded in parallel with the advance of weaponry. The superpowers began signing treaties in the late 1950s. Arms control, both nuclear and conventional, moved ahead more rapidly in the late 1980s and early 1990s, especially between Russia and the United States. Between their peak in 1987 and 1995, real global military expenditures dropped from about $1.36 trillion annually to about $860 billion. This phenomenal drop requires our attention. The collapse of the Soviet Union provides a very large part of the explanation. Nonetheless, a strengthened arms-control regime has contributed.

The Search for Standards to Control Arms   Among the most important types of standards for arms control are *qualitative arms limitations,* which focus on specific weapons or practices (Table 6.2). These often attempt to distinguish offensive and defensive weaponry, and to ban or limit the offensive ones (those that contribute most to the rivalry of the security dilemma).

One of many successful qualitative agreements was the U.S.-Soviet agreement in 1987 to eliminate intermediate nuclear forces (missiles with ranges between 500 and 5,500 kilometers). The superpowers considered those missiles especially dangerous because they would greatly reduce the warning time in a strategic attack. The West became alarmed in 1977 when the Soviets deployed a new missile in this class, the SS–20.

Table 6.2	Important Qualitative Arms Control Agreements	
Year	**Agreement**	**Provisions**
1963	Limited Test Ban Treaty	Bans nuclear tests in the atmosphere, outer space, and under water
1972	Biological Weapons Convention	Bans development, production, and stockpiling of biological weapons
1974	Threshold Test Ban Treaty	Limits underground tests of superpowers to 150 kilotons (not ratified)
1976	Peaceful Nuclear Explosions Treaty	Complements 1974 Test Ban Treaty by limiting peaceful explosions (not ratified)
1977	Environmental Modification Convention	Prohibits weaponry that could modify the environment
1981	Inhumane Weapons Convention	Prohibits certain fragmentation bombs, mines, booby traps, etc.
1987	Intermediate-Range Nuclear Force Treaty	Eliminates all missiles with ranges between 500 and 5,500 kilometers
1990	Underground Testing Verification	Adds protocol to 1974 and 1976 treaties specifying verification procedures
1992	Chemical Weapons Treaty	Multilateral agreement to cease production and eliminate stockpiles, and allow on-site inspections
1996	Comprehensive Test Ban Treaty	Bans all nuclear tests
1997	Convention on the Prohibition of Use, Stockpiling, Production, and Transfer of Anti-Personnel Mines and on Their Destruction	Bans antipersonnel land mines

Sources: Teena Karsa Mayers, *Understanding Nuclear Weapons and Arms Control,* 3rd ed. (Washington, DC: Pergamon-Brassey's, 1986), 90–91; Bruce Russett and Harvey Starr, *World Politics,* 4th ed. (New York: W. H. Freeman, 1992), 352–354; Stockholm International Peace Research Institute, *SIPRI Yearbook 1994* (London: Oxford University Press, 1994); assorted update materials.

More generally, in the mid-1980s a movement surfaced for restructuring Eastern and Western European forces according to a doctrine called **nonprovocative defense** (Hollins, Powers, and Sommer 1989). This concept was a direct response to the security dilemma, and the tendency of most military forces to threaten a potential opponent and engender an arms race. Looking at Swiss and Swedish force structures provides some suggestions concerning a nonprovocative approach to defense: Emphasize tank traps, and antitank and antiaircraft systems; build short-range fighter planes and helicopters in preference to long-range bombers; and stress civil-defense systems and economic-defense preparations. In 1990 top military officials of NATO and the Warsaw Pact met and jointly discussed such military doctrines.

Attempts to eliminate a particular category of weaponry sometimes depend less on the offensive-defensive categorization than on the particularly obnoxious character of the weapon. For instance, there was wide international support for the 1972 UN Convention on the Prohibition of the Development, Production, and Stockpiling of Bacteriological (Biological) and Toxin Weapons and Their Destruction. Under the conditions of that treaty, both the United States and the former U.S.S.R. reported several sites at which they conduct defensive research on biological agents. Iraq had an especially active program and had loaded missiles with biological agents before the U.S./UN invasion. This treaty is very important now, because recent advances in biotechnology, notably cloning and recombinant deoxyribonucleic acid (DNA) techniques, greatly increase the scientific potential for biological-weaponry development. Those same advances have frustrated the development of a convincing inspection scheme.

In 1992 states completed long-term negotiations on a multilateral convention on the Prohibition of the Development, Production, Stockpiling, and Use of Chemical Weapons and on Their Destruction (CWC). Although the Geneva Protocol of 1925 had banned the first use of such weapons, it had not prohibited their production. The CWC, which entered into force in 1997, after obtaining the necessary ratifications, allows "challenge inspections" on short notice with no right of refusal. Although these are significant efforts to reduce cheating (free riding), the treaty is hardly foolproof. When it entered into effect, U.S. intelligence believed that as many as 25 countries, including Libya, Syria, North Korea, Israel, and Iraq, had undeclared stores of weapons (*Christian Science Monitor,* April 28, 1997, 3). Nonetheless, China, France, India, and South Korea are among countries that acknowledged having had chemical-weapons programs and moved to destroy stockpiles.

Following the success with chemical weapons, a broad-based campaign began to ban antipersonnel landmines, which kill an estimated 25,000 people each year around the world, primarily civilians. Pushed by activist nongovernmental organizations and small states, 125 governments signed a treaty in 1997. The United States, Russia, and China were among the large powers refusing to do so, calling into serious doubt its long-term effectiveness. The United States cited the need to defend South Korea against the North as a primary motivation.

Weapon test-bans also fall generally into the category of qualitative approaches. In 1963 the United States, U.S.S.R., and Great Britain negotiated the Partial Test-Ban Treaty prohibiting atmospheric testing of nuclear weapons.[7] In 1974 a bilateral U.S.-Soviet agreement went one step further and banned underground explosions of more than 150 kilotons. Finally, a Comprehensive Test Ban Treaty that would prohibit all testing opened for signature in 1996. India refused to support the treaty because it did not require the declared nuclear powers to commit to eliminate their nuclear weapons. Although this blocked agreement in the Conference on Disarmament, which requires unanimity, Australia led a submission of the treaty to the UN Security Council where a two-thirds majority opened it for signature.

---

[7]Between 1945 and 1980 the five declared powers exploded 528 nuclear bombs in the atmosphere (Soroos 1998, 9).

Table 6.3	Important Quantitative Arms Control Agreements	
Year	**Agreement**	**Provisions**
1972	ABM Treaty (SALT I)	Limited superpower deployment of defense missile systems
	Interim Agreement (SALT I)	Froze superpower missile launcher numbers for 5 years
1979	SALT II Treaty	Limited superpower missile types and numbers (not ratified)
1990	Chemical Weapons Agreement	Committed superpowers to reduce chemical weapon stocks to 5,000 tons by 2002 and end production
	Troop Levels in Central Europe	Limited U.S./Soviet forces in Central Europe to 195,000 each
	Conventional Armed Forces in Europe (CFE)	Limited and substantially reduced NATO and Warsaw Pact arms levels
1991	Strategic Arms Reduction Treaty (START I)	Committed the United States and U.S.S.R. to reduce warheads to about 8,500 and 6,500 respectively
1992	Strategic Arms Reduction Treaty (START II)	Committed the United States and former U.S.S.R. to reduce warheads by 2003 to 3,500 and 3,000 respectively

Sources: Teena Karsa Mayers, *Understanding Nuclear Weapons and Arms Control,* 3rd ed. (Washington, DC: Pergamon-Brassey's, 1986), 90–91; Bruce Russett and Harvey Starr, *World Politics,* 4th ed. (New York: W. H. Freeman, 1992), 352–354; Stockholm International Peace Research Institute, *SIPRI Yearbook 1994* (London: Oxford University Press, 1994); assorted update materials.

Quantitative arms limitations (as opposed to total prohibition) constitute a second approach to standards for arms control (Table 6.3). The first Strategic Arms Limitations Talks (SALT I) led to an agreement in 1972 that obligated the United States and U.S.S.R. to restrict development of antiballistic-missile (ABM) defense systems to two sites. A 1974 treaty lowered the limit to one site per country. This treaty is now very important to Russia, because it will help protect the viability of their nuclear forces. Many U.S. legislators would like, however, to overthrow the agreement and aggressively pursue an antiballistic-missile defense system.

The SALT I agreements also placed five-year interim limits on the number of strategic launchers. The SALT II treaty in 1979 placed ceilings of 2,250 on the total numbers of Intercontinental Ballistic Missiles (ICBMs), Submarine-Launched Ballistic Missiles (SLBMs), heavy bombers, and Air-to-Surface Ballistic Missiles (ASBMs) of both sides, with specific limits within categories as well. (The box on "Nuclear Acronyms" explains nuclear weapons terminology.) In addition, that treaty limited the number of warheads on each missile to 10 for ICBMs and 14 on SLBMs (failure to reach agreement to restrict warheads per missile in 1972 had led to a multiple-warhead race). Carter withdrew SALT II from the U.S. ratification process

Nuclear Acronyms

Delivery Vehicles

ALCM	Air-launched cruise missile—*see* Cruise missile (CM)
ABM	Anti-ballistic missile system—a system designed to detect and destroy incoming nuclear missiles
CEP	Circular error probability—a measure of missile accuracy indicating the radius of a circle around a target within which 50 percent of missiles will fall
C^3I	Command, control, communications, and intelligence—the system for maintaining control over nuclear capabilities during both peace time and war
CM	Cruise missile—a pilotless air-breathing missile that flies relatively slowly and at low elevations
GLCM	Ground-launched cruise missile—*see* Cruise missile (CM)
ICBM	Intercontinental ballistic missile—range normally exceeds 5,500 kilometers
IRBM	Intermediate range ballistic missile—range between 1,850 and 5,500 kilometers
MIRV	Multiple, independently targeted reentry vehicle—a missile with two or more warheads that can be directed to separate targets
SLBM	Submarine-launched ballistic missile—either intercontinental or intermediate range
SLCM	Sea-launched cruise missile—*see* Cruise missile (CM)

Control Efforts

INF	Intermediate nuclear forces treaty—the U.S.-Soviet treaty that eliminated these weapons
NPT	Nonproliferation treaty—completed in 1968, it obligates the more than 100 signatories not to transfer nuclear materials or technology to nonnuclear powers
SALT	Strategic arms limitations talks (I and II)—the forum in which the United States and U.S.S.R. limited strategic missiles
START	Strategic arms reduction talks—the series of discussions in which the United States and U.S.S.R. agreed to reduce strategic forces

Sources: Christopher J. Lamb, *How to Think About Arms Control, Disarmament and Defense* (Englewood Cliffs, NJ: Prentice Hall, 1988), 267–278; Teena Karsa Mayers, *Understanding Nuclear Weapons and Arms Control*, 3rd ed. (Washington, DC: Pergamon-Brassey's, 1986), 90–91, 112–116; Richard Smoke, *National Security and the Nuclear Dilemma*, 2nd ed. (New York: Random House, 1987), 307–314.

after the Soviet invasion of Afghanistan virtually assured its defeat in the Senate. Nonetheless, both sides continued to adhere to the limits it established, while periodically leveling charges and countercharges of cheating.

The superpowers pursued the quantitative strategy further with the Strategic Arms Reduction Talks (START). The START Treaty, signed in 1991, committed

Figure 6.2   The Nuclear Warhead Balance

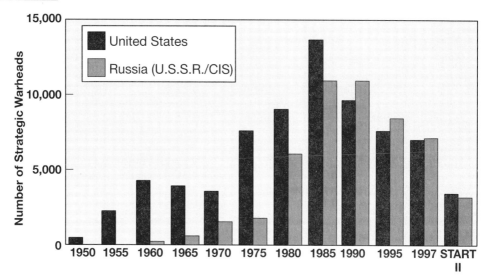

Note: The decline from 1985 to 1990 is a function of switch from SALT to START I counting rules. START II figures are treaty agreement levels for the United States and Russia.

Sources: John P. Holdren, "The Dynamics of the Nuclear Arms Race: History, Status and Prospects," in *Nuclear Weapons and the Future of Humanity,* eds., Avner Cohen and Steven Lee (Totowa, NJ: Rowman and Allanheld, 1986), 41–84; International Institute for Strategic Studies, *The Military Balance 1991–92* (London: International Institute for Strategic Studies, 1991), 219–220; Stockholm International Peace Research Institute, *SIPRI Yearbook* (New York: Oxford University Press, assorted years).

the United States and the former Soviet Union to reduce strategic warheads significantly over seven years. In 1993, with START not yet ratified, the leaderships of the United States and Russia agreed in START II to reduce their warhead totals to 3,492 and 3,044, respectively, by 2003 (see Figure 6.2). It also requires the elimination of ICBMs with multiple warheads. Although the United States ratified START II in 1996, the Russian Duma balked. Many in the Russian legislature felt that Russian conventional forces no longer provided adequate defense and that the West had taken advantage of Russian weakness by expansion of NATO. Leadership of the two countries nonetheless floated the idea of a START III, which would reduce warheads to around 2,000 on each side. Although the two nuclear superpowers no longer target their nuclear warheads at each other, missiles remain on constant alert and can be retargeted and fired in about 15 minutes. The value of further control agreements is obvious.

Quantitative arms control has also made headway on conventional weaponry. The signing of the Conventional Forces in Europe (CFE) Treaty in 1990 committed NATO and the former Warsaw Pact to much clearer accounting for and to substantial cuts in weaponry. The collapse of the Warsaw Pact and of the Soviet Union, and the shifting of tanks by Russia beyond the Urals where the counts would not apply to them, complicated that agreement immediately. But the 30

Table 6.4	Important Arms Control Agreements on Confidence and Security Building Measures	

Year	Agreement	Provisions
1963	Hot Line Agreement	Maintains communication link between the United States and U.S.S.R.
1971	Hot Line Modernization Agreement	Added two satellite circuits to ground cable teletype system
	Nuclear Accidents Agreement	Requires notification of other superpower of nuclear weapons accidents
1972	High Seas Agreement	Provides measures to prevent dangerous incidents on seas
1973	Agreement on Prevention of Nuclear War	Institutes measures to limit risk of war during crises
1975	Conference on Security and Cooperation in Europe	Requires notification of military maneuvers
1984	Hot Line Modernization Agreement	Adds facsimile transmission
1986	Confidence and Security-Building Measures and Disarmament in Europe	Establishes observers during military maneuvers
1987	Crisis Reduction Centers Agreement	Establishes communication centers in Moscow and Washington
1989	Accidental Confrontation Avoidance Agreement	Restricts provocative measures by peacetime military forces
1992	Open Skies Treaty	Permits unarmed reconaissance aircraft to overfly

Sources: Teena Karsa Mayers, *Understanding Nuclear Weapons and Arms Control,* 3rd ed. (Washington, DC: Pergamon-Brassey's, 1986), 90–91; Bruce Russett and Harvey Starr, *World Politics,* 4th ed. (New York: W. H. Freeman, 1992), 352–354; Stockholm International Peace Research Institute, *SIPRI Yearbook 1994* (London: Oxford University Press, 1994); assorted update materials.

countries agreed in 1997 to the outline of a follow-up agreement that would set limits by state and area rather than by alliance and would further reduce overall conventional arms in the region.

A third category of arms control consists of **confidence and security building measures** (Table 6.4). Largely because the superpowers recognized during the Cuban Missile Crisis that their communications via embassies were antiquated, the two countries agreed in 1963 to establish a "hotline" teletype system maintaining constant and nearly instantaneous contact. In 1986 the Stockholm Conference on Confidence and Security Building Measures and Disarmament in Europe (CDE), part of the Helsinki Agreement process, required NATO and Warsaw Pact members to undertake a variety of activities to improve communication in crises and thereby to reduce the risk of accidental or surprise attacks. In 1987 Moscow and Washington established risk reduction centers.

A fourth approach to arms control is *regional disarmament or nonmilitarization* (Table 6.5). For instance, the United States and Great Britain agreed in 1817

Table 6.5	**Important Arms Control Agreements on Regional Disarmament or Nonmilitarization**	

Year	Agreement	Provisions
1959	Antarctic Treaty	Prohibits all military use of Antarctic
1967	Outer Space Treaty	Prohibits placement of weapons in space, including on the moon
	Treaty of Tlatelolco	Prohibits nuclear weapons in Latin America
1968	Nonproliferation Treaty	Prohibits acquisition of nuclear weapons by nonnuclear signatories
1971	Seabed Treaty	Prohibits placement of weapons on the ocean floor
1985	South Pacific Nuclear Free Zone	Prohibits nuclear weapons in the South Pacific
1995	Southeast Asian Nuclear Free Zone	Prohibits nuclear weapons in Southeast Asia
	Nonproliferation Treaty Extension	Indefinite extension of treaty

Sources: Teena Karsa Mayers, *Understanding Nuclear Weapons and Arms Control,* 3rd ed. (Washington, DC: Pergamon-Brassey's, 1986), 90–91; Bruce Russett and Harvey Starr, *World Politics,* 4th ed. (New York: W. H. Freeman, 1992), 352–354; Stockholm International Peace Research Institute, *SIPRI Yearbook 1994* (London: Oxford University Press, 1994); assorted update materials.

to demilitarize the Great Lakes with the Rush-Bagot Treaty. Although violated in the nineteenth century, that agreement now represents one of the most successful regional treaties.

Most modern efforts have created nuclear-free zones. In 1959 the 12 countries most active on the continent signed the Antarctic Treaty, prohibiting all military use including nuclear testing and waste disposal. The Treaty of Tlatelolco in 1967 prohibited nuclear weapons in Latin America. The 1971 Seabed Treaty prohibited nuclear weapon placement on the ocean floor beyond the 12-mile territorial limit of states. In 1985 eight states signed an agreement creating a South Pacific Nuclear Free Zone. In 1995 ten countries agreed on the Southeast Asian Nuclear Weapon Free Zone (SEANWFZ). Neither the United States nor China supported the accord, which would restrict their transport of nuclear weapons through a large area.

Because of the fear that many states will obtain nuclear weapons, an especially important category of nonmilitarization measures is *nuclear-weapon nonproliferation.* International measures exist that seek to restrict the spread of nuclear capabilities. The International Atomic Energy Agency (IAEA), founded in 1957, requires reporting on nuclear-power installations by 100 member countries and relies on material audits and on-site inspections to verify that the facilities do not supply materials to weapons programs. The 1968 Treaty on Non-Proliferation of Nuclear Weapons (NPT) required signatories to accept IAEA controls.

Two difficulties face efforts to prevent nuclear-weapons proliferation. First, peaceful nuclear technology is very widespread. Second, nuclear weapons are not outrageously expensive. The United States devotes only about 10 percent of its total military expenditures to nuclear forces. Most of the Newly Industrialized

Countries (NICs) and essentially all developed countries have the wherewithal to become nuclear powers.

Thus it was not surprising that in 1993 North Korea, a country with quite advanced missile technology, aroused global concern when it announced that it would withdraw from the nonproliferation treaty. The immediate precipitant was a demand by the IAEA for inspection access to two undeclared nuclear waste–disposal sites. Following diplomacy by many parties, North Korea agreed in 1994 to abandon a very active nuclear program in exchange for U.S. agreement to build two nuclear power plants in North Korea that cannot produce plutonium for bombs. Implementation of the agreement has been unsatisfactory.

In 1995, 178 countries met to consider the fate of the nonproliferation treaty and decided to extend it indefinitely. Many nonweapons parties to the treaty, most vocally India, had long argued that it discriminated against them because it created two classes of global citizens: those allowed to maintain their weapons and those prevented from attaining them. As a price for continuation of the treaty they insisted on both serious arms reductions by the nuclear powers (a demand to which SALT and START were responsive but were considered inadequate by India) and a comprehensive test-ban treaty by 1996.

Unilateral Approaches: True Grit?   In addition to arms-control agreements, we sometimes see unilateral initiatives. Those who advocate unilateral measures believe that a single actor can initiate a dynamic of reciprocity by taking several unilateral, cooperative actions. Eventually, they argue, such actions will create an atmosphere of trust and elicit reciprocity from other states.

For example, Charles Osgood (1962) proposed "graduated reciprocation in tension-reduction (GRIT)." He suggested that the United States, while maintaining nuclear weapons and a strong second-strike capability, undertake some initial unilateral steps such as destroying all B-52s or undertaking a moratorium on building bombs. The government should announce a timetable for such actions and make them verifiable. It would then encourage a Soviet response in kind but proceed with at least several steps before abandoning the effort. Fundamentally, the proposal aimed to set in motion a process of diffuse reciprocity in arms control.

Would such an approach work? In 1963 President Kennedy announced a "Strategy of Peace," unilaterally stopping atmospheric testing of nuclear weapons (Hardin 1982, 210). Premier Khrushchev reciprocated, and the episode led to the nuclear test ban treaty. Oswald assassinated Kennedy later that year and the experiment ended as the Vietnam War escalated.

The demobilization that the United States undertook after the Vietnam War is another less-than-perfect example of the unilateral strategy (Figure 6.3). U.S. military spending dropped steadily after the peak of the Vietnam War, declining dramatically between 1968 and 1978 from 9.3 percent of GNP to 4.9 percent. Estimated Soviet spending continued to climb sharply, and the U.S.S.R. achieved significant leads in the numbers of nuclear missiles, in important categories of conventional weaponry (such as tanks), and in personnel. This led to the observation by many American military leaders that "when we build, they build—when we stop, they continue building." The substantial military buildup of the United States in the 1980s terminated this second episode.

Figure 6.3   U.S. and Russian Defense Spending

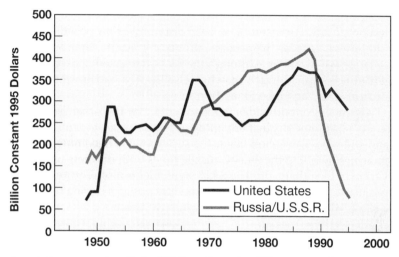

Sources: Assorted sources, primarily the U.S. Arms Control and Disarmament Agency, *World Military Expenditures and Arms Transfers* (Washington, DC: ACDA, assorted issues) and International Institute for Strategic Studies, *The Military Balance* (London: IISS, assorted issues).

Then the Soviet Union announced significant unilateral cuts in late 1988. NATO initially declared that those were necessary simply to redress the imbalance in conventional forces and would not affect NATO force levels. Many attributed the proposed Soviet reductions to domestic economic pressures, or even to the pressure generated by the U.S. buildup, rather than to an earnest desire for arms control.

In 1989 and 1990, several Central and Eastern European countries announced unilateral reductions in military spending, and Western states followed with their own cuts. Public opinion clamored for more. In the early 1990s the long-term dynamic of the East-West arms race collapsed completely. Instead of a continuing upward spiral with only limited pauses, members of NATO and the former Warsaw Pact began to rush toward substantial conventional and nuclear-arms cuts. U.S. defense expenditures dropped from 6.3 percent of GNP in the late 1980s to 3.8 percent by 1995. The United States also took a number of unilateral measures, including elimination of several weapons systems and removing nuclear bombs from alert. In some cases agreements ratified the process, but in many others, reciprocity dynamics and even unilateral measures appeared to drive it.

It might be possible to conclude that the new downward dynamic proves the utility of tit-for-tat and GRIT strategies. Obviously, however, the real force behind the process was collapse of communism throughout the East and quick downturns in military spending. These changes encouraged the West to believe that the East sincerely desired and economically needed ongoing reductions, and to respond in kind.

Problems of Arms Control   Protection of state interests precludes many arms-control efforts. For instance, several potential nuclear powers have believed it to be in their interest to protect the option of developing nuclear forces, and they have not signed the nonproliferation treaty. Yet even when states see agreement to be in their interest, problems may stymie them. Verification is always a key issue. Because the Soviets were long a closed society, they rejected most U.S. verification proposals. For instance, in 1955 Eisenhower proposed an "open skies" policy to allow regular inspection flights by each superpower over military installations of the other. Although the Soviets rejected it, observation by satellites began to accomplish much of what Eisenhower had in mind. In early 1992 24 countries signed an Open Skies Treaty.

Openness of both sides to examination by the other (some call this "transparency") has some distinct advantages. For instance, to remain within treaty limits and still modernize their fleets, the superpowers decommission nuclear-missile submarines by filling the empty missile tubes with concrete under the satellite observation of the other side. The SALT agreements also require each superpower to forgo encryption of information returned by missiles during tests, so that the other side can easily eavesdrop on the communications.

Yet electronic measures, called "national technical means," have limits. The Intermediate Nuclear Forces (INF) treaty of 1987 made breakthroughs concerning on-site or so-called intrusive inspections. These included initial inspections of all INF sites, observations of missile-elimination procedures, and short-notice inspections of INF-related sites during the three-year elimination period and for ten years thereafter (to assure that the opponent did not reconstruct the weapons). START I allows 12 types of on-site inspections, including surprise visits to strategic weapons sites.

Besides verification, the most significant problem of arms control is that of comparing "apples and oranges" in force structures. For instance, both sides generally accept that the United States has higher-quality weaponry and Russia had greater quantity. Exactly how one balances quality against quantity in reductions is complicated. Also, how does one compare tanks with fighter aircraft? A modern fable illustrates the problem. According to the story, the members of the animal kingdom met for a disarmament conference. The eagle called for abolition of fangs, the lion for controls on beaks and tusks, and the elephant for restrictions on the use of talons and teeth. The bear offered still another approach, the abolition of all weapons (general and complete disarmament). Instead, quarrels should be settled by hugging.

The world has built an impressive structure of arms-control agreements since World War II, even before the end of the Cold War. It impresses even realists. Yet these same realists would want to remind us that the agreements reflect state interests and that they could collapse as quickly as the Soviet Union did. An edifice of such agreements, built with great care by diplomats between the two world wars, proved useless in the face of fascist aggression. Why should we believe that these new agreements would survive a probable challenge of China to U.S. hegemony or even the accession of a militaristic government to power in Russia? That is a challenging question.

Conclusion

The realist worldview that has organized the last three chapters explains a great deal about world politics and constitutes a powerful initial basis for understanding. That it is frequently parsimonious (simple) in its portrayal adds to its appeal.

In its pure form it is too simple, however, and even realists recognize the need to relax some of its elements. Specifically, we need to relax, and in some cases to overturn completely, three elements of the basic realist world view. First, the characterization of states as rational, unitary actors is a frequently useful fiction, but it stands in the way of a fuller understanding of state behavior. The next chapter considers how forces inside states interact in the making of decisions and create state-specific and not always rational policy. Second, states are not the only actors in world politics. Chapter 8 documents the growing number and strength of *nonstate* actors. Third, as we have already seen in this chapter, power and security are not the only ends of world politics. Many subsequent chapters will turn our attention to freedom from governmental oppression, economic well-being, cultural identity, and even environmental preservation.

Some of the separate challenges to realism in these coming chapters are friendly amendments and extensions that realists readily accept. For example, even Thucydides noted that what happened within Greek city-states influenced their external behavior. Both Machiavelli and Morgenthau, although emphasizing the primacy of power motivations, also recognized the importance of ideals concerning justice and morality. Yet when we develop the full range of amendments and extensions, they will move our thought well beyond the simple realist world view.

Selected Key Terms

positivist (law)

naturalist (law)

diplomatic immunity

law-making treaties

soft law

just war

respondent superior

rivalry

congestion

nonexcludability

private goods

coordination goods

common property
 resources

externality

tragedy of the commons

public goods

collective good

free riders

privileged group

spoiler

side payments

regimes

shadow of the future

collective security

nonprovocative defense

confidence and security
 building measures

CHAPTER 7

Opening the State

On December 7, 1941, with no prior declaration of war or other warning, Japanese planes, ships, and submarines attacked Pearl Harbor, Hawaii, initiating four years of war between the United States and Japan. Japanese soldiers, loyal to the emperor, were notorious for their refusal to surrender and for their willingness to commit suicide in the execution of their missions. They also committed atrocities in many Asian countries that they occupied, including the brutal "Rape of Nanking" in which soldiers killed as many as 300,000 Chinese and raped up to 80,000 women. Three days after the United States declared war on Japan, it also declared war on Germany and Italy, entering the conflict in Europe. The conventional fire bombing of German cities by the United States and the United Kingdom completely destroyed some of those cities and the U.S. fire bombing on Tokyo killed perhaps 100,000 in one night. The United States ended the war in Asia by dropping two nuclear weapons on major cities of Japan. Only at the end of that conflict did the United States learn definitively that its European enemy had systematically organized the mass slaughter of more than 6 million humans.

KEY WEB LINKS

www.pipa.org/
www.gallup.com/
www.brook.edu/default.htm

Today Japan, Germany, and the United States are allies. Yet they remain three of the very most powerful military and economic actors in the world, and they compete aggressively in international trade. Should we not, based on realist theory of power relationships, expect that their alliance is temporary and that they will come again into military conflict? Many analysts, as well as citizens of those countries, are reluctant to give an affirmative answer to that question, not just because another war would be even more horrific than the last, but because they believe there have been fundamental changes. In particular, many believe that factors inside those countries, especially within Japan and Germany, are now fundamentally different than they were in 1941.

Levels of Analysis

Looking at world politics from the viewpoint of individual states, and from the perspective of the state system as a whole, helped us elaborate the realist worldview in the last three chapters. The individual state and the state system are two alternative **levels of analysis** for world politics. To better understand state behavior, however, it is useful to identify at least three additional levels of analysis (Singer 1961; Rosenau 1980) that collectively constitute an intrastate perspective: the society, individuals, and the government (which generally mediates between society and individuals, on the one hand, and the external environment, on the other).

Do societies differ in the extent and nature of their involvement in world affairs? How stable are such characteristics over time and what might cause them to change? What is the constellation of societal forces that helps give rise to the external orientation of a particular state? How important are the beliefs and personalities of specific leaders? How accurate is the perception by leaders of the external environment and how can they improve it? How do governmental structures translate pressures from society and the orientation of individual leaders into foreign-policy decisions? Do democracies differ from other governments in the nature of their interstate relations?

Moving inside the state draws these questions to our attention. When we finish considering them, we will return to the central issue of this chapter, the degree to which states are unitary, rational actors (and the importance of any deviations from that simplifying assumption).

Before considering each of the intrastate levels of analysis in detail, an example can convey the utility of bringing all to bear on global politics. The American occupation force drafted the post–World War II Japanese constitution of May 1947. Sometimes called the Peace Constitution, it set the stage for ongoing debates concerning defense spending and the appropriate use of Japanese military power. Article IX of that constitution states:[1]

> Aspiring sincerely to an international peace based on justice and order, the Japanese people forever renounce war as a sovereign right of the nation and the threat or use of force as a means of settling disputes.
>
> In order to accomplish the aim of the preceding paragraph, land, sea, and air forces, as well as other war potential, will never be maintained.

Interpretation of this article has changed with time. In 1950 General MacArthur, head of the occupation forces, authorized the creation of a 75,000-person Japanese National Police Reserve (McWilliams and Piotrowski 1988, 67). In 1954 the Japanese government decided that Article IX did not preclude a "minimal self-defense" and it created the Self-Defense Forces (SDF). In 1976 Japan made the decisions to increase military capabilities to allow defense against small-scale invasions, and to limit defense spending to 1 percent of GNP (that limit is *not* part of the constitution itself). In January 1987 Japan *slightly* exceeded the 1 percent limit.

---

[1]Niksch (1983, 59). Smith (1987) and Frost (1987) provided initial basis for this discussion of Japanese defense spending.

In fact, calculating the Japanese budget as most NATO countries do (with military pensions and R&D included) would put it at 1.6 percent of GDP (*The Economist*, October 12, 1996, 38). What determines the level of defense spending in Japan?

State System

We must seek much of the answer to that question outside of the country. The United States defeated Japan in World War II and, to assure itself that Japanese militarism would not be a threat again, insisted that the constitution demilitarize Japan. After several years of direct military occupation and rule, the United States convened a multilateral peace conference in San Francisco during September 1951 that produced a treaty ending the war. Forty-nine states signed (the U.S.S.R., Poland, and Czechoslovakia abstained).

The same day that the United States and Japan signed the peace treaty, which provided 90 days for removal of U.S. occupation forces, they also signed an agreement permitting U.S. troops to remain in assistance of Japanese defense (De Conde 1978, 333–334). Japan thereby moved under the umbrella of the defense system that the United States constructed in Asia and became a U.S. ally in the Cold War. In November 1952 Vice President Nixon visited Japan and declared that the United States had made "an honest mistake" in insisting on disarmament. In March 1954 the two countries signed a mutual defense agreement that required Japan to increase spending. In 1988 a Congressional amendment to the U.S. defense budget demanded spending at 3 percent of GDP (Chai 1997, 390). The growing power of China and the missile capability of North Korea add to pressure for higher spending.

Other systemic forces, however, restrain Japanese military spending. The most important may be the concerns of neighboring Asian countries such as China and Korea (see Map 7.1). They remember the Greater East Asia Economic-Coprosperity Sphere that Japan established before the war, ostensibly to free the region from Western imperialism but used to justify brutal imperial rule by the Japanese. To increase trade with China and other neighbors, Japan has felt it important to avoid raising any anxiety. In addition, the point at which American fears of renewed militarism would replace American pressure for increase is not clear.

These conflicting systemic pressures have contributed to the slow pace of change in Japanese spending levels. They also explain other aspects of Japanese defense behavior. For instance, in 1998 Japan contributed about $4 billion to the cost of American military personnel stationed at installations in Japan (37,000 in 1998, down from 260,000 in the 1950s). This and various in-kind contributions placate the Americans and diminish their perception of Japan as a free rider on defense.

The State

Japan is a geographically small, resource-poor island state. As it industrialized and its population increased, the need for raw materials and food imports rose; so, too, did its need for markets. This information is critical to understanding its prewar imperialism. Like European states before it, Japan saw the direct conquest and governance of external territories as a way of satisfying those needs. For instance, it

Map 7.1

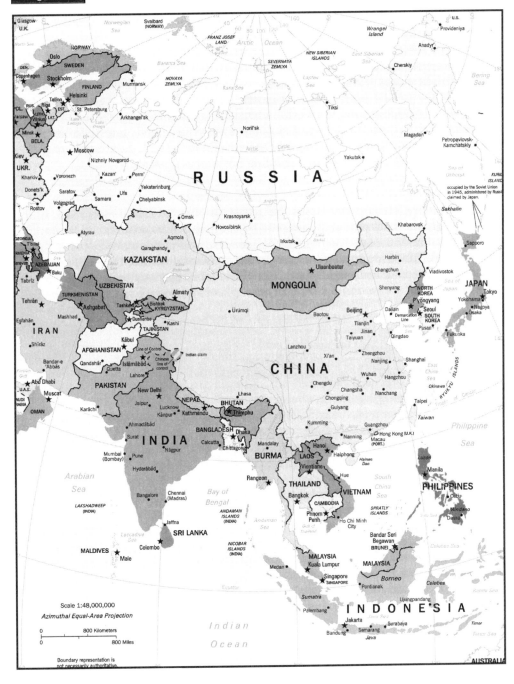

made the island of Formosa (now Taiwan) into a food-supplying colony. The Japanese need for oil, coal, and other raw materials helped lead it into additional imperialist adventures including the invasion of China in 1931 and creation of the puppet state of Manchukuo (Manchuria).

Since World War II, the development of an export capacity, sufficiently strong to guarantee the ability to buy food and raw materials, has satisfied these same needs. The alliance with the United States has simultaneously provided Japan access to raw materials, markets for industrial exports, and some guarantee of its freedom to trade around the world. A tension exists, however, between the Japanese drive for export earnings and its alliance with the United States, because of the large U.S. trade deficits with Japan. Japan continues to seek the strength of the alliance with as little damage to its trading position as possible.

Society

The Japanese society remembers the militarism that led it into World War II, the devastation of that war (including the two atomic bombs dropped on it), and the humiliation of defeat. The bulk of the Japanese population now displays a deep pacifism. Public support for increased military expenditures fell from 24 percent in 1969 to 6 percent in 1993. Support for revision of Article IX declined from 37 percent in 1955 to 13 percent in 1991 (Chai 1997, 403). Even recruitment for the Self-Defense Forces has sometimes been difficult.

The long-ruling Liberal Democratic Party (LDP) has supported the SDF and attempts to bolster them. The Social Democratic Party (formerly the Japan Socialist Party), the largest of the opposition parties in the late 1980s and early 1990s, steadfastly resisted those efforts. It is probable that many Japanese link their economic success (at least until the 1990s) to limitation of military spending. Americans certainly believe in such a linkage.

In the early 1990s a new and quite bitter debate arose concerning the use of Japanese forces in UN-sponsored peacekeeping missions abroad. Although Japan provided generous financial support for the UN-sanctioned war against Iraq, its Parliament stymied LDP efforts to send a small noncombatant "UN Peace Cooperation Corps." The LDP failed again in 1991 to pass legislation permitting units of up to 2,000 lightly armed troops to join UN missions like that in Cambodia. Even neighbors such as South Korea and Indonesia expressed readiness, however, to accept such deployment. Moreover, opposition in public opinion polls dropped from 78 percent in mid-1990 to 35 percent in mid-1992. Although the Social Democratic Party led an intense campaign against the measure again in 1992, the Buddhist-minded Komeito (Clean Government) party helped the LDP pass it that year.

At the same time it is important to note that a large segment of Japanese society retains a strong patriotism with clear elements of nationalism. That right-wing force (with growing power in the LDP) has prevented Japanese textbooks from rendering full accounts of Japanese behavior in World War II. When in 1998 the Iris Chang book *The Rape of Nanking* became a surprise bestseller in the United States, the Japanese ambassador to the United States criticized it; a film called "Pride," sympathetically treating the architect of World War II militarism

(General Tojo), swept Japanese theaters. In the late 1990s, support for the Socialists collapsed.

It is an important digression to note that Germans have similarly debated reinterpretations of their constitutional restrictions on the use of German forces abroad; they have also gradually expanded their willingness to do so. Like Japan, Germany kept its forces out of the Gulf War, arguing that its constitution forebade it. Thereafter, under the leadership of the Christian Democratic party, it sent minesweepers to the Gulf, army medics to Cambodia, and German marines to the Adriatic as part of UN efforts to monitor an embargo against Serbia. In 1999 it joined the air war in Yugoslavia.

Individual

Prime Minister Nakasone (1982–1987) was right-of-center in the Liberal Democratic Party and a nationalist. He had once served as defense minister and sought to propagate an image of Japan as an "unsinkable aircraft carrier." As prime minister, he actively advocated stronger security. In particular he emphasized the importance of protecting sea lanes, appealing to societal understanding of Japanese dependence on trade. His support was instrumental in the Diet's decision to exceed the 1 percent limit for the first time (although only to 1.004 percent in 1987) and to establish the precedent for higher spending. Similarly, in 1992 Prime Minister Miyazawa put his prestige at risk in an all-out effort to pass the bill allowing Japanese troops to serve in UN missions. And in 1996 Prime Minister Hashimoto supported a new National Defense Program Outline that strengthened forces.

Thus various prime ministers, in their personalized evaluations of the relationship with the United States and of the strategic situation facing Japan, have decided that they must lead in arguing for increases in spending and activism. In their role as primary representative of the state, they have probably weighed the external environment more heavily than did others in government. It is common that chief executives of countries visualize themselves as representing the interests of the state, and parliamentarians to a greater degree represent specific elements within society.

Government

The government and its decision-making process is the focal point of the various pressures from within and outside of the state. At least three factors peculiar to Japanese government have been important in decision making on defense spending. First, the existence of the Peace Constitution is a powerful factor reinforcing the societal desire to restrict spending.

Second, Japanese decision making traditionally lacks much of the pluralistic conflict found in Western European and North American democracies. Instead, an emphasis on consensus prevails. "To use a mischievous metaphor, the characteristic American response to a world crisis is to jump up on the table and make a speech, while the characteristic Japanese response is to crawl under the table and quietly build a consensus" (Frost 1987, 82). This contributes to a certain inertia in decision making and to a special reluctance to override the social majority opposed to higher spending. The issue of sending troops abroad evoked so much emotion in 1991 that a very uncharacteristic brawl broke out on the floor of the Diet (parliament), causing the leadership to retract the proposal. In a more characteristic act, after the LDP temporarily fell from power in 1994 the new Social Democratic prime minister rushed to reverse both his party's opposition to Japanese military participation in UN peacekeeping and its traditional support for North Korea.

Finally, among the competing groups within the government bureaucracy, the defense establishment has little clout. In their call on resources, the ministries related to economic development, such as the famous Ministry of International Trade and Industry (MITI) and the even more powerful Finance Ministry, carry much more weight. This is, of course, a "chicken-and-egg" situation. In countries where the military is strong, they invariably also have lobbying strength.

In summary, a levels-of-analysis approach facilitates our understanding of Japanese defense-spending policy and can similarly help us interpret other foreign policies. We turn now to a more extended discussion of intrastate forces: the society, individuals, and governments.

Society

One useful way of trying to understand the orientation of a society toward foreign affairs is through analysis of its public opinion. We will look inside the United States as a way of understanding its foreign policy. Yet we want to go beyond the public opinion polls and to understand what gives rise to expressed opinions. To do so, we will subsequently look in turn at the interests of various elements of the public and at the ideas that shape opinion.

Public Opinion

Realists look primarily to the state and state system for understanding of foreign policy. It is therefore not surprising that at the peak of realist influence on the study of world politics (in the first two decades after World War II) there was a general consensus that the public lacked knowledge about world affairs, that its opinions were volatile and poorly structured, and that (thank goodness) the public did not much affect policy. Evidence accumulated over many years supports a somewhat more liberal revision of that characterization (Holsti 1996; Eichenberg 1998): although knowledge is limited within a general public, volatility is mixed, and attitudes do have persistent structure. Moreover, there is considerable evidence that public opinion *does* affect policy.

Low Knowledge Level and Opinion Volatility   Polls regularly document how ignorant U.S. citizens are about geography, history, and contemporary foreign affairs. In one poll only 44 percent understood that the United States and the Soviet Union had been allies in World War II. In 1988 three-fourths could not name a single NATO country, and 16 percent believed the Soviet Union was a member. In 1989 fewer than half of American adults could locate Great Britain, France, South Africa, *or* Japan on a world map. One in seven could not locate the United States. In 1993, shortly before a Congressional vote on the North American Free Trade Agreement, 62 percent could not say what NAFTA was.[2] Other countries generally poll less heavily, but results are similar. Cohen (1995, 57) found that the uninformed public was larger in the Netherlands than in the United States.

Public opinion can also be volatile. In 1973 only 11 percent of Americans believed that the country was spending too little on defense. That percentage climbed to 27 percent in 1978 and soared to 56 percent in 1980. It plummeted again to 14 percent in 1985 (Schneider 1987, 43). Still, many studies conclude that such changes in opinion "appear to be 'reasonable, event driven' reactions to the real world, even if the information upon which they are based is marginally adequate at best" (Holsti 1992, 446). Not only had the Soviet Union's spending considerably outstripped that of the United States by 1980 (reversing the pattern of 1970), but it was acting aggressively in Afghanistan and Africa.

Attitudinal Structure Stability Although opinions on specific issues can change rapidly, studies repeatedly discover a large amount of underlying stability in the structure of basic attitudes and orientations (Russett, Hartley, and Murray 1994). With respect to engagement with the outside world, societies are generally **isolationist** or **internationalist** over quite long periods of time. The American public has been consistently internationalist since World War II (see Figure 7.1). The trauma of the Vietnam War led, however, to some retreat from that stance through the 1970s. More important, it gave rise to a differentiation among internationalists. Wittkopf (1990, 9) argued that we need to differentiate between cooperative internationalism (such as foreign aid or trade) and militant internationalism (such as military aid or intervention).[3] Blacks and women fall less often into the militant internationalist category. A Gallup poll in January 1991 found that 67 percent of men, but only 45 percent of women, supported war to expel Iraq from Kuwait (Russett and Starr 1992, 221).

Many have wondered if the end of the Cold War might give rise to another fundamental transformation in American attitudinal structures and a renewed isolationism. The preliminary evidence (as in Figure 7.1) suggests that the answer is "no." That may be a premature answer, however, simply because basic attitudes change slowly. For instance, support for foreign economic assistance appears to have dropped.

We should recognize also that for several decades American elites have been more committed than the broader public to both internationalisms. Studies have found this often true in other countries also. Table 7.1 presents data that indicate a fairly complex pattern of leader-public attitudinal differences in the mid-1990s. While leaders were especially supportive of preventing nuclear proliferation, securing adequate energy supplies, and defending allies, the public was particularly supportive of stopping the flow of illegal drugs, protecting American jobs, and

---

[2]*The Christian Science Monitor* March 20, 1989, 13, and November 15, 1989, 18. Rourke (1995, 117–118).

[3]Hughes (1978, 30) distinguished between military and nonmilitary internationalists. Holsti and Rosenau (1988) identified Cold-War internationalists, post–Cold War internationalists, and semiisolationists. Rosati and Creed (1997) labelled six orientations, none strictly isolationist.

Figure 7.1   Percent of U.S. Citizenry Favoring Active Role in World

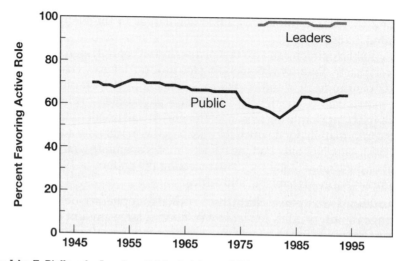

Source: John E. Rielly, ed., *American Public Opinion and U.S. Foreign Policy* (Chicago: The Chicago Council on Foreign Relations, 1991), 12; John E. Rielly, ed., *American Public Opinion and U.S. Foreign Policy 1995* (Chicago: The Chicago Council on Foreign Relations, 1995), 13. Reprinted with permission.

containing proliferation. Leaders accepted the end of the Cold War more quickly than did the public. They were quicker to call for reductions in arms spending as a result of its ending.

Putting together these pieces of information concerning knowledge level, opinion volatility, and stability of attitudinal structure, we can draw a general portrait of the American public (Almond 1950; Rosenau 1961). A group called the *general public*, constituting roughly 80 percent of the population, has limited knowledge of, or interest in, world affairs. A second segment, called the **attentive public,** and making up about 10–20 percent of the citizenry, is consistently tuned in to foreign affairs. Their attitudes have internal consistency and stability. A small subset of the attentive public, perhaps 1 percent, are **opinion leaders,** with considerable knowledge and interest, an ability to rapidly adapt and learn, and a willingness to communicate their understandings and beliefs to others. These individuals also, on the average, have been more internationalist in orientation.

Public Opinion and Policy   It is important also to note that public opinion appears to make a real difference in a democracy. Mueller (1973) traced how public opinion shifts toward the Vietnam War affected U.S. commitment to it. Figure 7.2 traces public opinion in the United States on defense spending (the percentage who favor increased spending of those with a preference for increase or decrease) and the size of the defense budget as a portion of GDP. It is obvious that the relationship is not terribly close and that the public does not control spending. Yet there is a relationship. In the first two decades of the Cold War (until the mid-1960s), a majority of the respondents who wanted

Table 7.1	Importance of Foreign-Policy Goals Differences Between Leaders and the Public (1994)	

Should Be an Important Goal	Public (percent)	Leaders (percent)
Stopping the flow of illegal drugs into the United States	89	57
Protecting the jobs of American workers	83	50
Preventing the spread of nuclear weapons	82	90
Controlling and reducing illegal immigration	72	28
Securing adequate supplies of energy	62	67
Reducing our trade deficit with foreign countries	59	49
Improving the global environment	58	49
Combating world hunger	56	41
Protecting interests of American business abroad	52	38
Strengthening the United Nations	51	33
Maintaining superior military worldwide	50	54
Defending our allies' security	41	60
Promoting and defending human rights in other countries	41	60
Helping to bring a democratic form of government to other countries	25	21
Protecting weaker nations against foreign aggression	24	21
Helping to improve the standard of living of less-developed countries	22	28

Source: John E. Rielly, "The Public Mood at Mid-Decade," *Foreign Policy,* no. 98 (Spring 1995), 82.

changed expenditures favored *higher* defense spending. Defense spending remained at or above 8 percent of GDP. By the peak of the Vietnam War in the late 1960s, the public had turned against defense spending. That sharp attitudinal shift preceded both de-escalation of the war and a subsequent decline in military spending throughout the 1970s. A majority of the public became supportive of greater spending again in 1977, the Soviets invaded Afghanistan in 1979, and defense spending rose in the early 1980s. Public opinion shifted against spending in the mid-1980s, and the government began to respond by the late 1980s. Public support for spending grew again in the late 1990s and spending may respond.

Interests

What gives rise to public opinion and to the differences within the public? One answer is that interests shape opinions. Another is that important ideas can have a life of their own beyond interests. We look first at interests, both the interest groups that are especially active in *interest articulation,* and the political parties that make a primary contribution to *interest aggregation.*

Figure 7.2   Public Opinion and Defense Spending in the United States

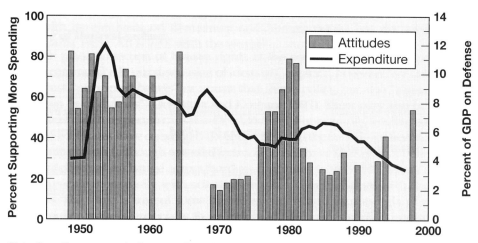

Note: Spending support is shown as those favoring more spending as a portion of those favoring more or less spending.

Sources: Barry B. Hughes, *The Domestic Context of American Foreign Policy* (San Francisco: W. H. Freeman, 1978), 112; Bruce Russett and Harvey Starr, *World Politics: The Menu for Choice,* 3rd ed. (New York: W. H. Freeman, 1989), 232; Gallup Report, assorted issues and releases (www.gallup.com); Arms Control and Disarmament Agency, *World Military Expenditures and Arms Transfers* (Washington, DC: ACDA, assorted editions); *International Institute for Strategic Studies, The Military Balance 1991–92* (London: IISS, 1991), 212; John E. Rielly, *American Public Opinion and U.S. Foreign Policy* (Chicago: The Chicago Council on Foreign Relations, 1991), 32; John E. Rielly, *American Public Opinion and U.S. Foreign Policy 1995* (Chicago: The Chicago Council on Foreign Relations, 1995), 34; *NATO Review* (Spring 1998), D15.

Economic Interest Groups   As implied by the label, self-interest generally directs interest groups. In all democratic countries, economic interest groups are among the most influential. Their chief concerns are the ease with which they can export, and the protection that they can obtain from external competition.

As a general rule, the orientation of an economic interest group toward trade depends on whether the factor of production it represents is relatively abundant or scarce.[4] **Factors of production** are those resources used in the process of production, most notably land, labor, and capital. When a factor like land is abundant, it will be inexpensive and activity based upon it will tend to produce goods competitive on the world market. In the United States land has always been abundant relative to other factors, whereas in Great Britain land has been relatively scarce and, since early in the industrial revolution, capital has been relatively abundant. Because of their factor balances, many British manufactured goods flowed to the United States in the 1800s and much U.S. agricultural output went to Britain. In

[4]Rogowski (1989) presented a very readable discussion of the Stolper-Samuelson theorem and its domestic political ramifications (see also Chapter 12). The specific-factors (Ricardo-Viner) approach takes the same logic down to specific sectors of the economy.

that century, British capitalists supported free trade, but British farmers could not compete with American farmers and desired protection against free trade. In contrast, American labor and capital (producers of manufactured goods) generally allied against freer trade while American farmers supported it. Those economic positions were very rational in self-interest terms.

The trade patterns that developed between the U.K. and the United States had impacts on their domestic economies. Between 1870 and 1913, when global markets were especially open, the ratio of wages to rents (on land) more than doubled in Britain and fell by half in the United States (*The Economist*, April 20, 1996, 68). This is because wages were relatively high in the United States (relative labor scarcity) and rents were high in the U.K. (relative land scarcity) prior to the compensatory surge in trade. Increased trade led to greater **factor price equalization** between the two countries, disadvantaging owners of the scarce production factor of both countries (at the same time that trade advantaged owners of plentiful factors).

By the end of World War II, American capital was also abundant and efficient. Although U.S. labor remained relatively scarce and therefore expensive, the export strength of the United States quite fully employed that labor, so that it did not oppose free trade. As long as the United States continued to export more than it imported, as it did from 1945 to 1971, interest groups based in land, labor, and capital largely continued to support free trade. The United States moved quickly after World War II to dismantle barriers to trade and to encourage other countries to do the same.

However, in most years since 1971 the United States has imported more than it exported. The abundance of U.S. capital and land continues to make those factors competitive around the world, and owners continue to support free trade. The relative scarcity of U.S. labor, however, makes it highly paid by global standards; therefore, U.S. labor is less competitive. As early as 1972 The American Federation of Labor and Congress of Industrial Organizations (AFL-CIO), the leading U.S. union organization, backed the Burke-Hartke Foreign Trade and Investment Act, which would have established quotas for all imports on a category-by-category basis and made it less profitable for multinational corporations to invest overseas (thus transferring American jobs abroad).

Because of the same self-interested logic, American agricultural and business interests have largely supported free-trade agreements like that between Canada, Mexico, and the United States, while American labor has opposed them. Debates over free-trade agreements make clear, however, that interest groups based on the same general factor of production will not always present a common front (Midford 1993). For instance, whereas American cereal producers stand to gain from freer agricultural trade with Mexico (U.S. grain land is plentiful), fresh produce growers could lose (U.S. land for winter produce is relatively scarce).

Intrafactor divisions will lead individual farmers, firms, and laborers to seek special advantage relative to their competitors. From the viewpoint of individual firms, the ideal situation would be freedom to export to open markets around the world (in fact, even bolstered by subsidies and credits to encourage exports), coupled with substantial barriers against access by foreign firms to the domestic market. Those owners of capital or land who step back and look at the "big picture," however, realize that domestic firms are unlikely to obtain access to foreign markets unless foreign firms have similar privileges.

This sets up a tension. Within the United States, individual businesses and farm interests frequently press for the protection of trade barriers, such as quotas that set maximum import levels. Cries of the automobile industry for protection against the Japanese market onslaught led in the 1970s and 1980s to a "voluntary quota" set by Japan on the total number of cars its manufacturers would ship to the United States. Had it not been done voluntarily, Congress would almost certainly have made it compulsory. Similarly, U.S. sugar producers have succeeded in obtaining a quota on sugar imports to the United States. Yet American business as a whole (represented, for example, by magazines like *Forbes* or *Business Week* or organizations like the National Association of Manufacturers) tends to support free trade. The U.S. shift to free trade after World War II was assisted by a movement in decision making—from a congressional aggregation of individual demands for protection to an executive-branch representation of the collective interest in reciprocal access to markets (Bauer, Pool, and Dexter 1972).

Noneconomic Interest Groups   Noneconomic interest groups also adopt foreign policy stances. For example, in the United States, more than in ethnically homogeneous democracies, groups that support or oppose particular foreign governments attempt to influence foreign policy. Sometimes they appear to have great success. The Committee of One Million Against the Admission of Communist China to the United Nations (the China Lobby) enrolled 97 members of the House of Representatives in 1956 and seemed capable of blocking any movement toward rapprochement with mainland China. Yet by 1969 more than one-half of the American public favored admission to the United Nations (Mueller 1973, 15–17), and in 1971 the UN did admit it. The following year Nixon visited China and began to reestablish relations.

Today the pro-Israel lobby is the most powerful of the ethnic lobbies, drawing on 6 million American Jews. An indication of the lobby's strength is that the United States annually provided about $3 billion in military and economic assistance to Israel throughout the 1990s. Other than Egypt (which received aid primarily because of its participation in an American-sponsored peace with Israel), no other country obtained more than one-fifth that amount (see again Table 4.4). In addition, the United States has frequently found itself voting with only a handful of other states against UN resolutions calling on Israel to proceed in discussions with Palestinian leaders. An objective, realist look at the state interest of the United States would almost certainly place it on the side of the oil-producing and (generally) anti-Israel Moslem countries of the Middle East. The United States has repeatedly risked offending those states and jeopardizing oil exports to itself and its allies through its support for Israel. In 1973 the Arab members of OPEC directed an oil embargo against the First World because of its support for Israel. Japan and many European countries capitulated and increased their support for the Arab states in the Mideast conflict. The United States remained firm in its commitment to Israel.

The **pluralist model** of decision making (Dahl 1956) portrays the competition among interest groups to translate their specific interests into policy. It represents domestic and, to a lesser degree, foreign policy as a *compromise outcome* of interest-group pressures. It has been said that a camel is a horse designed by a committee. To the degree that foreign policy similarly represents compromise among parochial interests, rather than clearheaded pursuit of a state interest, that process weakens the rational-state assumptions of realism.

Political Parties   Parties often draw together or *aggregate* the more diffuse interests within society. For instance, the Republican party in the United States has long aggregated many of the business interests in the country. It is thus not surprising that the Republican party was the party of protection during the early part of this century, when the mindset of business people still focused on protecting infant industries, whereas the Democratic party, historically more closely tied to agricultural interests (with plentiful land), supported tariffs only as a revenue-raising device (Bauer, Pool, and Dexter 1972, 26). Most Republicans in Congress continued, however, to oppose the Reciprocal Trade Agreements Act for many years after World War II. Congressional Democrats, although by then more closely tied to labor, were considerably more supportive of free trade. There is good reason to believe that an inertia of ideas often retards adaptation of policy orientation to underlying interests (Judith Goldstein 1988; Goldstein and Lenway 1989). Logically, positions of aggregative parties will change more slowly than those of the component interest groups. In the late 1960s and early 1970s, however, Congressional voting positions on protectionism reversed (Hughes 1978), and the parties came to more closely represent underlying economic interests.

A bipartisan consensus in American security policy characterized the era extending from 1948 to 1968 (Schneider 1987, 45). This consensus broke down, however, with the dissolution of the broader internationalist consensus within the general public. Beginning in the 1970s the Republican party generally better represented militant or Cold War internationalists, and the Democrats more often captured the support of cooperative internationalists. For instance, the Republicans became the party more likely to support military-spending increases, whereas the Democrats continued to give relatively greater backing to foreign aid. That differentiation persisted through the 1980s and the 1990s.

Party differences also characterize the foreign policy debate in other Western democracies. For instance, during the 1971 debate in Britain over entrance to the Common Market, Conservatives were more often pro-Market, and Labour Members of Parliament (MPs) more often anti-Market (Roskin 1989, 73). Margaret Thatcher's long rein over the Conservatives allowed her, however, to move the party to a more nationalistic, anti-integration perspective.

In the Federal Republic of Germany, the achievement of national power by the Social Democrats (SPD) preceded a strong enunciation of an *Ostpolitik* directed at improving relationships with the Soviet Union and Eastern Europe. The Christian Democrats (CDU) generally took a harder line toward the East, were less willing to negotiate, and were more reluctant to accept the division between East and West Germany (Joffee 1985).

Across Western democracies, the parties of the right (like U.S. Republicans, British Conservatives, and the German CDU) have been more likely to take a hard line against communists, to support nuclear and conventional military power, and in general to act like militant internationalists or realists. Eichenberg (1989, 180) found that in Britain, France, West Germany, and the Netherlands, the parties of the right consistently supported defense spending more than did parties of the left. The parties of the left are more often inclined toward cooperative internationalism or, like the Japanese Socialists, to relative isolationism.

Are Some More Equal Than Others?   The pluralistic competition of interest groups and parties does not preclude the possibility that the power of some interests to influence policy is considerably greater than that of others. Many social critics have identified potentially advantaged or dominant interests, giving labels to them such as military-industrial complex or power elite. Although emanating most often from the left, Republican President Eisenhower also raised such a possibility in his farewell address of January 17, 1961:

> Until the last of our world conflicts, the United States had no armaments industry. American makers of plowshares could, with time and as required, make swords as well. But we can no longer risk emergency improvisation of national defense. We have been compelled to create a permanent armaments industry of vast proportions. Added to this, three-and-a-half million men and women are directly engaged in the defense establishment. We annually spend on military security alone more than the net income of all United States corporations.
>
> Now this conjunction of an immense military establishment and a large arms industry is new in the American experience. The total influence—economic, political, even spiritual—is felt in every city, every state house, every office of the federal government. . . .
>
> In the councils of government, we must guard against the acquisition of unwarranted influence, whether sought or unsought, by the military-industrial complex. The potential for the disastrous rise of misplaced power exists and will persist. (Eisenhower 1961).

Exchange of money and personnel ties together the **military-industrial complex,** the legs of which are defense contractors, the defense bureaucracy, and Congress (Adams 1988).[5] Leading defense contractors contribute generously to federal election campaigns. In the 1980s more than 2,000 retired military personnel annually accepted jobs with defense contractors.

Do such linkages between government and industry affect national security policy? It is difficult to assess. A great deal of the influence wielded by contractors seeks to assure them of a bigger share of the pie. The more basic question is whether such politics alters the magnitude of defense spending—the size of the pie. As a percentage of the GDP, U.S. defense spending (shown earlier in Figure 7.2) has decreased significantly since Eisenhower's warning. External forces appear more important than defense lobbyists in determining the level of spending. After the U.S. defense buildup in the 1980s, the share of U.S. GDP taken by defense spending dropped from a peak of 6.1 percent in 1988 to about 3.6 percent in 1997,

---

[5]More radical observers of capitalist political systems argue that the military-industrial complex merely manifests, with respect to defense spending, the influence of a single, more comprehensive power elite (Mills 1956).

eliminating nearly half of the 1.4 million jobs in armaments industries. Would a truly powerful military-industrial complex allow such a decline?

Defense spending is, of course, not the only issue on which the defense industry lobbies. The world's largest defense contractor, Lockheed Martin, became a powerful advocate of NATO's expansion in the late 1990s. The recognition that new members would need to buy new and Western weapons obviously defined their interest in expansion. Also in the late 1990s, critics of the Clinton administration charged that campaign contributions from aerospace corporations facilitated government approval of sales of advanced missile technology to China. Some contributions may even have indirectly come from Chinese sources.

Ideas

It proved impossible in the above discussion of interests not to show also the power of ideas. The orientation of ethnic and religious groups to other countries very often lies in the concept of identity with those countries, not in any clear self-interest. Broad American support for Israel, in conflict with apparent self-interest, may similarly owe much to support for the idea of a democratic state built by a people that Nazism tried to destroy.

Even when ideas and interests appear to have an underlying connection, they can be out of phase. For instance, we saw that the Republican party's commitment to protectionist policies had an inertial life of its own, even after the businesses that had helped shape those policies redefined their own interests toward free trade. It may be that the continued support for free trade by many Democrats has similarly outlasted the support of the party's labor constituency for open markets. It may also be that the power of the idea of free trade is so great that it has fundamentally reshaped American beliefs, almost independent of interests.

National Character   One of the early manifestations of attention to the power of ideas was the concept of *national character.* An old joke says that you can differentiate the major powers of Europe on the basis of the relationship between what is permitted and what is forbidden: in Germany, what is not permitted is forbidden; in Britain, what is not forbidden is permitted; in France, what is forbidden is permitted; finally, in Russia, what is permitted is forbidden. Does that joke recognize a kernel of truth or simply reinforce prejudices? Many serious social scientists have looked for keys to the behavior of societies in national character. Weber identified the roots of European industrialization in the Protestant ethic of hard work, frugality, and achievement in this life. Perhaps the rapid economic growth of many Asian countries similarly has roots in a Confucian heritage that does not seek salvation in an afterlife but emphasizes societal contributions on earth (Palmer 1989, 332).

We should, however, be wary about sweeping societal characterizations, on two grounds. First, there is a fine line between identification of societal attributes and derogation. Is a society disciplined or militaristic? Are a people pragmatic or unprincipled? Is an orientation peaceful or cowardly? The values and goals of the observer frequently color characterizations and make labels into political tools rather than scientific assessments. Second, national characters, if they are meaningful, should be slow to change. Our perception of countries seems, however, to shift rather dramatically. Many believed before and during World War II that both Germany and Japan embodied expansionist militarism. Yet the peace movement in contemporary Germany ranks among the strongest in the world. Japan now appears almost isolationist (except commercially).

In short, national character is a thin reed on which to build a study of world politics. Although it is quite probable that at any given time societies do have distinctive aggregate orientations, they may be quite flexible and represent specific adaptations to a changing world.

Ideas and Foreign Policy   Recent studies have presented a more sophisticated portrait of how ideas and foreign policy may relate. Goldstein and Keohane (1993) draw our attention to three types of beliefs. *Worldviews* (much as defined in this text) fundamentally shape understandings of the world. *Principled beliefs* make ethical statements—such as whether or not slavery or torture is acceptable. *Causal beliefs* explain linkages in the world, such as that between carbon dioxide emissions and the greenhouse effect.

Each type of belief can shape policy in one of three ways. Beliefs can act as *road maps.* For instance, the Stalinist understanding of political-economic development shaped Chinese and Yugoslavian policy after World War II, even when Soviet troops did not occupy those countries. Similarly, Keynesian notions of international economics became imbedded in the postwar institutions that the United States and Great Britain established (Maynard Keynes had, himself, noted that economic policies often reflect the thought of some perhaps forgotten "scribbler").

Second, beliefs can provide *focal points* to resolve problems of coordination. Physical focal points, such as rivers and mountain ranges, can help define the boundaries between warring armies and even long-peaceful states (Schelling 1960). The United States stopped its advance through Germany near the end of World War II at the Elbe River and waited for the Soviets to arrive, in spite of limited resistance from the Germans on the other side. Ideas can similarly serve as focal points. The idea of one-state–one-vote has solved problems of decision making in almost all international organizations, in spite of the fact that both demographically and economically weighted alternatives clearly exist.

Finally, beliefs often achieve long-term influence through *institutionalization.* Democracy institutionalizes a full range of liberal beliefs: causal beliefs, principled beliefs, and, in fact, the entire liberal worldview. The state system as an institution carries with it a whole set of beliefs concerning sovereignty and nonintervention in the affairs of other states. In fact, it is the reality that fundamental institutional structures of world politics may be shifting that has given real impetus to the study of ideas and their power in world affairs. Subsequent chapters will return to the power of ideas.

Individuals

Students of world politics, especially historians, rely heavily on **great-person theories** to explain events. That is, they frequently explain history in terms of the preferences and actions of leaders. Obviously, explanations of the external behavior of totalitarian states and of dictatorships require attention to the personality of the leadership, especially when a leader has an abnormal personality.

> The key to an understanding of Hitler's invasion of Russia is more likely found in the realm of psychology than in political science or strategic thought. Hitler was not interested in just defeating Russia; it was not even important to him to conquer and incorporate her into the grand design of his Third Reich that was to last for a thousand years. What he really yearned to do, with all the passion of his demonic nature, was to destroy Russia altogether—to crush her government, pulverize her economy, enslave her people, and eliminate her as a political entity. (Stoessinger 1985, 27)

In wartime, democracies take on some of the character of dictatorships, delegating great power to individual leaders. Thus historians describe much of World War II in terms of the behavior of Roosevelt, Churchill, Mussolini, Stalin, and Hitler. Ralph Waldo Emerson claimed that "there is properly no history, only biography" (Kegley and Wittkopf 1991, 494).

Particularly in democracies during peaceful times, however, explanations of complex events in terms of the idiosyncrasies of individuals is often a lazy substitute for the search to find deeper, longer-term, and more generalizable explanations. Consider the common references to the "Reagan buildup" of the American military in the 1980s (or to the "Reagan revolution" in social policy or "Reaganomics" in economics). Although such terminology is sometimes simply shorthand to label an era, it frequently suggests causality. Reagan's personality, style, and beliefs certainly helped shape an era in U.S. history. The important question is, however, how much different would the period have been with other leaders in the presidency?

The "Reagan defense buildup" actually began under Carter, who reversed the decline in the percentage of GNP spent on defense following the Vietnam War. U.S. public opinion, as we saw earlier (see Figure 7.2), shifted by 1977–1978 toward favoring more defense spending. Soviet military outlays had increased steadily throughout the period of relative U.S. decline, and the U.S.S.R. had aroused Western fears by invading Afghanistan and supporting new Marxist governments in Africa; Congress and the public would have exerted tremendous pressure on *any* president for a continuation of the increase that Carter began.

Leadership and Vision

Our definition of statecraft in Chapter 4 required that a leader have an understanding of the world and a *vision* of desirable change. According to realists, leaders should base that vision in state interest. Might there be a "higher" morality, however, perhaps based on religious values or humanistic instincts, that should guide policy? U.S. leaders have grappled with that question and have embraced different balances between interests and moral visions, belying any simplistic realist interpretation of U.S. policy.[6]

[6]Stoessinger's (1979) account of eight twentieth-century American foreign-policy leaders conveyed their individual understandings of the world, visions, and ability to shape policy and outcomes accordingly. This discussion of leaders draws on his insights.

At the end of World War I President Woodrow Wilson's understanding of the bankruptcy of traditional power politics resonated in those who had suffered the horrors of the war. His vision of an interstate politics based on morality and conducted within the framework of the League of Nations aroused widespread excitement. He successfully imposed his will and that vision on the postwar settlement. He failed to transfer that same vision to a Senate or to a public that clung to an older, more isolationist image of the United States.

In the late 1930s Franklin Roosevelt understood the anachronistic character of U.S. desires to remain separate from the world economy and from the war that was beginning in Europe. By mid-1940 the Germans had sunk more than one-half of all British destroyers, but the United States remained on the sidelines. Roosevelt circumvented congressional opposition to an action that might involve the country in the war by trading, through executive order, American destroyers for British bases; he then sold the deal to the public. His worldview combined a realistic recognition of the dangers posed by Nazi Germany with some of the moralism that characterized Wilson. For instance, although the British prime minister, Winston Churchill, moved with typical realism to cooperate with Stalin after the German invasion of the Soviet Union, Roosevelt hesitated. After all, communism was a moral enemy, just as was fascism.

Harry S Truman became president on April 12, 1945, after the death of Roosevelt. As a senator earlier in the war, Truman had said that "If we see that Germany is winning we ought to help Russia and if Russia is winning we ought to help Germany and that way let them kill as many as possible. . . ." (Stoessinger 1979, 43). That was not just a statement of balance-of-power politics, because he held a strong moral antipathy to both fascism and communism. Although Truman developed some belief in his ability to work with Stalin during the wartime alliance with the Soviet Union, the failure of the Soviets to withdraw their troops, as promised, from Iran after March 2, 1946, evoked the earlier moral outrage. Truman's actions thereafter indicate a combination of pragmatism and moralistic anticommunism that is difficult to disentangle. In March 1947 Truman enunciated the Truman Doctrine, promising support anywhere to those threatened by communism. The Marshall Plan to rebuild Europe and the formation of NATO followed during the next two remarkable years.

The Cold War had begun. Subsequent U.S. presidents varied in the combination of realism and idealism they brought to the job. Under Eisenhower, for example, the moralistic anticommunism of his Secretary of State, John Foster Dulles, influenced administration policies. Dulles told the West German ambassador that "Bolshevism was a product of the Devil, but God would wear out the Bolsheviks in the long run" (Stoessinger 1979, 98).

The Vietnam War dominated the foreign policy of the Kennedy-Johnson administrations. Initially it brought together those who opposed communism on moral grounds and those who feared expansion of Soviet power. During the course of the conflict, however, both leadership and the U.S. public grappled increasingly with conflicting understandings of the moral basis of U.S. involvement.

The Nixon-Kissinger foreign policy team took over in 1968 and brought to the White House a self-consciously realist worldview and vision. Kissinger also believed, however, that nuclear weapons gave rise to a community of interest between the two countries, based on their need to avoid mutual destruction (Stoessinger 1976, 81). Nixon and Kissinger adopted a policy called **détente,** seeking to tie the two states to each other by a variety of bonds, without losing sight of the fundamental rivalry between them.

In 1976 Jimmy Carter put a liberal ideal at the center of his foreign policy vision. Specifically, he supported human rights of individuals everywhere. That support complicated the American-Soviet relationship and placed the United States in opposition to Israel on the treatment of Palestinians. Ronald Reagan again combined emphasis on power with a strong moralistic anticommunism, a belief that the Soviet Union was an "evil empire."

The collapse of the Soviet Union, the enemy of more than 40 years, left a vacuum in American foreign policy purpose. George Bush had difficulty articulating his worldview, which he called "the vision thing." In practice, he devoted increased attention to arms control, to trade relationships with Europe and Japan, to the Third World debt crisis, and to limiting nuclear proliferation in places such as Iraq and North Korea. William Clinton also found the world without a communist enemy to be complicated. He brought to both foreign and domestic policy a pragmatic desire for cooperation and compromise that some interpreted as lacking strong basis in either power politics or a moral vision. Yet he explicitly made free trade, support for democracy, and multilateral approaches to security the touchstones of his generally liberal foreign policy.

Any discussion of the implications of leadership and vision in the determination of recent foreign policy would be incomplete without comment on Mikhail Sergeyvich Gorbachev.[7] Although economic weakness and social evolution explain much of Soviet behavior in the late 1980s (regardless of leadership), no one can deny that Gorbachev played an exceptional personal role in transforming the foreign policies of the U.S.S.R. After becoming general secretary of the Communist party in 1985, his vision of the need to retrench and focus on domestic problems, combined with a strong belief in the value of cooperation with the West, dramatically reshaped external policy. He bombarded the world with a flurry of arms-control proposals containing much new flexibility (for instance, on verification). He trimmed Soviet commitment to foreign ventures around the globe, including Afghanistan. He encouraged complete transformations of Eastern European political systems at the expense of local Communist leaderships. In short, he brought cooperative internationalism to the leadership of the Soviet Union.

Gender and Foreign Policy

All American presidents have been male. Women play a growing, but far less than a proportional role in politics everywhere. In the twentieth century, no women served as elected heads of state until 1966. Between 1990 and 1998, however, voters elected 27 female heads of state (*Christian Science Monitor,* May 1, 1998, 5). This has great importance in and of itself, because it means that long-standing discrimination is

---

[7]Unfortunately, this limited treatment of individuals must omit discussion of other exceptional non-American leaders, such as Winston Churchill, Charles de Gaulle, Willy Brandt, and Anwar Sadat—not to mention more infamous ones like Muamar Khadafi.

retreating. There is debate, however, about its impact on world politics. The question often asked is "Will women, as they increasingly take their place in leadership, behave differently from men?"

Those who believe that women can change world politics point to the fact that women consistently express greater opposition to military force than do men (Reardon 1993). In December 1990, American men were fairly evenly split on whether attacking the Iraqi forces in Kuwait was a good idea; women opposed it by a margin of 73 percent to 22 percent (Tickner 1992, 152). They argue that women, because of their role in families and society, including their frequently subordinated position, seek to dampen or eliminate coercion, conflict, and violence. Liberals often find these claims attractive, although they can become uncomfortable when the arguments are pushed further. For instance, any suggestion that there are genetic, as well as environmental, bases for differences in female approaches to world politics is controversial.

Those who express skepticism about the "women-are-different" arguments point out that women in power do not clearly behave differently from men in power. Israeli Prime Minister Golda Meir was not "soft" on Jewish security; Britain's Margaret Thatcher oversaw the military operation in the Falklands; Indira Gandhi and Benazir Bhutto of India and Pakistan oversaw nuclear arms building programs; and Turkey's Tansu Ciller sent military forces into Iraq to fight Kurdish separatists. That is, removing women from their traditional social roles and placing them in positions of power and responsibility may eliminate their apparent attitudinal differences from men. Those whose thinking on world politics builds on the realist bases of power and its use will find this comforting.

There are still other perspectives on the impact that women may have on global politics that draw more on constructivism. Some observers point to the masculinization of the very concepts and language of world politics, especially realist versions. For example, realist discussions of security typically emphasize military prowess of self and the insecurity of others in zero-sum relationships, rather than freedom of all from fear and oppression. Constructivists suggest that an emphasis on power and force and an acceptance of conflict among states may be fundamentally related to an emphasis on power and force between genders and among social classes. This position argues that both domestic and global politics require transformations in relations so as to remove power and domination, force and conflict, from key roles. Thus the question should not be, "Will women in leadership behave differently from men?" The more fundamental questions are: "How should we structure world politics to significantly reduce conflict?" "How should we structure domestic society to fully involve women and men?" These questions redirect us to the clash of worldviews that organizes this book. Chapter 10 will return to constructivist perspectives.

Psychology and Foreign Policy

Our earlier promenade down the history of American leadership (with a digression to spotlight Gorbachev) emphasized competing and shifting visions. The quotation concerning Hitler's invasion of the Soviet Union, however, emphasized not vision but psychology.[8] Many in-depth analyses of individual leaders are largely psychological. For instance, Alexander George and Juliette George (1964) linked Woodrow Wilson's stern and punitive upbringing and inability to please his father to a need for self-esteem in later life. They explained his active idealism as compensation for fear of failure and rejection.

Barber (1985) suggested two categories for evaluation of personality characteristics relevant to how leaders perform in the presidency: their energy level on the job (active or passive), and their level of personal satisfaction with the job (negative or positive). For instance, active-positive presidents include Franklin Roosevelt, Truman, Kennedy, Ford, Carter, and Bush. Such individuals want results and behave flexibly to achieve them; Barber concluded that they generally handle challenges and crises well. Active-negative presidents strive to achieve and maintain power, and risk the danger of rigidly adhering to a failing policy. Barber characterized Wilson, Hoover, Johnson, and Nixon as active-negative presidents.[9]

Although psychological characterizations of personality convey useful insights, they sometimes appear subjective. We must be aware that, unless very carefully done, they may tell us almost as much about the policy preferences of the analyst as about the character of the foreign-policy maker.

Another potentially useful approach to characterizing personality is specification of the degree to which a belief system is "open" or "closed." Ole Holsti (1962) studied John Foster Dulles, Eisenhower's secretary of state. Investigating the childhood of Dulles as the son of a stern Presbyterian minister, and analyzing the content of his public pronouncements, Holsti found the belief system of Dulles to be moralistic and rigid. Dulles saw the Soviet leadership and Communist party as irredeemably bad. He held what Kissinger (1962) called an "inherent bad faith" model and could seemingly view no action on the part of the Soviets as positive. Dulles interpreted even reductions in Soviet troop strength negatively—to him they indicated diversion of personnel to more threatening uses.

Risk Aversion and Acceptance

Decision makers often face situations in which they stand to gain or lose stakes of significant value, including pieces of territory and lives. Willingness to take risks with respect to those gains or losses is a very important issue. One body of research, called **prospect theory,** investigates people's approach to situations in which outcomes or prospects are substantially uncertain (Levy 1997).

For instance, which do people prefer—the certainty of a smaller gain or the possibility of a larger one? Interestingly, most people are willing to accept $3,000 rather than to accept an 80 percent chance of winning $4,000, which statistically

---

[8]A sociological approach to the study of leadership also has merit. Leaders around the world are overwhelmingly middle-aged and older males, better educated than the general population, and economically well-to-do. Studies of American public opinion consistently show that those with such characteristics are more internationalist than the broader population. See Hughes (1978).

[9]Other categories of personalities include nationalists, militarists, conservatives, authoritarians, anti-authoritarians, and rigid personalities (Kegley and Wittkopf 1979, 378–379). It often proves difficult to classify presidents in such categories, which means the characteristics are not easy to define or measure.

should be worth 0.8 times $4,000 or $3,200. This means that they are **risk-averse** with respect to gains (Levy 1992, 174). At the same time, people overwhelmingly will risk an 80 percent chance of losing $4,000 rather than accept the certainty of losing $3,000. Statistically, this means that they will give up 0.8 times $4,000 or $3,200 rather than give up $3,000. Thus they are *risk-acceptant* with respect to loss avoidance.

From the point of view of world politics, these common characteristics have important implications (Levy 1997, 93). They suggest that typical leaders will avoid risk in the pursuit of improvements to their country's condition (e.g., free trade agreements that *might* enhance economic well-being, but risk social protest). They also suggest, however, that leaders would more often fight to avoid losing a piece of territory than fight to acquire it, and would, in fact, take excessive risks relative to expected rewards, to avoid losing territory.

Together these risk orientations also suggest potential strategies to influence behavior of others by *framing decision situations.* For example, a leader might sell a free trade agreement by reframing estimates that it had a 50 percent chance of creating 10,000 jobs to estimates that not signing created a 50 percent chance of losing 10,000 jobs.

Perception and Crisis

Individuals and their personalities are especially critical in periods of crisis. In crisis situations, the diversion of policy making to the highest levels, the stress induced by time pressures and threat, and the frequent inadequacy of information conspire to force individuals to the forefront of policy making and to compel them to reach inward for help in decision making. Here again the basic realist model fails to help us adequately understand the world, because many case studies of crises are analyses of irrational behavior (Jervis 1976).

More specifically, many studies of crises focus on the extent of *misperception.* For instance, social psychologist Ralph White (1985) studied the outbreak of World War I. Events proceeded quickly, at least by standards of the day, after a militant Serbian nationalist assassinated the Austrian Archduke Francis Ferdinand (heir to the throne) on June 28, 1914. On July 5 Germany assured Austria of its support for firm reaction in a telegram that became known as a "blank check." On July 23 Austria presented Serbia an ultimatum with demands. Two days later Serbia accepted all but one demand, which would have required Austrian participation in police activity within Serbia so as to bring the assassin to justice. Austria thereafter severed diplomatic relations and began war preparations. Feverish diplomatic activity followed, but on August 3 the Germans declared war on France, and the war quickly spread across Europe.

White analyzed the beliefs of the Austrian leadership and listed six areas of misperception and dysfunctional behavior. First, the Austrians held a diabolic enemy image, believing that the assassins threatened the very existence of the empire. The German Kaiser was perhaps even more subject to such enemy images. While the British were working to avert war, the Kaiser wrote on a diplomatic note:

The net has been suddenly thrown over our head, and England sneeringly reaps the most brilliant success of her persistently prosecuted, purely *anti-German world policy,* against which we have proved ourselves helpless, while she twists the noose of our political and economic destruction out of our fidelity to Austria, as we squirm isolated in the net. (White 1985, 233)

A second perceptual problem was a virile self-image on the part of the Austrians. They feared losing great power status by not acting appropriately and strongly. Simultaneously, and somewhat in contradiction, a third perceptual difficulty lay in maintenance of a moral self-image. Austrians viewed themselves as peace loving, civilized, and economically progressive, whereas the threatening forces exhibited opposite characteristics. A fourth misperception was that the Austrians saw the conflict as a local one and did not understand the growing concern of other powers until too late—a problem of selective attention.

A fifth difficulty was absence of empathy. The Austrians could not mentally put themselves in the place of the Serbians and see that Austrian demands appeared to be naked aggression. From the Russian viewpoint, the demands seemed a step toward annexation, like the Austrian absorption of Bosnia six years earlier. Sixth, and finally, the monarchy succumbed to military overconfidence. They believed that the combined Austrian-German power was adequate to deter conflict or win it.

An important reason for listing these six points should be obvious. Throughout the Cold War the danger of similar misperception by either the United States or the Soviet Union was high. Diabolic enemy images ("godless communism" versus "imperialistic capitalism"), virile and moral self-images, selective attention, absence of empathy, and military overconfidence all could have, under the right circumstances, transformed a cold war into a hot war. A British and Soviet double agent who defected from the KGB in 1985, Oleg Gordievski, reported that in 1983 there was growing fear in the Soviet Union that the United States was preparing to launch a surprise attack. Apparently the U.S. military buildup and rhetoric like Reagan's characterization of the Soviet Union as an "evil empire" created a near panic in Soviet leadership; some believed that NATO maneuvers planned for late in the year were to be a cover for attack (*Denver Post,* October 16, 1988, 19A). Although the Cold War may be over, dangers of such misperception continue within U.S.-Chinese, Russian-Chinese, Indian-Pakistani, Israeli-Syrian, and other relationships.

Crisis Management

Recognition that crises in the past, complicated by misperception, have led to devastating wars that none of the participants really wanted, have led policy makers to place great emphasis on crisis management. After the Cuban missile crisis, Secretary of Defense Robert McNamara declared that "Today there is no longer any such thing as military strategy; there is only crisis management" (Craig and George 1983, 205).

The desire to balance two sometimes incompatible objectives, winning in confrontations and avoiding war, complicates *crisis management* (Snyder and

Diesing 1977, 207–280). The first and most basic element of crisis management is to recognize that your own and your adversary's perception may be flawed. In general, states will often perceive the same stimulus as more threatening during a crisis than under more normal circumstances, even though the other side may not intend it to be more threatening. Therefore, to prevent an overreaction during a crisis, each side must consciously attempt to dampen their own reactions.[10]

A second and related element of crisis management is recognition *in advance* of the need for communication channels during crises so that each state can understand what the other side wants and how it views the current situation. During the Cuban missile crisis of 1962, Kennedy and Khrushchev relied on letters sent via embassies. In an era when the speed of missiles already provided a president only twenty minutes warning of an attack, and computer malfunctions or migrating geese could give rise to false signals, the United States and the U.S.S.R. exchanged messages that took six hours to deliver (Ziegler 1987, 241–243). In substantial part because the Cuban missile crisis spotlighted the problem, the United States and the U.S.S.R. established a "hot line" between them in June 1963. The United States and China also have a hot-line connection that President Clinton first used in 1998 when India tested a nuclear weapon.

A third contribution to crisis management is maximization of information quality. Iraq invaded Kuwait in 1990, based on grossly incorrect information about the possible U.S. response. Saddam Hussein relied perhaps too much on information from the local U.S. embassy. A good crisis manager recognizes the need for high-quality and redundant information conduits.

A fourth element is preservation of options. Sometimes defining an absolute commitment can force the other side to retreat. For instance, when the Soviets erected the Berlin Wall in 1961, any effort to knock it down would have almost certainly meant war. More often, however, it pays to start small, such as the embargo of Serbia, which did not fully preclude actions such as an air strike or invasion. In addition, it can be important to preserve options, especially escape routes, for the other side, allowing them to "save face" in any concessions they make. In the Cuban missile crisis, Kennedy "accepted" the proposal of Khruschchev to exchange a guarantee of noninvasion for the missile removal and was careful not to declare victory publicly. Privately, Secretary of State Dean Rusk said, when Russian ships turned back from the blockade, "we're eye-ball to eye-ball and I think the other fellow just blinked"—the United States perceived the outcome as its victory.

Individuals in Groups

This discussion of individuals has treated them as if single decision makers determined the direction of government, or as if groups of individuals acted much like single individuals. In reality, *group dynamics* can make outcomes quite different from decisions by single individuals. Some group dynamics create further departures from the goal of rationality in state behavior.

The history of interstate relations is littered with bad decisions. How, many have asked, could the invasion by Hitler catch the Soviet Union so much off guard?

---

[10]Wilkenfeld, Brecher, and Hill (1989) reinforced this finding by Holsti, North, and Brody (1968).

How could the United States have expected the invasion of Cuba at the Bay of Pigs in 1961 to succeed? How could Slobodan Milosevic not have expected Western reaction to his aggression in Bosnia and Kosovo?

Janis (1972) attributes many such failures of policy to **groupthink.** Decision-making groups frequently display much homogeneity of outlook. The age-old tendency of leaders to select advisors who agree with them reinforces this. Although new leaderships frequently accept substantial internal dissent (and even consciously recognize the need for it), over time those who fit in less well are more likely to leave. When there is no one who seriously and repeatedly questions basic assumptions, especially the outlook of the leader, then decisions may create new problems. There was, for instance, too little challenge by his advisors of the assumption of Lyndon Johnson that the United States could win the war in Vietnam. Highly authoritarian leaderships, like that of Muamar Khadafi in Libya, tend to exclude all opposing views from their leadership circle.

Government

Societal elements, individuals, and groups of decision makers all interact within the framework of government. In turning to the government, two questions are of special interest. First, how does governmental decision making bring together the various elements we have identified within the state? Second, do different types of government produce different international behavior?

Decision Making

Allison (1971) articulated three models that capture most understandings of foreign policy decision making. He argued that each helps us understand that complex process, and that none individually constitutes an adequate picture. His three models are rational actor, organizational process, and bureaucratic politics.

The **rational-actor model** is what civics courses teach us constitutes "good" decision making. The first step is identifying goals and objectives. The second is outlining alternatives or options. The third is assessing the potential consequences of each alternative. Finally, through evaluation of the potential consequences in light of goals, an optimal choice emerges.

The rational-actor model assumes sufficient information to identify policy options and assess consequences. It also often assumes a small and coherent decision unit (otherwise goals and objectives may not be clear and identifiable). In essence it is the simple realist model. Even when we doubt that this model consistently describes how decisions are made in our own country, we tend to fall back on it in describing the decision making of other countries (especially those with authoritarian political systems). In addition, we often believe it should be the way our own country makes decisions.

Herbert Simon (1957) argued that many preconditions of this rational-actor decision-making approach, which he called **optimizing,** are not present in reality. In the real world, information is often highly limited. Time for decisions, especially in crises, is short. Frequently, objectives are not clear even to an individual, and groups have great difficulties specifying a priority ranking. Simon suggests that most organizational decision making aims for satisfactory, not necessarily optimal, decisions, an approach he calls **satisficing.**

Allison's **organizational-process model** builds on these insights. It portrays decision making as relying heavily on standard operating procedures (SOPs) and inertia. Institutions seldom discard SOPs entirely, but instead modify them incrementally in reaction to what they learned from earlier decisions and what they understand to be the unique elements of the current situation. This description of decision making is familiar in budgeting, where allocations normally change slowly. It assumes limited information, time, and other resources for decision making. It also suggests that decision-making bodies may be unable to give a situation their full attention, and that they may bring limited imagination and flexibility to the decision-making process.

The third description of decision making is the **bureaucratic-politics model.** That model portrays the decision environment as one of groups (and individuals) in conflict. Each group may have a relatively clear set of values and objectives, but priorities differ across groups. Groups often have parochial, self-interested goals, captured in the expression "Where you stand depends on where you sit." Decisions are compromises among groups and reflect their relative strength.

Although observers of international politics regularly apply Allison's three models to investigations of decision making, we should recognize that these are by no means the only models with which to organize our thinking about it. For instance, Putnam (1988) proposed what he called a "two-level game" model. Foreign-policy decision makers often find themselves in two "games" at once, one internal to the country and one external. Consider, for instance, the efforts of the Salinas administration in Mexico simultaneously to negotiate a North American Free Trade Agreement with the United States and Canada and to sell that agreement to its public.

Differential Power of Decision-Making Models

The various decision-making models help in understanding a wide variety of foreign-policy decisions, but there is no reason to believe that they are equally apt in all situations. The rational-actor and organizational-process models provide more powerful descriptions within authoritarian systems, and the bureaucratic-politics model fits Western democracies better. The Soviet decision to withdraw from Afghanistan, for instance, unlike the U.S. decision to end the Vietnam War, did not reflect extensive media coverage of the war and widespread social protest (although the Soviet leadership began broader coverage of the war in support of its decision).

Within democracies, under what circumstances might the various models be most useful? In general, routine situations that have limited economic or security implications (such as the arrest of a citizen abroad or still another UN vote on sanctions against Iraq) are more likely to elicit organizational-process decision making. The rational-actor model better suits full-scale crises, such as reaction by Taiwan to Chinese missile tests off its coast. The bureaucratic-politics model becomes most appropriate when decision time is long and economic interests are great. Examples include the British decision not to adopt Europe's common currency or the size of the Indian defense budget. Table 7.2 provides additional examples of decision situations.

Table 7.2 A Typology of Foreign-Policy Issues, with Examples

Economic Considerations Important				Economic Considerations Relatively Unimportant			
Security Issue		Nonsecurity Issue		Security Issue		Nonsecurity Issue	
Decision Time Long (1)	Decision Time Short (2)	Decision Time Long (3)	Decision Time Short (4)	Decision Time Long (5)	Decision Time Short (6)	Decision Time Long (7)	Decision Time Short (8)
Size of defense budget	Marshall Plan	Tariff structure	Chile's copper nationalization	Support Nicaraguan contras	North Korean invasion of South	Policy on West Bank uprising	UN vote to oust South Africa
Vietnam War de-escalation	Foreign Oil Embargo	Adherence to Law of Sea Treaty	Peru's declaration of 200-mile fishing zone	Arms limitation treaty	Berlin blockade	Admission of China to UN	Arrest of American citizen abroad
Energy policy	Iraqi invasion of Kuwait	Eliminating CFC production		Iranian hostage affair	Cuban Missile Crisis	Japanese contribution to U.S. troops	
SDI deployment	Chinese missile testing off Taiwan	Adoption of European currency			Send ships to Persian Gulf	Adherence to World Court decisions	
Common model:	*Common model:*	*Common model:*	*Common model:*	*Common model:*	*Common model:*	*Common model:*	*Common model:*
Bureaucratic Political	Rational actor	Bureaucratic Political	Rational actor	Rational actor	Rational actor	Organizational process	Organizational process

Sources: Barry B. Hughes, *The Domestic Context of American Foreign Policy* (San Francisco: W. H. Freeman, 1978), 201; some additions from Bruce Russett and Harvey Starr, *World Politics: The Menu for Choice*, 4th ed. (New York: W. H. Freeman, 1992), 226.

Government Character and Foreign Behavior

Decision-making procedures other than rational actor throw into question the important unitary, rational-behavior assumptions of simplistic realism. Instead of hard, impenetrable states interacting according to physics-like laws, other models suggest "mushy," open states with behavior that will vary according to the organization of administrative structures, the leadership personnel, and the political strength of various groups within society.

Might the behavior of states vary *systematically* with the nature of their decision-making structures? Advocates of democracy, for example, propose that democratic states are less warlike than authoritarian states because the public, which would be required to fight the war and bear the economic cost, is less tolerant of war than is an elite leadership. In fact, the evidence is strong that no two democracies have ever fought one another (Ray 1989).

In addition to presence or absence of democracy, another key characteristic of governments is whether they are "weak" or "strong."[11] Single interest groups can heavily influence weak governments and the competition of many groups can paralyze them into inaction. Strong governments contain influential elements that set themselves apart from individual interest groups and pursue the interests, as they understand them, of the larger citizenry. Analysts generally characterize the U.S. government as weak and the French and Japanese governments as strong. Many governments in the developing world are so weak that leaders define security issues primarily in terms of internal stability. The external relations of such countries can become simply a search for allies to support internal stability and development (Levy and Barnett 1992), a dramatic contrast with traditional interstate theories of alliance.

Thus students of world politics increasingly portray a world in which what happens inside states, for instance whether they have democratic or nondemocratic governments and whether those structures are weak or strong, affects how they approach the outside world. Simultaneously, they see a world in which the external environment affects what happens inside states. For instance, we discussed earlier how the global economic system determines which domestic-production factors are in relative surplus or shortage and thereby strongly affects domestic politics on trade. One of the most important contemporary developments in the study of world politics is this moving beyond the study of states and their interaction to the study of politics within and across state borders.

On Rational, Unitary Actors

The simple realist model valuably provides a parsimonious "first-cut" description of world politics and also prescribes in general terms how states "should" behave in a complex world. By looking inside the state this chapter challenged the simple

---

[11]Krasner (1978, 53–61) provided definitional detail; the literature in this area somewhat confusingly refers to weak or strong states rather than governments.

realist *description* of the world, which assumes rational, unitary actors. It is obvious that the state is far from being a unitary actor. Is it possibly, however, still a rational actor?

To answer that question, we must first raise another: What is rationality? According to common definition, **rationality** requires means-end calculation like that which characterizes the rational-actor decision model: "behavior involving a choice of the best *means* available for achieving a given *end*" (Harsanyi 1986, 83).

The information for a sophisticated means-end calculation is seldom available. For example, we have seen how difficult it is to assess the capabilities of various states and how states sometimes conceal or misrepresent intentions. How calculating could even an absolute dictatorship be, when such basic information for linking actions to probable consequences is absent or highly inconsistent? Nonetheless, information limitations do not preclude rationality within those limits—a **bounded rationality** (Simon 1957).

Our review of decision process, however, suggests that decision makers do not always use even limited information in a means-end calculation. Groups, not individuals, make most decisions. When decision groups contain individual members urging rational pursuit of very different goals, it is not at all clear that the outcome of the process will be optimal for the state. The groupthink decision process that led to the invasion of Cuba at the Bay of Pigs was simply *irrational*—only group psychology, not means-end calculation, can explain it.

In addition, there are at least two reasons that means-end rationality, even when states achieve desired outcomes, may produce "nonrational" results. First, time horizons of decision makers may be relatively short, and they may sacrifice longer-term benefits for short-term gain. Second, individually rational action may lead to collectively unsatisfactory results. For instance, decisions to release increasing volumes of CO_2 into the global atmosphere provide economic advantage but are changing the global climate.

Where does this leave us? We still have some reason to believe that many decision makers (like the decision committee established during the Cuban Missile Crisis) strive to make decision making as nearly rational as possible—to apply a bounded rationality—and that outcomes are, on average, better when they do so. Thus the simple realist characterization is a helpful one. It is, however, incomplete. Extension of the simple realist model to consider the flaws that inadequate information, misperception, group interaction, and collective-action logic frequently introduce to decision making moves us toward a better understanding of world politics.

Challenges in this chapter to the assumption of means-end rationality by unitary actors have highlighted a weakness of the realist model. Challenges to the definition of actors and ends may, however, do realism even greater damage. People are the ultimate actors in global politics, and more than a struggle for security motivates people. Desires for freedom, demands for economic well-being, concerns about the environment, and abhorrence of war also motivate action. As we move into an extended discussion of liberalism in Chapter 8, we broaden our consideration of actors and their values.

Selected Key Terms

levels of analysis

isolationist

internationalist

attentive public

opinion leaders

factors of production

factor price equalization

pluralist model

military-industrial
 complex

détente

prospect theory

risk-averse

groupthink

rational-actor model

optimizing

satisficing

organizational-process
 model

bureaucratic-politics
 model

rationality

bounded rationality

CHAPTER 8

An Emergent Liberal World Order?

Throughout the 1980s, the Communist party of the People's Republic of China, under the leadership of Chairman Deng Xiaoping, undertook a broad range of changes in economic policy, encouraging entrepreneurial behavior domestically and facilitating a great expansion of trade and communication with the outside world. The leadership understood that the centrally controlled economy of earlier decades had failed to provide adequate supplies of food and other goods. Chairman Deng, in moving toward an open economy, argued that it "does not matter whether a cat is black or white, as long as it catches mice."

These successful economic liberalizations emboldened many Chinese to urge an extension of reforms to politics. In April, 1989, more than 100,000 students and workers camped in Tiananmen Square in Beijing (see Map 8.1). They even constructed a statue called the Goddess of Democracy (who looked remarkably like the Statue of Liberty). World television broadcast events in the square and accompanying protest marches in at least 20 Chinese cities. Faxes and voice phone connected the students with each other and the outside world.

KEY WEB LINKS

www.un.org/esa/coordination/
ngo/frame.htm

www.unhchr.ch

www.freedomhouse.org/

On June 3 and 4, army troops brutally crushed the protests, killing as many as 7,000, arresting perhaps 10,000, and subsequently executing 31. Although that leadership action stopped the protests and overt calls for political liberalization, it by no means quelled the desires. Brave actions of individuals and small groups continued, including periodic public petitions to the leadership calling for protection of human rights. Democratization in two other Chinese political systems, Hong Kong and Taiwan, continued after the military action. Economic liberalization continued in the People's Republic itself. In 1998 U.S. President William Clinton visited Tiananmen Square, and he called for Chinese protection of human rights in speeches and conversations that the Chinese media broadcast across the country. There can be

Map 8.1

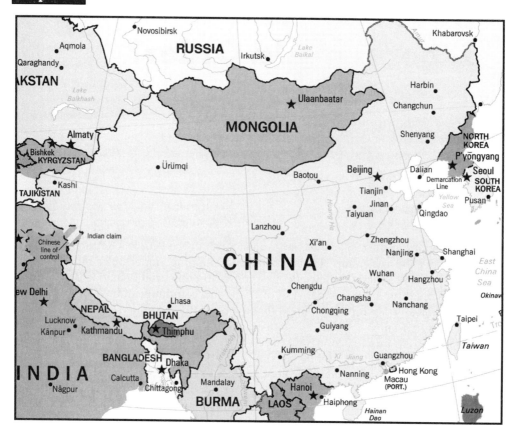

little doubt that the fundamental forces for political change not only remain, but are growing.

Nor is the democracy and human rights movement in China an anomaly. In 1980 Polish shipyard workers formed the Solidarity movement, insisting on the legal right to create labor unions and to strike. They extended their ultimately successful demands to include media access and free elections. In the early 1980s, mothers in Argentina marched in front of central government buildings carrying pictures of their children who had "disappeared" at the hands of a junta government; their actions helped bring about a change in government and trials in 1985 of junta members, including a former president, for murder and human rights abuses. In the 1990s the South African government released black leader Nelson Mandela from prison and scrapped the apartheid laws of strict racial separation. Voters elected Mandela president in 1994.

Chapter 1 reviewed some of the most important forces that continue to reshape human systems globally, including economic transformation and social/political mobilization. Liberals believe that many aspects of these forces, driven in part by the communications and transportation revolutions, have proven powerful forces in local and global liberalization. This chapter will paint a picture of global liberalization in three steps. First, it will consider the proliferation of nonstate actors. Second, it will examine development of a global "community." Finally, it will turn to the growth of international institutions.[1]

Actor Proliferation and Empowerment

States are only one of the forms in which human beings have organized themselves over the millennia. In fact, states have dominated world politics only since the 1600s. Although they may continue to dominate global political systems for another 100 or even 400 years, liberals believe that whether or not they do so will depend on how well they serve the interests of humanity.

That is not to say that states are likely to disappear from the political scene. They may, however, increasingly share political authority with other institutions, most notably local and regional governments within states and broader institutions that cross over state borders. As global democratization proceeds, individuals and their associations become increasingly able to demand the governance that best serves their needs.

Many individuals not playing official leadership roles influence the flow of international events. Mohandas Gandhi (the Mahatma or Great Soul) energized the nonviolent struggle for Indian independence from Great Britain (successful in 1947). Bishop Desmond Tutu won the 1984 Nobel Peace Prize for his work in South Africa against apartheid. Philanthropist George Soroos provided financial support in the 1990s for democratic and free market transitions in Central Europe and the former Soviet Union that rivaled that of Western States. Ted Turner, the founder of Cable Network News (CNN), pledged $1 billion to the United Nations, an amount approaching the $1.4 billion in unpaid U.S. dues. We ignore the critical role of specific individuals, either in key governmental positions or outside of them, at great peril to our understanding of global politics. Yet individuals are more effective in groups or organizations than alone. Certainly neither Gandhi nor Tutu would have played any historical role had they not mobilized important organizations behind them.

The *associational revolution* (Salamon 1994) is an important underlying basis for global democratization and presents reason to be optimistic about its further advance. More than 150 years ago de Tocqueville identified the associational proclivities of Americans as one of the foundations of their democracy. Today there are 21,000 nonprofit organizations in the Philippines and 10,000 have registered in Bangladesh; 100,000 Christian Base Communities with local action agendas function in Brazil; in India the Village Awakening Movement, with roots back to Gandhi, has spread to thousands of villages (Salamon 1994, 111). The phenomenon is even more widespread in developed countries. Britain has an estimated 275,000 charities controlling nearly 5 percent of the gross national product. The formerly communist countries of Central and East-

---

[1]Democracy, commercial liberalism, and international law/institutions all supported Immanuel Kant's vision of global peace (Russett, Oneal, Davis 1998 found that each does make individual and reinforcing contributions to peace). This chapter emphasizes the first and third bases, but adds a broader social context that draws on constructivism as well as liberalism (Price 1998).

Figure 8.1   Growth of International Nongovernmental Organizations

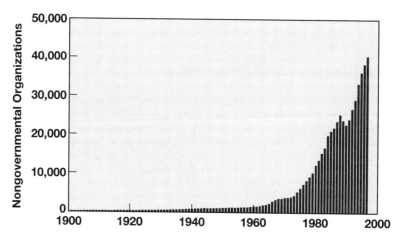

Note: Criteria for counting INGOs/NGOs were tightened in 1989 to exclude less active or less international groups.

Sources: Union of International Organizations (UAI), *Yearbook of International Organizations 1991/92, 1993/94, and 1997/98* (Brussels: UAI, 1991, 1993, and 1997).

ern Europe recognize the development of such a **civil society** as critical to their democratization.

The associational revolution and the development of civil society has progressed furthest at the domestic level. It also proceeds steadily, however, across state borders. **International nongovernmental organizations (NGOs or INGOs)** are organizations that draw on individuals or associations across states for their membership. Figure 8.1 shows how NGOs have proliferated. There were already 170 NGOs by 1914 (Wallace and Singer 1970). In the late 1990s, however, there were about 40,000 NGOs.

An important subclass of NGOs, **transnational social movement organizations (TSMOs),** "are *specifically* organized to carry out political goals which require globally oriented strategies. . . ."[2] For instance, Amnesty International (human rights) and Greenpeace (the environment) are TSMOs. In contrast, the Rotary Club International and the International Committee of Catholic Nurses play important roles in improving international communication and understanding, but do not pursue *political* goals. It is not at all clear that TSMOs directly improve relations among states. They may, in fact, increase tensions, as the human rights organizations sometimes do between the United States and China. What they clearly do is to make states more permeable to outside influences—often liberalizing ones. Thus their indirect and more fundamental impact may be in supporting transformations of domestic structures.

NGOs have become so numerous that they frequently create coalitions, networks, caucuses, and coordinating bodies linking multiple NGOs and domestic in-

[2]Leatherman, Pagnucco, and Smith (1994, 4). See also Keohane and Nye (1970) and Risse-Kappen (1994).

terest groups. The African NGOs Environmental Network counted 530 members based in 45 countries in 1990 (Princen, Finger, and Manno 1995, 43). The Women's Caucus, representing many groups, takes increasingly prominent roles at global conferences on social issues. The United Nations Non-Governmental Liaison Service has become a global coordinating organization for NGOs. NGOs even organized a World NGO Conference for 1999. States not only recognize the importance of NGOs, they increasingly work with them. For instance, states channel substantial amounts of foreign assistance through NGOs.

Another important transborder actor is the **multinational corporation (MNC)** or *transnational corporation (TNC),* a corporation that controls assets in two or more countries. Examples include Exxon, General Motors, and Nestlé. There are now over 7,000 MNCs. Like NGOs, they have proliferated much more rapidly than states. Whereas most NGOs promote a "principled idea," MNCs pursue their own economic gains.

There is much debate concerning the extent to which MNCs may influence or constrain state behavior. MNCs may pressure governments to resist any actions, including military hostilities, that would disrupt their transnational activities. Vernon (1971) raised the possibility that continuing growth in MNC strength might put "sovereignty at bay." One idealistic liberal elaborated the argument:

> In an important sense, the fundamental problem of the future is the conflict between the political forces of nationalism and the economic forces pressing for world integration. This conflict currently appears as one between the national government and the international corporation, in which the balance of power at least superficially appears to lie on the side of the national government. But in the longer run economic forces are likely to predominate over political. . . . (Harry Johnson, cited by Gilpin 1979, 355)

It is difficult to make definitive statements about the effect of actor proliferation on global politics. Yet individuals now have access to each other around the world via nearly instantaneous telecommunications linkages, both the passive linkages of the Herald Tribune or Cable News Network (CNN) and the active linkages of telephone, fax, and the Internet. Prices have dropped dramatically and Internet use is free for many. Amnesty International can now mobilize its global membership within days for a letter-writing campaign on behalf of a political prisoner anywhere in the world. The number of international congresses and conferences has grown from two or three per year in the mid-1800s to hundreds per year. MNCs link their subsidiaries in networks that make communication and financial flows between Bangkok and Frankfurt virtually equivalent to those within Frankfurt. States have lost the ability they once had to control substantial portions of interstate communication and exchange. They cannot insulate themselves from citizens of other countries or from the associations those citizens create.

Global Community

Liberals since Immanuel Kant (1724–1804) have argued that a process of global community building, rooted in the increased protection of human rights and the acceptance of democratic institutions, would ultimately provide a base for a predominantly peaceful world.

Globalization now drives the development of global community. Chapter 1 sketched the economic components of globalization, namely the rapid expansion of transborder trade and financial flows. Chapter 12 extensively elaborates the economic elements of it. Globalization is, however, a broader process.

Information flows are a key element of globalization. In 1998 the U.S. Commerce Department estimated that traffic on the Internet doubled every 100 days and that 100-million people were connected worldwide (compared to 3 million in 1994). In comparison, it took radio 38 years and television 13 years to reach 50 million people. The ratio of transborder telephone calls to domestic ones has increased steadily. In the Group of Seven countries, that ratio in the 1990s was seven times that of the 1960s (Walter, Dreher, and Beisheim 1997). A Colorado company named Earth Watch Incorporated has launched "civilian spy satellites." The company makes available detailed and relatively inexpensive photographs of even military targets over the Internet.

People also flow more freely than ever before. Tourism may be the world's largest industry. Although the United States is a magnet for immigrants, more than 250,000 of its citizens move abroad each year, a total of over 3 million in the late 1990s.

It is, of course, not just tourists, retirees, and business people who move easily across borders. Criminal networks of Italian mafia, Japanese yakuza, Russian mafias, Chinese triads, and Columbian drug cartels make activities of the past "look like mom-and-pop operations." Even the Hells Angels, which began as a motorcycle gang, have expanded from the United States into Brazil and Canada. The Russian mafia operated in 29 countries in 1994 and more than 80 by the end of the decade; it now threatens Italy as much as the home-grown mafia. Global trade in drugs, fueled especially by demand in the United States, accounts for a tremendous surge in such activity since 1970, more than offsetting revenues lost to crime from the legalization of gambling. One UN estimate put global criminal activity from drugs alone at $400 billion (just short of revenues from tourism), or almost 5 percent of the global economy.

Normative Community: Global Culture

Is a global community emerging as a result of these economic, informational, and personal movements across state boundaries? Many point to the infatuation of young people around the world with Coca Cola, blue jeans, and rock music, to the global sharing of movies and television, and even to the spread of English, as evidence of an incipient (and perhaps insipid) global culture. English is the basic language of the Internet (although rapid improvements in translation programs might change that). It is an official language of 58 countries with 460 million speakers (not counting India). Some estimates put total speakers globally at about 2 billion, one-third of humanity and more than twice the population of Mandarin speakers. Another important phenomenon is the increasing acceptance by countries around the world of dual citizenship. For instance, Mexico now allows adults who take U.S. citizenship to maintain Mexican citizenship.

Global culture would, however, consist of a great deal more than a veneer of pop culture, rapid information flow, increasing use of a common language, and multiple citizenship. It would require common values and attitudes. In analysis of public opinion data from 43 countries on 5 continents, Inglehart (1997) found that younger cohorts or segments of the population feel greater economic and physical security than their elders and have widely shifted their concerns to liberal (what he calls "post materialist") values: freedom, self-development, and quality of life. Inglehart relates this process to economic change and restructuring. Other observers, however, suggest that economic development does not promote a common set of values, but rather a renewed commitment to indigenous ones. Huntington (1996, 37) points, for instance, to a widespread Islamic resurgence and to East Asian rejection of Western individualism. Barber (1992) put it colorfully as Jihad (Islamic holy war) versus McWorld.

If there really is an emergent, liberal global culture and community, we would expect to see a variety of manifestations: recognition of the individual and of individual rights in law, both international and domestic; the spread of democracy; and the growth of a zone of peace among democracies. We look in turn for each.

Normative Community: Human Rights Law

Most of what writers normally call "international" law is, in fact, the interstate law that Chapter 5 discussed. Yet other and growing bodies of international law move beyond attention to the rights and obligations of states. The commercial law of trade and investment continues to grow with the volume of global economic transactions, and it defines the rights of individuals and companies. Many League of Nations and UN documents, resolutions, and declarations have defined the right to self-determination of peoples, affirming the right of ethnic groups to control their own destinies within their states. Efforts to establish and enforce this principle led to dismantlement of colonial empires, against the interest of many states. Of particular interest to us here, however, is the development of international law specifying the rights and responsibilities of individuals.

International human rights law has evolved slowly, but progressively. Consider, for instance, slavery. Philosophers from Aristotle through John Locke (1632–1704), one of the fathers of modern liberal thought, justified enslaving other human beings (Ray 1989). Great Britain prohibited the slave trade in 1807, however, and ended slavery in territories under its control in 1833. The Civil War of the United States emancipated slaves in 1865, and Brazil did so in 1888. Almost certainly, economic advance and ongoing social mobilization have contributed to the greater acceptance of the dignity of the individual, to the official global abolition of slavery (enshrined in a 1926 interstate convention), and to progress on other human-rights issues.

Even on such a basic issue as slavery, however, human rights are far more fully protected in law than in practice. As many as 100,000 traditional slaves labor in Mauritania (*Newsweek*, May 4, 1992, 32). In Nepal and Pakistan millions labor under bonded debts that can be sold to others and passed to the next generation (*The Economist*, September 21, 1996, 43). Around the world, such bondage-cum-slavery ties millions of children to carpet looms and brick factories, and it presses unknown numbers of girls and women into prostitution.

What are **human rights?** The Universal Declaration of Human Rights delivered the most powerful international statement in 1948. In addition to specifying the illegality of slavery and the right to a nationality, the declaration includes: a right to privacy; a right to emigrate from and return to one's country; protection

Table 8.1   UN Human-Rights Conventions

Convention (grouped by subject)	Year Opened for Ratification	Year Entered into Force	Number of Ratifications, Accessions, Successions Dec. 31, 1996
General Human Rights			
International Covenant on Civil and Political Rights	1966	1976	136
Optional Protocol to the International Covenant on Civil and Political Rights	1966	1976	89
Second Optional Protocol to the International Covenant on Civil and Political Rights, Aiming at the Abolition of the Death Penalty	1989	1991	29
International Covenant on Economic, Social, and Cultural Rights	1966	1976	135
Racial Discrimination			
International Convention on the Elimination of all Forms of Racial Discrimination	1966	1969	148
International Convention on the Suppression and Punishment of the Crime of Apartheid	1973	1976	100
International Convention Against Apartheid in Sports	1985	1988	57
Rights of Women and Children			
Convention on the Political Rights of Women	1953	1954	108
Convention on the Nationality of Married Women	1957	1958	65
Convention on Consent to Marriage, Minimum Age for Marriage, and Registration of Marriages	1962	1964	46
Convention on the Elimination of All Forms of Discrimination Against Women	1979	1981	154
Convention on the Rights of the Child	1989	1990	188
Slavery and Related Matters			
Slavery Convention of 1926, as Amended in 1953	1953	1955	92
Protocol Amending the 1926 Slavery Convention	1953	1955	58

| Table 8.1   UN Human-Rights Conventions (continued) | | | |

Convention (grouped by subject)	Year Opened for Ratification	Year Entered into Force	Number of Ratifications, Accessions, Successions Dec. 31, 1996
Slavery and Related Matters (cont.)			
Supplementary Convention on the Abolition of Slavery, the Slave Trade, and Institutions and Practices Similar to Slavery	1956	1957	115
Convention for the Suppression of the Traffic of Persons and the Exploitation of the Prostitution of Others	1950	1951	71
Refugees and Stateless Persons			
Convention Relating to the Status of Refugees	1951	1954	128
Protocol Relating to the Status of Refugees	1967	1967	128
Convention Relating to the Status of Stateless Persons	1954	1960	43
Convention on the Reduction of Statelessness	1961	1975	19
Other			
Convention on the Prevention and Punishment of the Crime of Genocide	1948	1951	122
Convention on the Non-Applicability of Statutory Limitations to War Crimes and Crimes Against Humanity	1968	1970	43
Convention Against Torture and Other Cruel, Inhumane, or Degrading Treatment or Punishment	1984	1987	101

Note: The number of ratifications, accessions, and successions include the participants that apply the treaty provisionally but does not include those states that have ceased to exist.

Source: Multilateral Treaties Deposited with the Secretary General, Status as of 31 December 1996, UN Document ST/LEG/SER.E/10.

against arbitrary arrest; a right to impartial trial; a right to ownership of property; freedom of thought, conscience, and religion; freedom of opinion and expression; freedom of peaceful assembly and association; a right to education; a right to leisure; a right to an adequate standard of living; and much more. Various UN covenants and conventions during the last 40 years spelled out many of these rights and freedoms (Table 8.1). The United Nations added a High Commissioner for Human Rights in 1994, charged with fact-finding and technical assistance.

Many Western states have been uncomfortable with the inclusion of various economic entitlements (such as a right to leisure and an adequate standard of living) alongside political rights and freedoms. Partly for this reason, U.S. ratification of these measures has been slow. It did not ratify even the Genocide Convention (formulated by the UN in 1948) until 1986, the UN Convention Against Torture until 1990, and the International Covenant on Civil and Political Rights until 1992.

The East-West conflict also politicized human-rights issues. Western states proceeded cautiously in endorsing multilateral human-rights measures, because they believed the East viewed them as propaganda instruments, to be ignored internally, whereas communist states simultaneously trumpeted any violations in the more open West. For example, the U.S.S.R. and other socialist states consistently and actively supported the self-determination principle, in part because they could use it to embarrass and harass the colonial powers of the Western world. Ironically, however, that principle undercuts any multinational state in which ethnic subgroups struggle for autonomy, and the Soviet Union proved its victim.

With respect to political and social rights of the individual, the West led the movement toward identification and acceptance of basic principles. The signing by 35 countries in 1975 of the Final Act of the Conference on Security and Cooperation in Europe (CSCE), better known as the Helsinki Agreement, intensified the pressure on the East. Although that agreement committed the West to accept the boundaries created by World War II (the territorial issue again), it also bound the Eastern signatories to respect human rights and fundamental freedoms. Citizen groups formed in Eastern Europe to monitor observance of human rights and to assist the West in drawing attention to violations: Helsinki Watch in Moscow and Charter 77 in Czechoslovakia. Although communist states long harassed, jailed, and exiled members for their activities, the groups maintained ties with Western media and continued to be outspoken.

With the collapse of communism and the fragmentation of the former U.S.S.R., the global human-rights effort moved from definition and monitoring to institutionalization of protection. The CSCE expanded from 35 members to 53 in 1992 and added institutional structure, including a permanent secretariat in Prague, a Conflict Prevention Center in Vienna, and an Office of Democratic Institutions and Human Rights in Warsaw. In 1995 the CSCE adopted a new name, the Organization for Security and Cooperation in Europe (OSCE). Remarkably, an organization that began in the Cold War has now joined the UN as one of the key bulwarks of human rights, struggling, for instance, with how to protect them in the former Yugoslavia (it suspended the Serbian-dominated government from membership in 1992 for its violations in Croatia and Bosnia). The Council of Europe, a somewhat narrower grouping of countries, reinforces the OSCE by taking an even tougher stance on human rights. Individuals in its member states who feel that governments have not respected their rights can appeal to the European Court for Human Rights in Strasbourg.

In the 1990s, another institutional support for human rights took form. In 1993 the UN set up an ad hoc war-crimes tribunal to prosecute genocide and other human rights violations in the former Yugoslavia. In 1998 delegates from 120 countries voted for a permanent International Criminal Court to address such crimes (the United States and six other countries opposed it). Because the International

Court of Justice of the UN handles only disputes among states, this will become the first global court that protects individual rights.

In addition to the key role of intergovernmental organizations such as the UN, OSCE, and the Council of Europe, many nongovernmental organizations add to the backbone of the evolving human rights regime. These include Amnesty International, Human Rights Watch, the International Commission of Jurists, the International League for Human Rights, the International Federation for Human Rights, and the World Council of Churches (Riggs and Plano 1994, 210). They work actively with the media to draw global attention to violations such as political arrests, torture, and death squads. Amnesty International, formed in London in 1961, won the 1977 Nobel Peace Prize. Human Rights Watch, established in 1978, is an umbrella organization for national groups like Helsinki Watch and Middle East Watch. Although such organizations hold no true enforcement power, there is little doubt that they have influenced governments.

Human-rights law scarcely existed at the end of World War II. Although the law has taken great leaps since then, one cloud continues to hang over it, much as during the Cold War. Are human rights truly universal or are they culturally relative? It is no longer communists who claim that Western views of human rights reflect cultural bias rather than universal rights, but Asian leaders and societies. In general they reject the strict attention of Western liberals to the individual and emphasize instead the importance of social values and orientation. In high divorce and crime rates, widespread drug use, and general social tension and conflict, the Asian critics see the weakness of Western liberalism and individual rights. Between radical universalism and radical relativism there is, however, much ground (Donnelly 1998). It is there that human-rights activists continue to build the global house of human rights, even as they leave the interior decoration of individual rooms to those who prefer particular cultural motifs.

Despite continued violations of human rights in practice, and ongoing debates about universality, the strength of the global human-rights movement and the strengthening of global respect for human rights nonetheless supports the liberal contention that a global community is developing:

> Carried to its logical extreme, the doctrine of human rights and duties under international law is subversive of the whole principle that mankind should be organized as a society of sovereign states. For, if the rights of each man can be asserted on the world political stage over and against the claims of his state . . . then the position of the state . . . has been subject to challenge. . . . (Bull 1977, 152)

Were the author of that paragraph to rewrite it today, he would almost certainly adopt gender-neutral language and change "mankind" to "humanity" and "each man" to "each individual." The developing global community also seeks equal status for women and men. The UN has sponsored global conferences on women and their rights: Mexico City in 1975, Copenhagen in 1980, Nairobi in 1988, and Beijing in 1995. The Women's Caucus, a collection of NGOs dedicated to women's issues, has grown steadily in influence within all global conferences. In fact, the *inclusive* norms of the emerging global community increasingly appear in the frequent conferences that focus on the rights of various individuals: the

Children's Summit in 1990, the Human Rights Conference of 1993, the Population Conference of 1994 (which gave women prominence as participants and actors on population issues), and the Social Development Summit of 1995.

Community of Understanding

Liberals place protection of human rights at the normative center of a potentially global community. In our discussion of ideas in Chapter 7, however, we noted that it is not just "principled beliefs" or norms that shape policy, but also "causal beliefs" and even "worldviews" (Goldstein and Keohane 1993). There may also be growing community with respect to causal understandings. For example, leading economists of almost all states have converged on liberal belief in the benefits of free markets for economic growth (although assorted financial crises have shaken that belief).

Intellectual exchange across borders continues to increase. Many scientists communicate more easily with scientists in other countries than with their fellow citizens. The same is true of some business leaders and increasingly of many national policy makers, especially those involved with issues such as environmental or energy policy. Large numbers of students study abroad for all or part of their education. Although it is difficult to measure, the result of all these connections must be an increasingly shared set of understandings of the world. The scientific methods that were so important to the Western Enlightenment period may transfer abroad most easily, but political and social philosophical systems also travel well.

In some issue areas, identifiable **epistemic communities,** informal groupings of individuals who share understandings and who remain in contact and act in concert on policy issues, have arisen (Haas 1989, 1992). They are perhaps most obvious on environmental issues, where they have played key roles in moving countries around the Mediterranean toward control of water pollution, in urging agreements to phase out chemicals that damage the ozone layer, and in mapping the Greenhouse Effect and possible policy approaches. There appears also an increasingly widespread communality of understanding on the dangers of unbridled population growth. Even the logic of collective action in the provision of public goods (see Chapter 6) is an increasingly shared understanding.

Global Governance: The Spread of Democracy

Political democracy builds on both a normative base and a set of causal beliefs. Democratization has advanced globally in waves:

> What could reasonably be called a democratic political system at the national level of government first appeared in the United States in the early nineteenth century. During the following century democratic regimes gradually emerged in northern and western Europe, in the British dominions, and in a few countries in Latin America. This trend, which Alexis de Tocqueville had foreseen in 1835 and which James Bryce documented in 1920, appeared to be irreversible if not necessarily universal. (Huntington 1985, 255)

Nonetheless, following World War I, the war to make the world safe for democracy, democracies fell during the 1920s and 1930s in Germany, Italy, Austria, Poland, the Baltic states, Spain, Portugal, Greece, Argentina, Brazil, and Japan. The second wave of democratization, immediately following World War II, restored democracy to most of those countries and extended it to new ones like India and Israel. Between the early 1950s and the early 1970s, there was again, however, some decline in the numbers of democratic countries. Military coups overthrew democracies in Peru, Brazil, Bolivia, Chile, Pakistan, Greece, and elsewhere.

The third wave of democratization (Huntington 1991) began perhaps in 1974 with a coup on behalf of democracy in Portugal. In the 1980s, a substantial transformation of Latin-American countries (including Argentina, Brazil, and Chile) from military rule to democratic rule advanced global democracy to a new plateau. So, too, in the late 1980s and early 1990s did the dramatic transformations of communist regimes into multiparty democracies in Eastern Europe and the impressive transformation in Africa of one-party states and dictatorships into multiparty systems. Altogether, more than 30 countries joined the democratic camp.

The prospects for further democratic transitions in the near future are uncertain. Many African, Asian, and especially Middle Eastern countries appear unlikely candidates. Moreover, debt, slow economic growth, and related crises could reverse many gains elsewhere. For instance, in 1992 a coup by its president set back democracy in Peru.

Nonetheless, democracy has made great gains globally. According to the Freedom House, in the early 1990s nearly 40 percent of humanity lived in free societies and another 30–35 percent lived in partially free societies. Figure 8.2 traces the number of democratic countries over a much longer period.

Figure 8.2   The Advance of Democracy

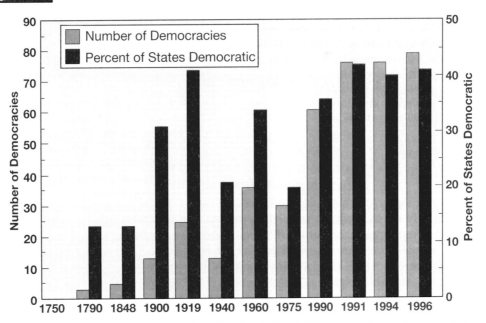

Note: Data from 1990 onward is taken from *Freedom in the World.* Democracies are those countries that are ranked as free by Freedom House. Percent democracies is calculated from the total number of countries surveyed by Freedom House.

Source: Francis Fukuyama, *The End of History and the Last Man* (New York: The Free Press, 1992), 49–50; Michael D. Wallace and J. David Singer, "Intergovernmental Organization in the Global System, 1815–1964: A Quantitative Description," *International Organization* 24, no. 2 (Spring), 239–287; McColm, Bruce, ed. *Freedom in the World: Political Rights and Civil Liberties* (New York: Freedom House, 1990, 1992, 1995, 1997).

Figure 8.3   Freedom as a Function of GDP per Capita

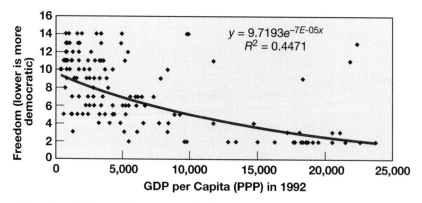

Source: International Futures (IFs) computer simulation, using data from World Bank and Freedom House. See Barry B. Hughes, *International Futures*, 3rd edition (Boulder, CO: Westview Press, 1999).

Is there reason to believe that global democratization will continue? One reason is that there appears a relatively strong relationship between democracy and economic development level. It is striking that nearly all democracies are economically developed. India is the most important exception. Figure 8.3 shows that relationship across all countries. If global economic development proceeds (see Chapters 12 and 13), there is considerable reason to expect further advance of democracy.

Global Community: Peaceful Interaction

Although community building on a global scale is still limited, it is not unrealistic to argue that considerably more has occurred at a regional level. In fact, there now exists a fairly extensive **zone of peace** among the economically developed, democratic countries of Western Europe, North America, and a few other parts of the world. Nearly 200 years ago, when modern democracies were just developing, Immanuel Kant predicted such a zone of peace. In his essay, "Perpetual Peace" (1795), he argued that:

> if the consent of the citizens is required in order to decide that war should be declared . . . nothing is more natural than that they would be very cautious in commencing such a poor game, decreeing for themselves all the calamities of war. . . . But on the other hand, in a constitution which is not republican . . . war does not require of the ruler . . . the least pleasure of his table, the chase, his country houses, his court functions, and the like. (Garnham 1986, 283)

In contrast, some have argued that democratic publics may be susceptible to waves of belligerency that the mass media sometimes stokes. The American public was long more stridently anticommunist than its leadership. Still another counterargument to Kant is that democratic governments use warfare as a distraction from domestic turmoil and a way of unifying their populations.

Are democracies more peace loving? Many empirical studies suggest just the reverse. Three large-scale research projects on warfare looked at the question. Quincy Wright concluded that:

Statistics can hardly be invoked to show that democracies have been less often involved in war than autocracies. France was almost as belligerent while it was a republic as while it was a monarchy or empire. Great Britain is high in the list of belligerent countries, though it has for the longest time approximated democracy in its form of government. (Wright 1965, 208)

Similarly, Small and Singer reported that, from 1816 to 1980, democracies were involved in 41.8 percent of all wars, although democracies seldom constituted more than one-third of all states. Even more telling, democracies actually initiated 57.1 percent of all the wars involving them.

There are two relationships between democracy and violence, however, that are remarkable (Rummel 1983, 1985, and 1988). First, democracies have not fought each other. It is possible to list only the War of 1812 (U.K.-United States), the American Civil War, the Peru-Ecuador war of 1994, and a few other partial or possible exceptions to the general rule. In each case the democracy of at least one party to the conflict had serious flaws.[3] For instance, only in 1828 could more than 50 percent of adult males in the United States vote (Huntington 1991, 16) and students of democracy do not date its arrival in England until still later. Monarchies and dictatorships fight each other often (as in the two world wars). Communist countries have gone to war against one another (the Soviet Union against Hungary, Czechoslovakia, and China; China against Vietnam). Although the statistics indicate the frequency with which democracies have battled these other forms of government and have taken possession of colonies, it is almost astounding that they do not fight each other.

Second, democracies do not kill their own citizens in extensive numbers. Unlike Nazi Germany, Stalinist Russia, and a wide variety of dictatorships that attack segments of their own citizenry (consider the "disappeared" under Latin-American military dictatorships), democracies do not generally so act. In fact, the "necessity" of strong action against internal groups (such as Jews, Armenians, bourgeois elements, or communists) serves often as the justification for overthrow of democracy by dictatorships. Consider two partial exceptions in the 1980s and 1990s to this second rule. Israel used substantial violence against Palestinians in the occupied West Bank. Yet the numbers killed during the Palestinian uprising were not high by the standards of national oppression; moreover, a debate within Israel seriously questioned and restrained the application of force, and the continued access of global media to the events further reinforced a measured response. The other exception is white South Africa, which directed a substantial level of violence against its black population. Again, while the outside world was able to watch and to a degree have some influence, an internal debate over the use of deadly force restrained its intensity.[4]

---

[3]Spiro (1994) suggested that liberals may define away troublesome cases and that, due to the limited number of democracies historically, the relationship of democracy to war is insignificant. Russett (1995) rebutted both arguments. Mansfield and Snyder (1995) suggested a much more important qualification to the democracy-peace relationship and an explanation for possible anomalies: transition to democracy may be sufficiently destabilizing as to increase warfare.

[4]It is also interesting that very few democracies maintain legal capital punishment (and Israel has only used it against the Nazi war criminal, Adolph Eichman). Almost all nondemocratic governments rely upon it. In 1998 the UN Human Rights Commission criticized the United States for applying the death penalty unfairly (over 50 percent of those executed from 1930 to 1990 were black).

Demonstrating Kant's notion of a zone of peace, Canada and the United States have not felt the need in a century to defend the long border between them. More generally, the Organization for Economic Cooperation and Development has come to be such a zone of peace. Organized in September 1961 to promote economic and social welfare, all of its members are democracies: most of the states of Western Europe, plus Australia, Canada, Japan, Mexico, New Zealand, South Korea, and the United States. There has not been a single war among organization members during its history.

Why do democracies not fight each other? For many years the existence of a common external threat to these countries from the Soviet Union and its allies *helped* explain their peacefulness and was also generally consistent with realist understandings of alliances. Yet the absence of that threat has not reduced their peacefulness nor broken their alliance.

Many liberals believe that increasing international economic ties, especially trade, have contributed to international political harmony (and have also reinforced democracy). For instance, the U.S. secretary of state at the end of World War II, Cordell Hull, argued forcefully in favor of a liberal international order as a means of linking countries through trade and financial ties and of making war less likely. The core of the argument is that as economic ties improve welfare, through mutually beneficial transactions, the cost of severing those ties increasingly exceeds any possible benefit of interstate conflict. Saburo Okita, the former president of the Japan Economic Research Center, agreed:

> We are living in a century when such military action is no longer viable. To build up military power just to protect overseas private property is rather absurd in terms of cost-benefit calculations. The best course for the Government in case of nationalization or seizure of overseas private Japanese assets is to compensate Japanese investors directly in Japan rather than to spend very large amounts of money to build up military strength. (Gilpin 1979, 356)

There is some empirical evidence for the belief that free trade and peace are linked. Domke (1988) investigated the relationship of democracy, trade, and membership in international organizations with war involvement. The strongest relationship he found was with trade: "governments of nations that are more involved in foreign trade are less likely to make decisions for war." Other research, however, finds that trade between a pair of countries actually increases conflict (Barbieri 1998).

Most explanations for peace among democracies look to democracy itself as the explanation and specifically emphasize either the structures/institutions of democracy or its norms/culture. Russett (1993) and Dixon (1994) analyzed the historic evidence and concluded that norms are the more important element.

There is one additional, if small, piece of evidence for a growing community norm of opposition to war (not simply an accidental absence of war), especially among the OECD countries, but extending beyond that region. A study of international legal texts since 1815 evaluated the permissibility of war, creating an index (see Figure 8.4) that ranged from 1.0 (war is generally legal) to 4.0 (war is generally

Figure 8.4   Legal Prohibition of War, 1815–1992

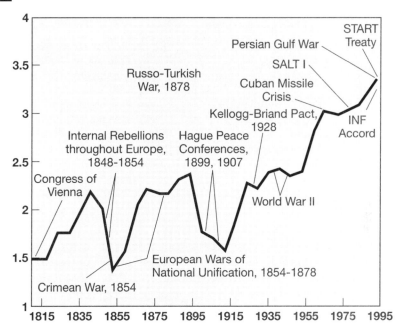

Source: Based on The Transnational Rules Indicators Project (TRIP), as described in Charles W. Kegley, Jr., and Gregory A. Raymond, *When Trust Breaks Down* (Columbia, SC: University of South Carolina Press, 1990). Courtesy of Charles W. Kegley, Jr., and Gregory A. Raymond.

illegal). Although the evaluation of legal texts of 1815 yielded a value of 1.5, and there have been many periods of regressive shift toward acceptance of war, the trend has clearly moved against war.

Institutional Development

Institutions are the formal and informal "rules of the game" within which politics take place (Keohane 1989, 3–4). Organizations like the OSCE or the Council of Europe are formal institutions. Regimes, like the arms-control regime and most other interstate law, are sets of explicit rules, which may exist even in the absence of formal institutions. Conventions, like reciprocity and the balance of power, are implicit rules and understandings that shape expectations and behavior.

One remarkable phenomenon of global governance and institutional development in recent decades has been the proliferation of **intergovernmental organizations (IGOs)** that build on states and their governments (Table 8.2). IGOs, like the United Nations, the World Bank, and NATO, are associations of states that have regularly scheduled meetings of representatives from their membership and a permanent secretariat.

Table 8.2	A Classification of Intergovernmental Organizations (IGOs)	
	Multiple Purpose	**Functional**
Universal	United Nations	United Nations Development Program
		International Civil Aviation Organization
		World Health Organization
Regional	European Union	Asian Development Bank
	Organization of American States	North Atlantic Treaty Organization
	Association of Southeast Asian Nations	Organization of Petroleum Exporting Countries
	Arab League	

Universal IGOs draw members from around the world. The United Nations and the International Monetary Fund are essentially universal. *Regional IGOs,* like NATO, draw on a limited geographic area. *Multiple-purpose IGOs,* like the European Union, address a combination of security, economic, environmental, or other needs of their members. **Functional IGOs,** however, serve only specific functions. For instance, the World Health Organization obviously emphasizes health.

Although the prevalence of intergovernmental organizations is a recent phenomenon in world politics, there are many historic prototypes. For instance, the Delian League linked Greek city-states for all but 26 years between 478 B.C. and 338 B.C. Although sometimes little more than a tool of Athenian power, it was at other times a genuine military alliance. Another example is the Hanseatic League, which facilitated trade among North German towns between the eleventh and seventeenth centuries (Jacobson 1984, 8–9). Perhaps the first modern IGO was the Central Commission for the Navigation of the Rhine, created at the Congress of Vienna to facilitate free navigation through the various political jurisdictions along the Rhine. In the count of Wallace and Singer (1970), there were 49 IGOs by 1914. In recent years, however, that numerical growth seems to have taken on a life of its own. By 1997 there were 6,115 IGOs. See Figure 8.5, which shows also how IGO growth rates parallel those of NGOs.

The growth rate of IGOs peaked in the mid-1970s and has slowed since then (Shanks, Jacobson, and Kaplan 1996, 598). In fact, between 1981 and 1992 perhaps 32 percent of IGOs "died," many as victims of the end of the Cold War and of reduced attention to developing countries. Most newly born IGOs are now "emanations," that is, they are creations of already existing IGOs. Although their growth rate has declined, the numerical growth of IGOs continues. The key questions, however, concern not their number, but their contribution to governance. Have they or will they increase their influence relative to states? The rest of this chapter explores the forces behind the growth of IGO numbers and influence. The next chapter will look in more detail at two important families of IGOs.

Figure 8.5 Growth of International Organizations

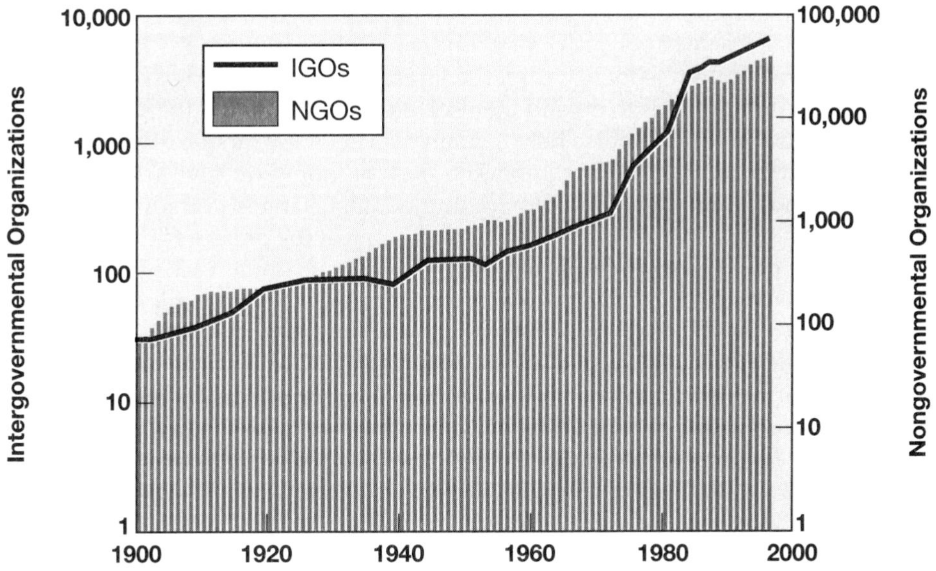

Sources: Union of International Organizations (UAI), *Yearbook of International Organizations 1991/92, 1993/94, and 1997/98* (Brussels: UAI, 1991, 1993, and 1997).

Beyond the State?

Is it possible that there could develop an international organizational structure that will in some significant way supplant the state? That is a favorite idealist and liberal theme. For instance, tapestries hung in the *Palais des Nations* in Geneva (of the old League of Nations) portray human beings moving progressively into larger, more comprehensive communities, beginning with the family and continuing through the tribe, the city-state, and the nation. This portrayal implies the existence of an underlying process that could ultimately culminate in a global society with global institutions (Jacobson 1984, 14). Is there an important long-term process underway that took human organization from smaller units to states and that might in turn supplant states?

If so, one of the long-term forces driving it has been technological advance. Consider briefly the implications of just two military technologies—gunpowder and nuclear weapons. Gunpowder was available in China by the ninth century and entered Europe in the fourteenth century.[5] The conquest of Constantinople by the Turks in 1453 benefited from cannon. Herz (1957) argued that the arrival in Europe of cannon made the small feudal units of medieval Europe, centered on a fort or

---

[5]Van Creveld (1989) said that the Chinese designed primitive grenades with bamboo tubes in the twelfth century. The technology of metal guns appeared in various places, including the Moslem world and Europe, by the early fourteenth century, initially only in handguns and cannon (rifles came later).

castle, indefensible. In doing so it changed the logic of security, putting a premium on larger geographic territories. These developments coincided generally with the rise of the modern state system in Europe. Herz argued further that the introduction of nuclear weapons and intercontinental delivery systems in the late twentieth century put in jeopardy even the largest states. By analogy he suggested that the inability of states to defend themselves would undercut the state system.[6]

Economic factors also help explain the rise of the modern state system. These include the demand for larger markets and for more extensive access to raw materials than feudal systems could accommodate. Changes in trading (such as shipping) and production technology created some of the pressures for more extensive economic units that gave rise to states. These forces remain active. In fact, no state, even the physically largest, can any longer satisfy the economic desires of its citizenry from within its own borders. Extensive interstate flows of goods, capital, and technology are now essential.

The importance of technological change in the military and the economy lead some to conclude that the state simply cannot maintain its position as the dominant institution of governance in world politics. If that assessment is correct, what might be the dynamics of movement toward suprastate actors? Let us consider two possible dynamics—federalism and functionalism.

Federalism   Some idealistic liberals look at the predicament of humankind, the inability of states to guarantee the security of their citizens except through a balance of terror that may ultimately be disastrous, and conclude that the only viable alternative is **federalism**—a governmental form that transfers most sovereignty from states to a central government. Following the same logic that led Hobbes to call for a social contract between citizens and a central government, the Leviathan, these idealists call for a voluntary global federalism.[7]

They can even point to historic precedent for abrogating sovereignty to deal better with threat. Colonies willing to overlook strong religious differences to achieve and maintain independence from England formed the United States. Switzerland represents a union among peoples with different religious, cultural, and even linguistic backgrounds, established in part to protect their mutual neutrality in European wars. Federalists argue that the threat now is the destruction of humanity in any future war. It gives new meaning to an old German proverb, "If thou wilt not my brother be, I'll smash thy skull most certainly" (Deutsch 1974, 181).

Plans for world federation have a remarkably long history.[8] Perhaps the first truly global government plan came from a French monk, Emeric Crucé, who presented in 1623 a proposal called *Le Nouveau Cynée* (Brown 1987, 116). Crucé suggested a council of ambassadors, with representatives from the European states, Turkey, Persia, India, China, and kingdoms in Africa, as well as representatives of

---

[6]In a subsequent reconsideration of his argument, however, Herz (1969) took the view that the state as an institution serves a number of other needs for human beings, such as manifesting a territorial imperative of the nation, which will give it longevity.

[7]Riker (1964, 11) defined federalism as "a bargain between prospective national leaders and officials of constituent governments for the purpose of aggregating territory, the better to lay taxes and raise armies."

[8]For reviews of many plans, see Jacobson (1984, 21–29) and Brown (1987, 111–123).

the Pope and of Jews. Majorities would prevail in votes of the council, a structure of voluntary negotiation and arbitration with a world court would settle disputes, and the council would have a military available to enforce decisions. The Crucé plan was remarkable in its anticipation of features of the global organizations of the twentieth century.

Yet, federalist plans still gain few adherents, for two reasons. First, even those observers who deem the end desirable often feel that there is "no way to get there from here." Second, many question whether such a world would, in fact, be a happy one. Although federalist plans invariably call for majority voting of some type, that principle by itself does not guarantee "good" decision making. Much of the world has never lived in a democratic society and has little commitment to protecting minorities from the power of the majority. In a world federation, for example, the poor majority would almost certainly call for significant income redistribution. That might be a happy world for the global South but would not excite many living in the North. In light of these problems, federalism poses a weak challenge to realism.

Functionalism   Federalists argue that "the worst way to cross a chasm is by little steps."[9] In essence functionalists propose exactly such an incremental strategy for bridging the chasms separating states. Instead of describing their strategy as one of "little steps," however, they would more likely represent it as one of throwing increasing numbers of rope bridges across the chasm rather than trying to put a superhighway in place immediately.

The individual rope bridges of functionalists consist of functionally specific intergovernmental organizations, each satisfying a common need of the member states that the organizations link. Functionalists argue that the number of these organizations will increase naturally with advances in interstate transportation and communication technology and with resultant growth in interstate trade and other transactions. Early examples were the Universal Postal Union (1874), the International Telecommunications Organization (1875), and the International Office of Weights and Measures (1875).

Functionalism avoids direct confrontation with the security issues of high politics. The proliferation of functional organizations is supposed instead to ensnare states within patterns of cooperation and raise significantly the stakes of any conflict that disrupts interstate ties. In David Mitrany's words:

> Every activity organized in that way would be a layer of peaceful life, and a sufficient addition of them would create increasingly wide strata of peace—not the forbidding peace of an alliance, but one that would suffuse the world with a fertile mingling of common endeavor and achievement. (Mitrany 1966, 70)

Although the dominant presence of states often leads functionalists to present their concepts and theory in the language of interstate politics, the underlying logic is very much a liberal one of attention to the needs of individuals. Humans have needs, including economic and security needs. States have long helped us satisfy those needs. If, however, other institutional structures will help us do so more

[9]Streit (1961); cited in Nye (1971, 50).

fully or more efficiently, liberals suggest that we will eventually build those other structures. The ultimate aim is to create institutions that will "deliver the goods."

One criticism of the functionalist approach to bridging the chasms between states is that it might result in many rope bridges but never produce a usable highway bridge. That is, functionalism may need a strategy that will ultimately move the process from the narrowly technical to the broadly political—and ultimately challenge the domain of states. In 1950 French Foreign Minister Robert Schuman stepped forward with a plan to unify the coal and steel markets of Europe that was intended to illustrate in practice, not just in theory, how that leap from the technical to the political, from low politics to high politics, could be made.

Based on the philosophical and practical work of Jean Monnet, the Schuman Plan was a conscious attempt to move toward the federalist goal, using a functionalist logic called **spillover**—a splashing of cooperation from one arena to another. Functionalists argue that transborder coordination and cooperation in one arena actually creates or intensifies problems resulting from failure to coordinate in other arenas and will give rise to pressures to extend cooperation. This process need not be limited to strictly economic or technical arenas of state interaction but can spill over into the very heart of politics. The continuing process is one of gradual *integration* of the societies involved in it.

Consider a simple example of the process of spillover. When European countries eliminated tariffs on goods crossing their borders, many trucks began to transport goods among them. Given border-crossing restrictions, however, such increased transport volume overloaded customs stations and led to long delays and high shipping costs. The producers and truckers exerted political pressure for the elimination or simplification of border-crossing procedures, thus extending integration. The same process is now happening between the United States and Mexico.

The partially automatic process of spillover helps states that initiate it move up a **scale of economic integration,** consisting roughly of five stages (Belassa 1961). A group of states that eliminate tariffs and border restrictions among themselves constitute a **free-trade area,** the first stage. At that point pressure grows to coordinate the tariffs of the member countries with respect to outside states, otherwise all goods from the outside flow into the organization through the member state with the lowest external tariffs. When states eliminate tariffs among themselves and establish a common external tariff, they create a **customs union.**

With reductions in intercountry barriers to goods, markets grow and manufacturers seek to establish production centers in other countries more easily. They want to buy foreign companies or to build new facilities closer to their expanded markets. They press to move capital and personnel more easily across state borders. A customs union that also allows free flow of labor and finance within it constitutes a **common market.** Because the European countries of the Schuman Plan established this goal for themselves, we still sometimes refer to them as the Common Market.

Should enough individuals begin to live parts of their lives in different member states of the common market as a result of expanded interstate corporate operations, pressures grow on the governments for coordination of retirement benefits and other social programs. With increased movements of goods, capital, and labor, it becomes increasingly difficult for individual states to pursue divergent policies dealing with inflation, interest rates, or unemployment. Pressure develops to coordinate such policies. When a common market harmonizes economic policies, it becomes an **economic union.** A single currency replaces those of individual states.

Now that Europe has reached this level, what might happen next? Pressures for increased coordination and cooperation will strain central institutional capabilities and require extensions and additions. As the central economic institutions become more powerful they will be able to dispense greater benefits and impose greater costs. The benefits will contribute to the building of loyalties to the structures, and the costs will shift domestic political activities toward them. At some point, central economic institutions become dominant over those of the state, and an economic union evolves into the fifth stage, total **economic integration.**

The higher stages of the economic integration process increasingly involve elements that everyone would characterize as highly political and near the core of state interests (for instance, control over money, taxing, and spending). It would still require a step of considerable size to move from economic integration to **political integration.** That last big step would require the transfer of the "locus of sovereignty" from states to the central institutional structures. That is, the states would no longer be the dominant decision-making elements, delegating authority to the common institutions; instead the central institutions would permit the residual state governments to maintain certain functions. A central military would replace the state militaries. When we consider that last step, the arguments of realists about the distinction between high and low politics resurface.

How might spillover occur between economic and political integration? For instance, European armament and aerospace manufacturers might recognize the economies of scale associated with sales to several member governments. With much overlap in weaponry and many common military interests, the states could begin to experiment with greater military coordination and joint military units. Desire may even arise among the peoples of the member states to exert more direct control, through a parliament, over both the economic and political-military elements of the process rather than to leave matters in the hands of existing state governments or European technocrats. Functionalists point out that much of this has, in fact, already happened in Europe.

This description of a process by which spillover could lead to ever higher levels of integration suggests that some of the steps up the scale, especially the last leaps to political integration, are quite large. **Neofunctionalists** argue that the process can never be as gradual and automatic as early functionalists argued and that it will require that elites, motivated by federalist ideals, personal glory, or service to citizens, periodically push the process forward with political action.

Europe, as Chapter 9 will detail, has moved quite steadily up the ladder of economic integration. Going back to our analogy of the chasm, solid bridges now link European countries. In reviewing this liberal logic, however, a realist could reasonably argue that the initial goal of a solid bridge across a chasm was an inadequate one—true political integration, if the goal is a superstate, is not a matter of building bridges but of *filling in the chasm.* Moreover, realists argue that the ties among states constructed by the functional process can lead to conflict as well as cooperation:

> Closer interdependence means closeness of contact and raises the prospect of at least occasional conflict. The fiercest civil wars and the bloodiest international ones have been fought within areas populated by highly similar people whose affairs had become quite closely knit together. (Waltz 1982, 81)

Nonetheless, Domke (1988, 151) found systematic empirical evidence that participation in limited membership organizations is associated with lower likelihood of involvement in wars. The functionalist web of interstate ties appears to constrain state behavior.

Conclusion

Although liberal theory is often less coherent, and certainly less simple, than realist theory, it is evolving rapidly into a meaningful portrait of global politics. This chapter reviewed the foundations of that theory in the proliferation and growing capabilities of nonstate actors and in the interests that both they and states share in increased regional and global cooperation. It went on to discuss some elements of global community that appear to be developing beyond basic interstate law, specifically human-rights law, the norm of democratic governance, and even the reluctance to use war among the countries where those norms are most developed. Finally, we moved into a discussion of institutional development upon the base of that emerging community. In particular, we elaborated the logic of functionalism and how a functional dynamic might lead to organizational structures that transcend the state. In the next chapter we turn to two specific and important organizations, the United Nations and the European Union. Are they simply creations of states and still fully under state control? Or are they embryonic structures for totally new patterns of global governance?

Selected Key Terms

civil society	human rights	scale of economic integration
international nongovernmental organizations (NGOs or INGOs)	epistemic communities	free-trade area
	zone of peace	customs union
	institutions	common market
transnational social movement organizations (TSMOs)	intergovernmental organizations (IGOs)	economic union
	federalism	economic integration
multinational corporation (MNC)	functionalism	political integration
	spillover	neofunctionalists
globalization		

CHAPTER 9

Organizations and Governance

Strasbourg, France, is the intellectual and commercial capital of the region of Alsace. As Argentoratum, Strasbourg was once an important Roman city in the province of Upper Germany. Bishops later ruled it as part of the Holy Roman Empire. For a considerable time in the Middle Ages burghers secured for it the status of a "free city." During the fourteenth century a revolution introduced corporative government, and the guilds held an important position. The city accepted the Reformation and in 1608 joined the Protestant Union. In 1681 King Louis XIV seized it for the relatively new state of France. German culture remains very evident, however, and Germany occupied it from 1871 to 1919 and 1940 to 1944. Strasbourg now hosts much activity of the European Union, including the European Parliament.

KEY WEB LINKS

www.unsystem.org/
www.un.org/
europa.eu.int/index.htm
www.itaiep.doc.gov/nafta/nafta2.htm
www.apecsec.org.sg/
www.g7.utoronto.ca/

Just imagine the kaleidoscope of changing identities or loyalties across the generations of a family that has lived in Strasbourg, France, over the centuries (Chapter 10 returns to the issue of identity). Imagine also the dynamism in forms of governance under which the citizens of Strasbourg have lived. Over two millennia, governance by states has actually been a relatively brief phenomenon. Moreover, over its three centuries of involvement in the modern state system, Strasbourg has witnessed two major transitions—from monarchy to democracy and from position at the crossroads of frequent Franco-German wars to major city of the European Union.

Human governance has evolved dramatically and continues to change. This chapter looks at the emergent phenomenon of regional and global organizations. There has been tremendous growth in such organizations, but this chapter devotes particular attention to two families of them: the United Nations and the European Union. What are the reasons for their growth? How have such international organizations begun to constrain the behavior of states? More specifically, how might such organizations be reshaping human governance patterns?

United Nations

The Allied powers fighting Germany and Japan wrote the charter of the United Nations in San Francisco during the spring of 1945, before the conclusion of World War II. The organization has five major components (see Figure 9.1; also www.un.org, April 23, 1998):

1. The *General Assembly,* the central organ, sets the budget, selects the secretary-general, and designates the nonpermanent members of the Security Council. Each state has one vote. "Important questions" (defined by the charter to include peace and security recommendations) require two-thirds majority, whereas simple majorities resolve other issues. In contrast, the League of Nations required unanimity on many votes. The General Assembly theoretically supervises a variety of functional agencies such as the United Nations Children's Fund (UNICEF), the UN Development Program (UNDP), and the UN Environmental Program (UNEP). In reality, many of these bodies maintain separate governing structures and rely heavily on contributions outside of the UN budget assessments.

2. The *Security Council* is a second legislative organ and its structure represents a conscious effort to learn from the failures of the league. The five permanent members of the council are the United States, the U.S.S.R., Great Britain, China, and France, which coincidentally became the first five declared nuclear powers. The General Assembly selects ten nonpermanent members with staggered two-year terms to join these great powers on the council. The permanent members wield vetoes on substantive matters, an arrangement that recognizes, as league institutions did not, that no action can be taken against a great power. Unlike the league, which allowed each member to decide on economic or other sanctions independently, the charter gives the Security Council the power both to identify an aggressor and to direct a military force. To provide such a military force, the charter theoretically obligates all members to make armed forces available to a Military Staff Committee. In reality, the UN has fielded only ad hoc military forces, under direct control of the Security Council rather than of the committee (Brown 1987, 158–159).

3. The *Secretariat* is the executive institution. At its head sits a secretary-general, charged for a five-year term with bringing appropriate issues to the UN institutions. The bureaucracy of the Secretariat, among many other duties, maintains an extensive global database, of substantial importance to anyone who wishes to understand the state of the world.

4. The judicial institution is the *International Court of Justice,* also known as the World Court. The Security Council and General Assembly elect the 15 justices, who serve staggered, 9-year terms. The court has jurisdiction only over disputes that states agree to submit. For instance, in the 1980s the United States rejected the right of the World Court to rule on Nicaraguan claims against it, including the mining of Nicaraguan harbors.

5. The *Economic and Social Council* (ECOSOC) coordinates many affiliated functional organizations (called specialized agencies) with varying amounts of autonomy. These include the Universal Postal Union (UPO), the World Health Organization (WHO), the International Monetary Fund (IMF), and the UN Educational, Scientific, and Cultural Organization (UNESCO). ECOSOC also oversees the activities of five regional economic commissions (by continent) and has consultative arrangements with more than 1,500 nongovernmental organizations.

Figure 9.1 United Nations System

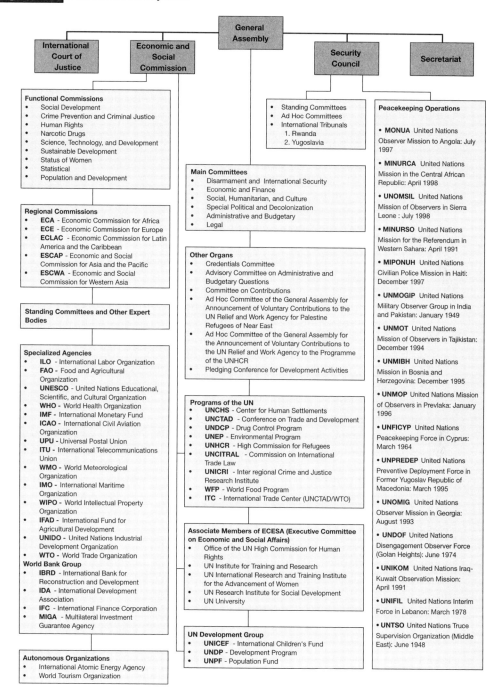

Note: The United Nations is a collection of many affiliated IGOs. This figure shows the system in operation at the start of 1999.

Source: www.un.org

Transformation

Although the basic structure of the UN has not changed since its founding, its functioning has changed significantly since 1945. First, power within the organization has shifted twice. Both power realignments came with expansions of membership from 51 states initially to 185 in 1998. UN members finally allowed the People's Republic of China to take its seat (replacing the government on Taiwan) in 1971, giving representation to one-fifth of humanity. Now only a handful of smaller states remain outside. Switzerland chooses nonmembership in protection of a strict definition of its neutrality. The expansion of membership, in the context of the Cold War, shifted power from majorities built around the United States to majorities that most often opposed the United States. From 1946 to 1950, 75 percent of roll calls agreed with the United States and only 34 percent supported the Soviet Union. The United States lost its majority position in the early and mid-1960s. From 1986 through 1990, the majority included the United States only 12 percent of the time but represented the Soviet position on 93 percent of all votes (Riggs and Plano 1994, 67).

How did that membership and power shift occur? Until 1955 the United States and the Soviet Union blocked most of the membership applications supported by each other, slowing membership growth and protecting the U.S. majority. In the thaw of superpower relations that followed Stalin's death, a package deal in 1955 allowed 16 states to enter. Thereafter, membership became virtually open, and with continuing decolonization large numbers of African countries entered. More than half of current members were colonies before World War II. Many LDCs voted consistently against the United States and the former colonial powers of Western Europe. Even the Latin American countries, on which the United States once counted heavily, shifted to frequent opposition.

The end of the Cold War and the break-up of the Soviet Union led to a second expansion of membership. Both North and South Korea joined in 1991, as did Estonia, Latvia, Lithuania, and two Oceanic micro-states. In 1992 other former republics of the Soviet Union joined and Russia took over the seat of the former U.S.S.R. In 1993 the Czech Republic and the Slovak Republic replaced Czechoslovakia, and Andorra, Eritrea, Macedonia (officially the Former Yugoslav Republic of Macedonia), and Monaco joined.

At the same time, however, the coalition of anti-U.S. and often anti-Western votes largely collapsed. On a wide variety of issues, including the sanctions imposed by the UN on Iraq after its invasion of Kuwait (1991) and on Libya for its failure to turn over two suspected bombers of a jetliner (1992), Russia and members of its former empire began to vote *with* the United States. In fact, while the UN could agree to impose sanctions only twice between 1945 and 1990, it imposed them four times in 1991 and early 1992 alone. Similarly, in its first 40 years, the UN undertook a total of 13 peacekeeping missions. By 1994 and 1995 the UN was running 17 missions simultaneously, with a total of about 70,000 soldiers.

A second and related transformation in the functioning of the UN has been significant shift in the weight placed upon different issues. At one time the key political-military agenda item for the UN was the self-determination of peoples. Assistance with decolonization is arguably one of the UN's greatest successes. The entrance of large numbers of newly independent but largely poor countries shifted the agenda more heavily toward development, economic and social. Then emergence of environmental issues in the 1970s and 1980s increased the weight placed on issues of global commons like the oceans and the atmosphere. For instance, the third and most extensive rounds of discussion on the Law of the Sea began in 1973 and ran until 1982. Although always on the UN agenda, the end of the Cold War greatly enhanced attention of the organization to human rights and democratization. That issue, in particular, challenges traditional realist concepts that the UN is a community of equal states and that states should not intervene in the domestic affairs of others. More generally, much of the UN agenda is clearly liberal. When we examine the functionalist side of the UN, the liberal orientation is especially obvious, because it emphasizes the condition of individuals: their health, the standards of their work places, their ability to communicate openly around the world, and their economic well-being.

Security has, of course, always been on the UN agenda and, in fact, at the top of it. The first purpose listed on the UN Charter is "To maintain international peace and security." This chapter cannot possibly review the performance of the UN on all of the issues it tackles. Fortunately, much of the rest of the book deals implicitly or explicitly with that performance. In Chapter 6 we discussed arms control—negotiation of treaties frequently occurs in UN forums and agreements become part of the "UN Legal Order" (Joyner 1997). In Chapter 8 we discussed human rights law. Later in the book we return to both economic and environmental treaties and agreements. Our discussion of performance here focuses on only two categories of issue: security and social development. Such focus is also appropriate because these issues build upon the two theoretical traditions that motivated the founders: collective security and functionalism.

Performance: Peace and Security

How has the United Nations done in enforcing the peace? Its inability to impose sanctions on great power aggression tore apart the League of Nations. The veto system of the United Nations, by recognizing the unreality of collective action opposed by one or more great powers, has preserved institutional integrity—no state has withdrawn as Japan did. That same system, however, greatly limits UN ability to act.

Collective Security   During the Cold War the UN supported only one **collective security** action. When the Korean War erupted in 1950, the U.S.S.R. was boycotting the Security Council in protest of its failure to seat the People's Republic of China (which took control of the mainland in 1949). The United States pushed through a resolution committing the United Nations to support South Korea. Yet only 22 of 60 member states offered forces to the United Nations command, and the United States and South Korea together supplied more than 90 percent of total personnel.

At the end of the Cold War, the United Nations undertook a second collective security action. In August, 1990, the Security Council voted 14 to 0 to demand Iraq's withdrawal from Kuwait. Following eleven intervening resolutions, the council set a deadline of January 15, 1991, for withdrawal, after which it authorized Kuwait's allies "to use all necessary means." On January 16, the United States led a 28-state force into attacks on Iraq. The United States provided approximately two-thirds of the personnel.

No UN enforcement action to date has occurred without a dominant U.S. role. Until that changes, UN military sanctions in the name of collective security merit some skepticism. Economic and other nonmilitary sanctions also have a complicated record. Between 1948 and 1955 a nonmandatory embargo on arms shipments to Israel and the Arab States of the Mideast was partially successful, but was ignored thereafter. UN members frequently violated both voluntary and mandatory sanctions against arms sales to South Africa during the 1960s and 1970s (Riggs and Plano 1994, 110). On the other hand, tightened economic sanctions in the late 1980s may have significantly influenced the dismantling of apartheid in the early 1990s. All in all, the UN record on collective security is limited.

Peace Keeping   The problems associated with collective security, especially the application of military sanctions, include (1) the inability to apply sanctions to great powers or over their strong opposition, (2) the difficulty of identifying aggressor states in many conflicts, and (3) the unwillingness of states to commit extensive resources. UN **peacekeeping** efforts have evolved to live within these significant constraints—they do not confront great powers, they often do not identify an aggressor, and the level of resource involvement is low. This often means placing small peacekeeping forces or observer missions between combatants who are ready to cease hostilities and can use some help in doing so. The United Nations personnel generally use force only in self-defense.

The UN supplied such a mission in 1947–1949 on the Northern border of Greece to monitor external support for leftist guerrillas. The UN first fielded larger peacekeeping military forces in 1956 during the Suez War. A United Nations Emergency Force (UNEF) took control of the area around Egypt's Suez Canal, so as to facilitate the withdrawal of British, French, and Israeli forces.

Still larger forces, backed by the full support of great powers, at least once blurred the line between peace keeping and collective security (peace enforcing). Both superpowers supported the early stages of an operation by a force in the Congo during 1960–1964 that was large enough, with 20,000 troops from 29 countries, to attempt active conflict termination rather than simple separation of weary belligerents. The forces backed an anti-Soviet faction in the struggle for control of the Congo, however, and the joint sponsorship disintegrated. The Soviet Union and France, among others, refused to pay, and the expensive mission precipitated a UN financial crisis. Unpopular peacekeeping missions subsequently created other financial crises for the organization. That history must serve as a warning whenever the UN moves toward more expensive and potentially unsuccessful or even divisive peacekeeping missions.

Since 1945 the United Nations has organized a total of 45 peacekeeping forces. More than 1,500 peacekeepers have lost their lives on missions. Most operations followed the end of the Cold War. The peak was in 1994 when there were 18 missions that cost $3.3 billion. By 1997 costs had fallen to $1.4 billion, even with 16 missions underway (see Figure 9.2).

The missions of the 1990s reflected the changing character of global conflict. The traditional peacekeeping role was policing a ceasefire between war-weary

Figure 9.2   United Nations Peacekeeping Expenditures and Arrears in Payment by Members

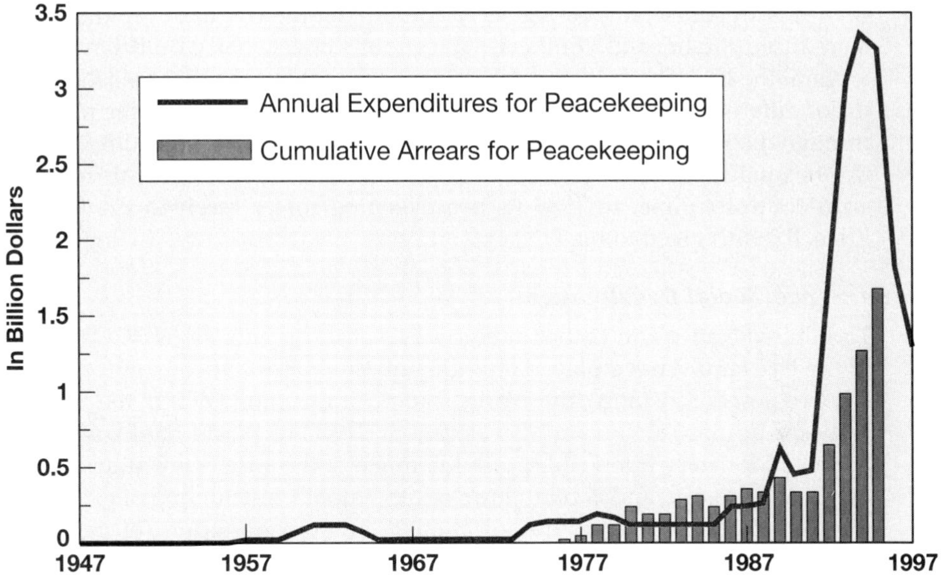

Source: Worldwatch Database Disk, 1998.

states. Of the 11 missions initiated in 1992–1994, however, 9 placed UN forces into domestic conflicts. Domestic missions tend to demand more active engagement of larger forces. In Somalia the force level grew to 36,000, and in Yugoslavia it reached 40,000. The effort in Somalia ended badly when U.S. troops were killed (with bodies dragged through the street on global television), and it withdrew from the mission in 1994. The Somalia tragedy traumatized many Americans and led to greatly reduced support for peacekeeping missions.

Dispute Resolution   The use of force is not the only method by which the United Nations contributes to global conflict resolution and by which we should judge its efforts. Article 33, Paragraph 1, of the charter lists other procedures, which collectively constitute **dispute resolution:**

> The parties to any dispute, the continuance of which is likely to endanger the maintenance of international peace and security, shall, first of all, seek a solution by negotiation, enquiry, mediation, conciliation, arbitration, judicial settlement, resort to regional agencies or arrangements, or other peaceful means of their choice. (Riggs and Plano 1994, 131–132)

The United Nations itself identified 172 regional conflicts that it has helped end through 1996. Haas (1986) concluded that the UN had great success in 23 percent of disputes and limited success in another 30 percent. The UN also addresses disputes, which may or may not involve conflict, via the International Court of Justice. Between 1946 and 1997 the court delivered 60 judgments and 23 advisory opinions on issues as disparate as land frontiers, hostage-taking, nationality, and rights of passage.

It is, of course, impossible to be certain that the UN has ever ended disputes or reduced fatalities in conflicts. We cannot know what would have happened without the UN. The evidence, however, is overwhelming that the UN has made a major difference, via collective security action, with its peacekeeping missions, and through dispute resolution. It has also provided a permanent forum for arms-control negotiations, and it has facilitated essentially all multilateral treaties in the arms-control regime. In 1988 its peacekeeping forces received the Nobel Peace Prize, the fifth given to the UN.

Performance: Social Development

The United Nations and other intergovernmental organizations (IGOs), many part of the UN family, have played an indisputably important role on many issues of low politics. For instance, the World Trade Organization (WTO), the International Bank for Reconstruction and Development (IBRD or World Bank), and the International Monetary Fund (IMF) provide much of the structure within which international trade, aid, and capital flows occur. Smooth functioning of global communications (mail and telecommunications) and transportation (of people and of goods) requires other IGOs such as the Universal Postal Union, founded in 1874, and the International Telecommunication Union, established in 1875.

The functional benefits of the UN do not always require an ongoing institutional framework; sometimes special conferences provide them. For example, the United Nations Law of the Sea Conferences (UNCLOS) in 1958, 1960, and 1973–1982 developed international policy on use of the oceans. Those meetings established the principles of 12-mile territorial seas (with guaranteed passage through navigable straits even within the 12-mile limit) and of 200-mile Exclusive Economic Zones (EEZs), within which states have sole rights to fishing and minerals.

We focus here, however, on the ways in which the UN has contributed to social well-being. It has made important contributions to human health. Most remarkably, WHO successfully eradicated smallpox from the world (except for samples in two laboratories). In 1974 WHO initiated the Expanded Program on Immunization (EPI) with the goal of vaccinating all children globally against diphtheria, measles, whooping cough, poliomyelitis, tetanus, and tuberculosis. At the time only 5 percent of children in LDCs received these vaccinations. In the 1990s that rate climbed to 80 percent, saving the lives of about 3 million children per year. For instance, global cases of polio fell from 400,000 children per year in 1980 to 140,000 in 1993, and eradication is imminent. Because disease can spread across borders and reinfect areas that have eliminated it, collective action of the kind that WHO organizes is necessary. For instance, the campaign to eliminate smallpox could have failed if even a single country refused to participate.

As with security, it is impossible to know exactly how much the UN has contributed to many social changes that state governments widely support. For instance, fertility rates per woman in developing countries declined from 6 births per woman in the 1960s to 3.3 in 1998. Use of effective family planning techniques grew from 10 percent of the world's families to 56 percent over the same period. UN agencies establish standards for safety on more than 200 food commodities. The UN has helped more than 1.3 billion people in rural areas obtain access to safe water. The UN has provided observers or other assistance to help guarantee free elections in Nicaragua, Haiti, Angola, El Salvador, South Africa, Mozambique, Eritrea, and more than 60 other countries. UN programs have helped female literacy rates in LDCs grow from 36 percent in 1970 to 62 percent in 1995.

In general, UN programs have devoted special attention to women and children. The 1990 World Summit for Social Development and the 1995 Fourth World Conference on Women exemplify this emphasis. More than 150 countries have ratified the 1979 UN Convention of the Elimination of All Forms of Discrimination against Women. Even when countries ratify it but fail to honor it, the convention provides support for those who fight against discrimination. Large numbers of people in developed countries come most directly into contact with the UN by buying Christmas cards from the United Nations Children's Fund (UNICEF), a Nobel Peace Prize winner in 1965.

Controversies Facing the United Nations

Even without a Cold War or domestically contentious issues like abortion, controversies remain around the UN. In some cases, the very *existence* of the UN is the source of controversy. The UN clearly has a liberal agenda and has facilitated economic and social globalization. Nationalists can fear the loss of local- or state-level control that globalization brings.

More often, of course, specific policies of the UN come under attack. The United States withdrew funding during the Reagan administration for the UN Fund for Population Activities (UNFPA), because it supported family planning efforts in countries that allowed abortion. (The Clinton administration resumed support of the organization.) Some critics raise concern about the support given by resolutions for Palestinian statehood and the criticisms directed at Israel. Others argue that the UN spends resources wastefully. It would not be surprising if large numbers of Serbs were very angry at the UN's intervention in Bosnia and its sanctions against Serb-dominated former Yugoslavia. The United States complains that it should not pay 25 percent of the total budget. Many states resent the veto power that the five permanent members of the Security Council wield and a few others (such as Germany and Japan) would themselves like permanent status.

With so many potential reasons for unhappiness with the UN, it is not surprising that various countries have periodically withheld their assessed contribution. Although they invariably plead poverty, withholding resources often constitutes an effort to control UN policies. In 1997 member states owed the UN a total of $2.3 billion, $1.6 billion for peacekeeping and most of the rest for the regular budget (see again Figure 9.2). The United States alone owed $1.4 billion.

The budget for the UN's core functions is $1.3 billion per year (about $1 billion less than that of Tokyo's Fire Department). Even the entire UN system (including the World Bank and all other specialized agencies and functions), has a total budget of only $18.2 billion (approximately the revenues of Dow Chemical). Thus unpaid dues of such magnitude have significant consequences for operations. The UN

Secretariat has downsized staff from 12,000 in 1984 to 9,000 in 1997, cut programs of all kinds, and borrowed from countries to pay peacekeeping expenses.

Nonetheless, the UN is now more than a half-century old. To most observers, even those who disagree with one policy or another, it has proven its worth. Although it only has a total of 53,000 employees (about the size of the city government of Stockholm), it plays an increasingly influential role in global affairs.

European Union

While the United Nations has close and explicit ties to both collective security and functionalism, the founders of the European Union had federalist aspirations but chose primarily functionalist means. Unlike the charter of the United Nations, there is no single document that defines the institutional structure of the European Union. From its beginning the organizations that ultimately became the European Union have been dynamic and subject to periodic transformation. The EU now has 10 governmental organs. They include (http://europa.eu.int May 6, 1998):

1. The citizens of the EU directly elect the *European Parliament.* Unlike the General Assembly of the UN, it represents people, not states. Representatives sit in political "groupings" (clusters of the many political parties throughout the member states), not by country. It has only a consultative role on legislation, but does amend and approve the budget. In addition, every fifth year it approves the Commission members and its President (in 1999 it threatened to fire all of them for mismanagement and they ultimately resigned).

2. The *Council of the European Union* represents the states and acts like a second legislative chamber. The fact that it is more powerful than the Parliament accounts for the **democratic deficit** (the relative inability of the European citizenry to directly control the EU's institutions and policy) to which some advocates of change point. Often known as the Council of Ministers, there are actually more than 25 different variations of the Council, each drawing together different ministers from the member states: foreign affairs, economic and finance, agriculture, and so on. Twice each year the heads of state from all members meet in a variation known as the European Council or European Summit. The Presidency of the Council rotates among member states every six months. The Council decides many issues through "qualified" majority voting (giving more votes to larger countries, but overrepresenting small countries), but makes the most important decisions (especially on foreign affairs and "Justice and Home Affairs") by unanimity. Some issues require codecision with the Parliament.

3. The *European Commission* is the executive branch of the EU. The Commission's 20 members serve 5-year terms. France, Germany, Italy, Spain, and the United Kingdom have two commissioners and all other states have one, but commissioners are supposed to represent the EU, not their home states. The Commission has a staff of 15,000 to help it propose legislation to the Parliament and Council and to enforce approved legislation. It also plays a key role in negotiating trade and cooperation agreements with countries outside of the Union.

4. The *European Court of Justice* is the judicial arm. Each state appoints one judge for renewable terms of six years. Whereas only states can bring cases to the World Court, states, individuals, companies, and the EU institutions can bring cases to the European Court. The court may even rule state law invalid because of conflict with community law. Between 1954 and 1998, 9,000 cases came before it.

There are additional governmental organs. For instance, the Economic and Social Committee represents interest groups, notably employers, workers, and various others. The Committee of Regions brings together regional presidents, mayors, and others who stand close to the citizens of the Union, for instance, to its regional ethnic groupings. The European Central Bank oversees the common European currency.

Transformation

The European Union exists as a result of a series of major transformations. Changes generally have involved either **deepening** (intensifying integration) or **widening** (expanding membership).

In terms of deepening, the roots of the EU lie in an organization called the European Coal and Steel Community (ECSC), established in 1952. The ECSC came into being as a conscious effort by European leaders to link Europe through free trade in two key economic sectors. The Treaty of Rome brought two additional organizations into being in 1958. The European Atomic Energy Commission (Euratom) coordinated the common development of nuclear energy including the sharing of research, investment capital, and specialists in that sector. The most famous element of the triad was the European Economic Community (EEC), better known as the Common Market because it set the creation of such a market as its goal. The structures of the three institutions merged into the European Communities (EC) in 1967.

Throughout much of the 1970s and early 1980s the functionalist process continued slowly—to many observers the process appeared moribund. In 1979 the Communities created a European Monetary System (EMS) loosely linking nine European currencies to each other. Although it failed, a European Currency Unit (ECU) came to serve as a unit of account for many EU transactions.

Then in 1986 European leaders took another large step up the integration ladder by adopting the Single European Act, an amendment to the Treaty of Rome. The goal was a true common market, and the EU largely achieved it by 1992. The Single Act removed remaining restrictions to movement in four categories: goods (primarily nontariff barriers, such as the quality requirements that kept almost all foreign beer out of Germany), services (such as barriers to the opening of bank branches across borders), labor (such as country-specific professional requirements for doctors and lawyers), and capital (such as currency exchange controls).

In late 1991 leaders of member states agreed via the Maastricht Treaty to still another set of substantial amendments to the Treaty of Rome. The treaty set a goal of joint foreign and security policy, and it targeted a common defense policy. It officially was a "Treaty on European Union." The 250-page accord also specified European Monetary Union (EMU), a joint currency under a single central bank. Eleven members subsequently agreed to introduce a joint currency for electronic transactions in 1999 and to issue joint bills and coins in 2002. It is important to understand that the European Monetary Union involves much more than just a common currency. In order to make it work, participating countries had to converge economically around very similar inflation rates, interest rates, government deficits, and government indebtedness.

Map 9.1

The Treaty of Rome itself, as well as the Single Act and the Maastricht Treaty, have demonstrated the principle of the periodic "big steps" that neofunctionalists claim are necessary to keep the integration process moving. As the EU gradually and irregularly moved up the scale of economic integration (deepening), it also expanded geographically (widening). The original six members of the organizations leading to the EU were Belgium, the Netherlands, and Luxembourg (known collectively as BENELUX), France, Germany, and Italy. After vetoes of British membership by France in 1963 and 1967, the EU accepted Britain, Denmark, and Ireland in 1973. Greece gained membership in 1981, and Spain and Portugal entered in 1986, doubling the initial number of states. In 1995 Sweden, Finland, and Austria joined, bringing the total to 15 states (see Map 9.1).

Further widening became more problematic, because it involved moving out of Western Europe and into the former communist countries, which did not have long experience with either democracy or free trade. In 1997 the EU leaders invited Poland, the Czech Republic, Hungary, Slovenia, Estonia, and Cyprus to negotiate entry. "Preliminary talks" began with Latvia, Lithuania, Romania, Bulgaria, and Slovakia. One problem that this round of widening caused was the anger of Turkey at being left out of even the second group and at having the Greek-dominated government of Cyprus included. The EU explained the decision in terms of the human rights record of Turkey (especially with its Kurdish minority). Turks saw it as the action of a Christian club.

Performance and Controversies

The deepening and widening of the EU are the best indicators of its performance and both point to the great success of the experiment in integration. The initial purpose of the foundational organization, the European Coal and Steel Community, was to help Europe end the frequent and devastating interstate wars that had raged across it, especially World Wars I and II. There has been no war among member states since 1945 and peace has deep support. Although Europeans still think of themselves first as Danish, Irish, Dutch, or German (perhaps as Bavarian), and only secondarily as European, the public support for the integration process has been extensive and consistent.

Although economic integration and peaceful relations were the primary goals, the EU has gone much further than that. It organizes its activities into three "pillars." Pillar One is very wide, including policy on agriculture, transport, environment, energy, and research and development. It also includes taxation, culture, and regional and social funds to help less-developed areas of the Union. Pillar Two is common foreign and security policy. Pillar Three is justice and home affairs. That includes asylum and immigration policy, external border control, and the fights against international crime, drug trafficking, and terrorism.

As in any political organization, there is contention. One problematic area is the Common Agricultural Policy (CAP). Put into place in the early years after the Treaty of Rome, the CAP pays heavy subsidies to farmers throughout the EU. Although a valiant effort to protect a depressed sector, those subsidies absorb about one-half of the EU's annual budget and result in large food surpluses. Attempts to export those surpluses create conflict with countries around the world.

Most of the rest of the EU budget goes to regional and social funds that support poorer members of the Union. The number of "poorer" members increased when expansion brought in less-developed European states like Spain, Portugal, and Greece. Because future candidates for membership are poorer than current members, both net donors to the EU budget (like Germany, Britain, and France) and current net beneficiaries (like Portugal and Greece) have concerns.

As in the UN, the larger and richer countries of the Union also complain about the voting rules. For instance, Germany has 22 percent of the EU population, but only 11 percent of the votes in the Council of Ministers, 16 percent in the Parliament, and 10 percent of the commissioners (*The Economist*, May 31, 1997, 12). At the other extreme, Luxembourg has 0.1 percent of EU population, 2 percent of the votes in the Council, 1 percent in the Parliament, and 5 percent of the commissioners. Discussions on voting rules (and contribution formulas) are regular and inevitable features in an evolving organization. With further expansion, these problems could intensify for larger members, as could the potential for deadlock in a system that requires large majorities or unanimity for decisions. The Treaty of Rome initially foresaw majority voting after 1966, but the French blocked it.

Most fundamentally, the controversies will continue to center on deepening and widening. Monetary Union will lead to debates about further coordination on fiscal policy. Cooperation on foreign policy and security are permanent issues. Some in Brussels liken the integration process to riding a bicycle—you must keep moving forward or you will fall over. Some in state governments believe that the process has gone far enough and that the analogy does not hold—the process can stop and still protect its gains.

Other Regional Economic Organizations

Many other regional economic organizations have come into existence during the postwar world. In fact, the World Trade Organization identified 76 such groupings since 1948, half of which came into being in the 1990s. Yet none has had the success of the EU. Members of the once competitive European Free Trade Association gradually joined the EU. In 1991 the former communist countries of Eastern Europe disbanded their Council for Mutual Economic Assistance (CMEA or Comecon). In 1961 Kenya, Uganda, and Tanzania established the East African Common Services Organization (EASCO), which became the East African Community in 1967, but collapsed in 1977. The disproportionate benefit reaped by Kenya was one factor that undercut that organization. The Latin American Free Trade Association (LAFTA) lasted from 1960 to 1980. Other efforts, including one in Central America, also faltered.

Two special problems plague all regional economic organizations, especially those that involve countries of the Third World. First, especially among LDCs, exports are frequently competitive (similar or identical raw materials) rather than complementary, so that the possibility of expanding trade can be limited. Second, differences in levels of development prove troublesome, and instead of economic well-being spreading to less-developed countries and equalizing incomes within an organization, resources (such as capital and skilled labor) often concentrate in more advanced areas and disparities intensify. That is, **backwash effects** (the concentration) prove stronger than **spread effects** (Myrdal 1957). This is similar to the concentration of industries like steel, automobiles, filmmaking and microcomputers in particular American cities.

In spite of a history littered with failure, regional associations have in recent years gained new life on all continents. In Africa, the Southern African Development Community (SADC) ties eleven adjoining countries to post-apartheid South Africa. This is the economically most dynamic area of sub-Saharan Africa and the SADC aims to eliminate tariffs and create a free trade area by 2004. Unfortunately, the 1998 war in the Congo deeply divided members.

In Asia, Indonesia, Malaysia, the Philippines, Singapore, and Thailand created the Association of South East Asian Nations (ASEAN) in 1967. Brunei joined in 1984 and Vietnam in 1995. Although primarily economic and relatively successful, the organization also considers issues of joint political importance. ASEAN members plan to phase out tariffs on most manufactured and agricultural goods by 2003. The Asia-Pacific Economic Co-operation forum (APEC) brings together leaders from North America and Asia, including Australia and New Zealand—but it is truly a forum rather than a regional association.

It is the Americas that have spawned the two economically largest and most ambitious regional associations outside of Europe. In 1988 the United States and Canada agreed to establish a free trade area, and Mexico joined in 1994. Negotiations to extend it to Chile began in 1995. In 1995 Argentina, Brazil, Paraguay, and Uruguay completed the initial agenda of the Southern Common Market or Mercosur (Mercosul in Portuguese). Although exempting many goods, Mercosur not only eliminated tariffs, but set common external tariffs, thereby becoming the second largest custom union in the world (after the EU). Its name indicates an aspiration to be a common market, but it has much to accomplish before it becomes one. Chile and Bolivia joined Mercosur in 1996.

At a Summit of the Americas in 1994, the United States proposed a Free Trade Area of the Americas (FTAA) that would incorporate the NAFTA and Mercosur countries, as well as other hemispheric members. To successfully negotiate such agreements, governments benefit greatly when their legislatures provide **fast-track authority.** Such authority means that an agreement subsequently brought to the legislature will receive an "up-or-down" vote not subject to amendments by special interests that would then require renegotiations with all foreign partners. The U.S. Congress declined to give fast-track authority to the Clinton administration, considerably complicating chances of success for the FTAA.

A Liberal Governance Model?

The changes in the United Nations and the European Union since the end of the Cold War have been so substantial and so rapid that it is difficult to keep up with them, much less to forecast where they might be leading those organizations and their member states. Do these developments indicate a coming triumph of liberalism over a state-centric order? More specifically, are states and interstate conflict losing their centrality in global politics? As Ferguson and Mansbach (1998) point out, humans have organized their sociopolitical lives through a variety of "polities," including families, citizens, firms, empires, and states. Over time various polities have risen and fallen in importance, and at any given point in time they coexist, overlap, layer, and nest.

There are many reasons to call for caution about assertions of fundamental change in our global governance systems. Most importantly, realist images of the world have a very long historic record upon which to draw, and that record suggests that the anarchy of the state system will invariably give rise to reassertion of state power and interstate conflicts. The period of euphoria about peace in the 1920s is a potential analogy to the current period. The League of Nations came into existence in January, 1920, with 24 members, growing to 48 by the end of the year (De Conde 1978, 91–96). Although the United States did not join the League, peace movements in the country boomed and a large disarmament contingent forced an initially reluctant U.S. administration to negotiate naval force limitations with other powers (naval forces were the strategic weapons of the day). Interstate agreements on arms control continued to grow throughout the decade, culminating in the 1928 Pact of Paris (Kellogg-Briand Pact) committing its 15 signatories to renounce war and to settle disputes by "pacific means." A World Disarmament Conference convened in 1932 and again in early 1934. Yet in spite of all that progress toward peace and global governance, in 1938 Germany annexed Austria and the slide into World War II began.

The United Nations is playing an increasingly important role in building a global community both through its activities with respect to peace and security and through its much broader, generally functionalist activities. The European Union, by deepening its cooperation and by broadening its membership, is re-shaping the European map. Together these and other international organizations are changing human governance in ways that affect not only Strasbourg, France, but potentially the world.

It is not, however, the creation of a "superstate" that we see in Europe. It is something that leaves states intact while it imbeds them in a more complex form of governance. Some portray it as a **Europe of concentric circles,** in which the innermost countries have proceeded furthest toward political integration, and the extent of integration drops as the circles become larger. For instance the "Schengen" group of European countries, which have abolished all border controls, began with only 7 members in 1995 (it reached 15 in 1998). Initially only 11 countries joined the European Monetary Union. Others suggest that such an image is too tidy, and that the circles of integration overlap, depending on the issue area. This last image carries labels such as **variable geometry** or Europe à la carte.

These concepts have increasing relevance beyond Europe. In economics there is one set of overlapping circles (see Figure 9.3). France, Germany, and the BENELUX countries are often seen as the core of Europe. They are joined in a central circle by the other members of the EU. A greater circle is the Organization of Economic Cooperation and Development (OECD), which adds non-European members. The Group of Eight major industrial states is a subcircle within the OECD overlapping with both NAFTA and the EU.

In security there is another set of circles, interacting with those in economics, and not particularly neat themselves. The four countries that have established a Eurocorps are at the center: France, Germany, Belgium, and Spain. Somewhat

Figure 9.3 Complex Governance

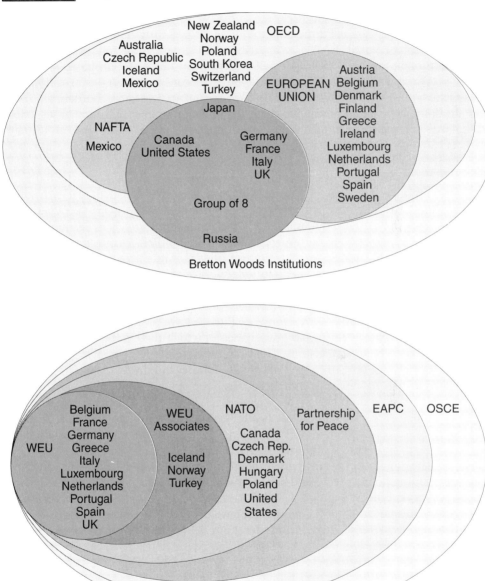

broader is the Western European Union, established in 1955 with the aim of creating a unified European military. It enrolls most EU members, but has failed to develop any significant institutional structure. NATO has a broader membership and also greater power. Its Partnership for Peace reaches further and the Euro-Atlantic Partnership Council (EAPC) even further. The Organization for Security and Cooperation in Europe (OSCE) adds all of Central and Eastern Europe.

We could identify still another set of partly concentric and partly overlapping circles with respect to environmental issues. For instance, countries bordering on both the Baltic and Mediterranean Seas have their own groupings. Still another set shapes global governance on human rights. The Council of Europe has grown from 10 members in 1949 to 40 in 1997; membership requires protection of human rights and democracy. The Council serves in part as a waiting room for the European Union.

Complicating further the image of evolving governance, substantial pressures for devolving authority to subunits of states have intensified rather than disappeared. Belgium adopted a federal constitution in 1979 providing considerable autonomy to Flanders, Wallonia, and French-speaking Brussels. A Basque regional government took power within Spain in 1980. In the 1980s France granted Corsica its own assembly and Spain allowed the Catalans, Andalucia, and Galicia to redevelop regional institutions. German federal government gives much power to 16 Länder (states). In 1997 Scots voted for their own parliament and increased regional autonomy. The list goes on and on.

Some of the nationality groups of Europe have advocated a truly "international" approach to European governance in which they, rather than traditional states, would be the basic units. The Committee of the Regions has 222 members and strongly supports the principle of **subsidiarity** in European governance. That principle calls for governmental functions to be pushed down to the lowest level at which they can efficiently be performed. Among the primary interests of the Committee of Regions are public health, education, youth, and culture. These issues are, of course, at the core of national identities, making the Committee in essence the protector of ethnicity.

The devolution of much government downward, as well as the movement of selected functions upward and beyond the state, has occurred in the United States as well as in Europe. Figure 9.4 shows the ratio of federal civilian employees to total federal, state, and local government employees in the United States over time. Although the relative increase of federal government in World War II is obvious, so is a long-term decrease in the share of the federal level.

In short, governance is becoming both variable in geometry and multilevel (Marks, Hooghie, and Blank 1996). States are sharing power with both subregions and multicountry organizations. We might call this evolving model, with both variable geometry and multiple layers, **complex governance** (Hughes 1993, 1995b). This complexity of organizational development suggests that it might be better to look at the European Union not as the embryo of a superstate or a supernation, but as one key organ in the embryo of an altogether new form of human governance. It is a form of governance compatible with functionalist expectations that humans will ultimately create government that "delivers the goods."

Figure 9.4 Federal Employment as Portion of Total U.S. Government Employment

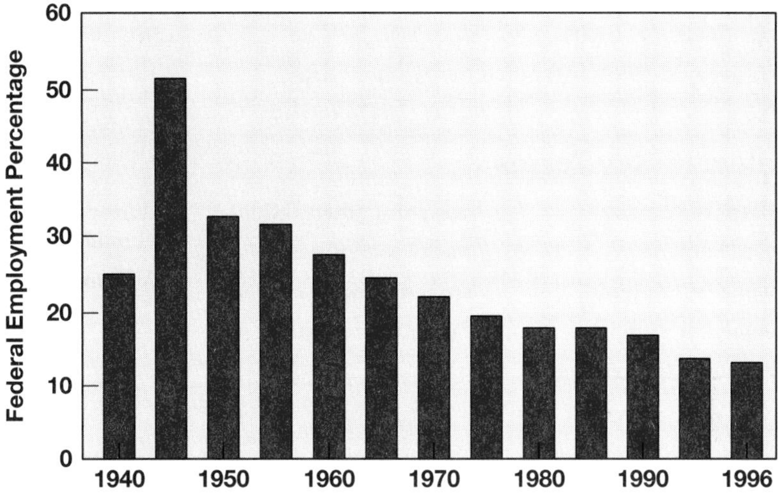

Note: Data are civilian employment, and the two series are not completely compatible.
Sources: Information Please Almanac 1998, 126; *The New York Times Almanac 1998*, 139.

It must be emphasized, however, that traditional states remain very much in charge of the gestation process and that we can see at most the outlines of a new world order. To put the process in context, consider the relative capacity of various levels of governance as indicated by the numbers of personnel and budgets at those levels. In 1998 the EU Commission employed only 15,000 people, of whom about one-fourth were translators. In contrast, nearly 3 million civilians served the U.S. federal government, and U.S. state and local governments had about 14 million employees. Only about 1.2 percent of the GDP of the EU flowed in the 1990s to EU institutions, compared with the 50 percent that European state governments took. The budget of the EU was about $90 billion, that of the entire UN system approximated $18 billion with all peacekeeping included, and U.S. federal expenditures were nearly $1,600 billion.

With respect to identities, in 1997 only 5 percent of the citizens of the 15 EU states reported that they felt "European only," while 45 percent reported that they identified only with their state (*Eurobarometer* no. 47, October, 1997). Still, another 51 percent reported feeling both European *and* the nationality of their state (including, presumably, many citizens of Strasbourg). And for at least two decades, large majorities of those with an opinion have supported European integration and their state's membership in the EU.

Conclusion

The United Nations today is stronger than any global organization of states has ever been. Global communication and transportation systems have undoubtedly created more of a global community than has ever existed among humans. The

European Union is a unique arrangement among states in which they have already and voluntarily given over considerable elements of sovereignty to a central body. Potential members clamor at the gate. The Cold War is over, and Western liberalism, with its emphasis on democracy and human rights, has declared victory (Fukuyama 1989). All is well with the world?

Selected Key Terms

collective security

peace keeping

dispute resolution

democratic deficit

deepening (integration)

widening (integration)

backwash effects

spread effects

fast-track authority

Europe of concentric circles

variable geometry

subsidiarity

complex governance

Constructing Global Society: Identities and Ideas

The Middle East is perhaps the most dangerous spot in the world. Domestic and international political turmoil are intense, and the region that cradled many ancient civilizations gave birth to the first major war of the post–Cold War era (that of UN-sanctioned forces against Iraq in 1991).

A power politics perspective helps us understand the Middle East. Five states in the region (Saudi Arabia, Kuwait, Iran, Iraq, and Abu Dhabi) collectively possess more than 60 percent of world oil reserves. Historically, Britain, France, and Germany extended their influence into the area to assure themselves a share of those energy resources. After World War II the United States became the primary external actor, seeking to continue the flow of oil to its allies and itself. For instance, it sent naval forces to the Persian Gulf during the Iran-Iraq war (1980–1988) to protect oil tankers. Many in the United States saw the war against Iraq after its take-over of Kuwait as necessary to protect the oil flow from the region by denying Iraq a doubling of its oil reserves to nearly 20 percent of the world total.

KEY WEB LINKS

www.ucis.pitt.edu/reesweb
www.departments.bucknell.
edu//russian/chrono.html
www.russiatoday.com/
www.arab.net/
www.israel-mfa.gov.il/
www.usis.usemb.se/terror/
index.html

States in the region have played the great powers against each other in efforts to assert their own independence. For instance, Egypt resisted early post–World War II pressures from the United States and Britain to enlist in anti-Soviet alliances, and in 1955 it turned to Czechoslovakia for arms. The United States responded by canceling its support of the project to build the Aswan Dam. Egypt subsequently turned to the Soviets for support in building the dam. In 1972 (after completion of the project) the Egyptians complained of inadequate Soviet support, threw their Soviet advisors out, and turned back toward the United States. Egypt effectively used the most important source of power it had, namely the desire of both superpowers to deny its allegiance to the other.

It is, however, impossible to understand the Middle East through the lens of interstate power politics alone. How, for instance, do we explain the series of wars (1948, 1956, 1967, and 1973) between Israel and its neighbors? Explanation requires understanding that Israel is a Jewish state, newly formed in 1948, in a region dominated by Moslem peoples (see Map 10.1). Even while dispersed throughout the world in what is called the **diaspora,** many Jews retained a sense of community, and the Holocaust of World War II greatly reinforced it. The Palestinians who lived in what is now Israel and the West Bank (there were only 60,000 Jews there in 1920 but 600,000 Arabs) also had a community identity (Boyd 1987, 114). They fought the international declaration in 1948 of the Jewish state called Israel (by which time there were 600,000 Jews and 1.1 million Arabs in Palestine) and enlisted neighboring Moslem states in their cause. Power has been important in creating and sustaining Israel, but the conflict is fundamentally one of competing religions and nationalisms.

Community identities and ideals also unite many peoples throughout the Middle East. For example, the predominantly Arabic inhabitants of the region share a culture and identity. Between 1958 and 1961, Egypt and Syria actually merged to create (temporarily) the United Arab Republic (UAR), abolishing national citizenship and labeling themselves simply Arabs.

In 1945 regional states formed the Arab League. The league has sponsored a common market, an Arab Development Bank, an Arab Press, and many other cooperative projects (Plano and Olton 1988, 324). The separate peace treaty that Egypt signed with Israel at Camp David in 1978 dealt a serious blow to Arab unity, and the league suspended Egypt until 1989. Nonetheless, a 1980 survey of people in Arab countries found that "eight out of ten respondents believed that the Arabs belonged to a single nation, and that they were culturally distinctive" (Dawisha 1986, 10). In 1991 the Iraqi army briefly captured the Saudi town of Khafji. Someone telephoned the town's hotel and the Iraqi soldier who answered declared "I am for the Arabs, for Arabism. . . . See you in Jerusalem." Ironically, even in a war pitting Arab states against one another, the ideal of pan-Arabism motivated soldiers.

Most of the Middle East is also Moslem, and the Middle East is the fount of Islam. Although a shared religion reinforces the common Arabic identity, Islam is sometimes also divisive. It has two main and competing sects, Sunni and Shiite. Iran is predominantly Shiite Moslem. Iraq's population is 60 percent Shiite and 35 percent Sunni, but the Sunnis control the government. Desire to overthrow the Sunni government of Iraq underlay the Iranian refusal to break off its war with Iraq, even after it pushed Iraq out of Iranian-claimed territory.

Why do the Palestinians and Israelis have such an enduring conflict? (Although the Oslo declaration of 1993 facilitated direct discussions, it did not bring peace.) Why has the Islamic Republic of Iran displayed such strong antipathy toward the United States? Why did the Egyptian leadership's signature on a peace treaty with Israel put it at odds with many of its own population? Why have many Palestinian and Israeli women joined forces in an attempt to end the conflict among their peoples? Identities and ideas help explain these and other aspects of politics in the Middle East.

Map 10.1

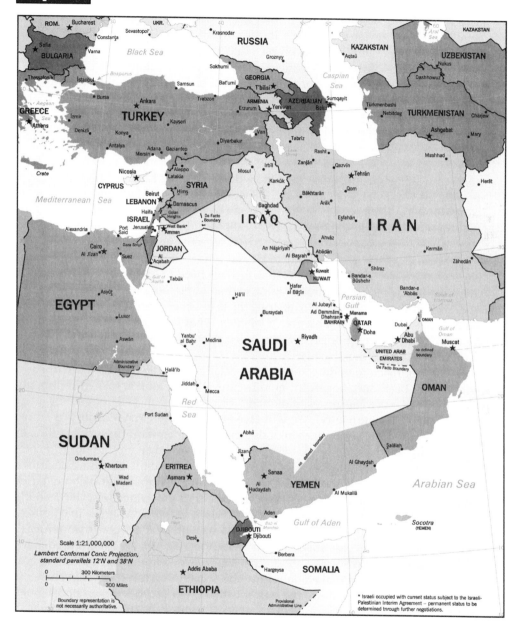

Social (De)Construction

The world is not simply states in interaction with each other. Nor is the world merely a collection of individuals interacting in the pursuit of enhanced well-being. The world is much more complex than these often useful simplifications of realism and liberalism. Our identities structure our interactions. It matters whether we are female or male, black or white, Kurdish or Greek, Jewish or Muslim. Our beliefs and values also structure our interactions. In politics (local and global) it matters whether or not we believe in slavery, whether or not we believe that females and males have equal rights to participate in politics, and whether or not we believe that there is one true religion.

To understand how identities and ideas shape global politics and how they come into being, we must first map the world in terms of them. To put it in a different way, we need to "deconstruct" the world in terms of identities and ideas. Instead of building a model of the world up from rationally interacting states or individuals, we need to look carefully at that world of identities and ideas in an attempt to understand what is there and how it came into being. That is not always easy, because we are part of that world, and our position in it can strongly influence what we see. Even our language, which we need to understand that world of identities and ideas, reflects our position in that world. Because those who attempt to deconstruct the world tend to mistrust the insights of others and even their own, such analysis can become obscure. "*Question:* What is the difference between the Mafia and a deconstructionist? *Answer:* A deconstructionist makes you an offer you can't understand." (Inglehart 1997, 20)

Our approach to understanding the socially constituted or structured world will be very basic and, hopefully, not obscure. We will look in turn at commonly recognized identity categories (nationality or ethnic group, religion, family, race, gender, class, and humanity). We will give extra attention to nationality or ethnic group, because of its importance in understanding contemporary world politics. In each case we will be attentive to two categories of ideas that are commonly associated with the identity category. First, we will look at "relational ideas." That is, we will consider the ways in which the various identity groupings draw boundaries around themselves and interact with other identity groupings (e.g., how ethnic groupings draw boundaries and interact). It is important to recognize that "difference" is a close relative of "identity." Second, we will look at "governance ideas" that often derive from particular identity categories (e.g., the way race-based identity led to apartheid in South Africa). After that survey, we will ask if there are any generalizations we can make about how the socially constituted world changes. Table 10.1 summarizes some of the concepts that the chapter discusses and should be a helpful reference.

Nations and Nationalism

The emergence in Europe of modern states, geographic units with relatively fixed territories and an independent government, interacted with the growth of nationalism. As the new states took shape, the appeal of political and religious univer-

Table 10.1	A Typology of Social Constructs	

Identity Grouping	Relational Ideas	Governance Ideas
Nation	Nationalism	States (nation-states)
	Self-determination	Fascism
	Nonintervention	
	Ranked and unranked ethnicity	
	Secession	
	Irredentism	
	Genocide/ethnic cleansing	
Religion	Imperialism	Theocracy
	Conversion	Empires
	Fundamentalism	
	Clash of "civilizations"	
	Culture wars	
Family	Nuclear/extended	Monarchy
	Family-based criminal groups	Confucianism
Race	Racism	Apartheid
	Slavery	
	Genocide	
Gender	Sexism	Gender-exclusive governance
	Engendered language	Gender-inclusive governance
	Labor division	
	Rights division	
	Feminism	
Class	Hereditary/social mobility	Feudalism
	Income/wealth distribution	Capitalism
	Class consciousness	Communism
Humanity	Ideologies	Liberal democracy
	Human equality	Socialism

sality, in the form of the Holy Roman Empire, declined, and peoples ceased looking outside the local environment for artistic and social standards (including the use of Latin for literature). **Nationalism** is a sense of collective identity or "we feeling," and a **nation** is a group of people bound together by nationalism.

What were the forces that supported the growth of European nationalism? Among other factors was the development of common languages, aided in turn by advances in printing and the spread of literacy. Before the thirteenth century, the Fancien dialect, which came to be the root of modern French, was spoken only in a relatively small area around Paris (Deutsch 1966, 43). The invention by Guttenberg of movable-type printing in 1436–1437 facilitated the adoption of selected dialects by broader populations; it would have been almost impossible to accommodate the wide variety of European dialects with individual written languages.

Sets of shared characteristics, such as language, literature, culture, race, or religion, reinforce collective identity. They do so in large part because they facilitate communication. It is no accident that "commun" serves as a root for both communication and community. Communication capabilities may or may not require a common language, but do require common concepts, shared experiences, and an essentially similar culture.

The French Revolution and the French Revolutionary and Napoleonic Wars (1789–1815) define an important period in the growth of modern nationalism, comparable to the position of the Thirty Years' War in the growth of the state. In an earlier era, Louis XIV (1643–1715) made his famous and egotistical pronouncement *L'État, c'est moi* (I am the state), differentiating the state from the people. During the French revolution, however, the larger population effectively captured the state. In 1789 the Declaration of the Rights of Man and Citizen decisively rejected the position of Louis XIV: "Sovereignty resides essentially in the nation; no body of men, no individual, can exercise authority that does not emanate expressly from it" (Rejai and Enloe 1981, 39). The character of the military illustrates one impact of this capturing of the French state by the French nation. Before the revolution, armies tended to be relatively small and to recruit mercenaries or those with a personal loyalty to the king:

> Foreign units of the French army were composed typically of Swiss Guards, and Irish units were also used when the French could recruit them. Scottish regiments were regularly found in the services of Holland. The French Army before the Revolution was half-composed of men who were not French; and the army of Frederick William I was one-third foreign. (Rosecrance 1963, 20)

In 1791 the French instituted mass conscription, the *levée en masse*, to protect and extend abroad the popular gains of the revolution. Those citizen armies went abroad for the greater glory of the French nation, not the French king. Napoleon's large armies helped accelerate the emergence of nationalism outside of France, making other states require the support of similarly popular armies.

Nationalism spread throughout Europe in the nineteenth century. The European revolutions of 1830 and 1848 reflected nationalistic passions (as well as commercial and aristocratic class antagonisms) and were advance warnings of the threat to the multinational Austrian empire. Before about 1800, state building most often preceded the creation of nations within Europe, but increasingly thereafter nationalism began to redefine states. The formation of a German state (in 1871 with the success of Prussia in the war against France) and an Italian state (roughly 1861 with the coronation of Victor Emmanuel II) followed the growth of nationalist fervor. This pattern has continued through to the current day as the Irish, Hungarians, Jews, Palestinians, Kurds, Croats, Tamils, and many others have acquired, or sought to acquire, control of their own state.

Although nationalism became a strong state-building force within Europe and around the Mediterranean, in the rest of the world many new states resulted from reactions against colonialism rather than from nationalism. The process in the Third World often has had more in common with the sixteenth- and seventeenth-century developments that created early European states like France and Britain than with the nineteenth-century emergence of Italy and Germany. One reason for the contemporary weakness and instability of many less-developed countries is their need *simultaneously* to build a modern state and to create a real nation.

The Modern Nation System

Nations pose some difficulties for the neat model of realists—states interacting with other states in a constant struggle for power and security. On one hand, nations reinforce states when the boundaries coincide; the loyalty and commitment of nations to their own states constitutes a source of tremendous power. On the other hand, nations can undercut and even destroy states in a manner that makes them global "actors" in their own right. As Conor Cruise O'Brien (1988) characterized nationalism, "the stuff is like fire; you need it to warm you, but it can destroy you if it gets out of control."

Some writers use the term **nation-state** interchangeably with country or state. The label implicitly recognizes the importance of nations and states to each other. To the degree that it implies a coincidence between nations and states, however, it is often misleading. We will therefore not use the term. Writers often inappropriately use the term *international system* as a synonym for interstate system (so regularly that this book fails fully to break the convention). When we think about it more carefully, however, there really does exist an **international system,** with nations as constituent elements rather than states. What does the modern international system look like?

Nietschmann (1987) estimated that there exist approximately 5,000 distinct "communities" in the current world of fewer than 200 states. This is consistent with the approach of linguists, who believe that 10,000 years ago, at the beginning of the Neolithic or agricultural revolution, there were about 15,000 languages, but that only 5,000–6,000 survive now (Krauss 1992). Many current languages do not exist outside of a single village. No more than 200 to 250 of them have a million or more speakers. Indigenous or native peoples, sometimes called the **Fourth World,** speak most of the endangered languages. For example, some of the roughly 560 tribal groupings of Native Americans in the United States no longer have any native language speakers. Roughly 300 million people around the world now fight a losing battle for cultural survival.

About 600 linguistic groups have more than 100,000 speakers and are therefore potentially viable nations in the modern world. In most cases, however, several coexist in single states. Nielsson and Kanavou (1996, 1) declared that "only about 30 of the world's 191 states would meet the test of near congruence between the members of a nation and the inhabitants of a state." Fifty-three states contain five or more significant ethnic groups. At least one-third of the members of 67 ethnic groups live outside of their primary state and members of 175 groups are dispersed across at least two states. Gurr (1997) identified 270 "politically significant" nonsovereign peoples whose rights are at risk in current states.

When the self-identification of a minority ethnic group is intense enough, that people often constitutes a nation wanting its own state. Some or many Basques in Spain, Sikhs and Muslims in India, Kurds in Iran/Iraq/Turkey, Uighurs in China, Dinkas in the Sudan, French-speakers in Canada, Scots in the United Kingdom, and Tamils in Sri Lanka do not consider themselves to be part of the nation dominating their state and do not want to be part of the state as currently constituted. These conflicts almost invariably spill over from one state to the larger state system. We look first at the intrastate issues and then return to those that affect interstate relations.

Nationalism Within States

International conflict in the international system is more pervasive than interstate conflict in the interstate system, and much contemporary conflict is at the intersection of the two systems (nationalism-based civil wars in states). Using a very inclusive definition of war, Nietschmann argued that 86 of 120 wars in the late 1980s pitted indigenous nations against states. He called that very messy conflict an undeclared *World War III.* In 1996 all but one of 27 armed conflicts in the world were internal to states (Sollenberg and Wallenstein 1997, 17). Frequently in such situations, nations seek to capture or create their own state in a process called **self-determination.**

In some cases the "we feelings" that drive nationalism give rise to a sense of superiority, however, and in turn, that gives rise to "they feelings," the identification of out-groups. When the bases of nationalism lie in common "race" or religion, intense nationalism sometimes becomes linked with racism and militant fundamentalism. Either can lead to efforts to conquer and subordinate, or even exterminate, inferior groups. **Genocide,** the systematic slaughter of a population group, is the most extreme form of nationalistic conflicts, but unfortunately it is not rare. In addition to the murders in Germany of 6 million Jews and others in World War II, there have been nearly 50 more episodes since 1945, taking the lives of 9–20 million people from 70 or more ethnic and religious groups (Gurr 1997, 16).[1]

The ideology of **fascism** glorifies the nation and the collective will, taking nationalism to an extreme that has led to genocide. The entire nation replaces individuals or classes as the fundamental social unit of importance. A powerful state is the political manifestation of the successful nation. In the words of World War II Italian dictator Benito Mussolini:

> The State is the guarantor of security both internal and external, but it is also the custodian and transmitter of the spirit of the people, as it has grown up through the centuries in language, in customs, and in faith. And the State is not only a living reality of the present, it is also linked with the past and above all with the future, and thus transcending the brief limits of individual life, it represents the immanent spirit of the nation. (Ingersoll and Matthews 1986, 231)

Basically fascist parties, calling themselves nationalist, grew throughout Europe in the 1990s in response to increased immigration and unemployment.

What causes nationalism to result in violence? It is important to remember that, although there may be an innate human tendency to identify in-groups and out-groups, nationality and relations among groups are social constructs. Although there are always some historic or cultural differences between nations, it often takes a political entrepreneur (like Hitler) to mobilize people around ethnicity and to turn them against others. One basis for mobilization of identity is a perception by a group of its deprivation relative to and often by another group. Germans before World War II believed themselves to be economically deprived relative to the Jewish population.

We should distinguish two more physical patterns of relationship between nations within a state (Horowitz 1985). One pattern is that of **ranked nations**—that is,

---

[1] Although the Holocaust is best known, other genocides are well documented. These include the deaths of about 1 million Armenians in Turkey at the turn of the century, of as many as 3 million in Kampuchea in the 1970s (Sivard 1987, 30; Harff and Gurr 1988, 364), and of unknown numbers of Kurds in Iraq and Dinkas in the Sudan during the 1980s.

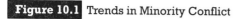
Figure 10.1 Trends in Minority Conflict

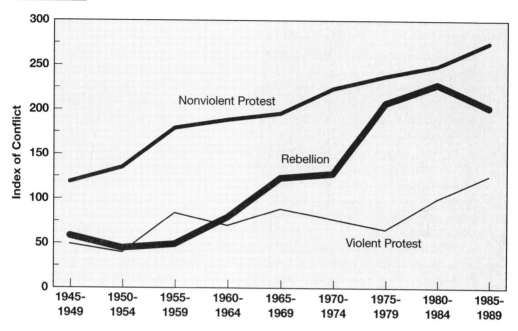

Source: Ted Robert Gurr, *Minorities at Risk* (Washington, DC: United States Institute of Peace, 1993), 101.

one group has a clearly higher social position than the other(s). The Tutsis in Rwanda and Burundi gained such a position relative to the Hutus via military conquest, as did the higher castes in India. In other cases, unranked nations coexist within a society more or less side-by-side. Like the French- and English-speaking Canadians, each grouping contains a full range of social strata. The economic and social interdependence of ranked ethnic groups *can* create a stable society, even one that evolves into a traditional class system like the Indian castes. On the other hand, when conflict does become overt in a ranked system, it can be an extremely violent battle for control, simply because the groupings cannot escape from each other. In contrast, unranked ethnic groups commonly have their own geographic bases and **secession** from the state to create a new one based on the nation is frequently a possibility. Conflict is very common, but like the "velvet divorce" between the Czechs and Slovaks, *can* also be mild. Of course many populations, like the Serbs and Muslims in Bosnia, exhibit a mixture of ranked and unranked relationships.

The triggers for feelings of relative deprivation may accompany modernization (Deutsch 1966). It is therefore not surprising that nationalistic conflict is increasing in this modernizing era (see Figure 10.1). Advances in literacy can spark conflict because it leads (as it did much earlier in Europe) to battles over the written language and over the language for education. Industrialization can also contribute to nationalism, because groups benefit differentially or because pressures for homogeneity of workers can create a backlash (Gellner, 1983). Even the early stages of democratization, as in Eastern and Central Europe, can remove repressive control that once dampened nationalistic conflict. Ultimately, however, democracy may become sufficiently strong to *accommodate* the tensions, as in Canada (Gurr 1993, 137).

Nationalism and Interstate Relations

Nonintervention in the affairs of other states is a principle closely tied to the sovereignty of states. It is, however, a (fundamentally realist) social construct and other principles compete with it. In particular, Woodrow Wilson presented his famous 14 points to structure the peace settlement at the end of World War I. He included the national self-determination principle in an attempt to defuse the problem of nationalism.

States regularly use the self-determination principle to thwart the nonintervention principle. In the name of self-determination a state controlled by a nation that recognizes fellow nationals in an adjoining state will frequently seek to incorporate those individuals and their land into the state, a desire known as **irredentism.** Before World War II there were Germans in Czechoslovakia and elsewhere, not just in Germany. German irredentism was a primary cause of the war. Self-determination and irredentism share the goal of identifying the state with the nation. Today, Hungarians express concern about their fellow nationals in Romania (specifically in Transylvania). Pakistan sees fellow Moslems in Indian Kashmir. NATO countries intervened in Bosnia and Yugoslavia during the 1990s in the name of both self-determination and the protection of human rights.

There are at least two other ways in which national conflict can spill across state boundaries, even in the absence of a multistate nation. First, refugees from nationalistic conflicts commonly move across boundaries. Gurr (1993, 92) estimated that more than half of the world's refugees in 1992 were in flight from ethnic conflict. Second, states can simply use national conflict as an excuse to intervene in other states. Libya sent forces into Chad over a 20-year period, nominally in support of Arabic populations in the north, but more fundamentally because it claimed a strip of Chadean territory.

Problem Cases

Failure of national and state borders to coincide has caused much of the greatest suffering in the twentieth century, including that in World Wars I and II. The catalyst of World War I was the assassination in Sarajevo of the Archduke Ferdinand, heir to the Austro-Hungarian throne. The reactive material into which that catalyst was thrown, however, consisted of a state incorporating various nationalities in addition to the Austrian and Hungarian: Serbian (national "brothers" of the assassin), Czech, Polish, Romanian, and so on.

Hitler's Germany justified its irredentist aggression before World War II as necessary expansion of the German state borders so as to include the entire German nation. Germans, it said, lived also in Austria, Czechoslovakia, and Poland, and wished to be part of the German state. A general acceptance by other states of the self-determination principle partly rationalized and even explained their failure to resist the naked aggression.

Israel and Palestine   World War II no more successfully extinguished the fires of nationalism than had World War I. On the contrary, the Holocaust reinforced a sense

Table 10.2	Location of Palestinian Refugees		
Location	**In Camps**	**Not in Camps**	**Total**
Jordan	238,188	1,050,009	1,288,197
West Bank	131,705	385,707	517,412
Gaza	362,626	320,934	683,560
Lebanon	175,747	170,417	346,164
Syria	83,311	253,997	337,308
Total	991,577	2,181,064	3,172,641

Sources: UNHCR, "UNHCR by numbers" (http://www.unhcr.ch/un&ref/numbers/table3.htm), June 15, 1998; Palestian Refugee ResearchNet, "Palestinian Refugees: An Overview" (http://www.arts.mcgill.ca/MEPP/PRRN/proverview.html, June 15, 1998).

of nationality among many Jews and intensified pressures for a corresponding state. Resistance of Arab Palestinians to the creation of the Jewish state of Israel and the eventual displacement of about three million Palestinians from traditional homelands (in the British mandate of Palestine) now fuels Palestinian nationalism.

Table 10.2 provides data that indicate the depth of the remaining problem. It shows where Palestinian refugees reside. Since the formation of Israel, Jordan has become a largely Palestinian state (they may ultimately dominate it). Although Palestinians lived throughout the Middle East even before the formation of Israel and prior to the 1973 Arab-Israeli war in which Israel occupied the West Bank and Gaza Strip, many in the Palestinian diaspora wish to return and most desire a Palestinian state. On the other side, there were 4.5 million Jews in Israel in 1997; the Israeli population has a density of 690 per square mile, relative to 332 in more fertile France. In 1987 riots in Gaza initiated the *intifada* or general uprising pitting the two claims for land against each other. The roots of the conflict run very deep.

The Former Soviet Union   Another area where nation and state borders fail to correspond is in the former Soviet Union, the last of the large European multinational empires. The others that divided much of the world among themselves in 1914, the Austro-Hungarian, the Ottoman, and the less formally integrated world empires of the British and French had fallen apart earlier in the face of the same divisive nationalism.

Approximately 100 ethnic groups uneasily made their home within the former Soviet Union. Only about half of its total population was Russian, and other ethnic groups were growing more rapidly (some Russians said, "They are winning in the bedroom"). Desire for full independence from the Soviet Union was especially strong in the Baltic Republics of Estonia, Latvia, and Lithuania, which have complex histories of independence and subordination. With *glasnost* in the Soviet Union, new nationalist organizations flowered in each of the Baltic republics. In 1989 Lithuania and Latvia passed laws moving the Republics toward economic sovereignty. In 1991 the Republics received independence and began the dissolution of the Soviet Union.

The newly independent states continue to have ethnic problems. Only in Russia, Azerbaijan, Lithuania, and Armenia do the native populations reach 80 percent

Table 10.3		Ethnic Republics of the Russian Federation		
Republic	**Population (thousands)**	**Native Population (percent)**	**Russian Population (percent)**	**Other Population (percent)**
Adygea	432	22	68	10
Baskortostan	3,943	22	39	39
Buryatia	1,038	24	70	6
Chechnya	1,270	58	23	19
Chuvashia	1,338	68	27	5
Dagestan	1,802	80	9	11
Gorno-Altay	191	31	60	9
Kabardino-Balkaria	754	48	32	20
Kalmykia	323	45	38	17
Karachay-Cherkessia	414	31	42	27
Karelia	790	10	74	16
Khakassia	567	11	80	9
Komi	1,251	23	58	19
Mari El	750	43	48	9
Mordovia	963	33	61	6
North Ossetia	632	53	30	17
Tartarstan	3,642	49	43	8
Tuva	309	64	32	4
Udmurtia	1,606	31	59	10
Yakutia	1,094	33	50	17

Note: Chechnya here includes Ingushetia.
Source: Courtesy of the Central Intelligence Agency, *Map 730319 (R00535) 11–93.*

of the total. In the former Soviet Union as a whole, 75 million people reside outside of their republics. The Russian Federation itself has ten republics in which Russians are a minority (see Table 10.3). A variety of nationality groups continue to protest or fight in support of greater autonomy or outright independence (as Armenians do in Azerbaijan and Chechnyans and Tartars do in Russia). Religious differences reinforce many ethnic divisions. For example, Christian Armenians in a region of the largely Muslem Azerbaijan Republic called Nagorno-Karabakh have demanded that the borders be redrawn to place them in the Republic of Armenia. War erupted in 1990.

Mass migration has been one consequence of nationality problems in the former Soviet Union. Between 1991 and 1995, more than 1 million Russians left Kazakstan, which is now a predominantly Kazak state.

Former Yugoslavia Yugoslavia's disintegration proved even more traumatic than that of the U.S.S.R. The former state consisted of six republics: Serbia, Mon-

Map 10.2

tenegro, Croatia, Slovenia, Bosnia-Herzegovina, and Macedonia (see Map 10.2). In 1991–1992 the last four of these declared their independence and other states soon recognized all but Macedonia (Greece protested that new state's use of the name). Slovenia, the most ethnically homogeneous of the group, won its independence with a spirited military campaign. Croatia, with a Serbian minority of less than 10 percent, fought an extensive civil war for independence. Ethnically complex Bosnia (formerly 44 percent Muslim, 31 percent Serb, and 19 percent Croat) broke down in especially vicious civil war, marked by Serbian expansion over 70 percent of the territory and **ethnic cleansing** (a combination of mass expulsions and genocide) of large areas. Religion again reinforced national divisions. Whereas Serbs are predominantly Eastern Orthodox, Croats accept Roman Catholicism. Muslim populations in Bosnia frequently became the victims of both. In 1998 protest began to grow within the Muslim and ethnically Albanian population of Kosovo, a province of Yugoslavia. The Serbs claimed Kosovo as the spiritual home of their own culture and suppressed the movement. Russia, with similar problems in Chechnya and historic ties to the Serbs, resisted military sanctions. In 1999, NATO attacked Yugoslavia on behalf of the Kosovars, in spite of Russian opposition.

Africa   No area in the world, however, can match the nationality problems of Africa. Colonial escapades of the Europeans drew state borders during the late nineteenth century with almost total disregard for national or tribal boundaries. In the Berlin Conference of 1884–1885, imperialists made adjustments to those borders simply with pen and ruler on a map of the continent. In a continent with many tribal groupings, this created multinational states and arbitrarily split nations by state boundaries. Only four sub-Saharan countries (Lesotho, Somalia, Cape Verde, and the Comoros Islands) are composed of single national groups. Other African countries contain as many as 126 tribes (Tanzania) and seldom

Figure 10.2   Ethnic Groups in Africa

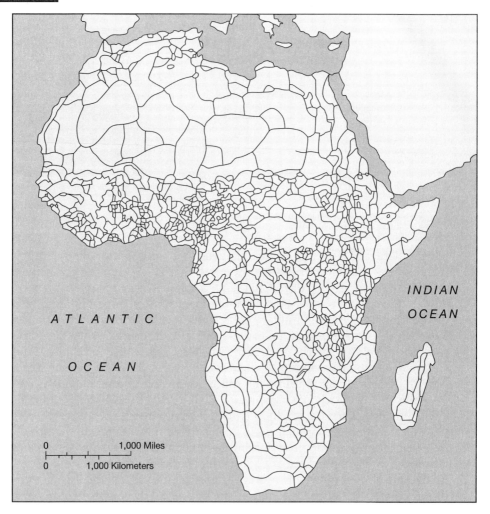

Source: Martin Ira Glassner and Harm J. de Blij, *Systematic Political Geography,* 4th ed. (New York: John Wiley and Sons, 1989), 532. Copyright © 1989 by John Wiley & Sons. Reprinted by permission of John Wiley & Sons, Inc.

encompass fewer than 3 or 4. Figure 10.2 shows the ethnic patterns on the continent, and it looks little like the political map of Africa in the front of this volume.

We could also have focused on *unsatisfied nationalisms* in India, China, Romania, or Kurdistan. The continuing and perhaps even increasing nationalism of the contemporary world, coupled with growing pressures in many arenas for interstate cooperation, led Lincoln Bloomfield to label ours the "Age of Nationalism Without Autonomy" (1988, 14).

Religion and World Politics

Stalin once disparaged the role of religion in world politics by asking about the Pope, "How many divisions does he have?" The fact is, however, that neither the history nor the contemporary state of world politics can be explained without interweaving the history of religion.[2] For instance, both military conflict between Christianity and Islam and their fruitful exchange of ideas frame much of European and Middle Eastern history since A.D. 622, the first year of the Islamic calendar. Within a century of its founding, Islam had swept through Spain and to within 100 miles of Paris, until Charles Martel's victory in the Battle of Tours arrested its northward progress. At the other end of the Mediterranean, Moslem forces laid siege in 716 to Constantinople, then the head of the Byzantine empire. They failed, but the city fell to Islam seven centuries later. In 1529 the Ottoman empire in the West reached the gates of Vienna. Even in 1878 much of the Balkans remained under its control.

This Islamic onslaught helped reverse the decentralization that had characterized Europe since the end of the Roman empire. The Catholic church took a leading role in reestablishing broader political-social order. It organized the first crusade in 1097–1100 to "recover" Jerusalem. By 1250 Christian forces had pushed Islam out of all of Spain except Granada. Governments on both sides were *theocratic*, basing their claim to power on divine sanction.

Christianity (like Islam) suffered internal schisms that frequently erupted into warfare. In 1517 the Augustinian friar Martin Luther posted 95 theses against indulgences on the door of the Wittenburg castle church. Thus began a revolution (the Reformation), challenging established church institutions, especially their control over doctrine and the conditions of salvation. The Thirty Years' War (1618–1648) had many interacting and overlapping causes: power struggles among leaders, personal loyalties and feuds, and even emerging nationalisms. The terms of settlement of the war, however, with the Peace of Westphalia, showed the primacy of religion:

> And as for the original cause of the war, religion, the delegates agreed merely to reestablish the principle laid down at the Peace of Augsburg in the previous century: each prince would determine the religion of his people now, even if he was a Calvinist. As a result the Hapsburgs drove all Protestants from their land, and many of the Lutherans and Calvinist princes compelled their Catholic subjects to choose between conversion and emigration. (Garraty and Gay 1981, 590)

The interaction of subsequent European imperialism and religion was also close. Although the superior technology and power of the Europeans would almost certainly have driven them abroad and to conquest regardless of religion, the cross and sword supported each other.

> Missionaries appear to have only indirectly imperial aims, but the conversion of souls in tribal societies often rested upon imperial protection and had imperial consequences. A Gikuyu proverb from East Africa reflects the relationship: "One White

---

[2]O'Brien (1988, 3) traced the linkages between nationalism and religion, going back to the Hebrew Bible in which "God chose a particular people and promised them a particular land."

Man gets you down on your knees in prayer, while the other steals your land."
Christianity appeared to many African tribes the ritual aspect of imperialism.
(Doyle 1986a, 170)

In contrast to Latin America and Africa, widespread *conversion* failed in
much of Asia, largely because of the stronger political systems that the Europeans
found there:

By late in the sixteenth century the number of Japanese Christians may have been as
high as 150,000. Whole domains of western Japan were converted when their daimyos
became Christians. . . . From the time of Hidyoshi [1582–1598], however, a reaction set
in. Japanese rulers . . . began to suspect that European missionary activity might be a
prelude to political conquest by the Spanish king [as they knew it had been in the
Philippines]. (Garraty and Gay 1981, 637)

The modern era appears to be characterized by a somewhat greater tolerance of
alternative religions (Table 10.4). There are many important exceptions, however. Despite the best efforts of Mohandas Gandhi, he could not bridge the gaps between the
Moslems and Hindus in India. When independence from Britain came in 1947, the
colony split into predominantly Hindu India and predominantly Moslem Pakistan.
Approximately 800,000 people died in the conflict accompanying partition and the resettlement of peoples across the new borders (Sivard 1987, 30).

The religious conflicts within India did not cease with partition. That country has a population that is 83 percent Hindu, 11 percent Moslem, 3 percent Christian, 2 percent Sikh, and 1 percent assorted other. One major problem currently is

Table 10.4   World Religions (by percent)

	Africa	Asia	Europe	Latin America
Christian	48.2	8.6	76.4	92.9
Muslim	41.3	22.2	4.4	0.3
Nonreligious	0.5	26.4	18.0	3.9
Hindus	0.3	22.4	0.2	0.2
Other	9.7	20.4	1.0	2.7
Total	100.0	100.0	100.0	100.0

	North America	Oceania	World Total
Christian	86.4	83.7	26.5
Muslim	1.9	1.3	15.3
Nonreligious	7.8	11.9	36.3
Hindus	0.5	1.1	10.8
Other	3.47	2.0	11.1
Total	100.0	100.0	100.0

Source: *The World Almanac and Book of Facts 1998* (New Jersey: K-III Reference Corp., 1998), 654.

in the Sikh community. Some nationalists seek to establish the new state of Khalistan, the "land of the pure." Sikhs in her own bodyguard assassinated Indian Prime Minister Indira Gandhi in 1984. A second problem for India is in Kashmir, which still has a Moslem majority and which is split between India and Pakistan. The two countries have fought two wars over Kashmir and come to the brink of others.

The ancient Christian-Moslem opposition continues in some regions of the world. One reason for the continued mutual antipathy of Greece and Turkey, and an obstruction facing Turkish efforts to draw closer to the European Union, is the fact that Greece is 97 percent Greek Orthodox and Turkey is 98 percent Moslem. In the Sudan, an effort by the majority Moslem population to impose Islamic law, the *sharia*, on the entire country initiated a civil war in the southern portion of the country, where animist and Christian minorities live. In 1995 the Secretary-General of NATO said publicly that Islamic fundamentalism posed the greatest threat to Europe.

In addition, however, religious divisions *within* Christianity and Islam also continue to fuel domestic and periodic interstate conflicts (seldom does a conflict that reaches the stage of a civil war remain completely free from the involvement of other states). Within Christianity, a civil war between Protestants and Catholics in Northern Ireland continued from the early 1970s into the 1990s, taking 3,600 lives. The conflict has roots in the incorporation by England of Ireland into the United Kingdom in 1801. Long rebellion led to the 1922 partition of Ireland into the independent Republic of Ireland (Catholic) in the south and British Northern Ireland (two-thirds Protestant). It is remarkable that Ireland and the United Kingdom have been able to maintain peaceful relations, even cooperative ones, while the passions of this conflict raged. Perhaps it illustrates the ability of democratic states to limit conflict among themselves. In 1985 the Anglo-Irish Agreement granted the Irish Republic a role in Northern Ireland and committed the British to protect the rights of both Protestants and Catholics, and to prevent discrimination. It reinforced the principle of majority consent for any changes in the status of Northern Ireland. In 1998 the Irish and British Prime Ministers brokered a peace settlement that would end direct British rule, arrange religious power-sharing in Northern Ireland, and institutionalize cooperation with the Irish Republic.

Why have we experienced a wave of fundamentalism in all parts of the world in recent years? Surely the end of the Cold War's clash of univeralisms (discussed later) and the collapse of communist governments that repressed both nationalism and religion are reasons. There are at least two others. First, fundamentalists can be populists who address needs that governments, particularly authoritarian ones, fail to meet. In Egypt fundamentalists assassinated President Anwar Sadat in 1981, but they also provided basic community services. By 1987 they had established 3,000 medical clinics and 6,000 schools. In Latin America the **liberation theology** of some Catholics is a comparable phenomenon. "Base communities" formed around local parishes to serve community religious, economic, and social needs.

Second, *fundamentalism* is in part a reaction against a secularizing liberalism:

Fundamentalists reaffirm the exclusive certainties of their own traditions, with a heightened sense of the boundaries of belonging that separate "us" from "them." Pluralists [liberals], without giving up the distinctiveness of their own tradition, engage the other in the mutual education and, potentially, the mutual transformation of dialogue. To the fundamentalist, the borders of religious certainty are tightly guarded; to the pluralist, the borders are the good fences where one meets the neighbor. To many fundamentalists, secularism, seen as the denial of religious claims, is the enemy; to pluralists, secularism, seen as the separation of government from the domination of a single religion, is the essential concomitant of religious diversity and the protection of religious freedom. (Eck 1993, 92).

In thinking about how the world might come to be structured after the Cold War, Samuel Huntington (1993) portrayed a **clash of civilizations** as the central organizing principle. He posited the solidification of seven or eight culturally based "civilizations," defined primarily by religion, but also by race and sociopolitical system: "Western, Confucian, Japanese, Islamic, Hindu, Slavic-Orthodox, Latin American and possibly African" (Huntington 1993, 25). The fault lines of the contemporary world appear, however, much more complex than that. It is, for instance, questionable to portray a monolithic "Islamic world," combining Indonesian and Iranian Muslims or modern and fundamentalist Muslims within Egypt into a single cultural category. In fact, Hunter (1991) suggested a world in which the orthodox or fundamentalist believers across religions increasingly find themselves in (at least informal, if not organized) opposition to the more secularized or liberal elements within each religious tradition. He referred to this very different cleavage pattern as the *culture wars.*

Family

Family is also a social construct. Consider, for example, how the cultural focus on the *extended family* (involving several generations and many ranks of cousins) has given way in more economically developed countries to the *nuclear family* (father, mother, and the kids). Although there is a great deal of rhetoric devoted to family values, the structuring of broader society based on the family is today often considered an anachronism and sometimes even a pathology. For instance, the disintegration of Somalia into a set of competing clans does not suggest that kinship is a good basis for social order in a modern state.

Historically it has not been long, however, since family dynasties ruled as monarchs in Europe. Even today, *Confucian* values are said to prevail in much of Asia. Confucius was a Chinese sage of approximately 500 B.C. whose system of precepts for the management of society focused on five relationships: parent and child, elder and younger brother, husband and wife, friend and friend, and sovereign and subject. Familial relationships dominate. The overseas Chinese community today is a dominant economic presence through much of Asia, and its strength continues to rely at least as much on family ties as on ethnic ones. Just as the Rothschild family was once able to dominate the European financial system, members of extended overseas Chinese families provide commercial support for each other.

More generally, family ties provide an especially strong basis for the trust necessary to overcome the Prisoner's Dilemma that afflicts relationships among individuals as well as those among states. It is hardly surprising that much transborder criminal activity, from the Italian mafia to the cocaine cartels of Columbia, has relied heavily on family connections. Interestingly, while the Italian mafia heavily use true familial connections, Chinese triads and Japanese yakuza rely on "fictive kinships," through which members "adopt one another as brothers and embrace the gang as their family" (Schaefer 1997, 324).

Race

Although there obviously are physiological differences between peoples, race itself is largely a social construct. Humans have socially defined differences among people based on race, including personality, behavioral, and intellectual ones, that considerably exceed any that genetics define. **Racism** is the social definition of those differences and the behavioral interactions of peoples based on those definitions.

Although treatment of those in other ethnic groups has often been brutal, treatment of those defined as being in other racial categories has been horrendous: dispossession from land and extensive killing of native American peoples, conveniently defined as "red-skinned savages"; pressing into *slavery* of many millions of those from "inferior races," including Africans; genocide or systematic slaughter of millions more somehow defined as racially distinct, including Jews.

Racism remains a very important contemporary social phenomenon. In the United States, where President Jefferson had written that "All Men are created equal" but kept his own slaves, President Truman did not end segregation of the armed forces until 1948. In 1954, when the Supreme Court struck down the practice, there were 17 states in the United States that segregated elementary schools by law. Although blacks had the legal right to vote in the United States as a result of a constitutional amendment that was ratified in 1870, it was in the 1960s that major drives were undertaken in several Southern states to end policies and behavior that denied the right in practice. Such action has tempered or weakened, but not ended racism in the United States. President Clinton's extensive African trip in 1998, the first by any U.S. president, had two overlapping purposes: to help bring Africa itself into the global community by celebrating its diverse cultures and its recent economic and political successes, and to make a statement against racism in the domestic community.

All those who have been defined as races have suffered from racism. The word for slavery comes from the word "Slav," because that people was enslaved by various other European peoples. Concerns about the rise of China and its possible challenge to the largely Caucasian West often do not deeply hide fears of the "Yellow Hordes." Many Japanese regularly indicate not only their prejudices about fellow Asians, but those towards Caucasians and, especially, black Americans. Throughout Latin America, there is a correlation between lighter skins and higher social position; the revolt in the Mexican state of Chiapas is in significant part a protest by native peoples of their treatment in the broader society.

Few have suffered from racism as much in recent years as black Africans. Some racism has been internal to the continent. One of the most rapid genocidal slaughters on record was the killing of perhaps 800,000 Tutsis and sympathizers by Hutus in Rwanda in April and May, 1994 (*The Economist,* October 12, 1996, 48). Although economic class and history contribute strongly to differentiating those two peoples, they both understand each other to be physically distinct. In light of the warnings that had circulated for months prior to that spasm of violence, why did the outside world not intervene in any significant way? And why did the UN forces give up in Somalia so relatively easily, also in 1994, when they were prepared to stay the course in Bosnia? For that matter, why did it take until 1990–1991 to end apartheid in South Africa? Racism may be a social construct, but its effects on world politics are real.

Gender

Women and men clearly are different, something that not only the French celebrate. But why did women not obtain the right to vote in the United States until 1920? Why are they still dramatically underrepresented among economic and political elites everywhere in the world (Scandanavian countries are a partial exception)? Why do women work longer hours than men everywhere in the world and receive less pay—or none at all for work in the home? Why did the Colorado state legislature fail in 1998 for the third consecutive year to enact legislation protecting girls from female genital mutilation? Why must women cover their heads in Muslim countries and risk being slain in Algeria if they do not? Why is there widespread infanticide of female babies in Asia and increasingly widespread selective abortion of female fetuses? Why does physical violence toward women and sexual exploitation of them remain so pervasive around the world?

The obvious simple answer to almost all of these questions is **sexism.** Just as racism defines differences that the definers use to justify mistreatment, sexism socially defines differences between the sexes, and again the definers discriminate on those bases. Sexism runs very deep, even in supposedly liberal traditions. For instance, the Enlightenment period in Europe celebrated the individual, laying the foundation for liberalism. Specifically, it celebrated the male individual. More specifically, it celebrated the white male individual, because even Voltaire believed black ones to be inferior. The (white male) Founding Fathers of the United States wrote a Declaration of Independence that declared that "all Men are created equal"; then they went on to write a Constitution that did not need explicitly to exclude women from suffrage because their exclusion in practice was obvious. Although it would be a mistake to glorify the role of women in precapitalist economies, the spread of capitalism separated men and women's work roles, effectively devaluing women in societies that measure worth in terms of income. Men became responsible for productive work, leaving for women the unpaid reproductive work.

Language reinforces the devaluation of women, in fact their exclusion from importance. It does matter that the commonly used, generic gender in English is masculine, that humanity is mankind, that diplomats or leaders are statesmen, and that even God is commonly portrayed as a man. Derogatory slang terms for racial or ethnic groups devalue those slandered; engendered language devalues those omitted.

Logic and research make clear that the devaluing and exclusion of women have great real social costs. In Japan (and to some degree in all countries) women can receive advanced education, but find it extremely difficult to move into productive jobs in private industry or government, imposing real losses on the economy.

Research on developing countries suffering from rapid population growth has demonstrated repeatedly that the most effective way of reducing birth rates is to educate women. Yet in 1995 the female literacy rate in developing countries was 61 percent, compared to 79 percent for males.

Female literacy rate has increased, and progress exists elsewhere. Microloans have become increasingly popular tools of economic development programs, because they provide small amounts of capital (perhaps $100–$200) to individuals who have business plans and high rates of success in repayment. Women often receive most of the money in such programs. Chapter 7 documented the election of a number of women as heads of state in the last decades of the twentieth century. Chapter 9 noted the Fourth World Conference on Women in Beijing in 1995. In 1998 the Women's Environment and Development Organization announced that 70 percent of governments had drawn up plans to further women's rights and 66 countries had created national offices for women's affairs. Although the global figure is only 13 percent, women now hold about 40 percent of the seats in Scandanavian parliaments. The world is moving slowly and painfully from governance that excludes women to gender-inclusive governance.

Feminism fights sexism. Feminists seek to value the experiences and contributions of women equally with those of men. Feminists vary greatly on their approach to fighting sexism. Liberal feminists believe that the human rights movement and liberal democracy provide the space within which women can obtain equal rights. Constructivist feminists believe that the problem is deeper.[3] They see the devaluation of women so deeply embedded in social constructions (including language, beliefs, and norms) that it is necessary to actively explore, explain, and confront those constructions (to deconstruct them) and, in essence, to reconstruct those elements of society. Moreover, they see close relationships between the social constructions that disadvantage women and those that disadvantage certain races and economic classes. Thus they often believe that the social change needed must be deep and pervasive.

Class

It has been said that the rich are different. They have more money. Class is another social construction that can build actual differences into chasms. If money alone defined class, it would be obvious that there are continuous scales of both income and wealth within societies and therefore gradations of class. Yet we have socially fastened on the terms "working" (sometimes "lower"), "middle," and "upper" as the divisions in U.S. society, labor- and capital-owning classes as the divisions in the Marxist social hierarchy (widely used in industrial societies), and a complex and hereditary caste system in Indian society. The type of jobs that people do generally interact with income and wealth in defining class. That is quite rigidly true in caste systems. The terms "blue collar," "white collar," and even "pink collar" (mostly female social service positions) similarly link employment to socioeconomic status.

Societies vary greatly in the degree of social mobility that exists across classes within and between generations. When British Prime Minister Tony Blair said that

---

[3]The variety of feminist perspectives is greater than that conveyed here. See, for example, Peterson and Runyan (1993), Marchand and Parpart (1995), and Pettman (1996).

he wanted to create a classless society in Britain, he was only one of a long line of British leaders that have recognized mobility in Britain to be limited, in part because of the dialect and educational differences that reinforce class divisions.

Governance and class have almost always been closely linked. Feudal societies, built on agricultural economies, rigidly reinforced hereditary divisions between the peasant class and the aristocracy that claimed ownership of the land. Capitalist societies, built initially on industrial economies, have governments in which money improves chances of both entering government and influencing it. Karl Marx helped identify the class-basis of government. He also urged the creation of class consciousness among those disadvantaged by their exclusion from power. While famous for that analysis, he is more notorious for having proposed a system of government, namely communism, that the working class theoretically would control. In the attempts to implement communism, a political "class" (called the nomenklatura in Russia) came to dominate.

The second part of this text will elaborate Neo-Marxist concepts and use them as one of the lenses by which we examine the global political economy. We therefore do not discuss class at length now.

Humanity: Universalisms

Each of the social constructs that we have discussed tends consciously to differentiate and divide humans from each other. Religion is a partial exception, because it is sometimes a nationalistic force that seeks to define the boundaries of the community and to establish control within those boundaries (as with the Sikhs in India) and sometimes a universal philosophy (consider the Christian missionaries) calling for all of humanity to unite under one set of beliefs.

In this section we focus specifically on universal philosophies, and although religious movements sometimes are universalistic, the universalisms of greatest importance today are secular, political **ideologies.** "A political ideology is a system of beliefs that explains and justifies a preferred political order, either existing or proposed, and offers a strategy (institutions, processes, programs) for its attainment."[4]

We distinguish ideologies from philosophies. Philosophy means love of wisdom. The theories of philosophy help us understand, whereas the strategies and goals of ideology propel us into action. Unfortunately, the distinction is not always so clear in practice. What constitutes a philosophy for one person, such as socialism, may be a call to arms for another. The distinction becomes blurred because ideologies invariably draw on philosophies for understandings of human nature, the relationship between the individual and the group, and the proper character of governance.

Ironically, universalisms tend to divide rather than to unite humanity. Not everyone wishes to march behind the same universalistic flag. For that reason, realists agree on the inappropriateness of basing the application of power on universalism—whether religious or secular:

> The Wars of Religion have shown that the attempt to impose one's own religion as the only true one upon the rest of the world is as futile as it is costly. A century of almost

[4]Herbert Waltzer's definition cited in Foster and Edington (1985, 34).

unprecedented bloodshed, devastation, and barbarization was needed to convince the contestants that the two religions could live together in mutual toleration. The two political religions of our time [liberalism and Marxism] have taken the place of the two great Christian denominations of the sixteenth and seventeenth centuries. Will the political religions of our time need the lesson of the Thirty Years' War, or will they rid themselves in time of the universalistic aspirations that inevitably issue in inconclusive war? (Morgenthau 1973, 542).

Historic Universalism

The French Revolution gave us one of the early secular ideologies. Although that Revolution was in part nationalistic and therefore exclusively French, it was also universalistic and, at least initially, liberal. It offered the promise to peoples throughout Europe that people rather than sovereigns could rule governments, that social justice could be an aim of government, and that the rationalist ideals of the Enlightenment could guide the application of law. Napoleon's armies initially went abroad to defend the Revolution against the efforts by the Prussians and Austrians to take advantage of French weakness during the unrest. They used propaganda decrees to assure foreign peoples that France stood behind their efforts to overthrow monarchies (Garraty and Gay 1981, 769). Although Napoleon subsequently installed monarchies in client states (relying heavily on his own relatives), he also brought the Napoleonic legal code and the revolutionary ideals of liberty, equality, and fraternity. The French Revolution thus gave rise to a secular and universalistic ideology that posed a grave threat to the monarchies of Europe. In general, peace will not prevail in a world with a revolutionary, expansionist, and universalistic power.

Modern Universalism: Roots of the Cold War(s)

At the end of World War II the Soviet armies that had defeated the Germans remained in much of Eastern and Central Europe as occupying forces. They supported the installation of communist regimes with leaderships highly subservient to Moscow. The West faced the question of whether these were the actions of a traditional state or the manifestation of aggressive universalism.

The interpretation of Soviet behavior as that of a traditional state rested primarily on the relative absence of natural boundaries to Russia and the difficulty of defense in such an exposed position. Russia historically reacted to its vulnerable position by creating buffers around it, either by incorporating other peoples into the empire or by establishing client states. According to this view, the Soviet expansion into Eastern Europe after World War II was not new but merely reflected the lesson of the Nazi invasion that even more extensive buffers were necessary.

The universalistic interpretation of Soviet behavior also had support. Lenin wrote that "As long as capitalism and socialism exist, we cannot live in peace: in the end, one or the other will triumph—a funeral dirge will be sung either over the Soviet Republic or over world capitalism" (Schlesinger 1967, 47). In 1919 the Soviet Union founded the Third International—the Comintern—to coordinate and control the communist parties around the world from headquarters in Moscow. Following World War II the Soviets established the Communist Information Bureau (Cominform) to organize control over communist countries and parties of Europe.

Among its assumptions were that "war with 'imperialism'—notably the United States—was inevitable" (Macridis 1986, 135)

As in religions, schisms and heresies developed. Albania did not join Cominform. Moscow expelled Yugoslavia in 1948 because President Tito defied Soviet supremacy. Militarized border disputes actually erupted in 1963 between the U.S.S.R. and China in Sinkiang and Mongolia. In 1964 the Chinese exploded their first nuclear bomb, sealing their independence from the Soviets. Yet the Soviet leadership did not give up the effort to maintain unity. The Brezhnev Doctrine declared the right of the U.S.S.R. to eliminate threats to "socialism" in any state, and thus it justified the invasion of Czechoslovakia in 1968 and the overthrow of its reformist regime.

In 1985, however, the party selected Mikhail Gorbachev as general secretary. He held summit meetings with Western leaders, greatly accelerated negotiations on arms control (see Chapter 6), and reduced domestic arms spending. His leadership withdrew all forces from Afghanistan and scaled back various foreign commitments, including those in Africa. Although many in the West maintained their image of the U.S.S.R. as a universalistic power until its collapse in 1991, some revised their portrait of the Soviets even well before the reforms of the 1980s. By 1967 Arthur Schlesinger was able to document a revisionist school of historians who rewrote history about the origins of the Cold War. He contrasted two interpretations:

> The orthodox American view, as originally set forth by the American government and as reaffirmed until recently by most American scholars, has been that the Cold War was the brave and essential response of free men to communist aggression. . . . The revisionist thesis is very different. In its extreme form, it is that, after the death of Franklin Roosevelt and the end of the Second World War, the United States deliberately abandoned the wartime policy of collaboration and, exhilarated by the possession of the atomic bomb, undertook a course of aggression of its own designed to expel all Russian influence from Eastern Europe and to establish democratic-capitalist states on the very border to the Soviet Union. (Schlesinger 1967, 23–25)

Revisionist analysis asks us to reconsider the U.S. approach to the world after World War II and to consider it today. Were (and are) Americans universalistic rather than defensive? Roosevelt had been a member of Wilson's subcabinet and had campaigned for the League of Nations. He and his secretary of state, Cordell Hull, rejected a postwar world redivided into spheres of influence, and they embraced both a global economy and the UN. There were also sphere-of-influence proponents in the United States, most notably the famous diplomat George Kennan, ambassador to the U.S.S.R. and developer of the *containment* doctrine. He argued that the United States should leave the Soviets alone in their sphere but deny them any possibility of expansion. It is easy to see, however, that the Soviets then (or the Russians today) could interpret a system of alliances pressing on their borders not as containment, but as instruments of universalistic aggression.

In the West it is common to claim that "the Cold War is over, and we won." A liberal idealism, with its image of interstate cooperation within a framework of institutions such as the United Nations, the European Union, the World Trade Organization, and a Westward-expanding NATO has gained even more strength than it had at the end of World War II. From one viewpoint, the consolidation of a liberal world order is the ultimate triumph of reason and humanity (Fukuyama 1989). From another, it is the perhaps premature declaration of victory by just another universalism, that of Western democracy and capitalism.

Terrorism: Instrument of the Disadvantaged

Humans appear to have strong needs for the identities that nationalisms and religions help establish. We must benefit in important ways from defining those who are in our family or ethnic groups and those who are outside of them. We establish hierarchies (even when we rail against them) based on race, gender, or class. We can become passionately attached to political ideologies. We construct and embrace those social categories.

Yet ideas do have consequences. These social constructions have been responsible for hundreds of millions of deaths. They have also been responsible for life-long oppression and exploitation of hundreds of millions of other humans. The cycle goes on in part because those who are (or feel) aggrieved cry out for a restructuring of the system, one that will give them their rightful place, perhaps at the top of the system. If they see no other or no easier way, the oppressed may turn to terrorism.

Foundations of Terrorism

Terrorism is not only a modern phenomenon. In the years A.D. 6–135, Jewish nationalists, calling themselves zealots, maintained a terrorist campaign against the Romans then ruling Palestine and against their Greek and Jewish collaborators. After a zealot uprising in A.D. 6, the Romans crucified two thousand Jews (Schlagheck 1988, 16). Zealots used violence, especially assassination, to disrupt Roman rule. Targets were unpredictable but generally public, so that fear would spread. One technique was to use small daggers against Roman officials in crowds and then to disappear into the crush. The Romans took increasingly strong measures to stamp out the decentralized movements, finally deciding after A.D. 135 to expel all Jews from Palestine. That created the scattered community of Jews in exile, the diaspora, which sought for two millennia to return to its homeland. Interestingly, what the Jews did was terrorism; the greater violence of the Roman authorities was "legitimate." It is a disquieting distinction that remains with us in the modern state system.

The techniques of **terrorism** are similar today, and definitions of it generally list several characteristics. Violence, especially against humans, is key. Of all terrorist attacks in 1988, 48 percent were bombings, and 28 percent were arson—in both cases the target is often human life, and the victims are indiscriminate (U.S. State Department 1989, viii). Publicity is necessary. Terrorism becomes a kind of theater, in which the need for media attention and the global spotlight is great. Should the media or public become inattentive or jaded, the level of violence must escalate. Unpredictability is important, as are symbolic targets. Terrorists seek to engender fear and reaction, especially overreaction, by their opponents. They want adherents to flock to their cause—they wish to sharply define community boundaries and to bring within them those who remain ambivalent.

Nationalists undertake a large portion of international terrorism. In terms of the earthquake analogy of Chapter 1, terrorism often reflects a pent-up and growing nationalism for which the state fails to provide any release. Among the most important national groups with terrorist factions today are Palestinians, Sikhs, Basques (in Spain and France), and Armenians (originally concentrated in Turkey but now dispersed in still another diaspora). Sometimes the motivation for terrorism is primarily religious, for instance that of the Shiite groups operating loosely under the guidance of Iran—including the Islamic *Jihad* (Hizballah), which killed 241 American and 56 French marines in a suicidal truck-bombing attack in Beirut during 1983. Still other terrorist groups have ideological motivations. These have included the Baader-Meinhof Gang or Red Army Faction and Red Brigades, both leftist organizations operating primarily in Germany and Italy.

Trends in Terrorism

Through the 1980s, the trends in international terrorism were disturbing. In 1968, 124 incidents occurred globally, but in 1987 the total reached 665 (Figure 10.3). The focal point for nearly half of the incidents in recent years has been the Middle East. Western Europe is the second most seriously afflicted region, followed by Latin America and Asia. Despite the alarm with which the public in Europe and in the United States viewed the trend, terrorism caused only 8,700 deaths globally between 1968 and 1995. Although significant, consider that 12,600 Americans died from falls and 43,900 died in automobile accidents in 1995 alone, and the firebombing of Dresden, Germany, by American forces in 1945 killed about 50,000 civilians in 24 hours (legitimate state violence). Moreover, terrorism declined in the 1990s—the PLO renounced it, and the former communist states quit supporting it.

A major fear is that terrorists will increasingly have access to devastating weaponry. They have already used poison gas on Japanese subways. Were they to gain access to a lethal pathogen (like anthrax) or to a small nuclear weapon, they could dramatically raise the casualty level.

Some states have supported terrorists in a manner analogous to the superpower use of proxy military forces. The United States has identified Afghanistan, Cuba, Iran, Iraq, Libya, North Korea, the Sudan, and Syria as countries that have supported terrorists with financial contributions, training, and even leadership. Terrorist-supporting countries are too weak to directly confront major Western powers (except on their own soil, as in the Iranian hostage crisis), making covert support for terrorism abroad a seemingly viable alternative. The great powers have difficulty retaliating because the terrorist group, rather than the state sponsor, normally claims responsibility. In one exception in 1998, the United States bombed a chemical factory in the Sudan and training camps in Afghanistan for which President Clinton said there was irrefutable proof of ties to the embassy bombings in Kenya and Tanzania.

Lesser powers have long argued that certain use of force against them by the great powers is, in essence, **state terrorism.** For instance, in the absence of a declaration of war, the United States mined harbors of Nicaragua in 1984. The International Court of Justice declared the action illegal. In such examples, too, force is in essence an instrument selected from weakness. Covert behavior indicates an un-

Figure 10.3   International Terrorist Episodes and Deaths

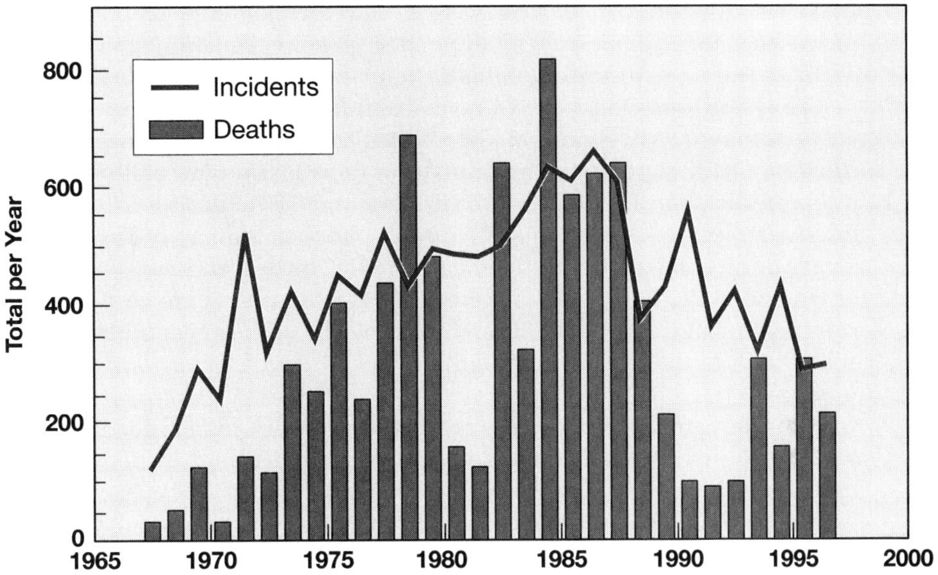

Source: Data courtesy of the U.S. Department of State, Office of the Ambassador at Large for Counter-terrorism, 1992; annual issues of *Patterns of Global Terrorism,* including Office of the Coordinator for Counterterrorism, *Patterns of Global Terrorism 1997* (Washington, DC: U.S. Department of State, 1998).

willingness to accept the brunt of domestic or international public criticism that would result from overt force.

Nearly all of these examples of violence, even those performed in the name of the state, can be attributed to some kind of identity-based idealism. This discussion should not end, however, by leaving the impression that all such idealism is bad. Even hard-core realists often have their favorites; one person's terrorist is another's freedom fighter or patriot. Instead we should conclude by noting once again that neither the simple model of power politics at the state level nor the more complex model of an evolving liberal order is adequate to a full understanding of world politics.

Social Construction

This chapter has mapped (or in a very general sense, "deconstructed") the social constructs or structures of the world, in terms of basic categories of identities, and the relational and governance ideas commonly associated with them. Social structures are highly dynamic. It is obvious that a fourteenth-century peasant from Bavaria would be amazed to be moved forward in time and to confront today's transportation and communications technologies. It should be equally obvious that she would find it easier to learn to drive a car and use a telephone than to comprehend that she was now a "citizen" of a "country" called "Germany," governed as a "democracy," in which she "voted" for a "party." Moreover, she might learn that she had an "occupation" as a "school teacher" and that today she is expected to take her children to a "day care center" and then join the "union strikers" on a "picket line" for "higher wages" and better "pension benefits." Our poor woman would, of course, confront all of this without even being able to read!

How did our world get from there to here? Although it is a gross exaggeration, there are two general approaches to the understanding of social construction. The first portrays that transformation as fundamentally idiosyncratic and unpredictable. The only way to understand it is to describe it in detail with "thick description." Unfortunately, doing so for our woman of Bavaria will give us very limited ability to predict the future for the descendents of another peasant woman in Burundi today, because the starting points are very different (for example, Burundi is already officially a republic with cars and phones) and because the potential alternative paths of social development are so incredibly numerous.

An alternative perspective suggests that there are, in fact, general patterns of social development, related to underlying technological and economic conditions. The philosophers of the Enlightenment believed in social "progress." Their liberal descendents today sustain that belief. Although currently unpopular in academia, this perspective gave rise to a model of developmental processes called **modernization theory** that posits generally similar relationships between economic, social, and political change in countries around the world. It is often said in exaggeration that in modernization theory "all good things go together": economic growth, social change, democratization, and even democratic peace.

Figure 10.4 shows the contemporary relationship between the GDP per capita of countries around the world and the position of women in society. It uses a Gender Empowerment Measure (GEM) to indicate the status of women, based on their representation in economic and political leadership relative to men. A value of "1.0" on the measure would indicate equal representation of women and men, so it is clear that women are not equal, even in the economically most advanced countries. It is also clear, however, that there is a strong relationship between economic level and gender empowerment.

Is it possible to conclude that, if economic growth continues around the world, the status of women will improve also, especially in currently less-developed countries? Those who take a more particularistic, path-dependent approach to understanding construction of social structures would say "no." Some might argue, for instance, that belief systems in the Islamic world are fundamentally different from those in the predominantly Christian countries that dominate the list of economically developed countries. Therefore, women in Islamic societies will not gain additional rights with economic growth. Those who see merit in modernization theory might say "yes," even social relationships in Islamic societies will change as incomes grow. The truth is that a relationship of two variables across countries at one point in time can give a suggestive but not definitive answer to the question about the dynamics of relationship over time (Hughes 1998). All we can know with certainty about social change is that it will be substantial and tumultuous.

Figure 10.4 Status of Women as a Function of GDP per Capita

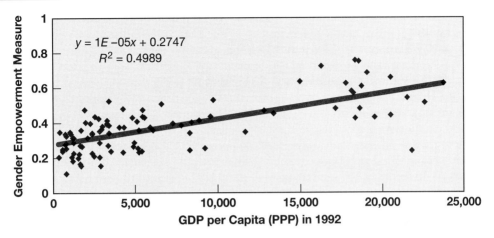

$$y = 1E-05x + 0.2747$$
$$R^2 = 0.4989$$

Source: International Futures (IFs) computer simulation, using data from World Bank and Freedom House. See Barry B. Hughes, *International Futures,* 3rd edition (Boulder, CO: Westview Press, 1999).

Conclusion

Ideas have consequences. Identities, relational ideas, and governance norms motivate individuals to great efforts on behalf of political movements. Realists and liberals may question the rationality of many such motivations and of actions based on them, but they should not doubt their power.

Selected Key Terms

diaspora	fascism	sexism
nationalism	ranked nations	feminism
nation	secession	ideology
nation-state	irredentism	terrorism
international system	ethnic cleansing	state terrorism
Fourth World	liberation theology	modernization theory
self-determination	clash of civilizations	
genocide	racism	

CHAPTER 11

Commercial Liberalism, Mercantilism, and Neo-Marxism

After adjustment for inflation, the world economy has grown at an average annual rate of about 3.6 percent since 1960, more than double the 1.7 percentage rate of growth in global population. The result is that the average human being now has a GDP per capita of more than $6,000[1]—not much different from that of the average U.S. citizen in 1900. Global life expectancy at birth also has risen from 55 to 65 years since 1960. In addition, global trade roughly doubled as a share of global GDP, to 20 percent of the total.

The poorest humans did not share in this economic advance. In 1960 the richest 20 percent of humanity had incomes 30 times those of the poorest 20 percent. By the 1990s the gap had grown to 60-to-1. For example, GDP per capita in Switzerland is over $26,000, but it is only $500 in Ethiopia. That poorest portion of the world remains almost entirely illiterate and largely malnourished.

KEY WEB LINKS

www.duc.auburn.edu/~johnspm/
glossind.html

www.helsinki.fi/WebEc/
WebEc.html

altaplana.com/gate.html

cep.lse.ac.uk/

csf.Colorado.EDU/gpe/
students.html

Do these economic facts have anything to do with world *politics?* Of course they do. Up to this point, however, we have devoted little attention to the world economy, directing our attention instead to issues of conflict, cooperation, institution building, and identify formation. This chapter, introducing Part III of the volume, broadens our perspective to a consideration of the interaction between world politics and economics—to the global **political economy.** Three worldviews, commercial liberalism (a subset of liberalism), mercantilism (an extension of realism), and neo-Marxism (a member of the social-constructivist family), organize most thought about the global political economy.

---

[1]Figures from Sivard (1996), the World Bank (1998), and United Nations Development Programme (UNDP) (1994).

Commercial Liberalism

The extended discussion of liberalism in Chapter 3 pointed out interacting and reinforcing traditions of liberalism: one that focuses on the individual, a second that directs our attention to interaction and exchange (including group interaction), and a third that investigates the development of institutions, formal and informal. Commercial liberalism falls within the second tradition, and even more specifically emphasizes economic interactions. Although large literatures elaborate the relationship between commercial liberalism and democracy (Hayek 1944; Friedman 1962) and between commercial liberalism and international cooperation (Morse 1976; Rosecrance 1986), our focus will be on the more strictly economic theory of commercial liberalism. Table 11.1 summarizes the conceptual and theoretical elements of the commercial liberal, mercantilist, and neo-Marxist worldviews; use it as a reference for the discussion of this chapter.

Concepts

Adam Smith (1723–1790) provided the classic statement of commercial liberalism in his *Inquiry into the Nature and Causes of the Wealth of Nations,* originally published in 1776. He argued that individuals act rationally to pursue their self-interests in trade. He began the discussion of exchange, involving firms (suppliers of goods and employers) and households (consumers and suppliers of labor), that occupies commercial liberal thought to this day.

Individuals (or their firm and household aggregates) come together in markets for **mutually beneficial exchange.** Firms seek to maximize profits, and households seek to maximize income and the utility of consumption based on it. If they act freely and in their rational self-interest, no party will enter into any exchange unless it benefits them. One of the most famous commercial liberals, Milton Friedman, described this mutually beneficial exchange process:

> In its simplest form a [free private enterprise exchange economy] consists of a number of independent households. Since the household always has the alternative of producing directly for itself, it need not enter into any exchange unless it benefits from it. Hence, no exchange will take place unless both parties do benefit from it. So long as effective freedom of exchange is maintained the central feature of the market organization of economic activity is that it prevents one person from interfering with another in respect of most of his activities. The consumer is protected from coercion by the seller because of the presence of other sellers with whom he can deal. The seller is protected from coercion by the consumer because of other consumers to whom he can sell. (Friedman 1962, 13–14)

Theory

Liberal economists draw on an extensive body of theory exploring production, trade, financial flows, and economic development.

Production   Production results from the use of some combination of **factors of production,** especially land (relatively unimportant outside of agriculture), phys-

Table 11.1	Political Economy Worldviews		
Worldview Name(s)	Commercial liberalism	Mercantilism	Neo-Marxism: World systems theory Dependency theory
Central Concepts: Agents/Structures	Individuals Firms-households Markets	States State system Anarchy	Classes (domestic and international) World system: Core and periphery
Values of Agents	Profits Utility	State interests: Power Wealth	Position Share
Central Concepts: Bases of Interaction	Mutually beneficial exchanges	Competition: Protection Subsidy	Class relationships: Hierarchy Domination
Theories: Systematic Descriptions	Production: Capital accumulation Labor productivity Technology Trade: Absolute and comparative advantage Dynamic gains Financing globalization Economic development: Stages of growth Structural transformation Modernization	Strategic trade theory: Externalities Excess returns Creation of comparative advantage	Technology-based production systems Class and social systems based on production Imperialism Cycles of expansion Dependence Dual economy development
Theories: Typical Forecasts	Continued growth Progressive spread of income	Trade wars	Continued crises System transformation
Values of Worldview Proponents	Efficiency Growth	Economic well-being and power of state	Equality Growth
Typical Prescriptions	Laissez faire Solution of market failure problems	Government targeting and protection of select industries	Revolution in the center Autarky or self-reliance

ical capital (buildings and machinery), labor, and technology. Producers reinvest a portion of their profits (earnings minus expenses) in additional physical capital to increase production efficiency, volume, and future profit. *Capital accumulation,* or reinvestment in excess of the wearing out of capital, drives growth. Capital accumulation facilitates *division of labor* and therefore greater efficiency in the production process. In Adam Smith's famous example of the pin factory, he argued that individuals could produce many more pins when they specialized— one drawing out thin wire, another cutting it, another producing pin heads, and so on. Today we can see division of labor at work both within factories and across country borders.

Another important force behind growth is increase in *labor productivity,* the amount of output that an hour of labor can generate. Both accumulation of physical capital and effective divisions of labor can increase productivity, but increased knowledge and skills of the work force also contribute greatly. We can therefore wisely invest in **human capital** via education and training—and even health care.

Liberals agree that investment in both physical and human capital enhances production. That liberal consensus pervades the thought of publics and leaders throughout the Western, developed world and makes those societies commercially liberal. Liberals can disagree bitterly among themselves, however, concerning the relative emphasis on policies that benefit capital or labor. Not surprisingly, the owners of physical capital favor policies that facilitate its further accumulation and the owners of labor support investment in human capital. This division shapes politics within liberal societies and our everyday political labels: modern American conservatives shade support toward capital, and modern American liberals shade it toward labor. Remember (as Chapter 3 made clear) that both modern conservatives and modern liberals in the American political environment share the emphasis on individual human rights and on markets that identify them as liberals, in the classical tradition that we elaborate here.

Trade   Adam Smith recognized that producers have differential access to capital, labor, and other factors of production. They advantageously specialize in the production of that which they can produce most efficiently and engage in mutually beneficial trade for that which they cannot so easily produce. If I am a good tailor (and already have a sewing machine) and you are a good vintner (and have a vineyard in the Napa valley), it hardly makes sense for me to grow my own grapes or for you to make your own clothing. I should make clothing, you should produce wine, and we should exchange our products. We both have an **absolute advantage** in the production of our own one good (that is, we can both produce one good less expensively than can the other).

To extend this example into global trade, consider the positions of England and Portugal. Assume initially that both countries produce only clothing and wine, and do not trade (the top of Table 11.2). Assume further that, using all of their resources, both England and Portugal can produce fifty units of each product. Thus, acting individually, the two countries could each deliver 50 units of clothing and 50 units of wine to their own populations. If the cost of clothing production in England were lower than that in Portugal, however, and England were to specialize in

| Table 11.2 | The Advantage of Trade | | | | | | |

No Trade

	Production		Trade		Consumption	
	Cloth	Wine	Cloth	Wine	Cloth	Wine
England	50	50	0	0	50	50
Portugal	50	50	0	0	50	50

Specialization and Trade

	Production		Trade		Consumption	
	Cloth	Wine	Cloth	Wine	Cloth	Wine
England	120	0	−60	+60	60	60
Portugal	0	120	+60	−60	60	60

clothing, it might produce 120 units. Similar cost advantage and specialization might allow Portugal to produce 120 units of wine. These results of specialization reflect hypothetical absolute advantages of the two countries (Portugal can more easily produce wine than England, because of its climate). If they were to so specialize (thereby increasing productivity) and then trade half of their production with one another, their populations would obtain 60 units of each product rather than 50 units. Obviously such trade is beneficial.

David Ricardo (1772–1823) recognized that in some cases one trading partner might have an absolute advantage in all production. Imagine that you own both the sewing machine and the vineyard. Thus (all else being equal) you can produce both wine and cloth at less cost than I can. Is trade with me still desirable? It is, because I should not sit idle (unless I intend to starve). Instead I should produce what I can produce with the lowest cost as a ratio to yours, because it is in that product that I have a **comparative advantage,** even if you retain the absolute advantage. Perhaps my comparative advantage will be in cloth because I have a needle and thread. Although I may be able to buy little of your wine with my cloth, trade still has value for both of us. Ricardo extended these insights into an understanding of the mutual benefits of trade, even if England could produce both wine and clothing more efficiently than Portugal (or the United States could produce both autos and wheat more efficiently than Mexico).

Modern theory recognizes that trade competition also leads to the adoption of improved technology, thereby creating **dynamic gains from trade.**[2] In fact, in a globalizing economy, dynamic gains may overwhelm the static ones that Ricardo described. Most economic theory and research in the United States and other developed market economies remain generally within this elaborated liberal worldview.

---

[2]Adam Smith speculated about such gains (Sachs 1998, 100).

Financial Flows   Production factors vary in their mobility. Land obviously does not move. Governments severely restrict labor flows across borders (although "electronic immigrants," for example, Indians writing software for Europe, have become common). The restrictions placed on capital flows rise and fall over time, but financial capital remains the most mobile factor of production. Financial capital flows pay for the physical capital of buildings and machinery. Because technology moves with machinery and management know-how, capital flows effectively make technology mobile as well.

Financial flows, absent political restrictions, respond to profit-margin differentials. In general, it makes sense to move capital from capital-surplus to capital-deficit regions. At least a portion of the tremendous gains of stock markets around the world in the 1980s and 1990s came from the higher rates of return that capital obtained as it moved across borders. Globalization is the tremendous surge of global capital flows since 1970, accompanied by lesser but substantial increases in trade volume. Although globalization has broader sociopolitical elements, trade and financial flows lie at its core.

Globalization has many critics (Mittelman 1996; Boyer and Drache 1996). Those with mercantilist perspectives fret about loss of state control, especially over the multinationals that dictate much financial movement. Critics from neo-Marxist perspectives point to growing inequalities when capital owners benefit relative to labor. They tend, of course, to emphasize the costs of capital flows to labor in countries of capital origin, and less often comment on the benefits of those flows to labor in countries that receive capital. Still, the criticism is damning within countries of capital origin, because it suggests that the market and globalization can undercut the very civil society on which, as we have seen, that political liberalism depends (Bell 1976). All critics suggest that massive capital flows, when easily reversible, can create serious economic and therefore broader sociopolitical instability.

Economic Development   Can the Less-Developed Countries (LDCs) transform themselves into more-developed countries? Liberals believe that they can. In general, liberals see the experience of developed, market-oriented countries as a model for development in additional countries. Rostow (1971b) portrayed the development process as consisting of several **stages of growth.** Increases in the rate of investment initiate limited growth, and further increases subsequently fuel the spread of it.

Liberal critics of the stages-of-growth portrayal argue that increased investment is a necessary condition for growth, but insufficient. Significant *structural transformations* must also occur throughout the economy, including a shift from primary goods production to manufactures, an increase in literacy, and often greater ties to the world economy (Chenery 1979). In the 1980s and 1990s liberals also frequently argued that LDCs need to free their economies from heavy state intervention as a prerequisite of economic growth. The broader modernization process in which economic development occurs will involve major structural changes in social, economic, and even political systems.

Liberals have also developed understandings of how the processes of economic growth interact with those of distribution. Simon Kuznets (1966, 217)

Figure 11.1   The Kuznets Curve

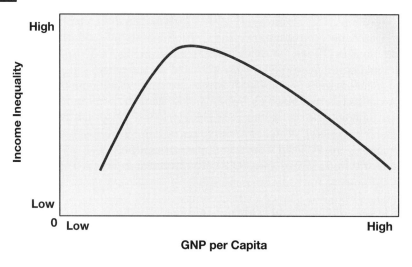

presented one such theoretical perspective. He argued that, in the early stages of industrialization, income inequality increases. One reason is that industrialization, and the benefits it confers, begins selectively, assisting perhaps one region of a country. Further, historically it has benefited the capitalists considerably more than farmers or workers, given large surpluses of labor and the low wages workers therefore have to accept. Over time and with continued industrialization, the income distribution begins to improve again. For instance, industrialization spreads throughout the country and draws in people from even the most backward sectors and geographic areas. This is the spread effect. As industrial employment grows and labor becomes scarcer, wages rise (as is happening in South Korea and Taiwan now). Kuznets also stressed the growing role of government in transferring income within the more economically developed countries. Evidence on the Kuznets theory is mixed and hotly debated.[3] Figure 11.1 presents what has come to be known as the **Kuznets curve.**

Kuznets developed his theory of income distribution and its improvement with continued growth to explain what happens within countries. The same logic might help explain, however, why global income distribution has worsened dramatically since the beginning of the industrial revolution but hope remains that, with time and international spread of industrialization, global income inequalities will lessen.

Values and Prescriptions

The topic of distribution creates difficulties for liberal theorists, in part because the core values of liberals are growth and *efficiency* (maximum production possible with given resources), looked at for the society as a whole. The classical liberal per-

---

[3]Stern (1995) found the right-hand side of the curve more empirically robust. For one of the most extensive analyses, see Adelman (1986). For a comparative test of several theories of distribution see Chan (1989). Stiglitz and Squire (1998) concluded that there is no relationship between growth and inequality.

spective continues to be that distributional issues are largely beyond the scope of economics and are a matter for social decision making and politics. Liberals are more likely to emphasize *equity* (impartiality and fairness) than *equality* (identical income or wealth shares). Classical liberals often argue that an emphasis on efficiency and growth best serves the interests of all, because it will help create a growing pie rather than diverting energy to redividing it.

Prescriptively, support for restraint of government has especially deep roots in liberalism. When Adam Smith developed liberal thought 200 years ago, he reacted against what he saw to be stultifying governmental control of the economy. He was, in essence, a spokesperson for the growing commercial or middle class and its desire for a free-wheeling capitalism against the remnants of the aristocratic and feudal perspective. As we might say today, he wanted to "get the government off our backs." The liberal prescription of *laissez faire* (French for "let do") calls for precisely that. As one joke at the expense of liberalism puts it: "How many politicians does it take to change a light bulb? None, the free market will do it."

Over the years liberals have identified several areas in which government activity may be appropriate, often in reaction to **market failures.** For example, pollution represents a market failure, because decisions by firms or households about production often do not consider the costs pollution imposes on broader society. Some economic sectors, like electricity distribution, are natural monopolies—another market failure. Economic activity in these fields requires such great capital investment that, when one firm is in place, it can manipulate prices so as to reap high profits and simultaneously prevent entry of other firms.[4] Such market failures call out for collective societal action through government.

In addition, society may decide that government should redress income or wealth inequalities. Even Adam Smith recognized the role that government can play in redressing income inequality. He suggested a tax on horse-drawn carriages so that "the indolence and vanity of the rich is made to contribute in a very easy manner to relief of the poor."

Mercantilism

Mercantilism extends the concepts and theories of realism (review again Table 3.1) into economics.[5] For mercantilism, as for realism, states are central actors and operate in an anarchical state system. They use power in the pursuit of security. In its extension to economic concerns, mercantilism elevates wealth to central conceptual status along with power:

> I believe that practically all mercantilists, whatever the period, country, or status of the particular individual, would have subscribed to all of the following propositions: (1) wealth is an absolutely essential means to power, whether for security or for

---

[4]More precisely, a natural monopoly exists when fixed costs are so high relative to variable costs that average cost declines over the entire range of demand (Weimer and Vining 1989, 61).

[5]Not all realists follow the path paved by their concepts into mercantilist economics. Many draw a sharp boundary between international politics and economics, adopting liberal thought in international economics.

aggression; (2) power is essential or valuable as a means to the acquisition or retention of wealth; (3) wealth and power are each proper ultimate ends of national policy; (4) there is long-run harmony between these ends, although in particular circumstances it may be necessary for a time to make economic sacrifices in the interest of military security and therefore also of long-run prosperity. (Viner 1958, 286; quoted in Gilpin 1987, 32)

The philosophy of mercantilism came of age with the modern state and state system, and it dominated political-economic thought during the sixteenth and seventeenth centuries. Adherence to mercantilist theory had consequences for both domestic and foreign policy. Domestically it led to state support for the manufacturing sector and the exports of it (which could secure bullion). For instance, Jean Baptiste Colbert (1619–1683), a leading French mercantilist with the ear of the king, used subsidies and tariff protection to encourage industry, while simultaneously building a large navy in support of commerce and colonization.

Externally, mercantilism required the development and protection of markets. For example, the British Navigation Act of 1651 forbade importation of many goods unless British ships carried them. Subsequent acts required that all goods shipped to the American colonies go through British ports. Parliament did not repeal the acts until 1849.

The linkages between classic mercantilism and imperialism are apparent. The typical colonizing country demanded that the colonies trade only with them. The colonizer dictated insofar as possible what the colonies could trade and at what prices. It used various mechanisms to extract the maximum economic benefit from exchanges with the colonies. The British colonies on the Atlantic coast of North America faced less onerous and complete control than did the Spanish colonies in South America, but they still resented the restrictions on their trade and the taxes (like that on tea) imposed by Britain.

In the post-colonial era, we speak frequently of **neomercantilism.** States no longer value bullion so highly, but they still value wealth in the form of large stocks of dollars, yen, and euros. Many of the modern methods for increasing state wealth are little changed from earlier years: support for research and development, infrastructure development, subsidies to select industries, tariffs, and assorted nontariff barriers to trade, so as to favor exports over imports. Box 11.1, entitled "Mercantilism and Neomercantilism," elaborates.

Neomercantilism, like realism, views the world as zero-sum and conflict prone. The primary source of tension between the United States and Japan today lies in U.S. claims that the Japanese protect their domestic economy while pursuing advantages abroad, in a self-centered effort to improve their own economic condition at the expense of others.

With the end of the Cold War and an increased emphasis on global trading relationships, **strategic trade theory** appeared as a variation of neomercantilism.[6]

[6]Krugman (1986) provided a classic statement, although he later decried the emphasis on interstate competitiveness (Krugman 1994). See also the emphasis on the "New View" in economics by Kuttner (1991) and the popularization of the theory by Fallows (1993). Fallows juxtaposed the German economist Friedrich List and the popularity of his perspective in Japan with Adam Smith and his popularity in North America.

Mercantilism and Neomercantilism

Classical mercantilism emphasized acquisition and retention of bullion as a store of wealth for the state. States could obtain bullion by maintaining trade surpluses with other countries, by plundering, and through exploitative relationships with colonies.

Today we more often view gold and silver as sterile, and we maintain wealth in the form of productive investments such as factories. "Neomercantilism is a trade policy whereby a state seeks to maintain a balance-of-trade surplus and to promote domestic production and employment by reducing imports, stimulating home production and promoting exports" (Blake and Walters 1987, 18).

Certain instruments of neomercantilism may target the domestic economy and only incidentally and even unintentionally improve the international positions of firms:

1. Development of infrastructure. More efficient transportation facilities assist exporting firms.

2. General assistance for industries. Support for research and development subsidies, and the provision of financing for firms provide advantages in both local and international markets.

Other measures clearly assist domestic firms in global competition, and states may adopt them specifically for that reason:

1. Tariffs (taxes on imports).

2. **Nontariff trade barriers (NTBs).** These include quotas, which limit the imports of a particular good. The United States limits sugar imports. States sometimes purposefully adopt health standards, like those the EU uses to exclude some American beef, as trade barriers. Japan has relied on bottlenecks at borders, such as inspection requirements and inadequate numbers of customs agents, to limit some imports. In addition, Japan has historically restricted bidding on many governmental contracts to domestic firms. Such NTBs are a considerably greater barrier to trade than tariffs.

3. Maintenance of an undervalued currency. Many LDCs keep the price of their currency low in order to make their goods inexpensive abroad and to make foreign goods expensive at home.

It is a relatively sophisticated theory with empirical base, and most of its proponents would decline the neomercantilist label. Nonetheless, strategic trade theory's emphasis on state intervention, and particularly on governmental support for selected industries, places it in that tradition. The theory presents several interrelated arguments that a government can improve the welfare of a particular country (quite probably at the expense of others) via intervention in the economy.

Almost all of the arguments of strategic trade theory build on understandings of market failures and efforts to take advantage of or to correct them (Krugman and Obstfeld 1997). First, some industries create externalities. A country might decide to subsidize a high-technology sector because firms within it create knowledge with spin-off benefits to other parts of the economy. Because the firms cannot obtain payment for these secondary benefits, without government help they would invest less than is socially desirable in the sector.

A second argument is that there can be **excess returns** in some industries. In general, profit margins tend to begin at high levels in new industries and then decline as competition grows. If a government could identify emerging industries of importance (such as consumer electronics in the 1960s), it might be able to provide initial and very rewarding advantages to its firms. Logically, as such products become commodities that firms around the world can produce, the governments should move their support to newer industries—like solar energy or biotechnology.

Another type of industry subject to excess returns is one that exhibits "increasing returns to scale." That is, the more a firm produces, the cheaper its unit costs become, because it can distribute very large development costs over more units produced. A number of modern, high-tech industries, including aircraft, exhibit this characteristic. In such an industry, a government can help a company establish a monopolistic position in the global market and, therefore, reap atypically large returns for its shareholders and workers. U.S. government contracts helped Boeing establish a major position in the global aircraft market. A fortunate contract with IBM helped Microsoft establish a similar position in operating systems for personal computers. Because of their increasing returns to scale, once they obtained great market power, it became very difficult for companies of other countries to challenge Boeing or Microsoft.

Other arguments in favor of government intervention in economies and trade tend to be political rather than economic. Perhaps the most common is that "other states do it." In fact, no matter how hard a country works at creating agreements on free trade and institutions to support it, other states continue to intervene in markets. The only way to encourage those states toward free trade may be the logic of tit-for-tat reciprocity. The threat or reality of one state's own trade interventions are necessary to discourage those of others.

The final argument looks to the domestic sociopolitical consequences of free trade. According to the **Stolper-Samuelson theorem,** free trade will reduce the returns to local factors that are relatively scarce (Chapter 7 discussed the domestic-political consequences of this). The gap in wages between skilled and unskilled workers within Britain, the United States, and other developed countries has grown over the last two decades. Because unskilled workers are relatively scarce in those countries (and thus overpaid in global terms), exposure to competition from other countries could explain why their relative incomes have fallen. Therefore government intervention to restrict trade could protect such workers and have social benefit. In direct contradiction of this argument, Jagdish Bhagwati, long one of the major opponents of strategic trade theory, argues that the real reason for the growing income gap is that technological change is transforming the entire global economy and reducing the demand for unskilled workers everywhere, regardless of trade—the knowledge economy requires skilled and professional workers. He argues that education and training are better responses than protectionist policies.

Together the arguments of the strategic trade theorists have shifted the discourse about trade in much of the developed world. The free-trade theory of the classical liberal economists continues to dominate the discussion, but the neomercantilist competition has become more sophisticated.

Neo-Marxism

A third political-economic worldview, a member of the social-constructivist family, is **neo-Marxism** (Holsti 1985). Constructivist thought generally rejects both the individual and the state as the appropriate basic unit of analysis and draws our attention instead to various identities and patterns of social relationship. In neo-Marxist constructivism, two principal units of analysis emerge: the *class,* and the global-political economy, or *world system,* as a whole.[7] Marxist thought, although always rooted in these concepts, has undergone considerable transformation as the world it describes has changed.

Marxist Conceptual Roots

Karl Marx (1818–1883) saw politics in terms of class structures and the interactions of classes within the political economy. He wrote:

> The proletariat and wealth are opposites. As such they form a whole. They are both products of the world of private property. The whole question is what position each of these two elements occupies within the opposition. (Tucker 1978, 133)

For Marx, history maps the ownership of the means of production and the opposition that property set up between the owners—whether slave holders, feudal aristocrats in control of the land, or capitalists—and all others. These economic divisions condition political and social relationships, even values, morality, and religion. More specifically, the dominant economic class controls important institutions, including the state and the church, and uses them to reinforce its position within society.

The system or mode of production changes over time. Marx identified "Asiatic (primitive communist, tribal societies), ancient (slave societies of Egypt, Greece, Rome), feudal, and capitalist" (Ingersoll and Matthews 1986, 137). Different "forces of production" (fundamentally the technology of the era and resources available to the society) characterize each system. So do different "relations of production," the relationships among people in the production process.

Marx argued that the relationships among people (class relations) change slowly, whereas the forces of production (and the technology underlying them) are quite dynamic. Sometimes the class relationships impede change in the forces of production, creating tensions or contradictions (much as we have stressed that tensions often build below the superstructures of world politics). In the face of tensions, class antagonisms harden, setting the stage for a revolution that will usher in a new mode of production. For instance, in the modern or capitalist era, Marx argued that the concentration of wealth in the hands

---

[7]Whereas neo-Marxists limit classes to as few as two and generally assume limited social mobility, liberals recognize multiple social ranks and considerable social flux (Watson 1993, 51).

of capitalists and the impoverishment of laborers frustrate the ability of new production techniques to satisfy the needs of all and will eventually lead to such a revolution.

That Marxist view of class relationships, and of hierarchy and domination in the political economy, differs sharply from the liberal view of economic interactions. Liberals portray individuals interacting in their self-interest, but doing so in a mutually beneficial milieu of market exchanges. Interactions are win-win or nonzero-sum; all can benefit. In Marxist analysis, however, the gains of one class generally come at the expense of another. The classes seek to maintain or enhance their position in the relationship and thereby their share of economic product. The game is win-lose or zero-sum. The world of Marxists is, in this sense, a harsher one than that of liberals and more akin to that of mercantilists.

Marx did, however, not doubt the strength of the forces for technological progress and welfare improvement that capitalism and capital accumulation set in motion. Marx foresaw the spread of capitalism around the globe and approved of it as a progressive force in societies dominated by more primitive modes of production and by feudal class relations. He also foresaw the inability of many capitalists to compete, therefore concentrating capital in a few hands. He further anticipated increasing impoverishment of the masses during the intense struggle for existence and dominance among capitalists. In the long run, only those capitalists who most effectively squeezed wage costs would survive. Ultimately this would lead to an uprising of workers against capitalists.

Imperialism

In the early 1900s, the Marxist forecasts of the spread of capitalism and the concentration of capital appeared to unfold. On the latter point, large firms with a global reach emerged, and absorbed smaller ones. The conditions of workers in many industrial countries, however, improved rather than deteriorated—a trend that both contradicted the Marxist supposition of increasingly antagonistic class relations and appeared unlikely to lead to revolution against capitalism. Those who wanted to build on Marxist theory needed to explain this phenomenon and why it was temporary.

John Hobson (1858–1940) provided the explanation. He argued, as had Marx, that the concentration of income and wealth in the hands of a few, and the removal of income and consumption power from the workers, set up a situation of surplus production. He saw the principal outlet for this surplus in *imperialism.* Such imperialism relieved the society of these surpluses, both through their export and by wasting them on associated militarism.

Lenin picked up many of the arguments of Hobson in his own study of *Imperialism, the Highest Stage of Capitalism,* published in 1916. He quoted Cecil Rhodes, the British industrialist, namesake of Rhodesia (now Zambia and Zimbabwe), and patron of Rhodes Scholarships:

> I was in the East End of London [a working-class quarter] yesterday and attended a meeting of the unemployed. I listened to the wild speeches, which were just a cry for "bread! bread!" and on my way home I pondered over the scene and I became

more than ever convinced of the importance of imperialism. My cherished idea is a solution for the social problem, i.e., in order to save the forty million inhabitants of the United Kingdom from a bloody civil war, we colonial statesmen must acquire new lands to settle the surplus population, and to provide new markets for the goods produced in the factories and mines. The Empire, as I have always said, is a bread and butter question. If you want to avoid civil war, you must become imperialists.[8]

Lenin linked such imperialism firmly to capitalism and saw it as the factor that explained the relatively good condition of workers in the more advanced capitalist states. As the world became divided among capitalist states so that outlets for the surpluses became scarce, however, Lenin foresaw inevitable clash among the imperialist states (like that of World War I, which erupted in 1914). In short, imperialism could prolong the era of capitalism—but not save it.

The truth of Lenin's link between capitalism and imperialism remains contested. Waltz (1979, 24–27) argues that noncapitalist powers such as Rome and Athens also relied on imperialism for various reasons. Thus capitalism is unnecessary for imperialism. Waltz also pointed out that, at the beginning of the twentieth century, England had about half of its capital invested outside of colonies, especially in the United States, implying that imperialism was not necessary for the disposal of surpluses by capitalist states.

Neo-Marxist Theory

Lenin foresaw the imminent end of capitalism in the clash of imperialisms around him. That did not happen, and imperialism, to the degree that it exists today, is very different in form from that of the early twentieth century. Thus Marxist theory again faced the necessity of adaptation.

An important recent development is *world-systems theory*. Although generally eschewing the Marxist label, world-system theorists adopt the basic conceptual framework of Marxism. André Gunder Frank described world-systems theory in terms of classes and an economic whole:

> This approach, which recognizes the exploitative class basis of past and present development, seeks to offer a historical perspective and an analytical approach to the examination of the past, present, and future development of the whole world within a *single modern world system.* (Frank 1983, 28)

World-system theorists argue that capitalistic development has proceeded in **cycles of expansion** rather than in the sudden surge that Lenin described. They see long waves of expansion and stagnation, or even contraction, beginning with the birth of the capitalist world system in feudal Europe (Wallerstein 1976 and 1980). These cycles have gradually expanded the scope of the world capitalist system from a small initial area to a global domain. Lenin wrote near the peak of one expansion cycle.

---

[8]Reported in Ingersoll and Matthews (1986, 169). Parts of this section draw upon their discussion.

Whatever the geographic scope of the world capitalist system, world-system theorists see within it a **core** of states and economies that dominate the system and a **periphery** of subordinate economies. They also identify a semiperiphery of countries such as Argentina at the turn of the century (it fell back to the periphery) and the newly industrialized countries today. In fact, most world-system theorists argue that the development of the more-advanced countries has occurred at the expense of the less developed. Frank called it the "development of underdevelopment." Contrast this with the thought of Marx, who saw the spread of capitalism to the less-developed countries as a progressive force.

This new understanding of the world economy helps neo-Marxists address several issues. The first is the submergence of conflict among the economically developed countries, the states that Lenin believed would inevitably fight over access to the developing world. World-systems theorists see continuing competition among those countries, but they also see shared interests, as members of the core collectively gain from the inexpensive labor, cheap resources, and large markets of the periphery, and from the investment profits generated there. Second, the world-systems perspective helps explain the *persistence* of the great gap between the North (core) and South (periphery). Third, the orientation explains why global crises of the capitalist system, such as that at the time of World War I, do not inevitably result in the triumph of socialism over capitalism. World-systems theory, although expecting continuing crises and an eventual transformation of the world capitalist system to a socialist one, does not attempt to identify which cycle and which crisis period will give rise to the **system transformation.**

The global economic downturn that began in the 1970s reinforced neo-Marxist belief in periodic capitalist crises and drew the attention of many academics in the First World to world-systems theory. The failure of global inequalities to narrow also supports neo-Marxism. In addition, the relative inattention of contemporary liberal theorists to the long term and to analysis of systemic change increases the attractiveness of world-systems theory.

Dependency theory, often called *dependencia* theory, offers another complementary variant of neo-Marxism. Dependency theory does not generally share the long-term horizon of world-systems theorists. Instead, it focuses on the contemporary relationship of core and periphery states, and the asymmetrical dependence that the latter have on the former (or the penetration of the latter by the former).

Dependency theorists question the mutual benefits of trade that liberal theorists associate with the logic of absolute and comparative advantage. They suggest instead that power relationships between countries in the global political economy influence the terms of trade or exchange so that less-developed countries generally obtain lesser benefit from trade.

Dependency theory further claims that interaction with developed countries of the core distorts the domestic economies and social-political systems of LDCs. Limited portions of the developing country come into contact with the core and its economy. This creates a **dual economy** within the developing country—one part superficially modern, international, and wealthy; one part traditional, domestic, and poor (Galtung 1964). The duality establishes a propensity to social and political instability. Some in the internationally linked portion of the economy develop close relationships with the core; they may seek and obtain support from the core in their effort to maintain a privileged position in their own countries.

Values and Prescriptions

The values of those espousing neo-Marxism remain largely unchanged from earlier Marxism. Marxists, like liberals, emphasize growth. They place much greater emphasis on equality, however, than do liberals.

How can greater equality be obtained? Historically, Marxists splintered when it came to prescriptions (even more bitterly than in analysis). Marxists of the right argued early in this century that the existence of extensive suffrage and fairly open political institutions in Europe made revolutionary action no longer necessary. Those of the left, like Lenin or Rosa Luxemburg, put much emphasis on continuing class antagonism and on the necessity of violent revolution.

Similar important divisions characterize neo-Marxist thought. World-systems theory and dependency theory are primarily analytical perspectives. The writing of many such theorists conveys an impression of inevitability in the movement to socialism. In contrast, some Marxists continue to believe that until workers overthrow capitalist institutions in the core, neither the developed nor the developing countries will break out of dependency relationships. Still other Marxists have found a model of self-reliance or autarky (economic independence) attractive. China, from the establishment of a Communist government in 1949 until its reentry into the global economy in the early 1980s, provided an example of such self-reliance. The admission of economic problems by that country greatly lessened the attractiveness of autarky. The movement of nearly all of Central and Eastern Europe toward free markets also dramatically undercut the appeal of central planning as a prescription. Neo-Marxists are in considerable disarray, but we should not ignore their arguments on class relationships, especially when inequality continues to rise around the world.

Worldviews and Methodology

Realists focus on states and the interstate system, commercial liberals on markets and participants within them. Realists and liberals recognize the historic existence of many interstate systems and markets. Scientists working within realist and liberal worldviews can search for patterns across the agents on which they focus, and across space and time with respect to the systems within which they interact. For instance, in their search for rules governing states, realists can compare the contemporary external behavior of India, the United States, and Croatia, and can further look at historic behavior of Athens or Prussia. They can compare the ancient Chinese state system with the global system of today.

The methodology that most often characterizes science within the realist and liberal worldviews grew from **positivism.** Scientists adopting positivist methods seek to put like phenomena into conceptual categories (for instance, Armenians, Palestinians, and Kurds are all nations) and attempt to generalize about relationships among concepts (for instance, nations not in control of states frequently pursue such control through various violent and nonviolent actions).

Another view of the world, often found in the thought of constructivists and some liberals, is that humans learn and society evolves in ways that make them unique across space and time. For instance, many neo-Marxists argue that there is only one world political economy (or world system), that it has unfolded over a long period, and that there has never been anything truly comparable in the past (Wallerstein 1976). If there is only one world system to examine, how can one search for generalizations and understanding? Methodology becomes more historical and holistic. It seeks to understand the dynamics of systemic evolution as an integrated phenomenon. Rules of repetition become less important than observations and insights.

Liberals face a similar problem of uniqueness when they look at the development of ideas and their interaction with global development. Consider how the concept of human rights has evolved over time as humans gradually proscribed slavery and torture (by no means fully eliminated) and as we began to believe that a certain level of material well-being (minimally access to food) is the right of all. Many idealistic liberals and constructivists turn to an examination of language (our definition of concepts like human rights, sovereignty, or power) to understand both the world around us and the way in which the evolution of language and ideas help structure that world (Ball 1988; Der Derian and Shapiro 1989). Because the methodology of positivism has links to the modern, scientific world (and worldview), they call for **postmodernism** in methodology.[9]

Critical theory provides one postmodern methodological orientation that we can contrast with positivism. In general it urges that we understand the world as a social construction. Critical theory takes positivism to task on two grounds in particular. First, critical theorists argue that positivists mistake time and culture-bound images of the world for objective understandings of it. This book illustrates the point. Each worldview has adherents who have difficulty seeing the world from other perspectives. Their location of birth (for instance, First or Third World), their status within society, and the time in which they live all conspire to provide the perspective from which they mentally organize the world. Even the choice one makes of "basic" concepts will reflect one's experiences. More strongly, theory will not only reflect one's experience, but support one's interests. Robert Cox (1981) said that "theory is always *for* someone *for* some purpose."

Positivists counter that there is still but one truth, even if some see only parts of it. They have difficulty understanding how their reproducible search for patterns across time and space is more likely to impose a particular and limited perspective on reality than is an approach that reaches deep inside oneself for analysis of particular instances.

---

[9]It is very difficult to generalize about postmodern methodology, within which there is much heterogeneity (George and Campbell 1990). Pauline Vaillancourt Rosenau (1994, 306–308) said that postmodernism draws on critical theory's "suspicion of instrumental reason," French structuralism's "suspicion of humanism," Nietzsche's and Heidegger's "skepticism about the possibility of truth, reason, and moral universals," hermeneutics' "critique of empiricism, rationality, universalistic science, and direct, mechanical causality," and much more. As this listing suggests, it can be easier to describe what postmodernism rejects than to explain what it proposes.

Critical theory's second criticism of positivists is that they downplay conscious human involvement in history and control of it, and therefore they are socially conservative. Positivists largely seek to understand society, and only secondarily to change it. Although some constructivists similarly place themselves outside of society and seek to understand it, many others want primarily to act on it. Contrast the commercial liberals who describe the regular and beneficent operation of the world economy, and who approve of it, with neo-Marxists who see instead an unjust and repressive class structure that inspires them to advocate change. Critical theorists want to bridge the gaps between philosophy, social observation, and social action.

This brief synopsis cannot do justice to the incredibly complex debate between positivists and their critics. An understanding of the depth of dispute between realists, liberals, and constructivists requires, however, realization that it often goes beyond facts, concepts, theories, and even values. It extends also to **epistemology,** to questions of how we study the world and how we understand it.

Selected Key Terms

political economy	market failures	cycles of expansion
factors of production	mercantilism	core
human capital	neomercantilism	periphery
absolute (trade) advantage	strategic trade theory	system transformation
comparative (trade) advantage	nontariff trade barriers	dependency theory
	excess returns	dual economy
dynamic gains from trade	Stolper-Samuelson theorem	positivism
stages of growth		postmodernism
Kuznets curve	neo-Marxism	epistemology

CHAPTER 12

The Globalization of the World Economy

I n early 1997 the economies of East Asia—Indonesia, Malaysia, South Korea, Thailand, Taiwan, Singapore, and China—began still another year of rapid economic growth. These "tiger" economies exemplified the possibilities available to less-developed countries in the world economy, requiring only an openness to world markets and a hard-working, high-saving population. For instance, the Republic of Korea had increased per-capita income of its citizens tenfold in just three decades.

By 1998 the tigers, especially the first four, looked more like wet kittens. Their stock markets had collapsed, along with the value of their currencies. They struggled to repay foreign debts. A new Korean Prime Minister apologized to his people, and riots in Indonesian universities brought down President Suharto after 32 years in power. Japan, in many respects the mother of these Asian tiger cubs, had completed still another year with minimal economic growth and deteriorating property and stock markets (which were about 50 percent lower than a decade earlier). Its markets then also fell sharply, and those of Russia collapsed. Analysts were asking what happened to the Asian miracle. Had the countries pursued internal policies that brought the wrath of global markets upon them? Had the markets simply panicked and temporarily interrupted brilliant economic advances? Were other countries, perhaps even Europe and the United States, subject to similarly humbling events? When might Asian growth resume? This chapter and the next move our attention to the globalization of the world economy and the implications of it.

KEY WEB LINKS

www.imf.org/
www.worldbank.org/
www.wto.org/
www.oecd.org/
www.adb.org/
www.stern.nyu.edu/~nroubini/
asia/AsiaHomepage.html

The Irregular Growth of an Open Global Economy

The power of Athens and later of Rome protected extensive long-distance trading relationships. Trade, and the military ability of the two cities to extract economic resources from their allies and empires, supported the comparatively elegant and rich life-styles of the imperial centers. The collapse of Athenian power reduced trade in the Aegean; the fall of the Roman empire preceded a restructuring of Europe into feudal units, which were largely self-contained political-economic systems with limited need for trade.

In 1500 Venice was the hub of an extensive early world-political economy, dominating shipping throughout the Mediterranean, to Britain and Scandinavia via the Atlantic Ocean, and to Asia on overland and land-sea routes. Genoa and Antwerp subsequently challenged the Venetians as the scope of European commerce continued to grow (Braudel 1979; Wallerstein 1976 and 1980). Many factors, including the expansion of the Ottoman empire, contributed to the relative decline of Venice and of Southern Europe more generally.

By 1650 Amsterdam and the United Provinces (now the Netherlands) had emerged as the clear center of an even more extensive capitalist world economy. In 1700 only 40 percent of the population in the Netherlands was engaged in agriculture, and the per-capita income was about 50 percent higher than that of England, its nearest rival (Maddison 1982, 14, 29). The scope of trade and political penetration had become global (Magellan's expedition circumnavigated the world in 1522).

In 1670 the Dutch owned more tonnage than England, France, Portugal, Spain, and the Germanies combined (Wallerstein 1980, 46). Their great naval superiority would seemingly have allowed them to dominate in free economic competition. In addition, Hugo Grotius, the Dutch jurist considered the father of international law, argued in the early 1600s that the seas of the world should be open to all. Yet instead of adopting the free-trade orientation of liberalism, the Dutch actively pursued mercantilist policies; that is, they sought to exclude others from principal roles in international trade and from their markets.

> The seventeenth-century world was still a place with limited markets, in which the success of trading countries depended on beggar-your-neighbour practices. Thus the Netherlands blockaded Antwerp's access to the sea from 1585 to 1795, taking over its entrepôt [import and re-export] trade and textile industry. Its successful struggle with Portugal was similarly responsible for Dutch monopolies in trade with large parts of Asia and Latin America. (Maddison 1982, 32)

England admired the Dutch success but chafed under it. For example, the efficient Dutch fleets could fish off England and deliver product to the English market at less cost than local fisherman. In addition, the Dutch dominated a large overseas empire, including Indonesia. England was larger than the Netherlands, however, with a more extensive internal market, partially protected by the English channel. It copied much of the Dutch technology and many of its policies, including a self-serving mercantilism. Most important, the industrial revolution began in England in the late 1700s and the early 1800s. With the English rise on the global stage, merchant capitalism (involving trade and transhipment) gave way to industrial capitalism (tied to efficient production).

Between 1820 and 1850, Britain moved from international policies based on mercantilism to those based on free trade. One of the most famous actions was the repeal in 1846 of the corn laws. In the early nineteenth century both consumers and manufacturers increasingly objected to the restrictions on low-cost grain imports (called "corn" imports in Britain), and eventually they succeeded in having the barriers dropped. The government also eliminated prohibitions on the export of machinery and the emigration of skilled labor.

The reasons for the movement of Britain from mercantilism to free trade remain relevant in debates on trade today. The shift of domestic power from the landed aristocracy to the growing industrial bourgeois gave support to free trade. Whereas the aristocracy benefited from high food prices, the bourgeois wanted low prices for their own consumption and for that of workers. Similarly, many in the bourgeois wanted to eliminate barriers to their import of inexpensive raw materials. They also wanted export markets for goods and machinery and were increasingly competitive in them. Other analysts posit that the theoretical arguments of liberals like Adam Smith convinced increasing numbers of Britons of the benefits that free trade would bring.

During 40 years prior to World War I, the openness of the world economy reached record heights. Capital, goods, and immigrants flowed across borders in a golden age of international economic integration (United Nations Conference on Trade and Development [UNCTAD] 1994, 119–131; Thompson and Krasner 1989). For instance, annual growth in world trade exceeded growth in world output by 1.4 percent between 1870 and 1913 and reached a ratio of global GDP that it did not surpass until the 1970s (see again Figure 1.7). Foreign direct investment stocks were 9 percent of global output in 1913, a level to which they recovered only in the early 1990s. Thirty-six million people emigrated from Europe between 1870 and 1915, mostly to the United States.

Although support for free trade grew throughout the global economy, often under British pressure, the United States did not join in opening its economy. The United States used tariffs in the nineteenth century to protect the growth of domestic industry and simultaneously promoted exports. While pursuing protectionist policies, the U.S. economy became increasingly important in the world. In 1870 Britain accounted for 24 percent of world trade compared with 8.8 percent for the United States (Lake 1987, 151). By 1900 the British share of world trade had dropped to 17.5 percent and the U.S. share had risen to 10.2 percent; in 1929 the U.S. share exceeded the British.

Other countries, faced with a growing American challenge restricted their markets. The United States, although protecting its domestic market, began to argue in support of liberal policies abroad. The United States increasingly offered reciprocity, that is, access to its markets in exchange for maintenance of access to those of others. In the concepts of Chapter 5, the United States moved toward specific reciprocity—it would cooperate to achieve immediate benefits.

Yet with the coming of the Great Depression, the United States did not stand behind its emerging liberal principles. Instead, the Smoot-Hawley Act of 1930 raised tariffs on all imports to 19 percent (on dutiable industrial goods to 60 percent). Other states reacted with similar sharp increases. Critics argue that U.S. policy turned the early stages of the depression into a downward spiral in global trade that greatly deepened and prolonged it (Kindleberger 1973). Only in 1934, after the collapse of world trade, did the United States become truly active in support of free trade. The Reciprocal Trade Agreements Act of that year encouraged the president to negotiate with other countries for reciprocal access to each others' markets and for lower tariffs. The act was part of Secretary of State Cordell Hull's liberal vision.

This new direction set the stage for post–World War II global leadership by the United States on behalf of liberal policies. It is to that era that we turn now. As we do so, we should carry two lessons from this historic review with us. First, although liberals prescribe a world of markets and limited state intervention, the reality has been and remains a world of substantial and important *intervention* in markets. Second, a single country has, depending on one's perspective, historically either led or dominated the world economy and thereby established the character of the global economic system. As this chapter surveys the period of U.S. leadership, we should consider whether that leadership remains strong and capable.

Liberalism Ascendant Again: Bretton Woods

At the end of World War II, the European and Asian economies on both sides of the conflict were in ruins. The United States, the only great power that escaped substantial attack and bombing, emerged stronger than before the war. In the earliest postwar days, the United States produced about one-half of the goods and services of the world. Tremendous demand chased those goods and sought U.S. dollars with which to buy them. In contrast to its withdrawal from responsibility in the 1920s and 1930s, the United States actively offered leadership. Even before the war ended, in July 1944, the United States hosted representatives of 44 countries in Bretton Woods, New Hampshire, for a discussion of the postwar economy. Collaborating with England, the country that had led the world economy for about two centuries, the Americans presented a plan for international public management of the global economy. The participating states accepted that plan, and the resultant structures and policies became known as the **Bretton Woods system.**

Institutions of Bretton Woods

Adopting a predominantly liberal outlook, the industrialized countries identified three principal international economic needs of the new era: stable exchange rates, international assistance to war-damaged economies, and low tariffs. Bretton Woods gave responsibility for meeting the first two needs to two new organizations: the International Monetary Fund (IMF) and the International Bank for Reconstruction and Development (IBRD), better known as the World Bank. It took until 1947 to establish a third organization, the General Agreement on Tariffs and Trade (GATT), charged with pursuing low tariffs. Both the IMF and the World Bank have headquarters in Washington, DC. Voting in each depends on capital contributions, and the United States has had a weight reflecting the relative size of its economy. GATT emerged without organizational structure, as a framework within which states conducted international trade negotiations. The eighth "round" of negotiations began in Montevideo, Uruguay, in 1986. It led to the creation of the World Trade Organization (WTO), which in 1995 incorporated GATT into a third Bretton Woods pillar more nearly comparable to the other two.

Concepts from Trade and International Finance

Exchange Rate

The **exchange rate** between two currencies is the number of units of one currency (for example, German marks) that it takes to buy a single unit of another (for example, the U.S. dollar) in the global marketplace. When the central banks of two states guarantee that the rate does not vary from day to day, there is a *fixed exchange rate*. When governments allow the rate to vary with supply and demand, there is a *floating exchange rate*.

Devaluation

Devaluation is downward change in the exchange rate of one country relative to the value of the currencies of its trade partners. States often purposely devalue their currency. An example explains the policy. If it costs two German marks (DM 2) to buy one U.S. dollar ($1), and $1 will buy a hamburger, a German can buy a hamburger with DM 2. It may also cost DM 2 (and therefore $1) to buy a bratwurst. If the German government wanted to discourage the purchase of hamburgers (which we will assume are imported from the United States) and encourage the purchase of German bratwurst, it could devalue the mark so that it cost DM 3 to buy $1. Germans would then find that it cost them DM 3 to buy a hamburger but still only DM 2 to buy a bratwurst. Both Americans and Germans would likely buy more bratwurst and fewer hamburgers.

Revaluation

Revaluation is the upward change in the nominal value of the currency of one country relative to the value of the currencies of its trading partners.

Balance of Trade

The balance of trade is the value of exports from a country minus the value of imports. There is a **favorable balance of trade** when exports exceed imports (reflecting mercantilist preferences for such a situation). The balance of trade is part of the balance of payments.

Balance of Payments

The balance of payments is international credits minus international debts. Credits include exports, earnings from tourists, profits from foreign investment, foreign aid receipts, and inflow of long-term capital investment. Debits include imports, tourist spending abroad, interest payments on foreign debt, foreign aid donations, and outflow of long-term investment. The balance is favorable when credits exceed debits. The market normally revalues floating currencies in response to favorable balances and devalues them in response to unfavorable balances.

The IMF and GATT were reactions to the collapse of world trade in the 1930s. Faced with trade imbalances at that time, countries raised tariffs to exclude foreign goods and devalued their currencies to make their export goods more competitive abroad. They thus used both restraint of imports and promotion of exports to keep domestic producers busier and employment higher. When many countries simultaneously pursued the same neomercantilist policies, however, they collectively reduced global trade. (The box entitled "Concepts from Trade and International Finance" explains some of the basic concepts of international trade and finance.) As in many other collective action situations, the pursuit of individually rational policies created a collectively irrational result.

The IMF encouraged stable exchange rates in two ways. First, no state could change the value of its currency without approval from the IMF (this is no longer the case, as we shall discuss later). Second, the IMF offers short-term financing for countries with financial imbalances, which at one time primarily indicated trade deficits. Each member country contributes to the financing of the IMF and initially draws against its own contribution when in need. As countries draw on greater shares of their own contribution, and especially when they draw beyond it, the IMF poses increasingly strict requirements or **conditionality** on the borrower. The IMF is *not* a foreign aid institution.

The WTO pursues free trade generally, and lower tariffs and nontariff barriers to trade specifically, through periodic rounds of multilateral negotiation. WTO members grant each other **most favored nation (MFN) status,** which means that they extend to all members the lowest tariff rates given to any state. They make some exceptions including preferential tariffs (lower than MFN tariffs) on selected goods from LDCs. Outside of the WTO, countries can put different tariff rates on the same good, depending on its source.

The MFN principle is a good example of diffuse reciprocity (see Chapter 5 on cooperation strategies). States open markets, and in some cases accept considerable economic costs by doing so, in the expectation that in the long run, similar actions of other states will compensate them.

The World Bank directed its initial efforts toward the countries of war-torn Europe. It is a lending institution, making loans on careful economic criteria and boasting a good record of loan repayment. During the 1950s it shifted attention from reconstruction of Europe to development of the Third World. In 1956 participating states created the International Finance Corporation as an affiliate of the Bank with the aim of supporting private companies in LDCs (Riggs and Plano 1994, 288). Reacting to criticism by recipients that loan terms were too demanding, the international community created still another affiliate in 1960, the International Development Association (IDA). The IDA makes "soft" loans, without interest and with easy repayment conditions. A convention established the Multilateral Investment Guarantee Agency (MIGA) as the fourth member of the World Bank Group in 1989.

The First World controls the IMF, the World Bank, and to a lesser extent the WTO. Many Third World countries have felt alienated from the Bretton Woods system (although most are members), arguing that it ill serves their interests; they have proposed, as we shall see in the next chapter, an alternative set of global economic institutions. The United States pressed the Soviet Union and Eastern European countries to join the new institutions in the late 1940s, but those countries chose to remain outside. By the end of 1992, however, nearly all of that region had joined the IMF and World Bank.

How successful have the Bretton Woods organizations been? Many give them considerable credit for the fact that world trade expanded from $77 billion in 1953

Figure 12.1   Exports as a Portion of GDP

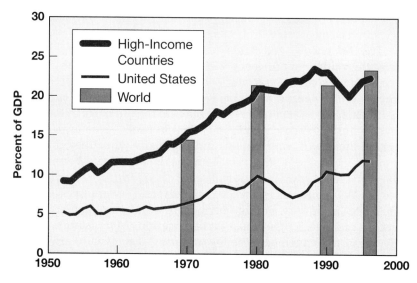

Sources: Courtesy of the Office for Development Research and Policy Analysis of the United Nations Secretariat, July 12, 1985; International Monetary Fund, *International Financial Statistics Yearbook* (Washington, DC: IMF, assorted years); World Bank, *World Development Report,* assorted issues (New York: Oxford University Press); World Bank, *World Development Indicators 1998* (Washington, DC: World Bank, 1998).

to $6,689 billion in 1996. Figure 12.1 shows that trade has expanded considerably faster than economies. In 1952 high-income countries as a whole exported goods equivalent to 9.1 percent of their GDP. In 1996 they exported 22 percent of GDP. Global trade has expanded as rapidly.

Early Challenge and Change

Already by 1947 the Bretton Woods system, as originally conceived, proved inadequate. The challenges it faced in the early years included very weak economic performance in Europe immediately after World War II and growing U.S. trade surpluses.

The immediate post–World War II demand for U.S. goods caused the U.S. trade surplus to grow, because other economies had little to export (substantial food and energy shortages still plagued much of Europe). The United States also held 70 percent of the world's monetary gold supply, making it impossible for most countries to buy those American goods with gold. They needed dollars—and the embryonic global institutions could not provide enough of them. These realities forced the United States to take a more unilateral role in managing the world economy from 1947–1960, basically by supplying dollars and thus the wherewithal to buy American goods.

Between 1948 and 1952, the United States provided 16 Western European countries with $17 billion through the European Recovery Program, known as the Marshall Plan. The United States spent billions more abroad by stationing its troops throughout a growing global defense system. The American government even encouraged some protectionist policies and devaluation of currencies in the recovering countries.

The outflow of dollars helped set in motion the European and Japanese economic miracles of the 1950s and 1960s. As the rest of the world recovered and began to compete in the world market, however, the hemorrhage of currency from the United States became a problem rather than a boon. By 1959 the dollars held abroad rose to $19.4 billion and the gold remaining in the country, at the official exchange rate of $35 per ounce, had a value of $19.5 billion. The United States had in essence committed all of its gold abroad. Throughout the 1960s the outflow of dollars continued, and a large "overhang" of dollars developed. The government encouraged allies like Germany to hold the dollars rather than to request gold. President de Gaulle of France argued, however, that this ability of the United States to print money to pursue its interests abroad was an "exorbitant privilege" not available to other countries, and he insisted on delivery of gold. Speculators increasingly did the same.

By 1971 U.S. foreign liabilities exceeded the value of its gold by more than five to one. In that same year, the United States imported more goods than it exported for the first time in the twentieth century. In August 1971 the Nixon administration decided without consultation abroad that it would no longer convert dollars to gold. In 1973 the United States devalued the dollar by 10 percent and put its exchange rate in the hands of the world market. Henceforth the dollar's value would float, depending on supply and demand forces. Other countries quickly followed that move.

Some thought then that the Bretton Woods system had ended. The United States had acted unilaterally in a world economic order supposedly based on cooperation within institutions, and many states abrogated the basic concept of fixed exchange rates linked to gold. The IMF, World Bank, and GATT/WTO remain in place, however, as do widespread commitments to free and orderly trade. A "Modified Bretton Woods" system thus continues to help manage the global political economy. The rest of the chapter outlines the many continuing and new challenges that it faces. In particular we focus on trade and finance.

Trade: The Shadow of Mercantilism

Perhaps the most fundamental ongoing challenge to the Bretton Woods system is neomercantilism. Although the philosophy of liberalism and the theoretical commitment to open global markets is widespread, the mercantilist belief persists that governments can improve the economic performance of their countries through *selective intervention*.

Bases of Neomercantilism

Mercantilism persists for at least two reasons. First, governments routinely intervene in their domestic economies for what they often see as purely domestic reasons. Such interventions can have unanticipated implications for trade. Even the British and Americans, historically committed to liberal principles, favor certain industries over others through tax benefits, research and development subsidies, infrastructure development, loans, and occasionally direct public ownership. For instance, developed countries provide various forms of support to their agricultural sectors, intending to ease the pain in farm households as that sector declines within the overall economy. A direct result of these policies, such as price supports, is agricultural surplus. The domestic policy has external consequences when, in their efforts to dispose of the surpluses, governments give food away abroad or sell it at reduced rates.

The second reason mercantilism persists in the global environment is that it appears successful. Not so many years ago President Charles de Gaulle of France refused to meet a Japanese Prime Minister, referring to him as a "transistor salesman." The Japanese government worked closely, however, with Japanese industry throughout the postwar period. It helped firms to acquire technology and finance and to penetrate foreign markets. At the same time it acquiesced in or reinforced various barriers to imports, the most effective of which were not tariffs, but rather customs procedures, standards requirements, exclusionary domestic distribution networks, government procurement policies, undervalued exchange rates, and others. Liberal theory strongly supports the argument that deviations from free trade internationally lessen the overall efficiency of the system and create welfare losses in the aggregate. It does not, however, preclude an individual country from taking advantage of a liberal economic order to strengthen its own relative position, and Japan appears to have accomplished that. Strategic trade theorists in other countries also believe it possible. Chapter 11 laid out the arguments of strategic trade theorists on behalf of government intervention. These include the possibility that a government can actually create comparative advantage, especially in an industry subject to economies of scale and thus monopolistic power (like aircraft), or it can bolster profits margins by investing in emerging industry.

Confronting the Challenge of Neomercantilism

Although liberals see global economics as nonzero-sum, mercantilists view it as zero-sum. Instead of focusing on the vast multitude of transactions among firms and households that result in increased system efficiency, production, and welfare, the mercantilist focuses on the gains and losses among states implied by their balances of trade. Every billion dollars of Japanese trade surplus creates a billion-dollar trade deficit elsewhere. The production of goods that generates a billion-dollar surplus employs many Japanese workers; were there no Japanese surplus, the same industries could potentially employ a comparable number in other countries. The belief that other countries (and especially Japan) take jobs away from locals leads to trade barriers in Europe and strong protectionist sentiment in the United States.

In sharp contrast, liberals worry little about the policies of other countries. They argue that other countries benefit if the Japanese produce goods below their real cost. Importing countries can accept the subsidy and devote their own resources to other goods. Moreover, a domestic industry that ultimately survives the onslaught of subsidized production (for instance, automobiles) will be especially efficient. However, even most liberals prefer "a level playing field." That is, they want all countries to play by the same free-trade rules.

In 1984 the United States decided that other countries supported their steel industries and dumped their surpluses on the U.S. market (Kline 1985, 208). Congress therefore approved a quota system restricting imports to 20 percent of the U.S. market. Going further, the Omnibus Trade and Competitiveness Act of 1988 *required* the U.S. Trade Representative to take retaliatory action to open foreign markets to U.S. goods. In 1995 the United States announced that it would levy 100 percent tariffs against Japanese luxury cars, because Japan was not moving aggressively enough to remove barriers to imports of U.S. auto parts. Although the measure violated WTO rules requiring use of dispute-resolution procedures, it had wide domestic support.

In a sense, such trade policies attempt to combine specific and diffuse reciprocity. They communicate the message that when other countries repeatedly take advantage of cooperative actions, and fail to deliver on their long-term obligations under diffuse reciprocity, the government will move to a specific reciprocity relationship with them. The danger some liberals see is that these *countermercantilist policies,* such as denying access to American markets for Japanese semiconductors in response to Japanese restrictions on American computers, might lead to trade wars that significantly restrict all markets. The line between countermercantilist and snow-balling protectionist policies is thin.

The problem is again one of collective action (see Chapter 6). It is possible to take advantage of the collective good of free trade (unimpeded access to markets around the world), while not contributing significantly to the provision of the good. Free riders can obtain individual gains at the expense of others in a liberal system. A few small free riders in a trade system with a strong leader may pose no problem. As noted earlier, the United States actually encouraged Europe and Japan to adopt some mercantilistic practices after World War II. Should the free riders become numerous, however, or the size of any one become large compared with the main provider(s) of the collective good, they become **spoilers** (Lake 1987). Spoilers hold the negative power of being able to disrupt the system and destroy the provision of collective goods. In contrast, **supporters** are countries like Great Britain that are not systemic leaders but make important contributions to collective-good provision.

The Fear of Spoilers

The danger of spoilers worries many liberals today. The threat comes from three quarters. The first is Japan. Japan ran trade surpluses with the United States throughout the 1990s of $40–70 billion. Japan sometimes appears to be opening its internal financial and goods markets and moving from many earlier mercantilist policies (see the box entitled "Is Japan Mercantilist?"). Access to its markets in wood products, medical equipment, telecommunications, and beef and citrus has improved. Nonetheless, the large trade surpluses of Japan still pose a threat to the system. In the United States these surpluses give rise not only to "Japan bashing," but to doubts concerning the value of liberal trade policies more generally.

The Newly Industrialized Countries (NICs) achieved rapid economic growth through promotion of exports, and they pose the second threat. They often rely on various neomercantilist policies, including undervalued exchange rates, to achieve rapid export growth. As other countries, including large ones like Brazil and India,

Is Japan Mercantilist?

Japanese tariffs are low, even by WTO-member standards. Japan uses decreasing numbers of implicit nontariff barriers to trade. Its currency has appreciated sharply, making imported goods less expensive. Yet it continues to run large surpluses with the United States and some other trading partners.

Why? One explanation is that Japanese businesses benefit from superior access to finance (the high Japanese savings rate); a well-trained, motivated, and socially cohesive labor force; and internationally aggressive marketing. A second explanation is that Japan does not have open domestic markets like those of the United States, and that even in the absence of easily recognizable neomercantilist barriers, its markets are largely impenetrable. Observers call Japan a "network state" or a "developmental state," referring to the close relationships among public institutions and private firms. Family, university, regional, corporate, and other social ties create personal relationships, trust, and reciprocal obligations that set up nearly insurmountable barriers to equal treatment of outsiders.

There is undoubtedly some truth in both explanations. The difficulty is in knowing which set of factors is stronger and how rapidly the Japanese networks may be opening to foreigners.

enviously examine the success of such policies, a danger arises of free riders that are too numerous or too large. For instance, the Chinese trade surplus with the United States climbed steadily from near zero in 1987 to $40 billion in 1996.

Some see an incipient third danger in the economic integration of the European Union. The common European currency can compete more strongly with the dollar in the global system than could the mark or yen. Heavy use of the euro as a reserve currency could increase its relative price and create competitive problems for Europe. If so, it would increase the danger of a "Fortress Europe," practicing free trade internally but raising barriers externally. Disputes between the EU and the United States are already common. In 1989 the EU ceased all imports of American beef, citing concerns about the human health effects of the growth hormones that U.S. producers often feed to cattle. The United States retaliated with bans on several European agricultural products. The 1989 episode differed little from other "spats" among the trading partners concerning pasta, wine, ham, and other goods, including the "banana war" of 1999.

The fear, however, is that the European Union will at some point create a fundamentally more protectionist Europe, and that the world could split into giant trade blocs (as in the 1930s), substantially closing their markets to each other. NAFTA constitutes a second potential regional trade bloc. Closer Japanese ties with East Asian neighbors could be the seed of a third. Figure 12.2 presents some basic data on these three potential trade blocs, of which the third is growing most rapidly.

Yet the historic and philosophic commitment to free trade in both Europe and North America is great enough that existing regional associations will not automatically become strong trade blocs. It would require a significant global

Figure 12.2 Regional Markets (1996)

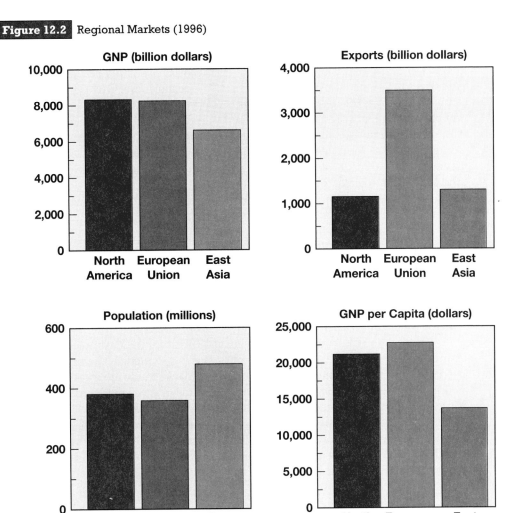

Note: East Asia defined as Hong Kong, Indonesia, Japan, Malaysia, Singapore, South Korea, Taiwan, and Thailand. GNP is at exchange rates.

Sources: World Bank, *World Development Indicators 1998* (Washington, DC: World Bank, 1998); CIA, *The World Factbook 1997* (Washington, DC: CIA, 1997).

economic downturn, with substantial and growing unemployment, to entice Western countries away from the liberal worldview and into policies of regional mercantilism.

The Heavy Trade Agenda

As the discussion to this point makes clear, protecting the gains of past trade liberalization challenges the global system and remains a top priority. Yet many other trade-related issues weigh heavily on the agenda (Schott 1996).

Geographic Widening   Expansion of WTO membership is one issue. Whereas GATT had only 91 members in 1986 when the Uruguay Round began, by 1998 the WTO had 132 members and 30 more aspirants, including China, which never entered GATT. The accession of more LDCs to the WTO has widened the reach of the liberal trade regime well beyond that of GATT. Furthermore, GATT had exempted some LDCs from full reciprocity in tariff reduction, but the WTO committed all members to the tariff reductions that the Uruguay Round mandated.

The communist countries refused after World War II to participate in the liberal economic order. Even now that the countries of Eastern and Central Europe have joined the WTO and seek integration into the world economy, those states find it difficult to make the transition. To understand why the transition is difficult for the Eastern economies, consider two problems they face: one, establishing market prices, and two, privatizing state-owned industries.

As a concession to the domestic consumer, the former Soviet Union set food and energy prices low. Russia has now moved such prices toward world levels. Several-fold increases in the prices of food and energy devastated those with little opportunity to increase low incomes (especially retired workers). Poland approached this painful process in 1989–1990 by adopting the "shock" approach—suddenly opening its borders to trade and freeing domestic markets from central control. Most countries in the region moved more gingerly.

Privatization of property has proven as difficult for the Eastern countries. Determining ownership of land and firms often poses a challenge. Governments have been loathe to sell all state-owned enterprises, because many are incapable of competing in free markets, and hundreds of thousands of employees would lose jobs. Moreover, increasing inequality of income and living standards almost invariably follows privatization because new entrepreneurs amass wealth. The former communist societies internalized socialist ideals of equality and protection of the downtrodden, and many citizens greatly resent the newly rich. That many have attained new wealth by use of old communist party connections only adds insult to injury.

Other Trade Issues   Widening the global-trade regime's membership has proceeded more smoothly than widening of its coverage of trade. Trade liberalization has historically focused on manufactured goods, bringing average duties below 5 percent in the biggest industrial countries. Protection of agricultural products remains very high with tariff and nontariff barriers averaging 40 percent globally. Although the General Agreement on Trade in Services (GATS) came into force with the WTO, trade in services also remains quite protected. Negotiations on trade categories like services continue, and WTO will devote future "rounds" of discussions (including the one in 2000) to such issues.

One important feature of the WTO not present in GATT is the dispute-settlement mechanism (DSM). Members can submit complaints about unfair practices by others to the WTO, which sets up panels to adjudicate disputes. Losers cannot veto rulings, and the WTO monitors compliance. Disputes lodged grew from about 30 in 1995 to more than 100 in 1998. The WTO has had difficulty handling the load. Therefore institutional and financial reform will become issues for the organization.

Various interests also push "trade-related" issues onto the global agenda. For instance, environmentalists watched both the North American Free Trade Agreement (NAFTA) and WTO discussions closely, with an eye to obtaining trade agreements that protect the environment. The Sierra Club opposed NAFTA, arguing that Mexico does not adequately enforce environmental protection. Other environmentalists criticize the WTO because it prevents a state from refusing to import a product for environmental reasons (that would be a nontariff barrier to trade). For instance, the WTO struck down a U.S. ban on Mexican tuna, implemented because Mexican fleets used techniques that imperiled dolphin. Other interests ask that social issues figure more prominently. For instance, the EU and the United States have urged definition of WTO standards on labor practices, including health and safety conditions. Not surprisingly, many LDCs resist that.

Some of the most difficult issues on the agenda, however, lie at the intersection of trade and finance. For instance, the Uruguay round approved the first trade-related investment measures (TRIMs) to oversee the use by countries of "carrots" and "sticks" on foreign investment. Although the discussions on the Multilateral Agreement on Investment (MAI) faltered, there will be further pressure for movement—both to open countries to investment and to protect investment made.

The movement to floating exchange rates in the 1970s introduced still another problem into the world financial system, namely exchange rate instability. Many economists argued that floating rates would be self-regulating. Should an economy develop a negative balance of payments, the net outflow of currency from that country would create a surplus of it in the global currency markets and depress its value. Changes in trade would bring the financial accounting of the country back into balance. After some initial adjustments to compensate for existing distortions in exchange rates under the old system, and after participants in the modified system learned the new rules of the game, liberals expected exchange rates to be quite stable.

In reality, movements of 50 percent in the value of a currency relative to other currencies have occurred in the space of a year or two, often to be quickly reversed in following years. Initially, central banks maintained a "hands off" policy with respect to these free-market fluctuations. In recent years, however, they have pursued coordinated and covert strategies to provide a more orderly currency market. Nonetheless, corporations and private parties can move hundreds of billions of dollars between currencies in hours, potentially swamping the resources of central banks. Instability is likely to remain a feature of the market (Figure 12.3).

Managing Explosive Financial Flows

The founders of Bretton Woods established institutions to deal with the trade-system problems of the 1930s (especially protectionism and competitive devaluations). In intervening years, however, transboundary financial flows have increased much more rapidly than trade. Increases in capital flows initially undercut the fixed exchange-rate system, and recent surges now lie at the root of several problems in the current system, including the instability of exchange rates. Whereas at one time most capital flows responded to the need to finance trade, in the contemporary environment the flows have become a very powerful force that affects exchange rates and therefore trade. What was once the tail now wags the dog. In the 1990s, more than a trillion dollars could move *daily* in

Figure 12.3 Effective Exchange Rate (Nominal)

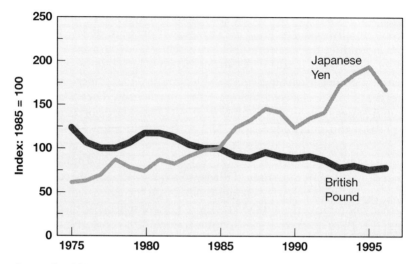

Source: International Monetary Fund, *International Financial Statistics Yearbook*, assorted years.

the financial markets, compared with annual global trade in the late 1990s of about $4 trillion.

Interstate financial flows take several forms. When investors buy partial or total ownership in companies abroad with the intention of participating in the management of those firms, it constitutes **foreign direct investment (FDI)**. When investors buy shares of stock in companies on a stock exchange without such an intention to manage, it constitutes equity investment. **Foreign portfolio equity investment (FPEI)** includes equity investment and other paper instruments such as treasury bills. In order to invest in firms or stocks abroad, one must normally first buy the currency of the target country. Such *foreign-exchange trading,* however, can also take place for more speculative reasons, simply because one believes that the value of the purchased currency will rise relative to the one sold.

The Volume and Pattern of Flows

Direct Investment   Worldwide direct investment *stocks* (that is, total amount in place) rose from $67 billion in 1960 to $3,200 billion in 1996 (United Nations Centre on Transnational Corporations [UNCTC] 1988 and UNCTAD 1997, 313). Annual direct investment *flows* (that is, the amount moving across borders in a given year) grew from less than $10 billion in 1970 to nearly $350 billion in 1996 (UNCTAD 1997, 303). During the 1980s and 1990s FDI grew especially fast, at a 14 percent pace. Foreign direct investment can substantially restructure economies. For instance, it potentially conveys an ability to compete in the world economy to recipients by building factories, filling them with advanced equipment, and orienting production toward world markets.

Where does FDI come from? Table 12.1 shows that the U.S. share of total stocks is decreasing steadily, falling from 47 percent in 1960 to 25 percent in 1996.

Table 12.1   Sources and Hosts of Foreign Direct Investment Stocks

Sources	1960	1980	1985	1990	1995	1996
United States	47.1%	42.9%	36.6%	25.8%	25.8%	25.0%
United Kingdom	18.3%	15.7%	14.6%	13.7%	11.7%	11.2%
Japan	0.7%	3.7%	6.5%	12.2%	11.1%	10.4%
Germany	1.2%	8.4%	8.7%	9.0%	8.6%	9.1%
France	6.1%	4.6%	5.4%	6.5%	7.4%	6.5%
Developed	26.6%	23.6%	25.1%	28.7%	27.5%	28.9%
Developing	—	1.2%	3.1%	4.1%	7.9%	8.9%
Total	100.0%	100.0%	100.0%	100.0%	100.0%	100.0%
Total (billions)	$67.0	$513.7	$685.5	$1,684.1	$2,730.1	$3,178

Hosts	1975	1980	1985	1990	1995	1996
United States	11.2%	17.2%	25.1%	23.0%	21.2%	19.9%
Western Europe	40.8%	41.6%	33.3%	44.2%	40.9%	40.3%
Other Developed Countries	23.1%	18.7%	14.8%	12.8%	10.6%	10.0%
Latin America	12.0%	10.0%	10.4%	7.1%	8.4%	9.8%
Asia	5.3%	7.9%	12.5%	10.2%	15.2%	16.6%
Africa	6.7%	4.3%	3.7%	2.4%	2.2%	1.8%
Other	1.5%	0.3%	0.2%	0.3%	1.5%	1.6%
Total	100.0%	100.0%	100.0%	100.0%	100.0%	100.0%
Total (billions)	$246.8	$481.9	$734.9	$1,717	$2,658	$3,233

Note: The discrepancy between total source and host values indicates measurement problems.
Sources: United Nations Centre on Transnational Corporations, *Transnational Corporations in World Development: Trends and Prospects* (New York: United Nations Centre on Transnational Corporations, 1988), 24–25; World Bank, *Global Economic Prospects and the Developing Countries* (Washington, DC: World Bank, 1991), 12; UNCTAD, *World Investment Report 1994* (New York: United Nations), 19; UNCTAD, *World Investment Report 1997*, 313–324.

Nonetheless, the United States still controls the most foreign investment, followed by Britain. The Japanese share of foreign direct investment stocks grew from 0.7 percent to 10.4 percent between 1960 and 1996, putting them in the top ranks. LDCs, traditionally only recipients of FDI, now are the source countries for 9 percent of total global FDI stocks.

Where does FDI go? About three-fourths of global investment finds its way from developed countries to other developed countries. Specifically, most investment flows among the United States, European Union, and Japan "triad."

For most of the twentieth century, Latin America hosted the largest share of FDI stocks in developing countries (see Figure 12.4 for total LDC and MDC stocks). Asia took the lead in the 1980s. Africa has also lost share to Asia. Although LDCs frequently complain about the pernicious impact of foreign capital, some observers say that "the only thing worse than being exploited by capitalists is not being exploited by them."

Figure 12.4   Annual Foreign Direct Investment (FDI) Inflows

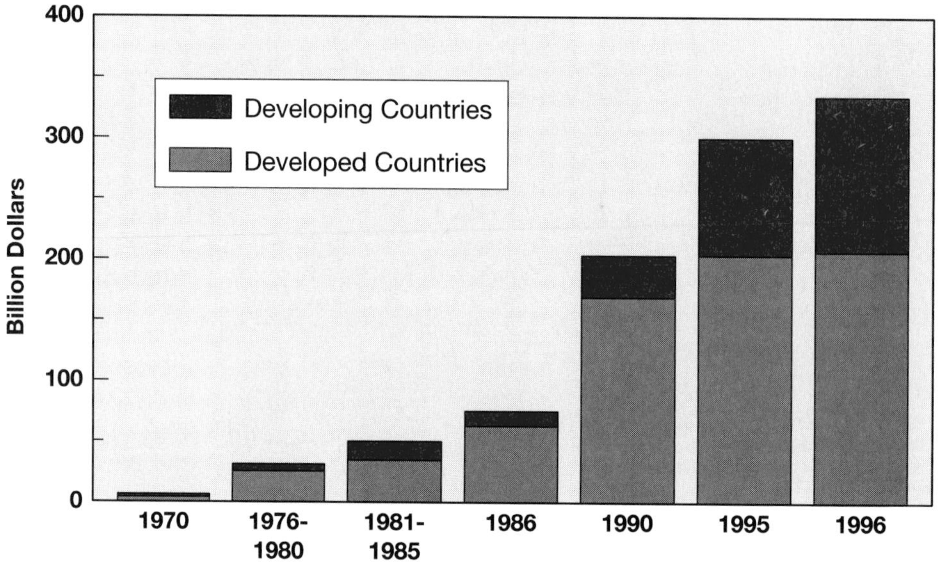

Note: 1976–1980 and 1981–1985 are annual averages.

Sources: UN Transnational Corporations and Management Division, *World Investment Report 1992* (New York: United Nations, 1992), 14; United Nations Conference on Trade and Development, *World Investment Report 1995* (New York: United Nations, 1994), 12; UNCTAD, *World Investment Report 1997*, 303.

To what sectors does FDI flow? Historically, much FDI was in the primary sectors (petroleum, minerals, and agriculture). Most FDI has flowed into manufacturing since World War II. Reflecting the transformation of the developed countries into postindustrial economies, however, FDI now increasingly appears in the service sector. By the mid-1980s, 50 percent of the world stock of FDI, and 55–60 percent of annual flows were in services (UNCTC 1991, 15).

And why does FDI matter? One reason is that, to be successful, large companies must increasingly take advantage of differences in comparative advantage by scattering parts of their production process around the world. Ford is truly a global automobile company that determines where it can most effectively produce engines, tires, electronic systems, and other parts, and where it can most effectively assemble those parts and design its new models. About one-third of cross-border merchandise trade now takes place within companies.

Portfolio Investment   The UN considers ownership of more than 10 percent of the shares in a foreign company to be direct investment. Ownership of fewer shares (or of bonds and other instruments) is foreign portfolio equity investment (FPEI). The rise of global stock market capitalization to more than $20 trillion in 1996 (from $6 trillion in 1986) greatly increased FPEI.

Whereas the LDC share of direct investment stocks has not significantly changed in the last two decades, developing countries have significantly enhanced their presence in global equity markets, moving from 4 percent of global markets

Figure 12.5 Capital Mobility and Foreign Direct Investment (FDI) Flows

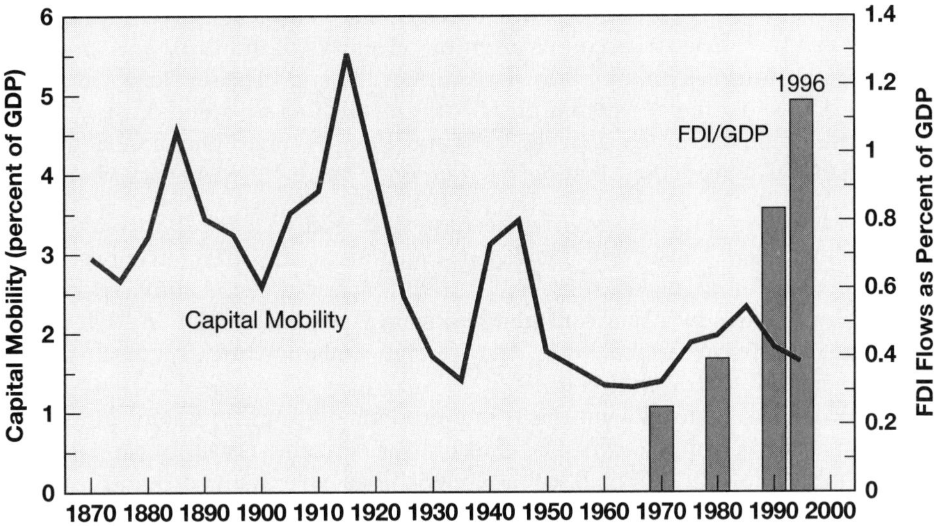

Note: Capital mobility represents only 9–12 countries over time. It is based on current account levels as a portion of GDP. Author calculations for 1990 and 1996 are weighted averages.

Sources: Alan M. Taylor, National Bureau of Economic Research, "International Capital Mobility in History: The Savings-Investment Relationship," *NBER Working Paper Series, No. 5743* (Cambridge, MA: 1996), 33; assorted issues of World Bank, *World Development Report* and *World Development Indicators;* UNCTAD, *World Investment Report,* assorted issues.

in 1986 to 11 percent in 1996. The International Finance Corporation classified only three emerging (LDC) markets as "free" to foreign stock investment in 1986, but 26 markets as free in 1995 (UNCTAD 1997, 114). International mutual fund investments in emerging markets rose from $4 billion in 1986 to $135 billion in 1996. Bond investments also rose dramatically. Annual flows, however, vary dramatically. Net portfolio flows to emerging markets rose from $0.6 billion in 1986 to $45 billion in 1993 and then fell to $32 billion in 1995 (UNCTAD 1997, 274). The East Asia crisis of 1997–1999 greatly curtailed equity flows.

Is Globalization Really New?   Economic historians often argue that attention to globalization of the contemporary world economy incorrectly suggests that the current era is unique. In fact, they say, the world economy was at least as tightly connected prior to World War I as it is today (Zevin 1992). Figure 12.5 shows the basis for that argument by tracing the net portion of 9–12 major economies available over time to finance, or to be financed by, external investment (the current account balance as a portion of GDP). That peaked before World War I at more than twice today's levels. For instance, in 1913 nearly 10 percent of British output was invested abroad each year. Those funds helped provide more than 30 percent of the total investment of such developing countries of the day as Canada and New Zealand. In the 1990s developing countries received only a bit more than 10 percent of their investment from abroad (International Monetary Fund [IMF] 1997, 234–241).

Much does, however, set the contemporary era apart from the earlier one. Bidirectional flows are massive today. The historic line on Figure 12.5 shows *net* flows. Those have actually decreased in the last two decades as countries have improved their external accounts after the oil shocks of the 1970s and, in the case of Europe, prepared for adoption of a common currency. The shorter-term bars in Figure 12.5 show the very rapid growth of *gross* FDI as a portion of the global economy. That quadrupled between 1970 and 1996. Whereas global GDP grew annually by 3.7 percent over that period, FDI grew by 10.4 percent each year.

Hot Money   FDI has grown in absolute and relative terms. Portfolio investment has exploded. Those flows increased at an annual rate of 25 percent between 1980 and 1996 (*The Economist,* October 18, 1997, 80). For instance, annual portfolio sales and purchases by Americans climbed from 9 percent of GDP in 1980 to 164 percent in 1996. On a global basis, daily foreign-exchange turnover rose from $15 billion in 1973 to $1.2 trillion in 1995.

Again, there is some historic precedent. In 1913, investors from the U.K., France, and Germany owned 80 percent of all securities issued by capital-importing countries (IMF 1997, 235). But at least two things have changed. Securitization of the global economy has advanced rapidly in recent years. Between 1988 and 1997 annual issues of asset-backed securities rose from tens of millions to nearly $0.5 trillion dollars (*The Economist,* May 9, 1998, 71). Consider how easy it is to buy global real estate assets today relative to earlier decades. It is even possible to buy bonds pegged to the fortunes of rock stars or to revenues from old Italian films. Second, modern computer and communications technology flashes buy and sell orders around the world 24 hours each day in ways that the telegraph and telephone technologies of the early twentieth century only began to allow.

Governments maintain reserves of foreign currency and gold in order to support the value of their own currency in the global market place (they can use those reserves to buy their own currency and therefore increase the price of it). As recently as 1977, the global values of those reserves were about 15 times as large as daily foreign exchange turnover (*The Economist,* July 13, 1996, 84). Now daily exchanges are of comparable size.

Consequences of Global Flows

Are massive financial flows instruments for the economic development of the world, or are they highly disruptive forces that will ultimately destroy the latest round of globalization? In the midst of the global trade and financial collapse of the 1930s, the famous economist John Maynard Keynes wrote:

> Speculations may do no harm as bubbles on a steady stream of enterprise. But when enterprise becomes the bubble on a whirlpool of speculation [and the] development of the country becomes a by-product of the activities of a casino, the job is likely to be ill-done. (*The Economist,* October 7, 1995, Survey 5)

In short, the answer is "yes." Financial flows bring development *and* disruption. Unfortunately, the disruption, like that of the Great Depression amidst which Keynes wrote, can have devastating political as well as economic consequences (see Figure 12.6). The Depression helped bring on World War II.

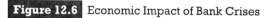

Figure 12.6 Economic Impact of Bank Crises

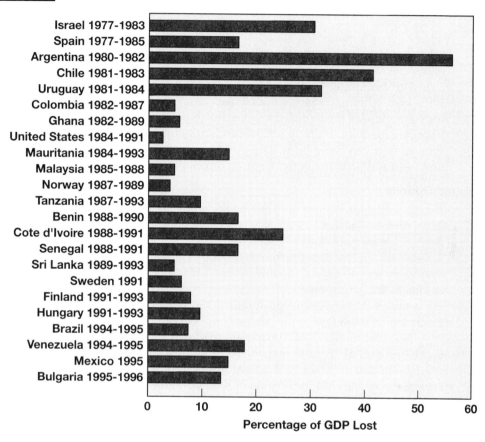

Source: World Bank, *World Development Report 1997* (Washington, DC: World Bank, 1997), 68; originally from Gerard Caprio, Jr., "Bank Regulation: The Case of the Missing Model," World Bank Research Working Paper No. 1574 (Washington, DC: World Bank Policy Research Department, 1996).

The fear is that financial flows can lead to excesses or bubbles, which then
will collapse around those who bought financial instruments believing that their
price could "only go up." One of the most famous bubbles was the Dutch Tulip-
mania of 1634–1637. At one time a single bulb could cost the modern equivalent of
$50,000; prices then collapsed more than 90 percent (IMF 1995, 179). Often the cur-
rencies and financial markets of entire countries suffer. At least three crises in the
United States and two in Brazil marked the period of globalization at the end of the
nineteenth and early twentieth centuries (IMF 1997, 238). That era ultimately
ended with the global collapse of stock markets in 1929.

The modern era of globalization has brought crisis, as well as development
capital, to many countries, even powerful ones. In the 1980s Japanese land and
share prices climbed rapidly, rising to values far above underlying fundamentals.
In 1989–1991 prices collapsed and then continued to erode throughout the decade.

Between 1990 and 1993, approximately one-fifth of all net capital flows to LDCs went to Mexico and the stock market more than quadrupled in dollar terms. Inflows peaked in late 1993 and early 1994, as the passage of NAFTA called forth what Keynes termed "the animal spirits" that drive markets. The crisis began in February, 1994, and stock prices fell 37 percent by April. In December the Mexican currency's value fell by more than half and a severe economic crisis began.

The beginning of this chapter already outlined the East Asian crisis of 1997–1998. Although each of these crises brought severe pain to individual countries or regions of the world, the larger fear is of another global collapse like that of 1929. Are markets similarly volatile and vulnerable now? Just as increased interstate contact can bring both cooperation and conflict, increased global financial flows can and do bring both increased development potential and vulnerability.

Policy Options

Two general approaches to addressing the problems associated with global financial flows surface. The more mercantilist and neo-Marxist analysts prescribe limiting the flows. Even many liberals entertain that option. Jagdish Bhagwati (1998) questioned whether the logic of benefits from comparative advantage and freer trade automatically carry over to capital mobility, particularly short-term flows. Nobel-prize winner James Tobin recommended that governments take back some control by imposing a tax on foreign-exchange transactions. For example, Chile requires that 30 percent of all inflows sit at the central bank without interest for one year.

Not surprisingly, IMF proposals reinforce rather than restrict free flows of goods and capital. In particular, the IMF emphasizes greater **transparency:** greater availability and accuracy of financial information. The Mexican government and several Asian ones hid the erosion of their currency reserves from investors in the early stages of their problems, setting the stage for massive capital outflows when investors discovered the truth. Government and banking industry "cronyism" (loans to relatives or friends) and poor regulation of stock market reporting requirements contributed further. The Bank of International Settlements (BIS) in Basle, Switzerland, serves as the "central bank for central banks," holding significant portions of the foreign-exchange reserves of states. In 1997 it issued "25 principles" of sound banking, many of which emphasize transparency. Other proposals, generally less popular, sit on the table. Economist Jeffrey Sachs called for a full blown international bankruptcy framework that would allow countries in crisis to "work out" loan repayment.

Whatever the proposals, policy development on trade and investment requires leadership. Does it exist in the global economic system?

The Leadership Question

The global political economy faces issues of protectionism in trade, volatility in financial flows, the reintegration of Eastern and Central Europe, and a gap between the rich and poor of the world that refuses to narrow (an issue for the next chapter). That is a large agenda. In addition, however, there is a critical question about leadership. Whereas the United States once unilaterally managed the institutions of Bretton Woods, there is increasingly a triad of important economic powers: the United States, the European Union, and Japan.

Yet there are questions about the leadership capability of all members of the triad. Japan's trade surpluses and lackluster growth in the 1990s undercut its contribution to leadership. The creation of the euro in 1999 positions the EU as the largest economy in the world. Yet major unemployment problems and continued attention to achieving integration of its member states distracts the EU from global leadership. The movement of the United States from the position of the world's largest creditor to that of the world's largest debtor, with large trade and payments deficits, sharply limits the leverage the United States can now exert within the global financial system. Although it has lost ability to unilaterally accomplish its objectives, the United States resists transfer of its dominant Bretton Woods power to Japan or Europe. Votes in the World Bank and IMF are proportional to capital contributions; the United States holds about 20 percent of the vote in each. To maintain that position in the World Bank, it has promoted the creation of "special" facilities that increase the relative contributions of other states without increasing their voting shares (Feinberg and Goldstein 1988, 7–2).

Diminished U.S. leadership capability in international trade and finance raises issues that Chapter 5 identified with the theory of hegemonic stability. Specifically, can a collective international grouping, rather than a dominant state, provide leadership on trade, finance, reintegration, and development issues? Even if that is possible, are Japan and Europe willing and able *co-leaders?* These are central questions of the next decade for the global political economy.

Selected Key Terms

Bretton Woods system

exchange rate

devaluation

favorable balance of trade

conditionality

most favored nation (MFN) status

spoilers

supporters

foreign direct investment (FDI)

foreign portfolio equity investment (FPEI)

transparency

CHAPTER 13

A World Divided

In the early 1900s, foreign interests, especially those just north of the border, owned large portions of the oil, mineral deposits, railroads, and even the land of Mexico. During the revolutionary period between 1910 and 1938, the Mexican government nationalized many of those resources and distributed land to the peasantry. Outside commercial interests and their home countries did not accept that gracefully. At one point the United States sent naval vessels to patrol the Gulf coast in order, according to the U.S. secretary of state, to keep the Mexicans "between a dangerous and exaggerated apprehension and a proper degree of wholesome fear" (Engler 1961, 194). Although Mexico had been the world's second largest oil producer in 1921, after nationalization the global oil companies shut the country out of the market, adding to the economic disruption caused by revolution.

KEY WEB LINKS

www.unicc.org/unctad/

www.undp.org/

nt1.ids.ac.uk/eldis/eldbr.htm

www.focusweb.org/index.html

www.sas.upenn.edu/

African_Studies/AS.html

Nonetheless, by the time world oil prices soared in the 1970s, Mexican oil exports supported an economic boom on the basis of which Mexicans borrowed abroad both to produce and to consume. In 1981, however, oil prices collapsed. Mexico could not meet its debt payments, and in 1982 the U.S. government stepped in with a loan package to save the country from default. After the 1982 collapse, and at the urging of the United States and the International Monetary Fund, Mexico liberalized its economy and embraced the forces of globalization. It swallowed the distasteful medicine of cutting government social expenditures and exposing its economy to strong international competition.

In the early 1990s the economy boomed again, especially when Canada and the United States accepted Mexico into the North American Free Trade Agreement. Investment flowed in from abroad, including purchase of government-issued bonds denominated in U.S. dollars. Yet in 1994 and 1995 the government once again found itself short of the foreign reserves necessary to meet debt payments.

Investment quickly abandoned the country. The Mexican currency collapsed, and the United States provided loans for another period of slow, painful retrenchment and recovery.

"Poor Mexico, so far from God and so close to the United States." How do poor countries like Mexico survive and attempt to advance in the presence of the overwhelming military, economic, and political power wielded by the wealthy of the world? It is a question that goes back at least to colonialism and that remains relevant today.

Imperialism and Decolonization

Two waves of empire building preceded World War I. In the sixteenth and seventeenth centuries, Portuguese, Spanish, Dutch, English, and French explorers claimed newly discovered territories in Asia and the Americas. Processes of looting, religious conversion, trading, and settlement followed, with the balance depending on the wealth, population, and political strength of the societies encountered (Doyle 1986a). The spread of empire suffered some important but partial reverses: the United States declared its independence in 1776 and the Latin American countries broke away from Spain and Portugal in the early 1800s.

The second wave targeted Africa and crested at the end of the nineteenth century.[1] The "Scramble for Africa" climaxed when the European powers finished dividing Africa into colonies at the Berlin West Africa Conference of 1884–1885. Only Ethiopia, Liberia, and South Africa were formally independent in 1914. Many explanations for this wave of imperialism emphasize dynamics of capitalist expansion. The competitive character of the process can, however, also support a more traditional realist interpretation. The acquisition of colonies may have preemptively denied possible advantage to other states. Whatever the reasons, European empires stretched across most of the globe by the end of the 1800s.

In 1900 the British empire was by far the largest. It covered one-fifth of the world's land surface and incorporated about a fourth of the world's population (Kegley and Wittkopf 1985, 77). The French empire ranked second in size. This global scope of imperialism changed little during the first half of the twentieth century, although the victors relieved Germany of its limited colonies at the end of World War I. Imperialism was violent and oppressive. When Gandhi was asked what he thought about Western civilization, he replied that "it would be nice."

Colonialism unraveled fairly quickly at the end of World War II, and the British, who had the most to lose, lost the most. India, the crown jewel of the empire, gained its independence in 1947. India had been a wealthy colony and the key to maintenance of much of the rest of the empire (Doyle 1986a, 236). Palestine, Sri Lanka, and Burma quickly followed India out of the empire. A nationalist government under Gamal Abdel Nasser took power in Egypt during 1952 and grabbed independence. The most troublesome colonies were those that had

---

[1]Counting former colonies, Headrick (1981, 3) traced the expansion of imperialism: "In the year 1800 Europeans occupied or controlled 35 percent of the land surface of the world; by 1878 this figure had risen to 67 percent, and by 1914 over 84 percent of the world's land area was European-dominated."

substantial European-settler populations, such as Malawi, Kenya, and Rhodesia. In these areas the fight for independence ultimately became a struggle with the settlers, rather than with Britain.

The French became involved in two substantial colonial wars that delayed independence for some of its colonies. The first began in Vietnam in 1945, when a nationalist movement that had fought the Japanese occupation declared independence—the French fought to recapture the colony, not abandoning the effort until 1954. The second began in Algeria during 1954; a large European-settler population together with the French attitude that Algeria was an integral part of the republic, not simply a colony, greatly complicated the eight-year war.

The remnants of Dutch, Belgian, and Portuguese empires fell away as well. The decolonization process in Africa was most dramatic because the continent had only 3 independent states in 1945 but counted 52 in 1970.

There are now about 110 states that fall into the Third World or LDC category, most of which are former colonies. They vary dramatically in per-capita income, economic and political structure, culture, the residual impact of colonialism, and prospects. Illustrating one extreme, when Belgium rather precipitously left the Congo (now the Democratic Republic of the Congo), in 1960, there were fewer than a dozen local people with university degrees (Papp 1988, 326). Large-scale racial violence broke out immediately and internal conflict flared repeatedly. Despite extremely rich mineral resources, the per-capita GNP in 1996 was still only $130. At another extreme is Hong Kong, a former British colony, now part again of China. It boasts a highly competitive industrial economy and a per-capita GNP in 1996 of $24,290.

Liberals expected that, after independence, Third World countries would follow in the economic and political footsteps of the First World (that is, they would modernize) and would catch up with the North. Liberals foresaw economic progress, including industrialization, and the development of pluralist societies with democratic institutions. They recognized that the widely varying conditions of LDCs would certainly mean that the process could take longer in some countries than in others, and that it might advance in fits and starts. W. W. Rostow (1971b) articulated the economic elements of this perspective and argued that all societies pass through stages of economic growth that have a largely unvarying logic across countries and over time.

Although few expected political development to so smoothly follow a pattern of stages, there was a strong belief that the political experience of the West was a road map for the newly independent states as well:

> The "progress" promised by the enlightenment—the spread of knowledge, the development of technology, the attainment of higher standards of material welfare, the emergence of lawful, humane, and liberal polities, and the perfection of the human spirit—now beckoned the third world, newly freed from colonialism and exploitation, and straining against its own parochialisms. The challenging question confronting the scholars of the 1950s and 1960s was how these new and developing nations would find their way into the modern world. . . . Some thought . . . that all good things go together, that science, technology, industry, and democracy were part of a seamless web. . . . (Almond 1987, 439)

Although Almond wrote this in the past tense, the fact is that more than a few scholars, and many citizens and leaders, continue to believe that, despite setbacks, the Third World will follow the lead of the industrialized, democratic countries, and that LDCs will close the economic and political gaps between them and the North.

Economic Gaps

The poor may always be with us, but their numbers change. In the last 200 years, and even in the last 20 years, their numbers have been increasing. Or have they? We need to consider the evidence.

North-South Gap

Little or no economic gap between North and South existed at the beginning of the industrial revolution. One estimate placed the per-capita GNP in Western Europe in 1800 at $212, whereas that in what we now call the Third World was $200 (Braudel 1979, 534). The gap, however, opened steadily thereafter:

> By 1850 the ratio between incomes in the industrializing societies and those in the rest of the world was perhaps two to one. In 1950 it had opened further, to about ten to one, in 1960 to nearly fifteen to one. If trends of the past decade continue, it may reach thirty to one by the end of the century. (Brown 1972, 42)

In fact, however, the trend documented by Brown did not continue after 1960. Figure 13.1 shows the ratio of per-capita GNP in the First and Third Worlds since then. Using slightly different categories than Brown did, the figure shows that the

Figure 13.1   North-South Gap: Ratio of per-Capita Incomes

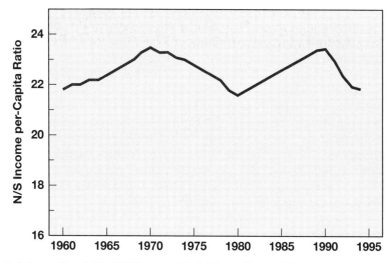

Source: Ruth Legar Sivard, *World Military and Social Expenditures 1996,* 16th ed. (Washington, DC: World Priorities, 1996), 44.

Figure 13.2 Percent of Global GDP

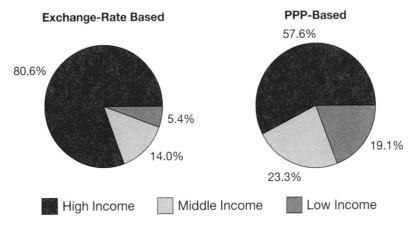

Source: World Bank, *World Development Indicators 1998* (Washington, DC: World Bank, 1998), 14.

ratio has fluctuated between 22 and 24 since 1960. Has the gap thus stabilized, and is it perhaps even on the verge of declining? That is a matter of great dispute.

Liberals have come to question the magnitude of the North-South gap that GNP figures normally produce. Those figures use official exchange rates to convert all GNPs to a common currency, and in the process they substantially understate the purchasing power that incomes in LDCs have (few could actually survive in an African country with a GNP per capita of $300 per year unless prices for goods there were substantially lower than in France). Official exchange rates indicate that the GNP per capita in China was $750 in 1996. Analysis of the spending power of the Chinese suggests, however, that it was as much as $3,330. Figure 13.2 compares the distribution of the world's GNP using exchange rates and using purchasing-power parity. Instead of accounting for 81 percent of the world's GNP, the industrial countries account for "only" 58 percent. Overall, use of purchasing-power parities would cut the North-South GNP per-capita ratio to about seven to one.

Some analysts reject this ratio analysis, whether based on exchange rates or purchasing-power parity, and argue that the gap is still increasing steadily. Instead of looking at the ratio of GNP per capita, they focus on the absolute gap between conditions in the North and South. In 1960 a $7,280 per-capita GNP difference existed between the $7,630 in the industrialized countries and $350 in the developing countries. By 1994 a $17,330 gap separated GNP per capita of $18,160 in the North from $830 in the South (Sivard 1996, 44). By this measure (using official exchange rates again) the gap more than doubled (Figure 13.3).

Some liberals suggest still another way of looking at the gap (Simon 1981). Income may be less important than what it does for our quality of life, and an excellent first measure of quality is length. Figure 13.4 shows that the average life expectancy in the South has been steadily closing on that in the North since 1960—the gap fell from 22 years to 10 years.

Figure 13.3 North-South Gap: Absolute per-Capita Income Values

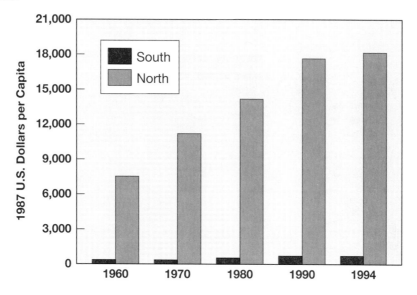

Source: Ruth Legar Sivard, *World Military and Social Expenditures 1996,* 16th ed. (Washington, DC: World Priorities, 1996), 44.

Figure 13.4 North-South Gap: Life Expectancy

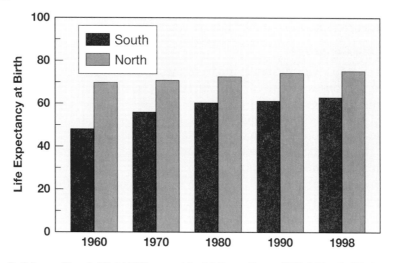

Sources: Ruth Legar Sivard, *World Military and Social Expenditures 1991,* 14th ed. (Washington, DC: World Priorities, 1991), 9; Population Reference Bureau, *World Population Data Sheet,* assorted years.

Justice in the World

THERE IS NO JUSTICE IN THE WORLD.

THERE IS SOME JUSTICE IN THE WORLD.

THE WORLD IS JUST.

Source: Drawing by Mankoff. Copyright© 1981 The New Yorker Magazine Inc.

Which measure is most appropriate? If your income is one-tenth that of your neighbor and you both succeed in doubling your income, should you focus on the fact that your income is still only one-tenth that of your neighbor, the reality that the neighbor increased her or his income ten times as much as you did, or the absolute benefits of your much-improved diet and quality of life? There is no inherently correct answer—it depends on your perspective.

Gaps Within Countries

Income gaps within countries add to the division of the world to which gaps between countries give rise. There are two especially notable characteristics of gaps within countries. First, they are larger in less-developed countries than in developed ones. This is illustrated in Table 13.1 by showing income shares taken by the richest and poorest 20 percent of various societies.

Second, income gaps within many countries rose in the 1980s and 1990s. For example, the median real (after inflation) income for families in the United States fell by 1 percent between 1979 and 1994. Moreover, while the richest 20 percent of families increased their incomes by 35 percent over that period, the poorest 20 percent of families saw their income fall by 12 percent. In short, income distribution worsened significantly during a period of rapid globalization.

Figure 13.5 shows that income distribution within countries deteriorated elsewhere in the world from the 1970s to the 1990s. The ratio of incomes in the top quintile (richest 20 percent) to the bottom quintile rose most significantly in formerly

Table 13.1   Income Distribution, Most Recent Year

	Percent of Income Received by				Percent of Income Received by	
	Lowest 20 Percent	Highest 20 Percent			Lowest 20 Percent	Highest 20 Percent
Selected Latin America				**Selected Africa**		
Bolivia	5.6	48.2		Cote d'Ivoire	6.8	44.1
Brazil	2.5	6.4		Ghana	7.9	42.2
Chile	3.5	61.0		Kenya	3.4	62.1
Colombia	3.1	61.5		Niger	7.5	44.1
Costa Rica	4.0	51.8		Nigeria	4.0	49.4
Guatemala	2.1	63.0		Rwanda	9.7	39.1
Mexico	4.1	55.3		Senegal	3.5	58.6
Panama	2.0	60.1		Tanzania	6.9	45.4
Peru	4.9	50.4		Tunisia	5.9	46.3
Venezuela	4.3	51.8		Uganda	6.8	48.1
				Zambia	3.9	50.4
				Zimbabwe	4.0	62.3
Average	3.6	51.0		Average	5.8	49.3
Selected Asia				**Selected Developed Countries**		
Bangladesh	9.4	37.9		Australia	7.0	40.9
China	5.5	47.5		Canada	7.5	39.3
India	9.2	39.3		Denmark	9.6	34.5
Indonesia	8.4	43.1		France	7.2	40.1
Madagascar	5.8	50.0		Germany	9.0	37.1
Malaysia	8.4	53.7		Finland	10.0	35.8
Pakistan	4.6	39.7		Italy	7.6	38.9
Philippines	5.9	49.6		Norway	10.0	35.3
Sri Lanka	8.9	39.3		Spain	7.5	40.3
Thailand	5.6	52.7		Sweden	9.6	34.5
Vietnam	7.8	44.0		Switzerland	7.4	43.5
				United States	4.8	45.2
Average	7.2	45.1		Average	8.1	38.7

Source: World Bank, *World Development Indicator 1998* (Washington, DC: World Bank, 1998), 68–70.

Figure 13.5   Quintile Ratios: Ratio of Income in Richest Quintile to Income in
Poorest Quintile

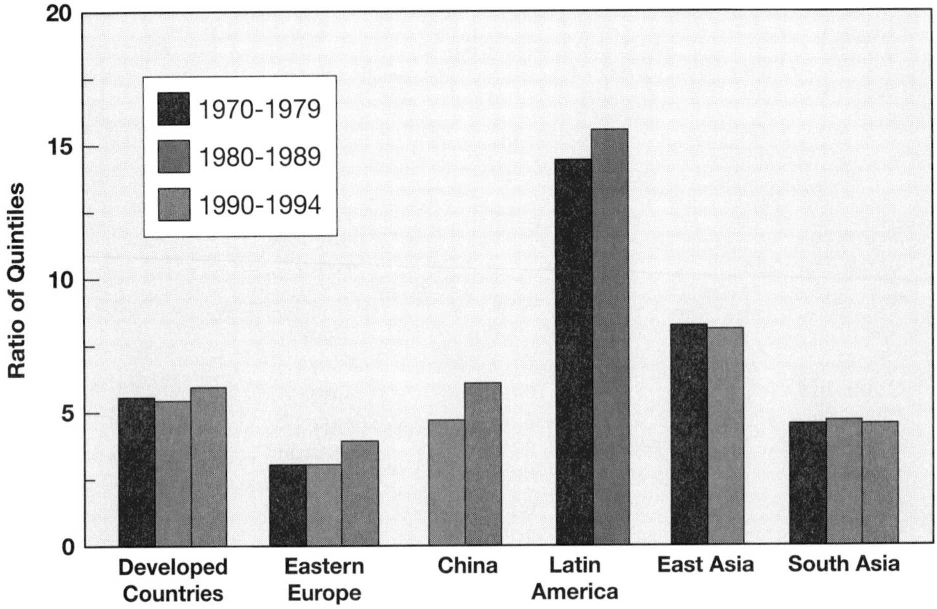

Note: Quintiles are 20-percent shares of population.

Source: United Nations Commission on Trade and Development, *Trade and Development Report,
1997* (Geneva: UNCTAD, 1997).

communist countries as they moved to market economies. It also rose in Latin
America, where ratios in the 1970s were already among the worst in the world.[2]

There is much debate among economists about whether the reason for worsening income distribution is globalization of trade and finance or global economic
restructuring with the technology of the knowledge revolution (Rodrik 1997; Sachs
1998). The former force may take jobs from workers in rich countries and move
them with global capital flows to poorer countries. The second force may put a premium on the skills held by the most educated in the world, and at the same time it
may destroy many of the production jobs of the less educated. Given mixed evidence, all that is truly clear is that interpretation of income inequality is once again
a matter of perspective.

Global Structures

The neo-Marxist perspective moves away from looking at the world as individual
states (or economies) and begins looking at it as a single economic system. When
England and France developed industrial economies and democratic institutions,

[2]The UNDP (1994, 35) calculated that on a global basis the ratio of top-to-bottom quintiles of humanity rose from 30 to 60 between 1960 and 1991. The fundamental reason was lack of economic growth
for the poorest 20 percent.

they did so as independent states with a high level of control over domestic economies. They used various mercantilist mechanisms to initiate their economic development before subsequently adopting liberal policies from positions of economic strength. "Bismarck insisted that free trade was the weapon of the dominant economy anxious to prevent others from following its path" (Kindleberger 1973, 303). Although Dutch incomes were once twice those of England, that advantage did not translate into significant political-economic penetration and control of England.

In contrast, LDCs today exist in a world in which they face actors much more politically, militarily, technologically, and economically powerful than themselves —actors that very strongly influence their political economies. There are four concrete structural manifestations of this relationship. The first is the existence of a global division of labor, a highly integrated world economy in which countries tend to specialize with respect to production. Second, the advanced countries have established international institutions (those of Bretton Woods) and regimes in international policy that LDCs cannot ignore. Third, powerful MNCs have evolved and, whether they are instruments of the developed countries or independent actors in their own right, they have great influence in LDCs, with respect to both financial and technological flows. Finally, the large military-power differentials of rich and poor countries make it inevitable that security policies of the rich will affect the poor. We look at each in turn.

Global Division of Labor

At one time, the economies of low- and middle-income LDCs depended heavily on the export of primary commodities (raw materials, both agricultural and mineral). In 1996, however, only 21 percent of the exports of low-income LDCs consisted of such goods. The bulk, 66 percent, were manufactures and the other 13 percent were services. The corresponding numbers for high-income countries were similar: 15 percent primary goods, 64 percent manufactures, and 21 percent services (World Bank 1998, 190, 198). Yet more than 50 percent of the export earnings of many LDCs still come from just one or two primary products: for example, Zambia (copper); Burundi (coffee); Ethiopia (coffee); Niger (uranium); Botswana (diamonds); Mauritania (fish and iron ore); and Malawi (tobacco). Most OPEC countries earn more than 75 percent of their foreign exchange from oil.

One problem with such dependence is that prices of raw materials are notoriously unstable. Although prices of manufactured goods might fluctuate 5 to 10 percent from one year to the next, it is not uncommon for commodity prices to double, triple, or fall by similar amounts. Imagine a government attempting to build roads, an electric grid, schools, and hospitals when the bases of its revenues fluctuate so dramatically.

A second problem associated with dependence on primary commodities in the global market is that, in addition to price fluctuations, the long-term trend in commodity prices has been downward. The **terms of trade** is the trade-weighted ratio of export and import prices, that is, the ratio of the prices of goods a country *sells* (considering how much of each good it markets) to the prices of goods it *buys*. If a developing country is dependent on primary goods exports and the prices of those goods in world markets decline while prices of manufactured imports remain stable, the terms of trade for the LDC deteriorate.[3] The evidence concerning trends in the terms of trade is mixed, complicated by our inability to evaluate and measure quality changes over time. Although a ton of copper today is no different from that of 50 years ago, automobiles and machine tools, although perhaps not priced so much higher in real terms, are much superior to those produced a half-century earlier. That could offset much of the apparently adverse trend in Figure 13.6.

The international division of labor is, of course, not static. Most LDCs now are industrialized countries, a label we once reserved for more-developed countries. Even here, however, they have a disadvantage in the global division of labor. It is not the most technologically advanced manufactures, with the highest profit margins, that move to LDCs. According to Vernon's (1987) **product cycle theory,** manufacturing moves South only when competition has squeezed profits and lower-cost production is needed. If true, and there is considerable supportive evidence, LDCs remain at a competitive disadvantage.

Political-Economic Institutions and Regimes

Colonialism is all but dead in today's world, and formal control by the countries of the North over the polities or economies of the South has evaporated. Nonetheless, high levels of influence by North over South remain through the exercise of political and economic power including that of institutions and regimes. Some call the modern pattern **neocolonialism.** The earlier review of the global economic order (in Chapter 12) emphasized primarily how that order structures trade and financial relationships among developed states. Let us focus now on the way it shapes the trade and financial relationships between Northern and Southern states. In particular we will focus on the trade issue of tariffs and on the financial issue of debt.

Trade and Tariffs   Tariffs illustrate how the global political structure can work against LDCs. Tariffs served two important functions in the development of most industrial economies. First, they provided state revenues. New governments could relatively easily collect them at borders. Effective income-tax mechanisms are much more complicated, are phenomena of the twentieth century even in developed countries, and are still not widespread in LDCs (countries as advanced as Italy continue to have difficulty enforcing collection). In 1995 taxes on trade still accounted for about 9 percent of middle-income LDC government revenues versus nearly zero in high-income countries (World Bank 1998, 228). Second, they protect **infant industries** (newly established and not always efficient and competitive firms) against external competition. France used tariffs for both purposes in its early development. And the United States surely did not pursue laissez-faire economic policies in its early push for development:

> In evaluating early American economic development, it should be recognized that there was *a great deal of government intervention and even public investment in the economy so as to develop industry and commerce. . . .* The most important federal measures di-

---

[3]Raul Prebisch argued that terms of trade deterioration is the long-term fate of LDCs. First, as global incomes rise, people spend higher portions of total income on manufactured goods and services, and smaller portions on primary products. Second, technological advance allows manufactured products to use less material input in total and to substitute increasing amounts of synthetic materials.

Figure 13.6   Terms of Trade

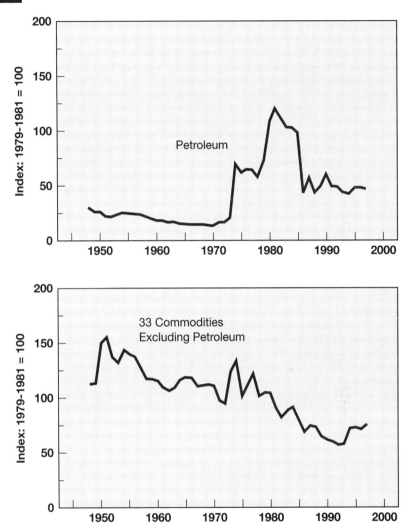

Sources: World Bank, *Commodity Trade and Price Trends 1987/88* (Baltimore: Johns Hopkins University Press, 1988), 46; British Petroleum, *BP Statistical Review of World Energy* (London: British Petroleum, 1992), 12; World Bank, *Global Economic Prospects and the Developing Countries* (Washington, DC: World Bank, 1991), 46; World Bank, *Global Economic Prospects and the Developing Countries* (Washington, DC: World Bank, 1995), 91; World Bank, *World Development Indicators 1998* (Washington, DC: World Bank, 1998), 324.

rectly supporting economic growth took the form of investment in the Bank of the United States and, more important, protective tariffs to encourage domestic industry against products manufactured in England. (Lipset 1963, 48)

In fact, every country that industrialized successfully after Britain in the nineteenth century used tariffs to protect infant industry (Doyle 1986a, 264).

In spite of protectionist histories during their own development, more-developed countries and their institutions like the IMF and World Bank now insist that exposure by the LDCs of their industry to tough world competition is the best policy. LDCs reasonably argue that the rich deny them the benefits of protective tariffs that developed countries once reaped. The central principle of the Bretton Woods tariff system, reciprocity, works against LDCs. Moreover, the WTO strengthened its demand for full LDC participation in trade liberalization, relative to its predecessor organization, the GATT.

MDCs do not always even apply the principle of reciprocity fairly. At the same time that they pressure LDCs to forgo the benefits of protective tariffs for more-advanced manufactured goods from infant industries, they frequently place unusually high tariffs on the less-advanced goods that LDCs already produce competitively. Although the rounds of GATT negotiations greatly reduced average tariffs, "the manufactured and semi-manufactured products of particular export interest to less developed countries (such as textiles and semi-processed metal or wood products) typically face tariff levels of two to four times this average" (Walters and Blake 1992, 40). Behind this phenomenon is the fact that the industries in which LDCs are competitive tend to be older industries, generally in decline within the advanced capitalist countries. Unemployment in those industries leads to pressures within the developed countries for support and protection. In the industrialized states, the lobbyists of LDCs seldom carry the clout of those from the domestic textile or shoe industries.

Finance and Debt   Financial help from abroad supported the development of many countries over the last 200 years. British capital built railroads, other infrastructure, and industry in the United States during the nineteenth century. The British invested directly and through debt issued by the U.S. government. Despite high levels of public debt in 1870, the private sector became so strong that the United States transformed itself from a net debtor into the world's largest creditor.

Liberal development theorists argue that this kind of progression is natural: a reliance on foreign capital to build an industrial base and then a use of that base to export, to retire foreign debt, and eventually to invest abroad. One obvious flaw emerges in this portrait, when examined from a systemic viewpoint: Not all countries can ultimately become creditor states (for every credit there must be a debit), and it may be extremely difficult for many LDCs to retire debt in a highly competitive, widely industrialized world.

The issue of debt became especially important after the global oil shocks of 1973–1974 and 1979–1980. Most LDCs depend heavily on imported oil and in those years world oil prices rose dramatically. To finance oil imports and to maintain economic growth in this period, they borrowed heavily from abroad. Credit was inexpensive during the 1970s, because the oil-exporting countries had large surpluses of cash. They recycled those surpluses to the global financial community through the burgeoning Eurocurrency markets.

Problems arose in the early 1980s for three reasons. First, in a war against inflation, waged by the more-developed countries, global real-interest rates rose. This made the debt burden more onerous. Second, the level of debt began to frighten private financial institutions, which then frequently refused to loan addi-

Figure 13.7   LDC Debt and Exports

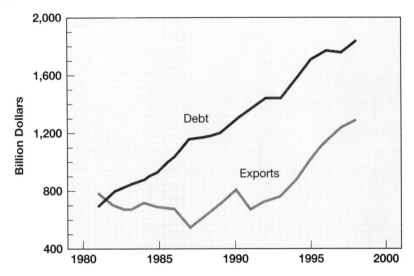

Note: LDCs exclude Eastern Europe and the former U.S.S.R.

Sources: International Monetary Fund, *World Economic Outlook* (Washington, DC: International Monetary Fund, 1989), 186; International Monetary Fund, *World Economic Outlook* (Washington, DC: International Monetary Fund, 1992), 171, 176; International Monetary Fund, *World Economic Outlook* (Washington, DC: International Monetary Fund, 1998), 204–205.

tional funds, previously a common practice. Third, the global economy weakened, and therefore markets for the exports of the LDCs contracted. Commodity prices fell sharply. Thus the export earnings of LDCs failed to grow as projected and as needed to repay indebtedness (Figure 13.7).

In 1981, before the widespread recognition of a debt crisis, LDC debt had reached $750 billion, and payments on it absorbed 16 percent of all LDC export earnings. By 1986 interest and principal payments required 22 percent of export earnings. Although exports resumed growth in the 1990s, rising interest rates kept debt service at about that level through the decade. Table 13.2 shows the debt levels for major debtors.

The first real evidence that the debt problem had become a debt crisis appeared in Mexico in 1982. Ironically, that country had not borrowed to finance oil imports, the most common pattern. Instead, major oil discoveries in the 1970s led it to borrow in anticipation of earnings and to aid development of the resources more rapidly. Oil prices peaked in 1981 and began to decline sharply thereafter, creating a severe predicament for Mexico.

Once banks came to perceive a debt crisis, *private* capital flow to the South collapsed, and the situation became even worse. Annual net private flows to LDCs exceeded $50 billion in 1981 but fell to about $8 billion in 1985. Between 1983 and 1988 commercial banks removed capital from LDCs, by receiving more in interest and principal repayments than they offered in new loans (Sewell and others 1988, 228–230).

Table 13.2	LDCs Whose Debt Service Exceeded 30 Percent in 1980 or 1996			
	Total Debt (billion dollars)		Debt Service/Exports (percent)	
	1980	1996	1980	1996
Argentina	27.2	93.8	37.3	44.2
Bolivia	2.7	5.2	35.0	30.9
Brazil	71.5	179.0	63.3	41.1
Burundi	.2	1.1	NA	54.6
Chile	12.1	27.4	43.1	32.3
Colombia	6.9	28.8	16.0	34.6
Côte d'Ivoire	7.4	18.7	38.7	26.2
Ecuador	5.9	14.5	33.9	22.6
Ethiopia	.8	10.1	7.6	42.2
Guinea-Bissau	.1	.9	NA	48.7
Hungary	9.8	27.0	NA	41.0
Indonesia	20.9	129.6	NA	36.8
Mexico	57.4	157.1	44.4	35.4
Morocco	9.2	21.8	33.4	27.7
Mozambique	NA	5.8	NA	32.3
Peru	9.4	41.2	44.5	35.4
Sierra Leone	.5	1.2	23.8	52.6

Sources: World Bank, *World Development Indicators 1998* (Washington, DC: World Bank, 1998), 238–244.

Because the World Bank is a lending, not an aid-giving institution, it cannot resolve the debt crisis. In fact, repayments to the Bank from 17 highly indebted, middle-income countries in 1988 exceeded new loans (World Bank 1988, 34). Similarly, the IMF is not a development or general lending institution. It did increase transfers to the Third World sharply in 1982 and 1983 as the debt crisis unfolded, but by 1986 it, too, was removing more capital from LDCs than it provided to them. Figure 13.8 shows that net transfers to LDCs were negative between 1984 and 1991. Net flows turned positive in the early 1990s because private flows (direct investment, portfolio investment, and private loans) returned.

The IMF assists more indirectly with resolution of debt problems by organizing refinancings of LDC private debt. It brings the lending banks into consortia to extend the repayment periods, to lessen the interest burden, and now and then even to offer additional capital to prime the dry economic pumps of the borrowers. To make any relaxation of terms palatable to lenders, it imposes, as it does with its own loans, conditions on the borrowers in the new agreements. This conditionality requires the LDCs to reduce government spending and deficits and to eliminate impediments to trade. Frequently, for instance, the IMF calls on LDC governments to rid themselves of money-losing, state-owned industry, to reduce subsidies and welfare expenditures, and to devalue local currencies so as to make

Figure 13.8   Net Lending to All Developing Countries

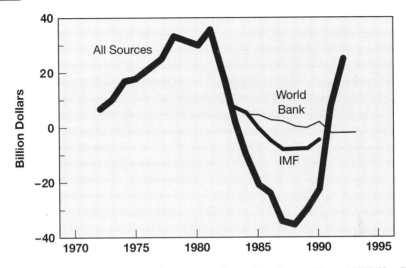

Sources: United Nations Development Programme, *Human Development Report 1992* (New York: Oxford University Press, 1992), 50–51; United Nations Development Programme, *Human Development Report 1994* (New York: Oxford University Press, 1994), 64.

exports more attractive. As liberals would say, it is necessary to "get the prices right"—to let the market work.

The domestic consequences in LDCs of acting to meet these conditions have been severe. They include increased unemployment, decreased support systems for the poorest in society, and increased consumer prices. The GNPs per capita in Africa and Latin America actually declined in the "lost decade" of the 1980s by annual averages of 1.7 and 0.4 percent, respectively. In the financial crises of the late 1990s, people in countries like Mexico and Indonesia suffered greatly under the terms that the IMF and other external financial agencies imposed. In 1998 hundreds died in riots in Indonesia against the Suharto government and against the economic retrenchment it implemented under external pressure. The IMF is now extremely unpopular in many LDCs. President Mubarak of Egypt called it the "International Misery Fund."

Even when successful in increasing exports and cutting imports, these policies have not lowered Third World external debt, which grew from $603 billion in 1980 to $2,095 billion in 1996 (World Bank 1998, 240, 244). The more-developed countries have moved only gradually to address the problem. In 1989 U.S. Treasury Secretary Brady proposed that the IMF and World Bank lead a plan by which private banks would forgive some indebtedness in exchange for guarantees on remaining loans. The first agreement under that plan reduced the Mexican commercial debt burden by about 20 percent. The Brady Plan subsequently helped a total of 18 countries. Although economic growth in Latin America turned positive in the early 1990s, severe financial problems remained throughout the Third World.

Multinational Corporations

We have discussed two elements of the global structure in which rich and poor countries interact: the global division of labor and the existence of interstate political-economic institutions dominated by First World countries and their philosophies. **Multinational corporations (MNCs)**, sometimes called *transnational corporations (TNCs)*, constitute a third element. The United Nations Conference on Trade and Development counted 45,000 with 280,000 foreign affiliates in 1997 (UNCTAD 1997, xv). Just the largest 100 of all TNCs controlled approximately $1.7 trillion in assets abroad, about one-fifth of all global foreign assets. The affiliates of all TNCs posted sales of about $7 trillion (about one-fifth of the global GDP).

Economic Impact of Multinational Corporations   Whether MNCs are agents of global capitalism, tools of the states from which they originate, servants of their stockholders, autonomous units acting on behalf of management, or some combination of these, there can be little doubt that their masters almost always exist outside of LDCs. The economic size of the larger corporations challenges that of the LDCs. General Motors, Ford, Royal Dutch Shell, and Exxon had annual sales in 1996 larger than the GNPs of Norway, South Africa, Poland, and Finland respectively (Table 13.3). Global merger activity grew from less than $100 billion in 1982 to about $1.7 trillion in 1997, further increasing MNC size (*The Economist*, May 2, 1998, 62).

Neo-Marxists point out that Britain, France, the United States, and Germany did not face such powerful external economic actors when they developed. MNCs have often imposed unfavorable economic terms on LDCs. For instance, about one-third of world trade consists of sales across state borders but between units of the same corporation (UNCTAD 1996, 103). In such internal corporate transactions, the companies have nearly complete control over **transfer pricing** (the prices one division of a corporation charges another division for a product). Critics frequently accuse them of setting transfer prices to avoid taxation or limitations on repatriation of large profits from LDCs. In the 1980s MNCs exported timber from a Pacific Island Country (unnamed), using "third-country invoicing" to avoid all local corporate income taxes. That is, the MNCs priced timber exports low from the country of origin, "sold" them at considerably higher prices in paper transactions in a country that charges little or no tax, and then delivered timber to market at the higher price (United Nations CTC 1988, 94–95). Similarly, the U.S. Internal Revenue Service reported in 1990 that more than half of the 37,000 foreign firms doing business in the United States paid no taxes—on gross sales of over $550 billion they reported net tax losses. Analysts cited transfer pricing as the reason.

The major reason LDCs desire the presence of multinational corporations is to obtain investment capital from the companies. However, MNCs often obtain large portions of their capital in the host country. Moreover, through repatriation of profits back to the home country, MNCs periodically set up net capital transfers from South to North (as they did in the 1980s). Nonetheless, the value of the technology, management skills, and production that LDCs gain is high. It is nearly impossible to assess the net economic impact of MNCs on LDC production levels, but one can reasonably ask if many LDCs would have *any* modern manufacturing without MNCs.

Table 13.3   The World's 100 Largest Economic Units, 1996 (million dollars)

#	Unit	Value	#	Unit	Value
1.	United States	7,433,500	51.	Colombia	80,200
2.	Japan	5,149,200	52.	*General Electric*	79,179
3.	Germany	2,364,600	53.	*Nissho Iwai*	78,921
4.	France	1,533,600	54.	*Nippon Telegraph*	78,321
5.	United Kingdom	1,152,100	55.	*IBM*	75,947
6.	Italy	1,140,500	56.	*Hitachi*	75,669
7.	China	906,100	57.	*AT&T*	74,525
8.	Brazil	709,600	58.	United Arab Emirates	72,900
9.	Canada	569,900	59.	*Nippon Life Insurance*	72,575
10.	Spain	563,200	60.	*Mobil*	72,267
11.	South Korea	483,100	61.	*Dalmer-Benz*	71,589
12.	Netherlands	402,600	62.	Chile	70,100
13.	Australia	367,800	63.	*British Petroleum*	69,852
14.	India	357,800	64.	*Matshshita Electric Industrial*	68,148
15.	Russia	356,000	65.	Venezuela	67,300
16.	Iran	343,500	66.	*Volkswagen*	66,528
17.	Mexico	341,700	67.	*Daewoo*	65,160
18.	Taiwan	315,000	68.	Egypt	64,300
19.	Switzerland	313,700	69.	*Siemens*	63,705
20.	Argentina	295,100	70.	Pakistan	63,600
21.	Belgium	268,600	71.	Ireland	62,000
22.	Sweden	227,300	72.	*Chrysler*	61,397
23.	Austria	226,500	73.	Ukraine	60,900
24.	Indonesia	213,400	74.	*Nissan Motor*	59,118
25.	Saudi Arabia	205,600	75.	Peru	58,700
26.	Thailand	177,500	76.	New Zealand	57,100
27.	Turkey	177,500	77.	*Allianz*	56,577
28.	Denmark	168,900	78.	*US Postal Service*	56,402
29.	*General Motors*	168,369	79.	*Philip Morris*	54,553
30.	Hong Kong	163,600	80.	*Unilevel*	52,067
31.	Norway	151,200	81.	*Fiat*	50,509
32.	*Ford Motor Company*	146,991	82.	*Sony*	50,278
33.	*Mitsui*	144,943	83.	*Dai-Ichi Mutual Life*	49,145
34.	*Mitsubishi*	140,204	84.	*IRI*	49,056
35.	*Itochu*	135,542	85.	*Nestle*	48,933
36.	South Africa	132,500	86.	Czech Republic	48,900
37.	*Royal Dutch/Shell*	128,175	87.	*Toshiba*	48,416
38.	Poland	124,700	88.	*Honda Motor*	46,995
39.	*Marubeni*	124,027	89.	*Elf Aquitaine*	46,818
40.	Greece	120,000	90.	*Tomen*	46,506
41.	*Exxon*	119,434	91.	*Bank of Tokyo-Mitsubishi*	46,451
42.	*Sumitomo*	119,281	92.	*Veba Group*	45,246
43.	Finland	119,100	93.	*Tokyo Electric Power*	44,735
44.	*Toyota Motor*	108,702	94.	*Texaco*	44,561
45.	*Wal-mart Stores*	106,147	95.	Hungary	44,300
46.	Portugal	100,900	96.	*Sumitomo Life Insurance*	44,063
47.	Singapore	93,000	97.	*Sunkyong*	44,031
48.	Israel	90,300	98.	*NEC*	43,933
49.	Malaysia	89,800	99.	Algeria	43,700
50.	Phillipines	83,300	100.	*Electricite de France*	43,659

Note: Figures for corporations are annual sales; those for countries are GNP at exchange rates.

Sources: Fortune August 4, 1997, F2–F28; World Bank, *World Development Indicators 1998* (Washington, DC: World Bank, 1998).

Capital is but one factor of production. Two others are labor and technology, and LDCs feel disadvantaged with respect to them as well. Hiring by MNCs contributes to a **brain drain,** in which many of the most educated individuals from the South move North. The other side of the brain-drain argument, however, is that remittances of workers back to families contribute substantially to the country of emigration. In Turkey, Egypt, Portugal, Pakistan, and Morocco, remittances have exceeded 5 percent of GNP. One study found that Mexican migrants send back more than twice what they can make at home (UNDP 1992, 56). The conventional wisdom has shifted from seeking solely to avoid brain drain of the educated to arguing also in favor of freer immigration for the less skilled.

Technology, like capital, is a key production factor that LDCs hope to attain from multinationals. LDCs have three primary complaints in this area. First, they believe that MNCs charge too much for existing technology. Second, they argue that MNCs maintain the research and development function in the home countries, and thus retard LDC efforts to develop their own innovation capabilities. Third, LDCs have concerns about the character of the imported technology. Industrial countries that are rich in capital but poor in labor often do not develop **appropriate technology** for LDCs that are poor in capital and rich in labor. The import of inappropriate technology can increase unemployment.

Power of Multinational Corporations   LDCs sometimes believe that they are relatively powerless compared with MNCs. Although both sides may gain, bargaining from a position of weakness often means obtaining an unequal bargain. Even governments in more-developed countries often question their ability to deal successfully with MNCs. States and cities within the United States often find themselves in bidding wars over the location of MNC plants. Those governments provide tax and other concessions that reduce the net benefits to them while increasing the benefits to the corporation. The competition among LDCs for corporate favor is equally fierce.

Raymond Vernon's concept of the **obsolescing bargain** can help us better understand bargaining positions—and the love-hate relationship between companies and countries. When MNCs first approach Third World countries (or, for that matter, First World countries), the states often actively pursue the MNC and the benefits it can bring. A courtship by multiple potential hosts allows the MNC to strike a favorable bargain. Countries may offer land, tax benefits, and favorable treatment under national laws. Once a corporation has invested its capital, however, power shifts to the host country. The country can hold the ultimate threat of nationalization over the company's corporate head, and short of that it can bring to bear the entire legal system it controls (including health and safety standards, environmental controls, and labor regulation). The government may request increased taxes, greater local ownership, higher levels of exports, or other concessions of interest to it.

The concern of neo-Marxists extends beyond the economic roles of MNCs, however, to their political ones. MNCs have interfered in the politics of states and have also attempted, sometimes with apparent success, to involve their home states on their behalf. There is as much debate over the political power of MNCs abroad as over their economic influence:

Dependencia [dependency theory] writers have tended to assert that multinational firms have solid local political alliances and great local political influence, with the margin for autonomous domestic policy action extremely thin. International business writers, in contrast, tend to argue that foreign companies are continuously buffeted by hostile local forces, discriminated against on a regular basis, and left to operate almost totally without domestic political clout. (Moran 1985, 15)

Specific examples of interference frequently involve bribery. United Brands has been accused of bribing local officials in Guatemala (Blake and Walters 1987, 108) and Honduras (Spero 1981, 240). A U.S. congressional inquiry found that one hundred MNCs had made improper foreign payments totaling more than $100 million (Kegley and Wittkopf 1989, 170).

A particularly notorious example of MNC political interference occurred in Chile. International Telephone and Telegraph Company (ITT), a U.S.-based MNC, worked actively to avoid the election of Salvador Allende, Socialist party leader, to the presidency in late 1970, because it feared nationalization (Krasner 1978, 303). It put $350,000 into the coffers of his conservative opponent. It also approached the CIA before and after the election with offers to support action against him. The U.S. government did undertake covert activity both to prevent the election and to foment the 1973 coup that overthrew and assassinated Allende. This example does not imply, however, that MNCs consistently behave in such a manner. Moreover, it appears that the U.S. government took action independently of pressure from ITT.

The rise of MNCs in the postwar period has been so dramatic that some perceive them as a growing international political force, eventually strong enough to undercut the sovereignty not only of LDCs but of economically developed states. Vernon (1971) wrote of "sovereignty at bay." Is there any evidence on the changing relative strength of MNCs and states? Figure 13.9 summarizes the relative economic size of the two categories of actors, building on several tables like Table 13.3. It traces over time the ratio of GNPs of states in the top 100 global actors to sales of MNCs in that set. Service corporations (e.g., banks, insurance companies, and fast-food chains) have become major global actors more recently than oil companies and industrial firms like automobile companies. It appears that MNCs gained in size relative to states in the 1970s (when oil companies benefited from higher prices) and again more recently as larger service firms have emerged.

Controls on Investment and Corporations   As FDI has grown and transnational corporations have flourished, both corporations and states increasingly call for policy on FDI. Corporations call for protection against expropriation of assets and for transparency in policies by host countries toward foreign investment. They also want barriers to transborder capital flows removed. Host countries want some control over repatriation of profits and capital and ensured access to technology. Both companies and hosts have interests in reducing bribery and in setting up acceptable dispute settlement mechanisms.

Lengthy multi-issue discussions in the 1970s on a Code of Conduct on Transnational Corporations failed, as did long talks in the 1990s on a Multilateral Investment Agreement. Yet other multilateral agreements, for instance on intellectual property rights and dispute settlement, have been successful. Also more than

Figure 13.9 Relative Size of States and Industrial MNCs in Largest 100 Global Economic Actors

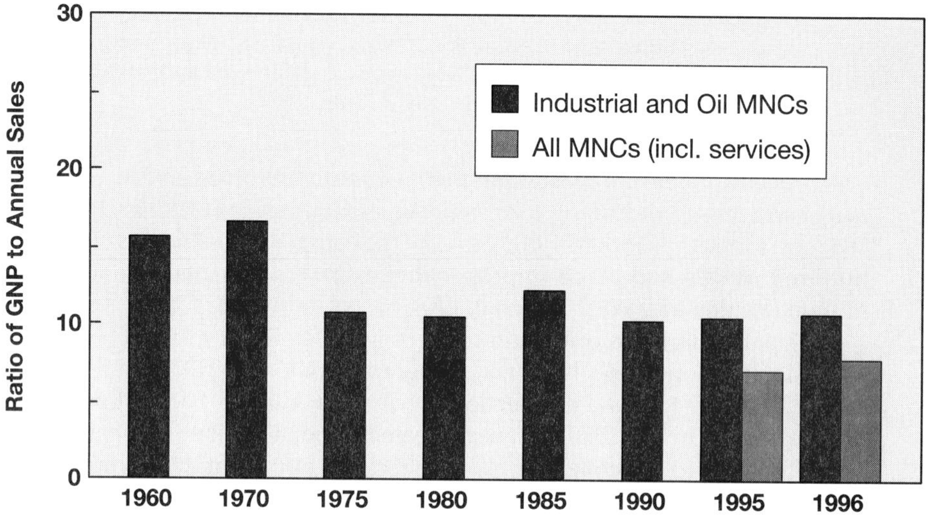

Note: Figure shows industrial and oil MNCs from 1960 to 1996. Only the "All MNC" bars include the financial and service sectors. *Fortune* began including service firms in 1994.
Sources: Assorted tables like Table 13.2.

1,100 bilateral investment treaties (BITs) have come into force, primarily in the 1990s (UNCTAD 1996, 147). Large numbers control double taxation, but they cover a wide range of other issues, including liberalization of entry. International law on trade and finance promises to be a growth industry for many years.

Military-Power Differentials

To this point we have discussed three elements of global structure that influence North-South relations: global division of labor, global institutions, and multinational corporations. We have left the most obvious until last: military-power differentials. Clearly those give the North substantial ability to intervene directly with force in the South. That ability has, however, sharply declined in the 40 years since decolonization. In 1960 the military expenditures of developed countries were 11 times those in developing countries and the armed forces of the developed world were larger (Sivard 1996). By 1995 the military expenditures of the developed world were only 3.4 times larger and the armed forces of developing countries were twice as large as those in developed countries. Although a solid preponderance of military power remains in the hands of developed countries, the world has changed substantially (Figure 13.10).

There have been some direct North-South conflicts in the last half century (e.g., the British-Argentine war over the Malvinas/Falklands). Yet the collateral damage that military tensions and conflict in the North inflict on the South exceeds damage rooted in purely North-South disputes. A Swahili proverb says it well: "When two elephants fight, the grass gets trampled" (Shepherd 1987, 1). After the

Figure 13.10   Military Sizes in North and South

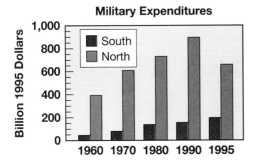
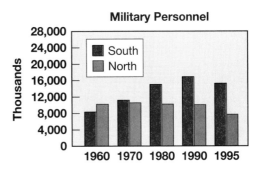

Sources: Ruth Leger Sivard, *World Military and Social Expenditures 1993* (Washington, DC: World Priorities, 1993), 42; U.S. Arms Control and Disarmament Agency, *World Military Expenditures and Arms Transfers 1996* (Washington, DC: US ACDA, 1997), 49.

breakdown of their World War II alliance, the superpowers moved rapidly to organize as much of the world as possible around them. LDCs quickly became objects of their interest and instruments of their power.

LDCs have often been proxies or stand-ins for the superpowers, creating **proxy wars.** Many proxy wars pitted one superpower against proxies of the other. Neither the United States nor the Soviet Union cheerfully watched any changes of government within their spheres of influence that appeared to give the other superpower an edge. For example, in June 1950 communist North Korean forces invaded the noncommunist South, converting the Cold War into a hot one. The United States led an alliance of 17 noncommunist powers under the banner of the United Nations. The United States and the U.S.S.R. avoided direct conflict, but China entered the war on the communist side.

Cuba was long a focal point for East-West tension. After the victory of Castro in Cuba in 1959, relations with the United States soured, and the Soviet Union backed the new Communist government. In reaction, the United States sponsored a disastrous invasion attempt by exile forces at Cuba's Bay of Pigs in 1961. The Soviets then attempted in 1962 to use Cuba as a platform for nuclear missiles, and the United States successfully forced the Soviets to cease construction of the installations during the Cuban missile crisis. The missile crisis was as close to direct conflict as the superpowers came in the Cold War.

Asia became the major battlefield once again, however. Simmering involvement by the United States in the Vietnamese civil war during the early 1960s escalated in 1964 to bombing attacks on the communist North. American troop commitment built rapidly to a peak in 1968 of about 1/2 million (more than 56,000 Americans died there). The last Americans finally withdrew in April 1975.

Between 1974 and 1979 the Soviets became especially aggressive in the Third World (Saivetz and Woodby 1985). The Soviets sponsored a Cuban intervention in the Angolan civil war in October 1975; there were 50,000 Cuban soldiers in the country when withdrawal finally began in 1989. In 1979 another Cuban force went

Figure 13.11 Arms Sales

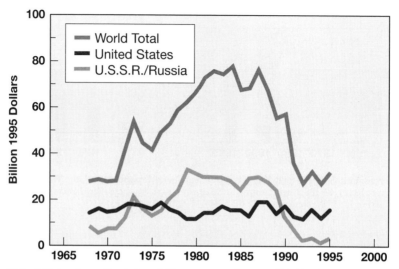

Sources: United States Arms Control and Disarmament Agency, *World Military Expenditures and Arms Transfers, 1968–1977* (Washington, DC: US ACDA, 1979), 113, 147, 151; United States Arms Control and Disarmament Agency, *World Military Expenditures and Arms Transfers, 1988* (Washington, DC: US ACDA, 1989), 69, 103, 104; United States Arms Control and Disarmament Agency, *World Military Expenditures and Arms Transfers, 1990* (Washington, DC: US ACDA, 1991), 89, 123, 127; United States Arms Control and Disarmament Agency, *World Military Expenditures and Arms Transfers, 1996* (Washington, DC: US ACDA, 1997), 100, 139, 147.

to Ethiopia as a Soviet proxy. In December 1979 the Soviets invaded Afghanistan. The involvement of about 115,000 troops lasted nearly a decade; it culminated in a retreat nearly as ignominious as that of the United States from Vietnam. This quick review only scratches the surface of overt and covert intervention by the Soviet Union and United States in the affairs of other countries—it leaves out Iran, Guatemala, Nicaragua, El Salvador, Libya, and many other venues.

The superpowers also long sparred in weapons support for client states. Early in the Cold War they provided gifts and sold inexpensive or obsolete equipment from their arsenals. In the 1980s they sold highly sophisticated military technology at high prices. In that decade the two superpowers accounted for about 60 percent of total global arms sales, and their NATO and Warsaw Pact allies provided most of the rest. (Third World suppliers like Israel, South Korea, and Brazil became important, however.) The United States was the world's largest supplier until the late 1970s, the Soviet Union took over that place of honor in the 1980s, and the United States regained it in the 1990s, after Soviet collapse demolished the appeal of Russian weapons (see Figure 13.11).

Since the end of the Cold War, global arms sales have fallen by more than half. And perhaps most important, Northern interventions have generally not been for the purpose of countering other great powers, but for humanitarian reasons. Only one interstate conflict has caused great loss of life: the UN action against Iraq in

1991 in a collective defense operation after Iraq's occupation of Kuwait. Russia and the United States both supported that action. The United States invaded Somalia in 1992 and Haiti in 1994 in efforts to restore order and protect human rights. In both cases the UN supported the intervention. The UN and NATO cooperated (with Russian support) to address the conflict in Bosnia.

A critical question for the next decade is how the end of the Cold War will, in the longer run, affect Northern participation in the creation and dampening of conflict in the South. There are many possible forecasts. Many realists would anticipate at most a brief respite in competition among great powers for the resources (including markets) of the South. Some of that competition will inevitably lead to military conflict—the oil resources of the Middle East will likely remain a focal point. Liberals would hope for, but not necessarily forecast, collective efforts by the North to reduce causes of Southern conflict. On this issue neo-Marxists are likely to agree with realists: the elephants have long trampled the grass throughout the Third World; they are unlikely to develop better manners.

Development Strategies

The existence of an international division of labor, well-established international political-economic institutions dominated by developed countries, powerful MNCs, and military-power differentials jointly support the contention that we must look at the world political economy as a whole, and that paths of development blazed by rich countries may be irrelevant to contemporary LDCs. Southern countries must somehow cope in the world they face, however, and the development strategy they adopt will depend on their perspective on that world. Three dominant sets of strategies exist: inward-looking policy, systemic reform, and participation. Neo-Marxists (and realists) have sometimes supported the first strategy, reform attracts attention from both selected neo-Marxists and liberals, and many liberals strongly recommend participation.

Inward-Looking Policy

When developed countries hammered together the Bretton Woods institutions, LDCs insisted on provisions to relax the conditions of free trade. They wanted to be able to use import controls, regional-preference systems, and commodity agreements (Spero 1981, 184). Fundamentally, however, GATT did not allow that flexibility for LDCs, imposing instead the same free-trade rules on all countries. Not having obtained what they wanted, many LDCs refused to join GATT. Instead, in the early decades after World War II, they pursued policies of import substitution.

Import substitution is a policy of producing domestically as much as possible of that which a country traditionally imported. Many LDCs, especially in Latin America, maintained their high prewar tariffs or added further barriers to imports so as to encourage local industry. In addition, governments provided support for their infant industries through subsidies and other policies (sometimes direct ownership). Some countries, like China and Albania, carried the strategy to real extremes; they literally withdrew from the world political economy.

By the late 1980s most countries had concluded that import substitution was not working (or had sheltered the nascent industries long enough). The strategy had often led to high-cost, inefficient domestic production, relatively little of which could be exported. Most countries have abandoned or weakened import substitution. Even China, with its huge resource base and internal market, and with the official maintenance of communism, concluded that it needed to reestablish economic ties with the outside world.

Countries adopting the inward-looking strategy today are more likely to frame it in terms of maximizing **self-reliance,** but maintaining involvement in the world economy. That is, they see relationships with the developed economies as inevitable, and even beneficial, but seek insofar as possible to approach transactions with them on their own terms and to obtain a greater share of the benefits.

Nationalization (state ownership) of foreign-owned assets was part of the inward-looking approach. At one time a large portion of the investments by MNCs in the Third World were in petroleum, mining, and plantation agriculture. LDCs nationalized most of these investments; takeovers of petroleum assets in the 1970s by the oil-producing countries largely completed the process. Western governments did not always accept that process gracefully, particularly because radical regimes often directed it. Several postwar U.S. foreign interventions, including those in Iran (1953), Guatemala (1954), and Chile (1971–1973), attempted to retard nationalization or to control the terms of it. In the subsequent movement toward more market-oriented economies, many LDCs privatized the industries again, but have maintained more local control.

Another important element of many inward-looking strategies is a focus on **basic human needs** (food, shelter, clothing, and education) of the poor and attention to income distribution. Neo-Marxists argue that waiting for the benefits of growth to "trickle down" is unacceptable (and may never happen). Mahbub ul Haq of Pakistan put it succinctly: "We were taught to take care of our GNP as this will take care of poverty. Let us reverse this and take care of poverty as this will take care of the GNP" (Todaro 1989, 144). Neo-Marxists reject both the necessity and desirability of allowing income distribution to worsen substantially in the early phases of growth.

Collective and Structural Reform

Even while alternating between more state-centric, inward-looking strategies and free-market policies, Southern countries have worked steadily to reform the liberal, Northern-dominated system and to maximize their collective leverage within it. In 1955 leaders of 27 states met in Bandung, Indonesia. From the Bandung Conference emerged the Nonaligned Movement (NAM) under the leadership of Tito from Yugoslavia and Nehru from India. It represented a collective effort to resist the superpower pressure. In truth the NAM never broke free of the very East-West tensions against which it sought to provide a united front. The movement proved unable to condemn the American war in Vietnam or the Soviet invasion of Czechoslovakia, because friends of the respective superpowers opposed such action.

As colonies began to achieve independence and form new states, especially around 1960, two developments logically followed. First, the United Nations gradually became a preferred focus for collective Southern efforts. By 1961 most of the 104 members were former colonies. Second, the focus of LDC interests and activities shifted to postcolonial or neocolonial economic relationships with the North. In contrast to earlier disengagement from the independence movements of colonial countries, Latin America shared an interest in these economic issues and took an active role in collective Third World efforts to reshape the Bretton Woods system.

Thus it is no coincidence that the new Third World majority established two organizations at the United Nations to represent them, and that the organizations quickly focused on economic interests. Both the Group of 77 (G-77), with 127 members by the 1990s, and the United Nations Conference on Trade and Development (UNCTAD) date from 1964. UNCTAD I in 1964 was a forum for the G-77 to propose a new international trade organization that would supersede GATT. The West resisted demands for such an organization and, as a compromise, UNCTAD itself became a permanent institution with meetings approximately every four years. Through it the South obtained a Generalized System of Preferences (GSP)—allowing some access to Northern markets through low tariffs, while permitting the South to protect their infant industries.

At a summit in Algiers in 1973, the Southern leaders called for a **New International Economic Order (NIEO).** Frustrated by Northern inaction and emboldened by the OPEC cartel's success in raising prices, the Third World pushed through the UN General Assembly resolutions that made specific NIEO proposals, clearly addressing the global structures this chapter has discussed. They included:

1. Creation of an Integrated Program for Commodities (IPC), using a Common Fund to finance international stocks of them, which would accumulate in periods of oversupply and be sold into the market during periods of scarcity. This would, hopefully, flatten price fluctuations.
2. Easier access to IMF credits, with lower interest rates and less conditionality.
3. Provision of foreign assistance equivalent to 0.7 percent of First World GNPs.
4. Development of a program for debt relief.
5. International regulation of MNCs to control some of their most negative impact on the Third World.

First World response was lukewarm. LDCs differed sharply with respect to how aggressively they wished to pursue confrontation to achieve the NIEO. The North is unlikely to *ever* address the proposals as a whole, but the ideas continue to frame much contemporary North-South dialogue.

Not all approaches to collective action have been global. OPEC appeared in the 1970s to offer LDCs still another model for collective action, vis-à-vis the North. In 1973–1974 the OPEC countries seemed to bring about a quadrupling in the price of oil and an even more dramatic increase in revenues, simply by holding a small percentage of this necessary commodity off the market after the 1973 Mideast war. In a show of Southern solidarity, OPEC members attempted to translate their success into increased bargaining power of the South. They insisted on a North-South conference, which took place in Paris in 1975–1977. The meetings discussed many of the NIEO proposals but accomplished little.

A producer **cartel** is a group of states (or firms) that operates in concert to restrain production in an attempt to raise market prices and increase profits. Other producer cartels gained interest in the glow of OPEC success and the boom of commodity prices during the 1970s. These include the Intergovernmental Council of Copper Exporting States (CIPEC), made up of four countries that dominate the world's copper trade: Zambia, Chile, Peru, and Zaire. The apparent success of almost all such organizations, including that of OPEC, evaporated in the global commodity-price downturn of the early and mid-1980s. The LDCs relearned a lesson about their position in the world division of labor—commodity prices are unstable. The boom-and-bust cycle of the 1970s and 1980s initially fooled many into thinking that this particular boom was a new phenomenon and would continue indefinitely.

Instead of the boom being the harbinger of a new era, the boom-and-bust cycle ultimately reinforced the arguments made by liberals concerning the power of market responses to foil price-manipulation efforts. The momentum that collective action by the South appeared to have in the 1970s dissipated almost completely in the 1980s. At UNCTAD IX in 1996, the developed countries even questioned whether, in light of the World Trade Organization, UNCTAD still serves a purpose. One additional factor, however, shaped the climate of North-South relations in the 1980s and 1990s—the great economic success of the handful of Southern countries known as the Newly Industrialized Countries (NICs). We turn next to their strategy.

The Liberal Rebuttal: Growth-Enhancing Participation

Liberals recognize that global structures now exist and that they influence development prospects of LDCs. They argue, however, that rather than retarding development, current global structures promote and facilitate it:

> Today we would expect the process [of economic development] to go much more rapidly in many of the developing nations, the central reason for this being the existence of the gap between the developed and the developing that many deplore as the source and cause of underdevelopment. (Kahn, Brown, and Martel 1976, 34)

Between 1830 and 1910 the industrial revolution in the British economy supported a "booming" growth rate of 1.2 percent per year (compared to 0.3 percent in the 1700s). At that rate the British doubled their GNP in 58 years. The United States subsequently did it in 47 years, the Japanese still later in 34 years, and the South Koreans recently in 11 years (*The Economist*, October 16, 1993, 84). In the 1980s and 1990s the Chinese economy grew at a rate that doubled it every seven to eight years.

This argument encompasses three principal subthemes about the advantages of backwardness (Gershenkron 1962). First, it costs less and takes less time to adapt technology than to develop it. The LDCs today can draw on 200 years of industrial revolution technology. For example, the rapid rise of the Japanese economy depended primarily on technology importation and adaptation, not on innovation. Second, capital is more widely available today than ever before. Just as British capital helped develop the United States, American, British, and Japanese capital bring modern technology (generally through the vehicle of MNCs and foreign investment) to the entire world. The transformation from predominantly agricultural to largely industrial economies occurs at a remarkable pace in LDCs as a result of Northern technology and capital (review Figure 1.6). The third theme is the existence of markets in the more advanced countries. What good, liberals ask, were vast African deposits of cobalt, copper, or uranium until the establishment of global industrial markets? Would resource-poor countries like Taiwan and South Korea have been able to make incredibly rapid progress and become industrial powerhouses without Western markets for industrial goods?

During the 1970s and 1980s, the most successful economies in the Third World combined substantial industrialization and heavy reliance on industrial exports to achieve high rates of growth. This combination generally characterizes the **newly industrialized countries (NICs).** Like many other country categorizations, this one is fuzzy. Even the name is uncertain, since many prefer newly industrialized *economies* (NIEs) to stress that the phenomenon is economic. Definition is often by example, and the countries cited include Hong Kong, Singapore, South Korea, Taiwan, Portugal, Spain, Argentina, Brazil, Chile, and Mexico. The first four are known collectively as the Four Tigers or Four Dragons and appear on all lists of NICs. China has now joined most lists of NICs and India is appearing.

Although the label emphasizes industrialization, the key policy prescription of liberals is involvement in the global economy. In fact, many observers of NICs point to their export-led growth patterns:

> They have all placed great emphasis on outward-oriented growth policies as a means of promoting rapid industrialization. Their policies typically include special tax incentives to local and foreign investors (especially for production of exportable goods); duty-free entry of imports (raw materials, intermediate goods, machinery) necessary for producing goods to be exported; currency devaluations to maintain a competitive position for national production in world markets; income policies designed to keep wages low; and maintenance of an hospitable environment for direct foreign investment. (Blake and Walters 1987, 172)

There are at least two problems, however, when liberals place such great weight on export promotion. First, export-promoting countries have not consistently adopted liberal policies, and with the exception of the British Crown Colony of Hong Kong, often exhibit a generally neomercantilist orientation. For example, they have maintained undervalued currencies so as to make their exports inexpensive to other countries. In addition a substantial role for the state is the general rule. For instance, Korean government spending and planning played a critical role in its rapid industrial growth. Singapore is notorious for strong governmental direction of the economy. In short, the countries the liberals often pointed to as exemplars did not consistently follow liberal policies.

The second problem is an obvious one of systemic logic. The Four Tigers together have a population about one-half that of Brazil. Their collective economy is only one-half larger than that of Brazil and only one-fifth as large as that of Japan. Yet the United States and Europe have voiced serious concern about their export strength and trade surpluses. Were a few countries the size of Brazil, China, or India to emulate their attention to exports seriously (as China began to do in the

WittyWorld's prize went to Igor Varchenko for this cartoon

Source: Drawing by Igor Varchenko. Reprinted by permission of Witty World
International Cartoon.

1990s), the effect on the global economy could be highly disruptive. It is possible that only relatively small countries, and only a few of them, can reasonably pursue such an aggressive international strategy.

In fact, the Asian economic crisis of 1997–1998 (with which we began Chapter 12) exemplifies this. Observers sometimes use a metaphor of flying geese to discuss Asian economic growth. Japan flies at the head of the V-shaped formation, using an export-led strategy, but moving its attention from lower- to higher-technology industries over time (the logic of strategic trade theory). Hong Kong, Singapore, South Korea, and Taiwan fly just behind the leader, drawing on slightly less-advanced technology, but also shifting industrial focus and emphasizing exports. Malaysia and Thailand follow further back in the formation, as do Indonesia and China. If, however, the global market can no longer tolerate this advancing and growing flock, they may be grounded.

Fortunately, the progress of many other LDCs in both manufacturing and economic growth, even if less dramatic than that of the Asian countries, indicates that successful participation in the world economy may not require intense promotion of exports. Turkey maintains fairly steady economic progress (with intermittent setbacks), and although open to the world economy, it does not promote exports fervently. The Latin-American countries that experts regularly list as NICs also participate actively in the world economy, without relying on large export surpluses to drive their growth.

Regardless of the success of the NICs in the last three decades, it is remarkable how skewed the world distribution of income remains (see Table 13.4) and how few countries have broken free of the cluster of those mired in poverty. Whether any strategy or combination of strategies can help large numbers of Third World countries close the North-South gap remains uncertain. Because of the great human costs of both absolute and relative poverty, it also remains a critical question for humanity as we move into a new millennium.

Conclusion

This chapter illustrated how each of the worldviews bring their intellectual arsenals to bear on the issues of North-South relations. We gave most attention to neo-Marxism, because we had not previously elaborated it in depth, and because many in the South see their relationship with the North to be one of dominance and subordination—a continuation of patterns established under colonialism. We saw also that liberalism, in its attention to remarkable long-term economic growth and socioeconomic transformation in the South, particularly on the part of NICs, provides a critical perspective. It offers a much more optimistic image of recent history and holds out real hope that the North-South gap will begin to narrow. Alert readers also saw the shadows of realism throughout this chapter. Realism, looking at North-South relations through a state-centric lens, drew our attention to military-power differentials and to the mercantilism of both Northern states and many NICs.

Although all of the perspectives thus provide some insights, one question probably building in your mind is how to judge the relative accuracy and contribution of the competing worldviews. One approach is to focus on the accuracy of

Table 13.4 The Global Distribution of Income, 1996	
GNP/Capita (dollars)	Population in Millions (number of countries)
0– 999	3,139 (54)
1,000– 1,999	582 (19)
2,000– 2,999	357 (10)
3,000– 3,999	209 (10)
4,000– 4,999	216 (5)
5,000– 5,999	3 (1)
6,000– 6,999	0 (0)
7,000– 7,999	0 (0)
8,000– 8,999	35 (1)
9,000– 9,999	2 (1)
10,000–10,999	56 (2)
11,000–11,999	10 (1)
12,000–12,999	0 (0)
13,000–13,999	0 (0)
14,000–14,999	39 (1)
15,000–15,999	10 (2)
16,000–16,999	0 (0)
17,000–17,999	4 (1)
18,000–18,999	0 (0)
19,000–19,999	146 (3)
20,000+	632 (14)

Source: World Bank, World Development Indicators 1998 (New York: Oxford University Press, 1998), 12–14.

their predictions. Early in this chapter we discussed understandings and predictions about the evolution of the North-South gap, and we ended by looking at forecasts that a substantial class of Southern countries, the NICs, might move from one side of the divide to the other. Liberals and neo-Marxists vary considerably in their expectations for the future of the world political economy, and in later chapters we will focus more specifically on the question of change.

Selected Key Terms

terms of trade

product cycle theory

neocolonialism

infant industries

multinational corporations (MNCs)

transfer pricing

brain drain

appropriate technology

obsolescing bargain

proxy wars

import substitution

self-reliance

basic human needs

New International Economic Order (NIEO)

cartel

newly industrialized countries (NICs)

CHAPTER 14

Modernism and Eco-Wholism

In 1990 and 1995 the Intergovernmental Panel on Climate Change (IPCC), sponsored by the United Nations Environment Programme and the World Meteorological Organization, issued reports on the global climate. To arrive at its findings, the IPCC drew on the contributions of more than 2,500 scientists around the world, using some of the most advanced technology available today, including extensive satellite studies and massive computer simulations. The experts now constitute an "invisible college" on a global basis, linked via the World Wide Web, to which they have posted their conclusions for the world (http://www.unep.ch/ipcc).

The IPCC's initial report was remarkable for the consensus of the scientists on the reality of a Greenhouse Effect that causes global warming. In June 1992, representatives of more than 150 countries attended the Earth Summit in Brazil, armed with conclusions from the panel's first study. They signed the UN Framework Convention on Climate Change, agreeing to reduce the emission of greenhouse gases. The second IPCC report refined the analysis and forecast that global average temperatures will increase more than 2°C during the next century and that sea levels will consequently rise by about half a meter. Governmental representatives met again in 1997, in Kyoto, Japan, to agree on specific reductions of greenhouse gases. Both the technology that underlay the IPCC's analysis and the pessimistic conclusions that the panel reached concerning global climate have become part of global politics.

This chapter initiates Part IV of the book. Part III extended our attention beyond traditional matters of interstate politics to the *global political economy.* Now we widen our horizons still further to global **political ecology,** the interaction of global politics with issues from the biological and physical environment. This chapter introduces the primary worldviews of political ecology; the next two elaborate the manner in which those views interact with understandings of world politics. The

---

KEY WEB LINKS

www.wri.org/
www.unep.org/
www.unfccc.de/
www.sustainable.doe.gov/

---

two worldviews of this discussion hold less inherent "political" content than do the others we have examined—but they interact with the earlier worldviews in important ways, adding essential flesh to understandings of world politics.

Modernism

Modernism emphasizes accumulated human progress in mastering the broader environment—in shaping and controlling it so as to improve human well-being, generation after generation. Technological advance is so important to this worldview that some refer to its adherents as "technological enthusiasts."

Sketch of the Worldview

Table 14.1 summarizes the modernist worldview, specifying concepts, theories, values, and prescriptions. At the core of the modernist worldview are humans in search of knowledge. Teilhard de Chardin coined the term "noosphere" (**knowosphere** is a better spelling) to refer to the accumulated body of knowledge on which humans draw and to which they add with time (Boulding 1981, 109). Humans use knowledge to control their environment. The environment is both adversary and resource; human ingenuity overcomes the obstacles it presents (for instance, disease) and uses the bounty it provides. Life expectancy and material comfort meas-

Table 14.1	**Political Ecology Worldviews**	
Worldview Name(s)	Modernism	Eco-wholism
	Technological enthusiasm	Neotraditionalism
Central Concepts:	Innovators	Species
Agents/Structures	Accumulated knowledge or "knowosphere"	Ecosystems
Values of Agents	Knowledge	Survival
		Propagation
Central Concepts:	Control of environment	Carrying capacity
Bases of Interaction		Delays
		Unanticipated consequences
Theories: Systematic	Knowledge accumulation	Tragedy of the Commons
Description	(virtuous cycle)	Externality creation
	Acceleration of progress	Free-rider behavior
	Technological innovation	
Theories:	Progressive control of	Overshoot and collapse
Typical Forecasts	environment	
Values of Worldview	Progress	Sustainability
Proponents		Quality of life
Typical Prescriptions	Laissez innover	Sustainable development:
	Support research and	Control population
	development	Minimize economic throughput
		Control technology

ure success in the effort. By these measures, as we shall see in the next chapter, humanity has been very successful indeed.

Knowledge is for modernists what capital is for liberals or power for realists. It is both a means and an end. It is at the center of a *virtuous cycle* or **positive feedback loop.** That is, just as states apply power to obtain more power, and entrepreneurs reinvest capital to yield additional capital, scientists and engineers utilize knowledge in the search for greater knowledge. The famous investment advisor John Templeton once illustrated this view in an interview with *Forbes* magazine:

> The world is now spending about $1 billion each business day on scientific research. Half of all the scientists who ever lived are alive today. . . . Two centuries ago 85 percent of the world's people were needed just to produce enough food. Now, in America, fewer than 4 percent are producing food, yet they produce such a surplus that they don't know what to do with it. That's going on in other nations, too. . . . Our studies indicate that the [world's] standard of living is going to quadruple again in the next forty years, instead of the next seventy years. We are living in the most glorious period of world history. We are looking ahead toward an extraordinary period of long-range prosperity. (*Forbes,* January 25, 1988, 81)

Templeton, like most humans, valued such progress highly.

Realists accept few restrictions on the rights of states to act in the world. Commercial liberals accept few restrictions by government on the rights of producers and consumers to interact in markets and codify that principle as laissez faire. Similarly, modernists prescribe **laissez innover** (McDermott 1972, 155), the freedom to innovate. Modernists do not, however, *proscribe* all government action with respect to technology; in fact, they *prescribe* strong societal support for research and development. Critics claim that certain technologies, such as the genetic engineering of new organisms, may hold great dangers and that society should carefully oversee them.

Are there global political ramifications of a focus on technological advance? Consider these two. First, the world of many modernists is predominantly nonzero-sum. All of humanity can benefit from a vast variety of technologies. Humans can share knowledge without losing it. Second, human interaction within and between states depends specifically on our communications and transportation technologies. As those technologies progress, they inherently alter and, many modernists would argue, enhance the nature of human interaction. Modernists less commonly consider negative implications of technological advance. For instance, although technology has a nonzero-sum character in the long run, it creates inequalities in the short run. The most obvious examples of the dangers of uneven advance lie in military technology. In the next chapter we explore both the positive and negative impact of technological advance on world politics.

Important Contributions to Modernist Thought

Modern science emphasizes concepts or categories (which group like phenomenon) and theoretical structures (which explore the relationships among concepts). Aristotelian science (of the ancient Greek Golden Age) also emphasized categorization, but often stressed identification of hierarchies and distinctions among categories rather than connections or relationships. At the center of the search for knowledge, in Aristotelian science, lay the desire to place things into categories, and to elaborate the attributes of things and categories. It extensively used the syllogism to do that. For instance:

> All living creatures are mortal.
> Humans are living creatures.
> Therefore, humans are mortal.

Such science has a limited ability to identify points at which humans can intervene. Its intent is to describe nature as it exists or as God created it (the science of the church in the Middle Ages built on the Aristotelian approach). *Modern* science, although retaining emphasis on categorization, devotes a great deal more attention to linkages among concepts, to *causality*. For instance, raising the temperature of a liquid can convert it into a gas and cause its volume to expand. Converting water to steam can drive a piston and a rod attached to it, thus creating a steam engine. When scientific knowledge is causal, it can be the basis for **technology**—knowledge adapted to human purposes.[1]

Near the beginning of the seventeenth century, science in Europe became more active in searching for explanations and dynamics and in adapting these to human purposes. Francis Bacon (1561–1626) helped develop the philosophy of this new science. He explicitly attacked the passive classificatory orientation of the old science.

Instead of syllogistic methods, Bacon suggested an experimental science involving active search for *new* information and truths. Bacon even stressed the importance of "rejections and exclusions," a fundamental component of modern scientific method, which constantly searches for instances to disprove theories. Those theories that have withstood attempts to contradict them are those to which we continue to adhere. Contradiction, if it occurs, intensifies the search for new or revised theory.

Others who contributed to this transformation of thought included Galileo, Hobbes, Descartes, Pascal, Spinoza, Leibniz, and Newton. They and their contemporaries initiated a scientific revolution and laid the foundations for the industrial revolution. Their Age of Reason ushered in the modern science and set the stage for the modernist belief system centered on knowledge accumulation and progress in the use of it. Bacon himself wrote *New Atlantis*, a utopian novel about an island on which a giant laboratory assured technological progress and the comfort of inhabitants. Jeffrey Hart described the period:

> Sometime during the fifteenth century, the great and glorious project of modernity was launched in earnest. To put it briefly: whereas ancient Greek and Roman culture, with their extention [sic] and modification in medieval Christian culture, sought to understand the world and live according to that understanding, the modern project sought not to understand the world in its totality but to control it and use it. (Hart 1988, 3)

---

[1]Actually, Heron of Alexandria, who lived near the time of Aristotle, understood the principles of steam and created a number of mechanical and pneumatic contrivances. Thus the discussion exaggerates the distinction between the basic science of the two periods. Nonetheless, the fact that Heron's work did not lead to a steam engine in his era reinforces the argument here with respect to application of knowledge.

The scientific advances of the seventeenth century built the foundations of Enlightenment thought in the seventeenth and eighteenth centuries. Faith in humanity's ability to master the environment gave rise to faith in humanity's ability to structure superior societies, both domestic and international. Hume, Locke, Rousseau, Voltaire, and many others contributed their varied ideas to this effort.

Eco-Wholism

Labels carry connotations or implications that can prejudice us favorably or unfavorably. Some call the challengers to modernism "pessimists" or "ecopessimists." Those labels implicitly convey a negative connotation, because most of us prefer optimists to pessimists—they are more fun to have around. Hence, those friendly to perspectives that challenge modernism have suggested alternative terminology. Pirages (1983, 1989) preferred "inclusionist" (one who stresses the position of humans within the environment) and juxtaposed that view with the "exclusionist" (one who places humans outside of, and in control of, their environment). Haas (1990, 66) proposed **eco-wholist** (spelling it "ecoholist"), emphasizing, like Pirages, the attention of the perspective to ecological wholeness. We adopt that term here. We sometimes interchangeably use *neotraditionalist* (Hughes 1985), because that term recalls the attitudes concerning the intimate and interdependent relationship of humans and their environment that characterized more traditional (premodern) societies.

Challengers in Brief

The eco-wholist begins with the concept of ecosystem. An **ecosystem** "is essentially a biotic community in interaction with its physical environment" (Dasmann et al. 1973, 29). For the eco-wholist, human beings are a part of that ecosystem, not above nor beyond it. Humans, like other species in the ecosystem, seek to survive and to propagate. No portion of the system can indefinitely expand, however, without damaging the system and therefore itself. A **carrying capacity** defines how large a species population can become before it overuses the resources available in the ecosystem. In reference to a species within the ecosystem that grows without respect for such bounds and thereby destroys its host, some eco-wholists suggest the analogy of a cancer within a human body.

Another important concept is that of **delays.** Significant time lags often separate an action that affects the environment from any noticeable impact. Movement of a pesticide like DDT through the food chain illustrates delays. Water and air systems take DDT applied on farmland to the ocean; it subsequently moves into plankton, into the fish that eat those organisms, and eventually into human fatty tissue. The concentration in fish and humans increases for many years after discontinuation of DDT use (Meadows et al. 1972, 89–94).

Eco-wholists also emphasize the possibility of *unanticipated consequences* of human action. No one predicted that the use of DDT would weaken eggshells of some birds, and eventually it would cause their population to decline. Even "environmentally friendly" action can have unanticipated negative consequences. In

1998 the U.S. Environmental Protection Agency announced that catalytic converters on cars, intended to reduce hydrocarbon emissions, create nitrous oxide, a particularly potent greenhouse gas.

Eco-wholists combine the concepts of carrying capacity and delay into a theory of **overshoot and collapse.** A limited ecosystem, like that on an island, provides a simple example. If a predator population, such as wolves, grows too large on an island, it will eventually exceed the carrying capacity limit defined by its prey, such as the rabbit population. It may continue to grow for some time beyond that limit (the overshoot), while it decimates the prey. That is, there will be a delay between the time when the predator population begins to reduce the prey and the time when the prey becomes so scarce that the predator can no longer survive. At some point the wolf population will collapse to the level that a much reduced rabbit population can sustain, and the cycle is complete. If the prey has not been driven to extinction, another cycle will begin as the prey population rebuilds.

The eco-wholist points to the collapse of the Central American Mayan civilization (possibly from damage to land fertility through overexpansion of maize cultivation), and to collapses of other agriculture-based civilizations around the Mediterranean, as evidence that human beings have not been immune historically to this logic of ecosystems. Has modern technology changed the rules? Not according to the eco-wholist. Instead, it temporarily relaxes ecosystem limits and leads us to overshoot them further without immediate consequences. For instance, humans are now in the process of using all of the readily accessible oil and natural gas in the world, something we could never have done in previous eras and which allows us (temporarily) to greatly expand agricultural production.

Many of the theories of eco-wholists focus specifically on the pattern of human interaction with the ecosystem. Several of these build on the concept of commons (common property-resource problems) and the tension between individual action and collective interest (you might wish to review the discussion of Chapter 6; the next two paragraphs quickly summarize some of it).

In the classic tragedy of the commons, each farmer individually decides to graze additional animals on a common field, and the resultant overgrazing destroys the vegetation and the ability of *all* farmers to make a living. Why does this happen, when it is so obvious that all farmers would benefit by limiting the number of animals to the carrying capacity of the land? One reason is that the individual farmer captures all of the benefit of the extra animal but externalizes much of the cost to other farmers. Although our individual behavior often damages the ecosystem, others will eventually bear many or all of the costs of damage. For example, those who cut the Amazonian rain forests to create homesteads for themselves reap the rewards individually, but may harm the global environment and negatively affect all of humanity.

No individual can solve the problem. For instance, a factory owner who restricts emissions, to protect the air or water, will pay all costs individually. The improvement in environmental quality, although marginally benefiting the factory owner, will be a positive **externality** that all others in society capture. That reality will encourage factory owners to urge other owners to reduce emissions, for the good of humanity and the ecosystem, but avoid doing it themselves. Everyone would prefer to obtain benefits without paying costs—to free ride.

Values and Prescriptions

Achievement of an acceptable quality of life, sustainable within carrying capacity limits over the long term, ranks high among the values of the eco-wholist. Many adherents of this worldview question the necessity or desirability of constantly expanding consumption. Many also define progress in terms of spiritual or intellectual achievement, rather than in material terms. They urge **sustainable development** rather than simply growth. Ultimately, sustainable development means goals like those set by the Dutch government for the long term: consumption of energy limited to solar capability and recycling of all waste material (World Resources Institute 1994, 239).

Foremost among specific prescriptions of most eco-wholists is population control. Should humans not act to limit their own numbers, the ecosystem will do it for them. In addition, they argue that we can manufacture and consume goods with much less pressure on resources and much less generation of waste than we currently accept. That is, for a given level of production and consumption, we should minimize *economic throughput* (Daly 1980). A more limited number of eco-wholists also favors restrictions on technological development, especially in areas such as genetic engineering, where the technology may alter and perhaps damage the ecosystem—or simply exacerbate the overshoot phenomenon (Rifkin 1984).

Eco-wholists disagree concerning the implementation of these prescriptions. Some favor voluntary individual action, informed by the knowledge that large-scale efforts are necessary. The Hunger Project mobilized millions internationally, asking each to make a contribution to eliminating world hunger based on their own definition of the problem and their own capacity for action. Other eco-wholists argue that the inherent individual tendency to ignore externalities (like a smoker in a room of nonsmokers) and the tendency to free ride (let George clean it up), means that only collective action, using coercion to enforce it, will succeed.

This debate extends to international policy issues. Will states act individually to limit damage to the global environment from acid rain, the greenhouse effect, or the depletion of atmospheric ozone? Can they agree to act in the numbers necessary, with the knowledge that other states may free ride on their sacrifices? Do such problems inherently require stronger global institutions, possessing instruments for policy enforcement? Those are the issues of Chapter 16.

Important Contributions to Eco-Wholist Thought

Traditional hunting and gathering or agricultural societies observed the limits on human population at close range. They experienced periodic famines and developed great respect and even reverence for their environment, the sphere of the gods. These traditional peoples sought harmony between themselves and their environment, although they did not always achieve it.[2] A letter that Chief Seattle

[2]The tendency to romanticize the relationship of traditional peoples with the environment is unfortunate and inaccurate. Early immigrants to the Western hemisphere may have exterminated 80 percent of large mammal species (*The Chronicle of Higher Education*, May 4, 1994, A56). Anthropologist Harris (1977) argued that the neolithic revolution and the beginning of fixed agriculture was a necessary response to increased population density and overhunting. Environmental historian J. D. Hughes (1994) documented extensive deforestation, overgrazing, and wildlife depletion by the ancient Greeks and Romans.

of the Suquamish tribe purportedly wrote to President Pierce in 1855 illustrates the reverence:

> The great Chief in Washington sends words that he wishes to buy land. . . . How can you buy or sell the sky—the warmth of the land? The idea is strange to us. Yet we do not own the freshness of the air or the sparkle of the water. How can you buy them from us? We will decide in our time. Every part of this earth is sacred to my people. Every shining pine needle, every sandy shore, every mist in the dark woods, every clearing and humming insect is holy in the memory and experience of my people.
>
>   We know that the white man does not understand our ways. One portion of the land is the same to him as the next, for he is a stranger who comes in the night and takes from the land whatever he needs. The earth is not his brother, but his enemy, and when he has conquered it, he moves on. He leaves his fathers' graves, and his children's birthright is forgotten. The sight of your cities pains the eyes of the redman. But perhaps it is because the redman is a savage and does not understand.[3]

The belief that an environmental carrying capacity limited humans was dominant until recently. Plato (427?–327? B.C.) recognized and deplored the destruction of the forests of Attica surrounding Athens:

> What now remains compared with what then existed is like the skeleton of a sick man, all the fat and soft earth having wasted away, and only the bare framework of the land being left. . . . Moreover, it was enriched by the yearly rains from Zeus, which were not lost to it, as now, by flowing from the bare land into the sea; but the soil it had was deep. . . . " [translated by Bury 1966, 273–275][4]

In fifteenth-century Italy, Niccolò Machiavelli defined the cost of reaching carrying capacity:

> When countries become overpopulated and there is no longer any room for all the inhabitants to live, nor any other place for them to go, these being likewise all fully occupied—and when human cunning and wickedness have gone as far as they can go—then of necessity the world must relieve itself of this excess of population . . . ; so that mankind, having been chastised and reduced in numbers, may become better able to live with more convenience. (Machiavelli 1940, 298)

Even in a period and society becoming increasingly permeated by modernist thought, Thomas Malthus (1766–1834) reiterated and elaborated this thesis. Based on his famous argument that population grows geometrically (what we would call exponentially), while food supply increases only arithmetically (linearly), he initially concluded that only war, famine, and disease maintained the balance between humans and their environment. In a later edition of *An Essay on the Principle of Population*, he signaled the eco-wholist emphasis on population control by

---

[3]Holister and Porteous (1976, 7–9). Apparently, Ted Perry, a film writer and professor, embellished Chief Seattle's words in an environmental film (*Denver Post*, April 22, 1992). Read the paragraphs as poetry, not necessarily accurate quotation.

[4]In China at about the same time, Mencius wrote about deforestation (translated by Lau 1970, 164–165).

Alternative Growth Patterns

Linear growth occurs when equal increments are added year after year. The graph shows growth of 0.2 units each year for 20 years.

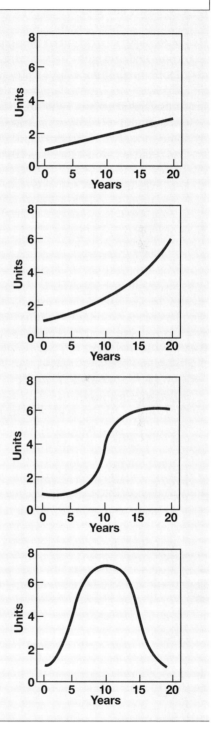

Exponential growth occurs with a constant percentage change each year to an increasing base. The graph shows growth by 10 percent each year (an initial increment of 0.1 units). Population and economic growth have been *super-exponential* in the last 200 years, because the percentage growth rates of each has increased over time. Positive feedback processes (both vicious and virtuous cycles) are exponential.

When exponential growth bumps up against limits, slows, and stops, it is *saturating exponential growth.* Demographers expect human population to follow this pattern in the twenty-first century.

When exponential growth exceeds sustainable levels, it creates an **overshoot and collapse.** Many environmental growth patterns take this form.

introducing "moral restraint" as a fourth mechanism for checking population (see box entitled "Alternative Growth Patterns").

The subsequent century-and-a-half appeared to repudiate Malthus's conclusions as human population globally increased more than fourfold from that of his time and average diets simultaneously improved. Malthusian argument resurfaced in the last half of the twentieth century, however, as global population growth rates reached historic highs. In the early 1970s the Club of Rome widely publicized the results of an analysis based on a computer simulation of global development. That study, released immediately before a two-year period of drought and famine in Northern Africa and parts of South Asia, became the focal point for an intense debate. It argued that:

> If the present growth trends in world population, industrialization, pollution, food production, and resource depletion continue unchanged, the limits to growth on this planet will be reached sometime within the next one hundred years. The most probable result will be a rather sudden and uncontrollable decline in both population and industrial capacity. (Meadows and others 1972, 23)

In the 1970s and 1980s political movements grew up around eco-wholism. Environmentalist movements appeared in most developed countries and gave rise to "green" parties around the world. Concern for the environment even proved a powerful unifying force for groups opposing communist leaderships in Eastern Europe. It appears probable that the extent of commitment to environmental protection will become a long-term political dimension throughout the world, adding to religious and economic divisions. Internationally, environmentally committed NGOs, like Greenpeace and the World Wildlife Fund, have gained membership rapidly, carrying a new set of issues to global forums. In 1989, UN Secretary-General Javier Pérez de Cúeller declared that "It is generally agreed that the environment has moved to the top of the world's political agenda."

Popular attachment to the competing perspectives varies over time and depends on the circumstances of the day. In general, international crises in the environment or in resource availability (as in the mid-1970s) strengthen the eco-wholist perspective, whereas periods free of immediate crisis reinforce the modernist view. Because we can expect continued alternation between such conditions, regardless of any dominant long-term trend, the relative popularity of the two worldviews is likely also to rise and wane cyclically. The next two chapters consider each perspective in more detail.

Selected Key Terms

political ecology	laissez innover	(environmental) delays
modernism	eco-wholist	overshoot and collapse
knowosphere	ecosystem	externality
positive feedback loop	carrying capacity	sustainable development

Technological Advance and Human Interaction

Stanley Kubrick's classic film, *2001: A Space Odyssey*, opens rather surprisingly with a scene showing prehistoric ape-humans. Although they have only begun to use tools, such as readily available animal bones, it is obvious that such primitive technology has already become important, both in their productive search for food and in conflict with each other. Through all the intervening years, technology has always had multiple implications for human interaction: it connects humans, it helps them meet their needs cooperatively, and it increases the lethality of their conflict. What has changed is, of course, technological sophistication. At the end of the scene a bone-club thrown into the air metamorphoses into a space ship, demonstrating the increased sophistication and also symbolizing the ability of technology to link humans across time and space.

This chapter explores the multiple faces of technology. We look first at how communications and transportation technology directly shape interaction, then at the contributions of technology to human well-being, and thereafter at technology and warfare. The relationships between humans and their technology, however, goes one important step further.

KEY WEB LINKS

www.sciam.com/
currentissue.html
www.compinfo.co.uk/index.htm

Technology does not merely connect or link individual humans; its character shapes the complex social structures that we build. There is, in fact, much speculation that recent advances in technology, particularly communications technology, may now position humanity for significant changes in political and social organization. Social structures, in turn, shape the process and focus of technological innovation. We need also to explore this mutually formative interaction of technology and society.

Intensity and Patterns of Interaction

For much of human history, the most lethal weapon system was the bow and arrow, delivering deadly force at a distance not far beyond rock-throwing range.

337

Similarly, drums and fires extended direct communication only somewhat beyond shouting range. The speed of runners and later of horses greatly limited transportation and indirect communication options.

Although the word "revolution" is overused, no other word can describe adequately nineteenth- and twentieth-century developments in these arenas. Artillery range grew to three miles in the first half of the 1800s. Today humans can kill each other in the millions from the far side of the world. A trip around the world in 1800 required several years by sailing ship. Jet aircraft can now circle the earth in one day and an orbiting spacecraft can do it in 90 minutes. Before the invention of the telegraph in 1840, nearly all messages traveled with human beings, so that communication speeds were the same as those in transportation. Morse demonstrated a telegraph message ("What hath God wrought?") from Washington to Baltimore in 1844. Today communications satellites transmit information between any two points in the globe almost instantaneously. Moreover, the cost of communications is increasingly insensitive to distance (de Sola Pool 1990, 34)—at the extreme, the cost to the sender of an e-mail message between London and Canberra is now the same as one between adjacent offices.

These three types of technology—military, transportation, and communications—are among the most important in determining our patterns of interaction. Earlier chapters have devoted considerable attention to military technology. We focus here primarily on means of transport and of communications. Commentators once commonly remarked that such technology was causing the world to shrink. It became such a cliché that people say it less often now. It is, however, even more true today.

Transportation

Native Americans and Australian Aborigines can attest to the social impact of transportation—and may well have reason to wish that Europeans had never developed long-distance sailing. Transportation technologies have not evolved as dramatically in recent years as those in communications, but nevertheless the advance has been very significant. For instance, the use of freight containers greatly facilitates and lowers the cost of intermodal connections among trains, trucks, and cargo ships. The development of supertankers similarly improved petroleum movement. Egypt can attest to its importance. Prior to the supertanker, most oil enroute to Europe moved through the Suez Canal. An interim closure of the canal in the 1950s encouraged the development of the supertanker, which now conveys most oil around South Africa.

Perhaps most impressively, new generations of aircraft continue to lessen the costs of passenger and freight movement around the world. Air-transport costs decreased by 60 percent between 1970 and 1990. As a result, global movement of people and goods has grown considerably faster than population. For instance, world tourism rose from a total of 25 million arrivals in 1950 to 587 million in 1996.[1] Its growth has averaged 7.2 percent, about five times that of world population. By some accounts it is the world's largest industry. Figure 15.1 conveys the pace of growth in international sea and air transport.

---

[1]World Tourism Organization, Madrid, and World Bank (1998, 358).

Figure 15.1   International Sea and Air Transport

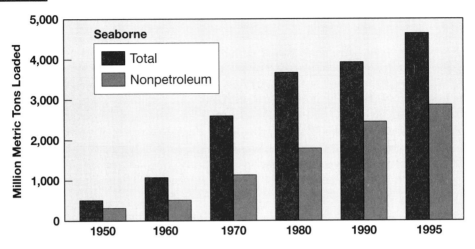

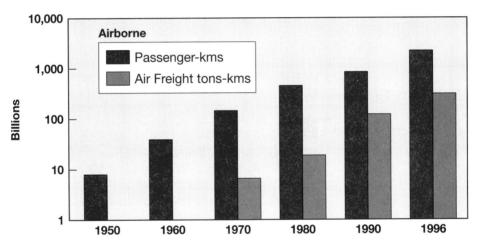

Sources: United Nations, *Statistical Yearbook* (New York: United Nations), (1985), 550; (1985), 1047; (1977), 591; (1966), 459. OECD, *Maritime Transport 1995* (Paris: OECD), 150. *ICAO Bulletin* (July 1997), vol. 52, no. 6; (July 1992), vol. 47, no. 7, 19; (November 1988), Vol. 43, No. 11, 12; (May 1972), vol. 27, no. 27, 18; (May 1959), vol. 14, no. 2, 56.

Communications

International telephone availability and cost illustrate the pace of change in global communication volume (Figure 15.2). The world now has about 150 telephone lines for each 1,000 people. In 1996 there were 28 mobile phones per 1,000 people globally. The cost of a three-minute call from New York to London dropped (in real terms) from $244.65 in 1930 to $31.58 in 1970 and $3.32 in 1990 (World Bank 1992b, 34).

Figure 15.2   Global and Regional Telephones

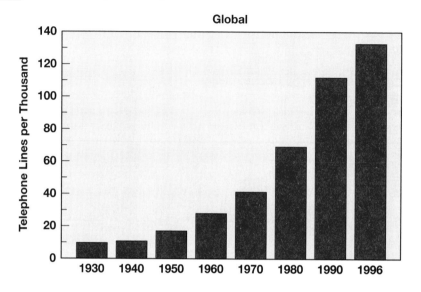

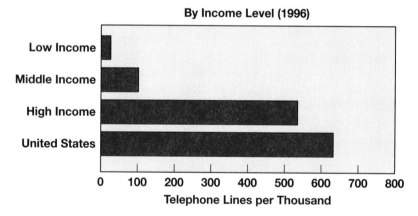

Sources: AT&T, *The World's Telephones: A Statistical Compilation as of January 1, 1992* (Morris Plains, NJ: AT&T, 1982); *AT&T, The World's Telephones* (Whippany, NJ: AT&T, 1989), World Bank, *World Development Indicators 1998* (Washington, DC: World Bank, 1998), 292.

Global communications have been growing 10 to 15 percent annually.[2] Although optic fiber cable linkages and microwave transmission have been critical, global satellite networks have now created truly worldwide connections of all human beings. The International Telecommunications Satellite Organization (INTEL-

---

[2]We should not underestimate the communications capabilities of earlier eras. By 1880 undersea telegraph cables (mostly British) connected Europe with North and South America, South Africa, India, and even Australia (Headrick 1981, 161).

SAT) put its first communication satellite in orbit in 1964; by 1995 the system offered 24 satellites. Mail among Third World countries, and later electronic communications such as telegraph messages, had passed for centuries through gateway cities in the more-developed countries. Satellites finally eliminated the barriers to direct communications among LDCs. (Many satellites are in geostationary orbit 22,300 miles above the equator. Increasingly, however, systems use low-earth orbiting (LEO) technology like that of Motorola's Iridium system. That allows approximately 66 satellites to provide point-to-point phone service anywhere in the world.)

The introduction of the rapidly improving equipment is far from complete, and the full impact will unfold over decades. It is difficult even to measure the progress of implementation. We measure cross-border phone traffic in billions of minutes, but connections now carry large volumes of data and compressed voice messages. Thus, the growth in information flows is phenomenal.

The convergence of communications and computing technology has made much of this advance possible. In 1946 scientists unveiled the first electronic computer, ENIAC, built around 18,000 vacuum tubes. Researchers invented the transistor in 1947. (Its inventor thought it might help develop a better hearing aid, so it initially received little press attention.) Integrated circuitry, combining many transistors on a single chip, emerged in 1959—the Japanese call these integrated circuits the "rice of the information age." Intel developed the microprocessor, basically a computer on a chip, in 1971. Widely distributed computers came of age with the desktop or personal computer in the early 1980s. The workstation of the late 1980s brought large amounts of computing power under the control of individuals for the first time. By 1985 output of the global electronics complex equaled that of the world automobile industry (about 4 percent to 5 percent of world product) and exceeded that of the world steel industry (Castells and Tyson 1988, 57). The number of computers in the world continued to climb from 4 million in 1981 to more than 300 million in 1997,[3] and the speed of invention and product innovation in the microelectronics industry has not slackened.

The day is essentially upon us when average citizens everywhere can pick up a telephone (or use their computer) and call or transmit significant volumes of data to nearly anyone in the world. Similarly, satellite dishes on rooftops throughout Latin America now receive cable television stations from North America, an excellent satellite telephone system ties together Indonesian islands, and even Indian villagers can obtain national television broadcasts on at least a single community-owned set. Moreover, Chinese citizens listen to radio broadcasts from the Voice of America, the British Broadcasting Corporation, and other Western sources, despite prohibitions, and they, too, rapidly install satellite dishes. The advance in these technologies and thus in the extent of human connection globally promises to be steady.

Technology and Human Well-Being

Technological advance not only brings humans into ever increasing contact with each other globally, it provides tremendous benefits. Life expectancy is an important summary indicator of how agriculture, sanitation, medical, and other technologies

---

[3]Brown, Lenssen, and Kane (1995, 132) and World Bank (1998, 296).

Life Expectancy

"You figure it. Everything we eat is 100% natural, yet our life expectancy is only 31 years."

Source: Reprinted with permission by John Jonik.

have collectively contributed to dramatic advances in well-being. In the England of 1800 life expectancy was only 32 years; in the Great Britain of 1995 it reached 76 years. In the developing world of the early 1950s it was 43 years; by 1995 Third World parents could expect their children to live an average of 64 years.

Chapter 1 documented a long-term increase in global food production per capita (with the exception of Africa). Famines, once common and inevitable in all societies, now occur rarely and appear to be preventable anomalies. Support from the Rockefeller Foundation helped initiate the **green revolution** in Mexico in the 1950s. It spread quickly around the world, with assistance from other foundations, international organizations, and national governments. No questions of national advantage delayed the dissemination of the new knowledge.

Biogenetic engineering will be the basis for a second "Green Revolution," which could have dramatic international consequences. The field is very new: researchers cloned the first gene in 1973; entrepreneurs established Genentech, the first company in the field, in 1976; and scientists did not express the first plant gene in another plant species until 1983 (Office of Technology Assessment 1986, 362). Imparting to grains such as wheat or rice the ability to fix nitrogen from the air, rather than requiring nitrogen fertilizers, might be one breakthrough in a second revolution. Greatly improved resistance to drought could be another. In the late 1990s genetically altered (not bred) soybeans, potatoes, and cotton came rapidly "on line." Consumers in many countries expressed anxiety about the safety of such food. A conference in Colombia during 1999 failed to reach agreement on standards concerning its trade. The industry may ultimately build advances on what have been called "designer genes." Such developments could markedly increase food production and economic prospects in currently food-deficit countries of the Third World.

Perhaps the most exciting single effort in the biotechnology field is the Human Genome Project, assigned the task of determining the function of all 50,000–80,000 human genes. The pace of such effort continues to accelerate. In 1998 a private company (Perkins-Elmer) announced a three-year effort to sequence the entire genome. In the twenty-first century such knowledge will lead to treatment for many genetic diseases; it will also lead to many highly controversial genetic engineering experiments.

Global income levels have also climbed as the world industrialized. Although the average per-capita GNP in some developing countries has grown only modestly, incomes in all countries have advanced. Fundamental to economic advance is energy technology. Watt's steam engine generated 40 horsepower in 1800, a dramatic improvement upon the 5.5 horsepower of Newcomen's steam engine in 1712 and on water mills and windmills (3 to 14 horsepower). A modern, large-scale electric power plant, either coal-fired or nuclear, delivers 1.5 million horsepower (Cook 1976, 29).

Figure 15.3 shows four indicators of human well-being over the last 200 years. Technological advance has been important to each one of them. Moreover, no one country could unilaterally have accomplished the progress made globally on these four indicators in the last 200 years. There is a very strong nonzero-sum character to such advance. Not only do those who make the discoveries benefit, but, as modernists emphasize, those to whom the knowledge is communicated also benefit.

This nonzero-sum character of technology might suggest that it should be easy to achieve international cooperation on technology and the benefits of it. Do not individuals from around the world who are better fed, clothed, housed, and educated increase their own contributions to technological advance and thus to our collective well-being? Impoverished and hungry Russians might not threaten anyone's military security, but they would also make limited contributions to global fusion. Richer and better-fed Indians might compete in world markets, but they would also push back technological frontiers and improve our own lives in ways we could never anticipate.

Technology and War

Military technology provides perhaps the most obvious exception to the argument about the advantages of technological diffusion. The United States is rapidly moving into an era of electronic warfare. In the 1991 Gulf War it demonstrated stealth bombers, laser-equipped bombs, and precisely controlled cruise missiles. In the late 1990s over Bosnia it deployed JSTARS, a surveillance system that can track all vehicles in all weather.

Figure 15.3 A Broad Spectrum of Global Progress

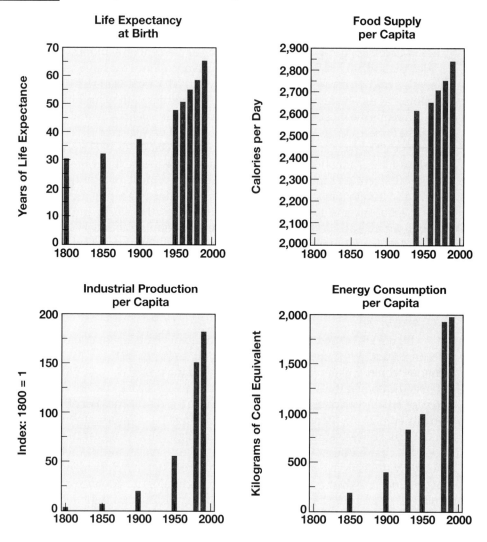

More generally, this new **revolution in military affairs** involves three elements. The first is intelligence gathering from satellites and various types of aircraft, some remote controlled. The second is information processing using advanced command, control, communications, and computing systems (C4). The third is the use of precision-guided weapons. Because of the importance of all these information systems to future war, the United States also seeks **information dominance,** the ability to disrupt similar systems of others while protecting its own.

Obviously, the United States would not want its potential and actual enemies to have any military technology it develops. Or would it? That depends in part on whether the technology appears to favor offensive or defensive action. One of the recurring themes of military technology throughout history has been the relative advantage of defensive or offensive systems. For instance, the invention of the machine gun gave a substantial advantage to the defense. Massive waves of men during World War I, even following large-scale heavy artillery attacks, could not often dislodge those in the trenches armed with machine guns—hundreds of thousands died in the attempt. One of the important miscalculations that led to World War I was the belief preceding it (based in part on Bismarck's earlier success against France) that modern military technology gave great advantage to the offensive, and that "it will all be over before you know it." The German Schlieffen plan mapped a war strategy involving quick mobilization and transport by railroad of soldiers.

An invention near the end of World War I—the tank (first used on the Somme in September 1916)—really did shift advantage to the offense. It became a dominant weapon in World War II and allowed Nazi Germany to achieve remarkable success in a technique called *Blitzkrieg*, combining the use of tanks to penetrate defensive lines with the assistance of paratroopers dropped behind them. Offensive tank assaults by Warsaw Pact forces in Europe long remained a primary concern of NATO planners.

Reviews of military history (Quester 1977; McNeill 1982) conclude that defensive superiority helps maintain the political status quo (and relatively quiet interstate relations), but periods of offensive superiority often coincide with attempts by some actors to overthrow the status quo. Jervis (1978) emphasized not just defensive or offensive advantage, but also ability to clearly differentiate defensive and offensive forces. The most stable world is one in which actors clearly recognize defensive technology to have the advantage.

There has been ongoing debate as to whether the contemporary advantage lies with offensive systems such as heavily armored tanks or with defensive ones like sophisticated antitank weaponry. The Iran-Iraq war ended in a stalemate, in part because of the successful antitank tactics of the Iraqis. The Afghanistan conflict illustrated also how the new antiaircraft missiles (like the Stinger) can protect otherwise inferior forces against helicopters and even bombing aircraft. Similarly, the war between the British and the Argentines over the Falklands-Malvinas proved that relatively inexpensive, electronically guided missiles could destroy very much more expensive and heavily armed warships. All of this may suggest a relative advantage for the defense in modern conventional weaponry (Barnaby 1986). U.S. progress in dominating the electronic battlefield, however, including its success in Iraq, suggests that the same systems can create devastating offensive capability (Orme 1997). Thus the United States is likely to continue efforts to protect that technology.

Technological Advance and Diffusion

Technology facilitates human interaction and enhances well-being, but simultaneously increases the lethality of, and in some cases even the potential of conflict. Thus it should not surprise us that the politics around technological advance and diffusion are complex, with states sometimes supporting both advance and diffusion, but sometimes opposing technological transfer. In addition, the advance and diffusion of technology is not simply a matter of what states do. Individuals make discoveries. They and their employers want to benefit from their efforts.

We look first at an argument that technological advance has its own, relatively predictable dynamics of advance and impact. Then we return to a discussion of the interaction of multiple actors, especially states, in the process.

Long Waves of Technological Advance?

Many economists have noted what they call **Kondratieff** (or Kondratiev) **cycles** of approximately 50 to 60 years in the world economy. These take their name from the Russian economist who identified them in the 1920s. Joseph Schumpeter proposed an explanation for these **long waves** in 1939. Schumpeter made distinctions among *invention* (identifiable technical change), *innovation* (the "introduction of new products, techniques and systems into the economy" [Freeman 1988, 38]), and *diffusion* (the widespread use of the new products in ways that clearly affect the growth of productivity and of the economy). For example, James Watt patented his invention of a steam engine in 1769. A stream of innovation used the engine to power textile production machinery, milling processes, and transportation systems (the first steamship was demonstrated on the Potomac in 1787). Diffusion took longer. In transportation applications, a ship powered only by steam finally crossed the Atlantic in 1838, initiating the large-scale replacement of sailing ships by steamships.

The History of Long Waves   According to Schumpeter "creative gales of destruction" or clusters of new inventions lead to periods of accelerated innovation and diffusion and thus to economic upswings. Observers have identified four such "long waves" historically:[4] (1) the early stages of the industrial revolution (beginning in the 1780s), led by innovation in cotton textiles, iron, and the steam engine; (2) the railroad era (after about 1842); (3) an era of growth dominated by electricity and chemical technologies, and by better and cheaper steel (after about 1898 and including the *belle epoque* before World War I); and (4) the post-World War II wave (beginning in the late 1940s), characterized by the automobile, advances in aviation, and an inexpensive, oil-based energy system.

The theory argues that after the initial surge of innovation, diffusion, and associated economic growth, a period of diminishing productivity improvements and slower growth follows. Although the technologies (as inventions) for a new upswing are often available throughout the downturn, they initially contribute little to productivity. In fact, their initial introduction may destroy employment and investment in old sectors faster than it creates new structures. Peter Drucker (1969, 24) noted that an inventor brought forward the first practical electrical generator in 1856 and that entrepreneurs established nearly all contemporary electric-apparatus companies before 1879. In that year Edison invented the electric light bulb and initiated the modern electric industry. That critical product innovation, and others like it, finally set in motion a new Kondratieff upswing at the beginning of the twentieth century.

[4]See Joshua Goldstein (1988, 32) and Freeman (1988, 54). Goldstein (1988) traced the cycles back to 1495. Students of the cycles admit that they become less clear-cut prior to the industrial revolution.

Computers have been available (as inventions) since the late 1940s. Drucker argued in 1969 that the computer-based innovations needed in order to set off another cycle of diffusion and economic upswing would be information systems capable of delivering knowledge cheaply and near universally. The development of microcomputers in the 1980s and extensive electronic networks in the late 1980s and 1990s may constitute the critical innovations for a new Kondratieff upswing. After a period of global economic slowdown, starting in the early 1970s,[5] global growth accelerated in the 1990s. Interestingly, until recently we still tended to measure economic capability in terms of steel produced or energy consumed (measures appropriate to earlier *long waves*). We now need measurements in terms of information available and efficiently organized.

We must emphasize, however, that evidence for the very existence of Kondratieff cycles is ambiguous. We also lack theoretical understanding, which has caused highly regarded economists like Kindleberger and Samuelson to refer to the cycles as "astrology" and "science fiction." (*Forbes*, November 9, 1981, 166; Goldstein 1988, 21) Most disconcerting for Kondratieff theorists is difficulty in clearly identifying and dating the economic cycles they attempt to explain. The cycles actually appear more clearly in price data than in production patterns (Figure 15.4).

[5]In the 1960s the world economy grew 5 percent annually; in the decade after 1973 growth averaged 2.7 percent.

Figure 15.4   Kondratieff Cycles in U.S. Price Data

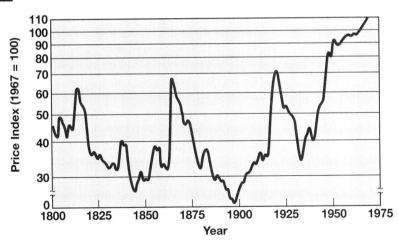

Note: The price data are derived by combining two time series for wholesale prices, one from 1800 to 1890 (series E52) and one from 1890 to 1970 (series E23). Data from U.S. Department of Commerce, Bureau of the Census, *Historical Statistics* (1975 ed.).

Source: Joshua S. Goldstein, *Long Cycles: Prosperity and War in the Modern Age* (New Haven, CT: Yale University Press, copyright © 1988), 35.

Long Waves and Global Politics   The potential relationship between technological-economic cycles (if they truly occur) and interstate conflict interests us also. Some scholars note a moderately strong association between intensified conflict and the upswing phase of the economic cycle (Imbert 1956; Thompson and Zuk 1982). Why would that be? The upswing could benefit some states more than others and thus change the interstate power balance, or it could cause an intensified struggle for resources. Goldstein (1988) generally accepted the upswing argument, and warned that, given a new upswing around 1995, the greatest danger of substantial conflict would be in the first 25 years of the twenty-first century.

Other scholars direct our attention to the potential relationship between the roughly century-long waves of hegemonic domination and the Kondratieff cycle of about half that length. They divide a hegemonic century into two waves. During the first upswing the hegemonic power is ascending, whereas during the second the mature power is approaching decline. Hopkins and Wallerstein (1980) argue that acute conflict is most likely during the first upswing (ascending hegemony) and the second downswing (declining hegemony).

We do best in conclusion to be cautious: technological advance *may* occur in long waves that *may* affect both economic performance and interstate conflict propensity. Although these are important research questions, the evidence is mixed.

State Efforts to Control Technology

States play a very complicated game with respect to technology. They seek to deny potential or actual enemies access to military technology. In addition, they often seek to deny dual-use technology, that is, knowledge that can produce both trucks and tanks or civilian and military aircraft. Some states even seek to deny their own citizenry access to considerable amounts of technology. At the same time, however, states attempt to foster the development of a wide range of technology, work to protect the property rights of their citizens who develop technology, and act to advance the flow of certain technologies to developing countries. Finally, they sometimes find themselves involved in extensive interstate cooperation to develop and extend technology. We look at several of these various activities in turn.

Denial of Military and Dual-Use Technologies   The U.S. Export Control Act of 1949 attempted to deny access by communist countries to interstate technology flows, particularly those with any military implications. After passage, the United States immediately set up the now defunct Coordinating Committee on Multilateral Export Control (Cocom) to coordinate Western policy on trade with the East. Cocom prepared a list of embargoed items. The Mutual Defense Assistance Control Act of 1951 further authorized the president to eliminate aid to any country providing strategic goods to the Soviet Union or Eastern Europe (Spero 1981, 294–296). These measures nearly shut down East-West trade at the peak of the Cold War.

The primary contemporary effort to control military technology flows centers on nuclear proliferation. Even during the Cold War the Western nuclear states managed to cooperate with the Soviet Union to limit flows of nuclear technology to nonnuclear states. And already before the 1968 signing of the Treaty on the Non-

Proliferation of Nuclear Weapons, nuclear states established the International Atomic Energy Agency (IAEA) in Vienna to monitor the flow of nuclear materials. In 1974 most nuclear states (including both superpowers) established a "trigger list" of equipment that they would export only if importers agreed to IAEA safeguards, restricting their use to peaceful atomic programs. In 1987 major Western states also created the Missile Technology Control Regime to limit the proliferation of delivery vehicles. Russia subsequently accepted its provisions and China has claimed to do so.

The end of the Cold War created problems for the nonproliferation regime for the following reasons: (1) the former communist countries faced urgent needs for export earnings; and (2) the weakening of government throughout much of Central and Eastern Europe made it easier for corrupt officials and other criminals to secure nuclear technology and materials for illegal sales. In the early and mid-1990s German authorities discovered several illegal shipments of nuclear material. In 1995 the United States mounted a major effort to prevent sales of nuclear power plant technology, possibly with weapons implications, by Russia to Iran. The United States also tried and failed to prevent Chinese provision of nuclear and missile technology to Pakistan and Iran.

Three problems frustrate any effort to deny technology to specific states. The first involves collective goods and free riders yet again. All members of the Missile Technology Control Regime benefit from the collective good of fewer states with such technology. Yet each individually can benefit by high-priced sales, and thus each has incentive to cheat on the collective policy. Cheating often does not take the form of blatant shipments of military goods, but rather of trading in categories in the large gray area of dual-use technology. For instance, the world learned in 1998 that U.S. companies (Loral Space & Communications and Hughes Electronics) provided technology to China that improved the guidance systems on the rockets that launch satellites for U.S. corporations. Unfortunately, the same technology can improve systems on China's nuclear-tipped missiles.

A second problem is that technology, although less fungible than commodities like oil or wheat, is still sometimes difficult to identify by origin. This further encourages cheating on the nonproliferation regime. For example, Pakistan covertly obtained an extensive range of prohibited nuclear technologies from a number of West German firms in the late 1980s (Spector 1988, 34–35).

Third, states circumvent restrictions with networks of economic and military technology espionage, using diplomatic missions, exchange students, and other personnel. In an early Cold War success, the Soviets obtained secrets that helped them build their own nuclear bomb. In the 1990s the Chinese stole information on warhead miniaturization from the United States.

Even allies squabble over military technology. In 1989 a bitter debate erupted in the United States over proposed cooperation between General Dynamics and Mitsubishi on the development of the F–22 fighter plane. The proposal was to provide the Japanese with the technology for the General Dynamics F–16, on which the F–22 was to be based, in exchange for advanced Japanese technology to be incorporated into the new plane. The allies were to share production.

Proponents pointed out that the Japanese Defense Agency's research and development institute called in 1985 for Japan to build such a plane alone, potentially taking from the United States one of the last clear areas of its technological advantage. Opponents claimed that the deal would help them do exactly that. The corporations signed the contract in 1990 and unveiled the first F–22 in 1995. Cooperation remained shaky throughout, with the Americans refusing to explain the details of some components.

Restriction of Access by Citizens   As Seyom Brown (1988, 174–178) argued, states erect the real barriers to movement of people and messages now through use of passport and customs requirements, overflight and landing restrictions, jamming of broadcasts, selection of nonstandard communications systems, and other conscious or unconscious actions that disrupt the constantly growing demand to use the available technology. The formerly communist governments of Eastern Europe and the Soviet Union extensively restricted what have come internationally to be considered two basic human rights: access to information and freedom of movement. The United States, in part because of its influence over international electronic media and partly because of its open society, has consistently supported Article 19 of the Universal Declaration of Human Rights, affirming the right "to receive and impart information and ideas through any media regardless of frontiers."

Increasingly, states recognize, however, that they themselves will be the greatest victims of efforts to deny technology. For instance, slowing economic growth in the Soviet Union and Eastern Europe became noticeable in the 1960s. Those countries lagged in the development and use of new electronic technology. The Soviet Union actually abolished the computer division of its Academy of Sciences in 1962; the U.S.S.R. long seemed as concerned about the potential dangers that distributed computing posed for social control as about the economic benefits of the technology.

The Soviet decision in the late 1960s and early 1970s to pursue détente with the West and to seek Western technology through trade had many bases, but recognition of a linkage between technological weakness and growth difficulties was important. The resulting infusion may have helped somewhat, but there remained reluctance to embrace the technology. Electronic technology in the West allowed smaller-scale, more flexible manufacturing, something that Soviet centralized planning could not efficiently oversee and which, therefore, threatened it.

Continued economic stagnation (relative to earlier rapid growth) increased pressures, not only to develop or import the technology, but to adopt a decentralized political-economic system better suited to its diffusion and effective use. This helps us understand the Gorbachev emphasis in the 1980s on "restructuring," or *perestroika.* That restructuring, once begun, proved impossible to control, and the communist system collapsed. The Chinese began similar restructuring in the 1980s.

Nearly all Southern countries have considerable labor surpluses, and they also look at the most advanced technology with ambivalence. On the one hand, they often cannot be competitive globally without it; on the other, it displaces labor. For instance, the introduction of robotics into the Japanese automobile industry made it impossible in 1980 for the South Koreans, with a wage rate of $1 per hour, to be competitive, even though the Japanese rate was $7 per hour (Castells and Tyson 1988, 70). The Koreans had to adopt the robotic techniques themselves.

Support for Technological Innovation   At the end of the seventeenth century England and France established the Royal Society for the Advancement of Science and the Académie Francaise, respectively, simultaneously demonstrating and solidifying their leadership in the emerging state system (Strange 1988, 121). Many countries now seek to develop a wide variety of technologies, especially those with military application, before their acquisition by other states, and act to maintain their monopoly as long as possible. The struggle for relative advantage gives rise to considerable interstate rivalry.

There is a definite character of **technological mercantilism** to the competition for economic advantage within the West. Japan, although beginning the post-World War II era in a position of inferiority, now helps set the pace for the technical competition. An important tool of Japan is cooperation between government and industry. The Ministry of International Trade and Industry (MITI) targets technologies of the future, stimulates research and development, and helps secure financing for Japanese industry. For example, the Japanese government and 45 corporations were at work in 1988 within a consortium on superconductor technology, even though scientists expected few significant applications for decades. Japan has also protected its domestic markets against high-technology imports such as supercomputers, while encouraging export growth in the same industries.

Europeans recognize that their individual states cannot compete with the United States or Japan. One facet of their response has been a series of collective efforts under the auspices of the European Union. Joint programs have sponsored research on energy, health, the environment, information and telecommunications, and raw materials. Programs have included the European Strategic Program for Research and Development in Information Technology (ESPRIT), Research and Development in Advanced Communications Technology (RACE), Basic Research in Industrial Technology for Europe (BRITE), and the Joint European Submicron Silicon program (JESSI). The European Research Coordinating Agency (EUREKA) reaches beyond the European Community and draws on the expertise of other European states. Interindustry consortia supplement governmental efforts.

Supplementing such precompetitive, EU-wide research cooperation, many high-technology projects in Europe lead to joint production activity. The French-British Concorde project is among the best known. More commercially successful is the five-country Airbus project (Kirchner 1988, 17-f). The same countries and firms developed and produce the Ariane rockets for satellite launching.

The seeming success of the Japanese and European models for government support to advanced-technology industries sparked a debate concerning industrial policy and government-industry cooperation in the United States. The U.S. government has taken several steps toward an industrial policy that will enhance the external competitive strength of its companies. For instance, in 1984 Congress revised antitrust laws to facilitate joint research by U.S. corporations. By 1990 more than 125 cooperatives had formed.

Semiconductor technology is of special interest in the United States (and at special risk of falling to Japanese leadership). In 1986 the U.S. government encouraged the establishment of Sematech, a consortium of U.S. electronics companies engaged in joint research. The Pentagon provided part of the funding. In 1989 a group of manufacturers announced U.S. Memories, Inc., a joint venture to manufacture advanced chips. Its collapse in 1990 triggered renewed American introspection with respect to its competitive position.

The U.S. government has sponsored new engineering and scientific research centers on college campuses, while also lowering the barriers between governmental research centers and companies able to commercialize their discoveries. In addition the U.S. government vigorously tries to protect the existing technological advantage of domestic corporations. For example, in 1983 it prosecuted Hitachi for stealing secrets from IBM (MacDonald 1986, 53–54). U.S. trade legislation in 1988 also took unilateral action to protect American firms by requiring the U.S. Trade Representative to provide a list of countries that "inadequately protect American goods from counterfeiting or infringement" (*Business Week,* May 22, 1989, 86). Failure to improve protection invokes automatic sanctions after six months.

In reality, U.S. government support for technological development has often been more extensive than recognized within the country. For instance, the U.S. military began a system called ARPANET in the 1970s that would connect computers so that the network might survive a nuclear attack. It then became a tool for universities and research organizations and evolved into the Internet in the late 1980s. Although it has gone global, the extensive early use of it in the United States was and remains an advantage for the country.

Intellectual Property Rights Protection   The global recognition of patents regulates the pattern of transfer of technology among states, corporations, and individuals. Innovators register patents within one state and thereby create a world monopoly on rights to the patented innovation. This allows the inventor to capture the benefits of invention for a period. Without patent protection, the invention would immediately be a public good, and this would encourage free riding rather than innovation. The intellectual property rights agreement of the Uruguay Round made great progress in unifying global standards beginning in 1995: It set global patent protection at 20 years and set copyright on computer programs, movies, and sound recordings at 50 years (Schott 1994, 115–123). LDCs have a phase-in period, but the same rules will apply.

At the same time that the global property rights regime attempts to protect rights, it also seeks to encourage the diffusion of technology. The individual, corporate, or state entity controlling the patent can use the technology abroad (one basic reason for the existence of multinational corporations) or license it to others. There are obvious incentives to exploit the technology during the period of patent protection and to establish a dominant market presence before the protection ends. This system facilitates rapid domestic development and worldwide transfer of new technology.

Pirating exists on an extensive scale and further hastens global flow of technology. Most pirating consists of violation of consumer-good trademarks; imitation goods flood global markets. Pirates also steal patented technologies, however, such as those in microprocessors at the core of personal computers. Large corporations use their patent and trademark registration rights to fight such infringement, but they face serious difficulties in enforcement abroad; small corporations have little chance to protect their technology. The Uruguay Round of GATT devoted special attention to this problem, requiring members to enforce property rights under domestic law. It also placed intellectual property rights under the Dispute Settlement Understanding of the World Trade Organization (WTO) and considerably increased enforcement after 2000.

Interstate Cooperation on Technology   By no means is all interstate interaction on technology competitive. Northern governments transfer some technology to the South through public programs, such as the British Colombo Plan, the Economic Development Fund of the EU, the U.S. Agency for International Development, the U.S. Peace Corps, and the Swiss Institute for Intermediate Technology. Public technology transfer heavily targets agricultural and medical technology.

In 1991, the EU, Japan, the United States, and Russia agreed to cooperate on a nuclear-fusion research project using magnetic confinement. Because it would cost about $1 billion to design and $4 billion to build, such an experimental facility increasingly exceeds the willingness of individual states to provide. In 1993 Russia and the United States agreed to merge core elements of their space programs. This led to a linking of the American shuttle to Mir, the Russian space station, in 1995. In 1997 Russia and the United States signed an agreement with 14 other countries to complete a space station early in the twenty-first century.

Are States Losing Control?

This discussion has indicated the importance of states in the development and diffusion or denial of technology. The long-term impacts of any technology are, however, always hard to predict. In World War II, scientists invented DDT to protect soldiers against insects—no one then thought of using it on crops and contributing to the great postwar advances in food production. Similarly, a forecast in the late 1940s concluded that the world market for computers in the year 2000 would be 1,000 at most (Drucker 1986, 214–216). Lawyers at Bell Labs hesitated to apply for a patent on the laser, not seeing any relevance to the phone industry. Both DDT and computers reshaped the post-World War II world, and lasers in combination with optic fiber are revolutionizing communications.

Such unpredictability raises an interesting question: might some of the very technologies that states help to sponsor ultimately undercut their own power in the world order? One interesting illustration of this possibility again comes from telecommunications. States established the International Telegraph Union in 1865 (by which time there were already 150,000 miles of cable around the world) to help them manage that relatively new technology.[6] The organization became the International Telecommunications Union (ITU) in 1932. From 1965 until the early 1980s the ITU served states in their efforts to manage new technologies like the telephone (invented in 1876)—often at the expense of making the new technologies widely available. More important to the ITU than diffusing technology was protection of

[6]Zacher with Sutton (1997, 163) and Deibert (1997, 117). See also Rutkowski (1995).

the state-controlled PTTs (post, telephone, and telegraph administrations) by which countries ran their domestic markets. Even in the late 1980s the cartel of PTTs priced cross-border calls at about three times their cost (Zacher 1997, 166) and used the excess profits to subsidize intrastate service.

The U.S. breakup of the AT&T monopoly and telecommunication liberalization in Britain began to destroy this system in the 1980s, partly under the pressure of companies that wanted to enter true global competition. Throughout the 1990s liberalization rolled ahead around the world as the PTTs in Europe and elsewhere grudgingly opened local markets to the foreign onslaught. Intelsat began to allow the launching of rival satellites. The Uruguay Round of GATT incorporated services into its discussion and a Telecommunications Annex into its GATS agreement, solidifying a shift of locus for future discussions away from the ITU to the new WTO. The combined result of all such change was a transformation of a global regime built around the norm of state control to one that emphasized liberalization.

Actually, of course, it was state action that initiated this transformation, and state action could bring it to a halt. Yet it appears possible that the unleashed technologies are now helping transform not just a global regime, but a world social and political order. We turn to that possibility.

Technology and Social Organization

Earlier chapters presented arguments that various technologies can reshape the global sociopolitical order. For instance, Herz claimed that gunpowder had created the states when it made feudal units indefensible and that nuclear weapons could ultimately undercut the dominant role of states for the same reason. And Marxist traditions argue that changes in economic technologies have repeatedly reshaped economic and political systems throughout history. Given the heavy emphasis of this chapter on technologies of interaction, we should consider contemporary argument that communications technology also determines the way humans organize themselves and that changes in that technology are reshaping global social structures. A first step in that argument is easy: Such technologies obviously penetrate states in ways that can undercut their sovereignty.

Penetration of States

During the 1980s the spotlight of media attention on human-rights violations in countries like Chile, South Africa, and the Soviet Union connected the victims with the global community and led to pressure on the governments (not always successful but steady) to undertake reforms. The communications media also regularly portrays hunger and malnutrition in Africa to the rest of the world. Just as humanity now collectively rejects human sacrifice and slavery, we appear to be moving toward collective condemnation of political violence and starvation. In June 1989, when the Chinese army brutally crushed the democracy movement, color film took the story to global news networks and ignited a storm of protest. UN Secretary General Boutros Boutrous-Ghali once said that CNN has become "the sixteenth member of the Security Council."

Modern transportation and communication make contemporary states permeable and increase *penetration* by external actors (Rosenau 1966). In a dramatic example, a German, Mathias Rust, penetrated Soviet air defenses in 1987 and landed his small private plane on Red Square. Penetration by communication is, of course, easier than by transportation. Under the Shah, Iran controlled the electronic media. Nonetheless, the Ayatollah Khomeini, an Iranian exile in Paris, developed and strengthened a network of support, in part by distributing cassette tapes throughout Iran. Opponents can sometimes even turn communications systems once controlled by repressive regimes against those regimes. For instance, the revolutionary regime in Romania in 1989 seized and initially governed from the Bucharest television station.

Similarly, one of the main information sources for millions of Chinese in prodemocracy protests during 1989 was Voice of America radio transmissions. The Chinese authorities therefore resumed electronic jamming of them for the first time since they restored diplomatic relations with the United States in 1979. They were unable or unwilling to cut telephone linkages, however, and the daily volume of calls between the United States and China rose from 10,000 to 30,000 during the protests. Worldwide telephone networks greatly increase permeability of societies, despite state restrictions. The commercial necessity of being tied into the global network has provided average citizens and political activists the technology to contact their peers around the world.

In the summer of 1990 an American foundation distributed in Central Europe what it called "Democracy Kits," each containing a copier, a computer, and a fax machine. If it were possible to add a radio, a television satellite dish, a cellular telephone, and an international airline ticket to the kit, it would truly symbolize the current interconnectedness of people globally, and it would signal their capabilities for collective self-defense against oppression.

Transformation of Global Order?

It is, of course, a significant step from arguing that new technologies penetrate states to arguing that they are transforming the global political system. Might that, however, be the case?

Marshall McLuhan popularized **medium theory** with the expression that "the medium is the message." Medium theory (Deibert 1997) argues that the manner of organizing and transmitting information strongly influences what comes to be knowledge and, ultimately, how we understand and therefore structure the world. As social constructivists argue, the process is bidirectional, and changes in fundamental communication technologies correspond to changes in social organization:

- The invention of writing coincides with the development of the first civilization in the form of the city-states of ancient Sumeria
- The development of the alphabet and the spread of literacy ca. 700 B.C. in ancient Greece coincides with the onset of the Greek enlightenment
- The development of movable type and the spread of printing in Western Europe coincides with the Renaissance and early Modernity (Deibert 1997, 2)

If the last few hundred years have been the era of printing, and that era helped give rise to a world order built around the state, into what communications era are we now moving, and how might it affect the world order? Deibert calls the emerging communications system one of "hypermedia." Hypermedia does not supplant printing, but overlays the World Wide Web and a more general planetary "central nervous system" onto it. Communications and access to information, supported by computerization, become global, ubiquitous, simple, instantaneous, and inexpensive.

One institutional consequence of this is the globalization of financial markets that Chapter 12 discussed. Multinational corporations gain great flexibility in locating production and other functions. Most large corporations have their own global "intranets," as well as access to the Internet. Ford Motor Company has "Fordnet," connecting 20,000 designers and engineers seamlessly to each other (Deibert 1997, 141). Although it would be foolish to think it irreversible, one consequence of such integration has been the convergence (and liberalization) of government economic and regulatory policies around the world, even in the face of much popular opposition to such change.

Another institutional consequence of hypermedia is the surge of transnational social movements and the development of a global civil society (see Chapter 8). The number of nongovernmental organizations focused on human rights rose from 38 in 1950 to 138 in 1980 and 275 in 1990 (Deibert 1997, 158). Environmental groups have created the EcoNet via the Internet. There is also a PeaceNet, WomensNet, and LaborNet (as well as a global neo-Nazi network).

What kind of political order might evolve to fit this emerging communications pattern? Few argue that the state will disappear, or even cease to be fundamentally important, in the foreseeable future. A complex pattern of governance like that evolving in Europe is a more likely model.

Conclusion

Technologies now spread quickly around the globe. Advancing microelectronic and communication techniques constantly accelerate that diffusion. In the last 200 years many new technologies have greatly improved collective human well-being, including our life expectancies. Much technological advance promises still greater average well-being and, perhaps, even the narrowing of gaps between rich and poor. Expectations of such developments are at the heart of the modernist worldview.

Advances in communication, transportation, and military technologies have integrated the world and made states more permeable. Transborder interactions, with potential for both good and harm, have intensified. Many modernists are also liberals or social constructivists and argue that advance in these technologies may now be bringing us to a cusp between old and new world orders. To them, new military capabilities make the old state-centric, power-politics relationships and behavior patterns unsustainable, at the same time that communication and transportation developments make possible new transnational relationships.

But in the short- and mid-run, the historic state struggle for relative position continues, even over technologies that ultimately hold the promise of global benefits. States remain key actors in the development and diffusion of technology. Most modernists fail to develop fully the mixed political ramifications of their technological optimism. Once again, we have seen that the realist worldview can also help us make sense of the world.

Selected Key Terms

green revolution	information dominance	dual-use technology
revolution in military affairs	Kondratieff cycles	technological mercantilism
	long waves	medium theory

CHAPTER 16

Environmental Context and Constraints

China has a population of about 1.3 billion and, although its demographic growth has greatly slowed, the total may reach 1.6 billion by 2025. On a land mass only slightly larger than the United States, China has somehow managed to improve the average diet of that huge and growing number. Between the mid-1970s and mid-1990s the portion of Chinese children under age 5 who are underweight (malnourished) fell from 26 percent of the total to 16 percent and calorie availability for the entire population grew to nearly 90 percent of that in European countries.[1]

Land under cultivation is falling in China, however, in part because of urbanization and in part from soil loss and other environmental problems. China also has some of the most severe water shortages in the world, both in terms of safe water for urban population and adequate water for agriculture. China is already one of the largest net importers of grain in the global market and by some estimates its demand on global markets in 2030 could be twice the size of all current exports. Yet China has also undertaken perhaps the largest reforestation program in the world (greatly reducing the dust storms sweeping into Beijing from the north), and the leadership expresses confidence in its ability to increase food production as needed.

China depends on coal for about 75 percent of its energy consumption. Because the burning of coal pollutes so badly, urban air quality in China ranks among the worst in the world. Beijing has, however, banned leaded gasoline, shut down or fined the dirtiest factories, spent over $1.2 billion in the last decade on the environment, and announced plans to replace high-sulfur coal with other energy forms.

KEY WEB LINKS

www.prb.org/
www.unfpa.org/
www.fao.org/
www.cgiar.org/IFPRI/index.htm
www.eia.doe.gov/
www.opec.org/
www.epa.gov/
www.wwf.org/
www.usgcrp.gov/

[1]Sources on China include the World Bank (1998), Population Reference Bureau (1997), UNDP (1997), Brown (1995), British Petroleum (1997), World Resources Institute (1998), and *The Economist*, April 11, 1998, 31.

In short, a report on China's environment includes both good news and bad news. Its future environmental prospects are uncertain. The aim of this chapter is to report, similarly, the good and bad news for the larger global environment. The focus of this chapter on the environment will help us understand the eco-wholist perspective, but the insights of other perspectives will be critical. Although our primary focus is the **macroenvironment** (population, food, energy, and pollution), we begin by considering the **microenvironment** (bacteria and viruses).

Microenvironment

William McNeill (1976) traced the long-term relationship between disease and human social development in his classic book, *Plagues and Peoples.* Between 1300 and 1700 Europe experienced a series of major plagues as it gradually established regular contact with the rest of the world and imported its diseases. Some historians believe that Bubonic Plague, which killed one-third to one-half of all Europeans between 1347 and 1350, cut back an unsustainably large population and helped set the stage for technological and economic growth in the next century.

By 1700 Europe had largely "domesticated" epidemic diseases from around the world and European population began a major and steady expansion (McNeill 1976, 224–225). Their adaptation to many diseases increased the edge of the Europeans over other populations to which they then carried a lethal combination of illnesses. McNeill points out that the Spanish conquest of Mexico, pitting 600 men under Cortez against the Aztec empire, benefited from superior military technology and the local alliances that Cortez formed. The Spanish also brought smallpox to the New World, however, and it ravaged the empire during the conquest. Old World diseases contributed much to the precipitous collapse of New World populations and civilizations.

Their own diseases, especially malaria, long protected the Africans from the outside world; malaria killed about one-half of all Europeans who attempted to penetrate the interior. The manufacture of quinine after 1820, and its widespread use by 1850, finally opened Africa to the Europeans and they proceeded to conquer and divide it (Headrick 1981).

The impact of disease on human relations is not necessarily a thing of the past. As late as World War I, a global influenza epidemic (1917–1918) killed 20 million or more (a greater number than the war killed), helped by the large troop movements of the war and the weakened condition of many peoples. McNeill concluded:

> Even without mutation, it is always possible that some hitherto obscure parasitic organism may escape its accustomed ecological niche and expose the dense human populations that have become so conspicuous a feature of the earth to some fresh and perchance devastating mortality. . . . Infectious disease which antedated the emergence of humankind will last as long as humanity itself, and will surely remain, as it has been hitherto, one of the fundamental parameters and determinants of human history. (McNeill 1976, 289–291)

Does AIDS, recognized only in 1981, perhaps constitute a modern version of the plagues that historically altered the course of human events? More than 33 million people carried the HIV virus in 1998 (about 1.0 percent of all sexually active people globally). AIDS killed 2.5 million in 1998. More than 16,000 people acquire the virus every day. More than 40 percent of all those infected globally are now women. The economic impact of AIDS is very great, because 90 percent of those who die are between 20 and 49 years of age (and thus are economically productive), and because the costs of treatment during the prolonged illness induced by AIDS are high.

AIDS incidence in Africa is especially high, with about two-thirds of cases worldwide on that continent. Those in developing countries are in especially great danger because other sexually transmitted diseases such as chlamydia, syphilis, and gonorrhea are more prevalent; genital sores from untreated diseases facilitate the spread of HIV. Because of this mode of transmission, and the socially vulnerable position of women in LDCs, AIDS is predominantly a heterosexual disease in the Caribbean and sub-Saharan Africa. More than 20 percent of the adult population in Botswana and Zimbabwe carries HIV and the rates in all countries of South Africa exceed 10 percent. Life expectancy at birth in Botswana fell from 61 in the late 1980s to 41 in 1998, and the U.S. Census Bureau says it may collapse to 33 by 2010.

Africa now has 8.4 million AIDS-orphans, a number that could grow to 40 million in 2010. Under such circumstances, social systems collapse, and we will see what have come to be called **failed states,** states no longer capable of organizing resources to provide basic social needs, including order. Thucydides documented long ago the consequences of such state failure:

> Athens owed to the plague the beginnings of a state of unprecedented lawlessness. . . . As for what is called honour, no one showed himself willing to abide by its laws, so doubtful was it whether one would survive to enjoy the name for it. It was generally agreed that what was both honourable and valuable was the pleasure of the moment. . . . No fear of god or law of man had a restraining influence. (Thucydides 1972, 155; cited in Lofdahl 1997, 75–76)

How might the continued spread of AIDS affect interstate politics? One early hypothesis was that it could give rise to a substantial program of global cooperation:

> But with farseeing leadership, this great human disaster could lead to rescue and interim management by some international consortium in the name of humanity. As more countries need help, this management could become a sort of new Marshall Plan, a stepping stone to a new global order. . . . In the next few years, the challenge of coping with AIDS at all levels could give the world a new sense of planet-wide interdependence and responsibility for human survival and for the future. (Platt 1988, 45)

Although there has been considerable global cooperation, individual states have organized most response to the epidemic. For example, competitive French and U.S. medical efforts identified the virus in 1983. Communication of results among such teams is very rapid—frequent global conferences help. Individual country costs of the disease are sufficiently great to justify high levels of individual state expenditure, the results of which are global collective goods. In addition, drug companies undertake their own research in the hopes of being able to capture, through patent protection, at least some of the good that an AIDS vaccine would produce.

The logic of collective action suggests that there is little incentive for many countries to make substantial individual contributions to AIDS research. Why should a small LDC spend a significant fraction of its governmental budget on AIDS research, when that expenditure might do no more than allow its scientists to keep up with the larger research programs of the United States or France? Thus a few large, developed countries with high incidence of AIDS undertake a disproportionate amount of AIDS research. In the terms of Chapter 6, the group of states served by a potential treatment for AIDS is privileged.

To put the worldwide AIDS epidemic in context, 3 million children die *every year* from diarrhea, measles kill 1 million children and adults, 2.5 million people die from malaria, and tuberculosis (TB) kills about 3 million (increasingly as a result of dual infection by HIV and TB). In total, infectious and parasitical diseases (IPDs) account for about 28 percent of global deaths (Olshansky et al. 1997, 4) and about 5 percent in developed countries. In spite of the AIDS epidemic and a major resurgence in malaria resistant to chloroquine, increasing portions of humans die of noncommunicable disease like heart disease and cancer. Smoking alone kills about 3 million annually.

Yet the AIDS epidemic has had a major psychological and physical impact globally. Just as the civil war in the former Yugoslavia reminds us that the suffering of war is not simply something in the history books, and just as recurrent LDC economic problems remind us that economic disasters are always possible, the AIDS epidemic is teaching humanity that it has not yet banished plague from the world. A resurgence of cholera in Latin America in the early 1990s reinforced the lesson, as did an outbreak of the deadly Ebola during 1995 in Zaire. Scientists have identified at least 28 previously unrecognized and possibly new diseases since 1973. Moreover, a new strain of staph bacteria, which infect more than two million people in the United States alone each year and kill up to 80,000, resists all known antibiotics.[2] Virulent TB resistant to multiple drugs has also appeared.

Recognition of human vulnerability in the face of the physical and biological environment increasingly extends also to the macroenvironment, the subject to which we now turn.

Population Pressures

More than any other single issue, eco-wholists draw our attention to the rapid growth of the world's population. Increased size of population places stress on the environment in two principal ways. First, a larger population demands increasing volumes of inputs from the environment: food, energy, and other raw materials. Second, the increasing economic activities of growing population produce outputs that affect the environment: soil erosion, deforestation, and air and water pollution. In the rest of this chapter we look in turn at the growth of global population and at its input requirements and output effects.

[2]Global antibiotic use can be appalling. Individuals fail to complete courses of treatment, facilitating development of resistance in bacteria. Farmers use half of all U.S. antibiotics to facilitate faster growth in animals and even to spray on fruit trees.

Chapter 1 identified the demographic transition as one of the most important contemporary global forces. That discussion made several points with respect to the growth of population:

1. Declining mortality caused an acceleration of population growth in Europe during the 1800s, and in the Third World since 1945. Fertility decreases have come more slowly, but are now underway almost everywhere.
2. The acceleration of global population growth rates reached a peak about 1970 (2 percent each year), and growth rates have declined to about 1.4 percent. Annual increments to global population reached 90 million in the late 1980s and have fallen to about 80 million.
3. Population growth rates are much higher in the global South than in the North, and that will remain true for many decades. Many Northern countries even have declining populations.
4. Rapid population growth increases the size of the dependent population under 15, whereas slow population growth increases the size of the retirement-aged population.

Competing Perspectives

A die-hard realist reaction to demographic trends might emphasize the growing share of global population located in the South and the contribution such population may eventually make to Southern power. Realists would also note how larger populations could affect the definition of state interests, especially if they force states to look externally for necessary food and resources. Will not some countries with powerful military forces use their power rather than risk slipping into economic or political chaos internally? For example, Iraq has one of the very highest annual rates of natural population growth in the world, nearly 3 percent, one reason it covets the resources of several neighbors. An astounding annual rate of increase of 4.6 percent in the Gaza strip promises continued problems for both Israel and the Palestinians.

From the perspective of political economy, both liberals and neo-Marxists point to the strong relationship between income level and family size. In a somewhat rare show of agreement, both argue that individuals *desire* larger families when children provide net economic benefits, through contributions to family income or support of parents in old age. These net benefits diminish as family incomes rise and children are more likely to require financial support for education than to augment family income. Moreover, as societal incomes increase, governmental programs begin to replace children in providing disability and old-age insurance. There is much truth in the slogan that "development is the best contraceptive."

The eco-wholist focuses on the environmental burden of population. Lester Brown (1988a) argued that a significant portion of the Third World may find themselves in a demographic trap. The rapid population growth in some countries places unsustainable demands on their food, resource, and environmental systems; they are destroying their support systems and their economic prospects. Rather than moving to higher incomes and lower birthrates, they may experience deterioration of incomes and higher death rates. That is, they may regress to the pretransition situation of traditional peoples, achieving a balance between number of births and death rates, only because both are high. In short, the **demographic**

trap is a vicious cycle of high population growth, environmental damage, economic and political failures, and high population growth again.

In our discussion of the microenvironment we have already discussed one of the major global policy issues tied directly to population, namely health. The global community has been very important in helping LDCs raise average life expectancy from 48 in 1960 to 63 in 1998. For instance, in 1980 only 20 percent of the world's children received vaccinations against six common childhood diseases. The WHO's Expanded Program on Immunization raised that to 80 percent in 1991. We move our attention now to two other population-based issues: migration and population control.

Migration and Refugees

On a day-to-day basis, population issues intrude on interstate politics primarily through the migration of people among countries. Population pressures and inadequate economic opportunities (even food scarcity like that in Ireland) *pushed* most of the Europeans who emigrated in the 1800s and early 1900s; war and social unrest drove many others from home. The wealth of the New World *pulled* many to the Americas. As a result of the same forces in the late 1990s, about 140 million people lived outside of their country of birth as legal immigrants, illegal economic immigrants, and *refugees* (those who have fled from actual physical danger). Civil war and ecological disruption displaced 30 million more within their own countries (World Resources Institute [WRI] 1998, 147–148).

In the 1990s the principal recipients of immigrants and refugees were the United States, Canada, Australia, and the European Union (especially Germany). Migration to Western Europe from the former communist countries and from Mediterranean states became a major issue in the 1990s. The inflow reached 3 million in 1992. In the late 1990s it fell to levels similar to those of the United States: roughly 1 million legal immigrants, another 200,000 asylum seekers, and perhaps another quarter million illegal immigrants. The opening of all internal borders among most European states has made it more difficult to keep out the illegals—Italy alone has 5,000 miles of coastline. Inflows remain large by historic standards, and one result has been the rise of nationalistic parties and party factions in all recipient countries.

Although immigrants clamor for admission to the developed countries, for much of the rest of the world, the issue is refugees—displaced peoples who at least initially hope to return one day to their own homeland—and other "peoples of concern" to the UN, including returnees and internally displaced peoples. The number of such people climbed from 1.5 million in 1951 to 2.5 million in 1970 and a peak of 27 million in 1995 (Figure 16.1). Numbers declined in the late 1990s (to 22 million in 1997), as conflicts in Afghanistan and Rwanda wound down. Table 16.1 shows the primary types of "peoples of concern" and their regional locations. It is very difficult to count such people, and official tallies can be low. For instance, the U.S. Committee for Refugees estimates that at least 30 million people are internally displaced.

In 1988–1995 the civil war in Afghanistan (with a combination of ethnic and religious roots) created the largest number of refugees. Nationalism explains the circumstances of many people uprooted from their homes (such as the Palestinians

Figure 16.1 Global Refugees

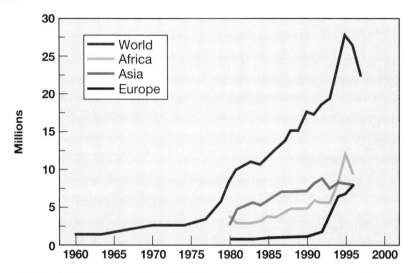

Sources: Worldwatch Institute Database (Washington, DC: Worldwatch Institute, January 1998); UNHCR & Refugees http://www.unhcr.ch/un&ref.htm (June 11, 1998).

and various peoples of the former Yugoslavia). In other refugee situations, such as Somalia and Ethiopia, environmental pressure is a primary factor. Even when civil war or nationalism is the apparent cause (as in Rwanda), population and resource pressures may fuel those fires.

Although the office of the UNHCR coordinates some of the global refugee relief effort, most refugees rely on the generosity of neighboring or otherwise interested states (such as the German efforts on behalf of former Yugoslavia). A few countries, including Australia, Canada, Germany, Sweden, the United States, Switzerland, Denmark, France, and New Zealand, have accepted especially large numbers of refugees for permanent resettlement, relative to their own populations. On the whole, however, as pressures to resettle refugees and immigrants have *grown*, willingness to accept them has *declined*.

Population Control Efforts

Fertility control is a second important global population issue. Many individual states have acted. India established perhaps the first family-planning program in the world, in 1952. By 1996, 95 countries had some family-planning effort, although it was significant in only 41 countries (Population Reference Bureau 1996). Surprisingly, many LDCs still have very weak programs—or none at all. It is interesting that the LDCs with the most active programs are primarily NICs (see Table 16.2). Commitment to family-planning programs continues to widen, however. In 1976, only one-third of African governments thought fertility was too high; by 1996 two-thirds of them had at least a formal program to reduce it.

Region	Refugees	Returnees	Internally Displaced	Others of Concern	Total January 1, 1997
Africa	4,341,000	1,693,000	2,058,000	—	8,091,000
Asia	4,809,000	1,241,100	1,719,000	156,000	7,925,000
Europe	3,166,000	308,000	1,066,000	1,209,000	5,749,000
Latin America	88,000	70,000	11,000	—	169,000
North America	720,000	—	—	—	720,000
Oceania	75,000	—	—	—	53,600
Total	13,200,000	3,311,000	4,854,000	1,365,000	22,729,000

Table 16.1   Persons of Concern to UNHCR (January 1, 1997)

Source: United Nations High Commissioner for Refugees (UNHCR) (http://www.unhcr.ch/un&ref/numbers/table2.htm, July 6, 1998).

Success of family-planning programs is not simple to measure, but there is little question that global contraceptive use has increased. The portion of married couples in Latin America using modern contraception grew from under 20 percent in 1960 to 58 percent in 1998; in Africa the rate went from 10 percent to 17 percent. Nonetheless, the unmet demand for contraception in much of the Third World remains very high, implying a potential for even greater success with more active programs. As many as 100 million women globally want to avoid pregnancy but do not use contraception because they cannot afford it or husbands pressure them not to. According to one UN estimate, the result from 1995–2000 will have been 120 million unwanted pregnancies, 49 million abortions, and 65,000 maternal deaths.

Northern states have supported family-planning programs of LDCs. The United States took a position early, when President Johnson made support for LDC programs an important component of the overall foreign aid effort in 1965. It provided about two-thirds of the total international effort between 1965 and 1975. Many other states followed that lead.

In 1967 the United Nations established its Fund for Population Activities (UNFPA). The UN has also sponsored World Population Conferences in every decade since 1954. The first two conferences in 1954 and 1965 brought together population experts and enhanced our understanding of global demographics (Ashford 1995, 6). The next three shifted the agenda to population policy. A major split characterized the 1974 meeting in Bucharest. More-developed countries stressed the urgency of attention to population control in the South. Some states in the South protested that Northern pressures for population control were an extension of colonialism, and a few even labeled it a form of genocide.

The 1984 UN conference in Mexico City differed dramatically. Most of the South had shifted to the viewpoint that population growth severely threatened their development prospects. China, which had taken an anti-North position in 1974, and which had thereafter adopted a one-child-per-family policy, exemplified the change. In essence, the eco-wholist view had come to influence the South strongly. Ironically, the leading early supporter of Southern family planning, the United States, changed its position in 1984. Under the influence of classical liberal

Table 16.2 Contraceptive Prevalence and Availability in LDCs

Country	Percentage of Married Couples Using Any Method	Country	Percentage of Married Couples Using Any Method
High Use		**Low Use**	
China	83	Philippines	40
South Korea	77	Syria	36
Costa Rica	75	Jordan	35
Mauritius	75	Botswana	33
Singapore	74	Kenya	33
Thailand	74	Guatemala	32
Colombia	72	Grenada	31
Cuba	70	Guyana	31
Brazil	66	Nepal	29
Sri Lanka	66	Lesotho	23
Turkey	63	Rwanda	21
Vietnam	65	Ghana	20
Panama	64	Swaziland	20
Jamaica	62	Haiti	18
Tunisia	60	Cameroon	16
		Uganda	15
Moderate Use		Iraq	14
Peru	59	Malawi	13
St. Vincent	58	Togo	12
Ecuador	57	Pakistan	12
Paraguay	56	Cote d'Ivoire	11
Indonesia	55	Benin	9
Antigua	53	Burundi	9
Lebanon	53	Sudan	8
Mexico	53	Senegal	7
Trinidad/Tobago	53	Mali	7
Algeria	52	Yemen	7
Morocco	50	Nigeria	6
South Africa	50	Liberia	6
Venezuela	49	Mauritania	3
Nicaragua	49	Afghanistan	2
Barbados	48		
Malaysia	48		
Zimbabwe	48		
Honduras	47		
Egypt	47		
Bangladesh	47		
Bolivia	45		
St. Lucia	43		
India	41		

Source: World Resources Institute, *World Resources 1998–1999* (New York: Oxford University Press, 1998), 252–263.

philosophy, and reflecting the Reagan administration's opposition to abortion (legal abortion is an element of population-control programs in many countries), the U.S. delegation declined to support active family-planning efforts. Instead, the United States argued that adoption of market-oriented economic policies would stimulate growth and thereby smaller family size. It also substantially reduced bilateral and multilateral economic support for family-planning programs in the 1980s and ceased it altogether for countries using abortion. For example, the United States eliminated all of its funding for the UNFPA between 1985 and 1993, ostensibly because of the organization's support for the Chinese family-planning effort, which had coerced abortion decisions.

The 1994 conference in Cairo again differed strikingly from earlier meetings, in participation, tone, and outcome (Ashford 1995). Delegates represented 180 countries and 1,200 participating NGOs (compared to 109 NGOs in 1974 and 139 in 1984, present only as observers). No significant actor in Cairo other than the Vatican questioned the global need to slow population growth. Moreover, the conference placed women at the center of the discussion and of the agenda. Dr. Nafis Sadik, Secretary-General of the conference, set the tone. Prime Ministers Brundtland of Norway and Bhutto of Pakistan played important supporting roles. All three of those women, and a Women's Caucus of 400 organizations, emphasized not just the direct role of women in childbearing decisions, but the importance of reproductive rights, female education, and economic and political empowerment of women (United Nations Non-Governmental Liaison Service [NGLS] 1994, 1). The 1994 conference represented a milestone: The global population discussion had moved from fact-finding by experts through rancorous interstate debate to substantial consensus on both issues and policies—even the Cairo debate on abortion could not derail the momentum.

As family-planning programs become established in LDCs, and population growth rates fall faster than earlier estimates, new population issues emerge. Across all 15 countries of the European Union the fertility rate is now only 1.5. In Italy it fell to 1.2 and the country became the first in the world in which the number of people over 60 exceeds that under 20. The burden on pension systems is growing steadily and such countries increasingly develop *pronatalist* (pro-birth) policies.

Resource Scarcities: Food

Which has been growing faster in the last 50 years, world population or world food supply? The discussion of food in Chapter 1 gave you the basis for an intelligent answer to that question:

1. For the world as a whole, food production has grown faster than population in the last half century. Per-capita increases slowed, however, throughout the 1990s.

2. Productivity growth has often led to large surpluses in many of the more-developed countries of the world, especially in Canada, Australia, the United States, and Western Europe.

3. Averages conceal much. In Africa, for example, especially in the countries of the Sahel, food production (up 130 percent between 1960 and 1995) has fallen short of population growth, causing increased malnutrition and increased dependence on food from the outside world. Even in the relatively prosperous states of Latin America, significant hunger persists.

These characteristics of the world food situation may suggest what seems a straightforward "solution" to world food problems. Given surpluses of food in the North and shortages in Africa, it is only necessary to transfer the food surpluses to where they are needed. Yet this book continually emphasizes that there are multiple sides to every issue; it is no different with respect to food.

Competing Perspectives on Global Food Supply

Not everyone believes that the world has a continuing ability to support the growing global population, even with food transfers. Many eco-wholists argue that the human population is running up against the carrying capacity of its environment. Many years ago Lester Brown (1981, 45) calculated that level to be 6 billion people, a limit the earth has now reached. Whether such a ceiling on population ultimately proves binding will depend on such factors as land availability, water supplies, and the quality of technology.

Land Availability   Brown argued that the global trend of increasing food per capita is unsustainable, because it is destroying the environmental base for food production. Historically, bringing additional land under cultivation, like the opening in the nineteenth century of the agricultural potential of the American Midwest, provided most of the per-capita increase in food production. For example, between 1950 and 1976 world land devoted to cereals expanded from 590 to 720 million hectares, or by 22 percent (Brown 1988b, 123). Where cultivation has expanded it has drawn upon marginal land with limited long-term productivity, often better suited for grazing or forest. The soil under the Amazonian rain forests of Brazil, for example, is of considerably lower quality than that of most temperate regions.

Since 1980, the area harvested has declined, and cultivated land *per capita* has declined significantly. Even with some continued expansion of cultivation into marginal areas, the global average of 0.27 hectares of cropland per capita will drop to about 0.17 hectares in 2025. Growth in food production now comes overwhelmingly from increased productivity per unit of land, from increased intensity of cultivation.

Both expansion of land under cultivation and more intensive use of it contribute to two problems. First, they destroy forests and grasslands, important biological resources. **Deforestation** (Table 16.3) has reduced global forest area to about 4 billion hectares, approximately half the forested area of 8,000 years ago (WRI 1998, 187). Forest cover in Haiti has fallen from 40–50 percent a century ago to 2 percent today. The primary assault now is on forests in LDCs, including rain forests, where annual losses run at about 14 billion hectares annually. Humans have also altered much of the remaining forest, often thinning it or creating plantations of identical, fast-growing trees.

Table 16.3   Deforestation, Worst Cases of the 1980s and 1990s

Regions and Countries	Total 1995 Forest Area (thousand hectares)	Average Annual Deforestation Percent Change 1980–1990	Average Annual Deforestation Percent Change 1990–1995
Africa			
Algeria	1,861	1.2	1.2
Angola	22,200	0.6	1.0
Congo, Dem. Republic	109,245	0.7	0.7
Cote d'Ivoire	5,469	7.7	0.6
Ghana	9,022	1.3	1.3
Guinea-Bissau	2,309	0.8	0.4
Liberia	4,507	0.5	0.6
Malawi	3,339	1.2	1.6
Mali	11,585	0.8	1.0
Mauritania	556	0.0	0.0
Niger	2,562	0.0	0.0
Nigeria	13,780	1.6	0.9
Sierra Leone	1,309	2.8	3.0
Sudan	41,613	1.0	0.8
Zambia	31,398	0.9	0.8
Latin America			
Argentina	33,842	0.6	0.3
Bolivia	48,310	0.8	1.2
Brazil	551,139	0.6	0.5
Colombia	52,998	0.6	0.5
Costa Rica	1,248	2.8	3.1
Ecuador	11,137	1.7	1.6
Guatemala	3,841	1.7	2.0
Honduras	4,115	2.1	2.3
Mexico	55,387	0.4	0.9
Nicaragua	5,560	1.4	2.5
Paraguay	11,527	2.5	2.6
Peru	67,562	0.3	0.3
Venezuela	43,995	1.1	1.1
Asia			
Indonesia	109,791	0.8	1.1
Malaysia	15,471	2.1	2.4
Myanmar	27,151	1.2	1.4
Nepal	4,822	0.9	1.1
Philippines	6,766	3.3	3.5
Sri Lanka	1,796	1.0	1.1
Thailand	11,630	3.1	2.6
Vietnam	9,117	0.9	1.4

Source: World Resources Institute, *World Resources 1998–1999* (New York: Oxford University Press, 1998), 292–293.

Table 16.4 Human-Induced Soil Degradation 1945 to Late 1980s		
	Total Degraded Area (million hectares)	Degraded Area as a Percentage of All Vegetated Land
World	**1,964.4**	**17**
Light Degradation	749.0	6
Moderate Degradation	910.5	8
Strong Degradation	295.7	3
Extreme Degradation	9.3	0
Africa	**494.2**	**22**
North and Central America	158.1	8
South America	243.4	14
Asia	748.0	20
Europe	218.9	23
Oceania	102.9	13

Source: World Resources Institute, *World Resources 1992–1993* (New York: Basic Books, 1992), 290.

Second, more extensive and intensive cultivation degrade marginal land, often irreversibly. About 38 percent of all cropland globally suffers some degradation (WRI 1998, 156), causing production losses of about 17 percent since 1945 (see Table 16.4). Some of the land becomes desert after initial vegetation is removed, a process called **desertification.**[3] In addition we appear to be mistreating even our high-quality agricultural land, through practices that allow substantial soil erosion. The U.S. Department of Agriculture estimates soil loss in the United States at 2 billion tons annually, twice the amount newly formed, and equivalent to 781,000 acres of cropland.[4] Another estimate puts net loss of soil in the formerly very fertile Ethiopian highlands at 1 billion tons each year.

Water Supplies   Productivity increases require inputs, two of the most important being water and energy. In 1900 the world irrigated 40 million hectares; in the mid-1990s the figure reached 230 million, and most of the increase has occurred since 1950. Agriculture accounts for about 70 percent of global fresh water consumption (WRI 1998, 189). Much water used in agriculture, however, comes from unsustainable sources. In the United States, total irrigated area is stable but is declining in some areas because farmers are depleting the aquifers that earlier sus-

[3]By one estimate, desertification annually claims an area twice the size of Belgium (Postel 1989, 21). Or does it? In 1991, studies using satellite measurement indicated that the Sahara expands and contracts much more each year than believed (*Science News,* July 20, 1991, 38).

[4]Brown (1981, 18); *Christian Science Monitor* (August 10, 1994, 14). No-till farming practices have, however, helped reduce that rate of loss in 1992 from 3 billion tons in 1982.

tained it, especially the Ogallala of the Great Plains. Finally, much irrigation has led to waterlogging and salinization of the land; perhaps 10–15 percent of the world's irrigated land suffers.

Water issues increasingly spill over into interstate politics. The word "rival" comes from the Latin "rivalis," meaning "one using the same stream as another." Conflicts in the Middle East are among the most serious. In 1990 Turkey shut off the flow of the Euphrates to fill the Ataturk Dam. Doing so brought protests from two downstream countries, Syria and Iraq. Syria and Iraq nearly went to war in 1975 over the waters of that river. Israel, Jordan, and Syria continue to argue about the Jordan river, which supplies most of Israel's water. The Mideast peace talks between Israel and Palestinians have raised critical water issues, because West Bank aquifers provide one-fourth of Israel's fresh water (Sosland 1997, 8). Future conflict between the Sudan and Egypt concerning the Nile is also possible.

Technological Advance Those who fall generally into the modernist category reject pessimism about land and water. Farmers have not yet planted the high-yielding varieties of green revolution rice and wheat on most grain-producing land globally. Productivity on a considerable portion of the world's land is little changed since early in the century. Thus the potential for production growth appears great, simply with the adaptation of improved techniques already available.

The Washington-based Consultative Group on International Agricultural Research (CGIAR) funds a network of 16 international research centers (Table 16.5) that strive continually to push back technological limits. But the next surge in agricultural productivity could owe much to the private sector. Biotechnologies, based on the development of recombinant DNA techniques in 1973, may promise food crops that need less chemical fertilizer and are more resistant to drought, soil salinity, and insects. In 1988 the U.S. Patent and Trademark Office issued the first patent in the world for a genetically altered animal (WRI 1988, 64). By 1988 Monsanto had already invested $100 million in biotechnologies, and in the late 1990s its chief executive spun off the older fertilizer and pesticide components to concentrate on biotechnology.

The emphasis on genetic manipulation places a premium on genetic raw material. The 1992 Earth Summit in Brazil produced the Convention on Biological Diversity. It simultaneously guarantees access by the firms of developed countries to genetic material globally, while recognizing the rights by developed countries to some compensation. A deal in 1991 between Merck, a large pharmaceutical company, and Costa Rica may be a model for cooperation in developing the genetic resources of tropical forests (WRI 1994, 124).

The Politics of Food Supply Although an examination of the physical and technological bases of food supply is important, political economists provide quite different analyses of why production is adequate in some parts of the world and inadequate elsewhere.

Liberals draw our attention to inappropriate state intervention, particularly the tendency of Third World governments to mandate food prices below those of a naturally functioning market. The reasons Third World governments set low food prices range from the humanitarian to the selfish. The humanitarian impulse

Table 16.5	International Agricultural Research Centers	
Year	**Center and Location**	**Focus**
1960	International Rice Research Institute (Philippines)	Improved rice varieties: germplasm collection bank
1966	International Maize and Wheat Improvement Center (Mexico)	Maize, wheat, barley, and triticale
1967	International Center of Tropical Agriculture (Colombia)	Beans, cassava, rice, and beef in the tropics of the Western hemisphere
1967	International Institute of Tropical Agriculture (Nigeria)	Cowpea, yam, cocoyam, sweet potato, cassava, rice, maize, beans, among others
1970	International Potato Center (Peru)	Potatoes in the Andes and lower tropics
1970	West Africa Development Association (Ivory Coast)	Rice in West Africa
1972	International Crops Research Institute for the Semi-Arid Tropics (India)	Improved quantity and reliability of food production in the semi-arid tropics
1974	International Plant Genetic Resources Institute (Rome)	Strengthened conservation and use of plant genetic resources
1975	International Food Policy Research Institute (United States)	Meeting food needs for LDCs
1977	International Center for Agricultural Research in the Dry Areas (Syria)	Rain-fed agriculture in arid and semiarid regions in North Africa and West Asia
1977	International Center for Living Aquatic Resource Management (Philippines)	Protection and management of aquatic resources
1977	International Center for Research in Agroforestry (Kenya)	Mitigating tropical deforestation
1979	International Service for National Agricultural Research (Netherlands)	National agricultural research systems
1984	International Irrigation Management Institute (Sri Lanka)	Irrigated agriculture
1992	Center for International Forestry Research (Indonesia)	Tropical forest ecosystems

Source: http://www.cgiar.org:80/centers.htm (June 12, 1998).

comes from a recognition that many of their people would be less well nourished, or even starve, should they allow prices to rise. This logic can also be self-serving, because governments seek to placate the urban dwellers of the capital and other major cities so as to defuse political instability. Whatever the motivation, low prices are literally counterproductive, because farmers facing them lack incentives to invest in higher production.

Government intervention in the market similarly aggravates the persistent food surpluses of the advanced capitalist states. Efficient production has created surpluses, depressed prices, and lowered farm incomes. Among the economic policies growing out of the Great Depression period of the 1930s were farm-price supports. In Europe the political compromises necessary to secure French participation in the EU resulted in a Common Agricultural Policy with especially strong protection for farmers. In both the United States and the EU, the subsidies to farmers allow them to remain on the farm and encourage them to overproduce. Japan's commitment to its farmers is even greater. In 1997 government direct or indirect subsidies provided more than 70 percent of the gross receipts of farmers.

The clear relationship between government policy and either underproduction or overproduction suggests a seemingly straightforward way out of the problem—allow prices to rise in regions with food shortages and slash subsidies where there is overproduction. That is not simple, however. When the Egyptian government tried to raise subsidized prices in 1977, large riots ensued, and officials retreated. The EU managed, however, to reduce agricultural expenditures from almost 90 percent of its budget in 1970 to under 50 percent in the late 1990s. It is trying to switch from subsidies to (temporary) income supplements for farmers.

Competing Perspectives on Food Distribution

Let us put aside for the moment the potential problems of unattainability or unsustainability of increase in global food production and focus directly on the distributional issue. Let us, at least temporarily, accept Griffin's (1987, 17) view that "there is no world food problem, but there is a problem of hunger in the world." Maldistribution of food itself, of income to purchase food, and of land and resources to produce food, all potentially contribute to the *hunger* problem. We begin with the distribution of food itself. Are global hunger problems easily resolved by food transfers?

The two categories of transfers are gifts (food aid) and sales (trade). Food gifts are a long-standing approach to the food distribution problem. In 1954 the U.S. Congress passed P.L. 480, better known as the "Food for Peace" act. This seemed to be the perfect solution to the asymmetrical problems of food surpluses in the United States and shortages in countries such as India. In 1960 the United States gave away, in this program, or sold on concessional terms, 27 percent of what it exported (Lewis and Kallab 1983, 236).

Such largesse subsequently decreased substantially, however, for three reasons. First, the U.S. surpluses nearly disappeared in the early 1970s when crop failures in Africa, Asia, and the Soviet Union combined to create a trade demand sufficient to absorb them. Second, those taking a look (especially liberals) at the economic impact on recipient countries of long-term food aid began to argue that

Table 16.6	Annual World Grain Trade (billion metric tons)						
	1934–1938	1950	1960	1970	1980	1990	1993–1995
North America	5	23	42	54	131	103	108
Latin America	2	1	(1)	4	(10)	2	(4)
Europe*	(10)	(22)	(25)	(22)	(16)	23	21
East Europe/Russia	1	0	1	(1)	(46)	(35)	
Africa	0	0	(5)	(4)	(15)	(26)	(31)
Asia	(1)	(6)	(19)	(37)	(63)	(79)	(78)
Oceania	3	3	6	8	19	14	13

Note: Parentheses indicate imports.

*Europe is Western Europe only until 1990 and all Europe thereafter.

Sources: Barry B. Hughes, *World Futures* (Baltimore, MD: Johns Hopkins University, 1985), 133; Lester R. Brown, "Reexamining the World Food Prospect," in *State of the World 1989*, ed. Lester R. Brown (New York: W. W. Norton, 1989), 45; World Resources Institute, *World Resources 1994–1995* (New York: Oxford University Press, 1994), 298; World Resources Institute, *World Resources 1998–1999* (New York: Oxford University Press, 1998), 288–289.

the assistance depressed local food prices and therefore the profits of local farmers. This economic disincentive to production retarded growth in indigenous supplies and thus perpetuated the very food shortages the aid was supposed to resolve. Third, global trade agreements now restrict much food aid. Whatever the reason, interstate food transfers increasingly consist of *trade* rather than *aid* (see Table 16.6).

In the 1970s and especially in the 1980s and 1990s Asia became the primary importing region. Africa also became an important importing region in the 1980s and 1990s. The Soviet Union and Eastern Europe avoided importing in the period between the Soviet collectivization of agriculture (the 1930s) and the early 1970s, primarily by belt tightening. For internal political reasons, and reflecting the more relaxed atmosphere of the détente period, Soviet shortages in the early 1970s led to a substantial movement into the world market. North American and Australian exports rose to meet the increased food demand from all of these regions. The green revolution technologies and the policies of the EU transformed Western Europe from significant net importer to substantial exporter.

The dramatically changed pattern of world grain trade in recent decades has political repercussions. Some realists began to see the control of food exports as a source of interstate power. Proposals surfaced in the 1970s to use food exports to the Middle East as a bargaining tool for obtaining oil at favorable prices—*food for crude*. Similarly, when the Soviets invaded Afghanistan in 1979, the Carter administration limited grain shipments to the Soviet Union. Two problems thus arise from food trade. The first is the political leverage it may provide exporters. The second is that many LDCs cannot afford imports over a long period.

The discussion of food distribution is not complete without discussing the distribution of income. If the citizens of Niger had higher incomes, they would have adequate food supply. The neo-Marxist perspective carries the argument one step further, however, positing that the problem is not limited to income distribution but extends to the distribution of land (the key production factor). Large land owners are much more likely to use their land for nonfood crops targeted to the export market. Colonial processes in much of the world concentrated considerable land in a few hands, and current political-economic structures often maintain those concentrations. Table 16.7 shows countries around the world with inegalitarian land distributions. Imagine the problems in Kenya, for instance, where the land is split primarily between very small and quite large land holdings, with few midsized properties. The worst regional pattern is that of Latin America, in which two-thirds of the land is in holdings greater than 50 hectares, but most farmers are on small and midsized holdings. Such conditions led to the political turmoil in the Chiapas region of Mexico, where many farmers can simply not survive on their small plots of marginal land.

Global Attention to Food Problems

What role can the global community play in ameliorating world food problems? A world food regime now exists to limit food shortages. We have already noted the network of research institutions under the sponsorship of the CGIAR. A cooperative effort of the Rockefeller Foundation and the Mexican government in 1941 successfully developed new wheat varieties that could triple traditional yields (with fertilizer, pesticides, and sufficient water). That led in 1960 to the founding of the first permanent center, the International Rice Research Institute in the Philippines. CGIAR itself came into being in 1971 and is an informal association of governments, IGOs, and foundations that supports the centers. The Rockefeller Foundation pioneered still another concept in 1985 when it began the Rockefeller Rice Biotechnology Network, seeking to expand the number of scientists from LDCs (WRI 1994, 124). Similarly, the Rockefeller Foundation began calling in the 1990s for a **doubly green revolution.** The concept is an environmentally sustainable green revolution, combining advance from biotechnology with integrated pest management.

The founders of the UN in 1945 established the United Nations Food and Agriculture Organization (FAO). It provides information and technical assistance to member states. In 1974 it sponsored the World Food Conference, organized in response to the global food crisis of 1972–1974. At that time the global community established the Global Information and Early Warning System (GIEWS) in an effort to reduce the risk of extensive, unanticipated food shortages. It also established the World Food Council to maintain attention to world food problems. It further set up an International Fund for Agricultural Development (IFAD), which began operations in 1977 with the charge of assisting the poorest LDCs. In 1996 the FAO sponsored the World Food Summit. Its declaration pledged reduction of the number of malnourished in the world by half before 2015.

The technical assistance and relief NGOs are also important forces. These include Oxfam, the International Red Cross, and Care. Increasingly, such organizations turn their attention to long-term initiatives for increasing food production capability rather than reacting only to the problems of immediate food scarcity. More than 1,200 organizations held an NGO Forum on Food Security in parallel with the World Food Summit in 1996.

Table 16.7   Land Distribution, Worst Cases of 1980

Regions and Countries	Agricultural Area: Distribution by Size of Holdings (percentage)		
	Less Than 5 Hectares	Between 5 and 50 Hectares	More Than 50 Hectares
Africa			
Algeria	14	63	23
Kenya	47	13	40
Liberia	36	35	29
Zaire	60	5	35
Zambia	34	19	47
Regional Average	60	26	15
Latin America			
Dominican Republic	13	30	57
El Salvador	20	31	57
Guatemala	13	24	63
Jamaica	28	17	55
Suriname	28	28	45
Regional Average	13	20	68
Middle East and Asia			
Cyprus	31	53	16
Israel	14	14	71
Jordan	19	53	28
Philippines	51	37	12
Saudi Arabia	10	32	58
Turkey	20	68	12
Regional Average	41	42	17
Western Europe			
Italy	16	39	45
Norway	16	55	29
Portugal	20	24	56
Regional Average	8	56	36
North America			
Regional Average	0	5	95

Source: World Resources Institute, *World Resources 1988–1989* (New York: Basic Books, 1988), 276–277.

Despite the effort by all of these IGOs and NGOs, periodic regional food crises still occur, on top of persistent malnutrition. For instance, in 1985 hundreds of thousands of Ethiopians starved; a dictatorial government compounded problems from famine. In 1992 famine put one-fifth of Somalia's population of 5 million at risk and by one estimate, at least 100,000 died. In 1998 approximately 35,000 Dinkas in the Sudan faced starvation. In each case political conflicts significantly exacerbated environmental and economic problems. One periodic proposal for dealing with famines is to maintain a global grain reserve. Calculations of the amount of grain needed to assure that 95 percent of all shortages could be met suggest quite modest costs for such a scheme—about $0.5 billion each year. To put that in context, U.S. citizens spend $10 billion annually on admissions to movies and theaters. Why then is the proposal not implemented? Producers in the grain exporting countries effectively maintain adequate reserves now—the problem has been distribution, not total food stores.

Resource Scarcities: Energy

A variety of raw materials support the world's economy in the same fundamental way that food supports the world's population. Chromium, cobalt, gold, manganese, nickel, petroleum, platinum, silver, tin, and tungsten are among the raw materials for which the world depends on a handful of major producers. For instance, Zaire, South Africa, Canada, and Malaysia provided more than 40 percent of the world's total production of cobalt, gold, nickel, and tin, respectively, at some time since 1970. South Africa is a major producer and exporter of several key commodities including chromium, diamonds, gold, manganese, and platinum. Are there dangers in the concentration of mineral production in the hands of a few states?

We should not ignore the damage that disruption of mineral exports, especially from countries like South Africa or Russia, could do to the world's economy. Metallic-mineral and precious-stone trades are remarkably small, however, compared with world trade in petroleum. Copper is the most heavily traded nonenergy raw material, but the value of global trade in copper is less than 3 percent that of oil. Moreover, the world economy is much more vulnerable to shortages in energy. Although energy constitutes only 5 to 10 percent of the GNP of most countries, without energy the economies would absolutely grind to a halt. Thus we focus our attention here on the *master resource*, energy.

Three general descriptive statements summarize the discussion of global energy trends in Chapter 1:

1. The world is in no imminent danger of running out of energy. World coal supplies alone are sufficient to carry a growing world economy through the twenty-first century (Figure 16.2).

2. The fossil supplies of conventional oil and natural gas are, however, more limited.[5] Although the world has not yet produced and consumed even 50 percent of the amounts that are accessible, it appears probable that peak global production will occur in the first

---

[5]Unconventional supplies, like those in tar sands or oil shale, could considerably prolong the contribution of petroleum to world energy. The costs, technology requirements, and global distribution of unconventional supplies are, however, so different from conventional sources that they are essentially different energy forms.

Figure 16.2 Lifetime of World Energy Reserves at Current Production Rates

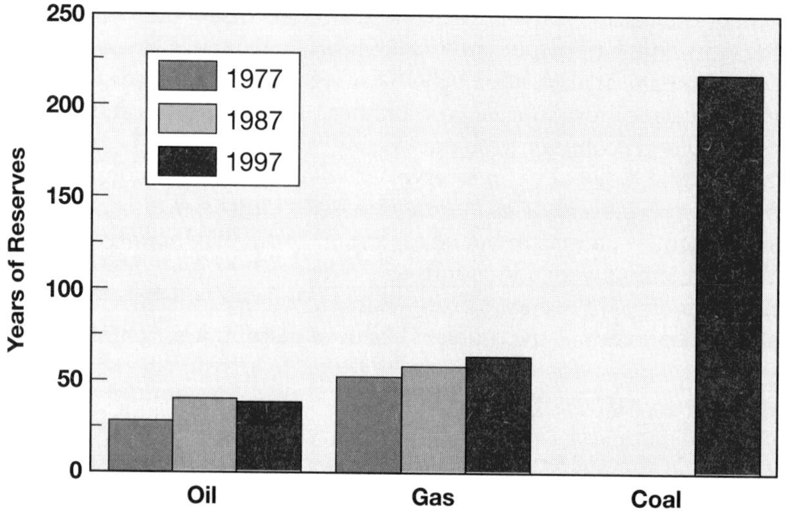

Source: British Petroleum, *BP Statistical Review of World Energy* (London: British Petroleum, 1998).

quarter of the twenty-first century and that the share of oil and natural gas in our total energy budget will generally continue the decline initiated in the 1970s. That is, we have entered a transition away from an energy system dominated by conventional oil and gas.

3. Oil and natural gas are unevenly distributed around the world. Just five OPEC countries (Kuwait, Saudi Arabia, United Arab Emirates, Iraq, and Iran) control approximately 65 percent of global reserves.

Competing Perspectives on Energy Supply

The power politics orientation of the realists serves us especially well in understanding the world energy situation. The global oil industry initially grew with the two superpowers to be, and both the United States and Russia claim the site of the first oil well (Odell 1983, 50). Even as we move into a new century, Russia and the United States produce more than any other country except Saudi Arabia.

The other great powers of the early twentieth century were hardly oblivious to the rise of oil and, given their limited domestic supplies, to the need for external sources. Britain created the Anglo-Persian Oil Company in 1913 to finance exploration in modern-day Iran. Great Britain, France, and the United States competed actively to secure oil concessions throughout the Middle East. Few better examples of geopolitics exist than the scramble for control of the region's resources, resolved at least temporarily in 1935 by an agreement among the external powers. As the great powers had earlier carved Africa into pieces of private property, they did the same in the 1930s with Middle Eastern oil. In both cases legal exclusion resolved the problems of what had earlier been treated as

Figure 16.3 U.S. Oil Production and Imports

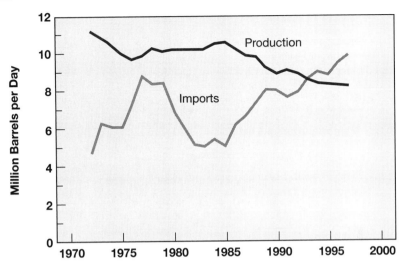

Note: Production includes natural gas liquids; imports includes refined products.

Source: Independent Petroleum Association of America, "United States Petroleum Statistics" (March 1995), Tables 7 and 9; Independent Petroleum Association of America, "United States Petroleum Statistics" (April 1998), Tables 7 and 9.

a contested common property resource. The United Kingdom retained a dominant position in the Mideast until the end of World War II, at which time the United States assumed a clearly preeminent role.

The major oil companies long reinforced the U.S. position in the global oil system. For many years after World War II the seven oil majors or "seven sisters" dominated Middle Eastern production and global oil distribution. Those corporations all rank among the largest in the world (see Table 13.3): Exxon, Mobil, and Chevron (all scions of the original Rockefeller Standard Oil monopoly, which the U.S. government dismantled in 1911), Gulf and Texaco (two additional U.S.-based corporations), British Petroleum (descendant of Anglo-Persian), and Royal Dutch/Shell (a Dutch-British corporation). Until the early 1970s the oil companies not only helped assure access by the United States and its allies to low-cost Middle Eastern oil, but returned healthy profits to the shareholders. Like Mexico in the 1920s (see Chapter 13), most LDCs with oil initially had little power and little alternative to accepting the terms that the advanced states and the big oil companies offered.

Several LDCs formed OPEC in 1960 in an effort to stem a downward slide in world oil prices, but control over the level of oil production within OPEC states remained in the hands of the oil companies. Power began to shift in the early 1970s, because the global oil market tightened as U.S. imports rose sharply in the early 1970s (see Figure 16.3). Libya nationalized oil properties within it between 1970 and 1973. Iran also began to assert greater control. In October 1973 war

Figure 16.4 World Oil Prices

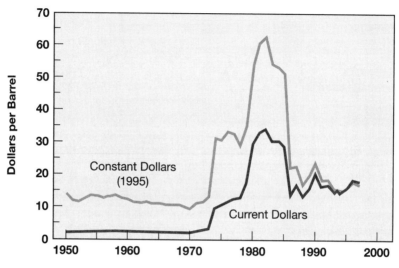

Sources: World Bank, *Commodity Trade and Price Trends,* 1987–1988 (Baltimore, MD: Johns Hopkins University, 1988), 80; British Petroleum, *BP Statistical Review of World Energy 1997* (London: British Petroleum, 1998), 14.

erupted between Israel and its Arab neighbors. The anger of Arab oil-exporting countries toward supporters of Israel rose simultaneously with the power those countries felt relative to the world oil market. They instituted an oil embargo against the United States and the Netherlands for their continued support of Israel (several other industrialized, oil-importing countries accepted demands for a policy realignment and avoided OPEC wrath).

The export restrictions imposed by the Arab oil-exporting countries caused the **first oil shock,** a nearly five-fold increase in global oil prices within a year. It convinced the OPEC countries that they had a tool available with which to increase their oil revenues dramatically and to achieve other ends, such as support for the Palestinians in their conflict with Israel. Joining realists in this emphasis on the use of interstate power, neo-Marxists saw in the events the possibility for the exercise of Southern power relative to the global North. As Mazrui (1988, 134) urged, "There is a crying need for other producer cartels, no matter how weak in the short run." Chapter 13 discussed the generally unsuccessful attempt by the South to use this newly discovered power.

Near the end of the 1970s, Iran was the second largest OPEC oil producer and exporter, following Saudi Arabia. The revolution in Iran during 1978–1979 sharply restricted production. This initiated the **second oil shock** or major increase in world oil prices (Figure 16.4), roughly another doubling. The Iran-Iraq War began in 1980, further restraining Iranian production and additionally lowering that of Iraq.

The response of economists (generally commercial liberals) to the two oil shocks was to analyze the economic basis for such increases in oil prices. They compared the new oil prices with the long-term costs of alternative energy sources such as coal, nuclear power, or solar energy. They concluded that the oil prices exceeded sustainable levels, because they would elicit new oil supplies (like those in the North Sea or the Alaskan North Slope) and encourage development of alternative energy sources. Eventually, increased global energy supplies would drive down oil prices. Important to understanding economic analysis is the concept of **elasticity,** the responsiveness of demand and supply levels to price changes. When the price of energy rises, market forces increase the supply of energy and decrease the demand for it. If these reactions are minor, then the price elasticities of supply and demand are low; if significant increases in supply and decreases in demand develop, the elasticities are high.[6] For a cartel to maintain higher prices (and thus profits) successfully, elasticities (reactivity of supply and demand) must be low; energy experts argued that they were *not* low.

It took longer than many energy economists predicted, but oil surpluses appeared in the early 1980s, and oil price then fell. Between 1985 and the end of the century, the price (after adjusting for inflation) irregularly eroded back to the level preceding the oil shock in 1973 (see again Figure 16.4). The **third oil shock** of the early 1980s created adjustment problems for oil-exporting countries (including Mexico) as great as those that the first two shocks posed for oil-importing countries.

Eco-wholists interpreted the first and second oil shocks as indicators of physically limited world oil supplies and the beginning of a transition away from an oil-based global energy system. Many exaggerated the shocks by arguing that the world had entered an **energy crisis,** a prolonged period of energy shortages. Discrediting of that exaggeration unjustly drew attention away from the significance of energy transition onset. Among likely consequences of the ongoing energy transition will be continued volatility in world energy markets. Additional oil shocks appear likely, and great power rivalry over vast stretches of desert real estate is unlikely to disappear in the near future. The embargo and war against Iraq in 1991–1992 caused a small upward shock, and a surplus of oil in the late 1990s caused a significant downward shock (big enough to again hurt Mexico, as well as Russia). Note again in Figure 16.3 the sharply increased U.S. dependence on imported oil in the 1990s and thus its vulnerability to shocks.

We should also not, however, ignore the potential of various renewable energy forms to substantially alter the global energy picture in the next two decades. Figure 16.5 shows dramatic drops in costs of solar energy and the resultant rise in photovoltaic shipments. Because sunlight is distributed globally much more evenly than oil and gas, a renewable energy system will someday fundamentally alter the political-economy of energy.

Energy Policy Issues

Most global actors view food availability as fundamentally nonzero-sum. Better nutrition can almost universally improve welfare. We therefore were able to talk about collective responses to food problems, namely a food regime led by organi-

---

[6]Specifically, the supply-and-demand elasticities are the percentage responses of supply and demand, relative to the percentage change in price. A greater than 1 percent change in supply or demand in response to a 1 percent change in price indicates an "elastic" commodity, and a less than 1 percent change means that it is "inelastic."

Figure 16.5 Solar Energy Costs and Sales

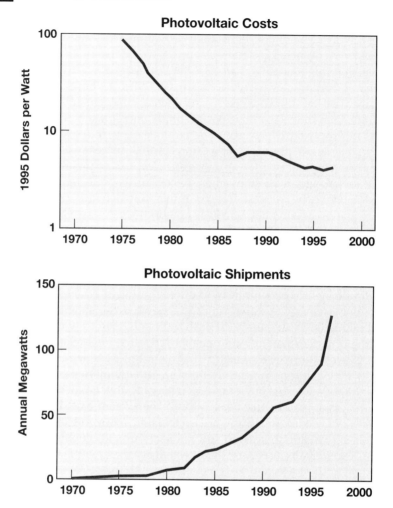

Source: Worldwatch Institute Database Diskettes (Washington, DC: Worldwatch Institute, 1998).

zations like the FAO, large numbers of NGOs, and the research network of CGIAR. Because they have surpluses, most high-income countries also see food as a "low-politics" issue, not bearing directly on national security. In contrast, energy issues have a more nearly zero-sum character and little collective global attention to them has emerged; the rule instead has been competitive responses. First World countries perceive energy as a "high-politics" issue, directly related to security. In 1977 President Carter went before the public to talk about the energy situation in the face of the first oil shock:

Tonight I want to have an unpleasant talk with you about a problem unprecedented in our history. With the exception of war, this is the greatest challenge our country will face in our lifetimes. . . . This effort will be the "moral equivalent of war." (Congressional Quarterly 1979, 1)

In response to the first oil shock, rich importers, in 1974, formed an organization known as the International Energy Agency (IEA). IEA membership largely replicates that of the OECD. The IEA countries agreed to share information concerning energy, to facilitate joint technological advance, and to decrease dependence on imported oil (although rivalry over access to oil supply creates competition in the short term, importers have common long-term interests). They even agreed to share oil supplies should another embargo or inadvertent supply disruption limit them. In reality, members expect little from the IEA in an emergency.

Most action by importing countries has, in reality, been more unilateral and less cooperative. The immediate response of the U.S. government to the first oil shock in 1973 was to declare Project Independence and set a goal of zero imports by 1980. That proved totally unrealistic. Subsequently, the United States acted more rationally, by establishing a strategic petroleum reserve to store oil when plentiful (it used releases from that reserve to calm world markets during the embargo against Iraq). Most importers have created some type of stockpile.

The United States additionally brought its military might to bear on the issue. Although the government resisted calls during the shocks of the 1970s for direct action in the Persian Gulf to secure supplies, it never fully precluded that possibility. In fact, the potential need for capability to intervene and secure oil supplies, reinforced by the impotence felt by the United States during the Iranian hostage episode, led it to develop a special Rapid Deployment Force (Hastedt 1988, 298). Moreover, in 1980 the United States stated the Carter Doctrine, namely that "an attempt by an outside force to gain control of the Persian Gulf region will be regarded as an assault on the vital interests of America and such an assault will be repelled by any means necessary, including military force" (Kegley and Wittkopf 1985, 335). The Reagan administration reiterated the Carter doctrine, verbally and in practice. In 1987 (during the Iran-Iraq War), it introduced naval forces into the Persian Gulf to protect tankers.

Although more Persian Gulf oil flows to Europe than to the United States, European allies decline most involvement in military action within the region. Except for Britain, they contributed little to the coalition that fought Iraq after its 1991 invasion of Kuwait. One explanation is that Europeans are less inclined to rely on military measures than are Americans—they more often seek diplomatic and multilateral mechanisms. A second is that they free ride on the leadership of the United States in providing a collective good, the continued flow of oil.

The formation of OPEC and the collective action of its members in the early 1970s may suggest that exporters have more common interest and perspective than importers. Below that surface, however, we again see a battle between self-interest and collective interest. OPEC countries all benefit from high oil prices—those prices are a collective good that translates into higher revenues. Individual members capture the benefits of those prices, however, whether or not they

Figure 16.6   OPEC Oil Production Levels, 1988 and 1997

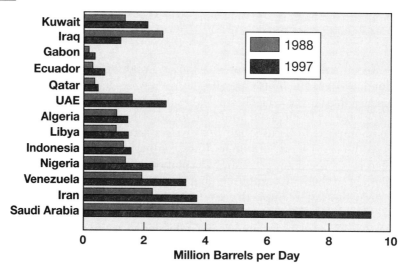

Source: British Petroleum, *BP Statistical Review of World Energy* (London: British Petroleum, 1998), 7.

contribute to maintaining them. Thus there is a natural inclination to cheat on the cartel or to free ride. Many OPEC producers, especially countries such as Indonesia and Nigeria with large, poor populations and nearly desperate needs for immediate additional revenues, regularly exceed the production quotas set for them in OPEC meetings.

A few OPEC countries like Saudi Arabia, Kuwait, and the United Arab Emirates have less urgent need for revenues and can reduce production (Figure 16.6), even below their quotas, to support higher prices. The weak world oil market of the 1980s, and the continued cheating by large numbers of OPEC members, gradually resulted in financial problems even for the economically stronger producers, however. In the late 1980s Saudi Arabia sought to restore price discipline by increasing production, flooding the market, driving down prices, and then dictating a return to quota observance as the price for renewed export restraint. Leadership in cartels, like leadership in the global market economy, is not always easy.

Although the Middle East remains critical, the immediate focus of global oil politics shifted a bit further north in the 1990s. Vast reserves of oil and gas exist in many states of the former U.S.S.R. Western energy companies, with the approval of their governments, have made huge investments, especially in countries around the Caspian Sea (including Azerbaijan, Kazakhstan, Turkmenistan, and Russia). The trick is getting the energy to Western markets when pipelines cross multiple competing and potentially unstable countries. For instance, in order to move natural gas from Turkmenistan to Turkey, the United States reluctantly approved a pipeline across Iran, a country it otherwise embargoed. Russia has become increasingly unhappy with the surge of production in states that it once controlled and with pipeline projects that bypass its territory. Energy exports earn most of Russia's foreign exchange. Because these developments threaten the Russian economy, they may do more real long-term damage to interstate relations than the expansion of NATO. Energy politics remain high politics.

Ecosystem Vulnerability

This chapter has focused until now on the extractive demands that human systems place on their environments, notably through the requirements of population for food and of economies for energy. We move now from input to output issues—to the impact that human activities have on the broader biological system and on such natural systems as climate.

The Range of Human Impact

It is common to review human impact on land, air, water, and perhaps biological systems. Although those categories are relatively tidy, our interest here is in the *politics* of the environment; we therefore use a typology of impacts with fuzzier, but more politically relevant boundaries. Some issues are primarily local, others are regional and cross-boundary, and still others are predominantly global.

Local Environmental Issues   At the local level, environmental issues and ones of economic development have a close relationship. Very often, developing countries face deteriorating urban-air quality, poor and worsening water quality, and generally unsanitary living environments. For instance, about 90 percent of sewage in LDCs is discharged without treatment (*The Economist,* March 21, 1998, 5). These immediate and local issues preoccupy both urban and rural areas. Diarrhea kills 2.5 million children each year, almost entirely in developing countries, and smoky indoor air from cooking and heating contribute to the respiratory infections that kill 4 million more (WRI 1998, 1).

Providing piped water must be one top policy priority. The large number of slum dwellers on the edge of all major LDC cities must now pay about 12 times what those with access to pipes pay for clean water, sometimes spending 20 percent of income. Another priority must be air quality. About 100 countries still allow leaded gasoline, a proven major health risk (historians believe that lead poisoning from plumbing contributed to the collapse of the Roman empire). In Bangkok, blood lead levels were about 20 times those in U.S. cities before Thailand switched to unleaded gasoline.

In contrast, the local air and water quality of developed countries has improved considerably since the early 1970s, suggesting that economic development and environmental policies very frequently reinforce each other. China enacted its first Environmental Protection Law in 1979 and began promulgating significant numbers of strictures only in the 1990s, as it became richer (WRI 1998, 123). Developed countries also suffer significant local problems, including air and water quality. Piped water, emissions restrictions, landfills, and sewage treatment have, however, reduced many of them.

Public-health authorities in high-income countries increasingly focus on life-style issues (exercise and diet) and on more esoteric environmental issues.

For instance, the ratio of male to female births, normally about 106 males per 100 females, has declined in Canada, Sweden, Germany, and elsewhere since 1970 (*Science News,* April 4, 1998, 212). Because males are more fragile in uterus than females (the ratio of conceptions is 125 to 100), this appears a possible sentinel indicator of environmental condition, like sperm count and frog populations (both of which are dropping). Scientists are looking for possible environmental explanations including hormone-like pollutants (e.g., dioxin).

Regional and Transboundary Issues   Because local environments have often improved in MDCs, attention in those countries focuses increasingly on issues of broader geographic scope. For instance, nitrogen pollution has become a significant issue. Humans "fix" nitrogen (convert it from the atmosphere into biologically useful forms) by planting legume crops and by creating fertilizer. Humans now *fix* more than do natural processes, so much that the nitrogen run-off from agricultural land heavily pollutes water supplies.

Both sulfur and nitrogen from fossil-fuel burning are air pollutants that also have regional, often cross-boundary impact and are major problems globally. They are what Soroos (1997, 53) calls transport and deposit problems. For example, sulfur emissions create the phenomenon known as acid rain, which causes interstate friction as well as domestic concern. Canada long accused the United States of significantly damaging its lakes and forests by failure to control acid-rain sources. A study by a highly politicized U.S. government group concluded in 1987 that there was little evidence for a significant acid-rain impact on lakes and streams in the Northeast United States (and by implication in Canada). Canada's environment minister labeled the report "voodoo science." The United States subsequently moved to address the problem.

It is difficult to apply the legal precedent of state responsibility for transboundary emissions that the Trail Smelter case established in 1941. For example, radioactive material, released from the Soviet nuclear plant at Chernobyl in April, 1986, spread around the world and measurably affected plants and animals in Central Europe and Scandinavia. Public outcry forced the U.S.S.R. to acknowledge the disaster, somewhat belatedly, but it is unlikely that any financial claims can be pressed against the Ukraine. Lives were lost in the episode, but the European victims will die only over time and without clearly drawn connections to the accident.

Again, developed countries are much further along in controlling most such problems (although they have by no means solved them). Average sulfur-dioxide levels in North American and Western European cities seldom exceed 25 micrograms per cubic meter. They exceed 50 micrograms in most major Chinese, Korean, and Turkish cities. The level in Rio de Janeiro is 129 (WRI 1998, 264–265). Total sulfur emissions in Europe peaked in the late 1970s and had already fallen by one-third in the mid-1990s. Similarly, deforestation has slowed dramatically in most developed countries, and regrowth of their temperate forests has been significant. It is the tropic forests of developing countries that are most at risk.

The richer countries have hopefully solved one transport and deposit problem completely. The last of 528 known atmospheric tests of nuclear weapons took place in 1980. Although underground tests, like those of India and Pakistan in 1998, have continued, the Nuclear Test Ban Treaty of 1963 now has very wide acceptance.

Radiation from fallout peaked at 7 percent of natural sources in 1963 (Soroos 1997, 106); it fell to 1 percent in the 1990s. One study suggests that the atmospheric testing will have caused a total of 430,000 cancer deaths by 2070.

The Case of Toxic Wastes   One particular problem of transport and deposit merits special attention because the transport has been deliberate. The world generates more than 350 million metric tons of hazardous waste each year (WRI 1998, 53). Because disposal costs are so high in developed countries, companies have significant incentive to ship the wastes to LDCs where disposal control is lax.

In 1992 the United States sent Bangladesh three thousand tons of "fertilizer." After one-third was spread on fields, it proved to be hazardous waste containing cadmium dust and lead from a South Carolina company. A Norwegian firm delivered 15,000 tons of "new materials for bricks" to Guinea. It proved to be toxic incinerator ash from Philadelphia. As a rule, poorer states do not have adequate treatment capability, and they also may have only inaccurate or inadequate information about the risks. Even when they do know the risks, the enticements for LDCs can be great. A Swiss firm offered Guinea-Bissau $600 million over five years to accept wastes, more than the country's foreign debt and 35 times its annual export earnings.

The EU now requires clear labeling and has some export restrictions, although operators seeking large profits continue to circumvent them. In March 1989 a UN treaty on toxic-waste exports bound 100 states to regulate them so as to stop clandestine commerce. Forty members of the Organization of African Unity refused to sign the treaty, calling for an outright ban on waste exports to Africa. In 1991 all African countries except South Africa signed the Bamako Convention banning such trade. A UN treaty in 1998 also now regulates exports of toxic chemicals, including pesticides.

Global Issues   Although it is again important to emphasize that developed countries are far from solving their local and regional environmental problems, it is in part a tribute to their progress that many citizens of high-income countries now focus on "global" problems. Unfortunately, it is also a recognition that such problems have become more threatening.

Thirty-nine percent of the ocean fish stocks with greatest commercial value are in decline, and 60 percent urgently need management (WRI 1998, 195). Nearly 60 percent of global coral reefs are at risk in the face of human activity. Increased world trade has dramatically increased "bioinvasions" by species from other habitats. Dependence on a handful of species for most global grain has significantly reduced biodiversity in the world's agricultural system.

Even some environmental problems that might be considered regional have such extent that we think of them as global. Soil loss is such a problem. Although tropical deforestation and its associated species' loss are taking place in the LDCs, essentially all of the world's tropic forests and biological diversity are at risk.

One environmental issue of central importance, the greenhouse effect, is not only global, but primarily a problem attributable to developed countries and their energy use. In 1995 global carbon-dioxide emissions were 22.7 billion metric tons (WRI 1998, 344). North America and Europe, with about 17 percent of global population, were responsible for over half of those emissions. The Kyoto agreement of 1997 requires those countries also to undertake a disproportionate effort to reduce emissions. There is real uncertainty about whether they will, and there will almost certainly be global warming and oceanic rise, even if they do slow growth in atmospheric carbon.

The twenty-first century *may* be the century in which humanity moves toward sustainability in its relationship with the environment. That is, however, by no means clear. Doing so will require a great deal of change in current behavior patterns around the world. It is to that prospect that we now turn.

Interstate Policy Approaches

As the scale of transboundary pollutants rises, states have come to see the need for collective action. European states fully realize that they can no longer individually protect their major water drainages (like the Rhine and Danube), their bordering seas (the Baltic and Mediterranean), or their air. In dealing with global problems such as ozone depletion and the greenhouse effect, individual states completely lose their ability to control the issues and policy approaches.

Clean water and air are collective goods, and the problems of providing them are problems of the commons (see again Chapter 6). Unlike food and energy, which states can largely secure for themselves, there is no alternative to collective action with respect to the ecosystem. Recognizing that a clean environment is a collective good helps us understand why it is so difficult to secure—because of free-rider problems, collective goods are normally underprovided. How then can humanity approach problems of the global commons? Three approaches to dealing with the tension between individual action and collective interest have surfaced again and again in this volume: voluntarism, privatization, and collective regulation.

Voluntarism Voluntarism, although naturally limited in a world strongly influenced by the self-interested behavior of states and economic actors, still has a role to play. Voluntarism often involves individuals, rather than states, and reflects a growing sense of global community. As in the strategy of GRIT, it involves unilateral action with the hope that others will eventually reciprocate. For example, an organization called the Programme for Belize began in 1988 to solicit funds from around the world to "endow" a tropical forest area in Belize, that is, to provide sufficient funds that the zone could remain intact indefinitely. Similarly, private organizations helped Bolivia retire some of its international debt in exchange for protecting a forest area.

Even states, those notoriously self-serving actors in world politics, have proven altruistic. Norway, Sweden, Canada, and the United States banned "nonessential" uses of CFCs in the late 1970s, prior to global rules about the substances (Soroos 1997, 225). We should not underestimate the importance of rising global consciousness on environmental issues and the contributions individuals are willing to make on behalf of the global community or press their states to undertake. Nevertheless, the voluntaristic approach by itself is inadequate.

Privatization Privatization is a second approach to problems of the environment. In the case of the ocean commons of the earth, the establishment of Exclusive Economic Zones (EEZs) by the United Nations Conference on Law of the Sea

III (UNCLOS III) extended control by states over ocean resources 200 nautical miles from their shores. That action transfers to state jurisdiction about 40 percent of the ocean area, containing 90 percent of the harvestable biological resources and all known commercial energy resources. Moreover, it gives more than 50 percent of the newly "fenced" area to only 13 states (Soroos 1986, 273 and 290). The action partially solves one common-property resource problem: It provides incentives for each state to manage the fish catch within their zones so as to maintain yields in the long run. Many states (including New Zealand, Chile, and Iceland) are now taking the next step of privatizing fish stocks *within* their zones, that is of selling transferable permits or quotas for quantitatively limited harvests each year.

Although the nine years of multilateral negotiations on UNCLOS III ended in 1982, it took until 1993 to obtain the 60 ratifications for it to enter into force one year later. Moreover, most ratifying states have been LDCs, and several key powers have not ratified. The treaty designated an International Sea Bed Authority to control exploitation of resources, including mineral deposits, beyond the 200-mile limits of EEZs. Countries believing they had the technical capability of exploiting such resources themselves objected to this establishment of a "common heritage of mankind."

For some, the example of EEZs may seem to provide an attractive approach to other environmental problems. Does privatization offer a general model? No. EEZs do not even resolve all of the commons problems of oceans, because much of that over which the states theoretically have control actually moves across state jurisdictions. For example, many fish, such as tuna, do not spend their lives only in the EEZ of Peru. Similarly, pollution drifts easily with ocean currents. Problems of movement are still greater in the atmosphere, and that common property resource cannot be privatized.

There is, however, great ideological commitment to both free markets and private property, and that can lead to some creative proposals for privatization. One example is tradeable pollution permits. Although it is essentially impossible to "privatize" any given volume of the global atmosphere, it is possible to privatize the actual emissions of pollutants into the atmosphere (because they can be attributed to individual sources at the time of emission). Many economists and a fair number of states have come to believe that the best way to control emissions of carbon dioxide, other greenhouse gases, and many other pollutants is to determine a total volume of such emissions that we will allow (in the complex trade-off between environmental and economic motivations); then states would sell or otherwise allocate "tradeable pollution permits." If China could replace inefficient coalfired electricity plants with efficient gas-fired ones at a lower cost than the United States could eliminate a comparable level of carbon-dioxide pollution (which is true), it would make sense for the United States to buy such pollution permits from China. China would use its earnings to invest in the new, environmentally better plants, and the United States would forgo some improvements involving higher expenditures. Between them the two countries together would achieve the greatest pollution reduction for a given investment.

Collective Regulation and Regime Elaboration   Still, the most common approach is for states to turn to the third approach, collective regulation. Figure 16.7 shows the steady growth in global environmental treaties. For example, the

Figure 16.7 International Environmental Treaties

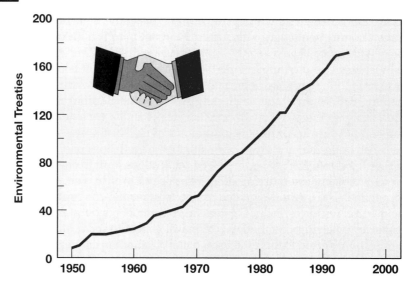

Sources: Worldwatch Institute Database (Washington, DC: Worldwatch Institute, 1998).

Antarctic Treaty of 1959 prohibits dumping of radioactive wastes there. A treaty of 1978 controls releases of oil and other substances by ships on the high seas. Such collective regulation will remain the central approach to many environmental issues.

A regime that organizes cooperation on a broad range of environmental issues, relying on a mixture of these three approaches to cooperation, especially collective regulation, is emerging slowly. Table 16.8 lists some of the primary global conventions that constitute the backbone of the regime. In an important early step, the United Nations held a Conference on the Human Environment in Stockholm during 1972. That conference symbolized for the first time global attention to the environment. It also created the United Nations Environment Programme (UNEP), with headquarters in Nairobi, Kenya. Most UNEP activities involve information gathering and environmental monitoring including a Global Environment Monitoring System (GEMS) and an International Register of Potentially Toxic Chemicals (IRPTC).

In 1992 attempts to reach agreement on reducing greenhouse emissions were high on the agenda at the United Nations Conference on Environment and Development (UNCED) or Earth Summit in Rio. Like the Stockholm Conference of 20 years earlier, it was an ambitious effort to reach agreement on many environment issues. In fact, with 118 heads of state attending, it was the largest summit meeting ever held. The United States initially resisted efforts to set mandatory reductions in greenhouse gases in spite of support from almost all other states, but Clinton committed the country to UNCED goals in 1993. In addition, two new global con-

Table 16.8	Principal Global Environmental Conventions		
Wildlife and Habitat	**Oceans**	**Atmosphere**	**Hazardous Waste**
Antarctic (1959–1980)	Ocean Dumping (1972)	Nuclear Test Ban (1963)	Biological and Toxin Weapons (1972)
Wetlands (1971)	Ship Pollution (1978)	Ozone Layer (1985)	Nuclear Accident Notification (1986)
World Heritage (1972)	Law of the Sea (1982)	CFC Control (1987)	Nuclear Accident Assistance (1986)
Endangered Species (1973)		Framework Convention on Climate Change (1992)	Hazardous Waste Movement (1989)
Migratory Species (1979)		Kyoto Protocol (1997)	Convention on Prior Informed Consent (1998)
Biological Diversity (1992)			

Source: World Resources Institute, *World Resources 1992–1993* (New York: Oxford University Press, 1992), 358–361. Updated.

ventions, one on Climate Change and the other on Biological Diversity, opened to signature. The forum also established a Sustainable Development Commission with the responsibility of monitoring adherence to other environmental agreements. It will draw on evidence gathered by NGOs (about 13,000 NGO representatives staged their own parallel meetings) and rely heavily on the pressure of public opinion, as does the UN Human Rights Commission.

Another important characteristic of the Earth Summit was the very explicit and strong linkage between the environment and development. The South argued that it needed help (side payments again) if it were to implement stronger environmental protection, including curbs on deforestation.

Evidence on the greenhouse effect, like that marshalled by the IPCC in its two reports, has increasingly convinced both leaders and a large portion of the public that the threat is real. Even substantial numbers of corporate leaders have added their voices to the call for action. In 1997 representatives of 160 countries met in Kyoto, Japan, and signed a protocol committing themselves to specific reductions in the emission of carbon dioxide and other greenhouse gases by 2012. Collectively, their pledged reductions are to a level 5.2 percent below 1990 emissions, with entities like the European Union (8 percent) and the United States (7 percent) making the largest cuts. Because LDCs will need to increase energy use and emissions in order to grow, they face no immediate restrictions. That may preclude U.S. ratification. If so, it raises the issue of leadership on global environmental issues.

The Importance of Leadership   Environmental policy has truly been a global effort, involving almost all states and countless NGOs. When leadership has emerged, it has often come from smaller countries, as when Malta took the lead in pressing for the Law of the Sea. States that traditionally have provided leadership on security and economic issues have less consistently done so on environmental

Figure 16.8 Annual Global Production of CFCs and Ozone Levels over Antarctica

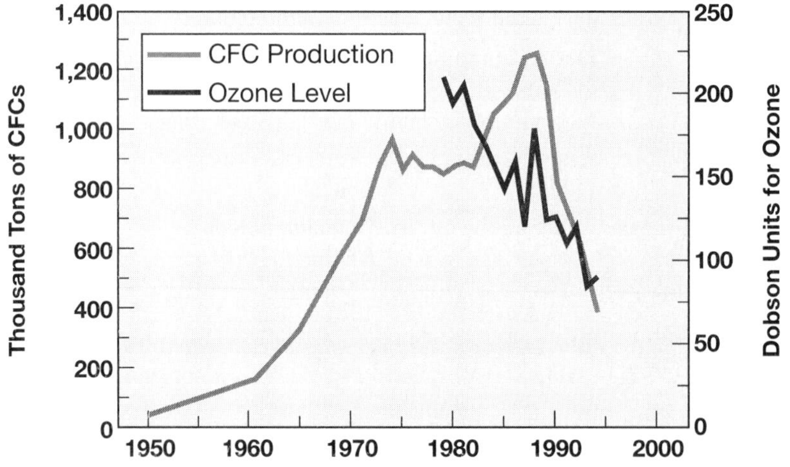

Source: Worldwatch Institute Database (Washington, DC: Worldwatch Institute, 1998).

ones. We have already seen the U.S. opposition to the Law of the Sea regime and its foot-dragging on action concerning greenhouse emissions.

Nonetheless, the situational logic of environmental issues, just as with security and environmental ones, often requires some leadership by large countries. The impact of North America and Western Europe on the global environment is so large that those countries *must* lead on many issues, or they will automatically be spoilers. At the same time, however, these countries are not as relatively large "environmentally" as they are militarily or economically. For instance, the United States manages only 6.1 percent of the world's forests and 9.2 percent of endangered species; it accounts for only 14 percent of global freshwater withdrawals and takes only 6.1 percent of the world's marine catch.

CFCs constitute one arena in which relative size of the rich countries has been much greater. Leadership by action was therefore possible on this issue. Twenty-two such disproportionately polluting countries agreed in Montreal in 1987 to reduce production of CFCs (Figure 16.8) by 50 percent before 1999. In London in 1990 a larger group agreed to a complete phase-out by 2000, and states agreed in Copenhagen in 1992 to stop production completely by January 1, 1996. Leadership by example alone, however, would have been inadequate. China planned to increase its production of CFCs or comparable substances tenfold by the year 2000 to allow its citizens to have inexpensive food refrigeration. Environmental leadership thus required side payments to countries like China that could otherwise spoil the effort to provide collective goods. The signatories of the 1992 Copenhagen agreement established a $340–500 million fund to help Third World countries introduce substitutes for CFCs.

The rich countries are also disproportionate polluters on greenhouse gases. Therefore, leadership on this issue remains possible. In 1991, the EU Commission pro-

Figure 16.9   Global Atmospheric Emissions

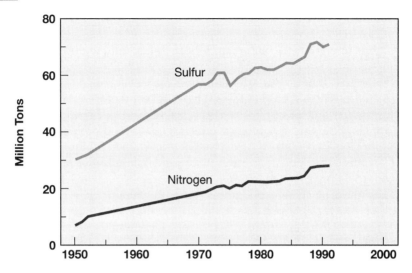

Sources: Worldwatch Institute Database (Washington, DC: Worldwatch Institute, 1998).

posed a "carbon tax," a tax on the emission of carbon from the burning of fossil fuels. Many experts argue that such taxes would provide private environmental benefits to the country that introduces them that would exceed economic costs. Specifically, reductions of other air pollutants (e.g., sulfur and nitrogen) can be side benefits of reductions in carbon emissions. Less dependence on imported fuels is another private benefit. Thus, a self-motivated leadership could emerge on greenhouse gas emissions.

Interstate action on acid rain has also been difficult to obtain because essential fossil fuel-burning electric plants release the chemicals that produce it, including nitrogen and sulfur oxides. Here, too, leadership has been weak. In 1988 24 countries agreed in Sophia, Bulgaria, to freeze nitrogen oxide emissions at current levels by 1995. For most of the 1980s, the United States did not actively support interstate agreements on the issue, because the Reagan administration claimed that research was incomplete. This was ironic, considering the scope and cost of efforts simultaneously taken within the United States. The rate of emission growth has slowed somewhat (Figure 16.9). Because control of emissions is expensive, however, large LDCs, such as India and China, and industrialized countries facing severe economic difficulties, such as those of Eastern Europe, are again likely to free ride on the global effort.

Conclusion

Several global forces interact to create increasing turbulence in global environmental politics: rapid population growth, slowing growth in food production, the ongoing energy transition, the global spread of industrial technology, and the increasing scope of biological and physical environmental damage caused by human systems. Issues related to the environment, such as famine in Africa, oil shocks, and the greenhouse effect, appear regularly on the front pages of our daily newspapers and have become focal points of world attention.

It is impossible to understand those issues fully without bringing to bear all of the worldviews presented in this book. Consider, for instance, famine in Africa. Eco-wholists draw to our attention the long-term change in rainfall patterns that explain drought and crop failures. They suggest that human activities have led to deforestation and desertification and contributed to climate change. Modernists inform us about the technological efforts to solve food problems including those at the four CGIAR centers in Africa (in Nigeria, Kenya, Ethiopia, and Liberia).

Commercial liberals contribute an understanding of how governmental decisions to set prices for consumers below market levels can lessen incentives for local farmers. They also explain how agricultural policies in the United States and Europe, which create surpluses there, distort the world market and further weaken incentives for African producers. Liberals document the international effort to satisfy immediate food needs and to assist in raising local long-term agricultural potential. Neo-Marxists clarify the historic connections between colonialism, plantation agriculture, and a contemporary emphasis on nonfood export crops at the expense of food production.

A social-constructivist perspective explains that nationalist and religious passions, such as those that divide the Islamic North and the Christian and animist South of the Sudan, rise in response to food shortages and contribute further to them. Realists (and neo-Marxists) see the difficulties that interstate power politics, especially the superpower rivalry, long created for local actors. For instance, outside powers fueled the civil wars in Ethiopia and the Sudan.

All of the issues in this chapter require a multiplicity of perspectives for a reasonably full understanding of both the problems and approaches to solutions. You should now have the tools to undertake more complete analyses than many that you will read in brief, journalistic accounts. Beware of single-cause explanations.

Selected Key Terms

macroenvironment	deforestation	second oil shock
microenvironment	desertification	elasticity
failed states	doubly green revolution	third oil shock
demographic trap	first oil shock	energy crisis

Continuity and Change in World Politics

In the year 2050 six major powers will dominate the world: the United States, a united Europe, China, a revitalized Russia, India, and Japan. They will each be seeking military advantage over the others via arms spending and via temporary and shifting alliances. In spite of power balancing, there will be periodic wars, most often among their proxies but sometimes directly among them. They will also be involved in intense economic competition.

In the year 2050 the world will have solved problems of food supply and largely eliminated malnutrition. Energy will be more plentiful and therefore more inexpensively available to humans than ever before. New energy technologies will also make both the production and the consumption of that energy less polluting than ever before in human history. Although environmental problems will still arise, humanity will have solved the primary air and water pollution issues.

KEY WEB LINKS

www.oecd.org/sge/au/
www.wfs.org/
www.inta.gatech.edu/peter/
globmod.html

Wait a minute! That first paragraph sounds suspiciously like a realist portrayal of the future. What about the growth of a zone of peace among democracies and the possibility that all of these countries may be democratic in 2050? What about the growing power of international organizations and international law? What about the proliferation of regimes in arms control, human rights, and the environment? And, what about the ethnic/religious tensions in India that may have torn that country apart by then and may have stripped the "autonomous provinces" of Tibet and Xinjiang from China? And that second paragraph sounds like the perspective of a modernist. We know that an eco-wholist sees global change very differently. Population will be putting increasing pressures on food supply. Fossil fuel resources will be increasingly scarce and expensive. Environmental degradation, especially of global oceanic and atmospheric commons, will have worsened.

It should not surprise you that world views served as the foundation for those two paragraphs of forecast. We have learned throughout this book that it is almost impossible to think systematically about world politics, past or present, without the lenses of worldviews and the concepts and theories associated with them. We want to turn now to the future, and we want to consider the insights that the perspectives give us. To do so, however, we once again need some additional tools.

Understanding Change

Chapter 2 introduced two analytical devices that shaped the presentation in this book. The first was division of the subject matter into three components: international political behavior (the concern of Chapters 3 to 10), the global political economy (Chapters 11 to 13), and the world political ecology or broader environment (Chapters 14 to 16). The second organizing device was a hierarchy of understanding. Primary worldviews organized thought within each subject matter (although variations of realism, liberalism, and constructivism appeared with special prominence throughout). Worldviews selectively rely on theoretical perspectives; theories in turn draw predominantly on a particular set of concepts; and any given set of concepts directs our attention to a specialized body of factual information.

We now need a third analytical device for understanding world politics, namely a categorization of approaches to describing change. There are four possible characterizations of dynamics in the interstate system: stability (or unpatterned change), cycles, progressive change, and fundamental system transformation (Holsti, Siverson, and George 1980). Table 17.1 shows how worldviews and associated theories (roughly) fit into the categories of change and into the three subject matters. Although scholars of world politics often move across perspectives and traditions and their thought can defy easy classification, Table 17.1 nonetheless helps us bring together all three of the organizing devices of the book. We need, however, to elaborate our new tool, the characterization of change. We look in turn at the four dynamics of change and the worldviews (with associated theories) that fall primarily, but not exclusively, within each dynamic.

Stability or Unpatterned Change

The perspectives in world politics that understand the past and future in terms of relative stability or unpatterned change are primarily realist, or variations thereof, like mercantilism and geopolitics theory.

Realism   Realism portrays an interstate system shaped by the struggle for security under conditions of anarchy. The security dilemma is perennial. The system maintains stability within fairly narrow limits primarily via the **balance of power.** That is not to say that the system is unchanging over time; actor numbers, relative power, and the technology of military and nonmilitary interaction evolve. Yet the basic structure remains intact and patterns of behavior vary little over long periods. Continuity and stability in a system indicate that the system is in **equilibrium** or balance; constant interaction and mutual cancellation of opposing powers gives rise to equilibrium. For the realist, the substructure forces and trends that Chapter 1 documented give rise to shocks that rattle the superstructure but cause no fundamental change in it.

Table 17.1   Summary of Worldviews and Theories

Dominant Subject Matter	Characterization of Change			
	Stability (and unpatterned change)	Cycles	Progressive Change	System Transformation
Political	Realism	Neorealism; Neoliberalism	Liberalism	Constructivism
	Security dilemma under anarchy Balance of power Statecraft Intrastate analysis (friendly challenge to realism) Collective goods	Hegemonic transition Hegemonic stability	Functionalism Neofunction- alism Growth of human rights and democracy Democratic peace	Construction of identity, relational norms, and governance norms
Economic	Mercantilism; Neomercantilism	Neoclassical Economics	Commercial Liberalism	Neo-Marxism
	Convertibility of power and wealth Strategic trade theory	Economic cycles	Capital accumulation Comparative advantage Stages of growth	Capital accumulation Imperialism System transformation
	Dependency	World Systems Theory		
	Dependence Dual economy Uneven development	Cycles of expansion		
Broader Environment	Geopolitics		Modernism	Eco-Wholism; Neotraditionalism
	Impact of technology and resources on power Imperialism		Technological advance	Overshoot and collapse Tragedy of commons Ecoconflict
	Predominantly zero-sum logic		Nonzero-sum logic	

Morton Kaplan, who identified alternative polarities of the interstate system, characterized these as "states of equilibrium of one ultra-stable international system" (1957, 21). The emergence of equilibrium from individual state action is comparable to the working of the invisible hand in economics, which translates the self-serving economic behavior of individuals and firms into an economic system that improves efficiency of production and distribution. The invisible hand of economics provides progressively greater volumes of goods, however, while the invisible hand of realist power politics can at best provide security most of the time and is subject to repeated failure.

Many realists, particularly those who are historically oriented, emphasize the importance of statecraft. **Statecraft,** the artful choice and application of the diplomatic, economic, and military tools available to the state, aids in the pursuit of state interest. Attention to statecraft suggests, however, a less deterministic view of state behavior than does an exclusive focus on the dynamics of power balances. In a friendly challenge to realism, some analysts go still further and look inside the state at a broad array of policy determinants—from interest groups to political parties to the personalities of leadership. There is, however, nothing in realism fundamentally incompatible with some **intrastate analysis** of states, as long as the macro or systemic assumptions of realism (especially systemic anarchy and the pervasiveness of the security dilemma) remain intact.

Kenneth Waltz elaborated the realist worldview in his *Theory of International Politics.* He, too, emphasized stability:

> The texture of international politics remains highly constant, patterns recur, and events repeat themselves endlessly. The relations that prevail internationally seldom shift rapidly in type or in quality. They are marked instead by dismaying persistence, a persistence that one must expect so long as none of the competing units is able to convert the anarchic international realm into a hierarchic one. (1979, 66)

Kaplan thought that some conscious attention to rules of behavior for states is required, whereas Waltz rejected the notion that states follow any system-serving rules; he argued that self-serving action within the balance-of-power structure will automatically (through coalitions) constrain even universalistic powers.

Although realist theory heavily emphasizes the conflict among states in an anarchic system, it also recognizes the possibility and even the prevalence of cooperation. In fact, states must cooperate if they are to "deliver the goods" for their citizens in terms of security and broader economic welfare. Theory on the provision of **collective goods** suggests how states interact under conditions of rivalry and uncertain ownership to satisfy those demands.

Although the roots of realism may be solidly in high politics (predominant emphasis on the political system) and in theories of stability and continuity, the branches of the worldview have spread widely. Some of those branches extend the scope of realist understandings into economic and broader environmental subsystems.

Mercantilism   States compete with other states for markets, investment outlets, and sources of raw materials. They seek maximum economic growth and full employment of their citizenry. These objectives lead them to stimulate technological advance through support for research and development and through direction of governmental spending to domestic industry. **Strategic trade theory** argues that these techniques can effectively improve well-being for a country. The objectives also cause states to expand their external market shares and to protect their domestic market, relying on various tariff and nontariff mechanisms to promote exports and restrict imports. Because states achieve gains with respect to many of these policies only at the expense of other countries, they correctly perceive their neomercantilist competition as zero-sum.

Like the mercantilists of old, neomercantilists believe in the *convertibility of wealth and power:* economic wealth can buy power (military, political, and economic) and states can convert power, through the appropriate policies, to wealth. The Achilles' heel of all mercantilist thought is that the competition of states over the size of their slices may reduce the total size of the pie. It is for this reason that liberals prescribe squelching the debate over slice size and devoting effort to baking a larger pie. Nonetheless, neomercantilists pose a serious real-world challenge to liberals.

Geopolitics   Geopolitics is an older extension of realism into issues of the broader environment. It is analogous to the mercantilist extension of realism into political economy in that interstate competition remains its primary dynamic. Morgenthau (1973) detailed the contribution of resource bases, broadly defined in terms of population, food, and raw materials, to power. Realists suggest that the environment motivates struggle as well as providing resources for the struggle. Theorists of *imperialism* (for example, Hobson and Lenin) have long argued that capitalist countries require markets and resources, and the requirement motivates expansion and conflict. Others suggest that all countries, regardless of economic system, face similar incentives for expansion (Choucri and North 1975). Waltz (1979) generalized the argument in discussing the motivation to imperialism of the "three surpluses": people, goods, and capital.

Neorealism and Cycles   Some analysts, in more recent formulations, carry systemically or structurally focused realist thought into an analysis of cycles within the world political economy. Although the state system exhibits long-term stability, polarity of the system varies, and there appears to be some regularity in that variation (see Chapter 4). At the end of his review of international politics in the Chou Dynasty, the Greek city-state system, Renaissance Italy, and the modern state system, Holsti argued that:

> These categories of international systems emphasize the recurrence of various power structures and interaction patterns in different historical contexts. . . . Each of the historical examples at some stage became transformed from the diffuse type to either the diffuse-bloc, multipolar, or polar type. Diverse conditions might be responsible for this phenomenon, but the trend is unmistakable. No system originally comprising a large number of roughly equal units, with power diffused among them, retained that structure for a very long period, and the usual direction of development was toward a polar structure.
>
> Even polar structures were not very stable. Starting with the anti-French coalition between the eighteenth and nineteenth centuries, polar structures have developed into diffuse structures, only to turn into polar or multipolar structures again. (Holsti 1983, 91)

Realists devote surprisingly little attention to the discovery of patterns in polarity transformation and explanations for it.

Instead of theorizing about polarity change, much recent thought within structural realism has focused on cycles of hegemony or leadership within unipolar systems. Three issues hold central place in theory surrounding hegemony: What explains the rise and fall of hegemons? How does the rise and fall of hegemons interact with interstate conflict? What are the implications for system management of the existence of a hegemon or of its decline?

Modelski (1978) and other observers of system leadership see not only a regularity in pattern of **hegemonic transition,** but also a constancy in period. Specifically, Modelski argued that the modern system has experienced five cycles of about 100 years. The systemic leader (Modelski avoided "hegemon") has been, in turn, Portugal, the United Provinces of the Netherlands, Great Britain (two centuries), and now the United States. Theorists propose several explanations for hegemonic decline (with implications for hegemonic rise): the costs of hegemony (including military expense), the shift of expenditures by a hegemon from investment to consumption (the third-generation effect), the rise of taxes and inflation (linked to the first two explanations), and the change of technological leadership in the world system. Major interstate conflicts generally mark the transitions between systemic leaders. Ironically, wars of transition often result in the relative fall of both leader and challenger, and the rise of a third state.

The theory of **hegemonic stability** explains some of the benefits that a hegemon may bring to the interstate system, including the development of trade regimes and, until the hegemon is challenged, an era of relative peace. For instance, British and American leadership have in turn supported free-trade regimes and eras free of great power war.

Progressive Change

Challenges to realism arise with respect to almost all of the elements of that perspective: the definition of states as rational, unitary actors; the predominant emphasis of realists on security and power rather than on other values; the almost exclusive emphasis on states and resultant inattention to important nonstate actors; and the focus on conflict rather than on the extensiveness of international cooperation.

Neither these challenges individually, nor the set of them collectively, fundamentally undercut the importance of the realist perspective. In fact most realists modify the basic worldview sufficiently to mollify many of the challengers. In particular, realists recognize the validity of suggestions that states cannot always be understood as unitary, rational actors. Realists readily admit that such a characterization is a prescriptive ideal for statecraft rather than a consistent reality. They accept "intrastate" analysis as a generally friendly challenge.

It is additional challenges, those that draw our attention to nonstate actors, to values other than power and security, to the advance of human rights law and democracy, to a considerable zone of interstate peace, and to extensive regional and global institutional development, that form the basis for an alternative, liberal view of world politics. With respect to the substructure forces of Chapter 1, liberals argue that increasing damage to the global environment (as a result of population growth and spreading industrialization) and rapid jumps in the lethality of weaponry create incentives for global community and institution building, while technological change (especially in communication and transportation), economic advance, and ongoing social mobilization provide energy and means for the processes.

Liberalism   Liberals portray a world experiencing a remarkable evolution in governance. Only the most idealistic of liberals deny the continuing dominance of states in the contemporary world and the power that realist understandings therefore bring to bear. Nor would most liberals suggest that change has only positive or progressive effects; as Samuel Johnson once said, "Change is inconvenient, even when it is for the better." Yet even the most analytical and cautious liberals claim that other structures are forming, enveloping states in patterns of interaction and governance that have begun to affect their relations.

The liberal world is pluralistic, both within states and among them. The interplay of interest groups in democracies determines policy. The interplay of nongovernmental organizations (which are also interest groups) across state borders has nowhere near that level of influence, but the rapid growth in numbers and energy of such groups has made them important actors. They press for the human-rights law, both within and across states, that gives individuals increasingly strong roles in governance structures. They support the spread of democracy.

The zone of democracy has spread during the Third Wave of global democratization. Most of humanity now lives in free or partly free societies. It would be foolish to argue that war is impossible within that zone. Substantial conflict, particularly over economic and ethnic issues, is prevalent within it and could always boil over into interstate conflict. Yet the remarkable record of **democratic peace,** of peace among the stable democracies in that zone, cannot but encourage liberal convictions.

Institutions, both formal and informal, are fundamental to governance. A considerable array of such institutions has developed and continues to evolve across state boundaries. Just as the number of NGOs has grown much more rapidly than the number of sovereign states, the number of IGOs has risen sharply. International institutions serve a variety of functions and liberals understand their proliferation in terms of **functionalist** and **neofunctionalist theory.** The economic institutions established at the end of World War II, in combination with multinational corporations (cousins of NGOs), have supported the growth of trade to levels considerably beyond those of previous eras. Other international institutions have addressed needs for health care, and many more tackle transborder environmental problems.

In elaborating the evolution of global governance, liberals stress the nonzero-sum nature of many issues. For instance, liberals argue that population, food, the environment, and natural resources present problems that often only collective action can solve; the solutions will provide benefits for all parties in excess of the costs. Perhaps most fundamentally, liberals perceive a pattern of progressive change in international politics. Since the beginning of the modern state system, agreements have regularly, and to a considerable extent cumulatively, enhanced the corpus of international law and added to the strength of international organization. That most advance has occurred only at the end of major global wars only adds to the urgency of the task in the nuclear age.

Commercial Liberalism   Early economists like Adam Smith, those who initially formulated the classical liberal worldview, identified accumulation of capital plus production specialization and trade (directed by comparative advantage in production) as the engines of *progressive* economic growth. They recognized, however, that population growth interacted with economic growth. Significant debates centered on the degree to which economic growth could outstrip that of population and allow net improvement in the condition of the citizenry. We must remember that Smith and his contemporaries wrote early in the industrial revolution, and that workers often faced miserable conditions. The literature of Charles Dickens told us how miserable. Many political economists believed that the forces of production growth would lift living conditions only temporarily, and that population growth would literally eat up the gains. Thomas Malthus was best known for his pessimism, but even Smith suggested such a long-term result:

> In a country fully peopled in proportion to what either its territory could maintain or its stock employ, the competition for employment would necessarily be so great as to reduce the wages of labour to what was barely sufficient to keep up the number of labourers. (Smith 1910, 138)

Analysts labeled such a dismal outcome the "iron law of wages"—wages will inevitably fall to the subsistence level.

After nearly two centuries in which global economic growth has exceeded that of population, most liberals now believe that economic growth is winning the race with population. Most liberals now view economic growth as a progressive force, capable of improving welfare for increasing portions of humanity over the long term. The forces of *capital accumulation* and **comparative advantage** drive that progressive growth. Theories about **stages of economic growth** and transformations of the economy outline its operation.

Neoclassical Economics and Cycles   In the last century the analysis of economics has increasingly taken long-term growth for granted and focused on the more immediate workings of the economy. Economists have developed a theory of demand to accompany the earlier dominant emphasis on production and have tied together their understandings of demand and supply in neoclassical theories of equilibrium in which the rise and fall of prices play a critical role. In addition, economists give considerable attention to the cycles that manifest themselves regularly in all countries. These include the 4-year business cycle, the 7-year Juglar cycle, the 20-year Kuznets cycle, and the much disputed 50-year Kondratieff cycle (Maddison 1982, 64–65). It is important to emphasize, however, that neoclassical economists understand those cycles to operate around an upward trend in growth (in contrast to neorealists who emphasize cycles in hegemony without progressive change).

Modernism   The concept of progress stands at the core of modernist thought. Modernists measure progress in terms of the human condition. For instance, Simon (1981) stressed the importance of nearly constant increases in life expectancy in the West during the last two centuries and around the world since World War

II. Herman Kahn (Kahn, Brown, and Martel 1976; Kahn 1979) heavily emphasized GNP per capita.

Technological advance is the driving force of such progress (see again Table 17.1). Modernists have, however, no particularly good theory of technological advance. It is a kind of *deus ex machina*[1] that has been on the stage for such a long time that we seldom think to ask where it came from or doubt its future contributions. General efforts to understand the march of technology fall into two categories (Ayres 1969, 29). One school holds that technology has its own, largely uncontrollable and unpredictable dynamics. Major inventions, such as the plow, the stirrup, or the transistor, may have been "inevitable" in a broad sense, but their timing was far from predictable. The other school sees a relationship between invention and the social, military, and economic needs of the time. In this view, humans control technological advance to a considerable degree. The Manhattan project to build an atomic bomb during World War II and the National Aeronautics and Space Administration project to put a human on the moon during the 1960s illustrate how decisions to develop technology can lead to its attainment.

Many liberal-modernists believe that by banishing material want and substituting abundance, modern technology progressively eliminates the major causes of war and creates a more peaceful world. H. G. Wells sketched just such a world in *Things to Come* (1936). Most modernists, however, devote remarkably little attention to the implications of technological advance for domestic or global politics, and there is sometimes a kind of political naïveté and wishful thinking in the approach of those who do. In contrast, another modernist, Herman Kahn (Kahn, Brown, and Martel 1976), saw no inherent problems in obtaining what humanity wants and needs from the environment, but felt strongly that both domestic mismanagement and interstate conflict were serious threats to its actually doing so. He was, in fact, a realist-modernist who believed that nuclear military technology could lead to nuclear war.

In addition to focusing on the power of modern weaponry in the hands of states unconstrained by superior force, there are at least two potential linkages between modernist thought and realism. First, the competition among states for technological advantage may be increasing with their growing state sponsorship of technological advance. Second, some neorealists seeking an explanation of hegemonic transition have adopted the long-wave theory of technological change to help explain the rise of new hegemons. For instance, Gilpin wrote:

> The clustering of technological innovation in time and space helps explain both the uneven growth among nations and the rise and decline of hegemonic powers. . . . Periods of slowing rates of growth appear to be associated with the shift from one set of leading industrial sectors and centers of economic growth to another and with the transition from one hegemonic leader to the next. (Gilpin 1987, 109)

Any loss of technological edge by the United States and weakening of its global leadership may usher in a dangerous period for interstate relations.

---

[1]Greek and Roman plays sometimes introduced a god by way of stage machinery to direct a certain course of events arbitrarily.

System Transformation

At seemingly unpredictable points in history, environmental, economic, and political systems undergo transformations. Equilibrium may persist for long periods of time, or it may appear that there is some kind of underlying progress in human systems. Yet the theory of **punctuated equilibrium** in biological evolution suggests that intermittently, perhaps as a result of comets striking earth or massive volcanic eruptions, the pattern of life on earth changes dramatically. Similarly, eco-wholists remind us that environmental systems can tip from one condition of relative equilibrium with the human population into another and very different equilibrium. Eden can become a desert. Marxists believe that political-economic transformation will shift the system from capitalism to socialism. Constructivists point to the ability of an ethnic group to turn suddenly to genocidal racism or, more hopefully, for the relationship between sexes to move from inequality and domination to equality.

Constructivism   Social constructivism is relatively theory poor. Although adherents direct our attention to important **identity groups, relational norms,** and **governance norms,** they tell us less than we would like about how those form or how they will shape world politics. We know that community or cultural identities will emerge or strengthen with effective communication (for instance, with a common spoken or written language) and with external pressure (for instance, threat by a larger community within a state to an ethnic group's cultural traditions or autonomy). We know that communities under pressure will engage in a mixture of measures including exclusion, conquest, or conversion of outsiders and that they will frequently seek to build or capture a state. Most fundamentally, the perspective emphasizes that humans construct their social systems. That opens at least the possibility that those systems can change fundamentally and profoundly, for better or worse.

Neo-Marxism   Most constructivist challenges to the basic liberal view share one feature: they emphasize the connections between, even inseparability of, economic and political systems. Marx's thought synthesized understandings of politics, economics, and the broader environment (especially technology). He found the basic motive forces of change in the economic production process, both its nature (rooted in the technology of production) and its organization (notably the ownership of the means of production). Social and political institutions are superstructures, growing out of the nature and organization of production. For instance, modern manufacturing technology requires capital, and a capitalist class controls that means of production. That class has developed institutions by which it also dominates society and government.

Traditional Marxists identify technological advance as the fundamental progressive force (with a very broad historic span), altering systems of production and thereby changing class structures. Thus Marxism shares, and in some ways more fully develops, the liberal belief in progressive change. It is thus not surprising that Marxists also foresee the kind of positive global political developments that pluralists identify. In the *Communist Manifesto,* Marx and Engels sometimes sound almost like liberals:

> National differences and antagonisms between peoples are daily more and more vanishing, owing to the development of the bourgeoise, to freedom of commerce, to the world market, to uniformity in the mode of production and in the conditions of life corresponding thereto.
>
> The supremacy of the proletariat will cause them to vanish still faster. United action, of the leading civilized countries at least, is one of the first conditions for the emancipation of the proletariat.
>
> In proportion as the exploitation of one individual by another is put to an end, the exploitation of one nation by another will also be put to an end. In proportion as the antagonism between classes within the nation vanishes, the antagonism of one nation to another will also come to an end. (Feuer 1959, 26)

Major differences obviously separate, however, the liberal and neo-Marxist worldviews. Liberals emphasize the mutually beneficial bargains of economic exchange and the spread of well-being throughout society. Neo-Marxists point to the ability of those with economic, social, and political power to expropriate the bulk of the benefits in economic transactions (including those generated by the employment bargain). Impoverishment of the workers in the same society that steadily increases its productive capacity creates serious tensions or contradictions. Although measures like exporting the capital and goods surpluses may ameliorate these problems for a time, such remedies face limits. Ultimately the tensions will become so great that they will lead to a transformation of the society—a socialist revolution in which the workers take control of the means of production.

World-Systems Theory and Cycles   World-systems theory is a variant of the neo-Marxist challenge to liberalism that elaborates the development of capitalism in Europe and its global expansion. It divides the world into the more powerful, economically advanced states of the core (or center) and the weaker states of the periphery. Although it retains the expectation of an ultimate transformation of capitalism to socialism, it focuses primarily on **cycles of capitalist expansion** and on the changing leadership (hegemony) of the capitalist state-system core throughout the expansion process.

> [World systems theory] constitutes a large-scale and long-term framework for the study of selected systemic structures, cycles and secular trends. Three central processes are stressed, the historic development of a core-periphery division of labor, the episodic rise and fall of hegemonic powers, and the gradual geographic expansion, coupled with the periodic growth and stagnation, of the world economy. (Thompson 1983, 11)

World-systems theorists explain the cycles of capitalist expansion and the rise and fall of hegemonic powers in terms that sound much like the explanations of neo-realist theorists of hegemonic stability.

Dependency Theory   Dependency theory provides still another variation of the neo-Marxist challenge to the liberal view. Traditional Marxism presents the broadest historical sweep, spanning major epochs and great system transformations, world-systems theory narrows the focus primarily to the emergence and cyclical development of capitalism, and dependency theory further focuses on the relationship between more- and less-developed countries in the contemporary era. Dependency theory identifies and investigates several consequences of the unequal relationship between core and periphery states. The local elite in many LDCs depends on and serves the interests of the multinational corporations, the bilateral and multilateral aid agencies, and other manifestations of the Northern elites. It is a two-way relationship in which the local elite receives economic rewards and political support, in an implicit exchange for a perpetuation of the existing, exploitative economic order. These divisions within LDCs grow from development of enclave or **dual economies,** in which only a portion of the LDC population enters the modern economy, while the rest remains a vast, disorganized army of inexpensive labor.

Like mercantilism, dependency theory draws our attention to the convertibility of economic and political-military power and to the zero-sum character of power relationships. Some dependency theorists (and world-systems theorists) argue that the hierarchical relationships are so strongly structured, and the core countries and LDC elites so greatly benefit from them, that the South can expect only highly *uneven development.* That is, development will privilege some, while disadvantaging many, and will suffer frequent setbacks from shocks transmitted by the global economy.

Eco-Wholism   Eco-wholists or neotraditionalists share with modernists a perception that important change is occurring in the broader context of world politics. They see that change not in technological advance, however, but in potentially irreversible environmental deterioration and resource depletion. In addition to proliferation of local pollution problems, they point to the global scope of environmental damage from atmospheric ozone depletion, increased atmospheric CO_2, and transboundary movement of the pollutants causing acid rain. Eco-wholists anticipate problems rather than progress.

Eco-wholists rely heavily on a systems perspective with some parallels to those of neorealists and neoclassical liberals. Eco-wholists believe that, within the ecosystem, some species increase in numbers, overextend themselves, and then decline. The logic of eco-wholists, because of the emphasis on repeated **overshoot and collapse,** can sometimes appear cyclical. Fundamentally, however, it is transformational—many environmental changes are basically irreversible.

Lester Brown drew our attention to the fate of the Mayans and to scholarship that suggests that the Central American civilization ran up against ecological limits before its still mysterious collapse:[2]

> Using the latest techniques of paleo-ecological research, scientists determined that the number of Mayans in the lowlands of Guatemala had expanded continuously over seventeen centuries, beginning about the time of Homeric Greece in 800 B.C. Doubling on the average of every 408 years, the population by A.D. 900 had reached

---

[2]Some recent studies of the Mayan collapse have emphasized climate change. Students of the rise and fall of civilizations disagree markedly about the reasons for their fall. In contrast to Brown's understanding, Toynbee (1972, 141) emphasized the loss of technological or creative impetus.

5 million with a density comparable to that of the most agriculturally intensive so-cieties of today. . . . Within decades, the population fell to less than one-tenth of what it had been. . . . As population pressure increased, soil erosion gradually ac-celerated. The topsoil was being washed into the area's lakes, draining the crop-land of its productivity and one of the world's early civilizations of its sustenance. (Brown 1981, 3–4)

One of the key mechanisms underlying overshoot is the clash between indi-vidual and collective interests. Popularized by Hardin (1968) as the **tragedy of the commons,** the argument is that the rational self-interest of individuals leads them to increase their exploitation of a public good. When all individuals make the same calculation, however, their actions become self-defeating. In this book we have dis-cussed the clash between individual and collective logic across a wide range of ex-amples including states erecting barriers to imports, despite believing in free trade; countries within OPEC cheating on other members of the cartel by producing above their quotas; states wanting to harvest a disproportionate share of ocean life; and humans jointly polluting the global atmosphere.

Although eco-wholists fear and even sometimes predict a transformation to a much worsened equilibrium with the environment, they prescribe a transforma-tion to sustainable development. Eco-wholists emphasize three possible ap-proaches to reconciling private and collective interests in the long term and post-poning, if not avoiding, disaster. The first, when physically possible, is to privatize the commons. The second is voluntary behavior changes. The third approach in-volves collective coercion.

Because it is very difficult to privatize many commons (e.g., the global at-mosphere), because voluntary behavior changes require self-sacrifice, and because there is no collectively coercive international order now in place, eco-wholists with a realist bent tend to be rather pessimistic about prospects for reaching an equilib-rium with the environment. Moreover, they believe that environmental problems will often translate into interstate conflict—what Pirages (1983, 251) calls **ecocon-flict.** Water problems in the Middle East illustrate the potential.

Cycles

We have seen that cycles are not so much a completely distinct form of change, but a variation on each of the other three. We therefore integrated discussion of cyclical perspectives with the discussion of the worldviews from which they stem. For instance, realists can point to cycle-like patterns in warfare that fun-damentally leave the system unchanged. Some neorealists (or structural realists or neoliberals) draw a cyclical portrait of world politics by describing the rise and fall of systemic hegemons. Neoclassical liberals point to cycles that operate around a progressive trend. They do so with respect to business cycles around the trend of economic growth. World-systems theorists have similarly traced cy-cles of expansion and contraction in the capitalist world economy, but like other neo-Marxists generally expect that at some point there will be a systemic trans-forming crisis of capitalism.

Putting the Perspectives Together

Once we understand the worldview(s) of a newspaper columnist or world leader, we can often anticipate how she or he will approach a new policy issue. In the 1980s, both British Prime Minister Margaret Thatcher and American President Ronald Reagan drew heavily on realist and commercial liberal understandings of the world and therefore often found themselves in agreement with one another—for instance, on the need to build strong security systems and to revitalize the liberal trading order. Reagan's predecessor, Jimmy Carter, drew in addition on more liberal and social constructivist perspectives. For instance, his emphasis on human rights grew out of a belief in an emerging global community, based on the rights of individuals, and his sensitivity to the Third World implicitly recognized the existence of global structures.

National leaders and analysts of world politics use worldviews in one of three very different ways. Some people follow the model of the child given a hammer for Christmas who hammers everything in sight. The intellectual version of the "law of the hammer" involves forming an extremely strong attachment to a single worldview, using it to understand as much as possible, and deciding that what the worldview cannot explain must be unimportant. We call such people "ideologues." Popular newspaper columnists and radio talk-show hosts often have a heavy anchor in one worldview.

The second approach is adoption of a combination of worldviews. Analogous to selecting food from categories on a menu (appetizers, entrées, and desserts) is the possibility of adopting one perspective on political behavior, another on political economy, and a third on the broader political ecology. Table 17.1 helps us understand why some combinations arise more often than others. Modernists frequently are liberals, because the perspectives share a belief in progressive change. Realists, mercantilists, and geopoliticians share an attention to zero-sum aspects of world politics and to continuity in interstate relations.

There are tensions inherent in any combination of worldviews. For instance, in recent years the realist, commercial liberal, and modernist worldviews have been dominant in the United States. An individual whose thought integrated these three perspectives would need to struggle with some important questions. Specifically, rapid advance in communication and transportation technologies (which the modernist anticipates) and increased capital, technology, and goods flows (the result of commercial liberal forces) inevitably intensify and complicate interactions across state borders. Do not these interactions, and the agents involved in them, at some point begin to undercut the traditional freedom of action and therefore sovereignty of the state (central to the realist perspective)? In thinking about a combination of worldviews, imagine the child at Christmas again, given a large pipe wrench, a small screwdriver, and a pair of plastic pliers. The tools complement each other—but crudely.

The third intellectual approach sees some value in each of the worldviews. The world is one of states, of actual and incipient communities, of markets, of social structures, of ecosystems, and of technological progress. There is no reason that theory concerning each of these elements should not be important to a complete understanding. Unfortunately, the synthetic approach can lead to analysis and action paralysis, symptoms of the disease, "on-the-other-handitis." A child who receives a complete adult's toolbox for Christmas may initially have little idea when to use the various hammers, screwdrivers, or wrenches, and may give up the whole enterprise in frustration.

The metaphor suggests that the trick is learning to know when to reach for one tool, or for a combination, or when others are appropriate. If the subject matter is nuclear strategy, realism helps us understand it, but when it is ethnic conflict, realist thought is of remarkably little use. If the subject matter is global cooperation in human rights, liberalism helps put Amnesty International into a proper context, whereas commercial liberalism and neo-Marxism combined provide a much better basis for comprehension of multinational corporations. We can thus imagine a more comprehensive understanding of world politics in which the worldviews of this volume *complement* each other rather than compete. In fact, this book has attempted to map the issues for which various worldviews contribute the most understanding.

Another step might be a more formal attempt to synthesize the views (Burton 1990). One approach to synthesis is to look for a unit of analysis or agent that is common to all perspectives (as physicists look to the basis constituent parts of matter for blocks on which to build unifying theories). Because individuals are the fundamental building blocks of communities, classes, and states, individuals could be the basis for synthesis. For example, Abraham Maslow (1970) argued that all humans have a hierarchy of needs: physiological (like food), safety, belongingness and love, cognitive (the desire to know or understand), aesthetic (craving for beauty), esteem (recognition and status), and self-actualization (the fulfillment of one's own potential). He suggested that humans require at least minimal satisfaction of more basic needs before they can move on to higher-level ones. It is possible to see connections between such needs and the values that we have associated with worldviews, for instance, between the security motivation underlying realism and Maslow's safety need, or between the identity and autonomy values of social constructivist perspectives and Maslow's higher values—belongingness, self-esteem, and even self-actualization. Clearly humans create states, build communities, participate in markets, become bound into hierarchical structures, pursue knowledge, and struggle to survive and propagate because such activities fulfill needs. If some needs are more basic than others, it might help us identify priorities among such activities.

Others have questioned, however, whether there is such a universal hierarchy of needs/values.[3] Remember that while Maslow said that physiological needs are most fundamental, many humans have unnecessarily starved or subjected themselves to the dangers of war in the name of nationalism and religion, or even for recognition and status. The idea of a single synthesis of worldviews is attractive, but it may also be remote.

---

[3]The field of anthropology has long embraced a cultural relativism, reluctant even to condemn practices such as genital mutilation. In 1947 the leadership of the American Anthropological Association withdrew from discussions that produced the Universal Declaration of Human Rights. Yet in 1994 the association's annual meeting theme was human rights and many attendees moved away from cultural relativism (Fluehr-Lobban 1995).

Each of us needs to develop our own understanding of the world, and that requires using worldviews (and associated theories and concepts), singly or in combination. Without worldviews, world affairs would seemingly consist only of random events, and knowledge would be simply a kind of trivia expertise. The worldviews presented here, variations of them and perhaps others not within the conception of this author, are fundamental to understanding world politics.

Conclusion

This book has now presented and elaborated multiple views of the world in some detail. There is only one world, however. Are you confused? Do you have trouble falling asleep at night because you cannot decide if you are a realist, liberal, constructivist, modernist, or eco-wholist? Probably not. The issue actually is a serious one, however, because your interpretation of world developments will influence how you vote, what organizations you join or give money to, and how you deal with individuals in other countries when you travel or work abroad. We all want to have as much self-knowledge as possible, and developing and understanding our own worldviews is an important part of that. The next chapter may help you clarify your own views.

Selected Key Terms

balance of power	functionalist theory	governance norms
equilibrium	neofunctionalist theory	cycles of capitalist expansion
collective goods	comparative advantage	
strategic trade theory	stages of economic growth	dual economies
hegemonic transition	punctuated equilibrium	overshoot and collapse
hegemonic stability	identity groups	tragedy of the commons
democratic peace	relational norms	ecoconflict

CHAPTER 18

Alternative Futures: The Clash of Perspectives

In 1995 scientists cooled atoms to a temperature so near absolute zero that the material formed something called a Bose-Einstein condensate, a new form of matter (neither gaseous, nor liquid, nor solid). Based on his theory of quantum mechanics, Albert Einstein had predicted the phenomenon decades earlier. Thus the scientists not only demonstrated the existence of the condensate—they added credence to Einstein's theory, which in turn built on work by Bose. Physical scientists regularly use their theories to predict outcomes that help to invalidate or add credibility to those theories.

This book has presented many competing social theories tied to larger worldviews. Should we not similarly be able to make predictions with such theories in order to help us choose among them? The answer is basically "yes and no." We can, but it is very hard. For instance, while physical scientists often make "point predictions" like the existence of the Bose-Einstein condensate, social scientists generally cannot. One reason is that carefully controlled experiments are essentially impossible at the macro level in the social sciences. We obviously cannot create experiments where war or economic depression are possible outcomes. When we rely instead upon the "real world" as our experimental test bed, so many variables are at play that assessment of causal relations proves extremely difficult, either in advance of a potential outcome or in retrospective assessment. Thus the results of analyzing social predictions tend to be much more ambiguous than in the physical sciences.

In addition, within the social sciences much theory development and testing takes place within rather than across worldviews. Thus realists gradually expanded their understanding of relationships between power balances and the potential for interstate conflict. Specifically, theories of the security dilemma, of power transition, and of hegemonic stability enriched earlier, simpler portrayals of interstate politics in terms of balances of power. Liberals similarly came to better explain transitions to or from democracy and the character of the democratic peace. Neo-Marxists learned from the failure of earlier predictions concerning the imminent transformation of political economies to socialism—they elaborated theory concerning repeated cycles of expansion and contraction in the world economy. The worldviews themselves, however, have largely adapted to changing theoretical content without losing their identities.

In spite of the difficulties, prediction in the social sciences does have two values. First, predictions do, indeed, help us test our theories. If, in the light of success or failure in sociopolitical prediction, observers with strong commitments to worldviews prove capable of reworking their theory accordingly, we improve our theory and our understanding. In the absence of carefully controlled experiments, decisive evidence in support of or in opposition to theories may seldom come. Yet there tends to be a slow accumulation of evidence in support or opposition. Even the relative credibility of entire worldviews rises or falls with evidence from the real world.

Second, developments in the global political system dramatically affect our lives, and we therefore must seek to anticipate them and even shape them as much as possible. Wars in the twentieth century took more than 110 million lives of soldiers and civilians. Short of overt warfare, the costs of military preparedness can also be staggering. Over a period of nearly 50 years the parties to the Cold War spent trillions of dollars on weaponry and personnel that could have supported health or education. Nor is the importance of global politics limited to security issues. World politics shapes global financial and trade flows and can determine whether the economies of countries grow steadily or collapse into depression. Global politics similarly affect the quality of the biological and physical environment and may ultimately determine whether humanity can live sustainably on the planet.

We will not make predictions here. Instead we use a related approach called *scenario analysis,* a technique that futurists and some social scientists use and which is generally consistent with the slow accumulation of information in support of or contradicting our expectations. Scenarios are basically stories about the future, weaving a number of interrelated tendencies together into what the developer hopes is an integrated, coherent, and theoretically based image of how the future might evolve. The rest of this chapter sketches several scenarios about the future. What gives them coherence? If you don't recognize worldviews in them, you need to go back and read this book again. If you do, then think seriously about the believability of these stories of the future (or variants of your own development). Those that seem especially credible probably tap into your own current worldviews. If your worldview structure is open, real-world developments that support these scenarios differentially over time may also gradually reshape your understandings and beliefs.

Many of the students reading this book will be near retirement age in the year 2050. You have every reason to believe that global change between now and then will prove as dramatic as that since 1945 (to which this book has given special attention). Heraclitus said that "Change alone is unchanging." What should you expect?

Business as Usual for States

Our world of 2050 is much more nearly multipolar than bipolar. China, India, and the United States clearly dominate the global system. Each has not only thousands of deep-sea-based nuclear warheads, but a full range of space-based offensive and defensive laser systems. Russia, Japan, and the European Union have second-tier status among the superpowers.

The European Union is the most questionable member of the so-called "superpower set." Although its members completed the establishment of a common market long ago (in 1992), several member countries dashed high hopes of movement toward economic union when, led by Britain, they refused to cede control of monetary and fiscal policy instruments. Spillover to even more highly politicized issues, such as the large joint military force that the BENELUX countries proposed in 2012, never materialized. The European integration process appears to be at a dead end, incapable of going beyond trade and selected environmental issues.

Although the superpowers naturally find their interests overlapping around the globe, the primary area of tension remains the "belt of conflict" stretching from Burma through Southeast Asia to Australia. China had clearly consolidated its hold on the South China Sea by 2035 when the United States backed off during the face-off over the Chinese invasion of Taiwan. By the same time India had clearly established its dominance of the Indian Ocean and its long-term rival Pakistan had collapsed economically under the weight of its regional competition with India. China and India then seriously began the cat-and-mouse competition in the belt of conflict that brought them near war in 2042. The United States and Japan continue, however, to play balancing roles that have prevented either India or China from consolidating their positions.

The major regional rivalry continues to be that of the Middle East. Iraq, Libya, Egypt, Israel, and Iran all have declared or undeclared nuclear forces and delivery vehicles putting other Middle Eastern countries (and in Israel's case, most of the world) within strike range. Development of nuclear strike doctrine was turbulent in the tense 2015–2035 period because the restricted geographic area made nuclear weapons in the Middle East into mutually destructive "doomsday machines." Israel's public mobilization of its nuclear weapons during its conflict with Syria in 2019 nearly plunged the region into nuclear war. An uneasy relative stability now exists in the Middle East.

Most of the competition among the superpowers remains economic, like that which erupted in the trade wars early in the century. Continued Japanese trade surpluses, coupled with growing surpluses in the NICs, especially China, intensified protectionist pressure around the world. Increased use of those surpluses to buy real estate and industrial facilities in the United States and Europe brought the issue to a crisis point. The U.S. Congress fired the first shot by passing legislation in 2008 that required the bilateral trade deficit with Japan to be completely phased out in five years, using a combination of U.S. tariffs and quotas to assure that result. The Japanese stock market collapsed, and the national economy contracted sharply, reducing its imports, triggering even sharper cutbacks in U.S. purchases from Japan, and setting in motion a downward trade spiral. World financial markets were in turmoil as capital sought safe havens.

After nearly a decade of global depression and increased global tension, negotiators succeeded in creating a new economic order that gradually initiated a new round of reduction in protectionist barriers. Global economic growth resumed and tensions eased.

Although states often do find bases for limited cooperation, the world remains one of anarchy and struggle for relative position. The historically great scholars of world politics, such as Thucydides, Machiavelli, and Morgenthau, would have little difficulty understanding the world of today. It may be a more dangerous place than ever, but the rules that guide its dynamics remain largely unchanged.

The Evolution of Global Governance

It is difficult to imagine the antagonism between the United States and Russia that threatened to destroy the world as recently as the 1980s. The major powers of today's world cooperate on most security, economic, and environmental issues. By far the greatest sources of conflict in the world remain pockets in the Balkans and Transcaucasia. Around most of the globe, however, nationalistic passions have cooled. Economic growth and global devolution of autonomy (even independence) for ethnic regions have largely eliminated the major source of warfare in the earliest twenty-first century.

The EU has continued to expand geographically and functionally. All of the Central European countries are now full members, as are Turkey, Israel, and Egypt. The new members have completed the substitution of the Euro, controlled by the European central bank in Frankfurt, for their historic local currencies. Many other Mediterranean states are associate members, as are Australia and New Zealand. Canada, the United States, Russia, and Japan have begun discussions with the EU about the creation of a World Economic Community, which would completely eliminate remaining economic barriers between those states and the EU.

China, the United States, Russia, and the EU have created what some call a condominium in their joint effort to limit remaining local conflicts in the Third World. They actively support the UN program of inspection to verify the bans on production and stockpiling of chemical and biological weapons. Even more important, they eliminated the last of their nuclear weapons in just the last five years. Through the United Nations, and its increasingly well-financed peacekeeping forces, they were also finally able to secure acceptance by the Israelis and Palestinians of a two-state solution to their conflict. The key was convincing many Israelis that the international guarantees of their borders and of Palestine's demilitarization could be enforced.

Economic leadership has come from a different combination of states: the EU, Japan, and the United States. After their joint success in resolving the African debt problems, they turned to reform of the world economic order. A key change was restructuring of the WTO, so that extensive trade preferences are routinely given to LDCs; the new Development Assessment Group (DAG) oversees the incremental process of graduation of NICs to developed status.

The principle of national self-determination, perhaps the most powerful of all world forces in the twentieth century, appears to have prevailed nearly everywhere in the twenty-first. China gave autonomy to Tibet after the widely publicized civil disobedience period, and, after lengthy violence, India and Pakistan accepted an autonomous Kashmir. There proved to be a strong interaction between willingness of states to support self-determination and the growth of a global community. As the pluralistic security community of the members of the Organization for Economic Co-operation and Development expanded into Asia, Central Europe, and Latin America, the security needs of most states became less pressing. In this generally safer world, the contemporary models of the EU and India, allowing great regional autonomy, while maintaining limited central governmental functions, have proven popular.

Global community continues to strengthen in several ways. For instance, the United Nations Human Rights Commission (HRC) now sends observer teams around the world offering technical assistance and undertaking assessment. The HRC recommends the application of economic sanctions against countries that it finds to hold political prisoners, use torture, reintroduce capital punishment, or otherwise violate global human rights standards. Although some countries still ignore the sanctions, failure to redress the problems identified by the observer teams (or refusal to admit them) now confers a pariah status on states that few are willing to accept. The continued spread of democracy facilitates this strengthening of global community. Freedom House now reports that 71 percent of the world's population lives in free societies, and another 23 percent are partly free (the numbers in 1990 were 39 percent and 22 percent).

In addition the global community has made some progress on environmental issues. The EU has been a leader in that arena as well. CFC production long ago ceased, and the ocean dumping regime has eliminated the most egregious sources of ocean pollution. The Mediterranean Action Plan was a useful early model. The Amazon for the Globe organization raised billions of dollars from governments, foundations, and individuals to compensate Brazil for conversion of extensive regions of the basin into national parks. The most central problem remains the increasingly obvious greenhouse effect. Although all major states now embrace carbon taxes (and raise extensive revenue from them), we have only begun to reduce global annual carbon emissions.

Human beings increasingly find themselves in communities with boundaries that they find comfortable and with institutions and policies they can control. The complexity of overlapping legal and institutional frameworks continues to grow in ways that Grotius, Kant, or Wilson might understand, but scarcely imagined. States have not disappeared, but they possess increasingly restricted freedom of action. The world has entered a new era.

The Clash of Peoples

After the Cold War ended in the 1990s, a rather surprising forecast gained some adherents (Huntington 1993). It foresaw that world politics would evolve into a global "clash of civilizations." It suggested, for instance, that Latin America, and perhaps even Africa, somehow constituted single "civilizations." Although dividing the entire world into a small number of civilizations or culture groups stretched credibility, and many textbooks on world politics derided or dismissed the argument, there proved some real validity to the insight. During the trade war in the second decade of this century, and the Long Depression that followed it, global groupings around roughly "cultural" lines became quite obvious.

The European Union had continued to exclude Turkey from membership as it expanded to incorporate more culturally similar countries in Eastern Europe. When the economic collapse came, a wave of anger and of Islamic and nationalistic sentiment swept across Turkey, and a government gained power that reversed a full century of secularization. The collapse hit the Turkish states in the southern region of the former Soviet Union even harder and, while the Western world was absorbed with bread lines and domestic turmoil, Turkey quickly established an empire of incorporated and associated states that swept east to the border of China. Large portions of Kazakhstan remained outside the empire only because of the Russian invasion. The West strongly protested the expulsion of millions of (Christian) Armenians from the new Turkish empire, but did nothing to stop it.

The Western world truly awakened to the reality of the situation when Turkey, newly in control of very extensive oil production, mobilized other Islamic states throughout the Middle East and Asia into the Islamic Petroleum Exporters Association (IPEA). The depression had caused oil prices to collapse, but restrictions of production by IPEA revived them sharply, adding to the economic pain in Western Europe and elsewhere. Western Europe found itself paying higher prices for desperately needed energy and therefore monetarily helping Turkey sponsor its war with Russia around the Northern Caspian, at the same time that Europe gave some support to Russia in that war. Because of the great benefits Iran received from the higher oil prices, it played a pivotal role by threatening to use its nuclear forces should Russia escalate to that level against Turkey.

In the same period, the devastating collapse of Japan's economy (in part because of the high prices it faced for oil) sharply shifted the balance of Asian power to China. China not only absorbed a demoralized Taiwan with limited resistance, it established a Greater Chinese sphere of influence throughout Eastern and Southeastern Asia. Although the United States blustered and threatened, it did nothing to stop the developments and the region dominated by China has now clearly become the world's most powerful.

Economic recovery in the West was terribly slow. Breakthroughs in solar technology helped. So, too, did the ultimate appearance of cleavages within IPEA, especially between Turkey and its southern neighbors over the highhandedness of Turkey on regional water supplies. Nor had Iran or Saudi Arabia ever really accepted more than general leadership by Turkey on issues related to oil prices. As Western recovery gained strength, cheating on oil quotas became more common and the cartel collapsed, followed shortly by the collapse of the "modern Ottoman empire."

Contemporary "cultural" issues are again more similar to those at the beginning of the century. Those who believed that various nationalisms would somehow succumb to economic growth or global liberalization have been decisively proven wrong. Localized conflicts in the Balkans, in Africa, and across the "arc of turmoil" from Turkey to India remain intense. It also remains obvious that racism continues as a strong force in world politics. That was particularly evident in the abandonment of Africa during and after the AIDS plague, which ultimately killed 60 million Africans, in spite of available, but expensive medicines that could have ended the dying. It is also apparent in the new bipolar tension between Greater China and the West.

Gender remains a major issue in global politics but its role varies dramatically around the world. Although some predicted that the Long Depression would cause a retreat from the gains of women in the West, it instead stopped progress. Studies show that women still earn only 85 percent of what men obtain in comparable jobs throughout the Western world. In Latin America the place of women in society remains even less nearly equal and only in recent years has the position of women in a few Islamic countries like Egypt begun to improve significantly. At the extreme, in spite of the three decades that now separate us from the collapse of the Turkish-Islamic empire, women in Turkey today can still neither vote nor hold political office.

The Global Market

Two primary forces have driven the continued integration of the global economy in the first half of this century: the magnetism of the Economic Union (formerly the European Union) and the dynamism of global corporations or GCs (once known as TNCs or MNCs). Let us consider each in turn.

The Economic Union (EU) is a multitiered structure of states progressively removing barriers to goods, capital, and labor flows among them. That process has gone the furthest in the 28 "inner tier" states of the EU, which have not only eliminated such barriers but have adopted the common currency. The second tier, the EU Associate Group, links the core to most of the other states of the old Organization for Economic Cooperation and Development and to the NICs of the early twenty-first century. These additional countries have eliminated tariffs among themselves, as well as with the core, but have yet to standardize economic policies fully. The third tier is the EU Preference Zone, and consists of states (now 62) that have undertaken to eliminate tariffs and to initiate the standardization of tax systems. In 2016 Brussels regularized the procedure for entry into the structure and for graduation across tiers. The scope and power of this complex structure is now so great that few states are likely to remain outside of it through this century.

Participation of Russia and its nearest Asian neighbors in the third tier was contingent on the economic reforms they began seriously early in the century. That process took much longer than many expected (and faced a variety of setbacks including the Eastern debt crisis) but eventually culminated in the establishment of stable currencies throughout the region. Now that those countries have truly joined the world economy, many expect several of them to progress rapidly into the first tier.

The GCs transmit the economic energy of the EU throughout the world. At one time they all had clearly established "home countries" (most originated in Europe, the United States, Japan, and the early NICs), whereas today the management of many companies is truly global and home offices commonly move across state borders. There has been slow and irregular evolution of world institutions capable of overseeing and controlling power of global corporations. The United Nations Global Corporation Center imposes uniform accounting standards on them and requires extensive public reporting. It is now reviewing charges of monopoly practices by World Visacorp in consumer financial services.

Latin America illustrates the role corporations have played in spreading economic growth around the world over the last 100 years. Early in the twentieth century most of the companies with important presence in the region were largely producers and exporters of primary materials (mineral and agricultural products). At the end of that century, and particularly after the debt crises of the 1980s and 1990s, global corporations brought massive amounts of capital into the region and transformed it into a center of global manufacturing. Critics point to the tremendous pollution problems of the early twenty-first century, but local and regional regulations gradually brought emissions under control. The same kind of industrialization process, driven by the capital and technology of the GCs, is now appearing in much of Africa, and the pollution in Nigeria and Zimbabwe is the worst in the world. In recent years, however, the large service companies have come to dominate the presence of global corporations in much of Latin America. This is particularly true in the newly postindustrial countries (NPICs), such as Chile, Mexico, and Colombia.

The impact of corporations on domestic and international political processes remains a source of debate, and many critics condemn their influence in politics. Cardenas (2032, 44–89) argues, however, that the industrialization of Latin America, with the assistance of the global corporations, was responsible for the growth of pluralism and the eventual destruction of the old land-owning elites. That in turn allowed the transformation of unstable democracies and authoritarian systems (subject to frequent military coups) into stable democracies.

The inner tier of the EU has now been free of interstate conflict for 50 years, and the possibility of it seems remote. The world is a more prosperous place than it has ever been. The same free markets that gave humanity such material benefit also encourage a pluralism that binds countries and dampens conflict.

Evolving Global Division of Labor

Although the global economy has evolved dramatically in the first 50 years of this century, there has been no change in the fundamental division of it into core and periphery. The most dramatic aspect of the evolution has been the marginalization of Russia, the Ukraine, Southeastern Europe, and the Turkish states of the former Soviet Union. As the economic and political reforms of those countries faltered at the turn of the century, and political unrest seemed to offer choice only between anarchy and intense repression, they turned to the West for help. The IMF and European banks organized consortia and provided nearly $200 billion by 2008. A stream of consumer and capital goods imports from the West fed the "economic miracles" of those countries.

Unfortunately, much of the lending sustained a high lifestyle for the new political and commercial elites in the East, without creating industrial facilities capable of facing global competition. The emergency restructuring of Ukrainian debt in 2006 staved off imminent default but began to make the scope of the problem clear. Banks quickly ceased to make additional loans and began to attempt recovery of their principal. During the next decade there was practically no growth in the region, and debt payments set up a substantial flow of capital from East to West.

As it had a generation earlier in Latin America, the IMF insisted on economic policy changes, particularly the dismantlement of the extensive welfare systems put in place during the era that aid was available. Social unrest followed, as did the establishment of military governments to keep order in several of the countries. Ironically it was the unpopularity of communism that set in motion this process of so-called reform and integration into the world economy in the 1990s; now there is a popular resurgence of communist parties throughout the region, although most governments repress the movement. In the last 20 years, growth has been irregular in the region, and political instability appears endemic.

The parallels between the region of the former communist countries and Latin America extend beyond the similarities of their debt crises. Although both are now heavily industrialized regions, little of that industry is high technology, and much of it (including steel, aluminum, chemicals, and automobiles) is both capital intensive and polluting. Levels of unemployment are high in both regions; air and water quality are poor. The core countries retain the headquarters and research and development centers of the TNCs that control industry in both regions and completely dominate the newer communications, biological, and space industries.

The Asian NICs, which showed such promise in the late twentieth century, have also had difficult times in the twenty-first century. Although Taiwan and Singapore made the transition to postindustrial economies and became part of the global core economy, South Korea, Thailand, and others were weakened by competition during the economic boom of the East, and then were hit hard by the global economic crisis of 2008–2012. The intensely nationalistic regime that came to power in Korea mismanaged the economy, and the Korean experience is now reminiscent of Argentina's twentieth-century fall from economic grace and political stability.

Africa remains at the bottom of the global division of labor. Only limited industrialization has taken root on the continent, and all efforts to implant it there face the problem of competition with already beleaguered industrial producers in Eastern Europe, Latin America, and Asia. Much of the world denies important export markets to semimanufactures from Africa, and other regions simultaneously seek to flood the limited domestic markets in Africa with their own goods. To add insult to injury, Africa has again become a dumping ground for industrial and household wastes from the industrial countries.[1] Although environmentalists in the core protest both the creation of pollution in the industrial countries of the periphery and the dumping of waste in Africa, there is little question that the core societies in which they live benefit from the inexpensive industrial goods available to them and from their privileged place in the global division of labor.

The political and economic structures that the core countries control appear stronger than ever. The understanding of the costs that those structures impose on the periphery, and the extent of opposition to them, has also strengthened, however. Marx and Engels or the world-systems theorists would have no difficulty identifying the contradictions and tensions in the contemporary system. The question is, will the capitalist world system once again prove capable of adapting and surviving, or will the pressures for drastic change this time prove too great?

[1]Some now refer to parts of the continent as "global sacrifice areas."

Technological Advance

Writers of the late twentieth century sometimes suggested that the pace of technological advance was accelerating. They did not anticipate, however, the degree to which the convergence of communications and artificial-intelligence technologies would further force that pace. By the turn of the century, an overlapping set of electronic networks integrated the scientific community globally and allowed simple and low-cost transmission of messages and data. Computerized language translation (still by no means completely bug-free but very serviceable) and the completion of library digitization now provide to scientists in all parts of the world essentially all books, articles, papers, and data from anywhere on the globe. Although political barriers to the free flow of such information were still common in 2000, the necessity of being tied into these networks to maintain the quality of domestic research convinced governments that it was technologically suicidal to restrict access.

Various artificial-intelligence techniques have rapidly increased the ease with which scientists can manipulate the otherwise overwhelming volumes of information and data available to them. Although these techniques still do not deliver on the promise, once felt to be inherent within them, of allowing computers to mimic human intelligence over a broad range of intellectual functions, specialized artificial-intelligence applications (such as information search and organization algorithms, elaborate simulation models, and expert decision-systems) continue to become more sophisticated and useful.

Biotechnology illustrates their importance. The mapping of the genetic structures of a wide variety of flora and fauna (including, of course, humans) would have been impossible without these systems. That mapping allowed an explosion during the last four decades in the numbers of genetically engineered plants and animals. In combination with slowing population growth, and despite considerably extended life expectancies, the new agricultural techniques put an end to food shortages around the world.

Technological advance in energy systems has been no less remarkable. New materials and techniques for construction of solar cells made those cells into what the Japanese call the "rice of the energy system." Ironically, many thought that the transition away from oil and gas would render the OPEC countries less important globally. Instead, the new solar technologies and the extensive desert surfaces of the Middle East have transformed Saudi Arabia and Iraq into large producers of solar energy (using a hydrogen transport system to the rest of the world). The astounding advances of the Russians in small-scale fusion power plants has, however, made it somewhat uncertain exactly which energy form will dominate the energy system of the future.[2]

Unfortunately, military technology has not stagnated either. Laser weapons make the successful delivery of nuclear warheads by missiles uncertain. At the same time, however, those laser weapons are capable of destroying cities and industrial facilities with incredible accuracy and speed. States are rushing to develop

---

[2]Theoretical physicists greatly advanced fusion research by discovering the Whippoorwillian Effect.

them. Although the joint (Russia, the EU, the United States, China, and Japan) mission to Mars illustrated the potential for the great powers to cooperate, the rivalry in military technology poses severe challenges.

Environmental Limits

The population of the world is now 9.2 billion, more than double that of 1970. Demographers early in the century told us that it would grow to 10 billion people before stabilizing near the end of the century. It appears now that global population will likely be less than 8 billion by 2100. The famines and plagues of the last decade in Asia, Latin America, and Africa have stopped population growth, and greater problems loom on the horizon. Global population clearly exceeds the carrying capacity of the global ecosystem. Consider two important pieces of evidence.

First, the greenhouse effect has raised the average global temperature by nearly 2°C and significantly damaged world agricultural capability. Many countries call for dramatic restrictions on the use of fossil fuels and therefore on the emission of CO_2; actual reductions have been minor, and the warming effect will inevitably intensify. Although scientists have done a remarkable job in producing plants capable of withstanding the changed conditions, and a select few countries of the world (like Canada) actually benefit somewhat from the higher temperatures, global grain production has stagnated in the last 30 years.

Exacerbating food production problems, the rising ocean levels (from ice-cap melting) have submerged many productive coastal areas around the world and caused extremely expensive relocation of people from coastal cities to still other once-productive agricultural areas inland. The war between India and Bangladesh resulted from the near elimination of the latter country (a former coastal delta) by higher ocean levels and from the desperate attempt by its peoples to find safe haven. Global refugees now number nearly 400 million, and the problem, especially in Asia, continues to worsen.

Second, attempts to compensate for the absence of growth in agricultural production led to often futile and even counterproductive efforts to increase land under cultivation. It appeared early in the century that Brazil had finally controlled the deforestation of rainforests. By 2010 demand for food reignited the process of forest clearing. The once-lush forests of Indonesia and the Philippines are essentially gone today. These actions, in addition to eliminating precious biological resources, have further accelerated the greenhouse effect. What were once grasslands in a belt across Africa known as the Sahel are now deserts, after disastrous efforts to raise more crops and animals there. The intensification of ocean fishing by fleets from a variety of Asian and Latin American countries led to substantial overfishing and a collapse of world ocean fish catch from 95 million metric tons in 2010 to 40 million tons last year. The dams that India built at such great expense on the watersheds of the Ganges, both for flood control and for irrigation purposes, have lost nearly one-half of their storage capacity already because of silt flows from the deforested slopes of the Himalayas; they could be worthless within ten years.

Population reduction is the top global priority of the more-developed countries. Many Asian, African, and Latin American LDCs are, however, caught in a demographic trap. High population has overstrained resources and led to environmental degradation. This has caused GNP growth per capita to decline for the Third World as a whole in the last ten years. Agricultural production per capita in the South has now declined for 25 years, and food imports and grants from the North are inadequate to sustain dietary standards. Death rates from malnutrition-related causes (such as diarrhea in the young, pneumonia in the old, and influenza and TB in all groups) are increasing sharply. In several countries (including India, Indonesia, Pakistan, Peru, Ecuador, Bolivia, and most of Africa), death rates per thousand population have risen substantially during the last decade, reversing declines that began nearly 100 years ago. Higher birthrates have followed increased death rates as parents seek to replace lost children. Thus even increased starvation has not yet reduced population. Several countries, including Ghana, now follow the path trod earlier by China, applying coercive social controls to reduce population. Many other countries have lost the political capability to undertake coherent social action.

Among the international political consequences of these developments is much greater conflict in the South and along the global North-South dimension. Although the North provides some food and technical assistance, developed countries increasingly feel overwhelmed by the scope of LDC problems, especially in light of significant difficulties of their own (especially coastal flooding and high energy prices).

Last Words

We cannot know the future. As this chapter suggests, however, that future will be critically important to us, because the range of potential scenarios for it is tremendous. Clearly, these scenarios vary not only in their possibility, but also vary greatly in their desirability. Because we humans do shape our world, we have choices to make. We cannot know the future, but we must act as if we do.

More specifically, we must keep asking ourselves three questions.[3] Where do trends and forces appear to be taking our world? Much of this book has drawn your attention to this question and provided tools to address it. What kind of world do we prefer? This book attempted also to provide you some help with this second question. The worldviews contain prescriptive and theoretical elements that certainly should help form your answers. Finally, what leverage do we have in bringing into being the world we prefer? For each of us it may be limited, but we have leverage. Whether and how you attempt to apply your leverage might influence local and even global developments. It will, without doubt, influence your own life.

---

[3]The book and computer simulation called International Futures (IFs) draw our attention to the study of the future and present these three questions as an organizing device (Hughes 1999). The computer simulation allows extensive study of the forces and trends that this volume sketches.

Glossary

Absolute Advantage   The ability to produce a particular good from fewer units of resources than can a trading partner. *See* Comparative Advantage.

Absolute Gain   An approach to cooperation, common in liberal analysis, emphasizing only one's own gain, not one's relative gain, in the interaction.

Acid Rain   Acidic precipitation caused by the release into the air of sulfur and nitrogen compounds from burning fossil fuels; it causes damage to lakes and forests, often across country boundaries.

Action-Reaction Dynamic   When one state attempts to improve or secure its position in the world system, another state takes reactive steps to maintain or improve its own position. The result of such efforts could be an arms race.

Aid Fatigue   Disillusionment by donors with the results of aid and a lessened commitment to it.

Anarchy   Absence of central governmental authority.

Appropriate Technology   Technology that in combination with a country's other factors of production can effectively employ most resources.

Arms Race   Competitive acquisition or production of armaments by two or more countries seeking security and protection against each other.

Associational Revolution   The rapid growth of nongovernmental organizations. It has fueled the global democratization trend.

Attentive Public   A segment of the population, approximately 10–20 percent, that has consistent interest in world affairs. *See* General Public.

Backwash Effects   The flow of capital and labor to more economically developed regions or countries from less-developed ones. *Contrast with* Spread Effects.

Balance of Power   A distribution of power among states in the interstate system. Definitions vary, but most require a relatively equal distribution among two or more states.

423

Bandwagoning   Jumping into support of an actor or coalition likely to win in order to share in the benefits of victory.

Basic Human Needs   Fundamental needs of all humans, including food, shelter, clothing, and education.

Bipolar System   A state system containing two dominant states of relatively equal strength. The system is "tight" when the two dominant states organize lesser powers into strong and opposing alliances. The system is "loose" when the two dominant states do not organize most of the lesser states into strong alliance structures.

Bounded Rationality   Rational decision making within the constraint of incomplete information.

Boycott   The refusal of one country to purchase exports from another country.

Brain Drain   The immigration of educated and professional workers from less-developed countries to more-developed ones, due to the lure of improved living conditions.

Bretton Woods System   The monetary and trade system created after World War II. Two pillars of the system are the International Monetary Fund and the World Bank.

Brinkmanship   When a state knowingly challenges the commitment by another state up to the brink of catastrophe with the expectation that the challenged state will back away from the commitment.

Bureaucratic-Politics Model   A description of decision making in which priorities vary across participating groups, and decisions become compromises in the conflict among those groups. *Contrast with* Organizational-Process Model; Rational-Actor Model.

Capital Accumulation   The buildup of investment, in excess of depreciation.

Carrying Capacity   A limit that indicates the size to which a species population can grow before it overuses the available resources in the ecosystem. *See also* Overshoot and Collapse.

Cartel   A group of actors that collaborate to restrict production of a commodity, attempting to raise market prices and increase profits.

Civil Society   The private and pluralistic world of individual and group interests and activities that operate peacefully within and increasingly among states.

Clash of Civilizations   A vision by Samuel Huntington of a world in which regions defined along cultural lines will become the principal bases for future conflict.

Class   A group of individuals defined by common economic interests. Marx saw in capitalism a tendency toward the formulation of two opposing classes, the bourgeoisie (capital owners) and the proletariat (workers).

Classical Liberalism   A variant of liberalism common in European politics and in academic writing that emphasizes limited government interference in the national economy. *Contrast with* Modern Liberalism.

Coercive Diplomacy   The conduct of diplomacy by stronger powers with the threat of force should weaker states not make concessions.

Cold War   A political and economic struggle between the former Soviet Union and the United States dating from the late 1940s to the collapse of the Soviet Union in 1991 that never resulted in "hot" war between the two states.

Collective Defense   An agreement among states to combine military capabilities and to defend any state under the security umbrella if an outside aggressor attacks that state.

Collective Good   A public good or partially public good, the provision or maintenance of which requires collective action.

Collective Security   An agreement to ensure state security among participating members by agreeing to restrain and punish any aggressive member.

Commercial Liberalism   A political economic perspective on world politics that, like liberalism, emphasizes individuals as the principal actors but focuses on their economic interactions.

Common Market   A group of states that have eliminated tariffs, established a common external tariff, and allowed the free flow of labor and finance among themselves. *See* Scale of Economic Integration.

Common Property Resources   Goods to which all actors have access and over which they compete. *See* Nonexcludability; Rivalry.

Comparative Advantage   The ability to produce a particular good at lower cost (in terms of opportunities lost for the production of other goods) than a trading partner. *See* Absolute Advantage.

Complex Governance   The development of multiple and shifting layers of government (*see* Subsidiarity and Europe of Concentric Circles), with differing depths of integration among different groupings of states (*see* Variable Geometry).

Complex Interdependence   Relations among states that rely upon multiple channels of communication connecting the two societies. Multiple issues, not simply security, reach the agenda, and the states do not resort to military force to resolve problems.

Comprador Class   The elites of less-developed countries that receive economic rewards and political support from multinational corporations and multilateral institutions in exchange for their involvement in the global political economy.

Concepts   Labels for general categories of phenomena.

Conditional Engagement   A foreign-policy orientation that combines containment when a state will not cooperate with engagement when it will. *See* Constrainment.

Conditionality   Specific monetary actions and government policy adjustments that the IMF requires when a country draws on its IMF contributions or when the IMF finances a bailout with loans.

Confidence and Security Building Measures   A method of arms control involving increased contact, information exchange, and cooperation (even joint military maneuvers).

Confucian   An Asian religious/philosophic system placing great emphasis on basic patterns of social relationship, including those between parent and child.

Congestion A characteristic of a good that involves increased competition over it as more actors demand more units of the good. *See also* Rivalry.

Constrainment A foreign-policy orientation that combines containment when a state will not cooperate with engagement when it will. *See also* Conditional Engagement.

Constructivism A worldview that portrays the world in terms of identity groupings and other social constructs or structures, including those of relationship and governance.

Containment A foreign policy orientation that seeks to deny another state the possibility of expanding its influence outside existing borders or sphere of interest. The United States once sought to contain the Soviet Union and has more recently sought "double containment" of Iraq and Iran.

Conversion The recruitment of peoples into a religion.

Convertibility of Wealth and Power A basic assertion by mercantilists that states can use power to attain wealth and draw upon wealth to augment power.

Cooperation under Anarchy A belief that within the anarchical interstate system, cooperation among states can still occur.

Coordination Goods Goods whose availability does not suffer with additional consumption of them (availability may even grow), but from which actors can be excluded. *See* Nonexcludability; Rivalry.

Coordination Power The strength that identity groups gain from their social connections. *See also* Exchange Power.

Core A term used to describe the high-income states that dominate the world system. *See* Periphery.

Core Interests The primary concerns of states, namely to protect their territorial boundaries, population, government, and sovereignty.

Countermercantilist Policies Retaliatory trade policies carried out against states that take advantage of cooperative trade agreements.

Crisis A circumstance or event that threatens high-priority goals, limits the time available for a response, and surprises the decision makers.

Crisis Management Reducing the risk of conflict in a crisis by recognizing that perceptions may be flawed, anticipating in advance the need for communication channels to minimize misunderstandings, maximizing information quality, and preserving options.

Critical Theory A mode of thought that steps away from the prevailing order of the world and asks how the particular order came about, often with the intention of suggesting change.

Cross-Cutting Cleavages The concept that in a multipolar world, countries can develop alliances with some countries on particular issues and other countries on different issues.

Crude Birth Rate Total annual births per thousand population.

Crude Death Rate   Total annual deaths per thousand population.

Culture Wars   Intrasocietal divisions between the more orthodox or fundamentalist adherents to religions and the more secularized or liberal adherents.

Customs Union   A group of states that have eliminated tariffs among themselves and created a common external tariff. *See* Scale of Economic Integration.

Cycles of (Capitalist) Expansion   A belief of world-systems theorists that capitalist development occurs in long waves of alternating growth and recession but with an underlying tendency for progressive waves to expand the size of the global system.

Deepening   Intensified integration within a set of countries. *See also* Widening.

Deforestation   The widespread elimination of forests.

Delay   The time lag between one activity and another, for instance, between an action that affects the environment and significant changes in the environment.

Democratic Deficit   Insufficiencies in direct control by citizens of the institutions and processes of the European Union.

Democratic Peace   The absence of war among states with democratic governments. *See also* Zone of Peace.

Demographic Transition   A shift from high fertility and mortality rates to low fertility and mortality rates.

Demographic Trap   Rapid population growth in developing countries that results in environmental degradation, economic poverty, political instability, and continued high population growth rates.

Demonstration Force   Limited force used by great powers to demonstrate capability and willingness to employ more power.

Dependency Theory   A variation of neo-Marxism focusing on the nature of contemporary relationships between core and periphery countries. The theory often focuses on the negative consequences of foreign penetration into the political economies of less-developed countries.

Dependent Population   The youngest and oldest portions of a population, which require health care, food, and education, while making little contribution to economic productivity.

Desertification   The process whereby land intended for agriculture becomes nonarable or turns to desert after natural vegetation is removed or poor soil-conservation methods are employed.

Détente   An easing of tensions among states, often specifically the period of tension reduction and engagement in the Cold War.

Diaspora   The dispersion of a religious or ethnic group to regions outside its homeland.

Diffuse Reciprocity   An exchange between two actors in which value given and received are not closely matched at any point in time, because a contextual relationship allows at least temporary imbalances. *See* Specific Reciprocity.

Diffusion (Technological)   The movement of a new technology, which initially has limited economic impact, into economic sectors where it definitively increases productivity; the third phase of a Kondratieff cycle.

Diplomacy   The conduct of foreign policy through the exchange of representatives, communication, and negotiation among states so as to influence each others' decisions and actions.

Diplomatic Immunity   Diplomats are not subject to prosecution for criminal action in a host country.

Dispute Resolution   Nonviolent activities, such as negotiation, mediation, arbitration, and judicial settlement, that diffuse tensions and reduce conflict.

Division of Labor   A specialization in the production of goods that increases the amount of output per hour of labor.

Doubly Green Revolution   A green revolution that increases agricultural production but is also "green" (environmentally friendly).

Dual Economy   An economy in which some sectors or regions have significant characteristics of a developed economy, but the rest of the economy remains traditional. *Compare with* Enclave Economy.

Dual-Use Technology   Technology that can have either civilian or military application.

Dynamic Gains from Trade   Improvements in production efficiency that result from the adoption of better technology to meet the competition of trade.

Ecoconflict   Interstate conflict over scarce resources or other environmental issues.

Economic Integration   (1) Ongoing and deepening economic cooperation among states; (2) the complete dominance of centralized economic institutions over those of the state. *See* Scale of Economic Integration.

Economic Throughput   The level of economic impact, as indicated by the consumption of resources and the output of pollutants, that is associated with a given level of human well-being. Eco-wholists urge minimization of throughput.

Economic Union   A group of states that have established a common external tariff; the free flow of goods, services, labor, and finance; harmony of economic policies; and a common currency. *See* Scale of Economic Integration.

Ecosystem   An integrated biological community in interaction with its physical environment.

Eco-Wholism   A worldview that believes environmental constraints on human systems to be very significant and that technological advance cannot ultimately eliminate those constraints.

Efficiency   Maximum production possible with given resources.

Elasticity (Price)   The responsiveness of supply or demand to changes in the price level.

Embargo   The refusal of one country to export goods to another country, combined normally with efforts to stop exports by others as well.

Enclave Economies   Geographical portions of a less-developed country's economy to which multinational corporations provide the luxuries of living in North America or Europe, while the surrounding economy remains relatively uninfluenced. *See also* Dual Economy.

Energy Crisis   A label given to the first and second oil shocks of the 1970s, when it appeared that they marked the beginning of a prolonged period of energy shortages.

Energy Transition   A shift in the predominant source of global fuel, such as from wood to coal or from coal to a combination of oil and gas.

Epistemic Communities   Informal and potentially global clusters of individuals sharing similar understandings on specific issues.

Epistemology   The study of the origins and nature of knowledge.

Equality   Similar income or wealth distribution. *Contrast with* Equity.

Equilibrium   A situation in which there is little tendency for change because opposing forces are roughly in balance. For example, a balance of power.

Equity   Impartiality and fairness in opportunities. *Contrast with* Equality.

Ethnic Cleansing   A term adopted by Serbs in Bosnia to imply mass expulsions and to mask the combination of expulsions with genocide.

Europe of Concentric Circles   A model of European integration that represents it as a core of states with a high level of integration and wider circles of states that exhibit decreasing levels of integration.

Excess Returns   Higher than normal profits.

Exchange Power   The strength that exchange or trade gives to those who engage in it. *See also* Coordination Power.

Expected Utility Theory   A theory that leaders of states weigh the costs and benefits of war, with or without allies on either side. If a state can expect a net positive utility, it will initiate war.

Exploitation of the Big by the Small   The tendency for smaller actors joining an organization (such as a military alliance) to obtain the benefits while contributing fewer resources than larger actors.

Extended Family   A family including more than the parents and children of a nuclear family.

Externality   A cost or benefit that does not accrue to those who produce or consume a good; for example, environmental pollution.

Factor Price Equalization   The convergence across countries of the prices of factors of production in the face of trade, financial flows, and information flows.

Factors of Production   Land, labor, capital, and technology, the basic components for production of goods and services.

Facts   Unpatterned, objectively verifiable information.

Failed States   Countries and governments that have lost the ability to organize coherent social response to internal or external threats.

Fascism   An ideology that glorifies the nation and its state and that supports authoritarian government and strong action against those outside of the nation-state.

Fast-Track Authority   Authorization given by a legislative body to an executive body allowing negotiation of an interstate agreement, such as a trade treaty, with the promise that the legislature will approve or reject the treaty without amendments.

Federalism   A system of government that divides authority between a central government and regional or subdivisional governments.

Feminism   The valuing of experiences and contributions of women equally with those of men and the movement for equal rights of women and men.

First Oil Shock   A dramatic increase in the price of oil in 1973, following OPEC's restriction on oil exports during the October 1973 war.

First Strike   When a state preemptively launches a nuclear attack against its opponent.

Fixed Exchange Rate   A relative value for the currencies of two countries that central banks do not allow to fluctuate from day to day. *See* Floating Exchange Rate.

Flexible Response   A U.S. retaliatory strategy toward the Soviet Union after 1957 that tailored threatened U.S. responses more closely in magnitude to Soviet provocations than had the policy of massive retaliation.

Floating Exchange Rate   Fluctuating exchange rates that supply and demand determine in an open market. *See* Fixed Exchange Rate.

Foreign Direct Investment (FDI)   Interstate capital flows through which a firm in one country acquires, creates, or expands a subsidiary in another country. *Contrast with* Foreign Portfolio Equity Investment.

Foreign-Exchange Trading   The buying and selling of currencies of other states.

Foreign Portfolio Equity Investment (FPEI)   The acquisition of financial assets in another state. *Contrast with* Foreign Direct Investment.

Fourth World   (1) Indigenous or native peoples fighting for cultural survival, generally living in poverty within states that incorporate their homelands; (2) those less-developed countries in the Third World that have exhibited least growth and development.

Framing Decision Situations   Presenting decision-making situations so as to increase the probability that actors will make particular decisions.

Free Rider   An actor that consumes a collective good but makes no contribution to the provision of that good.

Free-Trade Area   A group of states that has eliminated tariffs and border restrictions among themselves. *See* Scale of Economic Integration.

Functional IGOs   Intergovernmental organizations that address a specific issue.

Functionalism (Functionalist Theory)   A theory that interstate cooperation can productively begin on noncontroversial and technical issues and ultimately entangle states in a web of very extensive cooperation, perhaps even political integration. *See also* Neofunctionalism.

Fundamentalism A perspective characterized by rigid belief in basic principles, often rooted in religious text and traditional interpretation.

Fungible Easily converted from one form to another; for instance, a traded good, the units of which cannot be distinguished by origin.

General Public The approximately 80 percent of the population that has some knowledge of, or interest in, world affairs. *See* Attentive Public.

Genocide The systematic and/or widespread murder of people based on their ethnicity, religion, or other shared characteristic.

Geopolitics A school of thought dominant in the early twentieth century stressing the influence of geographic factors on state power and interstate relations.

Globalization Worldwide processes of increased technological, trade, financial, and informational flows that penetrate countries and affect domestic society.

Governance Norms Values and beliefs that define how the community should be organized and governed.

Great-Person Theories A belief that one individual's personality and actions can significantly influence states and global events.

Great Powers States that possess, pursue, or defend interests throughout the global system.

Green Revolution The development in the 1950s of new strains of grain, highly responsive to fertilizer, that substantially increased total yields.

Greenhouse Effect A rise in the global temperature due to emissions of carbon dioxide and other gases into the atmosphere. The greenhouse gases permit sunlight to penetrate the atmosphere but trap heat radiation from leaving the atmosphere.

Groupthink The tendency for members of a decision-making group to conform to the group's or leader's opinions.

Gunboat Diplomacy A great power's threat or use of military force, traditionally naval, in order to coerce another state.

Hegemonic Power or State A single state that has a dominant political and economic position in the world order.

Hegemonic Stability Theory A theory that a hegemonic power uses its military and economic strength in the world system to encourage a free flow of goods and technology and/or to promote peaceful cooperation among states on a wide range of issues.

Hegemonic Transition Theory A theory that explains why one hegemon replaces another hegemon and suggests that conflict typically arises when the challenging state forces the transition.

High Politics Politics surrounding military and strategic questions. *See* Low Politics.

Human Capital A work force's productive capabilities as expanded via experience, education, and maintenance of health.

Human Rights Those privileges that international agreements and documents such as the Universal Declaration of Human Rights declare due to all human beings.

Idealism   A less analytical variant of liberalism, whose proponents advocate extensive cooperation in the global system and who believe that interdependence among states makes possible extensive collaboration to solve common problems. In contrast to traditional realism, idealism posits a positive view of human nature.

Identity Group   A set of individuals with mutual affinity based on a shared perception of common characteristics and/or interests.

Ideology   A system of beliefs that explains and justifies a preferred sociopolitical order and that may offer a strategy for attainment of it.

Imperialism   A relationship of dominance and subordination through which one state controls the territory and people of another area.

Import Substitution   A development strategy whereby states set high tariff walls and provide heavy subsidies to protect infant industry growth. Production is intended for domestic consumption with the goal of eliminating dependence on imports.

Industrial Revolution   The extensive introduction of automated machinery, beginning in England in the late 1700s, that allowed mass production of goods.

Infant Industries   Start-up industries that do not produce goods as efficiently and competitively as previously established firms and often initially operate behind a tariff wall to prevent firm failure.

Information Dominance   The aim of countries on the modern battlefield to monopolize intelligence and weapon control information.

Information Revolution   The greatly increased reliance of the economy and society on information storage, flows, and use, beginning in the late twentieth century.

Innovation   The establishment of new products, methods, and practices in an economy; the second phase of a Kondratieff cycle.

Institutions   The formal and informal rules of the game within which politics take place.

Instrumental Interests   The objectives of states that arise from particular interpretations of how best to pursue core interests.

Integration   An ongoing and deepening process of political and economic linkage among states.

Interest Aggregation   The collection or summation of specialized interests in the political process, often by political parties.

Interest Articulation   The expression of specialized interests in the political process, often by interest groups.

Intergovernmental Organizations (IGOs)   Organizations whose members are states.

International Nongovernmental Organizations (NGOs or INGOs)   International organizations whose members are private individuals and groups from various countries.

International System   A term most often used to mean the interstate system, that is, the set of states and their political, economic, and social interactions. It could, however, more accurately refer to the world's nations and their interactions.

Internationalist   One who believes that states must continuously participate in the international system to pursue their basic interests.

Interstate System   The set of states and their interactions.

Intrastate Analysis   A focus on forces internal to states to explain world politics, an approach that realists accept to a limited extent.

Irredentism   The desire of a state controlled by a nation to incorporate fellow nationals in other states and the territory they occupy. Irredentism motivated the German annexation of portions of Czechoslovakia prior to World War II.

Isolationist   One who believes that more danger and risk than opportunity exist in engagement with other states. With limited resources, a state should focus its efforts on solving domestic problems and improving the livelihood of its own citizens.

Issues Linkage   The tying together of interaction and possible cooperation on multiple issues.

Just War   A view that some wars are just or moral, perhaps by reason of self-defense or redress of injury, or perhaps to do "God's will."

Knowosphere   The accumulated body of human knowledge.

Kondratieff Cycles   Fifty-to-sixty-year time periods in which the world economy completes a cycle that begins with technological **innovation,** moves to **diffusion** of new technology around the world, and results in economic upswings, before the technology matures and growth slows. *Compare with* Cycles of Expansion; Long Waves.

Kuznets Curve   A relationship suggesting that as GNP per capita rises in a country, income inequality rises initially and then gradually declines.

Labor Productivity   The amount of output that a unit of labor can produce.

Laissez Faire   A French term popularized by Adam Smith in the 1700s advocating a hands-off approach to government involvement in the economy.

Laissez Innover   A term used in conscious reference to laissez faire, meaning to advocate freedom for research and innovation with minimal government regulation or interference.

Law-Making Treaties   Multilateral agreements with widespread support. Signatory states may apply considerable pressure for acquiescence by nonsignatories. *See also* specific treaties.

Levels of Analysis   Categories of variables at the intrastate, state, and state system levels that explain how states act in the global system.

Liberalism   A worldview that focuses on individuals acting in a generally rational manner to seek more freedom, better living conditions, physical security, and other values.

Liberation Theology   A movement within Catholicism of Latin America to direct the efforts of the church toward economic and social as well as religious needs of practitioners. This can lead to active support for broader social-system change on behalf of the disadvantaged.

Long Waves   Often a synonym for Kondratieff cycles. Some political economists also use the term, however, to refer to a cycle in global system leadership that may run over two Kondratieff cycles or approximately 100 years.

Low Politics   Politics surrounding economic and environmental issues. *See* High Politics.

Lowest Common Denominator Principle   The making of decisions so as to satisfy those members of the group least willing to accept change or make sacrifice. Often said to characterize the European Union.

Macroenvironment   Large-scale environmental concerns, such as pollution, population size, food, and energy issues. *Contrast with* Microenvironment.

Major Powers   *See* Great Powers.

Market Failures   Structural impediments such as monopolies and externalities that prevent markets from determining true costs and benefits.

Massive Retaliation   A one-time American policy that threatened nuclear devastation of the Soviet Union, if it expanded beyond its already established sphere of influence. *See* Flexible Response.

Medium Theory   The argument that communications media themselves (not simply specific content) have social impact.

Mercantilism   An economic philosophy and practice of extensive government involvement in a country's economy so as to increase the power and security of the state. It is a variant of realism.

Microenvironment   Environmental concerns at the level of bacteria and viruses. *Contrast with* Macroenvironment.

Military-Industrial Complex   An interacting set of individuals from defense contractors, the defense bureaucracy, and the Congress, who are said to influence foreign policy.

Minimum Winning Coalition Principle   *See* Size Principle.

Misperception   Not seeing a situation objectively, but being influenced by one's own lack of information or psychological make-up.

Modern Liberalism   A variant of liberalism common in the United States that stresses the importance of the individual, but advocates significant government action on behalf of a more equal distribution of opportunities within society. *See also* Classical Liberalism.

Modernism   A worldview that emphasizes how technological advance and increased human knowledge improve the quality of life.

Modernization Theory   A theory of the transformation of countries from low levels of economic and political development to high ones that emphasizes the interconnectedness of various elements in the process.

Most Favored Nation (MFN) Status   Eligibility for the lowest tariffs granted to any trading partner of a state.

Multilateralism   An approach to foreign policy that relies upon collective rather than unilateral action.

Multinational Corporation (MNC)   A business organization with assets (foreign direct investment) in two or more countries.

Multiple-Purpose IGOs   Intergovernmental organizations that exist for cooperation on more than one issue.

Multipolar System   An interstate system in which a minimum of three states (frequently five or six powers) of relatively equal power dominate.

Mutual Assured Destruction (MAD)   A situation in which two states both possess the ability to survive a first nuclear attack and to launch a devastating retaliatory attack. Regardless of who attacks first, both sides would be destroyed, thus giving rise to great caution on both sides.

Mutually Beneficial Exchange (or Trade)   A statement of the principle that those who trade goods and services will do so only if they each gain.

Nation   A group of individuals who identify with each other based on ethnic, linguistic, and cultural similarities, and who believe they have a common heritage or destiny.

Nation-State   A term that implies the coincidence of state and nation boundaries, but which is often used loosely as a synonym for country.

National Character   Supposedly common characteristics or attributes of members of a nation.

Nationalism   The desire by people with a sense of self-identity as a nation to control their own affairs and possibly to exclude others from them.

Naturalist View of International Law   An approach that sees international law as fundamental principles that originate in divine law or human nature. *Contrast with* Positivist View of International Law.

Near Abroad   A term used by Russia to refer to the states surrounding Russia that once were republics in the Soviet Union.

Neocolonialism   Subtle, at least relative to imperialism and colonialism, domination of the South by the North via unequal exchange, economic penetration, and the institutionalized regimes of the world political economy.

Neofunctionalism   A school of thought that builds upon the logic of functionalism, but argues that elites need periodically to push the integration process forward in significant leaps.

Neo-Marxism   New or modern perspectives in the Marxist tradition, still focusing on class structures within and between countries, but less definitive than traditional Marxism about the transformation to socialism.

Neomercantilism   Mercantilism of the modern era, whose proponents argue that states should attempt to maintain a balance of payments surplus through promoting domestic production, reducing imports with tariffs and nontariff barriers, and encouraging exports.

Neorealism   A relatively theoretical branch of realist theory that, in explaining state behavior, emphasizes the anarchical structure of the interstate system and the distribution of capabilities among states, not human nature.

Neotraditionalist   *See* Eco-Wholism.

New Diplomacy   Diplomatic negotiations conducted overtly with significant media attention. *Contrast with* Old Diplomacy.

New International Economic Order (NIEO)   An agenda for change in the global political economy set by Southern leaders in 1973 that called for help, such as easier access to IMF credits, the development of a debt-relief program, and more foreign aid.

Newly Industrialized Countries (NICs)   Economies that have relied heavily upon exporting industrial products to achieve high rates of GDP growth. They include Hong Kong, Singapore, South Korea, and Taiwan.

Nonexcludability   A characteristic of a *good,* access to which cannot be restricted or denied to specific actors.

Nongovernmental Organizations (NGOs)   *See* International Nongovernmental Organizations.

Nonintervention   A basic legal principle in international law that denies states the right to interfere in the domestic affairs of other states.

Nonprovocative Defense   A method of national defense that reduces the probability of an arms race by restructuring military capabilities toward those that have negligible *offensive* potential.

Nontariff Trade Barriers (NTBs)   Attempts by states to limit imports of foreign goods through the use of measures like quotas, health standards, inspection requirements, and orderly marketing agreements.

Nonzero-Sum   A situation in which gains and losses across actors are not offsetting. *See* Zero-Sum.

Nuclear Family   A family involving parents and children only. *Contrast with* Extended Family.

Nuclear-Weapon Nonproliferation   A category of arms-control measures that seeks to prevent the spread of nuclear capabilities to nonnuclear states.

Nuclear Winter   The environmental repercussions following a nuclear war should a cloud of smoke from burning cities and forests prevent sunlight from entering the earth's atmosphere for a significant period of time.

Obsolescing Bargain   A shift in negotiating strength between host countries and multinational corporations. At the time of foreign direct-investment decisions, MNCs have relatively greater strength, but once investment is in place, power shifts to the host country.

Official Development Assistance (ODA)   Foreign aid that is concessional in character, with a grant component of at least 25 percent.

Oil Shocks   Rapid and substantial increases or decreases in oil prices that cause significant instability in financial and other markets.

Old Diplomacy   Covert diplomatic negotiations and treaties. *Contrast with* New Diplomacy.

Opinion Leaders   A very small segment, approximately 1 percent, of the population with significant knowledge and interest in world affairs and with the ability to communicate opinions and understanding to others.

Optimizing   Efforts to make decisions as in the rational actor model, thereby making the "best possible" decision.

Organizational-Process Model   A portrayal of decision making in which organizations rely primarily upon standard operating procedures and only slowly incorporate lessons learned from previous decisions. *Contrast with* Bureaucratic-Politics Model; Rational-Actor Model.

Overshoot and Collapse   The excess growth of a process (such as the growth of a species population) that continues until it overuses available resources and, after a lag period, collapses. *See also* Carrying Capacity.

Ozone Hole   A gap in the ozone level of the atmosphere over the Antarctic that appears to be growing due to the increased global use of chlorofluorocarbons (CFCs) and halons.

Paradox of Unrealized Power   The apparent victory of lesser powers over greater powers when the stronger fail to fully utilize all power resources, for example, the failure of the United States in Vietnam.

Partially Public Goods   Goods that exhibit nonrivalry (*see* Rivalry) or nonexcludability, but not both characteristics. *See* Public Goods.

Peace Keeping   United Nations efforts, generally using low levels of resources, to bring stability to war-torn regions without confronting great powers or identifying a particular aggressor.

Penetration   Intrusion into other societies via modern communications and transportation technology.

Periphery   A term used to describe the subordinate states of the world system, historically those that provided raw materials to the core economies.

Pluralism   The existence in modern society of numerous organizations and institutions that peacefully compete and cooperate.

Pluralist Model   A decision-making model that emphasizes competition among interest groups in the effort to influence policy decisions.

Pluralistic Security Community   A geographic region where established institutions and ingrained practices result in long-term peace and stability.

Polarity   A distribution of power in the state system, specified in terms of the number of major powers.

Polis   The ancient Greek city-state.

Political Ecology   A field of study that combines attention to politics, economics, and the natural environment.

Political Economy   A field of study that combines attention to politics, economics, and their interaction.

Political Integration The relinquishing by states of their sovereignty over political, economic, and security domains to central institutions.

Positive Feedback Loop A linked set of variables in which increases in one variable lead to increases in one or more others, which in turn "feed back" to increases in the first. Similarly, decreases "feed back" to decreases in the initiating variable.

Positivism A mode of thought in which knowledge is based on objective and reproducible observation, largely independent of time, place, and circumstance. Positivists believe that knowledge is generalized through concepts, laws, and theories about the external world. *Contrast with* Postmodernism.

Positivist View of International Law A generally realist position that international law is what states make it and that they will emphasize state sovereignty with voluntary and limited consent to international law. *Contrast with* Naturalist View of International Law.

Postmodernism A mode of thought, sometimes contrasted with positivism, in which knowledge is understood to be both relative to the perceptual framework of the observer and often not generalizable across time, place, and circumstance.

Power The ability to influence outcomes.

Power-Transition Theory An argument that the greatest possibility of war occurs when the balance of power is changing and the emerging state has eliminated the power differential between itself and the dominant state. *See* Hegemonic Transition Theory.

Prisoner's Dilemma A model used in game theory that indicates how seemingly rational individual action can lead to collectively irrational outcomes.

Private Goods Goods over which individuals or states compete and can exercise *exclusive* ownership.

Privatization Transfer of ownership from the public to the private sector. Privatization can create excludability (*see* Nonexcludability) for a collective good.

Privileged Group A group of consumers of a collective good who benefit because a subgroup has sufficient incentive to produce the good for all.

Product Cycle Theory Although profits are high in newly developed industries, increased competition subsequently drives them down. At some point, normally when profits have fallen, producers transfer operations to the South in an effort to reduce costs of production.

Propositions Statements of relationship linking two concepts.

Prospect Theory A set of propositions concerning how individuals make decisions when there is uncertainty in outcomes.

Proxy An actor working in the interest of others.

Proxy War A war in which a great power uses other parties to fight on its behalf in order to avoid direct military confrontation.

Public Goods Goods that anyone can access and over which there is no competition. *See* Rivalry; Nonexcludability.

Punctuated Equilibrium The theory that biological systems have long periods of relative stability (equilibrium) interrupted by periodic episodes of rapid change. Social change could occur in similar fashion.

Purchasing Power Parity A calculation of GDP and other economic variables that values goods and services at equivalent prices across countries. The IMF began using it in 1993.

Qualitative Arms Limitations A method of arms control that focuses on prohibiting possession or use of certain *categories* of weapons.

Quantitative Arms Limitations An approach to arms control that numerically limits specific weapons systems.

Quota A quantitative restriction on imports.

Racism The social definition of differences among peoples and the pattern of relationships that people build upon those definitions.

Ranked Nations A hierarchical social pattern that sometimes exists between ethnic groups within a state.

Rational-Actor Model An idealized portrayal of decision making in which sufficient information is available to identify policy options, assess the potential consequences of each option, and choose the option best able to attain a goal. *Contrast with* Bureaucratic-Politics Model; Organizational-Process Model.

Rationality The ability of decision makers to choose the best means to achieve a desired end.

Realism A worldview in global politics that sees states as the key actors in world affairs and as rational, autonomous, and unitary actors, whose behavior is shaped by the state of anarchy in the world system. Because states are fundamentally concerned with their security and their capabilities relative to other states, some conflict is inevitable.

Realpolitik Policies that attempt to maximize a state's security and power in an anarchical system with limited attention to issues of morality. Also known as "power politics."

Reciprocity A response in kind, either conflictual or cooperative.

Refugees Individuals who have fled their state in fear of physical danger.

Regime According to Krasner, the principles, norms, rules, and decision-making procedures around which actors' expectations converge in a given issue area.

Regional Disarmament or Nonmilitarization Treaties eliminating or prohibiting military armaments within a specific geographical region.

Regional IGOs Intergovernmental organizations comprised of states from a particular geographic region.

Relational Norms Values about interaction that characterize socially defined groups.

Relative Gain Within the neorealist tradition it is common to posit that a state will cooperate only if it gains as much as other states. *Contrast with* Absolute Gain.

Resistance Point   The minimally acceptable outcome for a party in diplomatic negotiation.

Respondent Superior   A defense against charges of war crimes based upon the claim that the defendant acted under orders of a higher officer or official.

Revolution in Military Affairs   The thrust toward combining intelligence gathering, information processing, and precision-guided weapons on the modern battlefield.

Risk-Acceptant   A willingness to accept the possibility of significant losses with the hope of receiving larger gains. *See* Risk-Averse.

Risk-Averse   An unwillingness to take actions that may result in losses of significant value. *See* Risk-Acceptant.

Rivalry   A characteristic of a good when only one state or individual can benefit from a specific unit of it.

Satisficing   A term coined by Herbert Simon to suggest that most organizations aim for satisfactory rather than optimal decisions.

Scale of Economic Integration   Five progressive stages of integration among states: free-trade areas, customs unions, common markets, economic union, and total economic integration.

Secession   The splitting off of a nation from a state to form its own nation-state.

Second Oil Shock   A second dramatic increase in the price of oil between 1979 and 1980, following a revolution in Iran and restricted oil production.

Second Strike   A state's reactive nuclear attack, after having absorbed a first strike.

Security Dilemma   The inability to protect oneself and enhance one's own security without threatening the security of others. *See also* Action-Reaction Dynamic.

Self-Determination   A doctrine proclaiming that a nation has the right to capture or create its own state and determine a political authority that will represent and rule it.

Self-Reliance   A strategy of less-developed countries that minimizes economic contact with developed economies and deals with those economies only on terms set by the less-developed countries so as to obtain a greater share of the benefits.

Sexism   The social definition of distinctions between genders and the patterns of relationship based on those definitions.

Shadow of the Future   State interaction (especially cooperation) in the present with the recognition that outcomes will affect interactions in the future.

Shuttle Diplomacy   Repeated travel among participating diplomatic camps by a negotiator in order to reach an agreement.

Side Payments   Exchanges among cooperating actors unrelated to the central issue, normally to help equalize costs and benefits of cooperation.

Size Principle   The tendency for alliances of states to be large enough to defeat an enemy yet not diminish shares in the victors' gains.

Slavery   The total subjugation of people via the definition of ownership by others.

Smart Sanctions   Sanctions intended to hurt the leadership of target countries rather than a broader population.

Social Capital   Social trust, networks, and norms that provide the basis for healthy and successful societies.

Social Constructivism   *See* Constructivism.

Social Constructs   Identities, relationships, and ideas that structure social relations.

Social Contract   A voluntary granting by individuals of the power to rule to a strong central authority in order to overcome anarchy in society.

Social Mobilization   The process of transforming the conditions and attitudes of people from those of traditional societies to those of modern ones.

Soft Law   International treaties and pronouncements that may significantly influence even states that are not signatories.

Soft Power   The influence of a state resulting from the appeal abroad of its culture and institutions.

Sovereignty   The principle that no authority exists above the state. The state is the supreme decision-making authority in the global system, and each is a legally equal player in the global environment.

Specific Reciprocity   An exchange between two actors in which value given is closely matched to value received. *See* Diffuse Reciprocity.

Specific Treaties   A treaty, often between two states, without regional or global ramifications. *See also* Law-Making Treaties.

Spheres of Influence   Geographic areas under the influence or domination of a great power.

Spillover   Increased cooperation among states in an issue area as a result of pressures that arise from cooperation in a prior issue area. A concept within functionalism.

Spoiler   A free rider in the consumption of a collective good that consumes so much that it undercuts efforts by others to provide the good.

Spread Effects   The diffusion of well-being from more- to less-developed areas and sectors within countries or regional economic organizations. This can be frustrated by backwash effects.

Stable Nuclear Balance   Neither nuclear power is likely to initiate a nuclear first strike knowing that the other side has a second strike capability and that both sides would therefore be destroyed. *See* Mutually Assured Destruction.

Stages of (Economic) Growth   A theory of economic development that outlined consecutive stages that would lead less-developed countries to advanced levels.

State   An entity occupying a definite territory, having an organized government with control over its territory and population, not answering to outside authorities, and recognized by other states as a legally equal actor.

Statecraft   A state's ability to understand the contemporary state system and to skillfully pursue its interests through diplomacy, economic instruments, and the use of force.

State Interests   The primary concerns of a country, namely to preserve its boundaries and system of government and to protect its population from outside forces. Secondary or more specific interests grow from these core interests.

State System   The collection of states in the world and their interactions. *See also* International System.

State Terrorism   The use by states of the tactics of terrorism, including attacks on property and life, meant to instill fear.

Status Discrepancy   A theory rooted in psychology, suggesting that if the perceived systemic position of a state is below the state's actual capabilities, frustration and dissatisfaction of the state will lead to interstate tension and perhaps conflict.

Stolper-Samuelson Theorem   Protection against imports helps the owners (within that country) of factors of production in which the country is poorly endowed and, conversely, hurts the owners of factors in which it is comparatively richly endowed. Protection frustrates full benefit from comparative advantage.

Strategic Trade Theory   A belief that government intervention in trade can improve the welfare of the people. For instance, states can create a comparative advantage for domestic industries.

Structural Realism   *See* Neorealism.

Structural Transformations   Changes in a state's economy with development, including a shift from production of primary to manufactured goods and then to services, increases in education levels, and often greater ties to the world economy.

Subsidiarity   A perspective on European integration that urges a decentralization of governmental functions toward the lowest level at which they can be performed efficiently.

Superpowers   States that possess extraordinary amounts of diplomatic, military, or economic power that enable them to pursue global roles in world affairs.

Supporters   Countries other than the systemic leader that make significant contributions to the provision of collective goods.

Sustainable Development   Economic growth that does not deplete the resources needed to maintain continued growth.

System   A set of units or actors and the interactions among them.

System Transformation   A neo-Marxist concept of the ultimate shift of the current capitalist order to a socialist system.

Tariff   A tax on goods imported from another country.

Technological Mercantilism   A variation of mercantilism focused on maximizing the technological advantage of a state. Tools include encouraging domestic cooperation between government and industry for the development of new technologies, and restricting the transfer abroad of technology.

Technology   The stock of knowledge and skills necessary to use resources in production; knowledge adapted to human purposes.

Terms of Trade   The ratio of the price of exports from one country to the price of exports from another. It is the change over time in the terms of trade that interests us.

Territorial States   States that seek territorial gains. *Contrast with* Trading States.

Terrorism   Activities of relatively weak social forces against strong states and governments. Terrorists target property and human life, seek media publicity for a particular cause, and often hope to create fear and overreaction of targeted communities through their unpredictable attacks on symbolic sites.

Theocratic   A governmental form involving religious control of government.

Theory   Clusters of interrelated propositions used to explain and sometimes to predict.

Theory of Hegemonic Stability   *See* Hegemonic Stability Theory.

Third Oil Shock   Significant oil surpluses sharply pushed down the price of crude oil in the late 1980s, forcing oil-exporting states to retrench economically.

Tied Aid   Foreign aid that requires the recipient to spend the money in the donor country.

Tit for Tat   A strategy in game theory in which an actor carries out the same actions in this round that the other player did in the previous round.

Trading States   States that seek gains through trade with others, in contrast with territorial states.

Tragedy of the Commons   A reference to the ancient tradition of a communal grazing area for livestock, on which privately rational decisions to use common resources lead to collectively irrational overuse.

Transaction Costs   The costs of a decision-making process, including bringing negotiators together, gathering information, and bargaining.

Transfer Pricing   The internal pricing for goods moved across borders, but within a corporation.

Transnational Corporation (TNC)   *See* Multinational Corporation.

Transnational Social Movement Organizations (TSMO)   International nongovernmental organizations motivated by the pursuit of a specific social goal.

Transnationalism   The proliferation of global interactions among multinational corporations, nongovernmental organizations, and international organizations, facilitated by advances in communication and transportation technology.

Transparency   Open and free availability of information.

Triad   The three delivery systems for nuclear bombs: land-based missiles, submarine-based missiles, and aircraft.

Turning Point   A point in an ongoing process at which the rate of growth reaches a maximum or minimum or changes sign. More colloquially, a significant transitional point in any ongoing process.

Unanticipated Consequences   In an environmental context, effects of action on the environment not foreseen by humans.

Unconventional Warfare   Force, including guerrilla warfare, involving hit-and-run tactics.

Uneven Development   The phenomenon of economic growth and transformation in only selected geographic areas or economic sectors. *See* Dual Economy; Enclave Economy.

Unipolar System   A state system dominated by a single great power.

Unit Veto System   A multipolar system in which all great powers have an absolute veto (such as that which nuclear weapons convey) over aggressive actions of others.

Universal IGOs   Intergovernmental organizations comprised of states from around the world.

Universalism   A subcategory of social constructivist perspectives that emphasizes global identities and relationships, often including forms of global governance.

Unstable Nuclear Balance   When one or both states lack the ability to launch a second strike and therefore have a special incentive to launch a first strike.

Utility   An economic term used to describe the level of satisfaction that a consumer derives from a particular basket of goods.

Variable Geometry   A pattern of integration in which the groups of states that have progressed furthest in the integrative process vary by issue area.

Virtuous Cycle   A process in which improvement in some condition facilitates further improvement. *See also* Positive Feedback Loop.

Widening   Expansion of membership within a set of countries undergoing integration. *See also* Deepening.

World System   Terminology preferred by neo-Marxists for the entire global political economy or global system.

World-Systems Theory   A theoretical approach with Marxist roots that attempts to explain the historic evolution and current status of the capitalist global political economy in terms of a systemic class division into core and periphery states.

World War III   An amalgamation of a large number of nationalism-based civil wars occurring for the most part within states. The term draws attention to the extensiveness of a phenomenon often seen as isolated and low-level conflicts.

Worldviews   Combinations of value preferences and theories that provide comprehensive understandings of social phenomena and bases for policy prescriptions.

Zero-Sum   A situation in which gain for one actor results in equivalent loss for another. *See* Nonzero-Sum.

Zone of Overlap   The range of possible outcomes framed by the minimal acceptable positions of parties to a negotiation.

Zone of Peace   A set of countries among which there has been no war for many years. *See* Democratic Peace.

References

Adams, Gordon. 1988. "The Iron Triangle," in *The Domestic Sources of American Foreign Policy*, eds. Charles W. Kegley and Eugene R. Wittkopf. New York: St. Martin's Press, pp. 70–78.

Adelman, Irma. 1986. "A Poverty-Focused Approach to Development Policy," in *Development Strategies Reconsidered*, eds. John P. Lewis and Valeriana Kalab. New Brunswick, NJ: Transaction Books.

Adler, Emanuel, and Beverly Crawford. 1991. *Progress in Postwar International Relations*. New York: Columbia University Press.

Adler, Emanuel, Beverly Crawford, and Jack Donnelly. 1991. "Defining and Conceptualizing Progress in International Relations," in *Progress in Postwar International Relations*, eds. Emanuel Adler and Beverly Crawford. New York: Columbia University Press, pp. 1–42.

Alker, Hayward R., Jr., and Thomas J. Biersteker. 1984. "The Dialectics of World Order: Notes for a Future Archeologist of International Savoir Faire," *International Studies Quarterly* 28, no. 2 (June), 121–142.

Allison, Graham T. 1971. *The Essence of Decision: Explaining the Cuban Missile Crisis*. Boston: Little, Brown.

Almond, Gabriel A. 1950. *The American People and Foreign Policy*. New York: Praeger.

Almond, Gabriel A. 1987. "The Development of Political Development," in *Understanding Political Development*, eds. Myron Weiner and Samuel P. Huntington. Boston: Little, Brown, pp. 437–478.

Almond, Gabriel A., and Sidney Verba. 1963. *The Civic Culture: Political Attitudes and Democracy in Five Nations*. Princeton, NJ: Princeton University Press.

Ashford, Lori S. 1995. "New Perspectives on Population: Lessons from Cairo," *Population Bulletin* 50, no. 1 (March), entire.

Axelrod, Robert. 1984. *The Evolution of Cooperation*. New York: Basic Books.

Ayres, Robert U. 1969. *Technological Forecasting and Long-Range Planning*. New York: McGraw-Hill.

Baily, Martin Neil, and Alok N. Chakrabarti. 1988. *Innovation and the Productivity Crisis*. Washington, DC: Brookings Institution.

Baldwin, David A. 1979. "Power Analysis and World Politics: New Trends versus Old Tendencies," *World Politics* 31, no. 2 (January), 161–194.

Baldwin, David A. 1985. *Economic Statecraft.* Princeton, NJ: Princeton University Press.

Ball, Terrence. 1988. *Transforming Political Discourse: Political Theory and Critical Conceptual History.* New York: Basil Blackwell.

Banfield, Edward. 1958. *The Moral Basis of a Backward Society.* Chicago: Free Press.

Banks, Michael. 1984. "The Evolution of International Relations Theory," in *Conflict in World Society,* ed. Michael Banks. New York: St. Martin's Press, pp. 3–21.

Barber, Benjamin R. 1992. "Jihad vs. McWorld," *The Atlantic Monthly* (March), 53–63.

Barber, James David. 1985. *The Presidential Character: Predicting Performance in the White House,* 3rd ed. Upper Saddle River, NJ: Prentice Hall.

Barbieri, Katherine. 1998. "International Trade and Conflict: The Debatable Relationship," paper delivered at the annual meeting of the International Studies Association, Minneapolis, MN, March 18–22.

Barnaby, Frank. 1986. "How the Next War Will Be Fought," *Technology Review* 89, no. 7 (October), 26–37.

Bauer, Raymond A., Ithiel de Sola Pool, and Lewis Anthony Dexter. 1972. *American Business and Public Policy,* 2nd ed. Chicago: Aldine Atherton.

Beck, Nathaniel. 1991. "The Illusion of Cycles in International Relations," *International Studies Quarterly* 35, no. 4 (December), 455–476.

Belassa, Bela. 1961. *The Theory of Economic Integration.* Homewood, IL: Richard Irwin.

Bell, Daniel. 1976. *The Cultural Contradictions of Capitalism.* New York: Basic Books.

Bennett, Robert William, and Joseph Zitomersky. 1982. "The Delimitization of International Diplomatic Systems 1816–1970: The Correlate of War Project's Systems Reconstructed," in *On Making Use of History,* ed. Joseph Zitomersky. Sweden: Esselte Studium, pp. 67–129.

Bergesen, Albert. 1983. "The Class Structure of the World-System," in *Contending Approaches to World System Analysis,* ed. William R. Thompson. Beverly Hills, CA: Sage Publications, pp. 43–54.

Bhagwati, Jagdish. 1998. "The Capital Myth," *Foreign Affairs* 77, no. 3 (May/June), 7–12.

Blainey, Geoffrey. 1988. *The Causes of War,* 3rd ed. New York: Free Press.

Blake, David H., and Robert S. Walters. 1987. *The Politics of Global Economic Relations,* 3rd ed. Upper Saddle River, NJ: Prentice Hall.

Blechman, Barry M., and Stephan S. Kaplan, with David K. Hall, William B. Quant, Jerome N. Slater, Robert M. Slusser, and Philip Windsor. 1978. *Force without War.* Washington, DC: Brookings Institution.

Bloomfield, Lincoln. 1988. "Foreign Policy—Backstage in an Election Year," *Christian Science Monitor* (March 14), 14.

Boulding, Kenneth E. 1981. *Ecodynamics: A New Theory of Social Evolution.* Beverly Hills, CA: Sage Publications.

Bower, Bruce. 1987. "Extinctions on Ice," *Science News* 132, no. 18 (October 31), 284–285.

Boyd, Andrew. 1987. *An Atlas of World Affairs,* 8th ed. New York: Methuen.

Boyer, Robert, and Danield Drache, eds. 1996. *States against Markets: The Limits of Globalization.* London: Routledge.

Braudel, Fernand. 1979. *The Perspective of the World.* Vol. 3 of *Civilization and Capitalism: 15th–18th Century.* New York: Harper and Row.

Brecher, Michael, and Jonathan Wilkenfeld. 1997. *A Study of Crisis.* Ann Arbor: University of Michigan Press.

Bremer, Stuart A., and Barry B. Hughes. 1990. *Disarmament and Development: A Design for the Future?* Upper Saddle River, NJ : Prentice Hall.

British Petroleum. 1997. *British Petroleum Statistical Review of World Energy.* London: British Petroleum Company.

Brown, Lester. 1972. *World without Borders.* New York: Vintage Books.

Brown, Lester. 1981. *Building a Sustainable Society.* New York: W. W. Norton.

Brown, Lester. 1988a. "Analyzing the Demographic Trap," in *State of the World 1987,* eds. Lester R. Brown et al. New York: W. W. Norton, pp. 20–37.

Brown, Lester. 1988b. "Sustaining World Agriculture," in *State of the World 1987,* eds. Lester R. Brown et al. New York: W. W. Norton, pp. 122–138.

Brown, Lester. 1995. *Who Will Feed the World?* New York: W. W. Norton.

Brown, Lester, Nicholas Lenssen, and Hal Kane. 1995. *Vital Signs 1995.* New York: W. W. Norton.

Brown, Seyom. 1987. *The Causes and Prevention of War.* New York: St. Martin's Press.

Brown, Seyom. 1988. *New Forces, Old Forces, and the Future of World Politics.* Glenview, IL: Scott, Foresman.

Bruckmann, Gerhart. 1983. "The Long Wave Debate," *Options* 2, 6–9.

Bueno de Mesquita, Bruce. 1981. *The War Trap.* New Haven, CT: Yale University Press.

Bull, Hedley. 1977. *The Anarchical Society: A Study of Order in World Politics.* New York: Columbia University Press.

Bull, Hedley. 1995. *The Anarchical Society: A Study of Order in World Politics,* 2nd ed. New York: Columbia University Press.

Burton, John W. 1985. "World Society and Human Needs," in *International Relations: A Handbook of Current Theory,* eds. Margot Light and A. J. R. Groom. Boulder, CO: Lynne Rienner, pp. 46–59.

Burton, John W., ed. 1990. *Conflict: Human Needs Theory.* New York: St. Martin's Press.

Bury, Reverend R. G., trans. 1966. *PLATO with an English Translation.* Cambridge, MA: Harvard University Press.

Caporaso, James A. 1993. "Global Political Economy," in *Political Science: The State of the Discipline II,* ed. Ada W. Finifter. Washington, DC: American Political Science Association, pp. 451–481.

Carr, Edward Hallett. 1964 (originally 1939). *The Twenty Years' Crisis 1919–1939.* New York: Harper and Row.

Cassese, Antonio. 1986. *International Law in a Divided World.* Oxford: Clarendon Press.

Castells, Manuel, and Laura D'Andrea Tyson. 1988. "High-Technology Choices Ahead: Restructuring Interdependence," in *Growth, Exports, and Jobs in a Changing World Economy: Agenda 1988,* eds. John W. Sewell, Stuart K. Tucker, and Contributors. New Brunswick, NJ: Transaction Books, pp. 55–95.

Central Intelligence Agency [CIA]. 1988. *The World Factbook 1988.* Washington, DC: Central Intelligence Agency.

Chai, Sun-Ki. 1997. "Entrenching the Yoshida Defense Doctrine: Three Techniques for Institutionalization," *International Organization* 51, no. 3 (Summer), 389–412.

Chan, Steve. 1984. "Mirror, Mirror on the Wall . . . : Are the Free Countries More Pacific?" *Journal of Conflict Resolution* 28, no. 4 (December), 617–648.

Chan, Steve. 1989. "Income Inequality among LDCs: A Comparative Analysis of Alternative Perspectives," *International Studies Quarterly* 33, no. 1 (March), 45–65.

Checkel, Jeffrey T. 1998. "The Constructivist Turn in International Relations Theory," *World Politics* 50, no. 2 (January), 324–348.

Chenery, Hollis. 1979. *Structural Change and Development Policy.* Baltimore: Johns Hopkins University Press.

Choucri, Nazli, and Robert C. North. 1975. *Nations in Conflict: National Growth and International Violence.* San Francisco: W. H. Freeman.

Cioffi-Revilla, Claudio. 1990. *Handbook of Datasets on Crisis and Wars, 1495–1988* AD. Boulder, CO: Lynne Rienner.

Cipolla, Carlo M., ed. 1970. *The Economic Decline of Empires.* London: Methuen.

Clark, Grenville, and Louis B. Sohn. 1960. *World Peace through World Law.* Cambridge, MA: Harvard University Press.

Claude, Inis L., Jr. 1962. *Power and International Affairs.* New York: Random House.

Cohen, Benjamin J. 1987. "A Brief History of International Monetary Relations," in *International Political Economy,* eds. Jeffrey A. Frieden and David A. Lake. New York: St. Martin's Press, pp. 245–268.

Cohen, Bernard C. 1995. *Democracies and Foreign Policy: Public Participation in the United States and the Netherlands.* Madison: University of Wisconsin Press.

Congressional Quarterly. 1979. *Energy Policy.* Washington, DC: Congressional Quarterly.

Cook, Earl. 1976. *Man, Energy, Society.* San Francisco: W. H. Freeman.

Couloumbis, Theodore A., and James H. Wolfe. 1986. *Introduction to International Relations,* 3rd ed. Upper Saddle River, NJ: Prentice Hall.

Council on Environmental Quality. 1981. *The Global 2000 Report to the President.* Washington, DC: Government Printing Office.

Cox, Robert W. 1981. "Social Forces, States and World Order: Beyond International Relations Theory," *Millennium* 10, no. 2, 128–137.

Craig, Gordon A., and Alexander George. 1983. *Force and Statecraft—Diplomatic Problems of Our Time.* New York: Oxford University Press.

Dahl, Robert. 1956. *Preface to Democratic Theory.* Chicago: University of Chicago Press.

Daly, Herman E., ed. 1980. *Economic, Ecology, Ethics.* San Francisco: W. H. Freeman.

Daly, Markate, ed. 1994. *Communitarianism: A New Public Ethics.* Belmont, CA: Wadsworth Publishing Company.

Dasmann, Raymond F., John P. Milton, and Peter Freeman. 1973. *Ecological Principles for Economic Development.* New York: John Wiley.

Dawisha, Adeed. 1986. *The Arab Radicals.* New York: Council on Foreign Relations.

De Conde, Alexander. 1978. *A History of American Foreign Policy,* 3rd ed., Vol 2. New York: Charles Scribner's Sons.

Deibert, Ronald J. 1997. *Parchment, Printing, and Hypermedia.* New York: Columbia University Press.

Der Derian, James, and Michael J. Shapiro, eds. 1989. *International/Intertextual Relations: Postmodern Readings of World Politics.* Lexington, MA: Lexington Books.

Desch, Michael C. 1998. "Culture Clash: Assessing the Importance of Ideas in Security Studies," *International Security* 23, no. 1 (Summer), 141–170.

de Sola Pool, Ithiel. 1990. *Technologies without Boundaries: On Telecommunications in a Global Age,* ed. Eli M. Noam. Cambridge, MA: Harvard University Press.

de Tocqueville, Alexis. 1945 (originally 1835). *Democracy in America.* 2 vols. New York: Vintage.

Deutsch, Karl W. 1961. "Social Mobilization and Political Development," *American Political Science Review* 55, no. 3 (September), 493–515.

Deutsch, Karl W. 1966. *Nationalism and Social Communication,* 2nd ed. Cambridge, MA: MIT Press.

Deutsch, Karl W. 1974. "Between Sovereignty and Integration: Conclusion," in *Between Sovereignty and Integration,* ed. Ghita Ionescu. New York: John Wiley and Sons, pp. 181–187.

Deutsch, Karl W. 1988. *The Analysis of International Relations,* 3rd ed. Upper Saddle River, NJ: Prentice Hall.

Deutsch, Karl W., et al. 1957. *Political Community and the North Atlantic Area: International Organization in the Light of Historical Experience.* Princeton, NJ: Princeton University Press.

Deutsch, Karl W., and J. David Singer. 1969. "Multipolar Power Systems and International Stability," in *International Politics and Foreign Policy,* 2nd ed., ed. James N. Rosenau. New York: Free Press, pp. 315–324.

Dixon, William J. 1994. "Democracy and the Peaceful Settlement of International Conflict," *American Political Science Review* 88, no. 1 (March), 14–32.

Domke, William K. 1988. *War and the Changing Global System.* New Haven, CT: Yale University Press.

Donnelly, Jack. 1998. *International Human Rights,* 2nd ed. Boulder, CO: Westview Press.

Dougherty, James E., and Robert L. Pfaltzgraff, Jr. 1986. *American Foreign Policy: FDR to Reagan.* New York: Harper and Row.

Doyle, Michael W. 1983. "Kant, Liberal Legacies, and Foreign Affairs," *Philosophy and Public Affairs* 12, 205–235, 323–353.

Doyle, Michael W. 1986a. *Empires.* Ithaca, NY: Cornell University Press.

Doyle, Michael W. 1986b. "Liberalism and World Politics," *American Political Science Review* 80, no. 4 (December), 1151–1169.

Drucker, Peter F. 1969. *The Age of Discontinuity.* New York: Harper and Row.

Drucker, Peter F. 1986. "New Technology: Predicting Its Impact," in *Technology and Man's Future,* 4th ed., ed. Albert H. Teich. New York: St. Martin's Press, pp. 214–218.

Eck, Diana L. 1993. "In the Name of Religions," *Wilson Quarterly* (Autumn), 90–100.

Eichenberg, Richard C. 1989. *Public Opinion and National Security in Western Europe.* Ithaca, NY: Cornell University Press.

Eichenberg, Richard C. 1998. "Domestic Preferences and Foreign Policy: Cumulation and Confirmation in the Study of Public Opinion," *Mershon International Studies Review* 42, no. 1 (May), 97–105.

Eisenhower, Dwight D. 1961. "Farewell Radio and Television Address to the American People," *Public Papers of the Presidents: Dwight D. Eisenhower, 1960–61.* Washington, DC: U.S. Government Printing Office, pp. 1035–1039.

Emmanuel, Arghiri. 1972. *Unequal Exchange: A Study of the Imperialism of Trade.* New York: Monthly Review Press.

Engler, Robert. 1961. *The Politics of Oil: Private Power and Democratic Directions.* Chicago: The University of Chicago Press.

Enloe, Cynthia. 1990. *Bananas, Bases, and Beaches: Making Feminist Sense of International Politics.* London: Pandora.

Etzioni, Amitai. 1988. *The Moral Dimension: Towards a New Economics.* New York: Free Press.

Fallows, James. 1993. "Looking at the Sun," *The Atlantic Monthly* (November), 69–100.

Feinberg, Richard E. 1985. "International Finance and Investment: A Surging Public Sector," in *U.S. Foreign Policy and the Third World: Agenda 1985–1986,* eds. John W. Sewell, Richard E. Feinberg, and Valeriana Kallab. New Brunswick, NJ: Transaction Books, pp. 51–71.

Feinberg, Richard E., and Gregg H. Goldstein. 1988. *The U.S. Economy and Developing Countries: Campaign 88 Briefing Papers for the Candidates.* Washington, DC: Overseas Development Council.

Ferguson, Yale H., and Richard W. Mansbach. 1988. *The Elusive Quest: Theory and International Politics.* Columbia: University of South Carolina.

Ferguson, Yale H., and Richard W. Mansbach. 1998. "Global Politics at the Turn of the Millennium: Changing Bases of 'Us' and 'Them,' " paper delivered at the annual meeting of the International Studies Association, Minneapolis, MN, March 18–22.

Feuer, Lewis S., ed. 1959. *Marx and Engels: Basic Writings on Politics and Philosophy.* New York: Anchor Books.

Finnemore, Martha. 1996. "Norms, Culture, and World Politics: Insights from Sociology's Institutionalism," *International Organization* 50, no. 2 (Spring), 525–547.

Fluehr-Lobban, Carolyn. 1995. "Cultural Relativism and Universal Rights," *The Chronicle of Higher Education* 41, no. 39 (June 9), B1–B2.

Foster, Richard H., and Robert Edington. 1985. *Viewing International Relations and World Politics.* Upper Saddle River, NJ: Prentice Hall.

Frank, André Gunder. 1983. "World System in Crisis," in *Contending Approaches to World System Analysis,* ed. William R. Thompson. Beverly Hills, CA: Sage Publications, pp. 27–42.

Freeman, Chris. 1988. "Diffusion: The Spread of New Technology to Firms, Sectors, and Nations," in *Innovation, Technology, and Finance,* ed. Arnold Heertje. New York: Basil Blackwell, pp. 38–70.

French, Hillary F. 1990. *Green Revolutions: Environmental Reconstruction in Eastern Europe and the Soviet Union,* Worldwatch Paper 99. Washington, DC: Worldwatch Institute.

Friedman, Milton. 1962. *Capitalism and Freedom.* Chicago: University of Chicago Press.

Frost, Ellen L. 1987. *For Richer, for Poorer: The New U.S.–Japan Relationship.* New York: Council on Foreign Relations.

Fukuyama, Francis. 1989. "The End of History?" *The National Interest* no. 16 (Summer), 3–18.

Gaddis, John Lewis. 1987. *The Long Peace.* New York: Oxford University Press.

Galtung, Johan. 1964. "A Structural Theory of Aggression," *Journal of Peace Research* 1, no. 2, 95–119.

Garnham, David. 1986. "War-Proneness, War-Weariness, and Regime Type: 1816–1980," *Journal of Peace Research* 23, no. 3 (September), 279–289.

Garraty, John A., and Peter Gay, eds. 1981. *The Colombia History of the World.* New York: Harper and Row.

Gellner, Ernest. 1983. *Nations and Nationalism.* Oxford: Blackwell.

George, Alexander L. 1991. *Forceful Persuasion: Coercive Diplomacy as an Alternative to War.* Washington, DC: United States Institute of Peace.

George, Alexander L., and Juliette L. George. 1964. *Woodrow Wilson and Colonel House: A Personality Study.* New York: Dover.

George, Jim, and David Campbell. 1990. "Patterns of Dissent and the Celebration of Difference: Critical Social Theory and International Relations," *International Studies Quarterly* 34, no. 3 (September), 269–293.

Gerschenkron, Alexander. 1962. *Economic Backwardness in Historical Perspective: A Book of Essays.* Cambridge, MA: Belknap, Harvard University Press.

Gilpin, Robert. 1979. "Three Models of the Future," in *Transnational Corporations and World Order,* ed. George Modelski. San Francisco: W. H. Freeman, pp. 353–372.

Gilpin, Robert. 1981. *War and Change in World Politics.* New York: Cambridge University Press.

Gilpin, Robert. 1987. *The Political Economy of International Relations.* Princeton, NJ: Princeton University Press.

Gochman, Charles S., and Zeev Maoz. 1984. "Militarized Interstate Disputes 1816–1976," *Journal of Conflict Resolution* 28, no. 4 (December), 585–615.

Goldstein, Joshua S. 1985. "Kondratieff Waves as War Cycles," *International Studies Quarterly* 29, no. 4 (December), 411–444.

Goldstein, Joshua S. 1988. *Long Cycles: Prosperity and War in the Modern Age*. New Haven, CT: Yale University Press.

Goldstein, Judith. 1988. "Ideas, Institutions, and American Trade Policy," *International Organization* 42, no. 1 (Winter), 179–217.

Goldstein, Judith, and Robert O. Keohane, eds. 1993. *Ideas and Foreign Policy*. Ithaca, NY: Cornell University Press.

Goldstein, Judith, and Stefanie Ann Lenway. 1989. "Interests or Institutions: An Inquiry into Congressional-ITC Relations," *International Studies Quarterly* 33, no. 3 (September), 303–327.

Grant, Lindsey. 1982. *The Cornucopian Fallacies*. Washington, DC: Environmental Fund.

Gray, Peter. 1993. *Briefing Book on the Nonproliferation of Nuclear Weapons*. Washington, DC: Council for a Livable World Education Fund.

Grieco, Joseph M. 1988. "Anarchy and the Limits of Cooperation: A Realist Critique of the Newest Liberal Institutionalism," *International Organization* 42, no. 3 (Summer), 485–507.

Grieco, Joseph M. 1990. *Cooperation among Nations*. Ithaca, NY: Cornell University Press.

Griffin, Keith B. 1987. "World Hunger and the World Economy," in *Pursuing Food Security*, eds. W. Ladd Hollist and F. LaMond Tullis. Boulder, CO: Lynne Rienner, pp. 17–36.

Gurr, Ted Robert. 1993. *Minorities at Risk*. Washington, DC: United States Institute of Peace.

Gurr, Ted Robert. 1997. "The Ethnic Challenge to International Security," *Futures Research Quarterly* 13, no. 1 (Spring), 11–23.

Haas, Ernst B. 1953. "The Balance of Power: Prescription, Concept, or Propaganda?" *World Politics* 5, no. 4 (July), 446–458.

Haas, Ernst B. 1986. *Why We Still Need the United Nations: The Collective Management of International Conflict*, 1945–1984, Policy Papers in International Affairs no. 26. Berkeley: University of California Institute of International Studies.

Haas, Ernst B. 1990. *When Knowledge Is Power*. Berkeley: University of California Press.

Haas, Peter M. 1989. "Do Regimes Matter? Epistemic Communities and Mediterranean Pollution Control," *International Organization* 43, no. 3 (Summer), 337–403.

Haas, Peter M., ed. 1992. *Knowledge, Power, and Policy Coordination*, special issue of International Organization 46, no. 1 (Winter).

Hampshire, Stuart, ed. 1956. *The Age of Reason: 17th Century Philosophers*. New York: Mentor Books.

Hardin, Garrett. 1968. "The Tragedy of the Commons," *Science* 162, no. 3859 (December 13), 1243–1248.

Hardin, Russell. 1982. *Collective Action*. Baltimore: Johns Hopkins University.

Hardin, Russell. 1995. *One for All: The Logic of Group Conflict*. Princeton, NJ: Princeton University Press.

Harff, Barbara, and Ted Robert Gurr. 1988. "Toward Empirical Theory of Genocides and Politicides," *International Studies Quarterly* 32, no. 3 (September), 359–371.

Harris, Marvin. 1977. *Cannibals and Kings*. New York: Vintage Books.

Harsanyi, John C. 1986. "Advances in Understanding Rational Behavior," in *Rational Choice*, ed. Jon Elster. New York: New York University Press, pp. 82–107.

Hart, Jeffrey. 1988. "Empiricism, Metaphysics and the Recovery of the Whole," *Essays on Our Times* 4, no. 1 (April), 3–21.

Hastedt, Glenn P. 1988. *American Foreign Policy: Past, Present, Future.* Upper Saddle River, NJ: Prentice Hall.

Hathaway, Oona A. 1998. "Positive Feedback: The Impact of Trade Liberalization on Industry Demands for Protection," *International Organization* 52, no. 3 (Summer), 575–612.

Hayek, Friedrich A. 1963 (originally 1944). *The Road to Serfdom.* Chicago: University of Chicago Press.

Headrick, Daniel R. 1981. *The Tools of Empire.* New York: Oxford University Press.

Hermann, Charles F. 1969. *Crises in Foreign Policy.* Indianapolis: Bobbs-Merrill Company.

Herz, John H. 1951. *Political Realism and Political Idealism.* Chicago: The University of Chicago Press.

Herz, John H. 1957. "Rise and Demise of the Territorial State," *World Politics* 9, no. 4 (July), 473–493.

Herz, John H. 1969. "The Territorial State Revisited," in *International Politics and Foreign Policy,* rev. ed., ed. James N. Rosenau. New York: Free Press, pp. 76–89.

Hinsley, F. H. 1986. *Sovereignty,* 3rd ed. Cambridge: Cambridge University Press.

Holister, Geoffrey, and Andrew Porteous. 1976. *The Environment: A Dictionary of the World Around Us.* London: Arrow Books.

Hollins, Harry B., Averill L. Powers, and Mark Sommer. 1989. *The Conquest of War.* Boulder, CO: Westview Press.

Holsti, K. J. 1983. *International Politics: A Framework for Analysis,* 4th ed. Upper Saddle River, NJ: Prentice Hall.

Holsti, K. J. 1985. *The Dividing Discipline: Hegemony and Diversity in International Theory.* Boston: Allen and Unwin.

Holsti, K. J. 1988. *International Politics: A Framework for Analysis,* 5th ed. Upper Saddle River, NJ: Prentice Hall.

Holsti, Ole R. 1962. "The Belief System and National Images: A Case Study," *Journal of Conflict Resolution* 6, no. 3 (September), 244–252.

Holsti, Ole R. 1992. "Public Opinion and Foreign Policy: Challenges to the Almond-Lipmann Consensus," *International Studies Quarterly* 36, no. 4 (December), 439–466.

Holsti, Ole R. 1996. *Public Opinion and American Foreign Policy.* Ann Arbor: University of Michigan Press.

Holsti, Ole R., P. Terrence Hopmann, and John D. Sullivan. 1973. *Unity and Disintegration in International Alliances: Comparative Studies.* New York: John Wiley and Sons.

Holsti, Ole R., Robert C. North, and Richard A. Brady. 1968. "Perception and Action in the 1914 Crisis," in *Quantitative International Politics,* ed. J. David Singer. New York: Free Press, pp. 123–158.

Holsti, Ole R., and James N. Rosenau. 1988. "A Leadership Divided: The Foreign Policy Beliefs of American Leaders, 1976–1984," in *The Domestic Sources of American Foreign Policy,* eds. Charles W. Kegley and Eugene R. Wittkopf. New York: St. Martin's Press, pp. 30–44.

Holsti, Ole R., Randolph M. Siverson, and Alexander L. George, eds. 1980. *Change in the International System.* Boulder, CO: Westview Press.

Hopf, Ted. 1998. "The Promise of Constructivism in International Relations Theory," *International Security* 23, no. 1 (Summer), 171–200.

Hopkins, Terence K., and Immanuel Wallerstein. 1980. "Cyclical Rhythms and Secular Trends of the Capitalist World-Economy," in *World Systems Analysis: Theory and Methodology,* eds. Terence K. Hopkins and Immanuel Wallerstein. Beverly Hills, CA: Sage Publications, pp. 104–120.

Horowitz, Donald L. 1985. *Ethnic Groups in Conflict.* Berkeley: University of California Press.

Hufbauer, Gary Clyde, Jeffrey J. Schott, and Kimberly Ann Elliott. 1990. *Economic Sanctions Reconsidered.* Washington, DC: Institute for International Economics.

Hughes, Barry B. 1978. *The Domestic Context of American Foreign Policy.* San Francisco: W. H. Freeman.

Hughes, Barry B. 1985. *World Futures: A Critical Analysis of Alternatives.* Baltimore: Johns Hopkins University Press.

Hughes, Barry B. 1993. "Delivering the Goods: The EC and the Evolution of Complex Governance," in Dale L. Smith and James Lee Ray, eds., *The 1992 Project and the Future of Integration in Europe.* Armonk, NY: M. E. Sharpe, pp. 45–69.

Hughes, Barry B. 1995a. "The Future of the Global Political Economy," in *The Politics of International Economic Relations,* ed. C. Roe Goddard and John Passe-Smith. Boulder, CO: Lynne Rienner.

Hughes, Barry B. 1995b. "Evolving Patterns of European Integration and Governance: Implications for Theories of World Politics," in *Controversies in International Relations Theory,* ed. Charles W. Kegley, Jr. New York: St. Martin's Press, pp. 223–243.

Hughes, Barry B. 1998. "Global Social Transformation: The Sweet Spot, the Steady Slog, and the Systemic Shift," paper presented at the annual meeting of the International Studies Association, Minneapolis, MN, March 17–21, 1998.

Hughes, Barry B. 1999. *International Futures: Choices in the Creation of a New World Order,* 3rd ed. Boulder, CO: Westview Press.

Hughes, J. Donald. 1994. *Pan's Travail: Environmental Problems of the Ancient Greeks and Romans.* Baltimore: Johns Hopkins University Press.

Hunter, James Davison. 1991. *Culture Wars: The Struggle to Define America.* New York: Basic Books.

Huntington, Samuel P. 1985. "Will More Countries Become Democratic?" in *Global Dilemmas,* eds. Samuel P. Huntington and Joseph S. Nye, Jr. Cambridge: Harvard University Center for International Affairs, pp. 253–279.

Huntington, Samuel P. 1988. "The U.S.—Decline or Renewal?" *Foreign Affairs* 67, no. 2 (Winter), 76–96.

Huntington, Samuel P. 1991. *The Third Wave: Democratization in the Late Twentieth Century.* Norman: University of Oklahoma Press.

Huntington, Samuel P. 1993. "The Clash of Civilizations?" *Foreign Affairs* 72, no. 3 (Summer), 22–49.

Huntington, Samuel P. 1996. "The West: Unique, Not Universal," *Foreign Affairs* 75, no. 6 (November/December), 28–46.

Imbert, Gaston. 1956. *Des Mouvements de Longue Durée Kondratieff* (Ph.D. dissertation). Aix-en-Provence: Office Universitaire de Polycopie. Cited in Joshua S. Goldstein. 1988. *Long Cycles: Prosperity and War in the Modern Age.* New Haven, CT: Yale University Press.

Information Please Almanac 1998. 1997. Boston: Information Please.

Ingersoll, David E., and Richard K. Matthews. 1986. *The Philosophic Roots of Modern Ideology.* Upper Saddle River, NJ: Prentice Hall.

Inglehart, Ronald. 1997. *Modernization and Postmodernization: Global, Economic, and Political Change in 43 Societies.* Princeton, NJ: Princeton University Press.

International Monetary Fund. 1995. *International Capital Markets.* Washington, DC: International Monetary Fund.

International Monetary Fund. 1997. *International Capital Markets.* Washington, DC: International Monetary Fund.

Jacobson, Harold K. 1984. *Networks of Interdependence,* 2nd ed. New York: Alfred A. Knopf.

Janis, Irving L. 1972. *Victims of Groupthink.* Boston: Houghton Mifflin.

Jervis, Robert. 1976. *Perception and Misperception in International Politics.* Princeton, NJ: Princeton University Press.

Jervis, Robert. 1978. "Cooperation under the Security Dilemma," *World Politics* 20, no. 2 (January), 167–214.

Joffee, Josef. 1985. "The Foreign Policy of the Federal Republic of Germany," in *Foreign Policy in World Politics,* 6th ed., ed. Roy C. Macridis. Upper Saddle River, NJ: Prentice Hall, pp. 72–113.

Joyner, Christopher S., ed. 1997. *The United Nations and International Law.* Cambridge, England: Cambridge University Press.

Kahn, Herman. 1979. *World Economic Development: 1979 and Beyond.* Boulder, CO: Westview Press.

Kahn, Herman, William Brown, and Leon Martel. 1976. *The Next 200 Years.* New York: William Morrow.

Kaplan, Morton A. 1957. *System and Process in International Politics.* New York: John Wiley and Sons.

Katzenstein, Peter J. 1985. *Small States in World Markets: Industrial Power in Europe.* Ithaca, NY: Cornell University Press.

Katzenstein, Peter J., ed. 1996. *The Culture of National Security: Norms and Identity in World Politics.* New York: Columbia University Press.

Keck, Otto. 1993. "The New Institutionalism and the Relative-Gains Debate," in *International Relations and Pan-Europe,* ed. Frank R. Pfetsch. Hamburg, Germany: Lit Verlag, pp. 35–62.

Kegley, Charles W., and Eugene R. Wittkopf. 1979. *American Foreign Policy: Pattern and Process.* New York: St. Martin's Press.

Kegley, Charles W., and Eugene R. Wittkopf. 1985. *World Politics: Trend and Transformation,* 2nd ed. New York: St. Martin's Press.

Kegley, Charles W., and Eugene R. Wittkopf. 1991. *American Foreign Policy: Pattern and Process,* 4th ed. New York: St. Martin's Press.

Kennedy, Paul. 1983. *Strategy and Diplomacy: 1870–1945: Eight Studies.* London: Allen and Unwin.

Keohane, Robert O. 1980. "The Theory of Hegemonic Stability and Changes in International Economic Regimes, 1967–1977," in *Change in the International System,* eds. Ole R. Holsti, Randolph M. Siverson, and Alexander L. George. Boulder, CO: Westview Press, pp. 131–162.

Keohane, Robert O. 1983a. "The Demand for International Regimes," in *International Regimes,* ed. Stephen D. Krasner. Ithaca, NY: Cornell University Press, pp. 141–172.

Keohane, Robert O. 1983b. "Theory of World Politics: Structural Realism and Beyond," *Political Science: The State of the Discipline,* ed. Ada W. Finifter. Washington, DC: American Political Science Association, pp. 503–540.

Keohane, Robert O. 1984. *After Hegemony, Cooperation and Discord in the World Political Economy.* Princeton, NJ: Princeton University Press.

Keohane, Robert O. 1989. *International Institutions and State Power.* Boulder, CO: Westview Press.

Keohane, Robert O. 1990. "International Liberalism Revisited," in *The Economic Limits to Modern Politics,* ed. John Dunn. Cambridge, England: Cambridge University Press, pp. 165–194.

Keohane, Robert O., and Helen V. Milner, eds. 1996. *Internationalization and Domestic Politics.* Cambridge, England: Cambridge University Press.

Keohane, Robert O., and Joseph S. Nye, Jr., eds. 1970. *Transnational Relations and World Politics.* Cambridge, MA: Harvard University Press.

Keohane, Robert O., and Joseph S. Nye, Jr. 1977. *Power and Interdependence: World Politics in Transition.* Boston: Little, Brown.

Keynes, John Maynard. 1936. *The General Theory of Employment, Interest, and Money.* New York: Harcourt, Brace.

Kindleberger, Charles P. 1973. *The World in Depression 1929–1939.* Berkeley: University of California Press.

Kirchner, Emil J. 1988. "Has the Single European Act Opened the Door for a European Security Policy?" paper delivered at the International Political Science Association Meeting, Washington, DC, August 28.

Kissinger, Henry A. 1962. *The Necessity of Choice.* Garden City, NY: Doubleday.

Klass, Rosanne. 1988. "Afghanistan: The Accords," *Foreign Affairs* 66, no. 5 (Summer), 922–945.

Kline, John M. 1985. "Multinational Corporations in Euro-American Trade: Crucial Linking Mechanisms in an Evolving Trade Structure," in *Multinational Corporations,* ed. Theodore H. Moran. Lexington, MA: Lexington Books, pp. 199–218.

Knorr, Klaus. 1975. *The Power of Nations: The Political Economy of International Relations.* New York: Basic Books.

Krasner, Stephen D. 1978. *Defending the National Interest.* Princeton, NJ: Princeton University Press.

Krasner, Stephen D. 1983. "Structural Causes and Regime Consequences: Regimes as Intervening Variables," in *International Regimes,* ed. Stephen D. Krasner. Ithaca, NY: Cornell University Press, pp. 1–21.

Krasner, Stephen D. 1987. "State Power and the Structure of International Trade," in *International Political Economy,* eds. Jeffrey A. Frieden and David A. Lake. New York: St. Martin's Press, pp. 47–66.

Krauss, Michael. 1992. "The World's Languages in Crisis," *Language* 68, no. 1, 4–10.

Krugman, Paul R., ed. 1986. *Strategic Trade Policy and the New International Economics.* Cambridge, MA: MIT Press.

Krugman, Paul R. 1994. "Competitiveness: A Dangerous Obsession," *Foreign Affairs* 73, no. 2 (March/April), 28–44

Krugman, Paul R., and Maurice Obstfeld. 1997. *International Economics,* 4th ed. Reading, MA: Addison-Wesley.

Kubálková, Vendulka, Nicholas Onuf, and Paul Kowert, eds. 1998. *International Relations in a Constructed World.* Armonk, NY: M. E. Sharpe.

Kugler, Jacek, and A. F. K. Organski. 1989. "The End of Hegemony?" *International Interactions* 15, no. 2, 113–128.

Kuhn, Thomas. 1970. *The Structure of Scientific Revolutions,* expanded ed. Chicago: University of Chicago Press.

Kuttner, Robert. 1991. *The End of Laissez-Faire: National Purpose and the Global Economy after the Cold War.* New York: Alfred A. Knopf.

Kuznets, Simon. 1966. *Modern Economic Growth: Rate, Structure and Spread.* New Haven, CT: Yale University Press.

Lake, David A. 1987. "International Economic Structures and American Foreign Policy, 1887–1934," in *International Political Economy,* eds. Jeffrey A. Frieden and David A. Lake. New York: St. Martin's Press, pp. 145–165.

Lapid, Yosef. 1989. "The Third Debate: On the Prospects of International Theory in a Post-Positivist Era," *International Studies Quarterly* 33, no. 3 (September), 235–254.

Lapid, Yosef, and Friedrich Kratochwil, eds. 1996. *The Return of Culture and Identity in IR Theory.* Boulder, CO: Lynne Rienner.

Lau, D. C. 1970, trans. *Mencius.* New York: Penguin.

Lauterpacht, H. 1985. "The Grotian Tradition in International Law," in *International Law: A Contemporary Perspective,* eds. Richard Falk, Friedrich Kratochwil, and Saul H. Mendlovitz. Boulder, CO: Westview Press, pp. 10–35.

Leatherman, Janie, Ron Pagnucco, and Jackie Smith. 1994. "International Institutions and Transnational Social Movement Organizations," Kroc Institute for International Peace Studies, University of Notre Dame, working paper.

Lebow, Richard Ned. 1981. *Between Peace and War: The Nature of International Crisis.* Baltimore: Johns Hopkins University Press.

Levy, Jack S. 1983. *War in the Modern Great Power System, 1495–1975.* Lexington: University of Kentucky Press.

Levy, Jack S. 1992. "An Introduction to Prospect Theory," *Political Psychology* 13, no. 2 (June), 171–186.

Levy, Jack S. 1997. "Prospect Theory, Rational Choice, and International Relations," *International Studies Quarterly* 41, no. 1 (March), 87–112.

Levy, Jack S., and Michael M. Barnett. 1992. "Alliance Formation, Domestic Political Economy, and Third World Security," *The Jerusalem Journal of International Relations* 14, no. 4 (December), 19–40.

Lewis, John P., and Valeriana Kallab, eds. 1983. *U.S. Foreign Policy and the Third World: Agenda 1983.* New York: Praeger.

Lipset, Seymour Martin. 1963. *The First New Nation.* New York: Basic Books.

Lofdahl, Correy L. 1997. *National Expansion and Natural Degradation.* Ph.D. dissertation, Department of Political Science, University of Colorado, Boulder.

Lopez, George A., and David Cartwright. 1998. "Making Targets 'Smart' from Sanctions," paper delivered at the annual meeting of the International Studies Association, Minneapolis, MN, March 18–22.

Lovins, Amory B. 1976. "Energy Strategy: The Road Not Taken?" *Foreign Affairs* 55, no. 1 (October), 65–96.

Luce, R. D., and Howard Raiffa. 1957. *Games and Decisions.* New York: John Wiley and Sons.

Lynch, Cecelia. 1994. "Kant, the Republican Peace, and Moral Guidance in International Law," *Ethics and International Affairs* 8, 39–58.

MacDonald, Stuart. 1986. "Controlling the Flow of High-Technology Information from the United States to the Soviet Union," *Minerva* 24, no. 1 (Spring), 39–73.

Machiavelli, Niccolò. 1886 (originally 1513). *The Prince,* trans. Henry Morely. London: George Routledge and Sons.

Machiavelli, Niccolò. 1940. *The Discourses.* New York: Modern Library.

Macridis, Roy C. 1986. *Contemporary Political Ideologies: Movements and Regimes,* 3rd ed. Boston: Little, Brown.

Maddison, Angus. 1982. *Phases of Capitalist Development.* Oxford, England: Oxford University Press.

Maddison, Angus. 1995. *Monitoring the World Economy 1820–1992.* Paris: OECD.

Maghroori, Ray, and Bennett Ramberg, eds. 1982. *Globalism versus Realism: International Relations' Third Debate.* Boulder, CO: Westview Press.

Mandel, Robert. 1986. "The Effectiveness of Gunboat Diplomacy," *International Studies Quarterly* 31, no. 1 (March), 59–76.

Mansfield, Edward D. 1994. *Power, Trade, and War.* Princeton, NJ: Princeton University Press.

Mansfield, Edward D., and Jack Snyder. 1995. "Democratization and the Danger of War," *International Security* 20, no. 1 (Summer), 5–38.

March, James G. 1966. "The Power of Power," in *Varieties of Political Theory,* ed. David Easton. Upper Saddle River, NJ: Prentice Hall, pp. 54–61.

Marchand, Marianna H., and Jane L. Parpart, eds. 1995. *Feminism/Postmodernism/Development.* London: Routledge.

Marks, Gary, Liesbet Hooghie, and Kermit Blank. 1996. "European Integration from the 1980s: State-Centric v. Multilevel Governance," *Journal of Common Market Studies* 34, no. 3 (September), 341–378.

Maslow, Abraham. 1970. *Motivation and Personality,* 2nd ed. New York: Harper and Row.

Mazrui, Ali. 1988. "International Stratification and Third World Solidarity: A Dual Strategy for Change," reprinted in *Global Issues 88–89,* ed. Robert Jackson. Guilford, CT: Dushkin Publishing Group, pp. 132–136.

McCalla, Robert B. 1996. "NATO's Persistence after the Cold War," *International Organization* 50, no. 3 (Summer), 445–475.

McDermott, John. 1972. "Technology: The Opiate of the Intellectuals," in *Technology and Man's Future,* ed. Albert Teich. New York: St. Martin's Press, pp. 151–177.

McKinlay, R. D., and R. Little. 1986. *Global Problems and World Order.* Madison: University of Wisconsin Press.

McNeill, William H. 1976. *Plagues and Peoples.* Garden City, NY: Anchor Press.

McNeill, William H. 1982. *The Pursuit of Power.* Chicago: The University of Chicago Press.

McWilliams, Wayne C., and Harry Piotrowski. 1988. *The World Since 1945.* Boulder, CO: Lynne Rienner.

Meadows, Donella H., Dennis L. Meadows, Jorgen Randers, and William W. Behrens III. 1972. *The Limits to Growth.* New York: Universe Books.

Meadows, Donella H., Dennis L. Meadows, and Jorgen Randers. 1992. *Beyond the Limits to Growth.* Post Hills, VT: Chelsea Green Publishing Company.

Mearsheimer, John J. 1990. "Back to the Future: Instability in Europe after the Cold War," *International Security* 15 (Summer 1990), 5–56.

Merquior, J. G. 1991. *Liberalism: Old and New.* Boston: Twayne Publishers.

Meyer, John W., Francisco O. Ramirez, Richardson Rubinson, and John Boli-Bennett. 1979. "The World Educational Revolution, 1950–70," in *National Development and the World System,* ed. John W. Meyer and Michael T. Hannan. Chicago: University of Chicago Press, pp. 37–55.

Midford, Paul. 1993. "International Trade and Domestic Politics: Improving on Rogowski's Model of Political Alignments," *International Organization* 47, no. 4 (Autumn), 535–564.

Midlarsky, Manus I. 1988. *The Onset of World War.* Boston: Unwin Hyman.

Mills, C. Wright. 1956. *The Power Elite.* New York: Oxford University Press.

Mingst, Karen A., and Margaret P. Karns. 1995. *The United Nations in the Post-Cold War Era.* Boulder, CO: Westview.

Mitrany, David. 1966. *A Working Peace System.* Chicago: Quadrangle, 1966. Originally published as *A Working Peace System: An Argument for the Functional Development of International Organization.* London: Royal Institute of International Affairs.

Mittelman, James H., ed. 1996. *Globalization: Critical Reflections.* Boulder, CO: Lynne Rienner.

Modelski, George. 1978. "The Long-Cycle of Global Politics and the Nation-State," *Comparative Studies in Society and History* 20, no. 2 (April), 214–235.

Modelski, George, ed. 1987. *Exploring Long Cycles.* Boulder, CO: Lynne Rienner.

Modelski, George, and William R. Thompson. 1987. *Seapower in Global Politics: 1494–1993.* London: Macmillan.

Moran, Theodore H. 1985. "Multinational Corporations and the Developing Countries," in *Multinational Corporations,* ed. Theodore H. Moran. Lexington, MA: Lexington, pp. 3–24.

Moravcsik, Andrew. 1997. "A Liberal Theory of International Politics," *International Organization* 51, no. 4 (Autumn), 513–554.

Morgenthau, Hans J. 1973. *Politics among Nations: The Struggle for Power and Peace,* 5th ed. New York: Alfred A. Knopf.

Morse, Edward. 1976. *Modernization and the Transformation of International Relations.* New York: Basic Books.

Mueller, John. 1973. *War, Presidents and Public Opinion.* New York: John Wiley and Sons.

Mueller, John. 1989. *Retreat from Doomsday: The Obsolescence of Major War.* New York: Basic Books.

Myrdal, Gunnar. 1957. *Rich Nations and Poor.* New York: Harper and Row.

Naisbitt, John. 1982. *Megatrends.* New York: Warner Books.

National Science Foundation. 1991. *International Science and Technology Data Update: 1991.* Washington, DC: National Science Foundation.

Nau, Henry R. 1990. *The Myth of America's Decline.* New York: Oxford University Press.

Nielsson, Gunnar, and Angeliki Kanavou. 1996. "Dispersed Nations and Interstate Relations," paper presented at the 1996 meeting of the International Studies Association, San Diego, CA, April 16–20.

Nietschmann, Bernard. 1987. "The Third World War," *Cultural Survival Quarterly* 11, no. 3, 1–16.

Niksch, Larry A. 1983. "Japanese Attitudes toward Defense and Security Issues," *Naval War College Review* 36, no. 4 (July/August), 57–72.

Nixon, Richard. 1962. *Six Crises.* Garden City, NY: Doubleday.

Nye, Joseph S., Jr. 1971. *Peace in Parts.* Boston: Little, Brown.

Nye, Joseph S., Jr. 1990. *Bound to Lead: The Changing Nature of American Power.* New York: Basic Books.

O'Brien, Conor Cruise. 1988. *God Land: Reflections on Religion and Nationalism.* Cambridge, MA: Harvard University Press.

Odell, Peter R. 1983. *Oil and World Power,* 7th ed. New York: Viking Penguin.

Office of Technology Assessment. 1986. "Commercial Biotechnology: An International Analysis," in *Technology and Man's Future,* 4th ed., ed. Albert H. Teich. New York: St. Martin's Press, pp. 360–385.

Olson, Mancur. 1965. *The Logic of Collective Action.* Cambridge, MA: Harvard University Press.

Olson, Mancur. 1982. *The Rise and Decline of Nations: Economic Growth, Stagflation, and Social Rigidities.* New Haven, CT: Yale University Press.

Olson, Mancur, and Richard Zeckhauser. 1966. "An Economic Theory of Alliances," *The Review of Economics and Statistics* 48, no. 3 (August), 266–279.

Onuf, Nicholas Greenwood. 1989. *World of Our Making.* Columbia: University of South Carolina Press.

Oppenheim, Lassa. 1908. "The Science of International Law," *American Journal of International Law* 2, 313–351.

Organski, A. F. K. 1968. *World Politics.* New York: Alfred A. Knopf.

Organski, A. F. K., and Jacek Kugler. 1980. *The War Ledger.* Chicago: University of Chicago Press.

Orme, John. 1997. "The Utility of Force in a World of Scarcity," *International Security* 22, no. 3 (Winter 1997/98), 138–167.

Osgood, Charles E. 1962. "Reciprocal Initiative," in *The Liberal Papers,* ed. James Roosevelt. Garden City, NY: Doubleday, pp. 155–228.

Oye, Kenneth A. 1987. "Constrained Confidence and the Evolution of the Reagan Foreign Policy," in *Eagle Resurgent? The Reagan Era in American Foreign Policy,* eds. Kenneth A. Oye, Robert J. Lieber, and Donald Rothchild. Boston: Little, Brown, pp. 3–40.

Palmer, Monte. 1989. *Dilemmas of Political Development,* 4th ed. Itasca, IL: F. E. Peacock Publishers.

Pape, Robert A. 1997. "Why Sanctions Do Not Work," *International Security* 22, no. 2 (Fall), 90–136.

Papp, Daniel S. 1988. *Contemporary International Relations: Frameworks for Understanding,* 2nd ed. New York: Macmillan.

Pei, Minxin. 1998. "Is China Democratizing?" *Foreign Affairs* 77, no. 1 (January/February), 68–82.

Peterson, V. Spike, and Anne Sisson Runyon. 1993. *Global Gender Issues.* Boulder, CO: Westview Press.

Pettman, Jan Jindy. 1996. *Worlding Women: A Feminist International Politics.* Sydney, Australia: Allen and Unwin.

Pirages, Dennis. 1983. "The Ecological Perspective and the Social Sciences," *International Studies Quarterly* 27, no. 3 (September), 243–255.

Pirages, Dennis. 1989. *Global Technopolitics.* Pacific Grove, CA: Brooks/Cole Publishing.

Plano, Jack C., and Roy Olton. 1988. *The International Relations Dictionary,* 4th ed. Santa Barbara, CA: ABC-CLIO.

Platt, John. 1988. "The Future of AIDS," reprinted in *Global Issues 88–89,* ed. Robert Jackson. Guilford, CT: Dushkin Publishing, pp. 40–47.

Pollins, Brian M. 1992. "International Order, Cycles, and Armed Conflict 1816–1976," paper presented at the annual meeting of the International Studies Association, Atlanta, March 31–April 4.

Pollins, Brian M. 1994. "Global Political Order, Economic Change, and Armed Conflict," unpublished Mershon Center paper, Ohio State University (June).

Population Reference Bureau. 1996. *Monitoring Family Planning Programs 1996.* Washington, DC: Population Reference Bureau.

Population Reference Bureau. 1997. *1997 World Population Data Sheet.* Washington, DC: Population Reference Bureau.

Population Reference Bureau. 1998. *1998 World Population Data Sheet*. Washington, DC: Population Reference Bureau.

Postel, Sandra. 1989. "Halting Land Degradation," in *State of the World 1989*, ed. Lester R. Brown and others. Washington, DC: Worldwatch Institute, pp. 21–40.

Press, Frank. 1987. "Technological Competition and the Western Alliance," in *A High Technology Gap? Europe, America and Japan*, ed. Andrew J. Pierre. New York: Council on Foreign Relations, pp. 11–43.

Price, Richard. 1998. "Reversing the Gun Sights: Transnational Civil Society Targets Land Mines," *International Organization* 52, no. 3 (Summer), 613–644.

Princen, Thomas, Matthias Finger, and Jack Manno. 1995. "Nongovernmental Organizations in World Environmental Politics," *International Environmental Affairs* 7, no. 1 (Winter), 42–58.

Putnam, Robert D. 1988. "Diplomacy and Domestic Politics: The Logic of Two-Level Games," *International Organization* 42, no. 3 (Summer), 427–460.

Putnam, Robert D. 1993. *Making Democracy Work: Civic Traditions in Modern Italy*. Princeton, NJ: Princeton University Press.

Quester, George H. 1977. *Offense and Defense in the International System*. New York: John Wiley and Sons.

Rasler, Karen, and William R. Thompson. 1989. "Ascent, Decline and War," paper delivered at the annual American Political Science Association meeting, Atlanta.

Rasler, Karen, and William R. Thompson. 1994. *The Great Powers and Global Struggle 1490–1990*. Lexington: University Press of Kentucky.

Ratner, Steven. 1998. "International Law: The Trials of Global Norms," *Foreign Policy* 110 (Spring), 65–80.

Ray, James Lee. 1987. *Global Politics*, 3rd ed. Boston: Houghton Mifflin.

Ray, James Lee. 1989. "The Abolition of Slavery and the End of International War," *International Organization* 43 (Summer), 405–440.

Ray, James Lee. 1990. *Global Politics*, 4th ed. Boston: Houghton Mifflin.

Reardon, Betty A. 1993. *Women and Peace: Feminist Visions of Global Security*. Albany: State University of New York Press.

Rejai, Mostafa, and Cynthia H. Enloe. 1981. "Nation-States and State-Nations," in *Perspectives on World Politics*, ed. Michael Smith, Richard Little, and Michael Shackleton. Chatham, NJ: Chatham House.

Richardson, Lewis F. 1960a. *Arms and Insecurity*. Pittsburgh, PA: Boxwood Press.

Richardson, Lewis F. 1960b. *Statistics of Deadly Quarrels*. Pittsburgh, PA: Boxwood Press.

Rifkin, Jeremy. 1984. *Algeny*. New York: Penguin.

Riggs, Robert E., and I. Jostein Mykletun. 1979. *Beyond Functionalism: Attitudes toward International Organization in Norway and the United States*. Minneapolis: University of Minnesota Press.

Riggs, Robert E., and Jack C. Plano. 1994. *The United Nations: International Organization and World Politics*, 2nd ed. Belmont, CA: Wadsworth Publishing Company.

Riker, William H. 1962. *The Theory of Political Coalitions*. New Haven, CT: Yale University Press.

Riker, William H. 1964. *Federalism: Origin, Operation, Significance*. Boston: Little, Brown.

Risse-Kappen, Thomas. 1991. "Did 'Peace through Strength' End the Cold War?" *International Security* 16, no. 1 (Summer), 162–188.

Risse-Kappen, Thomas, ed. 1994. *Bringing Transnational Relations Back In: Non-State Actors, Domestic Structures and International Institutions*. Unpublished manuscript.

Rodrik, Dani. 1997. *Has Globalization Gone Too Far?* Washington, DC: Institute for International Economics.

Rogowski, Ronald. 1989. *Commerce and Coalitions: How Trade Affects Domestic Political Alignments.* Princeton, NJ: Princeton University Press.

Rosati, Jerel, and John Creed. 1997. "Extending the Three- and Four-Headed Eagles: The Foreign Policy Orientations of American Elites during the 80s and 90s," *Political Psychology* 18, no. 3, 583–623.

Rosecrance, Richard N. 1963. *Action and Reaction in World Politics.* Boston: Little, Brown.

Rosecrance, Richard N. 1986. *The Rise of the Trading State: Commerce and Conquest in the Modern World.* New York: Basic Books.

Rosenau, James N. 1961. *Public Opinion and Foreign Policy.* New York: Random House.

Rosenau, James N. 1966. "Pre-Theories and Theories of Foreign Policy," in *Approaches to Comparative and International Politics,* ed. R. Barry Farrell. Evanston, IL: Northwestern University Press, pp. 27–92.

Rosenau, James N. 1980. *The Scientific Study of Foreign Policy,* rev. ed. London: Frances Pinter.

Rosenau, Pauline Vaillancourt. 1994. "Health Politics Meets Post-Modernism: Its Meaning and Implications for Community Health Organizing," *Journal of Health Politics, Policy, and Law* 19, no. 2 (Summer), 303–333.

Roskin, Michael G. 1989. *Countries and Concepts,* 3rd ed. Upper Saddle River, NJ: Prentice Hall.

Rostow, W. W. 1971a. *Politics and the Stages of Growth.* Cambridge, England: Cambridge University Press.

Rostow, W. W. 1971b. *The Stages of Economic Growth,* 2nd ed. Cambridge, England: Cambridge University Press.

Rourke, John T. 1995. *International Politics on the World Stage,* 5th ed. Guilford, CT: Dushkin Publishing.

Ruggie, John Gerard. 1983. "Continuity and Transformation in the World Polity: Toward a Neorealist Synthesis," *World Politics* 35, no. 2 (January), 261–285.

Ruggie, John Gerard. 1998. *Constructing the World Polity.* London: Routledge.

Rummel, Rudolph J. 1983. "Libertarianism and International Violence," *Journal of Conflict Resolution* 27, no. 1 (March), 27–71.

Rummel, Rudolph J. 1985. "Libertarian Propositions on Violence within and between Nations," *Journal of Conflict Resolution* 29, no. 3 (September), 419–455.

Rummel, Rudolph J. 1988. "From Political Systems, Violence, and War," *The United States Institute of Peace Journal* 1, no. 4 (September), 6.

Russett, Bruce. 1993. *Grasping the Democratic Peace: Principles for a Post-Cold War World.* Princeton, NJ: Princeton University Press.

Russett, Bruce. 1995. "And Yet It Moves," *International Security* 19, no. 4 (Spring), 164–175.

Russett, Bruce, Thomas Hartley, and Shoon Murray. 1994. "The End of the Cold War, Attitude Change, and the Politics of Defense Spending," *P.S.* 27, no. 1 (March), 17–20.

Russett, Bruce, John R. Oneal, and David R. Davis. 1998. "The Third Leg of the Kantian Tripod for Peace: International Organizations and Militarized Disputes, 1950–85," *International Organization* 52, no. 3 (Summer), 441–467.

Russett, Bruce, and Harvey Starr. 1985. *World Politics: The Menu for Choice,* 2nd ed. New York: W. H. Freeman.

Russett, Bruce, and Harvey Starr. 1989. *World Politics: The Menu for Choice,* 3rd ed. New York: W. H. Freeman.

Russett, Bruce, and Harvey Starr. 1992. *World Politics: The Menu for Choice,* 4th ed. New York: W. H. Freeman.

Rutkowski, Anthony M. 1995. "Multilateral Cooperation in Telecommunications," in *The New Information Infrastructure,* ed. William J. Drake. New York: Twentieth Century Fund Press, pp. 223–250.

Sachs, Jeffrey. 1998. "International Economics: Unlocking the Mysteries of Globalization," *Foreign Policy* 110 (Spring), 97–111.

Sagan, Carl. 1983. "Nuclear War and Climatic Catastrophe: Some Policy Implications," *Foreign Affairs* 62, no. 2 (Winter), 257–292.

Saivetz, Carol R., and Sylvia Woodby. 1985. *Soviet-Third World Relations.* Boulder, CO: Westview Press.

Salamon, Lester M. 1994. "The Rise of the Nonprofit Sector," *Foreign Affairs* 73, no. 4 (July/August), 109–123.

Samuelson, Paul A. 1955. "Diagrammatic Exposition of a Theory of Public Expenditure," *Review of Economics and Statistics* 37, no. 4 (November), 350–356.

Schaefer, Robert K. 1997. *Understanding Globalization.* New York: Rowman and Littlefield Publishers, Inc.

Schelling, Thomas C. 1960. *The Strategy of Conflict.* Cambridge, MA: Harvard University Press.

Schlagheck, Donna M. 1988. *International Terrorism.* Lexington, MA: Lexington Books.

Schlesinger, Arthur, Jr. 1967. "Origins of the Cold War," *Foreign Affairs* 46, no. 1 (October), 22–52.

Schneider, William. 1987. " 'Rambo' and Reality: Having It Both Ways," in *Eagle Resurgent? The Reagan Era in American Foreign Policy,* eds. Kenneth A. Oye, Robert J. Lieber, and Donald Rothchild. Boston: Little, Brown, pp. 41–74.

Schott, Jeffrey J. 1994. *The Uruguay Round: An Assessment.* Washington, DC: Institute for International Economics.

Schott, Jeffrey J. 1996. *WTO 2000: Setting the Course for World Trade.* Washington, DC: Institute for International Economics.

Schweizer, Peter. 1996. "The Growth of Economic Espionage," *Foreign Affairs* 75, no. 1 (January/February), 9–14.

Segal, Gerald. 1996. "East Asia and the 'Constrainment' of China," *International Security* 20, no. 4 (Spring), 107–135.

Sewell, John W., Stuart K. Tucker, and contributors. 1988. *Growth, Exports and Jobs in a Changing World Economy: Agenda 1988.* New Brunswick, NJ: Transaction Books.

Shanks, Cheryl, Harold K. Jacobson, and Jeffrey H. Kaplan. 1996. "Inertia and Change in the Constellation of International Governmental Organizations, 1981–1992," *International Organization* 50, no. 4 (Autumn), 593–627.

Shepherd, George W., Jr. 1987. *The Trampled Grass.* New York: Greenwood Press.

Simon, Herbert A. 1957. *Models of Man.* New York: John Wiley and Sons.

Simon, Julian. 1981. *The Ultimate Resource.* Princeton, NJ: Princeton University Press.

Simpson, Smith. 1987. *Education in Diplomacy: An Instructional Guide.* Boston: University Press of America.

Singer, J. David. 1961. "The Level of Analysis Problem in International Relations," in *The International System,* eds. Klaus Knorr and Sidney Verba. Princeton, NJ: Princeton University Press, pp. 77–92.

Singer, J. David, and Thomas Cusack. 1981. "Periodicity, Inexorability, and Steermanship in International War," in *From National Development to Global Community: Essays in Honor of Karl W. Deutsch,* eds. Richard L. Merritt and Bruce M. Russett. London: Allen and Unwin, pp. 404–422.

Sivard, Ruth Leger. 1987. *World Military and Social Expenditures*, 12th ed. Washington, DC: World Priorities.

Sivard, Ruth Leger. 1991. *World Military and Social Expenditures*, 14th ed. Washington, DC: World Priorities.

Sivard, Ruth Leger. 1993. *World Military and Social Expenditures*, 15th ed. Washington, DC: World Priorities.

Sivard, Ruth Leger. 1996. *World Military and Social Expenditures*, 16th ed. Washington, DC: World Priorities.

Small, Melvin, and J. David Singer. 1982. *Resort to Arms: International and Civil Wars, 1816–1980.* Beverly Hills, CA: Sage Publications.

Small, Melvin, and J. David Singer. 1985. "Patterns in International Warfare, 1816–1980," in *International War,* eds. Melvin Small and J. David Singer. Homewood, IL: Dorsey Press, pp. 7–19.

Smith, Adam. 1910. *An Inquiry into the Nature and Causes of the Wealth of Nations.* London: Dent.

Smith, Marjorie S. 1987. "Japanese Defense Spending: A Levels-of-Analysis Approach," unpublished paper, University of Denver.

Smith, Michael Joseph. 1986. *Realist Thought from Weber to Kissinger.* Baton Rouge: Louisiana State University Press.

Snidal, Duncan. 1985. "Coordination versus Prisoner's Dilemma: Implications for International Cooperation and Regimes," *American Political Science Review* 74, no. 4 (December), 923–942.

Snyder, Glenn H., and Paul Diesing. 1977. *Conflict among Nations: Bargaining, Decision-Making and System Structure in International Crisis.* Princeton, NJ: Princeton University Press.

Sollenberg, Margareta, and Peter Wallensteen. 1997. "Major Armed Conflicts," *SIPRI Yearbook.* Stockholm: SIPRI, pp. 19–30.

Sorokin, Pitirim A. 1937. *Social and Cultural Dynamics,* Vol. 3, *Fluctuations of Social Relationships, War, and Revolution.* New York: American Book Company.

Soroos, Marvin S. 1986. *Beyond Sovereignty: The Challenge of Global Policy.* Columbia: University of South Carolina Press.

Soroos, Marvin S. 1987. "Global Commons, Telecommunications, and International Space Policy," in *International Space Policy,* ed. Daniel S. Papp and John R. McIntyre. New York: Quorum Books, pp. 139–156.

Soroos, Marvin S. 1997. *The Endangered Atmosphere.* Columbia: University of South Carolina.

Soroos, Marvin S. 1998. "Preserving the Atmosphere as a Global Commons," *Environment* 40, no. 2 (March), 7–13.

Sosland, Jeffrey K. 1997. "Cooperating Rivals: The Water Scarcity Threat in the Arab-Israeli Arena, the Yarmouk River Case," paper presented at the annual meeting of the International Studies Association, Toronto, Canada, March 21.

Spector, Leonard S. 1988. *The Undeclared Bomb.* Cambridge, MA: Ballinger Publishing.

Spector, Leonard S., with Jacqueline R. Smith. 1990. *Nuclear Ambitions.* Boulder, CO: Westview Press.

Spero, Joan Edelman. 1981. *The Politics of International Economic Relations,* 2nd ed. New York: St. Martin's Press.

Spiro, David E. 1994. "The Insignificance of the Liberal Peace," *International Security* 19, no. 2 (Fall), 50–81.

Stern, Nicholas. 1995. "Measures of Development," in *Leading Issues in Economic Development,* 6th ed., ed. Gerald M. Meier. New York: Oxford University Press, pp. 13–22.

Stiglitz, Joseph E., and Lyn Squire. 1998. "International Development: Is It Possible?" *Foreign Policy* 110 (Spring), 138–151.

Stockholm International Peace Research Institute [SIPRI]. 1997. *SIPRI Yearbook 1997.* New York: Oxford University Press.

Stoessinger, John C. 1976. *Henry Kissinger: The Anguish of Power.* New York: W. W. Norton.

Stoessinger, John C. 1979. *Crusaders and Pragmatists: Movers of Modern American Foreign Policy.* New York: W. W. Norton.

Stoessinger, John C. 1985. *Why Nations Go to War,* 4th ed. New York: St. Martin's Press.

Stoll, Richard J. 1989. "State Power, World Views, and the Major Powers," in *Power in World Politics,* eds. Richard J. Stoll and Michael D. Ward. Boulder, CO: Lynne Rienner, pp. 135–157.

Strange, Susan. 1988. *States and Markets.* New York: Basil Blackwell.

Streit, Clarence. 1961. *Freedom's Frontier—Atlantic Union Now.* Washington, DC: Freedom and Union Press.

Thompson, Janice E., and Stephen D. Krasner. 1989. "Global Transactions and the Consolidation of Sovereignty," in *Global Changes and Theoretical Challenges,* eds. Ernst-Otto Czempiel and James N. Rosenau. Lexington, MA: Lexington Books, pp. 195–220.

Thompson, William R., ed. 1983. *Contending Approaches to World System Analysis.* Beverly Hills, CA: Sage Publications.

Thompson, William R., and L. Gary Zuk. 1982. "War, Inflation, and the Kondratieff Wave," *Journal of Conflict Resolution* 26, no. 4 (December), 621–644.

Thucydides. 1972, trans. *History of the Peloponnesian War.* New York: Penguin Books.

Tickner, J. Ann. 1992. *Gender in International Relations.* New York: Columbia University Press.

Tickner, J. Ann. 1997. "Identity in International Relations Theory: Feminist Perspectives," in *The Return of Culture and Identity in IR Theory,* eds. Yosef Lapid and Friedrich Kratochwil. Boulder, CO: Lynne Rienner, pp. 147–162.

Tilly, Charles. 1985. "War Making and State Making as Organized Crime," in *Bringing the State Back In,* eds. Peter B. Evans, Dietrich Rueschemeyer, and Theda Skocpol. New York: Cambridge University Press, pp. 169–191.

Todaro, Michael P. 1989. *Economic Development in the Third World,* 4th ed. New York: Longman.

Toynbee, Arnold. 1972. *A Study of History.* New York: Weathervane Books.

Tucker, Robert C., ed. 1978. *The Marx-Engels Reader,* 2nd ed. New York: W. W. Norton.

United Nations. 1973. *The Determinants and Consequences of Population Trends,* Vol 1. Department of Economic and Social Affairs, Population Studies No. 50 (ST/SOA/SER.A/50).

United Nations. 1980. *The World Population Situation in 1979.* Department of International Economic and Social Affairs, Population Studies No. 72 (ST/ESA/SER.A/72).

United Nations Centre on Transnational Corporations [UNCTC]. 1988. *Transnational Corporations in World Development.* New York: United Nations.

United Nations Centre on Transnational Corporations [UNCTC]. 1991. *World Investment Report: The Triad in Foreign Direct Investment.* New York: United Nations.

United Nations Conference on Trade and Development [UNCTAD]. 1994. *World Investment Report 1994.* New York: United Nations.

United Nations Conference on Trade and Development [UNCTAD]. 1996. *World Investment Report 1996.* New York: United Nations.

United Nations Conference on Trade and Development [UNCTAD]. 1997. *World Investment Report 1997.* New York: United Nations.

United Nations Development Programme [UNDP]. 1992. *Human Development Report 1992.* New York: Oxford University Press.

United Nations Development Programme [UNDP]. 1994. *Human Development Report 1994.* New York: Oxford University Press.

United Nations Development Programme [UNDP]. 1997. *Human Development Report 1997.* New York: Oxford University Press.

United Nations Environment Programme [UNEP]. 1979. *The United Nations Environment Programme.* Nairobi, Kenya: United Nations Environment Programme.

United Nations Non-Governmental Liaison Service [UN NGLS]. 1994. *NGLS Roundup: International Conference on Population and Development* (October).

United States Department of State. 1989. *Patterns of Global Terrorism 1988,* Department of State Publication 9705. Washington, DC: Ambassador-at-Large for Counterterrorism.

Van Creveld, Martin. 1989. *Technology and War.* New York: Free Press.

Van Deelen, Wim. 1988. "Nuclear Fusion Research in Europe," *Europe,* no. 274 (March), 26–28.

Van Dinh, Trans. 1987. *Communication and Diplomacy in a Changing World.* Norwood, NJ: Ablex Publishing.

Vasquez, John A. 1983. *The Power of Power Politics: A Critique.* New Brunswick, NJ: Rutgers University Press.

Vernon, Raymond. 1971. *Sovereignty at Bay.* New York: Basic Books.

Vernon, Raymond. 1987. "International Investment and International Trade in the Product Cycle," in *International Political Economy,* eds. Jeffrey A. Frieden and David A. Lake. New York: St. Martin's Press, pp. 174–186.

Viner, Jacob. 1958. *The Long View and the Short: Studies in Economic Theory and Policy.* New York: Free Press.

Wæver, Ole. 1997. "Figures of International Thought: Introducing Persons Instead of Paradigms," in *The Future of International Relations,* eds. Iver B. Neumann and Ole Wæver. London: Routledge, pp. 1–37.

Wallace, Michael D., and J. David Singer. 1970. "Intergovernmental Organization in the Global System, 1815–1964: A Quantitative Description," *International Organization* 24, no. 2 (Spring), 239–287.

Wallerstein, Immanuel. 1976. *The Modern World System,* Vol 1. New York: Academic Press.

Wallerstein, Immanuel. 1980. *The Modern World System,* Vol 2. New York: Academic Press.

Walt, Stephen. 1998. "International Relations: One World, Many Theories," *Foreign Policy* 110 (Spring), 29–47.

Walter, Gregor, Sabine Dreher, and Marianne Beisheim. 1997. "Globalization Processes in the OECD World," paper delivered at the annual meeting of the International Studies Association, Toronto, Canada, March 18–22.

Walters, Robert S., and David H. Blake. 1992. *The Politics of Global Economic Relations,* 4th ed. Upper Saddle River, NJ: Prentice Hall.

Waltz, Kenneth N. 1959. *Man, the State and War: A Theoretical Analysis.* New York: Columbia University Press.

Waltz, Kenneth N. 1969. "International Structure, National Force, and the Balance of World Power," in *International Politics and Foreign Policy,* 2nd ed, ed. James N. Rosenau. New York: Free Press, pp. 304–314.

Waltz, Kenneth N. 1979. *Theory of International Politics.* New York: Random House.

Waltz, Kenneth N. 1982 (originally 1973). "The Myth of National Interdependence," in *Globalism versus Realism: International Relations' Third Debate,* eds. Ray Maghroori and Bennett Ramberg. Boulder, CO: Westview Press, pp. 81–96.

Wang, Kevin, and James Lee Ray. 1994. "Beginners and Winners: The Fate of Initiators of Interstate War Involving Great Powers Since 1495," *International Studies Quarterly* 38, no. 1, 139–154.

Watson, Adam. 1992. *The Evolution of International Society*. Routledge: New York.

Watson, George. 1993. "Millar or Marx?" *Wilson Quarterly* (Winter), 50–56.

Weimer, David L., and Aidan R. Vining. 1989. *Policy Analysis: Concepts and Practice.* Upper Saddle River, NJ: Prentice Hall.

Wendt, Alexander. 1992. "Anarchy Is What States Make of It: The Social Construction of World Politics," *International Organization* 46 (Spring), 391–425.

White, Ralph K. 1985. "Misperception in Vienna on the Eve of World War I," in *International War*, eds. Melvin Small and J. David Singer. Homewood, IL: Dorsey Press, pp. 231–239.

Wilkenfeld, Jonathan, Michael Brecher, and Stephen R. Hill. 1989. "Threat and Violence in State Behavior," in *Crisis, Conflict and Instability*, eds. Michael Brecher and Jonathan Wilkenfeld. New York: Pergamon Press, pp. 177–193.

Will, George F. 1983. *Statecraft as Soulcraft: What Government Does*. New York: Simon & Schuster.

Williamson, Oliver E. 1985. *The Economic Institutions of Capitalism: Firms, Markets, Relational Contracting*. New York: Free Press.

Wittkopf, Eugene R. 1990. *Faces of Internationalism: Public Opinion and American Foreign Policy*. Durham, NC: Duke University Press.

Wolf, Edward C. 1988. "Raising Agricultural Productivity," in *State of the World 1987*, eds. Lester R. Brown and others. New York: W. W. Norton, pp. 139–156.

World Bank. 1979. *World Development Report 1979*. Washington, DC: World Bank.

World Bank. 1988. *Annual Report*. Washington, DC: World Bank.

World Bank. 1992a. *World Development Report 1992*. New York: Oxford University Press.

World Bank. 1992b. *Global Economic Prospects and the Developing Countries*. Washington, DC: World Bank.

World Bank. 1997. *World Development Indicators 1997*. Washington, DC: The World Bank.

World Bank. 1998. *World Development Indicators 1998*. Washington, DC: The World Bank.

World Resources Institute [WRI]. 1986. *World Resources 1986*. New York: Basic Books.

World Resources Institute [WRI]. 1988. *World Resources 1988–89*. New York: Basic Books.

World Resources Institute [WRI]. 1994. *World Resources 1994–95*. New York: Oxford University Press.

World Resources Institute [WRI]. 1998. *World Resources 1998–99*. New York: Oxford University Press.

Wright, Martin. 1991. *International Theory: The Three Traditions*. Leicester, England: Leicester University Press.

Wright, Quincy. 1965. *A Study of War*, 2nd ed. Chicago: University of Chicago Press.

Young, Oran R. 1986. "International Regimes: Toward a New Theory of Institutions," *World Politics* 39, no. 1 (October), 104–122.

Young, Oran R. 1994. *International Governance: Protecting the Environment in a Stateless Society*. Ithaca, NY: Cornell University Press.

Zacher, Mark W., with Brent A. Sutton. 1997. *Governing Global Networks: International Regimes for Transportation and Communications*. Cambridge, England: Cambridge University Press.

Zacher, Mark W., and Richard A. Matthew. 1995. "Liberal International Theory: Common Threads and Divergent Strands," in *Controversies in International Relations Theory,* ed. Charles W. Kegley, Jr. New York: St. Martin's Press, pp. 83–106.

Zeigler, David W. 1987. *War, Peace and International Politics,* 4th ed. Boston: Little, Brown.

Zevin, Robert. 1992. "Are World Financial Markets More Open? If So, Why and with What Effects?" in *Financial Openness and National Autonomy,* eds. Tariq Banuni and Duliet B. Schor. Oxford, England: Clarendon Press, pp. 43–83.

Author Index

A

Adams, Gordon, 166
Adelman, Irma, 262n
Adler, Emanuel, 49
Alker, Hayward R., Jr., 53n
Allison, Graham T., 177, 178
Almond, Gabriel A., 56, 160, 298–299
Ashford, Lori S., 365
Asimov, Isaac, 66n
Axelrod, Robert, 105, 106
Ayres, Robert U., 21, 403

B

Baldwin, David A., 82, 85, 92
Ball, Terrence, 272
Banfield, Edward, 56
Banks, Michael, 35n
Barber, Benjamin R., 189
Barber, James David, 173
Barbieri, Katherine, 198
Barnaby, Frank, 345
Barnett, Michael M., 180
Bauer, Raymond A., 164, 165
Beck, Nathaniel, 100
Behrens, William W., III, 331, 336
Beisheim, Marianne, 188
Bell, Daniel, 261
Bennett, Robert William, 63n

Bergesen, Albert, 64
Bhagwati, Jagdish, 266
Biersteker, Thomas J., 53n
Birdsall, Nancy, 5
Blainey, Geoffrey, 125
Blake, David H., 265, 308, 315, 323
Blank, Kermit, 224
Bloomfield, Lincoln, 240
Boli-Bennett, John, 22n, 23
Boulding, Kenneth E., 328
Bower, Bruce, 11
Boyer, Robert, 261
Braudel, Fernand, 275, 299
Brecher, Michael, 102, 176n
Bremer, Stuart A., 87
Brody, Richard A., 176n
Brown, Lester R., 13, 299, 341n, 358n, 362, 368, 370n, 374, 406–407
Brown, Seyom, 139, 202n, 208, 350
Brown, William, 322, 403
Bryce, James, 194
Bull, Hedley, 58, 130, 193
Burton, John W., 54, 409

C

Campbell, David, 272n
Caporaso, James A., 51n
Caprio, Gerard, Jr., 293
Cardenas, 418

Carr, Edward Hallett, 41*n*
Cartwright, David, 84
Cassese, Antonio, 126
Castells, Manuel, 341, 351
Chai, Sun-ki, 154, 156
Chan, Steve, 49, 111, 129
Chang, Iris, 156
Checkel, Jeffrey T., 53*n*
Chenery, Hollis, 261
Choucri, Nazli, 399
Cioffi-Revilla, Claudio, 98*n*
Claude, Inish L., Jr., 111*n*
Cohen, Avner, 144
Cohen, Benjamin J., 138
Cook, Earl, 343
Couloumbis, Theodore A., 125, 128, 129
Cox, Robert, 272
Craig, Gordon A., 63*n*, 66, 175
Crawford, Beverly, 49
Creed, John, 159*n*
Cusack, Thomas, 63*n*, 99

D

Dahl, Robert, 164
Daly, Herman E., 333
Daly, Markate, 53*n*
Dasmann, Raymond F., 331
Davis, David R., 185*n*
Dawisha, Adeed, 228
de Blij, Harm J., 240
De Conde, Alexander, 154, 222
Deibert, Ronald J., 353*n*, 355–356
der Derian, James, 272
Derrida, Jacques, 58
Desch, Michael C., 53*n*
de Sola Pool, Ithiel, 164, 165, 338
Deutsch, Karl W., 22, 23, 75, 113, 202,
    231, 235
Dexter, Lewis Anthony, 164, 165
Diesing, Paul, 176
Dixon, William J., 198
Domke, William K., 198, 206
Donnelly, Jack, 49, 193
Dougherty, James E., 79
Doyle, Michael W., 49, 242, 297, 307
Drache, Daniel, 261
Dreher, Sabine, 188
Drucker, Peter F., 346, 347, 353

E

Eck, Diana L., 244
Edington, Robert, 103*n*, 248*n*
Eichenberg, Richard C., 158, 166
Eisenhower, Dwight D., 166
Elliott, Kimberly Ann, 83
Engler, Robert, 296
Enloe, Cynthia, 57
Etzioni, Amitai, 53*n*

F

Fallows, James, 264*n*
Feinberg, Richard E., 295
Ferguson, Yale H., 35*n*, 55, 221
Feuer, Lewis S., 405
Finger, Matthias, 187
Finnemore, Martha, 57
Flavin, Christopher, 134
Fluehr-Lobban, Carolyn, 409*n*
Foster, Richard H., 103*n*, 248*n*
Foucault, Michel, 58
Frank, André Gunder, 269
Freeman, Chris, 346
Freeman, Peter, 331
Freeman, W. H., 100
French, Hillary F., 32
Friedman, Milton, 257
Frost, Ellen L., 153*n*, 157
Fukuyama, Francis, 195, 226, 251

G

Galtung, Johan, 270
Garnham, David, 196
Garraty, John A., 241, 242, 249
Gay, Peter, 241, 242, 249
Gellner, Ernest, 235
George, Alexander, 63*n*, 66, 81, 173, 175, 396
George, Jim, 272*n*
George, Juliette, 173
Gershenkron, Alexander, 322
Gilpin, Robert, 42, 114–115, 117, 187, 198, 264,
    403, 487
Glassner, Martin Ira, 240
Gochman, Charles S., 102, 104
Goldstein, Gregg H., 295

Goldstein, Joshua S., 100, 346*n*, 347, 348
Goldstein, Judith, 165, 168, 194
Gray, Peter, 107
Grieco, Joseph M., 48
Griffin, Keith B., 373
Gurr, Ted Robert, 233–236

H

Haas, Ernst B., 111*n*, 213, 331
Haas, Peter M., 194
Hannon, Michael T., 23
Hardin, Garrett, 133, 407
Hardin, Russell, 54
Harff, Barbara, 234*n*
Harris, Marvin, 333*n*
Harsanyi, John C., 181
Hart, Jeffrey, 330
Hastedt, Glenn P., 383
Hayek, Friedrich A., 257
Headrick, Daniel R., 297*n*, 340*n*, 359
Hermann, Charles F., 101
Herz, John H., 201, 202
Hill, Stephen R., 176*n*
Hinsley, F. H., 62*n*
Holdren, John P., 145
Holister, Geoffrey, 334*n*
Hollins, Harry B., 141
Holsti, K. J., 35*n*, 37*n*, 64, 80, 127, 128,
        267, 399
Holsti, Ole R., 113, 158, 159, 173, 176*n*, 396
Hooghie, Liesbet, 224
Hopf, Ted, 53*n*
Hopkins, Terence K., 348
Hopmann, P. Terrence, 113
Hufbauer, Gary Clyde, 83
Hughes, Barry B., 51*n*, 87, 159*n*, 162, 165, 173*n*,
        179, 196, 224, 254, 255, 331, 374, 422*n*
Hughes, J. D., 333*n*
Hunter, James Davison, 244
Huntington, Samuel P., 18*n*, 57, 189, 194, 195,
        197, 244, 415

I

Imbert, Gaston, 348
Ingersoll, David E., 234, 267, 269*n*
Inglehart, Ronald, 188, 230

J

Jacobson, Harold K., 200, 201, 202*n*
Janis, Irving L., 177
Jervis, Robert, 174, 345
Joffee, Josef, 165
Johnson, Harry, 187
Joyner, Christopher S., 211

K

Kahn, Herman, 322, 403
Kallab, Valeriana, 373
Kanavou, Angeliki, 233
Kane, Hal, 341*n*
Kaplan, Jeffrey H., 200
Kaplan, Morton, 398
Kaplan, Morton A., 63*n*, 112
Katzenstein, Peter J., 53*n*
Keck, Otto, 138
Keeling, Charles D., 13
Kegley, Charles W., 169, 173*n*, 199, 297, 315, 383
Kennan, George, 250
Kennedy, Paul, 78
Keohane, Robert O., 42*n*, 51*n*, 52, 106, 116, 168,
        186*n*, 194, 199
Keynes, John Maynard, 55–56, 168, 292, 294
Kindleberger, Charles P., 117, 276, 305
Kirchner, Emil J., 351
Kissinger, Henry, 89, 111, 173
Klass, Rosanne, 127
Kline, John M., 283
Kowert, Paul, 53*n*
Krasner, Stephen D., 180*n*, 276, 315
Kratochwil, Freidrich, 53*n*
Krauss, Michael, 233
Krugman, Paul R., 264*n*, 265
Kubalkova, Vendulka, 53*n*
Kugler, Jacek, 18*n*, 117
Kuhn, Thomas, 35*n*, 44*n*
Kuttner, Robert, 264*n*
Kuznets, Simon, 261, 262

L

Lake, David A., 276, 283
Lamb, Christopher J., 144
Lapid, Yosef, 37*n*, 53*n*

Lau, D. C., 334*n*
Lauterpacht, H., 125, 128
Leatherman, Janie, 186*n*
Lebow, Richard Ned, 103
Lee, Steven, 145
Lenssen, Nicholas, 341*n*
Lenway, Stefanie Ann, 165
Levy, Jack S., 98, 99*n*, 173, 174, 180
Lewis, John P., 373
Lipset, Seymour Martin, 307
Lofdahl, Correy L., 360
Lopez, George A., 84
Lovins, Amory B., 10
Luce, R. D., 136
Lynch, Cecelia, 57*n*

M

McCalla, Robert B., 113
McDermott, John, 329
MacDonald, Stuart, 352
Machiavelli, Niccolò, 45, 334, 414
McNeill, William H., 345, 359
Macridis, Roy C., 250
McWilliams, Wayne C., 153
Maddison, Angus, 15, 17, 275, 402
Mahan, Alfred, 78
Manno, Jack, 187
Mansbach, Richard W., 35*n*, 55, 221
Mansfield, Edward D., 118, 197*n*
Maoz, Zeev, 102, 104
March, James G., 92
Marchand, Marianna H., 247*n*
Marks, Gary, 224
Martel, Leon, 322, 403
Maslow, Abraham, 409
Matthew, Richard A., 51*n*
Matthews, Richard K., 234, 267, 269*n*
Mayers, Teena Karsa, 141, 143, 144, 146, 147
Mazrui, Ali, 380
Meadows, Dennis L., 331, 336
Meadows, Donella H., 331, 336
Mearsheimer, John J., 122
Merquior, J. G., 47
Merrick, Thomas W., 6
Meyer, John W., 22*n*, 23
Midford, Paul, 163
Midlarsky, Manus I., 114

Mills, C. Wright, 166*n*
Milton, John P., 331
Mitrany, David, 52, 203
Mittelman, James H., 261
Modelski, George, 62, 65, 68, 70, 118, 400
Moran, Theodore H., 315
Moravcsik, Andrew, 48*n*, 52
Morgenthau, Hans J., 41*n*, 45, 54*n*, 71, 111*n*,
    249, 399, 414
Morse, Edward, 257
Mueller, John, 49, 99*n*, 160, 164
Myrdal, Gunnar, 221

N

Naisbitt, John, 25*n*
Nau, Henry R., 18*n*
Nielsson, Gunnar, 233
Nietschmann, Bernard, 233
Niksch, Larry A., 153*n*
North, Robert C., 176*n*, 399
Nye, Joseph S., Jr., 52, 78, 186*n*, 203*n*

O

O'Brien, Conor Cruise, 233, 241*n*
Obstfeld, Maurice, 265
Odell, Peter R., 378
Olshansky, 361
Olson, Mancur, 115, 135*n*
Olton, Roy, 228
Oneal, John R., 185*n*
Onuf, Nicholas Greenwood, 53*n*
Oppenheim, Lassa, 126
Oppenheimer, Frank, 34
Organski, A. F. K., 18*n*, 117
Orme, John, 345
Osgood, Charles, 106, 148

P

Pagnucco, Ron, 186*n*
Palmer, Monte, 167
Papart, Jane L., 247*n*
Pape, Robert A., 83
Papp, Daniel S., 298

Pearson, Lester, 79
Perry, Ted, 334n
Peterson, V. Spike, 247n
Pettman, Jan Jindy, 247n
Pfaltzgraff, Robert L., 79
Piotrowski, Harry, 153
Pirages, Dennis, 331, 407
Plano, Jack C., 193, 210, 212, 213, 228, 279
Pollins, Brian M., 100
Porteous, Andrew, 334n
Postel, Sandra, 370n
Powers, Averill L., 141
Prebisch, Raul, 306n
Price, Richard, 185n
Princen, Thomas, 187
Putnam, Robert D., 56, 178

Q

Quester, George H., 345

R

Raiffa, Howard, 136
Ramirez, Francisco O., 22n, 223
Randers, Jorgen, 331, 336
Rasler, Karen, 115
Rattner, Steven, 128
Ray, James Lee, 35, 49, 75, 76, 91, 92, 180, 189
Raymond, Gregory A., 199
Reardon, Betty A., 172
Renner, Michael, 134
Richardson, Lewis Fry, 97, 98
Rielly, John E., 160–162
Rifkin, Jeremy, 333
Riggs, Robert E., 193, 210, 212, 213, 279
Riker, William H., 112, 202n
Risse-Kappen, Thomas, 186n, 297
Rodrik, Dani, 304
Rogowski, Ronald, 162n
Rosati, Jerel, 159n
Rosecrance, Richard N., 48, 232, 257
Rosenau, James N., 159n, 160, 355
Rosenau, Pauline Vaillancourt, 272n
Roskin, Michael G., 165
Rostow, W. W., 14, 261, 298
Rourke, John T., 159n

Rubinson, Richardson, 22n, 23
Ruggie, John Gerard, 53n, 58n, 138
Rummel, Rudolph J., 49, 197
Runyan, Anne Sisson, 247n
Russett, Bruce, 135n, 141, 143, 146, 147, 162,
    179, 185n, 197n, 198
Rutkowski, Anthony M., 353n

S

Sachs, Jeffrey, 260n, 294, 304
Sagan, Carl, 22
Saivetz, Carol R., 317
Salamon, Lester M., 185
Samuelson, Paul A., 131
Schaefer, Robert K., 245
Schelling, Thomas C., 168
Schlagheck, Donna M., 251
Schlesinger, Arthur, Jr., 249, 250
Schneider, William, 159, 163
Schott, Jeffrey J., 83, 285, 352
Segal, Gerald, 118
Sewell, John W., 309
Shanks, Cheryl, 200
Shapiro, Michael J., 272
Shepherd, George W., Jr., 316
Simon, Herbert, 177, 181
Simon, Julian, 300
Simpson, Smith, 79
Singer, J. David, 63n, 98, 99, 113, 125, 127, 186,
    195, 197, 200
Sivard, Ruth Leger, 22, 91, 92, 94, 95, 100, 101,
    116, 234n, 242, 256n, 299, 300, 301,
    316, 317
Siverson, Randolph M., 396
Small, Melvin, 63n, 98, 99, 125, 127, 197
Smith, Adam, 402
Smith, Jackie, 186n
Smith, Marjorie S., 153n
Smith, Michael Joseph, 45, 46
Smoke, Richard, 144
Snidal, Duncan, 132, 136
Snyder, Glenn H., 175
Snyder, Jack, 197n
Sollenberg, Margareta, 234
Sommer, Mark, 141
Sorokin, Pitirim A., 97, 98, 100, 134
Soroos, Marvin S., 130n, 142n, 386–389

Sosland, Jeffrey K., 371
Spector, Leonard S., 106, 349
Spero, Joan Edelman, 315, 319, 348
Spiro, David E., 197n
Sprout, Harold, 21
Sprout, Margaret, 21
Squire, Lyn, 262n
Starr, Harvey, 135n, 141, 143, 146,
    162, 179
Stern, Nicholas, 262n
Stiglitz, Joseph E., 262n
Stoessinger, John C., 81, 169, 170, 171
Stoll, Richard A., 63n
Strange, Susan, 351
Streit, Clarence, 203n
Sullivan, John D., 113
Sutton, Brent A., 353n

T

Tans, Pieter, 13
Taylor, Alan M., 291
Thompson, Janice, 276
Thompson, William R., 70, 115, 348, 405
Tickner, J. Ann, 55, 172
Tilly, Charles, 62
Todaro, Michael P., 320
Toynbee, Arnold, 406n
Tucker, Robert C., 267
Tucker, Stuart K., 309
Tyson, Laura D'Andrea, 341, 351

V

Van Creveld, Martin, 201n
Van Dinh, Trans, 79
Verba, Sidney, 56
Vernon, Raymond, 187, 306, 314, 315
Viner, Jacob, 264
Vining, Aidan R., 131, 263n

W

Waever, Ole, 53n
Wallace, Michael D., 186, 195, 200
Wallenstein, Peter, 234
Wallerstein, Immanuel, 272, 275, 348
Walt, Stephen, 53n
Walter, Gregor, 188
Walters, Robert S., 265, 308, 315
Waltz, Kenneth N., 42, 46n, 71, 112, 114, 206,
    269, 398, 399
Waltzer, Herbert, 248n
Wang, Kevin, 91
Watson, Adam, 58, 65
Watson, George, 267n
Weimer, David L., 131, 263n
Wendt, Alexander, 53n, 54
White, Ralph K., 174, 175
Wilkenfeld, Jonathan, 102, 176n
Will, George, 58
Williamson, Oliver E., 53n
Wittkopf, Eugene R., 169, 173n, 297, 315,
    383
Wolfe, James H., 125, 128, 129
Woodby, Sylvia, 317
Wright, Martin, 51n, 58
Wright, Quincy, 98, 99n, 197

Y

Young, Oran, 137n, 138

Z

Zacher, Mark W., 51n, 353n, 354
Zeckhauser, Richard, 115
Zevin, Robert, 291
Ziegler, David W., 176
Zitomersky, Joseph, 63n
Zuk, L. Gary, 348

Subject Index

A

Abortion, 215, 246, 367
Absolute (trade) advantage, 259
Absolute gain, 48
Abu Dhabi, 227
Académie Francaise, 351
Acheson, Dean, 79
Acid rain, 11, 386, 393
Action-reaction dynamic, 43, 105
Afghanistan, 89
    refugees from, 363
    Soviet invasion of, 91, 92, 99, 112, 127, 128,
        144, 318, 374
    Soviet withdrawal from, 178, 250
Africa
    AIDS incidence in, 360
    decolonization in, 297, 298
    family planning in, 364, 365
    food production in, 7
    imperialism in, 131–32, 241–42, 297
    nationality problems of, 239–40, 245–46
    rain forests in, 11
    regional economic organizations in, 220,
        221
    waste exports to, 387
Age of Reason, 330
Agriculture, 11, 282, 371. See also Food
Aid fatigue, 87
AIDS (acquired immune deficiency
        syndrome), 359–61

Airbus program, 351
Air pollution, 18, 385, 386, 388
Air transport, 338, 339
Albania, 27, 30, 82, 139, 250
Algeria, 298
Allende, Salvador, 315
Alliances, 77, 112–13
Ambassadors, 127
American Federation of Labor and Congress
        of Industrial Organizations (AFL-
        CIO), 163
American Revolution, 27
Amin, Idi, 91
Amnesty International, 25, 186, 187, 193
Analysis
    elements of, 27–40
        competing worldviews, 36–39
        structure of understanding, 33–36
        subject-matter categories, 28–33
    levels of, 153–58. See also Government;
        Individuals; Society, analysis of U.S.;
        State(s); State system(s)
Anarchy, 42–44, 51, 54, 56
Andalucia, 224
Andorra, 210
Anglo-Persian Oil Company, 378
Angola, 84, 89, 215, 317
Animal Farm (Orwell), 126
Antarctic Treaty of 1959, 132, 147, 390
Antibiotics, 361
Apartheid, 83, 130, 184, 230, 246

Appropriate technology, 314
Arab League, 228
Arbitration, 65
Argentina, 14, 99, 108, 184, 194, 195, 270, 316,
    323, 345
Ariane rocket, 351
Aristotelian science, 329–30
Armenia, 94, 237
Arms control and disarmament efforts, 50,
    124, 139–50, 171, 222, 348–49
  collective security, 139–40
  confidence and security building measures,
    146
  nonproliferation, 147–48
  nonprovocative defense, 141–42
  problems of, 149–50
  qualitative, 140–42
  quantitative, 143–46
  regional disarmament or nonmilitarization,
    146–47
  unilateral approaches, 148–49
Arms race, 105, 106
  players and their equipment, 21–22, 106–8
Arms sales during Cold War, 318, 348–49
ARPANET, 352
Asia-Pacific Economic Co-operation Forum
    (APEC), 221
Associational revolution, 185–86
Association of South East Asian Nations
    (ASEAN), 221
Aswan Dam, 227
Ataturk Dam, 371
Atomic bomb, 1, 20
AT&T Company, 354
Attentive public, 160
Attitudinal structure stability in U.S., 159–60
Augustine, St., 125, 128
Australia, 14, 67, 142, 221
Austria, 62, 102, 174–75, 194, 219, 236
Austria-Hungary, war fatalities in, 100
Autarky, 78, 271
Automobile industry, 9, 164
Azerbaijan, 94, 237, 238, 384

B

Baader-Meinhof Gang, 252
Backwash effects, 220–21

Bacon, Francis, 50, 330
Balance of payments, 278
Balance of power, 44, 110–11, 170, 396
  advocacy of, 111
  alliances, 112–13
  definition of, 111
  state behavior and, 112
Balance of trade, 278
Balkans, balance of power system and, 111
Baltic Republics, 30
Bamako Convention, 387
Bandung Conference of 1955, 320
Bandwagoning, 113
Bangladesh, 69, 185, 387
Bank crises, 293
Bank of International Settlements (BIS), 294
Bargain, obsolescing, 314
Barter trade, 138
Basic human needs, self-reliance strategies'
    focus on, 320
Basic Research in Industrial Technology for
    Europe (BRITE), 351
Bay of Pigs, U.S. invasion of, 177, 181, 317
Begin, Menachem, 81
Belarus, 107
Belgium, 15, 111, 115, 116, 219, 224
Beliefs
  causal, 168, 194
  principled, 168, 187, 194
Belize, 388
Bentham, Jeremy, 51, 52
Berlin Conference of 1884–1885, 132, 239, 297
Berlin Wall, 176
Beyond War, 25
Bhutto, Benazir, 172, 367
Bilateral analysis, insights from, 104–6
Bilateral investment treaties (BITs), 316
Biogenetic engineering, 342–43
Biological weapons, 142
Biotechnology, 371, 420
Bipolar system, 63, 65
Birth rate, 4, 362
Births, ratio of male to female, 386
Bismarck, Otto von, 305, 345
Blair, Tony, 247–48
Blitzkkreig, 345
Blue-collar jobs, 15
Bodin, Jean, 62
Bolivia, 195, 388

Borlaug, Norman, 7
Bosnia, NATO's role in, 119, 246
Bosnia-Herzegovina, 54, 58, 90, 130, 175, 192, 215, 235, 238, 239, 343
Botswana, 305, 360
Bounded rationality, 181
Boutrous-Ghali, Boutrous, 354
Boycotts, 82, 139
Brady Plan, 311
Brain drain, 314
Brandt, Willy, 171*n*
Brazil, 14, 69, 108, 185, 189, 194, 195, 323
Bretton Woods system, 277–80
    inadequacy of, 280–81
    institutions of, 277–79
Brezhnev Doctrine, 250
Bribery by multinational corporations, 315
Brinkmanship, 103
Britain. *See* Great Britain
British Broadcasting Corporation, 80, 341
British Navigation Act of 1651, 264
Brundtland, Prime Minister, 367
Brussels, 224
Bubonic Plague, 359
Bulgaria, 28, 32, 94, 139, 219
Bureaucratic-politics model of decision making, 178
Burke-Hartke Foreign Trade and Investment Act, 163
Burkina Faso, 69
Burma, 297
Burundi, 235, 305
Bush, George, 82, 120, 171, 173

C

Cambodia, 91, 128, 156, 157
Canada, 14, 21, 198, 386
Cape Verde, 239
Capital accumulation, 259, 268, 402
Capitalism, 38–39, 268
    cycles of expansion of, 405
    imperialism and, 268–69
Capital punishment, 197*n*
Carbon dioxide (CO_2), increase in atmospheric, 12, 13
Carbon-dioxide emissions, 387–89, 391
CARE, 86, 375

Carrying capacity, 331, 332, 334
Cartels, 322
    Organization of Petroleum Exporting Countries (OPEC), 164, 321, 322, 379, 380, 383–84
Carter, Jimmy, 81, 143, 169, 171, 173, 382–83, 408
Carter Doctrine, 383
Caste system, 235
Castro, Fidel, 83
Catalans, 224
Categorization, 329–30
Causal beliefs, 168, 194
Causality, 330
Central Commission for the Navigation of the Rhine, 200
Central Intelligence Agency (CIA), 81, 89, 315
CFCs (chlorofluorocarbons), 12, 136, 388, 392
Chad, 91
Change
    cycles, 407
    forces of. *See* Forces of change
    progressive, 400–403
    summary of worldviews and theories, 397
    system transformation, 404–7
    unpatterned, 396, 398–400
Charles VIII, King of France, 45
Charter 77, 192
Charter of the United Nations, 126
Chechnya, Republic of, 88, 118–19, 239
Chemical weapons, 142
Chernobyl, nuclear accident at, 386
Child labor, 189
Chile, 195, 294, 315, 322, 323
China, People's Republic of, 62–63, 71, 142, 274, 323, 325
    admission to UN, 164, 210
    CFC production, 136, 392
    economic growth in, 18, 322
    economic liberalizations in, 183
    environmental concerns in, 358–59, 385
    exclusion from UN, 126
    external assertiveness of, 119, 121
    food production in, 358
    human rights issue in, 121, 183, 186
    industrialization of, 15
    Japan and, 140
    military spending and personnel, 75, 121
    Nixon's visit to, 68, 164

China (*cont.*)
  nuclear weapons, 21, 68, 107, 108, 349
  one-child-per-family policy, 365
  population of, 20, 73–74, 358
  post–Cold War systemic role of, 121–22
  power
    aggregate, 76
    demographic, 72–73, 76
    military, 20, 75
  self-reliance or autarky of, 319, 320
  Soviet Union and, 68
  Taiwan and, 104, 121–22
  Tiananmen Square, 183
Chinese-Indian border dispute of 1962, 99, 399
Chinese system of Chou Dynasty period, 64, 65
Chlorofluorocarbons (CFCs), 12, 136, 388, 392
Cholera, 361
Christian Base Communities in Brazil, 185
Christianity, 241–43
Churchill, Winston, 94, 111, 169, 170
Ciller, Tansu, 172
City-state system, Greek, 64, 65, 399
Civilizations, clash of, 244, 415
Civil society, 52, 186, 356
Civil War (1861–1865), 14, 100–101, 189, 197
Clash of civilizations, 244, 415
Class, 55, 247–48
  Marxist view of, 267–68
Class consciousness, 58, 248
Classical liberalism, 37, 47, 48
Climate, 327
Climate patterns, 11, 12
Clinton, William, 122, 171, 183, 245, 252, 390
Cloning, 142
Club of Rome, 336
Cobden, Richard, 52
Code of Conduct on Transnational
      Corporations, 315
Coercion, collective, 135, 407
Coercive diplomacy, 81–82
Colbert, Jean Baptiste, 264
Cold War, 20, 63, 96, 101, 175
  arms sales during, 318, 348–49
  defined, 1–2
  post–Cold War uncertainties, 118–22
  proxy wars during, 317–18
  roots of, 249–50
Collective action, 283, 333
  and problems of underprovision, 135–36
  trade and logic of, 136–37

Collective coercion, 135, 407
Collective defense organizations, 139
Collective goods. *See* Goods
Collective reform, 320–22
Collective regulation, 389–90
Collective security, 139–40, 211–12
Colonialism. *See* Imperialism
COMECON, 220
Cominform, 249, 250
Comintern, 249
Commerce. *See* Trade
Commercial liberalism, 38, 257–63
  concepts, 257
  summary of, 397
  theory, 257, 259–62
  values and prescriptions, 262–63
Committee of One Million Against the
      Admission of Communist China to
      the United Nations, 164
Committee of the Regions, 224
Common Agricultural Policy (CAP), 219, 373
Common Market, 165, 204, 217. *See also*
      European Union (EU)
Common market, 204
Common property resources, 132–33
Commons, concept of, 133–34, 332, 407
Commonwealth of Independent States (CIS),
      120. *See also* Russia; Soviet Union
Communication technology, 16, 188, 339–41,
      355
Communism, 170, 248. *See also* Marxism;
      specific communist countries
  Central and Eastern European revolutions
      of 1989–1991 against, 27–32
  evolution of communist thought, 30
Communist Information Bureau (Cominform),
      249, 250
Communist Manifesto (Marx and Engels), 404–5
Communitarian perspective, 53*n*
Community(ies)
  epistemic, 194
  global. *See* Global community
Comoros Islands, 239
Comparative (trade) advantage, 260, 282, 294,
      402
Complex governance, 223, 224–25
Comprehensive Test Ban Treaty of 1996, 142
Computers, 16, 132, 341, 347, 353
Concepts in hierarchy of understanding, 34–36
Concert of Europe, 66

Conciliation, 65
Concorde project, 351
Conditional engagement, 122
Conditionality, 279
Conference on Security and Cooperation in
      Europe (CSCE), 192
Confidence and security building measures,
      146
Conflict. *See also* Warfare
   patterns of, in state systems, 97–104
Confucianism, 244
Congestion of goods, 131, 132, 139n
Congo, 212, 298
Congress of Vienna (1815), 66, 68, 127, 129, 200
Constitution of the United States, 51, 246
Constrainment, 122
Constructivism, 37–38, 404
   concepts of, 43, 53–56
   important contributions to, 58–59
   summary of, 397
   theory of, 43, 56
   values and prescriptions of, 43, 56–58
Consultative Group on International
      Agricultural Research, 371
Containment doctrine, 250
Contraception, 365, 366
Conventional Forces in Europe (CFE) Treaty of
      1990, 145
Convention on Biological Diversity, 371
Conversion, 242
Convertibility of wealth and power, 399
Cooperation, 46, 124–51. *See also* Global
      community
   under anarchy, 44
   arms control. *see* Arms control and
      disarmament efforts
   framework of, 125–30
      obligations of states, 127–30
      rights of states, 126–27
   goods and. *See* Goods
   reciprocated, 105–6
Cooperative internationalism, 159
Coordinating Committee on Multilateral
      Export Control (Cocom), 348
Coordination goods, 132, 133
Coordination power, 54
Core interests, 71
Core states, 270, 271
Correlates of War Project (University of
      Michigan), 75, 98, 99

Council for Mutual Economic Assistance
      (CMEA or Comecon), 220
Council of Europe, 192, 224
Council of the European Union, 216
Countermercantilist policies, 283
Covert operations, 89
Criminal networks, 188, 244–45
Crisis(es), 101–4
   perception and, 174–75
Crisis management, 175–76
Critical theory, 272–73
Croatia, 11, 30, 192, 238, 239
Cross-cutting cleavages, 113–14
Crucé plan, 202–3
Crude birth rate, 4
Crude death rate, 4
Cuba
   Bay of Pigs invasion, 177, 181, 317
   missile crisis, 90, 103–4, 124, 146,
      176, 317
   U.S. economic sanctions against, 83
Culture, global, 188–89
Culture wars, 244
Customs union, 204
"Cyber-terrorism," 89
Cycles, 407
Cycles of expansion, 269
Cyprus, 94, 219
Czechoslovakia, 27–29, 62, 89, 91, 127, 227,
      236, 250
Czech Republic, 120, 210, 219

D

DDT, 331, 353
Death rate, crude, 4
Debt crisis, LDC, 308–11
Decision making, foreign policy, models of,
      177–78
Declaration of Independence, 246
Declaration of the Rights of Man and Citizen,
      232
Decolonization, 1, 297–98
Defense, collective, 139
Defense spending. *See* Military spending
Deforestation, 11, 334, 368–69, 386, 387
De Gaulle, Charles, 68, 117, 171n, 281, 282
Delays, environmental, 331
Delian League, 65, 200

Democracy
protection of human rights in, 49
spread of, 183–84, 194–96
warfare and, 196–97
Democratic deficit, 216
Democratic party, U.S., 165
Democratic peace, 49, 401
Democratic Republic of Congo (Zaire), 4
Democratic Republic of the Congo, 298
Demographic transition, 3–7, 39, 362
Demographic trap, 362–63
Demonstration force, 89
Deng Xiaoping, 183
Denmark, 115, 219
Dependency theory, 270, 271, 315, 405–6
Dependent population, 6
Descartes, René, 50, 330
Desertification, 370
Designer genes, 343
Destructive potential, growth of, 20–22
Détente, 171, 350, 374
Devaluation, 278, 281
Development, sustainable, 333. *See also*
Economic development
Development Assistance Committee (DAC),
85
Diabolic enemy image, 174, 175
Diaspora, 228, 251
Dickens, Charles, 402
Diffuse reciprocity, 106, 279
Diffusion of technology, 346
Diplomacy, 79–82
coercive, 81–82
defined, 79
gunboat, 89
negotiation, 81–82
new vs. old, 82
reporting, 80–81
representation, 79–80
shuttle, 81
Diplomatic immunity, 128
Disarmament. *See* Arms control and
disarmament efforts
Diseases, 359–61
vaccination programs and, 12, 363
Dispute resolution
by United Nations, 213–14
by World Trade Organization, 286, 353
Division of labor, 259
global, 305–6, 418–19

Dollar, value of, 280–81
Doubly green revolution, 375
Drug trade, 188
Dual economy, 270, 406
Dual-use technology, 348, 349
Dulles, John Foster, 170, 173
Durkheim, Èmile, 58

E

Earth Summit (1992), 327, 371, 390, 391
East (category of states), 69
East African Common Services Organization
(EASCO), 220
East African Community, 220
Eastern Europe. *See also* specific countries
revolutions of 1989–1991, 27–33
East Germany, 28
formation of, 67
Ebola virus, 361
Ecoconflict, 407
Economic development
commercial liberalism on, 261–62
North-South gap in, 299–302
Economic espionage, 81
Economic integration, 205
scale of, 204
Economic interest groups, 162–64
Economic power, 74–75, 82–87
Economic restructuring, global, 13–18
Economics
neoclassical, 402
politics and, 38–39
revolutions of 1989–1991 and, 31–32
Economic throughput, 333
Economic union, 205
Economy(ies)
dual, 270, 406
global. *See* Global economy
political. *See* Political economy
Ecosystem, 331–33. *See also* Environmental
constraints
vulnerability, 385–93
Eco-wholism, 39, 331–36, 406–7
important contributions to, 333–34, 336
on population pressures, 362
summary of, 397
values and prescriptions, 333
Education, social mobilization and, 22

EEZs (Exclusive Economic Zones), 214, 388–89
Efficiency, defined, 262
Egypt, 81, 86, 164, 227, 228, 243, 297, 338, 371, 373
Eichman, Adolf, 197*n*
Einstein, Albert, 411
Eisenhower, Dwight D., 79, 150, 166, 170
Elasticity, 381
El Salvador, 215
Embargoes, 82, 84, 139, 140
Emerson, Ralph Waldo, 169
Energy, 377–85
    competing perspectives on, 378–81
    consumption per capita, 344
    lifetime of world reserves at current production rates, 378
    policy issues, 381–85
    revolutions of 1989–1991 and, 32
Energy transitions, 9–11
Engels, Friedrich, 404–5, 419
England, 14, 62, 275–76. *See also* Great Britain
ENIAC, 341
Enlightenment, 50–51, 246, 331
Environmental constraints, 358–94, 421–22. *See also* Political ecology
    ecosystem vulnerability
        interstate policy approaches, 388–93
        range of human impact, 385–88
    on food sufficiency, 7
    increased environmental impact, 11–13
    microenvironment, 359–61
    population pressures, 361–67
        competing perspectives on, 362–63
        migration and refugees, 363–64
        population control efforts, 364–67
    resource scarcities
        energy, 377–85
        food, 367–77
    revolutions of 1989–1991 and, 32
Environmentalist movement, 286–87, 336, 356
Epistemic communities, 194
Epistemology, 273
Equality, defined, 263
Equilibrium, 396, 398
Equity, defined, 263
Eritrea, 91, 210, 215
Espionage, 80–81
Essay on the Principle of Population, An (Malthus), 334, 336

Estonia, 30, 210, 219, 237
Ethiopia, 11, 83, 91, 139, 256, 297, 305, 318, 364, 377
Ethnic cleansing, 130, 239
Ethnic groups, 233–35, 237–39, 245
Euro-Atlantic Partnership Council (EAPC), 224
European Atomic Energy Commission (Euratom), 217
European Coal and Steel Community (ECSC), 217, 219
European Commission, 216
European Communities (EC), 217
European Court of Justice, 216
European Economic Community (EEC), 217
European Free Trade Association, 220
European Monetary System (EMS), 217
European Monetary Union (EMU), 217
European Parliament, 207, 216
European Recovery Program. *See* Marshall Plan
European Research Coordinating Agency (EUREKA), 351
European revolutions of 1830 and 1848, 232
European Strategic Program for Research and Development in Information Technology (ESPRIT), 351
European Union (EU), 55, 96, 118, 207, 284
    agricultural policies, 373
    budget and employees, 225
    CFC production, 136
    Common Agricultural Policy (CAP), 219
    deepening and widening of, 217, 219
    economic growth of, 18
    governmental organs of, 216–17
    performance and controversies, 219–20
    population of, 20
Europe of concentric circles, 222
Excess returns, 266
Exchange, mutually beneficial, 52
Exchange power, 55
Exchange rates, 277–79, 283, 287
Exclusive Economic Zones (EEZs), 214, 388–89
Expanded Program on Immunization (EPI), 214
Expansion, cycles of, 269
Exploitation of the big by the small, 115
Exponential growth, 335
Exports. *See* Trade

Extended family, 244
Externalities, 133, 265, 332, 333

F

F-22 fighter plane, 349–50
Factor price equalization, 163
Factors of production, 162, 257, 259
Facts in hierarchy of understanding, 34–36
Failed states, 360
Falkland Islands, 99, 172, 316, 345
Family, 244–45
Family planning, 214, 215, 364–67
Family size, 362
Famines, 342, 377
Fascism, 57, 170, 234
Fast-track authority, 221
Federalism, 202–3
Female infanticide, 246
Feminism, 56–57, 247
Ferdinand, Frances, Archduke, 102, 174, 236
Fertility control, 364–67
Fertility rates, 4–7, 214
Fertilizers, 7
Feudal system, 50, 61, 62, 248
Financial flows, 261
     managing explosive, 287–94
Finland, 219
First-strike capability, 109
First World, 69
Fishing, 133, 134, 275, 389, 392
Fixed exchange rates, 278
Flanders, 224
Floating exchange rates, 278
Focal points, 168
Food
     growing sufficiency of, 7–9, 342
     production, growth of, 367–68
     revolutions of 1989–1991 and, 32
     scarcities
          distribution of food, 373–75
          global attention to problems, 375, 377
          global supply of food, 368–73
     transfers, 373–74
Food for Peace Act of 1954 (P.L. 480), 373
Forces of change, 1–26
     demographic transition, 3–7
     destructive potential, growth of, 20–22

energy transitions, 9–11
environmental impact, increased, 11–13
food sufficiency, growing, 7–9
global economic restructuring, 13–18
social mobilization, increased, 22–25
Soviet Union, collapse of, 2, 20, 27–30, 68,
     70, 113, 171, 237, 250
uncertain implication of trends, 25
U.S. decline, 18
Ford, Gerald, 173
Foreign aid, 82, 84–87
Foreign direct investment (FDI), 288–91
Foreign-exchange trading, 288
Foreign policy
     attitudinal structure stability and, 159–60
     decision making, 177–78
     gender and, 171–72
     ideas and, 168
     interest groups and, 164
     political parties and, 165–66
     psychology and, 172–73
Foreign portfolio equity investment (FPEI),
     288
Fossil fuels, environmental impact of burning,
     11–12
Fourth World, 69, 233
Framing decision situations, 174
France, 14, 15, 62, 66, 111, 142, 219
     Académie Francaise, 351
     AIDS research by, 360
     colonial wars, 298
     energy and energy policies, 378
     imperialism and, 297
     nuclear weapons, 21, 68, 107, 109
     political parties, 166, 167
     war fatalities, 100
     withdrawal from NATO, 68
Franco-Prussian War (1870–1871), 14
Freedom House, 195, 415
Free rider, 116, 135, 283
Free trade, 138, 198, 284
     areas, 96, 204
     history of global economy and, 275–77
     Stolper-Samuelson theorem of, 162n, 266
     U.S. interests and, 163–65
Free Trade Area of the Americas (FTAA), 221
French Revolution, 232, 249
Functional intergovernmental organizations
     (IGOs), 199

Functionalism, 203–5, 401
Fundamentalism, religious, 94, 243–44
Fungible goods, 84

G

Galicia, 224
Galileo, 330
Gandhi, Indira, 172, 243
Gandhi, Mohandas, 185, 242, 297
GATT. *See* General Agreement on Tariffs and
    Trade (GATT)
Gaza Strip, 237, 362
Gender, 55
    foreign policy and, 171–72
    human rights and, 193
    sexism and, 246–47
Genentech, 342
General Agreement on Tariffs and Trade
    (GATT), 277, 278, 286, 308, 319
General Agreement on Trade in Services
    (GATS), 286
General Assembly of United Nations, 208, 209
General Dynamics, 349
Generalized System of Preferences (GSP), 321
General public, 160
General system of preferences (GSP), 124
Genetic engineering, 333
Geneva Accords, 90
Geneva conference of 1949, 129
Geneva Protocol of 1952, 142
Genocide, 234, 239, 245
Geopolitics, 78, 399
Germany, 15, 62, 66, 194, 219, 232
    industrial revolution in, 14
    nuclear weapons, 21
    reunification of (1989), 28, 30, 73
    World War I and, 67, 90–91, 174–75
    World War II and, 67, 78, 90–91, 129, 152,
        170
Glasnost, 237
Global community, 187–206. *See also*
    Cooperation
    community of understanding, 194
    culture, 188–89
    democracy, spread of, 194–96
    human rights law and norms of, 189–94
    information technology and, 188

institutional development and, 199–206
    peaceful interaction and, 196–99
    transportation and communications
        technology, 16, 188, 338–41, 355
Global division of labor, 305–6, 418–19
Global economy, 274–95, 417–18
    Bretton Woods system, 277–80
    contemporary challenges, 280
        in finance, 287–94
        leadership question, 294–95
        in trade, 281–87
    irregular growth of open, 274–77
    restructuring of, 13–18
Global Environment Monitoring System
    (GEMS), 390
Global Information and Early Warning
    Systems (GIEWS), 375
Globalization
    challenges, 18
    defined, 17
Global postal and telecommunications system,
    132
Global warming, 12, 327, 388
Golden Rule, 105
Gold supply, U.S., 280, 281
Goods, 135, 398
    basic characteristics of, 130–31
    categories of, 131–35
    collective action and problems of
        underprovision, 135–36
    trade and logic of collective action,
        136–37
Gorbachev, Mikhail, 34, 36, 172, 250, 350
    foreign policies of, 171
    on human rights, 30
    movement into power, 29, 68
Gordievski, Oleg, 175
Governance
    complex, 223, 224–25
    gender-inclusive, 247
    global, 414–15
    norms, 404
Government, 177–80. *See also* State(s)
    character, foreign behavior and, 180
    foreign-policy decision making by,
        177–78
Graduated reciprocation in tension-reduction
    (GRIT), 106, 148, 149, 388
Grass-roots organizations, 24–25

Great Britain, 66–68, 111, 117, 219
    arms control, 142, 146
    economic growth in, 322
    energy and energy policies, 378, 379
    Falklands conflict, 99, 316, 345
    foreign direct investment, 291
    hegemonic leadership of, 69–70
    imperialism and, 297
    loss of empire, 297–98
    mercantilism and, 264
    nuclear weapons, 21, 107
    Partial Test-Ban Treaty, 142
    political parties, 166, 167
    Royal Society for the Advancement of
        Science, 351
    trade policies, 138, 275–76
    trade with U.S., 162–63
    war fatalities, 100
Great Depression, 276, 292
Great-person theories, 168–69
Great (major) powers, 63
Greece, 14, 80, 94, 95, 104, 139, 194, 195, 200,
    219
Greek city-state system, 64, 65, 399
Greenhouse effect, 12, 194, 327, 387–88, 391
Greenhouse gases, 327, 391–93
Greenpeace, 25, 186, 336
Green revolution, 7, 342, 371, 374, 375
Grenada, 91, 128
Grotius, Hugo, 51, 125, 275, 415
Group of 77, 321
Group of Eight, 121, 222
Groupthink, 177, 181
Growth patterns, alternative, 335. *See also*
        Economic development; Population
Guatemala, 315
Guerilla (unconventional) war, 88
Guinea-Bissau, 387
Gunboat diplomacy, 89
Gunpowder, 201–2, 354
Guttenberg, Johannes, 231

H

Hague conferences of 1899 and 1907, 129
Haiti, 11, 69, 83, 215, 368
Hanseatic League, 200
Hapsburg family, 61
Hashimoto, Prime Minister, 157

Havel, Vaclav, 28
Health issues, 12, 359–61, 363
Hegemonic leadership, 68–70
    advantages of, 116–17
    character of regime imposed by hegemon,
        138
    hegemonic analysis, insights from, 114–18
    hegemonic power, defined, 20
    historic, 65–66
    open markets facilitated by hegemon,
        68–70, 137
    rise and fall of hegemons, 114–16
    transition of hegemons, 117–18
    of U.S., 64, 68, 70
Hegemonic stability, theory of, 116–17, 400,
    411
Hegemonic transition, theory of, 117–18, 400
Heidegger, Martin, 272n
Hellenic League, 65
Helsinki Agreement, 146, 192
Helsinki Final Act of 1975, 30
Helsinki Watch, 192, 193
Heraclitus, 412
Heron of Alexandria, 330n
Hierarchy
    of needs, 409
    of understanding, 34–35
High politics, 33
Hinduism, 242
Hiroshima, 1, 20, 107
Historic universalism, 249
Hitler, Adolf, 37, 46, 169, 171, 176
HIV virus, 359
Hizballah, 252
Hobbes, Thomas, 45–46, 139n, 202, 330
Hobson, John, 268, 399
Holocaust, 129, 152, 228, 234, 236
Holy Roman Empire, 61, 66, 231
Honduras, 315
Hong Kong, 14, 183, 298, 323, 325
Hoover, Herbert, 173
Hotlines, 146, 176
Hull, Cordell, 198, 250, 277
Human capital, 259
Human Genome Project, 343
Human nature, 45–46
Human needs, basic, 320
Human rights, 49, 354
    China and, 121, 183, 186
    defined, 189, 191

institutional support for, 192–93
UN conventions, 190–91
universal, 30
Human Rights Watch, 193
Hume, David, 331
Hungary, 27–29, 31, 32, 91, 120, 219
Hunger, 7–9, 373
Hunger Project, 333
Hussein, Saddam, 71, 89, 176
Hypermedia, 356

I

Iceland, 115
Idealism, 49, 51. *See also* Liberalism
religious, 55
Ideals and communities. *See also* Nationalism
in Middle East, 228
religion and world politics, 241–44
universalism, 57, 248–51
Ideas, 167–68. *See also* Ideals and communities
Ideational liberalism, 59*n*
Identity groups, 54–55, 404
Ideologies, 248–50
Ideologues, 408
IMF. *See* International Monetary Fund (IMF)
Immunizations, 214
Imperialism, 131–32, 232, 241–42, 306, 399
capitalism and, 268–69
decolonization and, 297–98
mercantilism and, 264
Imperialism, the Highest Stage of Capitalism
(Lenin), 268–69
Import substitution, 319–20
Income distribution
in developed vs. less-developed countries,
302–4
food distribution and, 374–75
industrialization and, 262, 343
India, 7, 71, 142, 185, 194
independence, 297
industrialization of, 15
nuclear weapons, 21, 84, 104, 107–9, 148,
349
population, 73–74
power of, 72–73
religious conflicts in, 242–43
territorial disputes involving, 71, 104, 124,
243

U.S. economic sanctions against, 83
Village Awakening Movement, 185
Individuals, 168–77
in groups, 176–77
liberalism's focus on, 47, 50, 51
Indonesia, 274, 311, 325, 384
Industrialization
environmental impact of, 11–13
income distribution and, 262, 343
nationalism and, 235
requirements of, 14–15
Industrial revolution, 13–14, 275, 322
Infant industries, 306, 307
Influenza epidemic, 359
Informal institutions, 56
Information dominance, 344
Information revolution, 14, 15–16, 188
Innovation, 346
*Inquiry into the Nature and Causes of the Wealth
of Nations* (Smith), 257
Institutional development, 199–206. *See also*
European Union (EU); United
Nations (UN)
Institutionalization, 168
Instrumental interests, 71, 72
Intellectual exchange, 194
Intellectual property rights protection,
352–53
Intelligence operations, 80–81
INTELSAT, 340–41
Interdependence, 52
Interest aggregation, 161
Interest articulation, 161
Interest groups, 162–64
Interests, 161–67
state, 42, 70–72, 78
Intergovernmental Council of Copper
Exporting States (CIPEC), 322
Intergovernmental organizations (IGOs),
199
Intergovernmental Panel on Climate Change
(IPCC), 12, 327
Intermediate Nuclear Forces (INF) Treaty of
1987, 150
International agricultural research centers, 372
International Atomic Energy Agency (IAEA),
147, 148, 349
International Bank for Reconstruction and
Development (IBRD). *See* World Bank
International Commission of Jurists, 193

International Committee of Catholic Nurses, 186
International Court of Justice (World Court), 208, 209, 213, 252
International Covenant on Civil and Political Rights, 192
International Criminal Court, 192
International Development Association (IDA), 279
International Energy Agency (IEA), 383
International environmental treaties, 389–90
International Federation for Human Rights, 193
International Finance Corporation, 279, 291
International Fund for Agricultural Development (IFAD), 375
Internationalism, 159, 165
International law, 125–30
    defined, 125
    human rights law, 125
    obligations of states, 127–30
    positivist versus naturalist views of, 125
    rights of states, 126–27
International League for Human Rights, 193
International Monetary Fund (IMF), 28, 126, 200, 208, 214, 277–79, 294, 295, 310, 311
International nongovernmental organizations (NGOs or INGOs), 186–87
International Office of Weights and Measures, 203
International Red Cross, 375
International Register of Potentially Toxic Chemicals (IRPTC), 390
International Sea Bed Authority, 389
International system, 233
International Telecommunications Organization, 203
International Telecommunications Satellite Organization (INTELSAT), 340–41
International Telecommunications Union (ITU), 353
International Telegraph Union, 132, 353
International Telephone and Telegraph Company (ITT), 315
International Whaling Commission (IWC), 134
Internet, 187, 188, 352
Interstate system structure. *See* State system(s)
Intifada, 237

Intrastate analysis, 398
Invention, 348
Iran, 21, 77, 80, 83, 89, 91, 94, 108, 227, 355, 378, 379
Iranian hostage crisis, 252, 383
Iraq, 21, 54, 77, 81–82, 84, 89, 94, 96, 107, 142, 171, 371, 380, 381
    invasion of Kuwait, 71, 83, 90, 91, 95, 108, 120, 128, 139, 172, 176, 210–12, 227, 318–19, 383
Irish Republic, 243
Irredentism, 236
Irrigation, 7, 370–71
Islam, 94, 228, 241–43, 254
Isolationism, 159, 168
Israel, 14, 21, 69, 71, 81, 82, 86, 104, 107, 108, 142, 164, 194, 197, 228, 237, 371, 380
Italian Renaissance system, 65, 399
Italy, 83, 139–40, 194, 219, 232, 363, 367

J

Japan, 14, 38, 62, 194
    China and, 139
    defense treaties, 67
    dispute over Kurile Islands, 71
    economic growth in, 322
    F-22 fighter plane technology and, 349–50
    foreign aid from, 85
    foreign direct investment, 289
    government in, 157–58
    Manchuria and, 139, 156
    military spending, 115, 153–54, 156, 157
    Ministry of International Trade and Industry (MITI), 158, 351
    nuclear weapons, 21, 108
    Pearl Harbor attack, 152
    post–World War II constitution of May 1947, 153
    power
        aggregate, 76
        economic, 74–75
        technological, 74
    society of, 156–57
    state of, 154, 156
    state system of, 154
    trade policies, 164, 265, 282–84
    U.S. occupation of, 153, 154

women in, 246–47
World War II, 152
Jefferson, Thomas, 245
Jewish diaspora, 228, 251
Jiang Zemin, 122
Johnson, Lyndon B., 103*n*, 173, 177, 365
Johnson, Samuel, 401
Joint European Submicron Silicon program
    (JESSI), 351
Jordan, 237
JSTARS, 343
Just war, 128

K

Kant, Immanuel, 49, 50–52, 57*n*, 185*n*, 187, 196,
    198, 415
Kashmir, 71, 104, 236, 243
Kazakhstan, 107, 238, 384
Kellogg-Briand Pact of 1928, 50*n*
Kennan, George, 250
Kennedy, John F., 148, 173, 176
Kenya, 220, 298
Keynes, John Maynard, 55–56, 168, 292, 294
KGB, 81
Khadafi, Muamar, 89, 171*n*, 177
Khmer Rouge, 91
Khomeini, Ayatollah, 355
Khrushchev, Nikita, 67, 148, 176
Kissinger, Henry, 68, 81, 89, 111, 170–71
Knowledge level of U.S. citizens, 158–59, 160
Knowosphere, 328
Kondratieff cycles, 100, 346, 347
    of warfare, 100
Korean War, 79, 91, 99, 101, 211
Kosovo, 82, 88, 90, 121, 239
Kurds, 54, 89, 94–96
Kurile Islands, 71
Kuwait, Iraqi invasion of, 71, 83, 90, 91, 95,
    108, 120, 128, 139, 172, 176, 210–12,
    227, 318–19, 383
Kuznets curve, 262
Kyoto agreement of 1997, 388, 391

L

Labor, division of, 259
Labor productivity, 259
Ladakh, 71
Laissez faire, 33, 38, 263, 306
Laissez innover, 329
Land availability, 368–70
Land distribution, 375, 376
Landmines, 142
Language, 188, 231, 246, 272
Lasers, 353
Latin America. *See* specific countries
Latin American Free Trade Association
    (LAFTA), 220
Latvia, 30, 210, 219, 237
Law
    international. *See* International law
    liberal focus on, 51
Law-making treaties, 128
Law of the Sea, 132, 211, 391
LDCs. *See* Less-developed countries (LDCs)
Leadership, 169–71
    gender and, 171–72
    hegemonic. *See* Hegemonic leadership
    personality, 173
    psychology and, 172–73
Lead poisoning, 385
League of Nations, 66, 67, 82–83, 139, 170, 189,
    208, 211, 222
Lebanon, 11
Leibniz, Gottfried Wilhelm, 330
Lenin, V. I., 249, 268–71, 399
Lesotho, 239
Less-developed countries (LDCs), 69
    debt crisis in, 308–11
    deforestation in, 11
    family planning in, 364, 365
    fishing fleets, 134
    foreign aid to, 85, 289
    immunizations in, 214
    literacy in, 22
    multinational corporations in, 312–14
    oil industry in, 379–80
    toxic waste disposal in, 387
    UN and, 210
Levels of analysis. *See* Analysis, levels of
Leviathan (Hobbes), 45
Liberalism, 46
    American vs. European usage of term,
        46–47
    classical, 37, 47, 48
    commercial. *See* Commercial liberalism
    concepts of, 43, 47

Liberalism *(cont.)*
  on development strategies, 322–23
  ideational, 59*n*
  important contributions to, 50–52
  modern, 47
  progressive change and, 401
  realism compared to, 48–49, 53
  realist, 60*n*
  summary of, 397
  theory of, 43, 48–49
  values and prescriptions of, 43, 49–50
Liberal world order, emergent, 183–206
  actor proliferation and empowerment,
    185–87
  global community. *See* Global community
Liberation theology, 243
Liberia, 297
Libya, 80, 89, 91, 108, 142, 210, 379
Life expectancy, 3, 256, 301, 329, 341–42, 344,
    363, 402
Limited Test-Ban Treaty of 1963, 124
Linear growth, 335
Literacy, 22, 235, 355
  female, 247
Lithuania, 30, 210, 219, 237
Locke, John, 51, 189, 331
Long waves of technological advance, 346–48
Louis XIV, King of France, 207, 232
Low-earth orbiting (LEO) technology, 341
Low politics, 33
Lusitania (liner), 103
Luther, Martin, 50, 61, 241
Luxembourg, 115, 116, 219
Luxemburg, Rosa, 271

M

Maastricht Treaty of 1991, 217, 219
Macedonia, 210, 238
Machiavelli, Niccolò, 45, 128, 151, 334, 414
Machine gun, invention of, 345
Mackinder, Sir Halford, 78
McLuhan, Marshall, 355
McNamara, Robert, 175
Macroenvironment, 359
Madison, James, 51
Magellan, Ferdinand, 275
Mahabharata, 128

Mahan, Alfred, 78
Mahbub ul Haq, 320
Malaria, 12, 359
Malawi, 298, 305
Malaysia, 274, 325
Malnutrition, 7–9
Malta, 124, 391
Malthus, Thomas, 334, 336, 402
Malvina Islands, 99, 316, 345
Manchuria, 139, 156
Mandela, Nelson, 184
Market failures, 263
Marshall, George, 85
Marshall Plan, 84–85, 87, 170, 280
Marx, Karl, 58, 248, 267, 268, 270, 404–5, 419
Marxism, 57, 267–68, 404–5
Mauritania, 189, 305
Mayan civilization, 332, 406–7
Media, exposure to, 22
Medium theory, 355
Meiji Restoration, 14
Meir, Golda, 172
Mercantilism, 38, 138, 256, 263–66, 399. *See also*
    Neomercantilism
  summary of, 397
  technological, 351
Mercosur, 221
Methodology, worldview and, 271–73
Metternich, Prince, 68
Mexican War, 101
Mexico, 14, 69, 245, 287, 296–97, 309, 323, 375
MI-6, British, 81
Microenvironment, 359–61
Middle East. *See also* specific countries
  community identities and ideals in, 228
  oil industry in, 9, 378–80, 384
Middle East Watch, 193
Migration, population pressures caused by,
    363
Militant internationalism, 159
Military-industrial complex, 166–67
Military personnel, state power measured by,
    72–73, 75
Military power, 20, 74–75, 87–92
  differentials, 316–19
Military spending
  by China, 75, 121
  by Japan, 115, 153–54, 156, 157
  state power measured by, 72–73

by United States, 20, 115, 148, 154, 160–62, 166–67, 169
Military technology, 343–45, 348–49
Mill, John Stuart, 51
Mineral production, 377
Minimum winning coalition principle, 112, 113
Ministry of International Trade and Industry (MITI), 158, 351
Mir space station, 353
Misperception, 174
Missile Technology Control Regime, 349
Mitsubishi, 349
Miyazawa, Prime Minister, 157
Modernism, 39, 328–31
    defined, 328
    important contributions to, 329–31
    progressive change and, 402–3
    summary of, 328, 397
    technology and, 329
Modernization theory, 254
Modern liberalism, 47
Modern universalism, 249–51
Mongolia, 250
Monnet, Jean, 204
Monroe Doctrine, 79
Monsanto, 371
Montenegro, 238
Moore's law, 16
Morality of realists, 44
More-developed countries (MDCs), 69
Mortality rates, 3–5, 7
Mossad, Israeli, 81
Most favored nation (MFN) status, 279
Mozambique, 215
Mubarak, Hosni, 311
Multilateral Agreement on Investment (MAI), 287, 315
Multilateral analysis, insights from, 110–13
Multilateral Investment Guarantee Agency (MIGA), 279
Multilateralism, 120
Multinational corporations (MNCs), 187, 356
    controls on, 315–16
    economic impact of, 312–14
    power of, 314–15
Multipolar system, 63–65, 68
Mussolini, Benito, 169, 234
Mutual assured destruction (MAD), 109, 110

Mutual Defense Assistance Control Act of 1951, 348
Mutually beneficial exchange process, 257

N

Nagasaki, 107
Nagorno-Karabakh, 238
Nakasone, Prime Minister, 157
Napoleonic Wars, 232
Nasser, Gamal Abdel, 297
Nation(s), 54
    defined, 231
    modern nation system, 233
    nationalism and, 231–40
National Aeronautics and Space Administration (NASA), 403
National character, 167–68
Nationalism, 54, 57, 230–40
    defined, 231
    interstate relations and, 236
    modernization and, 232
    problem cases, 236–40
    refugees and, 363–64
    social mobilization and, 23–24
    within states, 234–36
    terrorism, 252
Nationalization, 320
National Security Agency (NSA), 81
Nation-state, use of term, 233
Native Americans, 233, 333–34, 338
NATO. *See* North Atlantic Treaty Organization (NATO)
Naturalist view of international law, 125–26
"Near abroad," 119, 121
Needs, hierarchy of, 409
Negotiation, diplomatic, 81–82
Nehru, Jawaharlal, 320
Neoclassical economics, 402
Neocolonialism, 306
Neofunctionalism, 205, 401
Neo-Marxism, 38–39, 248, 256, 269–71, 304, 325, 404–5
    summary of, 397
Neomercantilism
    bases of, 281–82
    confronting challenge of, 282–83
    defined, 264, 265

Neorealism, 46, 53*n*, 54, 399–400
   summary of, 397
Neotraditionalism. *See* Eco-wholism
Nepal, 189
Netherlands, 61, 62, 66, 68, 114, 115, 117, 166, 167, 219, 275
New Atlantis (Bacon), 330
New diplomacy, 82
New International Economic Order (NIEO), 321
Newly industrialized countries (NICs), 69, 148, 283, 323
Newton, Isaac, 330
New Zealand, 67, 221
Nicaragua, 89, 215, 252
Niebuhr, Reinhold, 46
Nietzche, Friedrich, 272*n*
Niger, 305
Nigeria, 384
Nitrogen pollution, 386, 393
Nixon, Richard M., 68, 154, 164, 170–71, 173
Nomenklatura, 248
Nonaligned Movement (NAM), 320
Noneconomic interest groups, 164–65
Nonexcludability of goods, 131–33, 139
Nonintervention, 127, 236
Nonmilitarization, 146–47
Non-Proliferation of Nuclear Weapons, Treaty on (1968), 124, 147–48, 348–49
Nonprovocative defense doctrine, 141–42
Non-tariff trade barriers (NTBs), 265
Nonzero-sum orientation, 47, 282, 343, 401
North (category of states), 69
North American Free Trade Agreement (NAFTA), 158–59, 178, 222, 284, 286–87, 294
North Atlantic Treaty Organization (NATO), 2, 95, 113, 141
   formation of, 67, 170
   members and expenditures, 115–16
   Partnership for Peace, 120, 224
   post–Cold War role of, 119–20
Northern Ireland, 243
North Korea, 21, 79, 108, 142, 148, 158, 171, 210
North-South relations. *See also* Multinational corporations (MNCs)
   economic gap, 299–302. *See also* Economic development
   global division of labor, 305–6

   military-power differentials, 316–19
   over population control, 365, 367
Nuclear energy, 10
Nuclear family, 244
Nuclear Non-Proliferation Treaty of 1977, 108
Nuclear Test Ban Treaty of 1963, 386
Nuclear weapons, 20–22, 102, 202. *See also* Arms control and disarmament efforts; Arms race
   acronyms, 144
   strategic capabilities, 107–8
   strategic concepts and theory, 109–10
   testing, 386–87
   undeclared nuclear powers, 107–8
Nuclear winter, 22
Nuremberg trials, 129

O

Obligations of states, 127–30
Obsolescing bargain, 314
Oceanic rise, 388
Official development assistance (ODA), 85
Oil and gas industry, 9, 377–78
Oil embargo, 164
Oil prices, 379–80, 383–84
Oil shocks, 10, 308, 380–83
Okita, Saburo, 198
Old diplomacy, 82
Oligarchy, 65
Omnibus Trade and Competitiveness Act of 1988, 283
One-child-per-family policy, 365
Open markets, logic of collective action for, 136–37
Open skies policy, 150
Open Skies Treaty of 1992, 150
Opinion leaders, 160
Optimizing, 177
Organizational-process model of decision making, 178
Organization for Economic Cooperation and Development (OECD), 198, 222, 383
Organization for Security and Cooperation in Europe (OSCE), 192, 224
Organization of African Unity, 387
Organization of Petroleum Exporting Countries (OPEC), 164, 321, 322, 379, 380, 383–84
Orwell, George, 126

Osisraq nuclear reactor, 107
Oslo declaration of 1994, 82, 228
Ottoman empire, 94, 111, 241, 275
Overshoot and collapse behavior, theory of, 332, 335, 406
OXFAM, 86, 375
Ozone hole, 11–12, 388

P

Paine, Thomas, 52
Pakistan, 71, 189, 195, 236, 242, 243
    nuclear weapons, 21, 84, 104, 107–9, 349
    territorial disputes involving, 71, 104, 124
    U.S. economic sanctions against, 83
Palestine Liberation Organization (PLO), 82, 252
Palestinians, 82, 104, 164, 171, 197, 215, 228, 237, 252, 363, 371
Palmerston, Lord, 71
Panama, 91, 128
Papal authority, 61
Paradigms, 44n. *See also* Worldviews
Partially pure public goods, 135
Partial Test-Ban Treaty of 1963, 142
Partnership for Peace, 120, 224
Pascal, Blaise, 330
Patents, 352–53
Peacekeeping by UN, 210–13
Pearl Harbor, 152
Peloponnesian League, 65
Peloponnesian Wars, 45, 82
People's Republic of China (PRC). *See* China, People's Republic of
Perception, crisis and, 174–75
Perestroika, 350
Pérez de Cúeller, Javier, 336
Periphery states, 270. *See also* Less-developed countries (LDCs)
Persian Gulf War. *See* Kuwait, Iraqi invasion of
Personality of leaders, foreign policy and, 173
Persona non grata, 128
Peru, 195, 322, 389
Pesticides, 7
Philippines, 67, 185
Philosophies, 248
Pirating, 352–53
Plagues, 359
Plato, 334

Pluralist model of decision making, 164–65
Poland, 31, 89, 120, 194, 219, 236
    Solidarity movement in, 27, 28, 184
Polarity, 42, 44, 63–64, 66–68
    change in, and its consequences, 113–14
Polio, 12
Polis, 65
Political ecology
    defined, 327
    worldviews
        eco-wholism, 331–36
        modernism, 328–31
Political economy, 256
    worldviews. *See* Commercial liberalism; Mercantilism; Neo-Marxism
Political integration, 205
Political participation, social mobilization and, 23
Political parties, 165–66
Politics
    high, 33
    low, 33
    revolutions of 1989–1991 and, 28–31
Pollution, 7, 18, 385, 386, 388
Population, 421
    demographic transition of, 3–7, 39, 362
    dependent, 6
    growth, 2, 4
    Malthus on, 334, 336
    pressures, 361–67
    state power measured by, 72–73
    U.S., 20
Portugal, 14, 62, 66, 68, 115, 117, 194, 219, 323
Positive feedback loop, 329
Positivism, 125–26, 271–73
Postmodernism, 58–59, 272
Power. *See also* Hegemonic leadership
    aggregate capabilities and, 75–76
    definition and measurement of, 72
    demographic size and, 72–74
    economic, 74–75
    instruments of, 79–92
        diplomacy, 79–82
        economic, 82–87
        military, 87–92
    military, 20, 74–75, 87–92
        differentials in, 316–19
    other capabilities contributing to, 77–78
    paradox of unrealized, 92
    in realism, 37, 42

Power *(cont.)*
    state interests and, 78
    technological, 74
    territorial, 78
Power-transition theory, 117–18
Prague Spring, 127
Prices
    oil, 379–80, 383–84
    transfer pricing, 312
Principled beliefs, 168, 187, 194
Printing, invention of, 231, 355
Prisoner's dilemma, 109–10, 244
Private goods, 131–33
Privatization, 131, 137, 286, 388–89
Privileged groups, 135–36
Product cycle theory, 306
Production, 257, 259
    factors of, 162, 257, 259
Productivity, 15
Progressive change, 400–403
Project Independence, 383
Propaganda, 80
Property rights, intellectual, 352–53
Propositions in hierarchy of understanding, 35
Prospect theory, 173
Prostitution, 189
Protectionism, U.S., 165, 282, 287
Proxy wars, 89, 92, 317–18
Psychology, foreign policy and, 172–73
Public opinion, 158–61
Punctuated equilibrium, 404
Purchasing power parity, 74
Pure public goods, 133, 135

Q

Qualitative limitations on arms, 140–42
Quantitative limitations on arms, 143–46
Quotas, 82

R

Race, 55
Racism, 57, 245–46
Radio Marti, 80
Rain forests, 11, 368–69
Raison d'état, concept of, 128

Ranked nations, 234–35
Rational-actor model of decision making, 177, 178
Rationality, in decision making, 181
Reagan, Ronald, 34, 169, 171, 175, 408
Realism, 37, 38. *See also* State(s); State system(s)
    concepts of, 41–43
    continuity and change in political behavior, 396, 398
    important contributions to, 45–46
    liberalism compared to, 48–49, 53
    structural, 42*n*, 46
    summary of, 397
    theories of, 42–44
    values and prescriptions of, 43, 44
Realist liberalism, 60*n*
Realpolitik, 112
Reciprocal Trade Agreements Act of 1934, 165, 277
Reciprocity, 105–6, 276, 308
Recombinant deoxyribonucleic acid (DNA), 142, 371
Red Brigades, 252
Red Cross Societies, 86
Reformation, 241
Refugees, 363–65
Regimes, 137–38
Regional disarmament, 146–47
Regional economic organizations, 220–21. *See also* European Union (EU)
Regulation, collective, 389–90
Relational norms, 404
Relative gain, 48
Religion, world politics and, 241–44
Religious idealism, 55
Renaissance Italy system, 65, 399
Reporting, diplomatic, 80–81
Representation, diplomatic, 79–80
Republican party, U.S., 165
Republic of China (ROC). *See* Taiwan
Research, agricultural, 372
Research and Development in Advanced Communications Technology (RACE), 351
Resistance point, 81
Resource scarcities
    energy, 377–85
    food, 367–77

Respondent superior, 129
Revaluation, 278
Revolution(s)
    associational, 185–86
    Central and Eastern Europe, of 1989–1991,
        27–33
    European, of 1830 and 1848, 232
Revolutionary War, 101
Revolution in military affairs, 344
Rhodes, Cecil, 268–69
Rhodesia, 298
Ricardo, David, 260
Rights
    human. *See* Human rights
    property rights, intellectual, 352–53
    of states, 126–27
Risk aversion and acceptance, 173–74
Rivalry, 130–33, 137, 139
River blindness, 12
Road maps, 168
Robotics, 351
Rockefeller Foundation, 7, 342, 375
Romania, 27, 31, 32, 219, 236, 355
Rome, Treaty of (1958), 68, 217, 219, 220
Roosevelt, Franklin D., 169, 170, 173, 250
Roosevelt, Theodore, 78
Rotary Club International, 186
Rousseau, Jean-Jacques, 51, 139n, 331
Royal Society for the Advancement of Science,
    351
Rush-Bagot Treaty of 1817, 146–47
Rusk, Dean, 176
Russia, 62. *See also* Soviet Union
    arms control, 143, 145
    dispute over Kurile Islands, 71
    energy policy, 384–85
    food and energy prices in, 286
    invasion of Chechnya (1994), 118–19
    military spending, 78
    "near abroad" of, influence in, 119, 121
    nuclear weapons, 107, 108
    post–Cold War systemic role of, 120–21
    space program, 353
    United Nations and, 210
    war fatalities, 100
Russian Foreign Intelligence Service (IVR), 81
Russian Revolution, 27
Rust, Mathias, 355
Rwanda, 235, 245–46, 363, 364

S

Sadat, Anwar, 81, 171n, 243
Sadik, Nafis, 367
Salisbury, Lord, 70
SALT I and II treaties, 124, 143
Satellites, 21–22, 341
Satisficing, 178
Saturating exponential growth, 335
Saudi Arabia, 77, 227, 228, 384
Save the Children Fund, 86
Scale of economic integration, 204
Scenario analysis, 412–22
Schlieffen plan, 345
Schuman, Robert, 204
Schuman Plan, 204
Schumpeter, Joseph, 346
Science, 329–30
Seabed Treaty of 1971, 147
Seapower, 70, 78
Sea transport, 338, 339
Secession, 235
Second-strike capability, 109
Second World, 69
Secretariat of United Nations, 208, 209
Security
    as central value of states, 42–45
    collective, 139–40, 211–12
    confidence and security building measures,
        146
    post–Cold War security issues and
        structures, 118–22
Security Council of United Nations, 208, 209
Security dilemma, 42–43, 45, 46, 105, 139, 411
Selective intervention, 281
Self-determination principle, 234, 236
Self-reliance strategy, 320
Sematech, 352
Semiconductor technology, 352
Separation of powers, 51
Serbia, 30, 54, 82, 83, 90, 102, 111, 121, 174, 175,
        177, 192, 215, 238
Service sector, 15
Sewage, 385
Sexism, 246–47
Sexually transmitted diseases, 360
Shadow of the future, 138
Sharia, 243
Shiite Moslems, 228, 252

Shuttle diplomacy, 81
Side payments, 136
Sierra Club, 287
Sikhs of India, 242–43, 252
Singapore, 14, 69, 274, 323, 325
Single European Act of 1986, 217, 219
Sinkiang, 250
Six Books on the State (Bodin), 62
Six-Day War of 1967, 124
Size principle, 112, 113
Slavery, 189, 245
Slovakia, 219
Slovak Republic, 210
Slovenia, 30, 219, 238, 239
Smallpox, 12, 214, 359
Smart sanctions, 84
Smith, Adam, 33, 38, 52, 257, 259, 263, 276, 402
Smoot-Hawley Act of 1930, 276
Social capital, 56
Social class, 55, 247–48
Social constructivism. *See* Constructivism
Social constructs, 53
Social mobilization, increased, 22–25
Society, analysis of U.S., 158–68
    crisis management, 175–76
    ideas, 167–68
    individuals, 168–69
        in groups, 176–77
    interests, 161–67
    leadership and vision, 169–71
    perception and crisis, 174–75
    public opinion, 158–61
    risk aversion and acceptance, 173–74
Soft law, 128
Soft power, 78
Soil loss, 370, 387
Solar energy, 382
Solidarity movement, 27, 28, 184
Somalia, 58, 213, 239, 244, 246, 364, 377
Soros, George, 86, 185
Soros Foundation, 86
South (category of states), 69
South Africa, 14, 58, 83, 107, 130, 184, 197, 215, 230, 246, 297
South China Sea, 119, 121
Southeast Asian Nuclear Weapons Free Zone (SEANWFZ), 147
Southern African Development Community (SADC), 221

South Korea, 14, 38, 67, 69, 79, 108, 142, 210, 211, 274, 323, 325
South-North gap. *See* North-South relations
South Pacific Nuclear Free Zone, 147
Sovereignty, 126
    defined, 62
Soviet Union
    arms control, 124, 140, 142, 144, 149, 150
    Brezhnev Doctrine, 250
    Chernobyl nuclear plant, 386
    China and, 68
    Cold War, 1–2, 20
        arms sales during, 318
        proxy wars during, 317–18
        roots of, 249–50
    collapse of, 2, 20, 27–30, 68, 70, 113, 171, 237, 250
    conflicts since World War II, 91–92
    Cuban missile crisis, 90, 103–4, 124, 317
    de-Stalinization campaign, 67
    electronic technology development in, 350
    energy and energy policies, 32
    ethnic groups and nationalism in, 237–38
    food distribution, 374
    glasnost, 237
    industrialization of, 14, 31
    invasion of Afghanistan, 91, 92, 99, 112, 127, 128, 144, 178, 250, 318, 374
    nuclear weapons, 21–22
    perestroika, 350
    postwar management of power, 67
    power
        aggregate, 76
        following World War II, 28–29
        military, 20, 76
    rewriting of constitution (1988), 27
    Sputnik launch, 21
    trade policies, 138
    United Nations and, 210
    United States and, 171, 175, 176
        alliance against Nazi Germany, 112, 113
        embassies, 80
        hotline teletype system, 146, 176
    Vietnam War, 124
    World War II, 168, 170
Space program, 353, 403
Spain, 14, 62, 66, 117, 194, 323
Spanish American War, 99, 101
Specific reciprocity, 106, 276
Specific treaties, 128

Spheres of influence, 67
Spillover, 204, 205
Spinoza, Baruch, 330
Spoilers, 136, 283–84
Spread effects, 221
Sputnik, 21
Sri Lanka, 297
Stability, realism and, 396, 398
Stable nuclear balance, 109
Stages-of-growth approach to economic
    development, 261, 402
Stalin, Josef, 46, 67, 169, 170, 241
START I and II treaties, 144–45, 150
State(s)
    as agent in realism, 42–44
    categories of, 69
    defined, 62
    level of analysis, 154, 156
    obligations of, 127–30
    periphery, 270
    rights of, 126–27
Statecraft, 79–92, 398
    defined, 79
    diplomacy, 79–82
    economic instruments, 82–87
    military instruments, 87–92
State interests, 42, 70–72, 78
State power. *See* Power
State system(s), 94–123
    bilateral analysis, insights from, 104–6
    defined, 42
    hegemonic analysis, insights from, 114–18
    level of analysis, 154
    modern, 66–70
    patterns of conflict, 97–104
    polarities in, 63–64
        change in, and its consequences, 113–14
        multilateral analysis, insights from,
            110–13
        post–Cold War uncertainties, 118–22
State terrorism, 252–53
Stimson, Henry, 80
Stockholm Conference on Confidence and
    Security Building Measures and
    Disarmament in Europe of 1986, 146,
    390
Stolper-Samuelson theorem, 162n, 266
Strasbourg, France, 207
Strategic Arms Limitation Talks (SALT I), 124,
    143

Strategic Arms Limitation Talks (SALT II), 143
Strategic Arms Reduction Talks (START I),
    144–45, 150
Strategic Arms Reduction Talks (START II),
    145
Strategic trade theory, 264–67, 282, 399
Structural realism, 42n, 46
Structural transformations, economic
    development and, 261
Submarines, missile-launching, 109
Subsidiarity, 224
Sudan, 7, 55, 252, 371
Suez Canal, 212, 338
Suharto, President, 274, 311
Sulfur emissions, 386, 393
Sumer, 65
Sunni Moslems, 228
Super-exponential growth, 335
Superpowers, 63. *See also* Soviet Union; United
    States
Supporters, 283
Sustainable development, 333
Sweden, 219
Switzerland, 210, 256
Syria, 81, 94, 142, 228, 371
System, defined, 42
System transformation, 270, 404–7

T

Tadzhikistan, 120
Taiwan, 14, 62–63, 69, 104, 108, 121–22, 156,
    183, 274, 323, 325
Tanks, 345
Tanzania, 91, 220, 239
Tariffs, 82, 204, 276–78, 284, 306–8
Technological mercantilism, 351
Technology, 340–57
    agricultural, 371
    appropriate, 314
    communication, 16, 188, 339–41
    dual-use, 348
    fall of hegemons and, 115
    future developments in, 420–21
    human well-being and, 341–44
    intellectual property rights protection,
        352–53
    long waves of, 346–48
    military, 343–45, 348–49

Technology *(cont.)*
    modernism and, 329
    multinational corporations and, 314
    progressive change and, 403
    restriction of access by citizens, 350–51
    social organization and, 354–56
    support for innovation, 351–52
    transportation, 338–39
Teilhard de Chardin, Pierre, 328
Telephone, 339–41, 353–54
Templeton, John, 329
Terms of trade, 305–7
Territoriality, principle of, 127, 129
Territorial states, 48
Terrorism, 71
    foundations of, 251–52
    trends in, 252–53
Thailand, 274, 325, 385
Thatcher, Margaret, 165, 172, 408
Theocracy, 241
Theory in hierarchy of understanding, 35, 36
Things to Come (Wells), 403
Third International (Comintern), 249
Third World, 69. *See also* Economic
        development; Less-developed
        countries (LDCs); North-South
        relations
Thirty Years' War, 62, 66, 232, 241
Thucydides, 45, 151, 360, 414
Tiananmen Square (1989), 183
Tied aid, 85
Tit-for-tat interaction, 105, 106, 149
Tito, Marshal, 250, 320
Tlatelolco, Treaty of (1967), 147
Tocqueville, Alexis de, 52, 73, 74, 185
Tourism, 188, 338
Toxic waste disposal problem, 387
Trade
    China and, 121
    commercial liberalism on, 259–60
    global economy and, 281–87
    laws of international, 128
    logic of collective action and, 136–37
    restrictions, 82–84
    tariffs, 82, 204, 276–78, 284, 306–8
    terms of, 305–7
Trade deficits, 18
Trading states, 48
Tragedy of the commons, 133–34, 332, 407
Trail Smelter case of 1941, 386

Transaction costs, 138
Transfer pricing, 312
Transistors, 341
Transnational corporations (TNCs). *See*
        Multinational corporations (MNCs)
Transnationalism, 52
Transnational social movement organizations
        (TSMOs), 186
Transparency, 294, 315
Transportation technologies, 338–39, 355
Transylvania, 236
Treaties, specific and law-making, 128
Triad (nuclear delivery system), 108
Truman, Harry S, 61, 170, 173, 245
Truman Doctrine, 79, 170
Turkey, 94–96, 104, 111, 219, 371
Turkmenistan, 384
Turner, Ted, 185
Turning point, demographic, 4
Tutu, Desmond, 185

U

Uganda, 91, 220
Ukraine, 107, 121
Unanticipated consequences, 331–37
Unconventional (guerilla) warfare, 88–89
Undeclared nuclear powers, 107–9
Understanding, hierarchy of, 34–35
U.S.S.R. *See* Soviet Union
Unipolar system, 63
United Arab Emirates, 384
United Arab Republic (UAR), 228
United Brands, 315
United Kingdom, 15
United Nations (UN), 28, 208–16
    budget and employees, 215–16
    charter of, 126
    collective security and, 211–12
    components of, 208–9
    controversies facing, 215–16
    dispute resolution, 213–14
    economic sanctions used by, 83
    establishment of, 67
    membership of, 68, 210
    peacekeeping by, 210–13
    social development, 214–15
    transformation in functioning of, 210–11
    veto system, 211, 215

United Nations Children's Fund (UNICEF), 208, 215
United Nations Conference on Disarmament, 142
United Nations Conference on Environment and Development (UNCED), 390
United Nations Conference on Trade and Development (UNCTAD), 124, 321, 322
United Nations Convention against Torture, 192
United Nations Convention of the Elimination of All Forms of Discrimination against Women, 215
United Nations Development Program (UNDP), 208
United Nations Economic and Social Council (ECOSOC), 208, 209
United Nations Educational, Scientific, and Cultural Organization (UNESCO), 208
United Nations Environmental Program (UNEP), 208, 390
United Nations Food and Agricultural Organization (UNFAO), 8, 82, 134, 375
United Nations Framework Convention on Climate Change, 327
United Nations Fund for Population Activities (UNFPA), 215, 365, 367
United Nations Genocide Convention, 192
United Nations Law of the Sea Conferences (UNCLOS), 132, 137, 214, 388–89
United Nations Non-Governmental Liaison Service, 187
United States
    acid rain issue, 386
    agricultural policies, 373
    agricultural sector, 15
    AIDS research by, 360
    arms control, 124, 140, 142–50
    Bay of Pigs invasion, 177, 181, 317
    Cold War, 1–2, 20
        arms sales during, 318
        proxy wars during, 317
    conflicts since World War II, 91–92
    Cuban missile crisis, 90, 103–4, 124, 317
    decline of, 18
    defense treaties, 67
    energy and energy policies, 9, 378, 379, 383

European Union and, 284
exports and imports, 18
family planning programs and, 365, 367
federal employment as portion of total employment, 224, 225
food production in, 7
foreign aid from, 85, 86, 88, 164
foreign direct investment, 288–89
hegemonic leadership of, 64, 68, 70, 114, 118
immigration, 363
industrialization of, 14, 15
as largest debtor, 295
Marshall Plan, 84–85, 87, 170, 280
Mexican debt crisis and, 296–97
military spending, 20, 115, 148, 154, 160–62, 166–67, 169
military technology, 343–45
nuclear weapons, 21–22, 107, 108
occupation of Japan, 153, 154
political parties, 165–66
population, 20, 73–74
postwar management of power, 67
power, 79
    aggregate, 75–76
    economic, 74
    military, 20, 75
society. See Society, analysis of U.S.
Soviet Union and, 171, 175, 176
    alliance against Nazi Germany, 112, 113
    embassies, 80
    hotline teletype system, 146, 176
space program, 353
terrorism and, 252
trade policies, 83, 138, 162–63, 265, 276–77, 282–83
United Nations and, 210
Vietnam War, 20, 91, 92, 103, 124, 127, 148, 317
war casualties, 100–101
U.S. Environmental Protection Agency, 332
U.S. Export Control Act of 1949, 348
U.S. Information Agency, 80
Unit veto system, 63–64
Universal Declaration of Human Rights, 189, 350
Universal intergovernmental organizations (IGOs), 199
Universalism, 57, 248–51
Universal Postal Union (UPO), 132, 203, 208, 214

Unrealized power, paradox of, 92
Unstable nuclear balance, 109, 110
Uruguay Round of GATT, 286, 287, 352–54
Utility, 47
Utopianism, 49
Utrecht, Treaty of (1713), 66

V

Vaccination programs, 12, 363
Values, worldviews and, 35. *See also* specific
     worldviews
Variable geometry, 222
Venice, 65, 68, 275
Vietnam War, 20, 91, 92, 99, 101, 103, 124, 127,
     148, 159–61, 170, 177, 317
Village Awakening Movement in India, 185
Virtuous cycle, 329
Vision, 169–71
Voice of America, 80, 341, 355
Volatility of public opinion, 159, 160
Voltaire, François, 35, 246, 331
Voluntarism, 388
Voluntary organizations, 25

W

Wallonia, 224
Warfare, 2, 52–53
     biological and chemical, 142
     cyclic occurrence of, 99–100
     democracy and, 196–97
     electronic, 343
     frequency of, 98–99
     guerilla (unconventional), 88
     initiators of, 90–92, 118
     intensity of, 100–101
     international law of, 129–30
     just war, 128
     Kondratieff cycle of, 100
     legality of, 128, 198–99
     proxy wars, 89, 92, 317–18
     studies of, 97–101
     transition of hegemons, 117–18
War of 1812, 101, 197
Warsaw Pact, 2, 28, 113, 141, 145
Warsaw Treaty Organization, 67

Water pollution, 7, 385, 388
Water supplies, 370–71, 407
Watt, James, 346
Wealth of Nations, The (Smith), 33
Weaponry, 91. *See also* Arms control and
          disarmament efforts; Arms race
     biological and chemical, 142
     destructive potential, growth of, 20–22
     military technology, 343–45, 348–49
     nuclear. *See* Nuclear weapons
Weber, Max, 58
Wells, H. G., 403
West (category of states), 69
West Bank, 228, 237
West Germany
     formation of, 67
     political parties, 166, 167
Westphalia, Treaty of (1648), 62, 66, 241
White-collar jobs, 15
"White papers," 79
Wilson, Woodrow, 170, 173, 236, 250, 415
Wittgenstein, Ludwig Josef Johann, 58
Women. *See also* Gender
     status of, as function of GDP per capita,
          254, 255
Women's Caucus, 187, 193
World Bank, 28, 126, 214, 277, 279, 295, 310
World Council of Churches, 193
World Food Council, 375
World Food Summit of 1996, 8, 375
World Health Organization (WHO), 137, 208,
     214
World Meteorological Organization, 327
World Population Conferences, 365, 367
World-systems theory, 64, 267, 269–71, 405
World Trade Organization (WTO), 121, 138,
     214, 277, 286, 308, 353
Worldviews, 168, 194. *See also* Commercial
          liberalism; Constructivism; Eco-
          wholism; Liberalism; Mercantilism;
          Modernism; Realism
     in hierarchy of understanding, 35–36
     hypothetical futures based on, 412–22
     methodology and, 271–73
     overlapping, 59–60
World War I, 66, 90–91, 99, 101–3, 106, 111, 174,
     236, 345
World War II, 1, 46, 67, 90–91, 99, 101, 152, 170,
     236, 345

World War III, 101, 234
World Wide Web, 16, 132, 135
World Wildlife Fund, 336
Wotton, Sir Henry, 81
Writing, invention, 355

Y

Yeltsin, Boris, 28
Yugoslavia, 14, 27, 30, 31, 139, 213, 236, 238–39,
    250

Z

Zaire, 322, 361
Zambia, 305, 322
Zealots, 251
Zero-sum perspective, 47, 139, 282
Zhikov, 32
Zimbabwe, 360
Zone of overlap, 81
Zone of peace, 196, 198